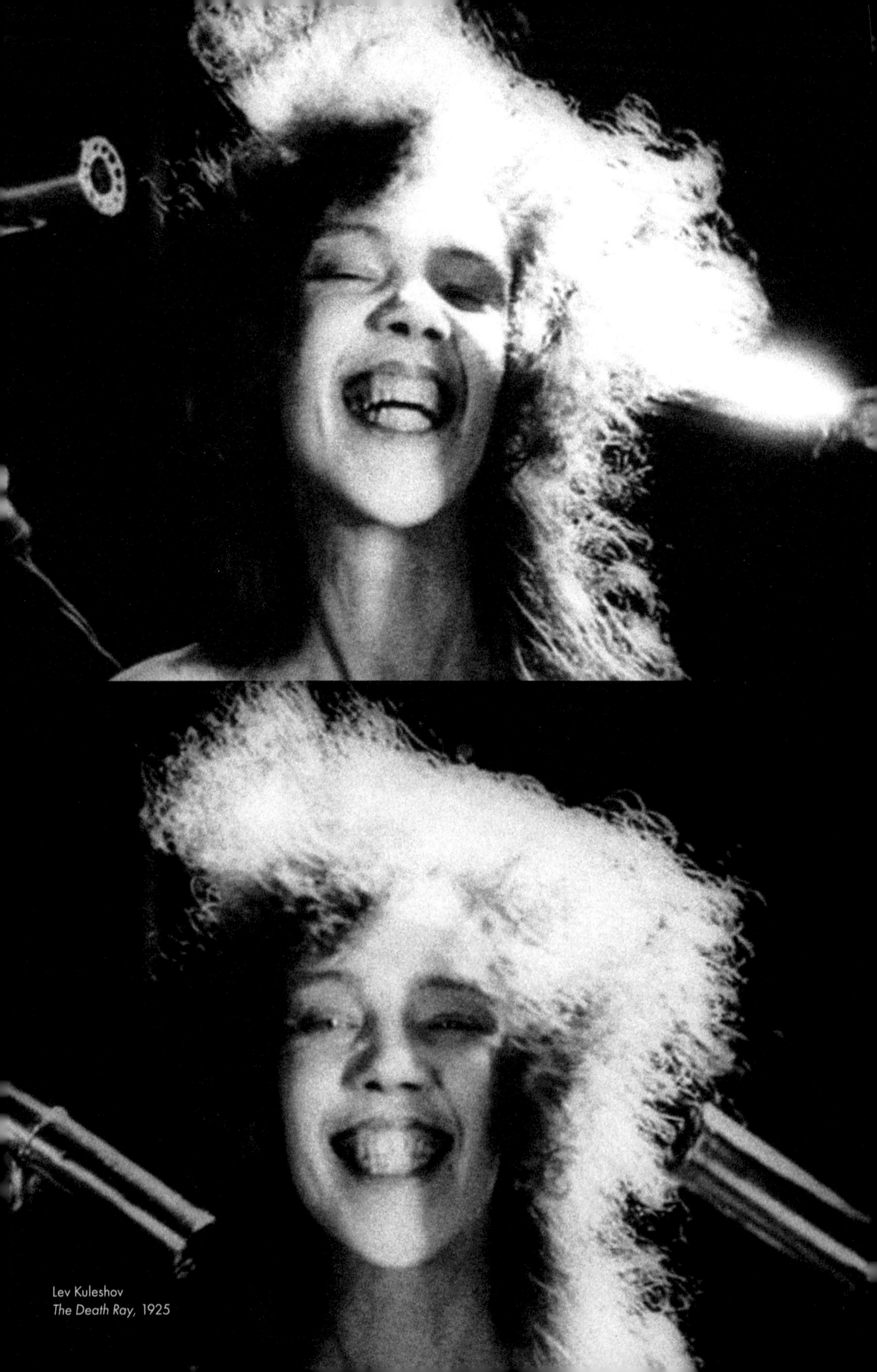

Lev Kuleshov
The Death Ray, 1925

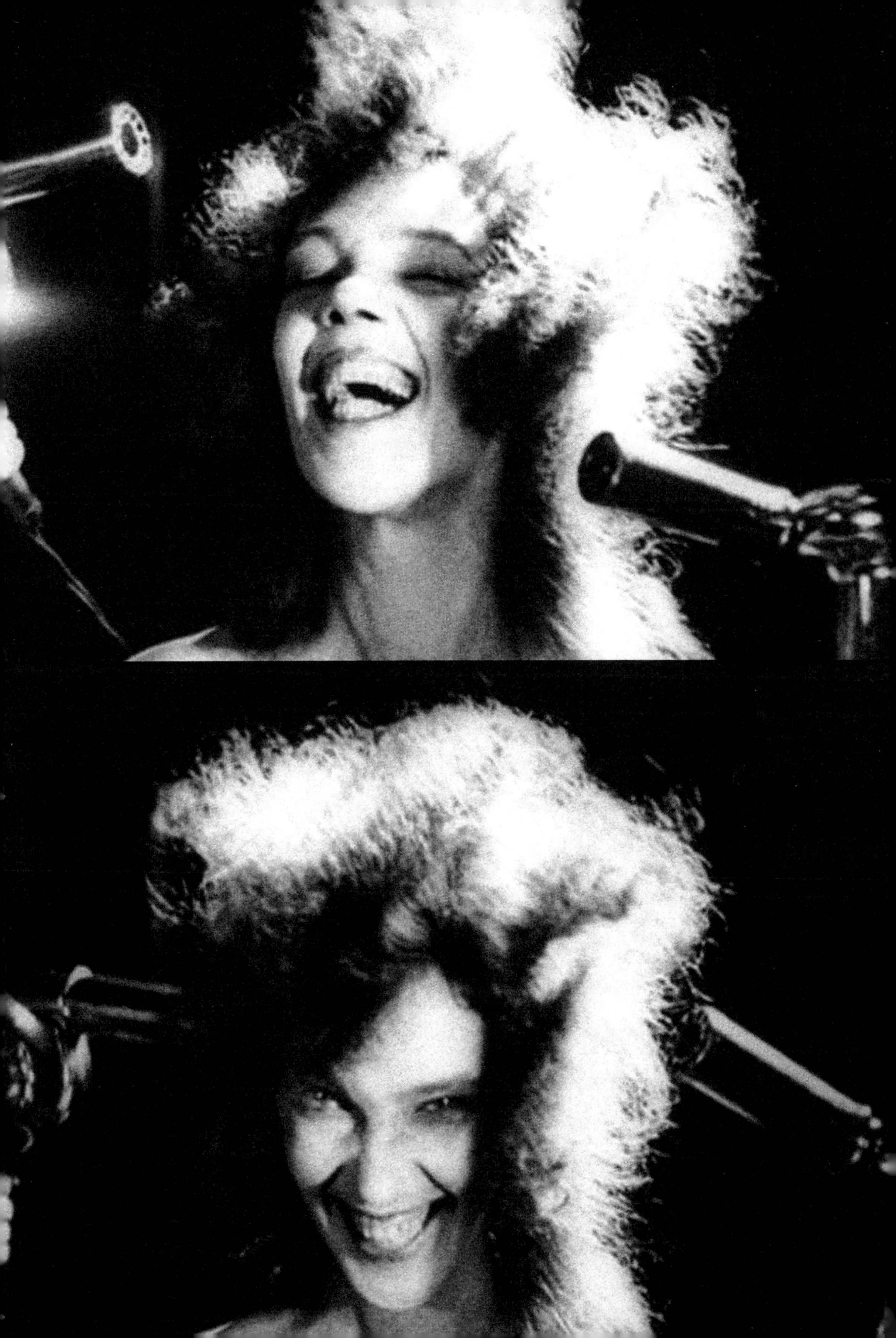

RUSSIAN

Da

1914—1924

Da

EDITED BY MARGARITA TUPITSYN

MUSEO NACIONAL CENTRO DE ARTE REINA SOFÍA • MADRID
THE MIT PRESS • CAMBRIDGE, MASSACHUSETTS • LONDON, UK

In the exhibition *Russian Dada 1914–1924*, the Museo Nacional Centro de Arte Reina Sofía focuses on an episode that is little known in Spain but was extremely influential for the development of artistic modernism: the impact of Dadaism in Russia during the years leading up to the Revolution and immediately following it.

In a context of enormous social and political upheaval both before and after the outbreak of revolution, a radical modernism germinated in the Russian artistic milieu and permeated the rest of the continent. These tendencies have already received attention from the Museo Nacional Centro de Arte Reina Sofía in exhibitions such as *Rodchenko and Popova: Defining Constructivism* (2009) and *The Russian Avant-Garde Book* (2013).

Dada was born in 1916 as a disorderly response rather than a movement with a sense of purpose, something that undoubtedly distances it from the programmatic nature of both the artistic avant-gardes and the political proposals that fed the totalitarianisms of the time. It emerged in a Zurich that was sheltering exiles, war refugees, deserters, and conspirators, one of them Vladimir Lenin, whose home was just yards from the Cabaret Voltaire, the nerve center of the origins of Dada.

The chronology of this exhibition thus starts with the outbreak of the Great War in 1914, continues with the birth of Dada, and ends with the death of the Bolshevik leader, an event that was to lead on to the origins of Stalinism and its subsequent demand for an academicist, realist, and antimodernist propaganda, far removed from the artistic production that had put Russia at the most radical forefront of the avant-garde.

The transnational character of the Dada experiment responds to a loss of confidence in the values established by the nationalist movements of the nineteenth century. It proceeds by challenging logic, established verbal and visual languages, and the values they represent. Its members therefore declared, “The signatories of this manifesto live in France, the United States, Spain, Germany, Italy, Switzerland, Belgium, etc., but have no nationality.”

Nevertheless, the various local branches of the movement were to have characteristics of their own, and it was from this specificity that they made their contributions to a modern art defined precisely as a response to the debates on identity inherited from the previous century, and as a result of weariness at forms of art seen as the products of a world in decline.

In the case of Russia, several critics of the time pointed out the Dadaist tendencies of the Russian avant-garde in its radical separation of form and content. Even Roman Jakobson came to speak of the October Revolution as the culmination of the political aspirations of Dada.

What is beyond doubt is that there was a creative seedbed in Russia, where the pioneering antiacademic experiments of Kazimir Malevich, El Lissitzky (the pseudonym of Lazar Markovich Lissitzky) and Aleksandr Rodchenko served as a spur for those who were drawn to negation, irony, and the absurd as radical forms of response in a period marked, to use Friedrich Nietzsche's term, by the "transvaluation of all values."

With more than two hundred paintings, drawings, collages, photographs, books, and films, the exhibition presents an in-depth survey of the period, arranged in several sections: abstraction, collage, and the readymade as mechanisms for contesting reason; revolutionary themes and the movement toward internationalism; and the interactions between Russia and the European Dadaists, with special reference to the groups in Berlin and Paris.

Russian Dada 1914–1924 comes at a most opportune moment. With the new century, the commemoration in 2018 of the end of the World War I, and the reactivation of the debate on the October Revolution with its centenary in 2017, the context seems ripe for using today's instruments and methods to rethink the contribution of the arts in the agitated Russian scene of the first decades of the twentieth century.

ÍÑIGO MÉNDEZ DE VIGO Y MONTOJO
MINISTER OF EDUCATION, CULTURE AND
SPORT AND GOVERNMENT SPOKESMAN

Perhaps it is the disappearance of grand narratives that has brought certain chronicles out of the shadows where they previously lurked. It may be that Russian constructivism, socialist realism, and the trail left by both throughout the twentieth century have left earlier experiments in a no-man's-land, even though they were laden with significance at a particular point in history. One such case is without doubt the revelation of the political component of the absurd in Russian Dadaism during the first decades of the last century.

"Dada," despite its legendary aleatory origin, means literally "yes yes" in Russian, a fact that appears above all to announce a Nietzschean affirmation in the initial formulation of Russian Dadaism. Its sense seems to be that of a forthright and radical declaration, a transformative harbinger of Bergsonian vitality. However, in the canonical narratives that locate the emergence of Dada in various cities (Zurich, New York, Paris, Berlin, Cologne, Hanover, and even a brief episode in Barcelona) sufficient attention has never been paid to the phenomenon in the context of pre- and postrevolutionary Russia. Nevertheless, the Dadaist reaction to bourgeois culture, which elevates a subordinate language to the forefront precisely amid the tragic context of the First World War, is something inherent to the October Revolution. The politicization of avant-garde culture was already imminent and inevitable in the 1910s, as was soon to be demonstrated by surrealism. Roman Jakobson would situate Dada at the origin of the political vindications from which the revolutionary phenomenon arose. However, the paradoxical Dada simultaneously denied this trust in the Revolution. The movement was, in a way, stillborn. As Victor Tupitsyn points out in the current volume, "in the cultural space, Dadaism is a kind of death drive, and in that sense it is not without its appeal, especially when combined with the 'theatrical drive' that balances the relationship between Eros and Thanatos. And if that is the case, theatricality in moderate doses is still necessary for visual art—at least so it can 'seem' alive. This might already have become a part of the postmodern cultural landscape, especially since nostalgia for Dadaism manifested itself in the second half of the twentieth century."

Dada is inevitably read from the perspective of the recovery of its strategies from the late 1950s onward in various contexts, especially the United States. Those experiments with aura, object, language, and the disappearance of the author under the impenetrable aegis of Duchamp might have overshadowed others that were silenced by the passage of time and the weight of historical events (Stalinism and its deviation from the destiny of the October Revolution), appearing too isolated, ultralocal, or derivative to be taken into consideration. And yet a whole series of practices is found in Russian Dada that undoubtedly revitalize and offer a more polyhedrous vision of a certain face of modernism, possibly—yet another paradox—the most antimodern of them all and the one that most violently denied the idea of progress inherited from the Enlightenment.

Russian Dada had first to escape from the watertight avant-garde compartment that futurism and its local evolution, cubo-futurism, had become. And while the urge to "create something new out of those residues" (Kurt Schwitters) found its pulse in international Dadaism through collage, one of the chief contributions of the Russian variant was undoubtedly the development of photomontage as a means of retrieving the literal image from the hegemony of the pictorial. In Russia, as Kazimir Malevich recalled in his 1933 autobiography, everything that was not assimilated to nature was regarded as futurism. In this respect, the experience of the reception of the avant-garde in Russia was not so different from that in Spain and Portugal (recently analyzed at the Museo Reina Sofía in the exhibition *Pessoa: All Art Is a Form of Literature*), where the penetration of avant-garde discourses soon drifted into a confusion of heteronyms and isms, with a tendency to simplify phenomena originating beyond the national borders and, at the same time, to complicate them with local nuances and ramifications, a case in point being ultraism in Spain.

Photomontage, developed in Germany's Weimar Republic by the likes of George Grosz and John Heartfield, meanwhile gave a new impulse and significance to the extraordinary proliferation of images in the context of an incipient culture of mass consumption. The photomontages of El Lissitzky, Aleksandr Rodchenko, and Gustav Klutsis represent the capacity of these images to intervene with timely and renovatory urgency in the public sphere, revealing the extent to which Russian Dada, which originated in 1914 and so predated the expatriate experiments centered on the Cabaret Voltaire in Zurich, also precedes the later axiom that art must be useful, new, and revolutionary. The Dada experiment is thus a laboratory, a testing ground onto which graphic design, painting, photography, magazine editing, stage design, advertising, architecture, and illustration all come into play in a huge upheaval or, as Hans Arp put it, "total pandemonium." This ability to move among media, together with the attempt to integrate art and life within the doubly affirmative "yes yes," allows us to speak of Russian Dada as a local and derivative phenomenon that was nevertheless extraordinarily influential in its context. The path traced by Russian Dada from 1914 to 1924 is the one leading from the upheaval to the project and from the tabula rasa to the new order.

It is surprising to discover in this exhibition how many different prefigurations of Dada existed in Russia under different denominations. On the one hand was the transrationalism and "shiftology" of Aleksei Kruchenykh, who gave a pioneering assessment in 1912 of the way in which the experience of the emotions was moving faster than human thought and speech. The first metamorphoses of this new panorama emerged precisely from poetry, so that the origins of Bolshevism, that attempt to reach a degree zero in history, can be located in the analysis of language and its reduction to minimal units. The members of the "41°" group thus presented themselves as "the founders of the word" in 1919 at the Fantastic Pub in Tbilisi, a Caucasian emulation of the Cabaret Voltaire. On the other hand, the "everythingism" of Mikhail Le Dantiu and Ilia Zdanevich and the apparently contradictory "nothingism" of the TvorNichBuro (Creative Office of the Nothingists) decried that it was in the paradox between the visual and the verbal, "where words fail," that the strategies of established power were revealed, with the slow penetration of discourses to the innermost core of each human being. This was an experience of totality, a positive and affirmative overcoming of reason as it had so far been understood, and an enshrining of change as a radical value. Dada, that is, but imbued with a confident pragmatism alien to its Central European kin, which concentrated more on a nihilism that even led to complacency and, on occasion, to the reactionary.

With this exhibition, the Museo Reina Sofía embarks on a noncanonical narrative inserted in a peculiar context. Russian Dada must be understood in its specificity as an exceptional participant in what Immanuel Wallerstein and Boaventura de Sousa Santos have more recently termed the "semiperipheries," or those spaces able to mediate in contacts between the center and the periphery. While Russia lay after 1917 at the heart of the debates and the most atavistic fears of the triumphant bourgeoisie that had emerged from the revolutions of the nineteenth century, it remained one of the historically most complex spaces for negotiation between East and West, between opposed cosmogonies and antithetical worldviews, and between reaction and revolution. For what other than this is the role that Russia has occupied, and continues to occupy, in the collective unconscious of Central and Southern Europe? How can it possibly still be regarded from Western Europe as an "other," threatening and at the same time seductive? If Jakobson considered that the October Revolution was the culmination of the political aspirations of Dada, how should we read the legacy of that initial moment from the standpoint of the present?

The advances that had taken place in nonobjective painting in the years before the chronological period of this exhibition were the result, on the one hand, of the dead end facing a cubism and futurism that had turned academic and, on the other hand, of the lyrical derivations of expressionism. While they had managed to undermine age-old principles of the representation of reality and the emotional implications of relations between apparently autonomous colors and forms, the Dadaists were moreover able to criticize their self-absorption and their surrender to the dynamics of taste, both components of bourgeois ideology. We therefore wish now to transcend the cultural logic of early socialism, materialized in the grand image and discourse of the omnipresent constructivism, through the analysis of the illogical, the negation of the inherited logos, which appears as one of the key elements in the founding moments of what Jorge Semprún described as the most influential experiment of the twentieth century.

MANUEL BORJA-VILLEL
DIRECTOR OF THE MUSEO NACIONAL
CENTRO DE ARTE REINA SOFÍA

Osip Brik
Scrapbook "Dada," ca. 1923–1924
Marcel Duchamp's *Fountain*, 1917

avec un tuyau sur la tête, se dandinaient en un exercice appelé *noir cacadou*. Tzara inventait des poëmes chimique et statique.

Le poëme statique se composait de chaises sur lesquelles étaient posées des pancartes avec un mot écrit dessus et qu'on déplaçait, après chaque baisser de rideau, en intervertissant l'ordre des mots. Janco dessinait, pour ses représentations, des costumes en papier, en carton, en chiffons, de toutes les couleurs, fixés avec des épingles, tout de spontanéité, offrant à tous le moyen « d'en faire autant », non seulement ne relevant d'aucune esthétique mais luttant contre l'apparence même de l'établissement d'un art quelconque avec tout ce qu'il comporte de règles d'un idéal formel. Périssables, volontairement laides autant qu'absurdes, ces matières choisies au hasard de l'œil et de l'esprit, symbolisaient en haillons splendides la révolte perpétuelle, le désespoir qui refuse de se laisser aller au désespoir.

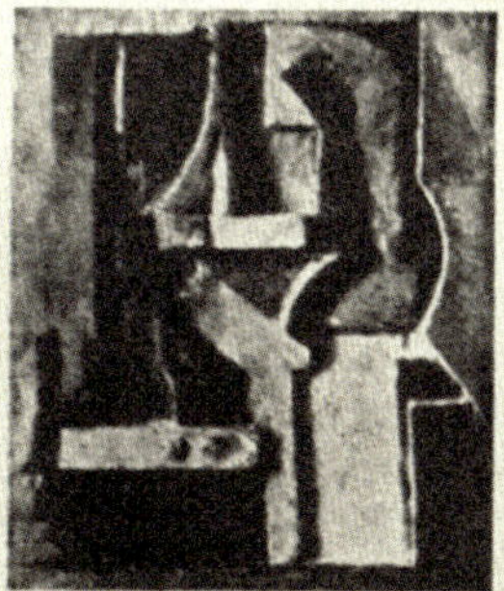

MARCEL JANCO, RELIEF EN PLATRE, ZURICH, 1918.

Dada III, en plus de son aspect extérieur qui détruisait tous les canons du bon goût de la typographie et de la mise en page et qui sapait le bon goût en général sous les lauriers de la raison et de la logique, apportait des noms nouveaux : Picabia, Reverdy, Birot, Dermée, Soupault, Huidobro, Savinio... Dada faisait tache d'huile.

Pour l'*Anthologie Dada* (N°s 4 et 5), Arp avait composé une couverture singulière, importante, et qui marque, malgré des intentions tendant vers un art abstrait evidemment opposé à Picasso dont toute l'œuvre jusque là partait d'un emprunt fait à la nature, la première cassure entre Dada et le modernisme, cassure que Picabia accentuera bientôt et qu'achevera, en 1920, l'esprit dada de Berlin, de Hanovre et de Cologne, représenté par Grosz, Heartfield, Schwitters, Baargeld et Max Ernst, auxquels se joint Arp. On peut presque dire, malgré le désir d'ordre qui la caractérise, que la couverture de *Dada* 4-5 est au cubisme ce que sont les mots sortis d'un chapeau de Tzara à la poésie du début du XXe siècle, assez sottement appelée elle aussi : poésie cubiste. Dans le papier collé de Picasso, et aussi dans ses sculptures-objets en carton et dans les matériaux qu'il avait introduits dès 1913 dans ses peintures (dont certaines sont reproduites dans les *Soirées de Paris*) le journal, le faux marbre et le faux bois sont des éléments lyriques et qui n'avaient jamais encore perdu de vue la réalité, tandis que chez Arp, et davantage encore chez Ernst, le journal, le papier peint, la photographie et la vignette, utilisés dans leurs lignes de hasard, dans leur structure toute faite adoptée telle quelle et déformée, transposée, désituée, par la facilité et l'inconnu font intégrer l'emprunté dans une recréation de l'objet, la réalité dans une réalité supérieure qui a déjà, depuis près d'un siècle un nom qui prendra, plus tard, à peine réformé, une importance capitale au point d'être la seule forme d'une nouvelle poésie. C'est en 1920, à Cologne, que les collages de Ernst ou dus à la collaboration de Arp et de Ernst atteindront leur intensité sous le nom global qui réunit une petite série d'objets et de collages, de *Fatagaga* (fabrication de tableaux garantis gazométriques).

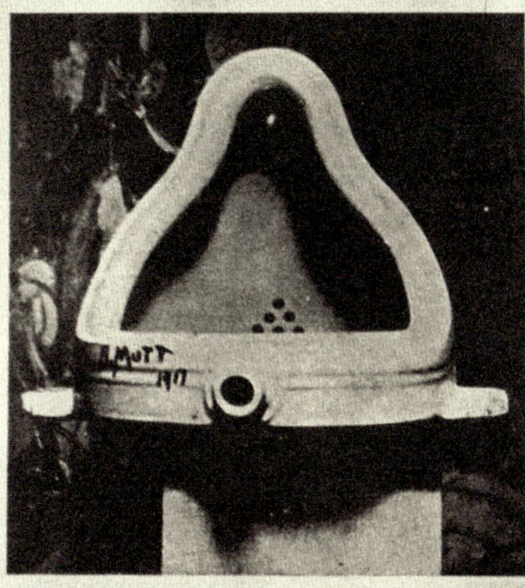

« FONTAINE », PAR R. MUTT (MARCEL DUCHAMP), EXPOSÉE AU PREMIER SALON DES INDÉPENDANTS A NEW-YORK, 1917. (PHOTO STIEGLITZ).

En dehors de quelques papiers collés comme celui que publia le *Cabaret Voltaire* et de la couverture de l'*Anthologie Dada*, qui est un journal collé sur le cartonnage, où se trouve un dessin suivi de cette mention : dada, les œuvres de Arp les plus significatives, dans la mesure où elles amorcent une destruction opérante qui entre dans l'état d'esprit dada, sont des illustrations pour deux livres de Tzara : *25 poëmes* et *cinéma calendrier du cœur abstrait*, beaucoup plus libres que celles du livre de Richard Huelsenbeck, rigides, formelles, aspirant à la pureté de la forme. Pour Arp, l'art abstrait qui était sa préoccupation et qui ainsi le séparait un tant soit peu de Tzara et de Huelsenbeck, partisans du désordre systématique et de la confusion des arts pour leur destruction, se réduisait à une volonté continuelle de ne jamais rappeler la nature. Pourtant il convient de signaler ici certaines expériences auxquelles se livra Arp, qui ont une portée d'autant plus grande qu'elles concordent avec des préoccupations qui jouèrent plus tard un rôle important dans la théorie des prospections à travers le domaine de l'inconscient. Arp traça sur le papier, chaque matin, le même dessin et obtint ainsi, inspiré ou non, une suite de dessins dont les variations lui marquaient les courbes de l'automatisme. Il s'en remit aussi au hasard en plaçant sur un carton des papiers découpés sans attention et coloriés : ces papiers étant posés sur leur face en couleur, Arp secouait le carton et les disséminait, puis il les collait sur le carton en respectant l'ordonnance de la disposition et des couleurs qu'il avait ainsi obtenue par le concours du hasard.

En 1919, il se forma alors, à Zurich, sous l'instigation de Hans Richter, sortant du groupe expressionniste allemand *Die Aktion* qui déjà durant la guerre, avait établi comme principe que l'artiste doit prendre part d'une façon active à la politique, c'est-à-dire, à l'époque, s'inscrire contre la guerre et aller avec la révolution, s'est formé un groupe de peintres de tendances disparates, sous le nom de *Association des Artistes révolutionnaires*. Cette association, guidée par la crainte que la révolution ne laissât de côté les artistes, voulait tenter d'incorporer à la révolution, à l'heure même où elle éclata à Munich et à Budapest, les artistes esthétiquement révolutionnaires. Certains peintres dada crurent bon de s'inscrire à cette association et d'y souscrire, qui eut une existence éphémère ne dépassant pas quelques semaines. Cette tendance spirituelle et artistique, reprise à peine plus tard par des artistes russes sous le nom de constructivisme q

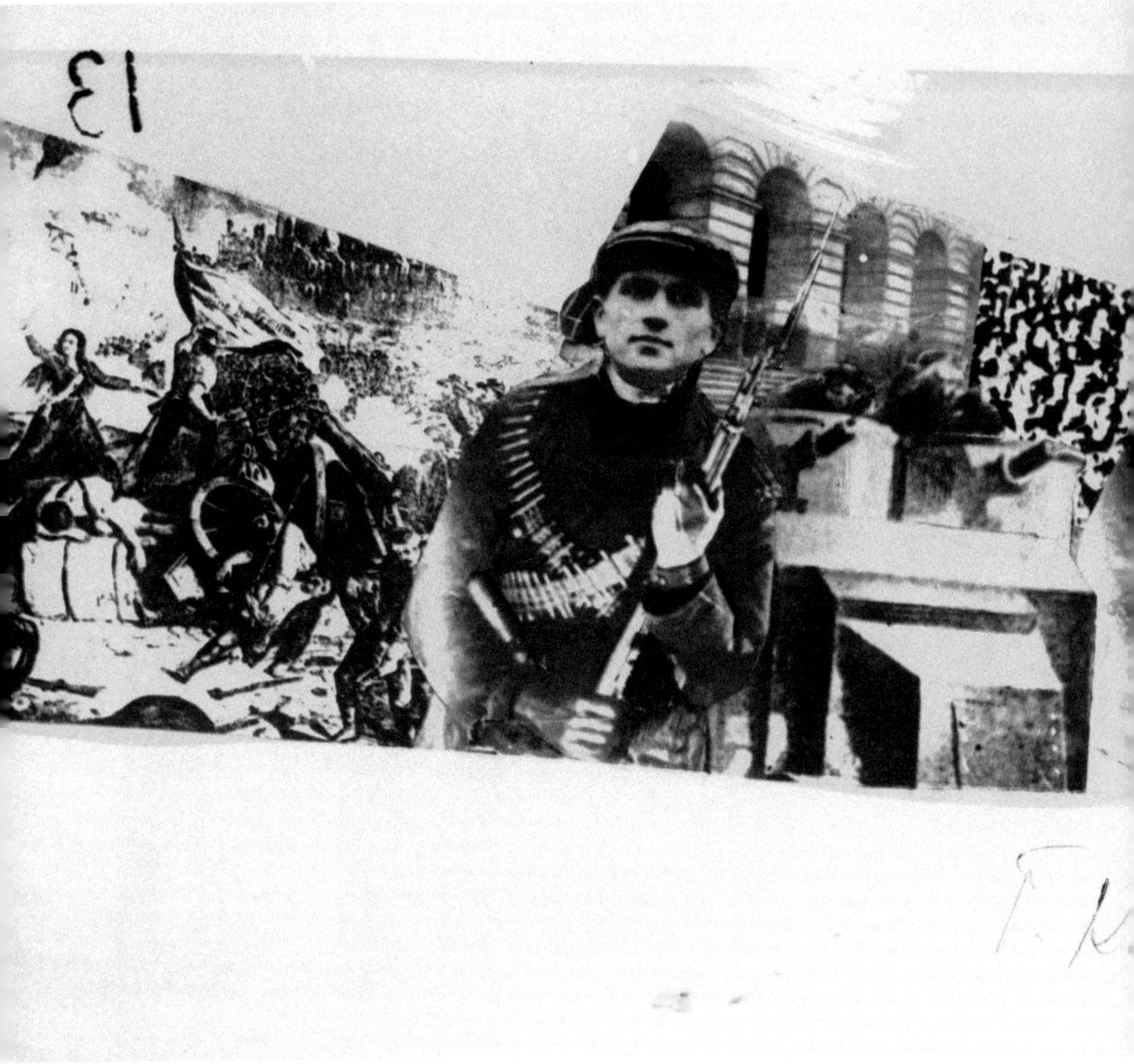

Gustav Klutsis
Design for the billboard *Storm: Strike on Counterrevolution*, ca. 1918

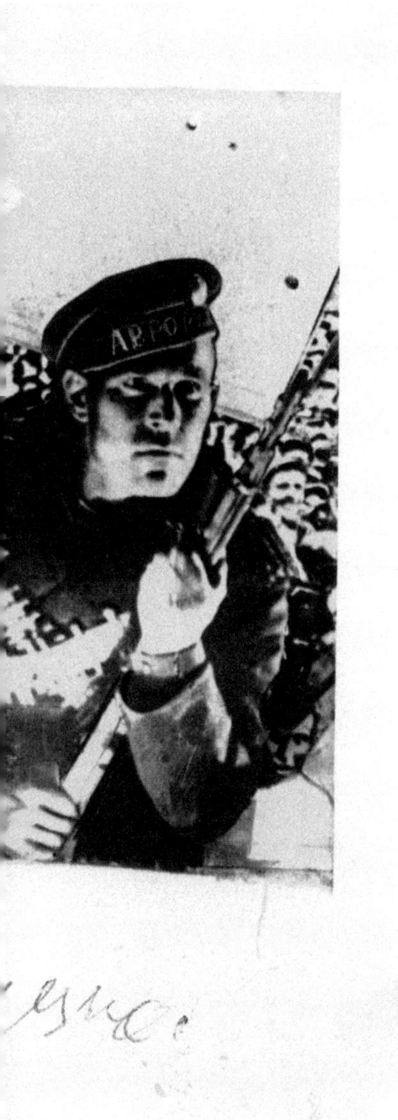

PREFACE

Russian Dada is the first major exhibition to approach Russian avant-garde art from the perspective of the canons associated with the international Dada movement. The exhibited works gathered from Russian and European museums and private collections were produced at the height of Dada's flourishing, between World War I and the death of Vladimir Lenin in 1924. Like the Dadaists, the selected Russian artists strove for internationalism, fused the verbal and visual, and engaged in eccentric practices and pacifist actions, including outrageous performances and antiwar campaigns. The exhibition emphasizes the art's multimedia character and its political implications during the world war, the two Russian revolutions, and the change in leadership from Lenin to Joseph Stalin.

In his seminal book *Dada: Art and Anti-Art*, Hans Richter states, "Curiously enough, Dada tendencies seem to have made their first appearance in Russia, where the Futurist influence was still very strong."[1] A decade later, the first Western publication of works by critic Nikolai Khardzhiev, a contemporary of Kazimir Malevich, would reverberate with Richter's account by identifying the proto-Dadaist characteristics in the first transrational opera, *Victory over the Sun* (1913). Much earlier in the century, the formalist critic Roman Jakobson and art historian Abram Efros had linked the aesthetic radicalism of Dada, as manifested in Marcel Duchamp's *Fountain* of 1917, with the October

1. Hans Richter, *Dada: Art and Anti-Art* (London: Thames and Hudson, 1965), 198

Revolution of the same year. And yet, despite these acknowledgments of what Leah Dickerman designates "dada tactics,"[2] as well as Filippo Tommaso Marinetti's conclusion (during his visit in 1914) that Russians were "false futurists," the term *futurism* has stuck to the prerevolutionary avant-garde.

Russian Dada begins by picking up on these references to the proto-Dadaist strategies of those avant-gardists who adamantly refused to associate with Italian futurism. They replaced futurists with *budetliane* (men of the future) and engaged in a critique of Italian futurism's fidelity to urbanism, rationality, and technological progress. Alogical and transrational creativity, saturated with laughter and perverse parody, became the operational devices they used to shock the public, disparage traditional artistic and social values, and mock technical skills. Perhaps the *budetliane*'s most important gesture was their rejection of Western modernism's celebration of originality and individual authorship, values they replaced with a proto-Dadaist model of multistylistic and collective practice coined *everythingism*. In the atmosphere of this theoretical strategy, Ivan Kliun, Mikhail Larionov, Malevich, Aleksei Morgunov, Ivan Puni, Olga Rozanova, Vladimir Tatlin, Kirill Zdanevich, and Ilia Zdanevich exhibited together in the first resonant, antiacademic exhibitions, introducing nonobjective art, paintings with assemblage, reliefs made from found objects, and installation works built using readymades. These forms of production proved to be instrumental for Dada.

Like the European Dadaists, Russian avant-gardists loathed and suffered from World War I, whose outbreak in 1914 intensified the awareness of the political significance of their cultural revolt. Aleksei Kruchenykh, Malevich, Vladimir Mayakovsky, and Rozanova prompted antiwar campaigns, creating posters and collages that denounced militarism and German brutality. The February and October Revolutions, which took place in the last phase of World War I, unshackled the leftist and anarchist factions to which many avant-gardists belonged. Together they could now fertilize real politics and reach out to members of the international art community who shared their views. Among these, the Dadaists were frontrunners. In the revolutionary period, the artists and poets who are united in *Russian Dada* engaged in parallel practices based on reason and antireason, sense and nonsense, rational design and chance-based collages, absurdist and political theater, mocking and

2. Leah Dickerman, "Introduction," in *Dada: Zurich, Berlin, Hannover, Cologne, New York, Paris*, ed. Leah Dickerman (Washington, DC: National Gallery of Art, 2006), 7.

propagandistic cinema. In this kind of formal and semantic dichotomy, Russian *da, da* (yes, yes) was converted into *nyet, nyet* (no, no), averting the clear-cut consumption of Bolshevik ideology and the political specificity of public spectacles as well as refracting an uncritical submission to positivist constructivism and to a purist form of suprematism.

Before Lenin returned to Russia in 1917, he was a frequent visitor to Cabaret Voltaire in Zurich, the founding site of Dada. His death in 1924 coincided with the end of Dada and the beginning of surrealism. In Russia, this was a turning point from the hyperproductive and multifaceted revolutionary epoch to the rise of cultural and political rivalry, the consequences of which were no laughing matter. The *budetliane* concept of a ray as a metaphor of gushing new visions, converted by Mayakovsky into a disseminator of the revolutionary spirit, was reshaped into "the death ray," a device of danger and suppression.

Russian Dada also builds a long, protracted bridge between the Dadaists and those Russian artists who visited or lived in Paris, Berlin, and New York in the early 1920s. Natalia Goncharova, El Lissitzky, Larionov, Puni, Sergei Sharshun, and Ilia Zdanevich joined various Dadaist factions, exhibited in Berlin's Der Sturm gallery (a staunch promoter of Dada), and organized and participated in key Dadaist events, such as the soirée *The Bearded Heart* (1923). Lissitzky commenced his activities by mechanically reproducing *Prouns* as well as the designs he made at the time of *Victory over the Sun*, restaged in Vitebsk in 1920. As a result, he was able to effectively popularize Malevich's and his own mode of nonobjectivity and globalize the characters of this iconic proto-Dadaist performance. Tatlin's *Monument to the Third International* became the Dadaists' epitome of antiart, and Mayakovsky and critic Osip Brik's European trips made Dada publications and reproductions of key works available in Russia. Katherine S. Dreier, the legendary collector committed to promoting Dada in New York, considered the Soviet avant-garde highly relevant and influential for her agenda. The iconoclast David Burliuk, who arrived in New York in 1921 after escaping the Bolsheviks' purge of anarchists, joined Dreier and her artists, and soon his paintings were displayed in her apartment next to Duchamp's. These and other examples of the Russians' integration into Dada milieus, along with their correspondence with Tristan Tzara, Paul Éluard, and Francis Picabia, compellingly demonstrate the legitimacy of Russian Dada.

MARGARITA TUPITSYN
GUEST CURATOR AND EDITOR

CONTENTS

PUTTING RUSSIA ON THE DADA MAP

Margarita Tupitsyn

Marcel Duchamp
L.H.O.O.Q., illustration on the cover of
the journal *391*, no. 12, Paris, March 1920

391

Au pluriel

“ Une définition n'a jamais été qu'un mot pour un autre — et le commun des mortels l'appelle erreur ”.

De plus en plus, de moins en moins, Trois cent quatre vingt onze est un oiseau à poils, la Vierge satisfaite le tient dans ses bras, la pluie des grands jours, un biceps bien tendre, une ombre à plusieurs, les paupières comme des ongles ou les ongles comme des heures ou.

Petit, petit trois cent quatre vingt onze de ma mère et des liqueurs de dessert, de plus en plus, de moins en moins, une lumière derrière un coup de poing, un coup de poing sur une lumière.

Je suis comme les autres, je vais au café. Aussitôt, j'entends : “ Garçon un 391 des dimanches ”. Je suis discret, je ne répète jamais ce que j'écoute dans les water-closets.

Un aimable désordre simili or n'étant qu'un effet de l'art, j'ai pu enjamber deux ou trois fois dans ma vie une belle religieuse aux cornes d'ivoire, une belle, très belle.

Le livre sur lequel j'écris est ouvert à la page 202.

En le lisant, les Cubistes ont bien pleuré.

PAUL ELUARD.

Eh bien non, la lettre signée Paul Eluard n'était pas de Reverdy ! Je m'excuse infiniment auprès de celui-ci, d'une réponse qui ne peut s'adresser à lui mais bien au véritable auteur de la lettre. Ce dernier n'aura qu'à relire deux fois la note parue dans “ *Proverbe* ”, en remplaçant le nom du sympathique Reverdy par le sien, il sera frappé de voir combien cette note lui est facilement applicable !

FRANCIS PICABIA.

TABLEAU DADA par MARCEL DUCHAMP

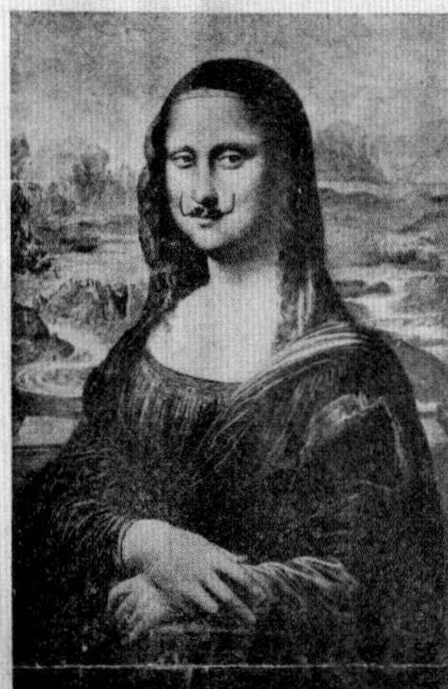

L H O O Q

Manifeste DADA

Les cubistes veulent couvrir Dada de neige ; ça vous étonne mais c'est ainsi, ils veulent vider la neige de leur pipe pour recouvrir Dada.
Tu en es sûr ?
Parfaitement, les faits sont révélés par des bouches grotesques.
Ils pensent que Dada peut les empêcher de pratiquer ce commerce odieux : Vendre de l'art très cher.
L'art vaut plus cher que le saucisson, plus cher que les femmes, plus cher que tout.
L'art est visible comme Dieu ! (voir Saint-Sulpice).
L'art est un produit pharmaceutique pour imbéciles.
Les tables tournent grâce à l'esprit ; les tableaux et autres œuvres d'art sont comme les tables-coffres-forts, l'esprit est dedans et devient de plus en plus génial suivant les prix de salles de ventes.
Comédie, comédie, comédie, comédie, comédie, mes chers amis.
Les marchands n'aiment pas la peinture, ils connaissent le mystère de l'esprit..........
Achetez les reproductions des autographes.
Ne soyez donc pas snobs, vous ne serez pas moins intelligents parce que le voisin possèdera une chose semblable à la vôtre.
Plus de chiures de mouches sur les murs.
Il y en aura tout de même, c'est évident, mais un peu moins.
Dada bien certainement va être de plus en plus détesté, son coupe-file lui permettant de couper les processions en chantant “ Viens Poupoule ”, quel sacrilège !!!
Le cubisme représente la disette des idées.
Ils ont cubé les tableaux des primitifs, cubé les sculptures nègres, cubé les violons, cubé les guitares, cubé les journaux illustrés, cubé la merde et les profils de jeunes filles, maintenant il faut cuber de l'argent !!!
Dada, lui, ne veut rien, rien, rien, il fait quelque chose pour que le public dise : “nous ne comprenons rien, rien, rien”.
“ Les Dadaïstes ne sont rien, rien, rien, bien certainement ils n'arriveront à rien, rien, rien ”.

Francis PICABIA
qui ne sait rien, rien, rien.

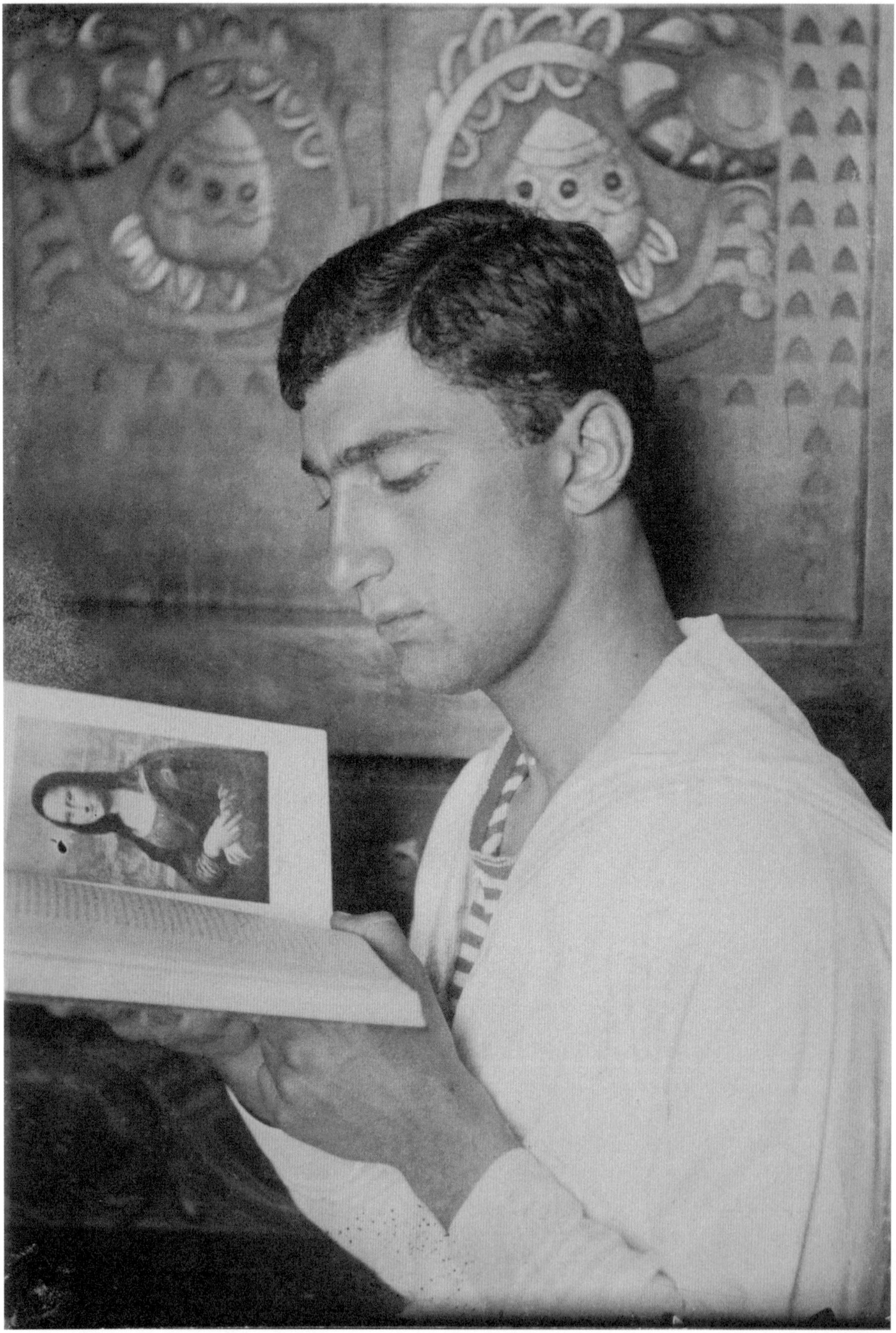

Anti-futurism, Proto-Dadaism, and Everythingism

In Russia everything that did not resemble nature was considered futurism.[1]
—Kazimir Malevich, "Autobiography," 1933

Anonymous
Ilia Zdanevich, 1912

A 1912 photograph shows Ilia Zdanevich, at the time a law student in Saint Petersburg, posing for a camera while gazing at a book reproduction of Leonardo da Vinci's *Mona Lisa*.[2] p. 22 Stolen from the Louvre in 1911, the painting had become a lost original, prompting both lament and mockery. Having read Filippo Tomasso Marinetti's first manifesto, from 1909, in translation, and several years ahead of Marcel Duchamp's *L.H.O.O.Q.* (1919), p. 21 Zdanevich chose the *Mona Lisa* as a target for theatrical defamation when, on January 18, 1912, during his first public lecture in the Troitsky Theater, he stated that the painting was not worth finding and claimed that a cheap ready-made such as a shoe should supersede it.[3] "Art must reflect contemporaneity, in my opinion, a pair of contemporary shoes is more precious, more elevated and useful than all Leonardo da Vincis. Giaconda, go to hell, Giaconda! We should represent a big city. We should paint slaps and street fights."[4] Two years after these proto-Dadaist manifestations in Russia, Zdanevich elaborated on the significance of mass-produced objects for twentieth-century art in the lecture "Adoration of a Shoe," which took place at the Saint Petersburg cabaret Wondering Dog on April 17, 1914 (three months after Zdanevich's meeting with Marinetti in Saint Petersburg).[5] p. 24

1. Unless otherwise noted, all translations are the author's.

2. Ilia Zdanevich scholar Gayraud Régis, in an email to me on June 30, 2017, confirmed the date of this image as 1912 and explains that the reason it is dated 1919–1920 in the exhibition catalogue *Iliazd* (Paris: Centre Georges Pompidou, 1978) was the organizers' reluctance to believe the photograph was taken before Marcel Duchamp's *L.H.O.O.Q*.

3. The lecture was organized by Saint Petersburg's Union of Youth, a society of artists and writers formed in 1909, the same year Marinetti's first manifesto was published. The union was a financial and logistical umbrella for the first exhibitions and public appearances of the avant-garde.

4. Zdanevich's speech was recounted by a contemporary critic, N. Breshko-Breshkovsky, in the newspaper *Peterburgskaia gazeta*. See I. E. Vasil'ev, "Il'iazd: vekhi zhizni i tvorchestva I. M. Zdanevicha," *Izvestiia ural'skogo gosudarstvennogo universiteta*, no. 24 (2002): 178.

5. See Zdanevich to Marinetti, January 28, 1914 [see p. 263 of the present catalogue]; and Marinetti to Zdanevich, June 1922.

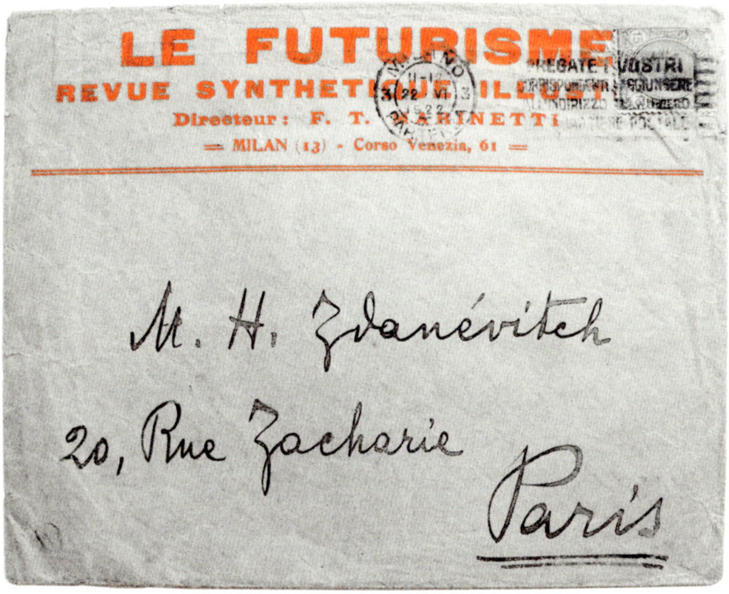

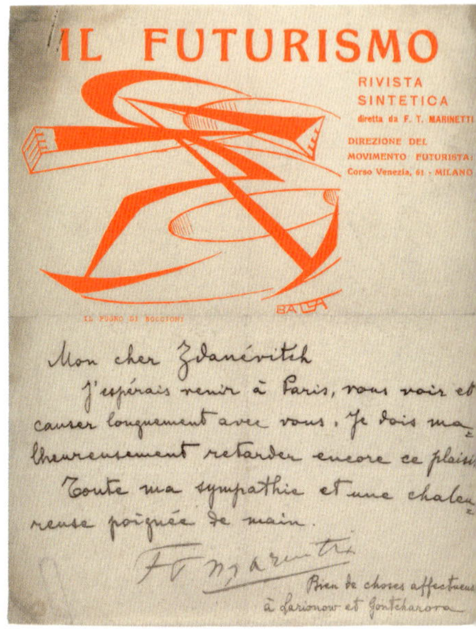

Challenging Italian futurism's fascination with progress and technology, Zdanevich hailed "common, mass-manufactured" object as "a symbol of today," forecasting that "in thousands of years, to those who think of the twentieth century there will appear a specter not of an airplane . . . not of futurism . . . not of wireless telegraph . . . not of Marinetti or of Tolstoy, but of a shoe."[6]

Through his brother Kirill, Zdanevich met and joined forces with Mikhail Larionov, the outrageous avant-gardist who formed groups and organized exhibitions with such scandalous names as *Donkey's Tail* (1911–1912) and *Target* (1913). Larionov's fixation on negation for the sake of negation turned him into a detractor of the absurdities of contemporary life, which he deconstructed with what the German Dadaist Hans Richter called "daemonic humour" and graffiti-like writing within the space of his paintings.[7] Larionov and the poet Velimir Khlebnikov, another friend and collaborator, shared Richter's awe at the creative power of laughter. Khlebnikov's short poem "Incantation by Laughter" (1908–1909) amply corresponds to Richter's eventual claim that laughter was "the only guarantee of the seriousness with which, on our voyage of self-discovery, we practiced anti-art."[8]

Together with Natalia Goncharova, his partner and equally an advocate of primitivism, p. 25 Larionov launched rayonism (*Luchizm*), which

Filippo Tommaso Marinetti
Envelope and letter to Ilia Zdanevich,
Paris, June 1922

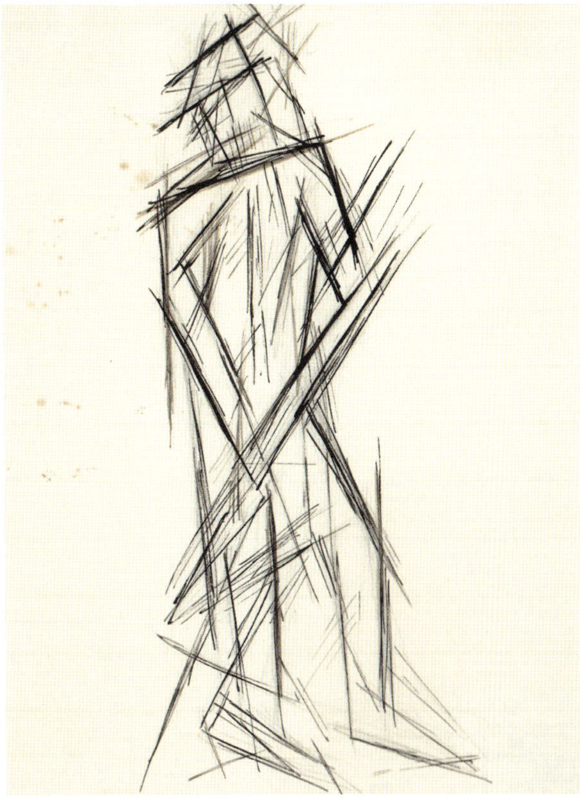

Mikhail Larionov
Man, 1913

Kirill Zdanevich
Composition, 1916

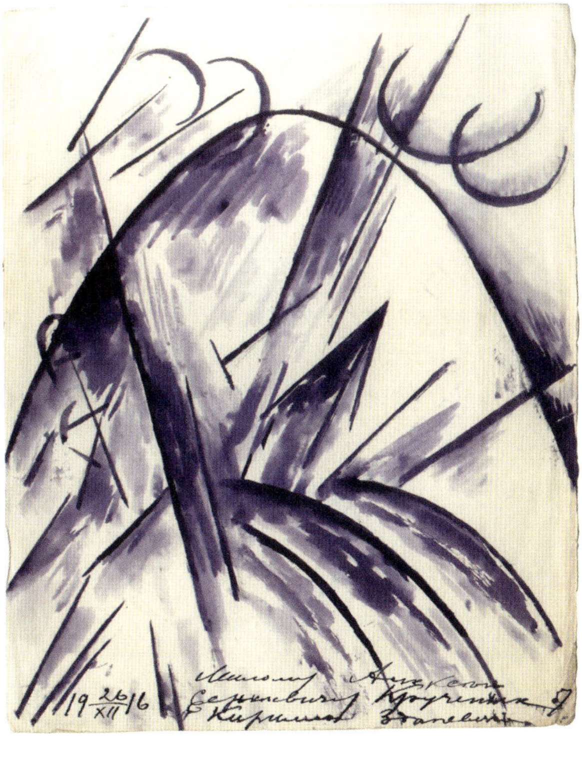

6. "Poklonenie boshmaku," in Il'ia Zdanevich, *Futurizm i vsechestvo, 1912–1914*, ed. A. V. Krusanov, 2 vols. (Moscow: Gileia, 2014), 1:17.

7. Hans Richter, *Dada: Art and Anti-Art* (London: Thames and Hudson, 1965), 182.

8. Ibid., 65.

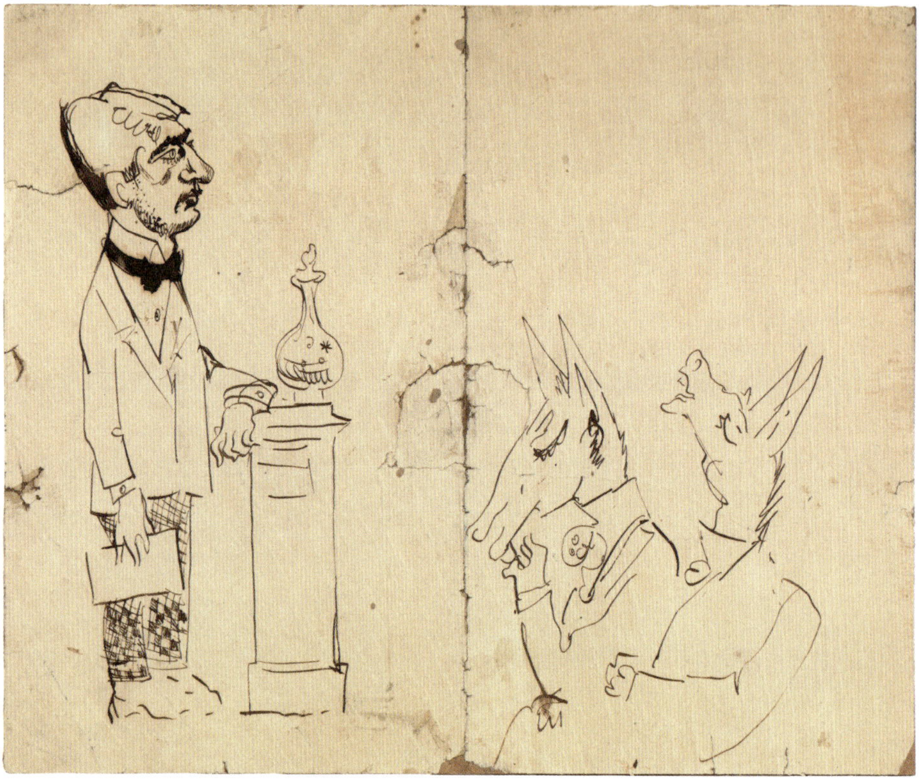

operated through an array of radiant lines. Zdanevich and artist Mikhail Le Dantiu—who, along with Goncharova, Kazimir Malevich, Vladimir Tatlin, Aleksei Morgunov, and Kirill
p. 26 Zdanevich, took part in *Donkey's Tail* and *Target*—helped Larionov theorize his inventions into a broader aesthetic system dubbed "everythingism" (*vsechestvo*).[9] Zdanevich's often scandalous promotion of everythingism is smartly interpreted in two 1915 sketches by Sigizmund Valishevsky that show Zdanevich lecturing to a group of donkeys. In the more detailed version, the donkeys are undersigned with the names of local leading conservative artists and critics as well as Marinetti (whom Larionov had similarly reproached during the former's visit to Russia in early 1914).[10]

9. Tristan Tzara's Dada manifesto of 1918 also uses the metaphor of crossing light rays as the guardians of time.

10. On Marinetti's visit to Russia, see N. I. Khardzhiev, "'Veselyi god' Maiakovskogo," in *Stat'i ob avangarde*, ed. Rudol'f Duganov, Iurii Arpishkin, and Andrei Sarab'ianov, 2 vols. (Moscow: RA, 1997), 2:18–31; and Aleksandr Parnis, "Benedikt Lifshits i F. T. Marinetti: k istorii odnoi polemiki," in *Terent'evskii sbornik: 1996*, ed. S. Kudriavtsev (Moscow: Gileia, 1996), 225–49.

11. Richter, *Dada*, 65.

12. On this subject, see my "Collaborating on the Paradigm of the Future," *Art Journal* 52, no. 4 (Winter 1993): 18–24.

Sigizmund Valishevsky
Untitled (Ilia Zdanevich lecturing donkeys), 1915

Ilin (Nal)
Futurism in a Village, 1914

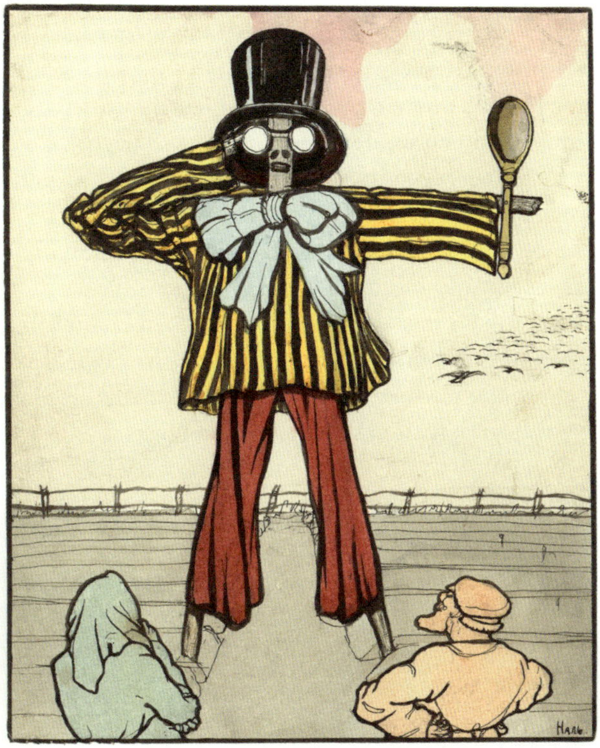

The drawings' iconography is a reminder that Larionov's *Donkey's Tail* referred to an occasion in 1910 when French critics praised a picture submitted to the Salon des Indépendants that turned out to have been made by a donkey (whose tail art students had tied a paintbrush). Valishevsky expanded on this stunt as an example of old-fashioned critics' inability to evaluate modern art. In the detailed version Larionov is also included as a donkey-waiter, preferring a common profession to the phony highbrow community. Valishevsky's spoofs evoke another comment by Richter on the self-deprecating tactics of Dada: "We laughed at ourselves just as we laughed at Emperor, King and Country, fat bellies and baby-pacifiers."[11]

Striving to undermine European modernists' fixation on originality and authorial significance, everythingism was an unrestrained amalgamation of all other styles. It announced that pastiche and copying result in an independent artwork.[12] On an unconscious level, this paradigm of appropriation liberated Russian avant-gardists from accusations of Western modernism's influence. According to art historian Rosalind Krauss, "pastiche mocks the modernist project of a self-realization achieved through control of what is internal to the medium itself . . . pastiche asserts an almost endless access to 'style' as a series of personal and capricious choices open to the artist-subject as a kind of consumer browsing among compositional options."[13] Thus, everythingism's act of negation through an acceptance of everything suggests an equation between the Russian *nyet* (no) and *da* (yes) and predates similar Dadaist equations, as in the leaflet *Dada Raises Everything* (1921), which also includes the phrase "Futurism is dead."[14]

Like the Dadaists at Cabaret Voltaire in Zurich, members of the radical avant-garde milieu acted not only through exhibitions but public disputes and performances such as Zdanevich's *Mona Lisa* lecture. In fact, Malevich later claimed "Futurism was mostly expressed in behavior in relation to the given condition of society. This is why Futurism manifested itself much more in performances than in artworks. Artists and poets smash everything."[15] This was an effective tool to explode the bourgeois society and to create the kind of public disorder conveyed in Nikolai Kulbin's 1913 cover for the book *Vzorval,* a neologism that
p. 29 best translates to "Explodity." (Earlier Kulbin had founded the cabaret Wondering Dog, depicted as a corporate body in Le Dantiu's 1914 draw-
p. 30 ing *Igor Severianin's March to Berlin.*) Kulbin's doodle for the *Explodity* cover shows a fervent speaker and an agitated audience about to topple him. It could easily be an illustration for a debate that took place on March 23, 1913, at Moscow's Polytechnic Museum, organized in conjunction with the *Target* exhibition, which ended with a fistfight and police involvement. There is little doubt, however, that the "exploder" is Larionov, for inside the book appears his portrait, also by Kulbin.

These kinds of theatrical disputes led to efforts to revolutionize theater and adopt cinema for broader dissemination of avant-garde performances. The now-classic absurdist opera *Victory over the Sun* (1913) was a first step in this direction. The idea came from the Union of Youth and immediately caught Larionov's attention. In a contemporary newspaper interview he revealed his concept for an avant-garde theater without a stage, where viewers would sit "on a wire grid under the ceiling."[16] He emphasized that the music should sound like "an orchestra tuning up its instruments"; in such a theater, "actors would play not only people but also props, costumes . . . it will not be so much a staging of plays . . . as hoaxing theater."[17] The next move was the issuing of the manifesto "Why We Paint Ourselves" (1913), signed by Larionov, Goncharova, Le Dantiu, and Ilia Zdanevich, and claiming that painting one's

Nikolai Kulbin
Cover of the book *Explodity*
by Aleksei Kruchenykh, Saint
Petersburg, 1913

body frees the artist from isolation and ego and allows for life's invasion. The phrase "Our painting is the newsman" envisions the artist as a walking kiosk committed, in opposition to the official press, to delivering an independent message.[18] Painted, Larionov and Goncharova played in Vladimir Kasianov's silent (now lost) film *Drama in the Futurists' Cabaret no. 13* (1913), launched nearly concurrently with *Victory over the Sun*. A spoof of crime films, it positions the avant-garde in terms of an aesthetic of risk and criminality.

Larionov's concept of transgressive theater and his readiness to abandon easel art positioned him as a prime candidate to manage the stage design of *Victory over the Sun*.[19] Yet

13. Rosalind E. Krauss, *The Picasso Papers* (New York: Farrar, Straus and Giroux, 1998), 17.

14. Although Mayakovsky first visited Paris in 1922, he most likely received this leaflet directly from Tzara, whom he met in Paris during his second visit (November 2–December 20, 1924). He also returned with Tzara's *7 Dada Manifestos*, published in 1924.

15. Kazimir Malevich, "Avtobiografiia," in *Malevich o sebe, sovremenniki o Maleviche: pisma, dokumenty, vospominaniia, kritika*, ed. I. A. Vakar and T. N. Mikhienko, 2 vols. (Moscow: RA, 2004), 1:39.

16. Larionov is quoted as saying this during an interview with *Moskovskaia gazeta* on September 9, 1913, in I. E. Vasil'iev, "Il'iazd: vekhi zhizni i tvorchestva I. M. Zdanevicha," 180–81.

17. Ibid.

18. Ilya Zdanevich and Mikhail Larionov, "Why We Paint Ourselves: A Futurist Manifesto, 1913," in *Russian Art of the Avant-Garde: Theory and Criticism, 1902–1934*, ed. and trans. John E. Bowlt (New York: Viking Press, 1976), 82.

19. Sergei Diaghilev would soon after invite Larionov to design his theatrical productions in Paris.

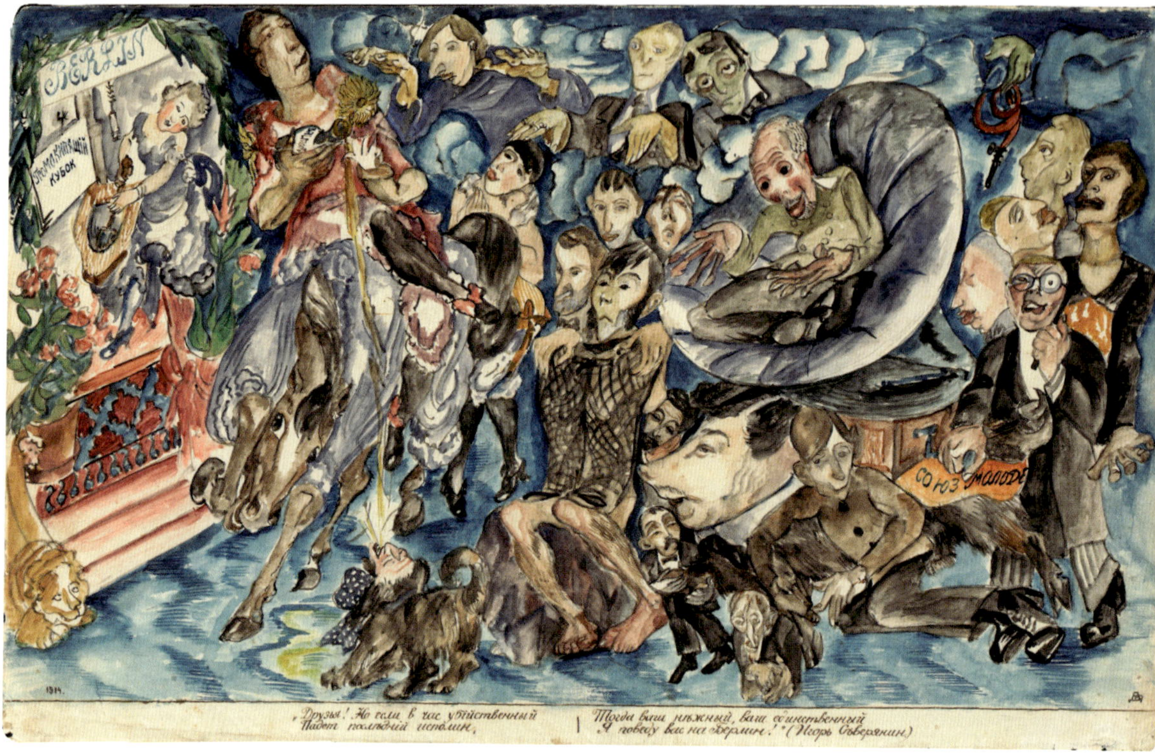

it was Malevich who got the job. Having known Larionov since the organization of *Donkey's Tail*, Malevich in his peasant series shared Larionov's and Goncharova's regard for primitivist sources and renditions. Yet Malevich lacked Larionov's parodying audacity, a quality that fits pp. 32, 44, 45 more amply *Victory over the Sun*'s overall "alogic extremism" and the transrational language (*zaum*) of its prologue and libretto, written by poets Khlebnikov and Aleksei Kruchenykh respectively.[20] The iconic costumes Malevich made for the opera animated the silent and frozen peasants of his paintings and converted them into loud and mechanical strongmen enfolded in multicolored geometric shapes and heralding "imminent political change."[21] The historian of the Russian avant-garde Nikolai Khardzhiev, who had a chance to discuss the opera with Matiushin, provides an invaluable sketch:

> After lifting a curtain, action did not start. Behind the lifted curtain there was another curtain made from the white calico and against its background the author read a prologue. Then two "colorful" characters appeared from behind the curtain, tearing it in half. Calico tore with a rattle, the curtain

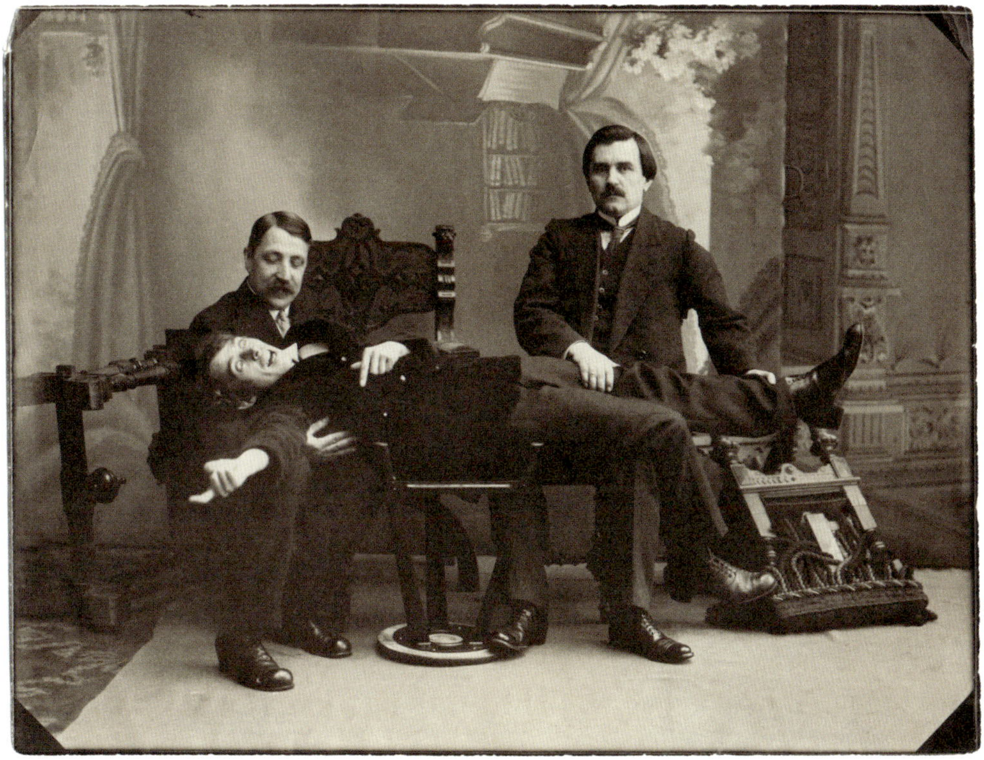

Mikhail Le Dantiu
Igor Severianin's March to Berlin, 1914

Karl Bulla
Mikhail Matiushin, Aleksei Kruchenykh, and Kazimir Malevich, 1913

20. Nikolai Khardzhiev, "Sud'ba Kruchenykh," in *Stat'i ob avangarde*, ed. Duganov, Arpishkin, and Sarab'ianov, 1:302. In 1914, Malevich publicly defied Larionov's scandalous methods of publicity and asked that he not be associated with "the Rayonist Larionov." Khudozhnik K. Malevich, "Otmezhevavshiesia ot Larionova, pismo v redaktsiiu," *Nov'*, no. 12 (1914).

21. Khardzhiev, "Sud'ba Kruchenykh," 1:302.

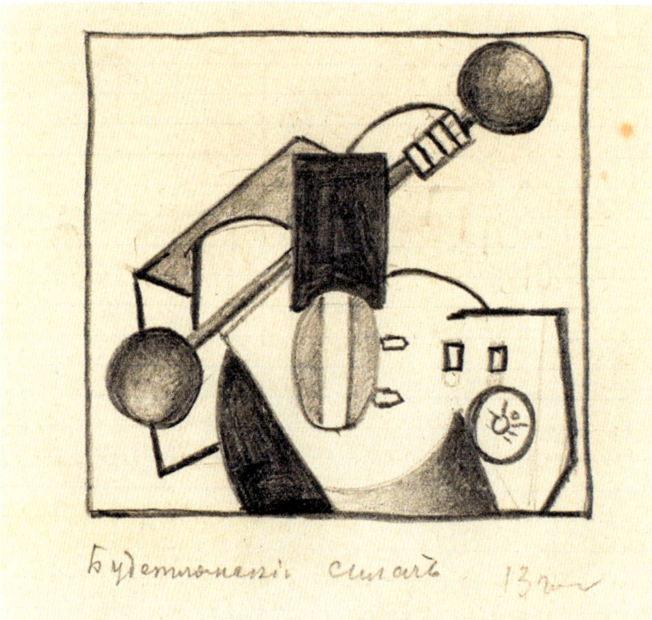

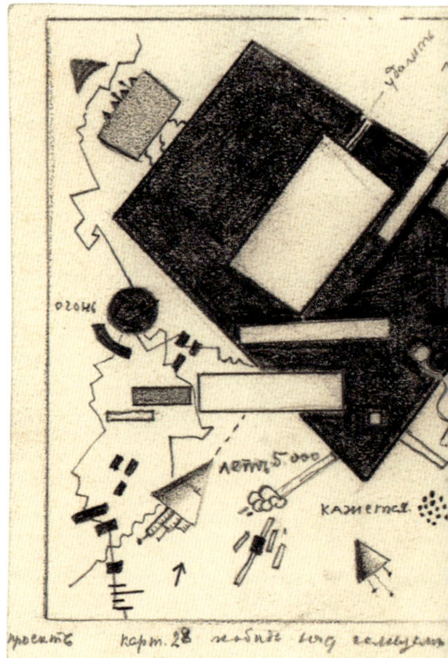

Kazimir Malevich
Alogic Composition, design for *Victory over the Sun* (*Budetlianin Strongman*), 1913

Kazimir Malevich
Stage design for *Victory over the Sun*, 1913

Kazimir Malevich
Design for the curtain for the opera *Victory over the Sun*, 1913

was pushed apart and "*budetliane* strongmen" appeared on a stage dressed in space-like suits. Their wide shoulders were at the level of a top of a head, over which towered an attached cube. Two *budetliane* strongmen moved like robots and in accordance with the author's remarks, spoke "vulgarly and downwards."[22]

Khardzhiev dubbed *Victory over the Sun* "antimilitarist" and thus "diametrically opposite to the theory and practice of Italian futurists," which endorsed the "triumph of machine and electricity" and "propagated imperialist expansion."[23] Khardzhiev concluded that the opera's librettist, Kruchenykh, could "be called 'the first Dadaist,' forerunning by three years the formation of this trend in Western Europe."[24] He does not mention a seminal
p. 33 black square drawn on a calico curtain, linking

22. Ibid., 303–4. *Budetliane* or *budetlianin*, a neologism coined by Khlebnikov, means "men (or a man) of the future."

23. Ibid., 302–3.

24. Ibid., 302, 305.

25. Mikhail Larionov and Il'ia Zdanevich, "Nashe prazdnichnoe interv'iu s futuristami," *Teatr v karikaturakh*, no. 1 (1914): 19.

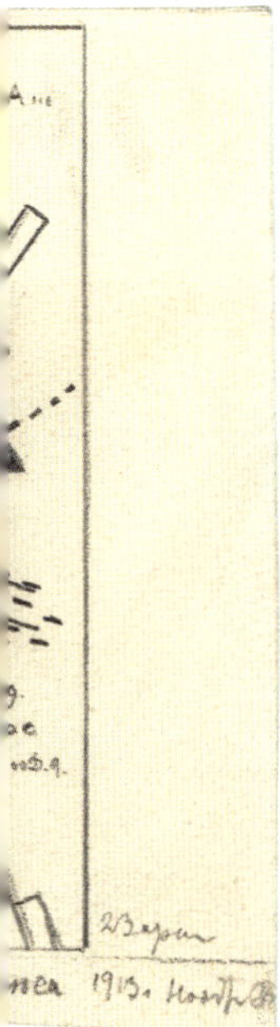

nonobjectivity and nonsense. Born as a theatrical prop, *Black Square* was rooted in theater and created a new kind of a modernist painting, void of autonomy.

In 1914, Zdanevich and Larionov published "Our Festive Interview with Futurists," a laconic exchange riddled with contradictions and subverting the program of rationality Marinetti had spelled out during his visit in January.[25] Published in a magazine with a suitable name, *Theater in Caricatures*, and eventually dubbed the "Yes-Manifesto" (*Da-Manifesto*), the interview is a game of mutually exclusive negative and affirmative declarations, such as saying "yes" to the inquiry "are you futurists?" and negating it directly after. Such dissonance based on the equation "yes = no" predates the Dadaists' declared postulate "Dada is anti-Dada."

In 1915, several pivotal exhibitions pursued everythingism's dynamic creativity and consolidation of art movements groomed in Russia and Europe. Endorsement of nonobjectivity, primitivism, the use of ready-made materials and objects, recitals of unconventional poetry, and readings of scandalous manifestos matched social and artistic intentions of the first Dada group, formed in early 1916 in Zurich. Ignoring local resistance to Italian futurism, artists Ivan Puni and Ksenia Boguslavskaia subtitled *Tramway V*, which opened on March 3, 1915, "the first futurist exhibition." Puni was of Italian descent and lived and studied in Paris before the war—hence, he was not so much concerned with separating himself from either cubism or futurism. Larionov and Goncharova's equivalence of an artist with a housepainter ("We march hand in hand with our ordinary housepainters") mirrored formalist critic Viktor Shklovsky's portrait of Puni as a masked troublemaker ("A housepainter is walking with a long ladder on his shoulder. He is modest and quiet. But his ladder hits people's hats, breaks glass, stops trams, destroys houses.").[26]

Tramway V was a meeting place for international isms (everythingism), as its eleven participants included Russian artists who had studied in Europe or visited the Continent before the war and others who had been responsible for developing local stylistic paradigms. What they shared was an aggressive mood, a desire to "spit every day on art's
p. 36 altar."[27] Among such "spits" inaugurated in
Tramway V were Malevich's alogic canvases
p. 41 *Englishman in Moscow* (1914), *Woman at Ad-*
p. 39 *vertising Column* (1914), and *Cow and Violin*
(ca. 1913–1915).[28] In all of them Malevich created "alogical juxtaposition[s]" in order to play out "a struggle with logism, naturalness, a

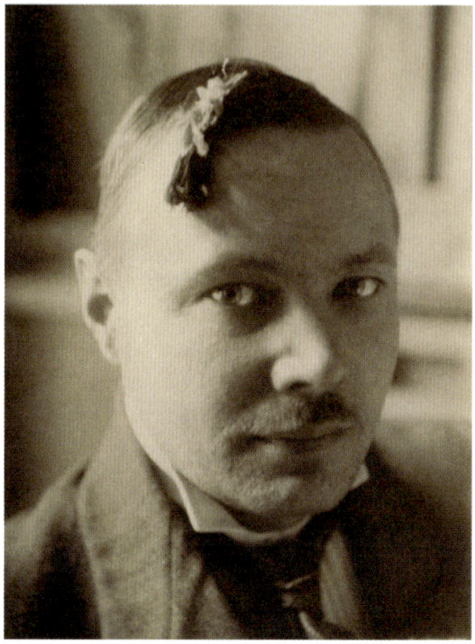

Anonymous
Mikhail Larionov, 1913

26. Mikhail Larionov and Natalya Goncharova, "Rayonists and Futurists: A Manifesto, 1913," in *Russian Art of the Avant-Garde*, ed. and trans. Bowlt, 90; and Viktor Shklovskii, *Gamburgskii schet: stat'i, vospominaniia, esse (1914–1933)* (Moscow: Sovetskii pisatel', 1990), 224. Puni's cover for the book *Futurists: Roaring Parnassus* (1914) was particularly obscene and along with the drawings p. 174 by other artists resulted in censors' decision to withdraw the edition.

27. This expression of Marinetti's was used as an epigraph by one of the reviewers of *Tramway V*. See Imanuil Saf'ianov, "Tramvai V ili ocherednoi plevok," *Sinii zhurnal*, no. 12 (1915).

28. See Aleksandra Shatskikh, *Black Square: Malevich and the Origin of Suprematism*, trans. Marian Schwartz (New Haven: Yale University Press, 2012), 6.

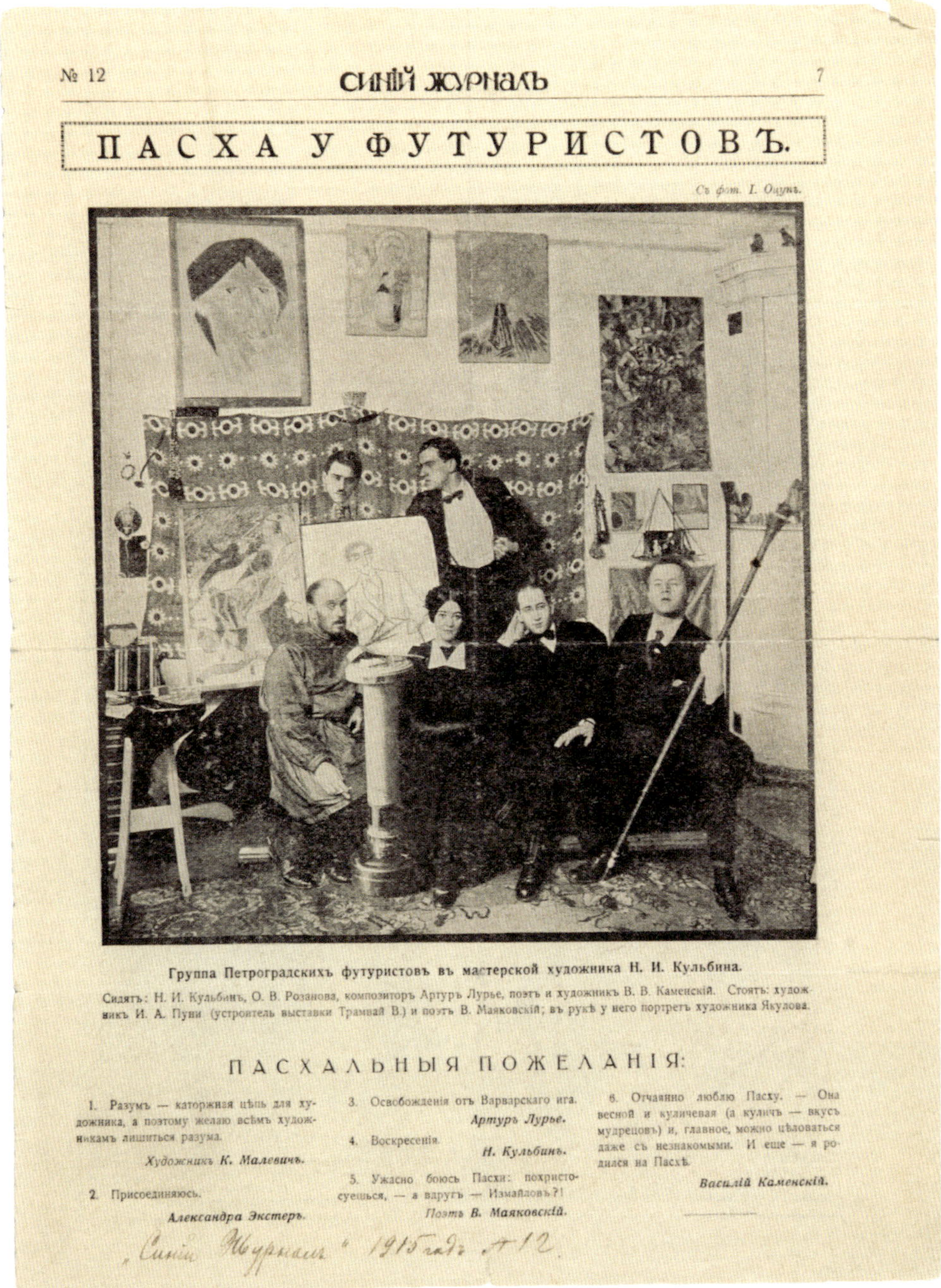

№ 12 СИНІЙ ЖУРНАЛЪ 7

ПАСХА У ФУТУРИСТОВЪ.

Съ фот. І. Оцупъ.

Группа Петроградскихъ футуристовъ въ мастерской художника Н. И. Кульбина.

Сидятъ: Н. И. Кульбинъ, О. В. Розанова, композиторъ Артуръ Лурье, поэтъ и художникъ В. В. Каменскій. Стоятъ: художникъ И. А. Пуни (устроитель выставки Трамвай В.) и поэтъ В. Маяковскій; въ рукѣ у него портретъ художника Якулова.

ПАСХАЛЬНЫЯ ПОЖЕЛАНІЯ:

1. Разумъ — каторжная цѣпь для художника, а поэтому желаю всѣмъ художникамъ лишиться разума.

Художникъ ***К. Малевичъ.***

2. Присоединяюсь.

Александра Экстеръ.

3. Освобожденія отъ Варварскаго ига.

Артуръ Лурье.

4. Воскресенія.

Н. Кульбинъ.

5. Ужасно боюсь Пасхи: похристосуешься, — а вдругъ — Измайловъ?!

Поэтъ ***В. Маяковскій.***

6. Отчаянно люблю Пасху. — Она весной и куличевая (а куличъ — вкусъ мудрецовъ) и, главное, можно цѣловаться даже съ незнакомыми. И еще — я родился на Пасхѣ.

Василій Каменскій.

„Синій Журналъ" 1915 годъ № 12.

Anonymous
"Easter at Futurists," illustration in the journal *Blue Journal*, no. 12, 1915

ТРАМВАЙ В. или ОЧЕРЕДНОЙ ПЛЕВОКЪ.

„Нужно плевать каждый день на Алтарь Искусства".

Ф. Маринетти.

Миланъ
11 мая 1912 г.

Когда наша петроградская публика отправляется на выставку футуристовъ, она испытываетъ обычно крайнее недоумѣніе и даже негодованіе. Чувства эти являются результатомъ очевиднаго недоразумѣнія.

Недоразумѣніе это является слѣдствіемъ предположенія, что футуристы хотятъ служить искусству. На самомъ же дѣлѣ они преслѣдуютъ совсѣмъ иныя цѣли. Цѣли противоположныя, о чемъ и заявляетъ во всеуслышаніе предводитель и изобрѣтатель футуризма Маринетти.

Футуризму ненавистно искусство. Его завѣтомъ является требованіе, поставленное въ видѣ эпиграфа нашей замѣтки. И если подойти съ этой точки зрѣнія къ пресловутой выставкѣ картинъ „Трамвай В", то все станетъ сразу яснымъ. Исчезнетъ и недоумѣніе и негодованіе.

Въ самомъ дѣлѣ, вся выставка, очевидно, служитъ вполнѣ ясной, единой цѣли, является исполненіемъ завѣта учителя — плевать на Алтарь Искусства. И задачей любого изъ этихъ вовсе не претендующихъ на художественность (совсѣмъ наоборотъ!) произведеній является изыскиваніе способовъ наиболѣе цѣлесообразнаго отрицанія, оплевыванія искусства, его принциповъ и стремленій.

Чѣмъ враждебнѣе искусству данное произведеніе, чѣмъ интенсивнѣе плевокъ, тѣмъ оно, съ футуристской точки зрѣнія, талантливѣе, pardon, „геніальнѣе" (у футуристовъ, вообще, геніи преобладаютъ надъ талантами).

* * *

Въ манифестѣ итальянскихъ футуристовъ живописцевъ отъ 11 февраля 1910 года, между прочимъ, сказано: „Портретъ **не долженъ походить** на свою натуру".

И еще сказано: „Чтобы нарисовать человѣческую фигуру, **не нужно ее рисовать**".

И еще сказано: „Пространство не существуетъ".

Если подойти къ нашимъ футуристамъ съ футуристской же точки зрѣнія, то произведенія ихъ не только не удивляютъ и не поражаютъ, но производятъ впечатлѣніе довольно мелкотравчатое. Плевки, съ позволенія сказать, не изъ удачныхъ.

Въ концѣ концовъ, если разобраться хорошенько, то по существу всѣ эти полотна и „живописные рельефы" никуда не ушли отъ настоящаго натурализма. Въ нихъ нѣтъ никакого **принципіальнаго** отличія отъ произведеній хотя бы Владиміра Маковскаго и Бодаревскаго. Они совершенно безсильны нанести дѣйствительный ущербъ тому искусству, которое они стремятся уничтожить и унизить.

Эммануилъ Сафьяновъ.

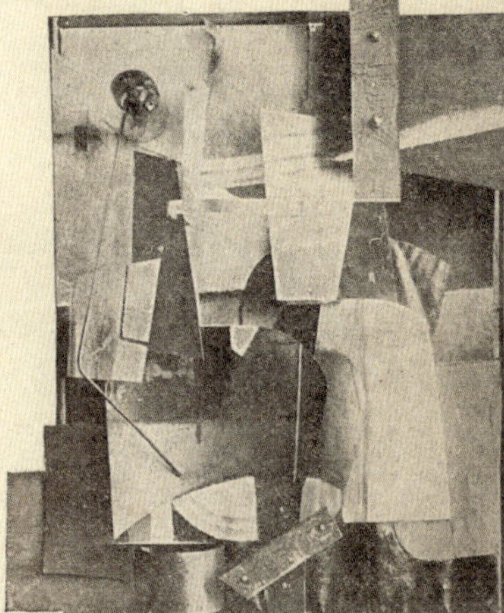

И. Пуни, „Игрокъ въ карты".
(Дерево, обои, жесть и др. матеріалы.)

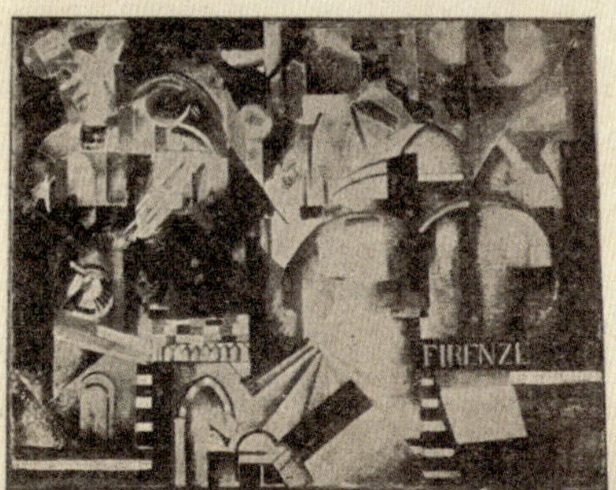

А. Экстеръ, „Флоренція".
(Масляныя краски.)

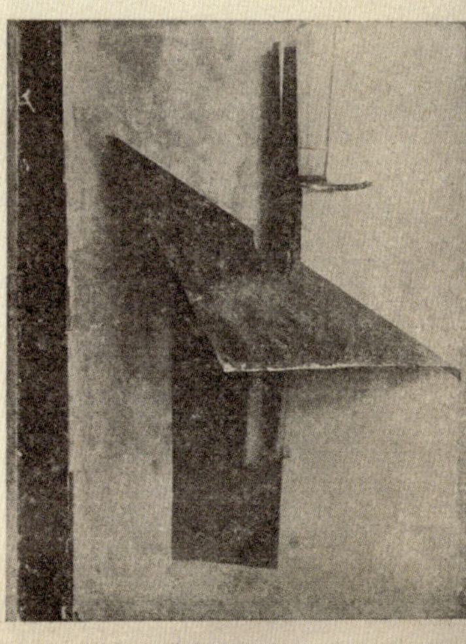

В. Татлинъ, „Живописный рельефъ"
(Дерево, жесть, проволока.)

„Синій Журналъ" 1915 годъ №12

"Tramway V or a Familiar Spit," illustration in the journal *Blue Journal*, no. 12, 1915 petty-bourgeois meaning, and prejudice." This antiestablishment agenda, inscribed on the back side of the piece of wood on which *Cow and Violin* was painted, advanced the concept of everythingism from that of synthesis to that of differentiation within the concept of synthesis. *Englishman in Moscow* (1914) also demonstrates Malevich's attitude toward foreignness in its title and nonsensical kaleidoscopic mixture of images potentially shocking to an outsider. An antagonistic saw and sword assert a semantic gap that a foreigner, Marinetti, conveyed to formalist critic Roman Jakobson in Saint Petersburg by saying that the Russians are "false Futurists" and that Russian poetry is "not futuristic."[29]

Malevich's close associate Morgunov similarly stressed a clash with Marinetti's passion for urbanism and technological progress in the painting *Aviator's Workroom* (1913), which juxtaposes an airplane, one of the favorite modern images of the Italians, with an axe, a primitive instrument of rurality, of "Futurism in a village," and a symbol of archaic life. But the axe is also a metaphor for the radicality of transrational practice. As Kruchenykh states, "Painters-*budetliane* like to use parts of bodies, and cuts, and speech creators *budetliane* use severed words, half-words."[30]

p. 49

In *Tramway V*, Tatlin met Malevich's painterly transrationality with *Painterly Reliefs* (ca. 1914–1915), which combine dissimilar, found materials such as glass, iron, wire, and wood.[31] Nikolai Punin, art critic and admirer of Tatlin, conveyed the theatrical and playful atmosphere of collectivity in which "Tatlin's constructivism" was first made: "They sawed and shaved, they cut and polished, they stretched and bent; painting was almost forgotten. . . . From the outside, this could all look like a

p. 58

29. Quoted in Roman Jakobson, "Art and Poetry: The Cubo-futurists, an Interview with David Shapiro," in *The Avant-Garde in Russia: New Perspectives, 1910–1930*, ed. Stephanie Barron and Maurice Tuchman (Cambridge, MA: The MIT Press, 1980), 18.

30. Vladimir Poliakov, *Knigi russkogo kubo-futurizma* (Moscow: Gileia, 1998), 198.

31. Most of these Tatlin works are available only in photographic reproductions. One of the *Counter-Reliefs* was acquired by Puni and Boguslavskaia.

mania."[32] The result—coarsely executed whimsical constructions, comprised of materials previously not used in art, and without concern for duration—automatically acquired anti-art status.

As an organizer of and participant in *Tramway V*, Puni was thrown into a pool of formal innovations and conceptual possibilities. The result was a series of assemblages that combine Malevich's roughly painted monochromes with Tatlin's use of common materials and everyday ob-
pp. 58–59 jects. In *Relief* (1915), Puni juxtaposed several planks of wood assembled as a blue monochrome with their painted imitation, conspicuously demonstrating the relation between a real object and its representation. *Relief* also affirms Jakobson's point that "in the nonobjective approach to objectness and the object-oriented attitude toward a nonobjective thematic—to the thematic of planes, paint, and space."[33] Puni's *Card Players* (ca. 1915), reproduced in a contemporary magazine review of *Tramway V* next to a now lost glass-and-iron *Painterly Relief* by Tatlin, recontextualizes Paul Cézanne's *Card Players* (1894–1895) not only by abstracting its content but by assembling wood and iron pieces to such a degree of density that the artwork's internal and external borders are perceived as severely breached. Onto this composition-without-boundaries Puni affixed a piece of wood to an outer edge, positioning *Card Players* as a springboard for Kurt Schwitter's *Merzbau*, an "expansive collage project . . . related to dadaism" and initiated in the early 1920s.[34] Shortly after *Tramway V* opened, Malevich and Morgunov announced that they would appear in the center of Moscow in "a fool's outfit with wooden spoons in buttonholes."[35] Although the two artists showed up in regular coats, the fact that they irritated the public with a readymade—that is, a dismantler of traditional concepts of artistic creativity—positioned their appearance as a prelude to the next scandalous show.[36]

The title of that show, *1915 Painting Exhibition*, is somewhat misleading, for its exhibits far exceeded the medium of painting. According to Khardzhiev, *1915* "was a parade of formal experimentation" and included "Tatlin's *Counter-Reliefs*, Malevich's and Morgunov's alogical canvases, Kandinsky's nonobjective compositions, Larionov's plastic rayonism."[37] The exhibition also featured several pieces involving ready-mades, including Vladimir Mayakovsky's "provocative 'Self-Portrait': half of a top hat and a black glove nailed or glued to a wall that was painted in black stripes" and "Larionov's 'kinetic' construction and a 'wall composition' with a mousetrap and alive mouse—a parody on naturalist tendencies in art."[38] To Khardzhiev's description, art historian Aleksandra Shatskikh adds that the "'kinetic' construction" was an installation of a fan on the

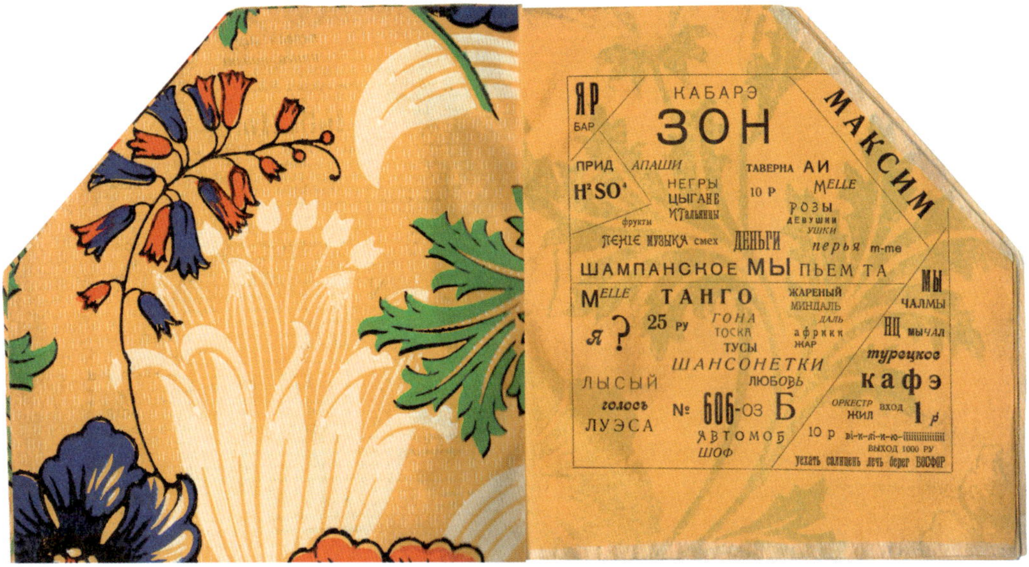

Vasily Kamensky, David Burliuk, Vladimir Burliuk
Tango with Cows: Ferro-concrete Poems
by Vasily Kamensky, 1914

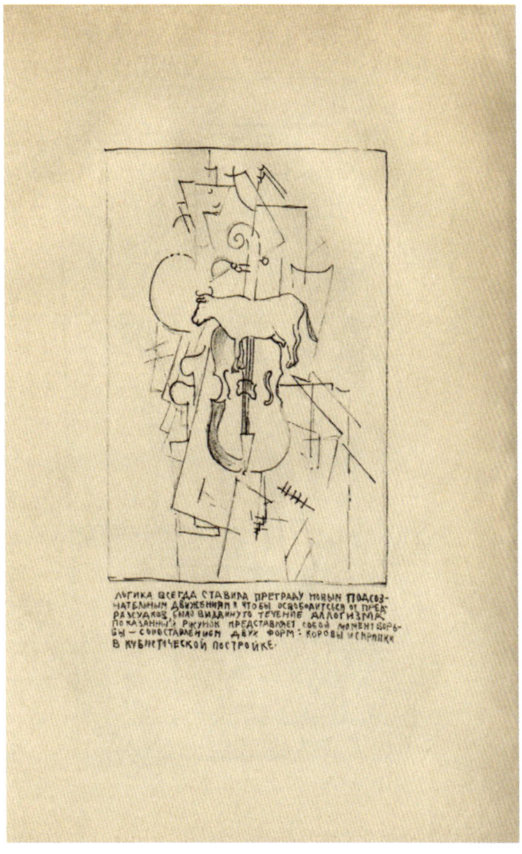

El Lissitzky and Kazimir Malevich
Illustration of Malevich's painting *Cow and Violin* (ca. 1913–1915) in the book *On New Systems in Art,* 1919

32. Nikolai Punin, "Apartment No. 5," on pp. 271–272 of the present catalogue. I believe Punin makes the attribution "Tatlin's constructivism" to distinguish it from a more scheming model of constructivism worked out from 1920 to 1922 by the Institute of Artistic Culture.

33. Roman Iakobson, "Vospominaniia," in *Malevich o sebe*, ed. Vakar and Mikhienko, 1:126.

34. Dorothea Dietrich, "Hannover," in *Dada: Zurich, Berlin, Hannover, Cologne, New York, Paris*, ed. Leah Dickerman (Washington, DC: National Gallery of Art; New York: Museum of Modern Art), 2005, 173.

35. The event was announced in the newspaper *Early Morning* (*Pannee utro*). See N. N. Punin, "Pervye futuristicheskie boi," in *Malevich o sebe*, ed. Vakar and Mikhienko, 2:146.

36. Malevich, "Avtobiografiia," 1:39.

37. Nikolai Khardzhiev, "Poeziia i zhivopis," in *Stat'i ob avangarde*, ed. Duganov, Arpishkin, and Sarab'ianov, 1:27. A checklist includes glass objects by Sofia Dymshits-Tolstaia.

38. Ibid.

wall next to Larionov's rayonist painting. As it "turned on sporadically, [it] stir[ed] a woman's lopped-off braid."[39] The poet and artist David Burliuk's installation included "calzones, a soup, and his calling cards," which matches well with Larionov's and Mayakovsky's ready-made objects in *1915*.[40]

Malevich's proto-Dadaist painting *Com-*
p. 54 *position with Mona Lisa* was first exhibited in *1915*.[41] For this canvas and other alogical compositions, he used the term *fevralism*. Although positioned as "rayonism's rival," fevralism effectively added another ism to Larionov and Zdanevich's everythingism.[42] Punin cites the following statement by Malevich as relating mistakenly to an exhibition in 1913 instead of to *1915*: "It was decided to prepare something special. I bought a reproduction of Giaconda at 'Avantso' and after gluing it on a canvas, made a cubist background, pasted in the place of the lips a cigarette butt, and made an inscription, 'apartment is for rent,' across the whole thing."[43] This description promised a picture much closer, in its degree of naughtiness, to Duchamp's *L.H.O.O.Q.* But instead of applying the kind of mockery Duchamp performed several years later in *L.H.O.O.Q.*, in *Composition with Mona Lisa* Malevich decided not to recycle old art into a new modernist icon but to negate it by means of eclipse. For Malevich, it became the best ready-made for performing a theater of replacement, of victory over the old. The words *partial eclipse* partially overlap a black rectangle looming over the *Mona Lisa*'s image like "a curtain in an act where victory had occurred."[44] The painting *Black Square*, born of a black square on a curtain and anno-
p. 33 tated by Malevich as "no. 1," carries the *Mona Lisa*'s spell. Like Leonardo's canvas, it is enigmatic; it has too many, in T. J. Clark's words,

Kazimir Malevich
Alogic Composition 3 (study for the painting *An Englishman in Moscow*), 1914

Aleksei Morgunov
Study for *The Barber Set Off for the Bathhouse*, 1915

39. Shatskikh, *Black Square*, 22.

40. Ibid.

41. Shatskikh concludes that the hitherto accepted date of 1914 for *Composition with Mona Lisa* is "erroneous." She dates it to 1915. See Shatskikh, *Black Square*, 18.

42. This painting was not exhibited again until 1980. On fevralism, see ibid., 1–33.

43. Punin, "Pervye futuristicheskie boi," 145.

44. Malevich to Matiushin, ed. Vakar and Mikhienko, May 27, 1915, 1:66.

45. On the stormy reception of *Black Square* by Malevich's colleagues, see my *Malevich and Film* (New Haven: Yale University Press, 2002), 9–13.

46. Malevich to Matiushin, ca. early June 1915, in *Malevich o sebe*, ed. Vakar and Mikhienko, 1:67.

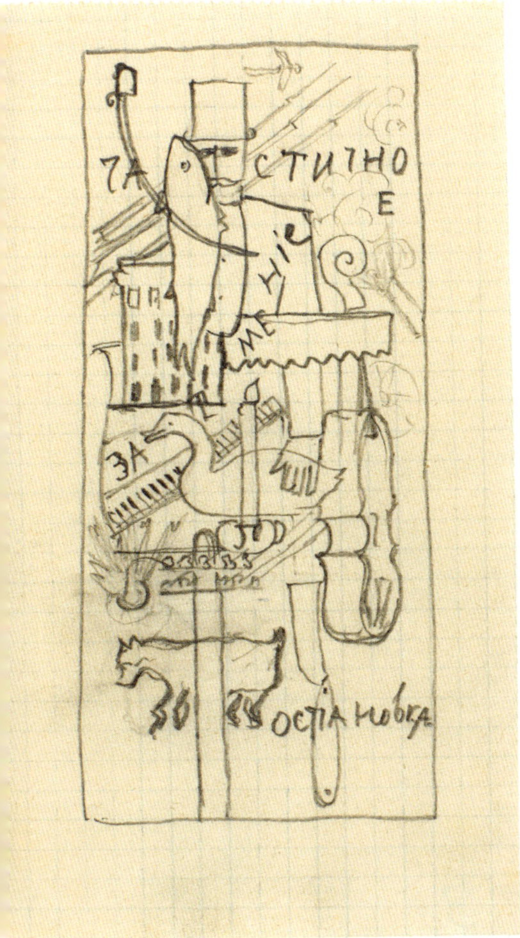

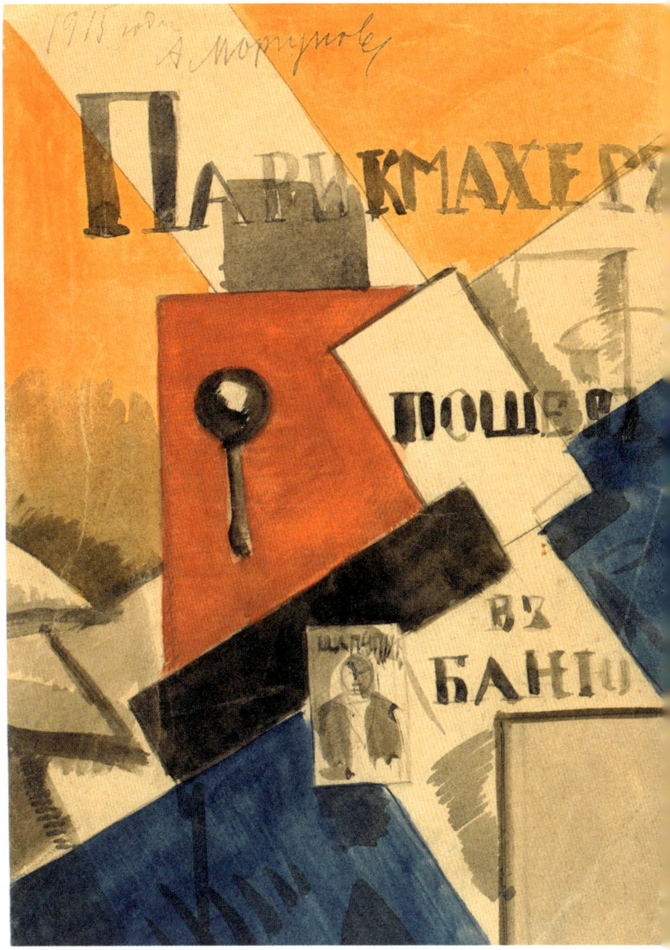

"undecidables" and is coded with a desire for, multiplying and permission for copying.[45] pp. 55, 57

That the painting *Black Square* (1915) was executed in July, shortly after *Composition with Mona Lisa*, is thus only logical. In a letter written about this time, Malevich complains that "no one had noticed" his "new" concepts for *Victory over the Sun*.[46] His dissatisfaction could easily have prompted him not only to turn compositions developed for *Victory over the Sun* into paintings but to dub the term *suprematism* as an act of separation from the equivalence of multi-isms, of everythingism, and ultimately from Larionov's *supremacy* in the Russian avant-garde. Shortly before the opening of the exhibition *0,10: The Last Futurist Exhibition of Painting*, in which *Black Square* was first shown,

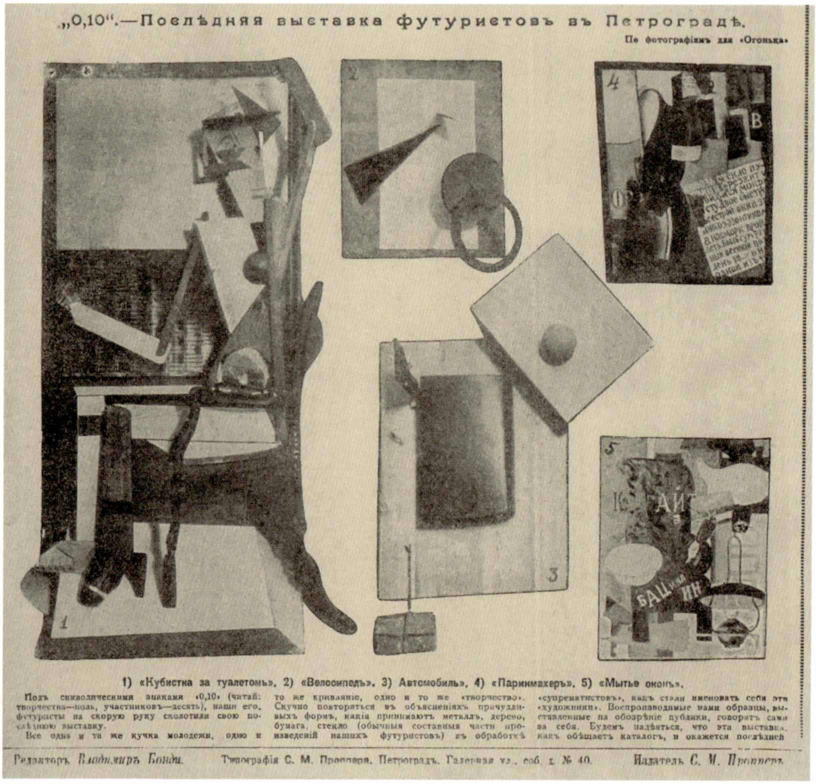

„0,10“.—Послѣдняя выставка футуристовъ въ Петроградѣ.

По фотографіямъ для «Огонька»

1) «Кубистка за туалетомъ», 2) «Велосипедъ». 3) Автомобиль», 4) «Парикмахеръ». 5) «Мытье оконъ».

Подъ символическими знаками «0,10» (читай: творчества—ноль, участниковъ—десять), наши его. футуристы на скорую руку сколотили свою послѣднюю выставку.

Все одна и та же кучка молодежи, одно и то же кривляніе, одно и то же «творчество». Скучно повторяться въ объясненіяхъ причудливыхъ формъ, какія принимаютъ металлъ, дерево, бумага, стекло (обычныя составныя части произведеній нашихъ футуристовъ) въ обработкѣ «супрематистовъ», какъ стали именовать себя эти «художники». Воспроизводимые нами образцы, выставленные на обозрѣніе публики, говорятъ сами за себя. Будемъ надѣяться, что эта выставка, какъ обѣщаетъ каталогъ, и окажется послѣдней

Редакторъ *Владиміръ Бонди.* Типографія С. М. Проппера. Петроградъ. Галерная ул., соб. д. № 40. Издатель *С. М. Пропперъ*

Malevich was still referring to the concept of a black square as a curtain rather than a composition: "a curtain that depicts a black square is the embryo of all possibilities and in its development acquires a powerful force; it's a precursor of a cube and a sphere, its disintegrations carry an amazing culture in painting, in the opera it signified the beginning of victory."[47] Malevich's use of the Russian word *shar* (sphere or globe) suggests he thought of the black square as a global "trademark" open to multiplication ad infinitum.

Black Square was installed theatrically in a corner in *0,10*, separate from Malevich's otherwise densely hung canvases, thus emphasizing its objectness and positioning it to compete with another seminal invention: Tatlin's *Corner Counter-Reliefs*. In his leaflet for *0,10*, Malevich writes, with a dose of anarchic egocentrism, "I have transformed myself in the zero of form and have fished myself out of the *rubbishy slough of*
p. 43 *academic art*."[48] He thus refers to *Black Square*'s status, to paraphrase Roland Barthes, as "painting degree zero."[49] Accordingly, Malevich planned to call a periodical associated with his group Supremus, newly

Anonymous
"0,10: The Last Futurist Exhibition in Petrograd"
Illustration in *Ogonek*, no. 1, 1916

Kazimir Malevich
I the Apostle of New Concepts in Art, 1916

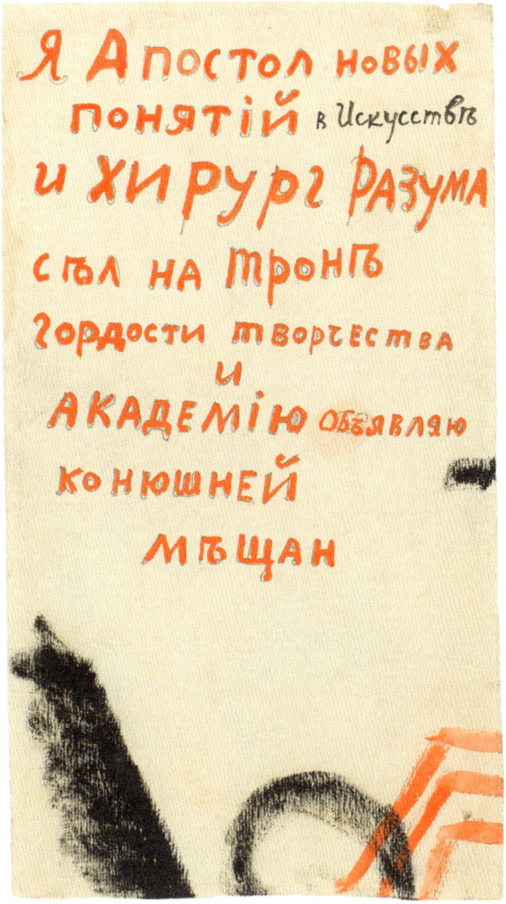

launched in 1916, *Zero*.[50] This and Punin's eloquent conclusion that "in Suprematism European painting converged in order to die" landed Malevich on the same ground as the Zurich Dadaists, who chose the term *Dada* for "its appropriateness as an emblem for 'beginning at zero.'"[51] And they shared this ground with Duchamp's *Fountain* (1917)—painting's ultimate gravedigger. p. 13

47. Ibid. On *0,10*, see Charlotte Douglas, "0-10 Exhibition," in *The Avant-Garde in Russia*, ed. Barron and Tuchman, 34–40.

48. Malevich, "From Cubism and Futurism to Suprematism: The New Painterly Realism, 1915," in *Russian Art of the Avant-Garde*, ed. and trans. Bowlt, 118; emphasis in original.

49. In introducing the concept of "writing degree zero," Barthes had in mind a true revolutionary writing rather than the obedient writing of revolutionaries.

50. Malevich to Matiushin, May 29, 1915, in *Malevich o sebe*, ed. Vakar and Mikhienko, 1:66. The periodical ended up being called *Supremus*. The controversy between Malevich and Tatlin and associates Popova and Udaltsova resulted in Malevich's appearance at Tatlin's exhibition *The Store* (1916) with "0,10" on his forehead and a note on his back that read, "I the apostle of new concepts in art and the surgeon of reason sat on the throne of pride in art and declare the Academy a stable of philistines." See Varvara Stepanova, "V epitsentre avangarda," in *Chelovek ne mozhet zhit bez chuda: pis'ma, poeticheskie opyty, zapiski khudozhnitsy* (Moscow: Sfera, 1994), 61.

51. Nikolai Punin, "Vykhod Malevicha," in *O Tatline*, ed. I. N. Punina and V. I. Rakitin (Moscow: RA, 1994) 52; and Leah Dickerman, "Zurich," in *Dada*, ed. Dickerman, 33.

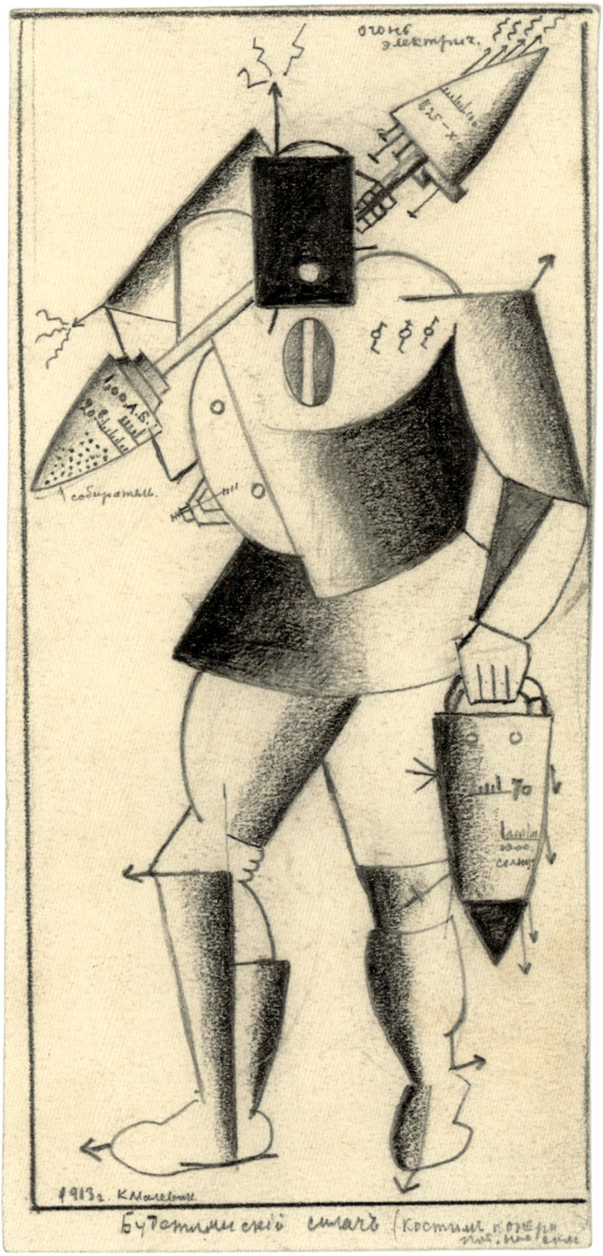

Kazimir Malevich
Costume design for *Victory over the Sun*, Budetlianin Strongman, 1913

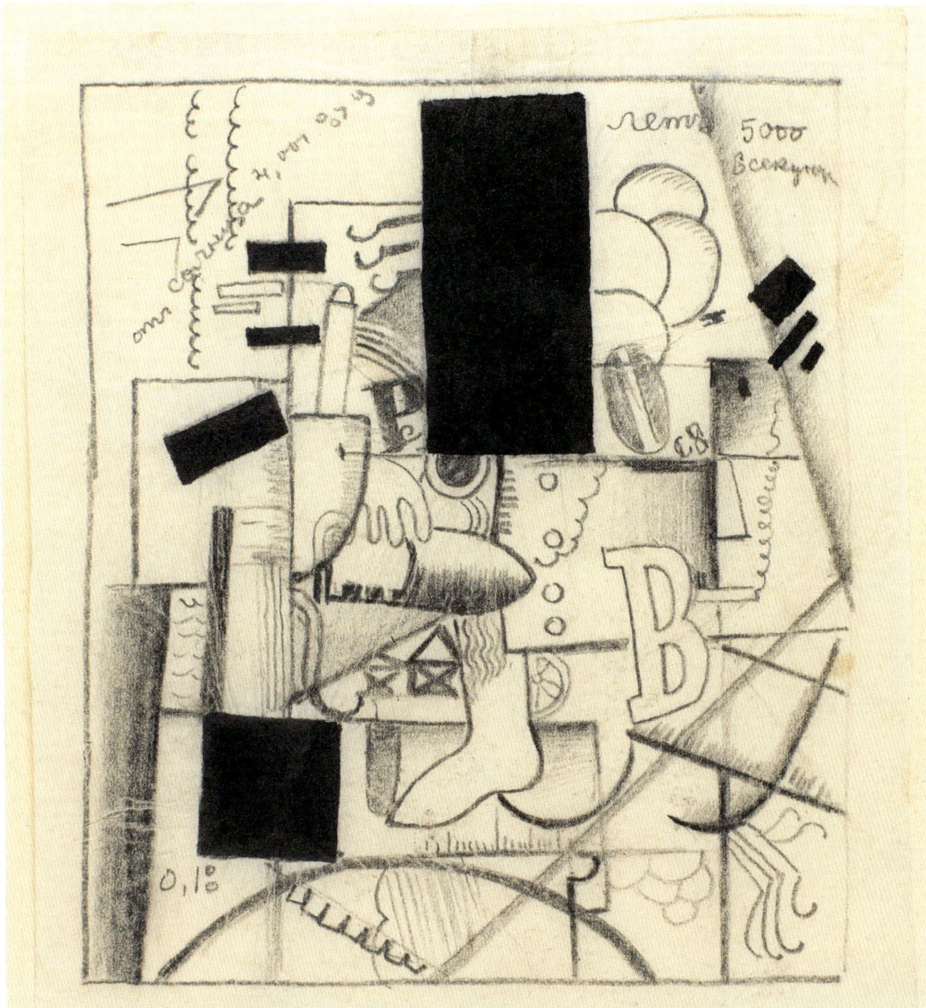

Kazimir Malevich
Curtain design for the opera
Victory over the Sun, 1913

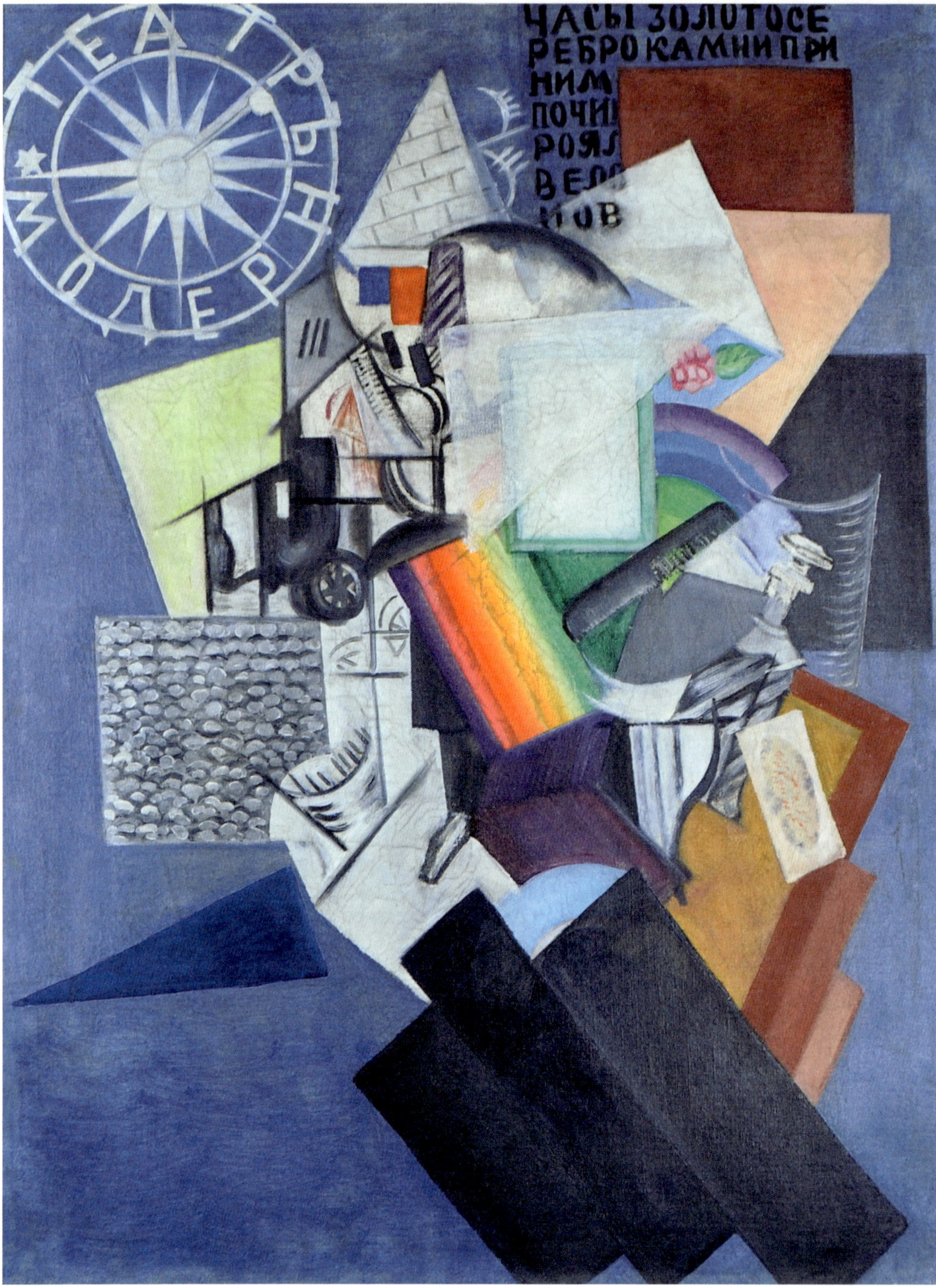

Olga Rozanova
In the Street, 1915

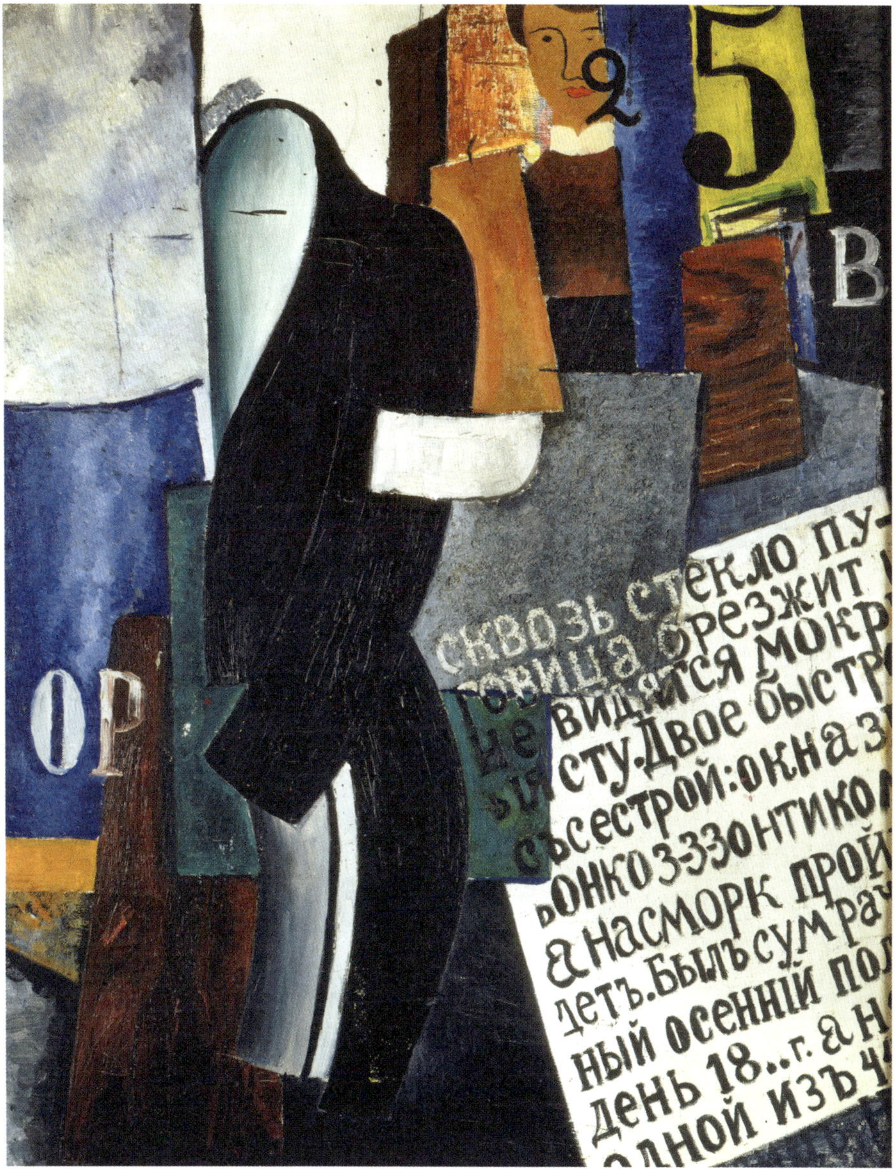

Ivan Puni
Barber, 1915

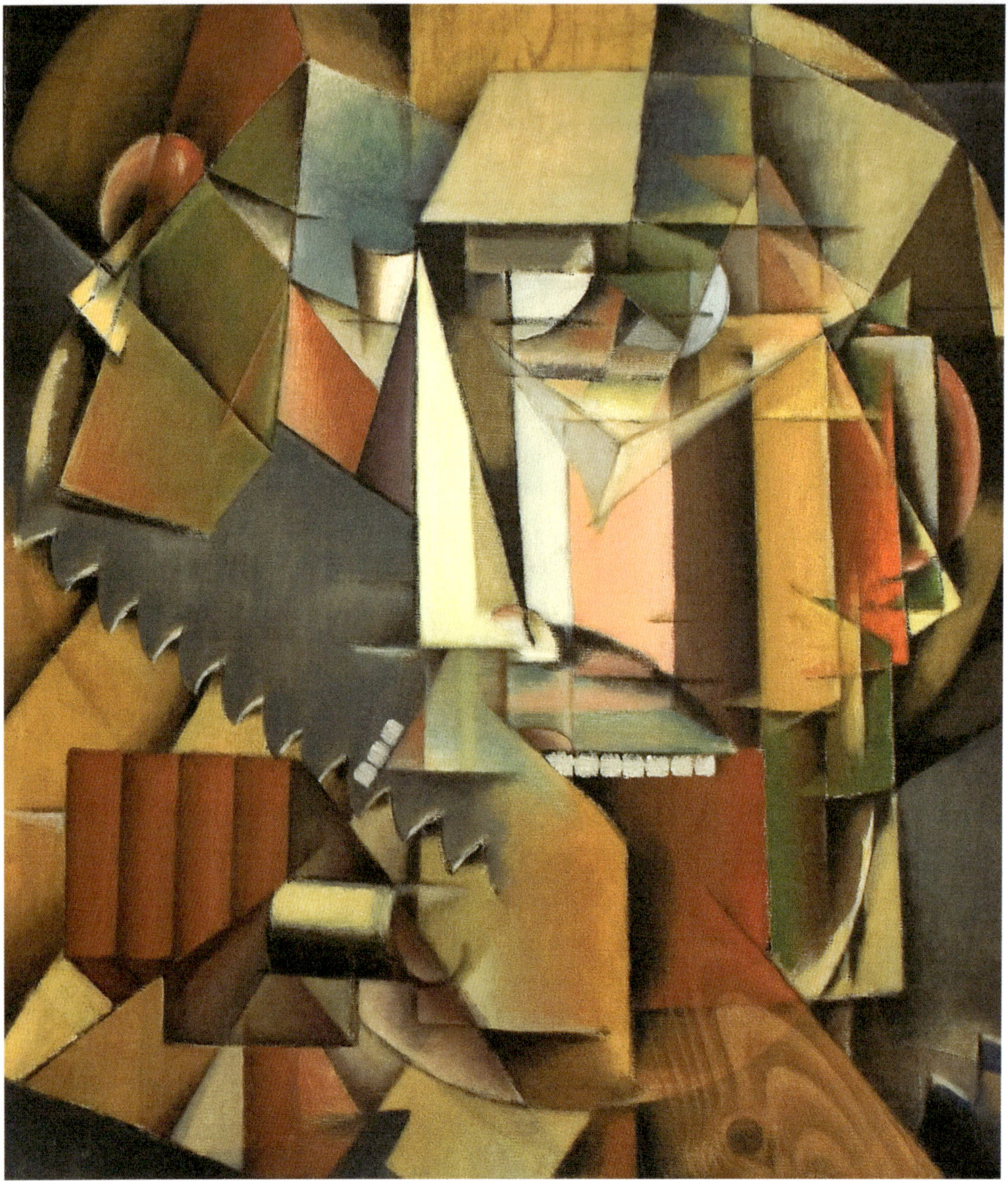

Ivan Kliun
Self-Portrait with a Saw
(Nonobjective Composition), 1914

Aleksei Morgunov
Aviator's Workroom, 1913

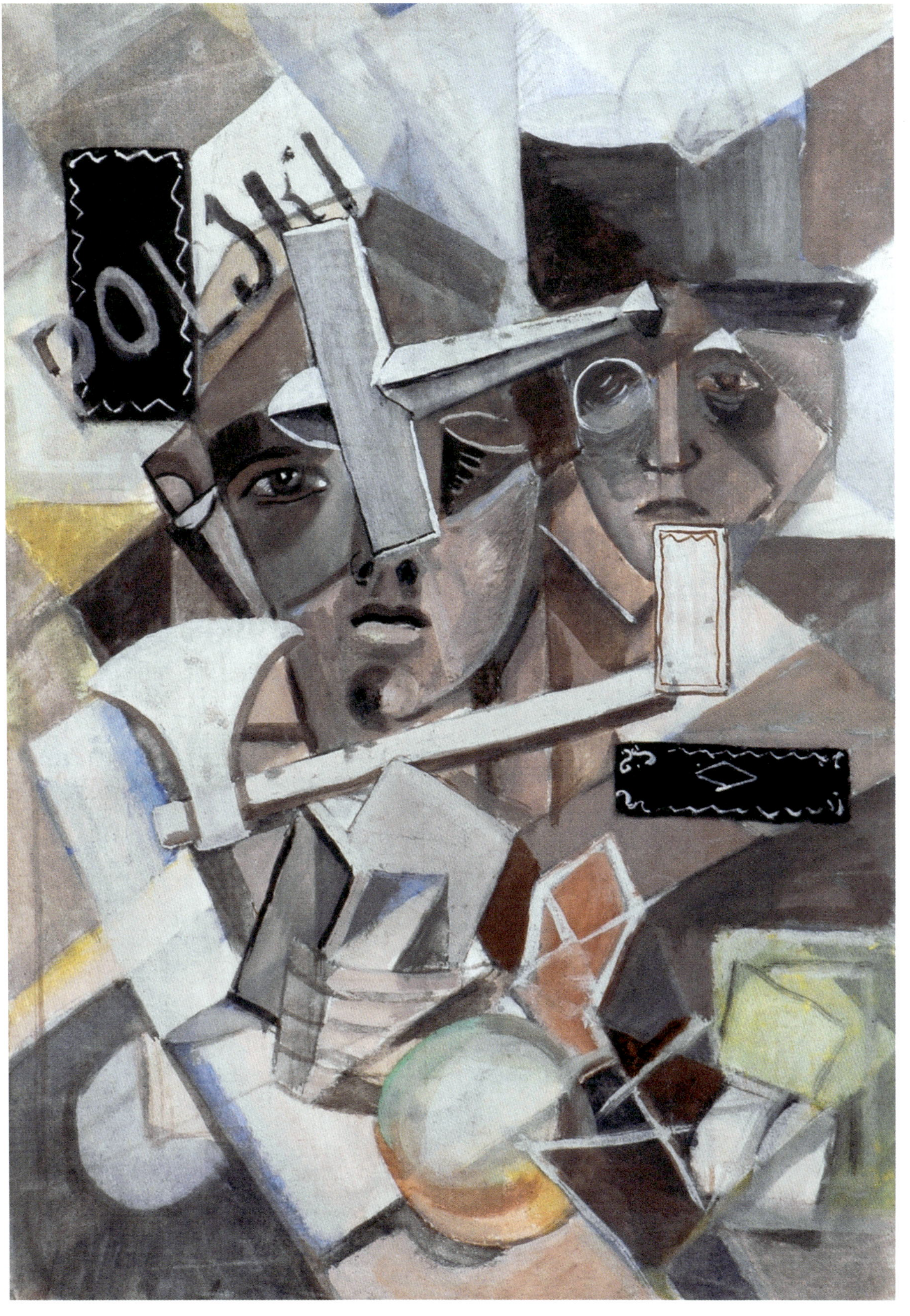

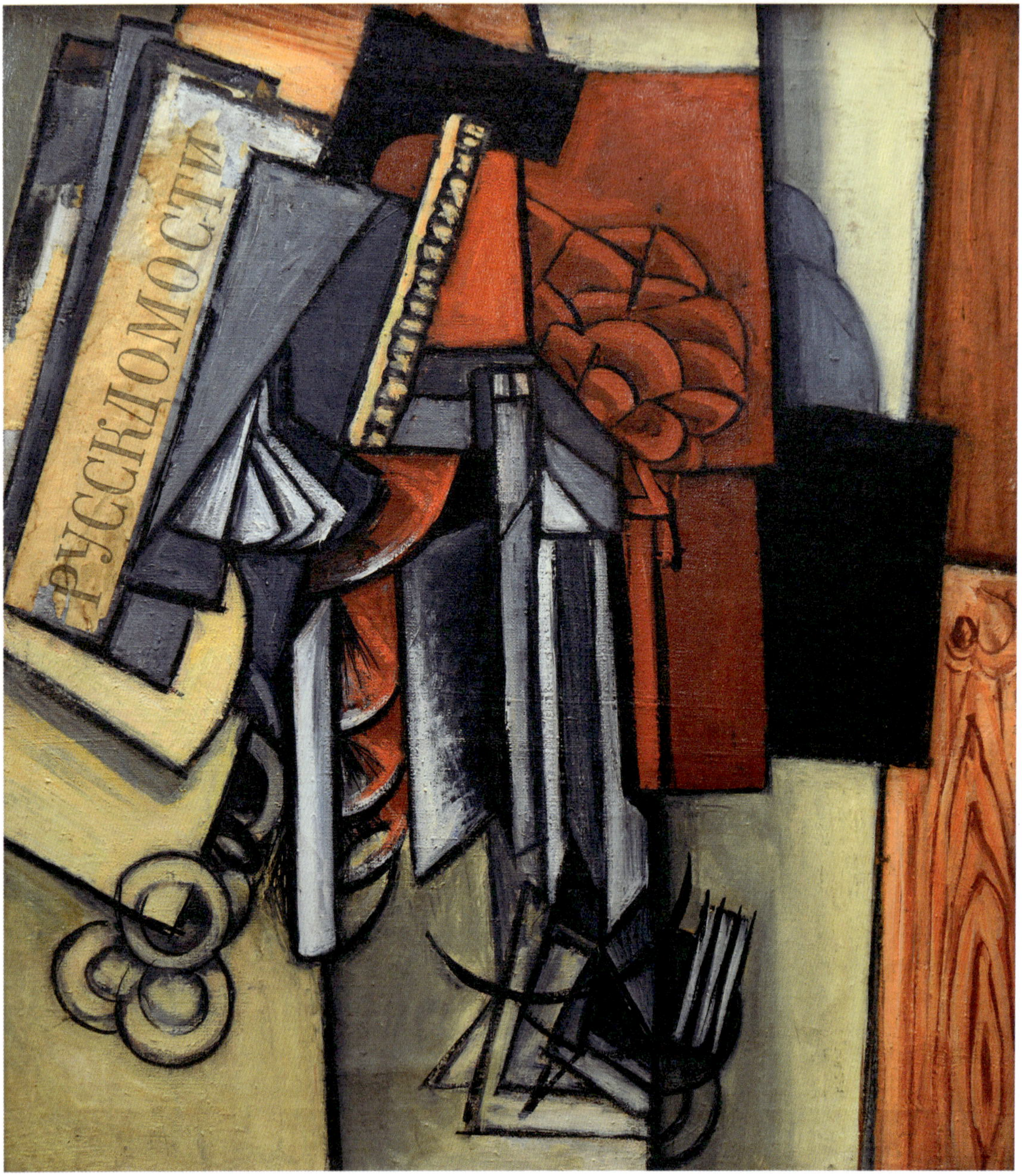

Vera Pestel
Still Life with Red, 1915–1916

Mikhail Menkov
Tramway 6, 1914

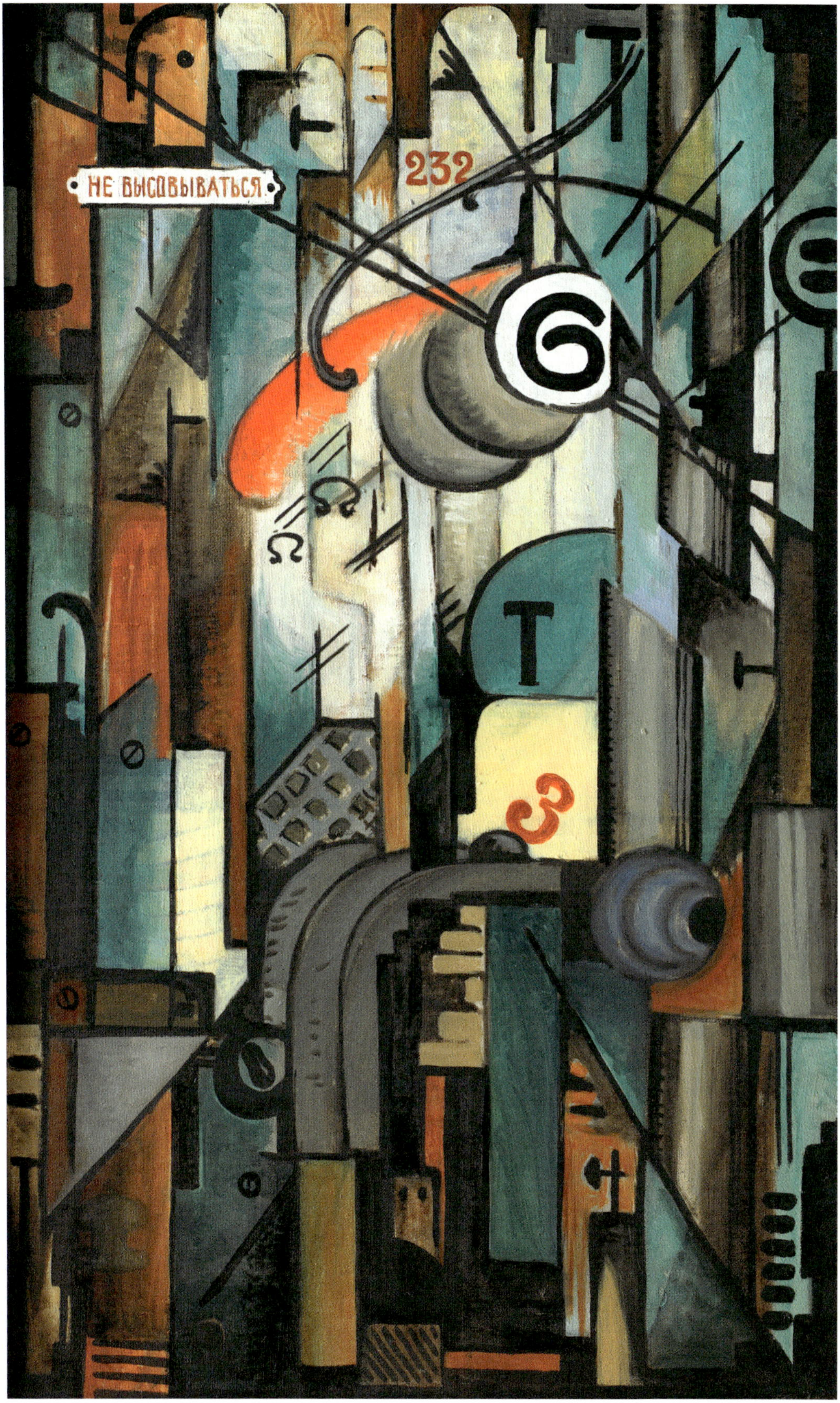
НЕ ВЫСОВЫВАТЬСЯ
232

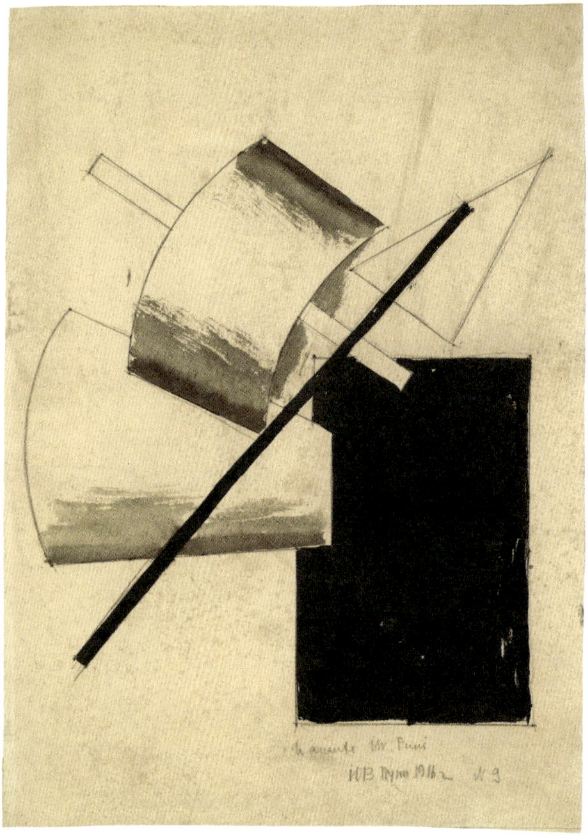

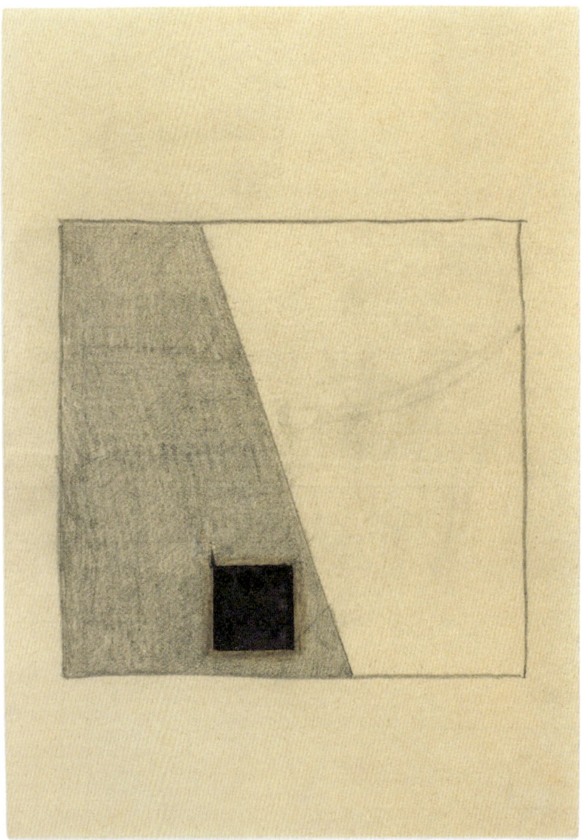

Ivan Puni
Composition, 1916

Kazimir Malevich
Suprematism: Square on a Diagonal Surface, 1915

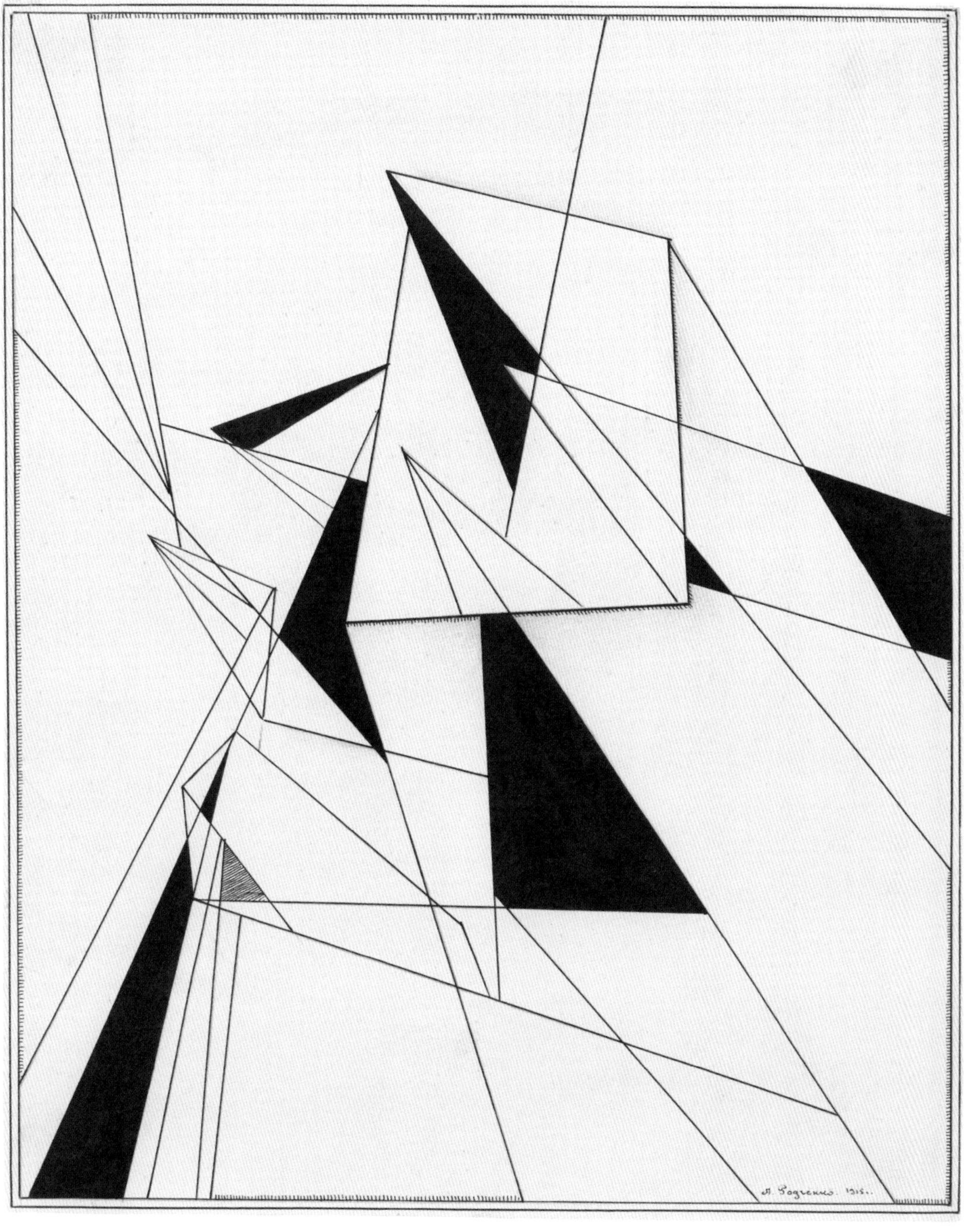

Aleksandr Rodchenko
Line and Compass Drawing, 1915

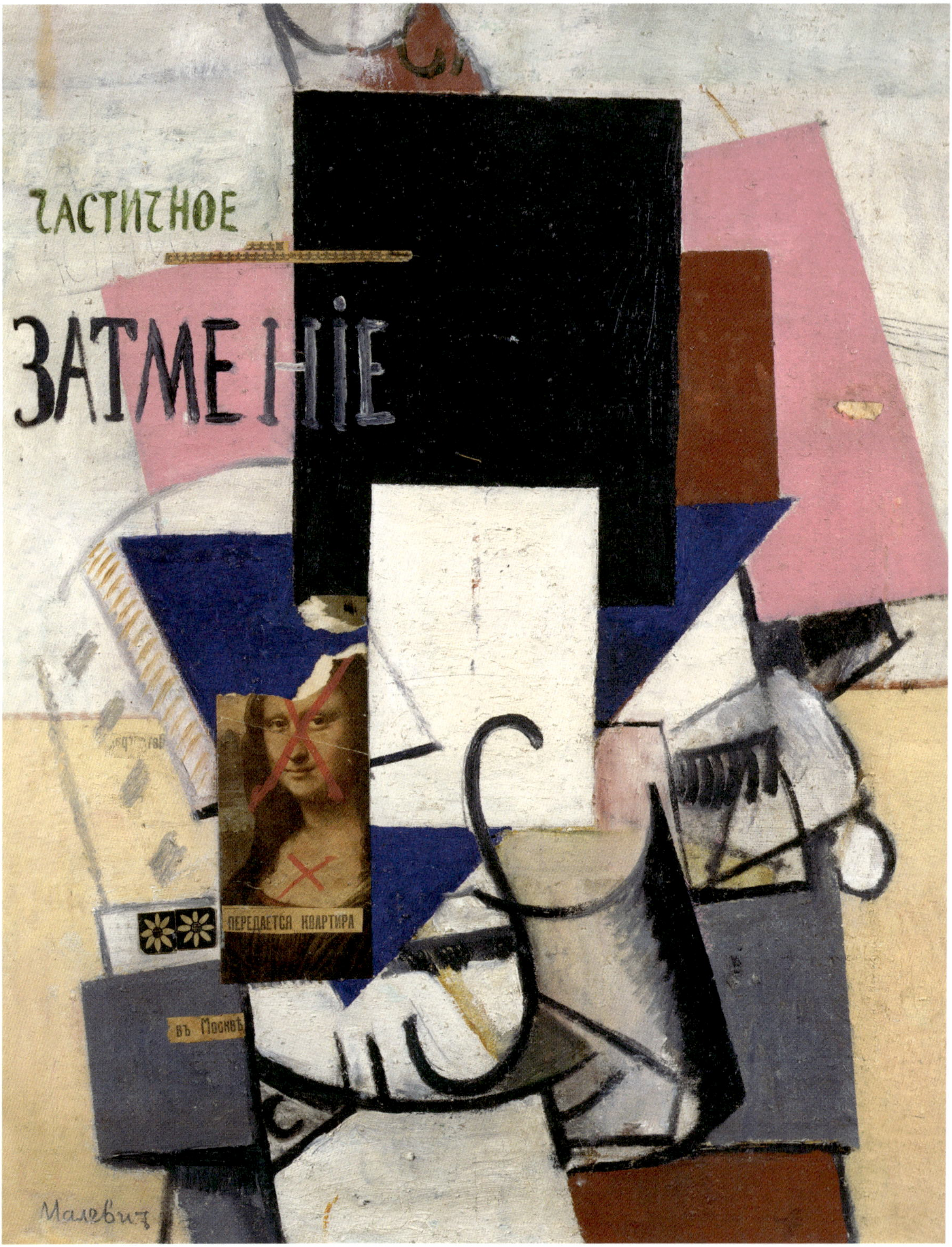
ЧАСТИЧНОЕ
ЗАТМЕНІЕ
ПЕРЕДАЕТСЯ КВАРТИРА
въ Москвѣ
Малевичъ

Kasimir Malevich
Composition with Mona Lisa, ca. 1914–1915

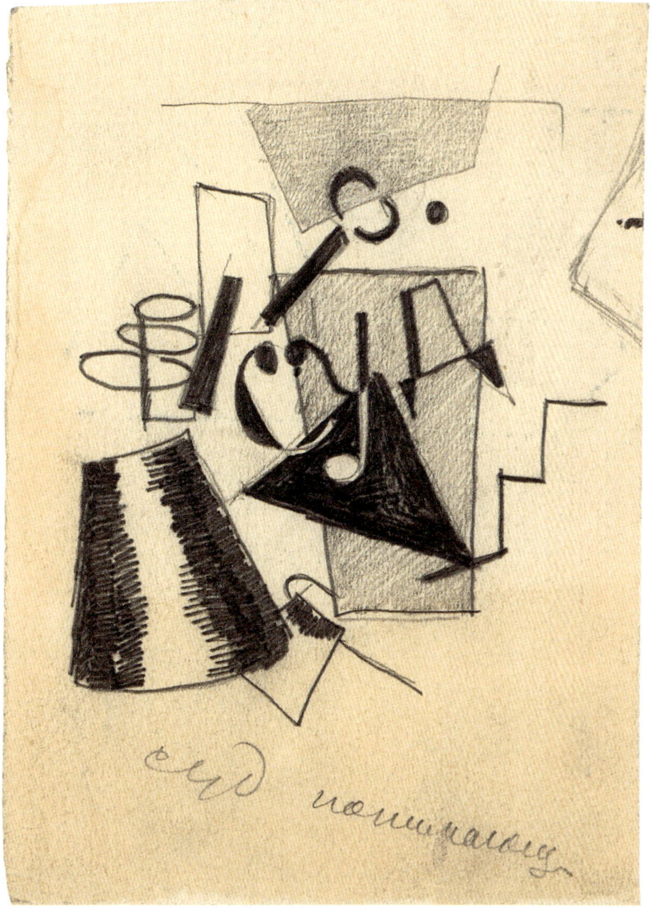

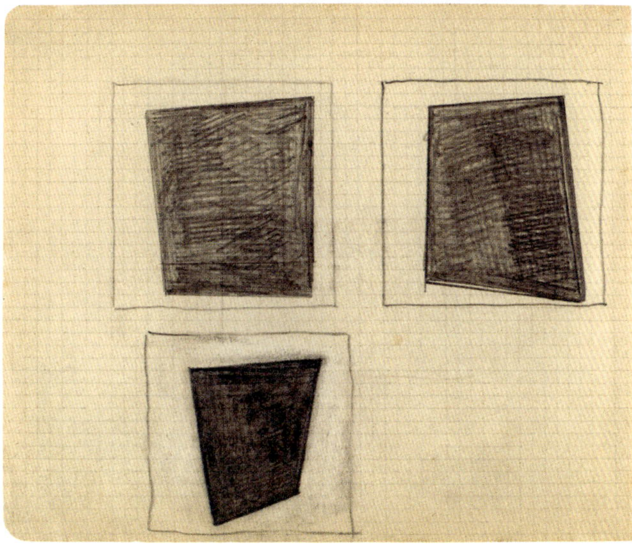

Ivan Puni
Composition (The Understanding Court), 1915–1916

Kazimir Malevich
Three Irregular Quadrangles, ca. 1915–1916

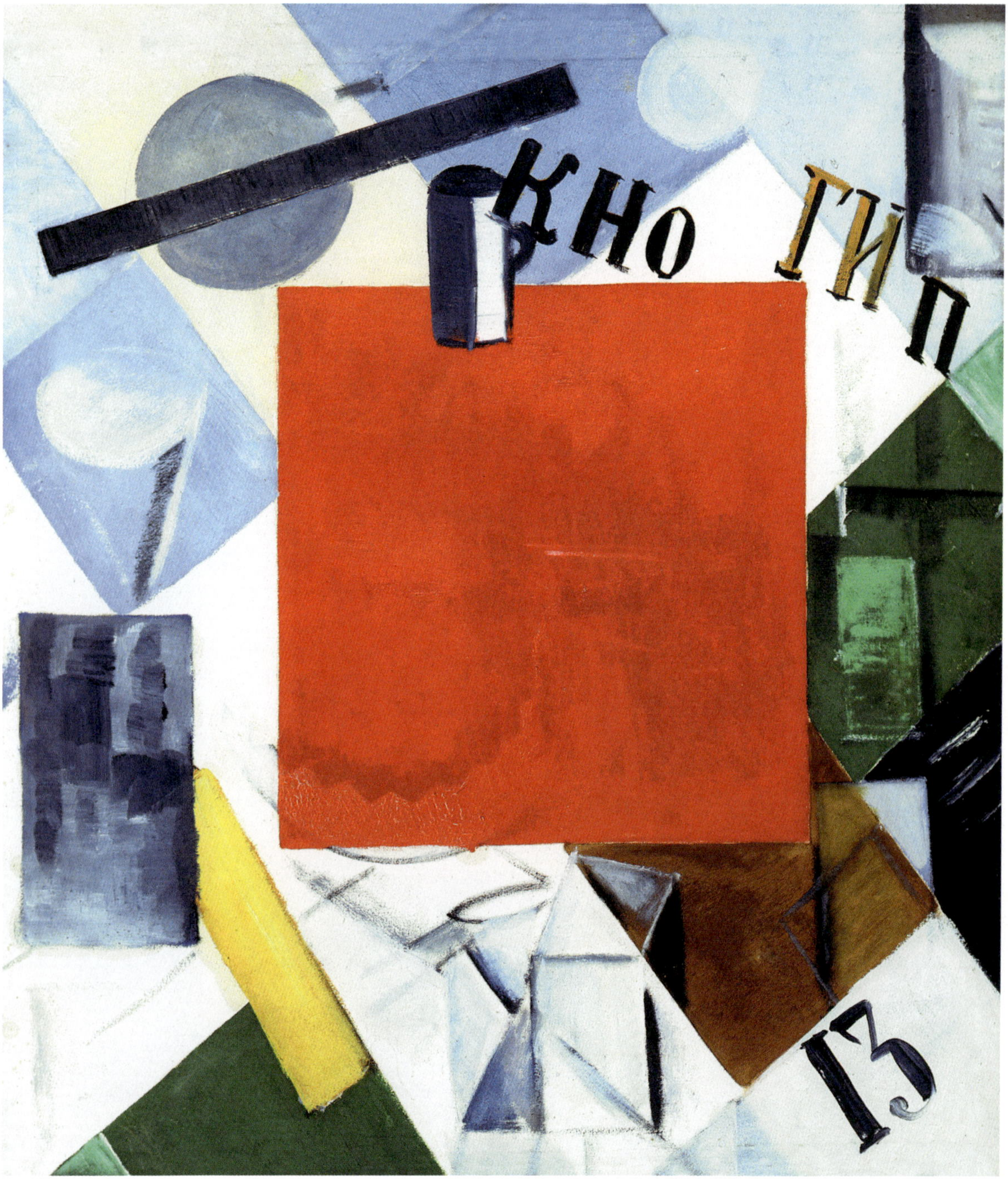

Aleksei Morgunov
Composition no. 1, 1916–1917

Kazimir Malevich
Four Squares, 1915

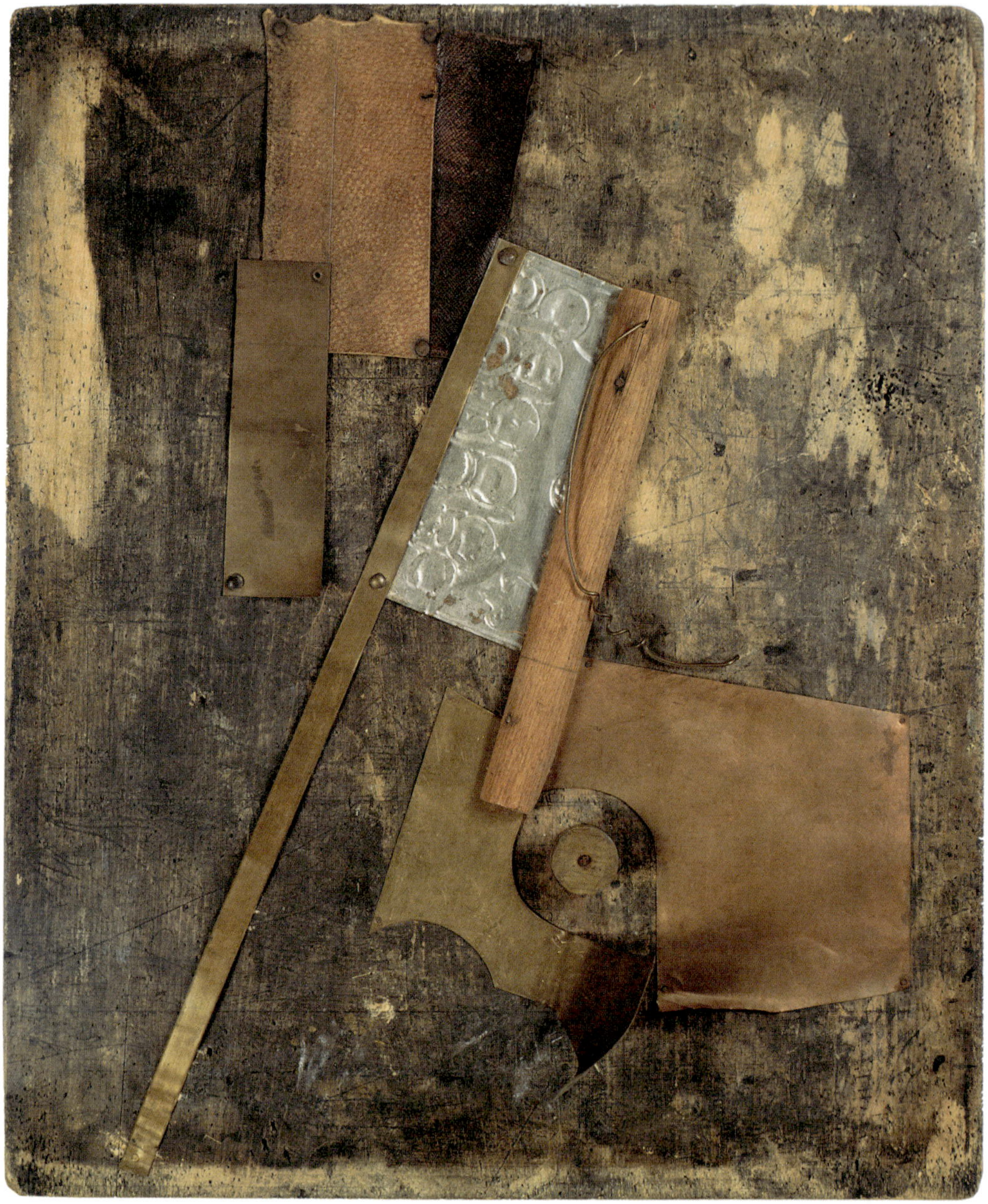

Vladimir Tatlin
Painterly Relief, ca. 1914

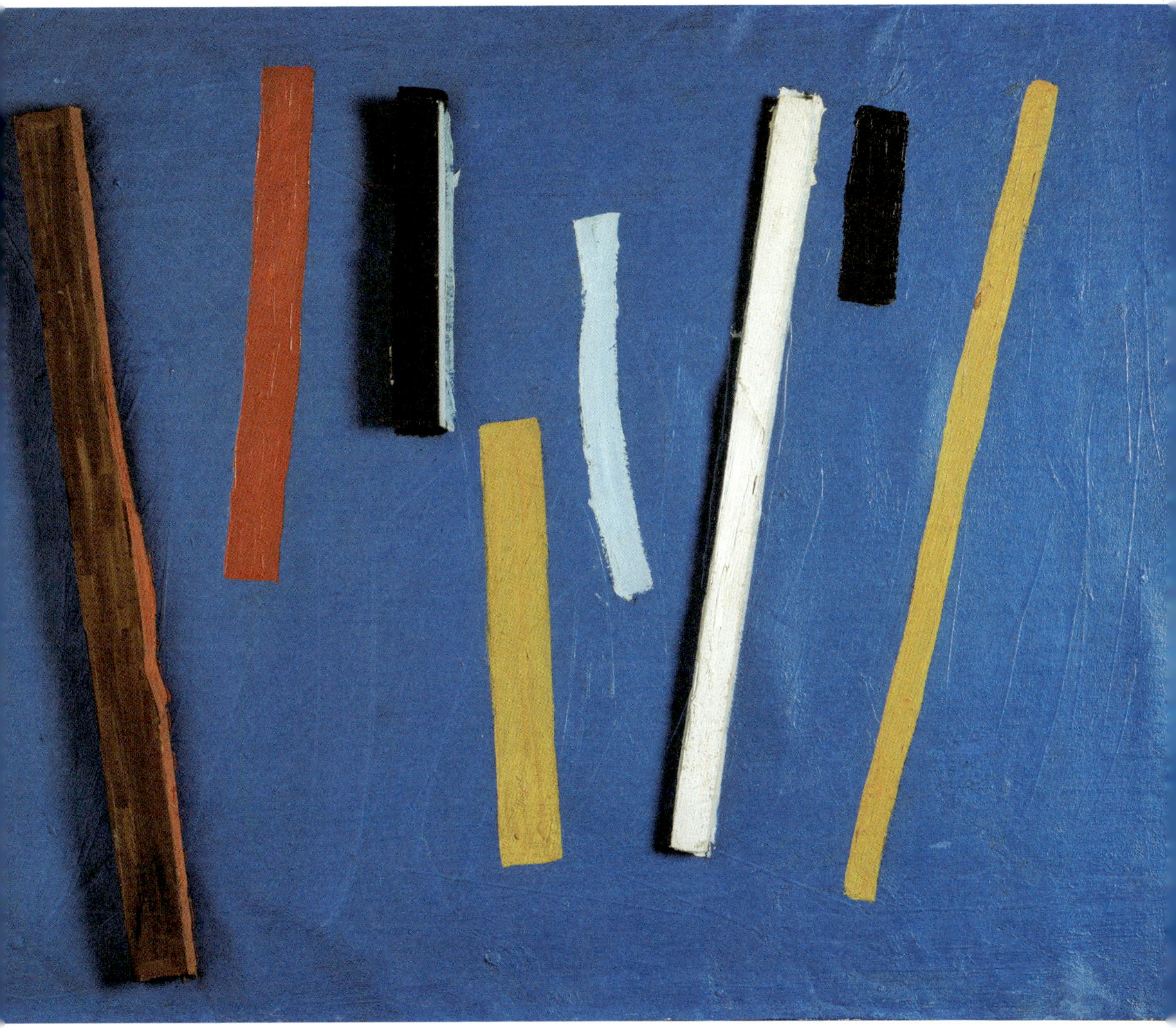

Ivan Puni
Relief, 1915

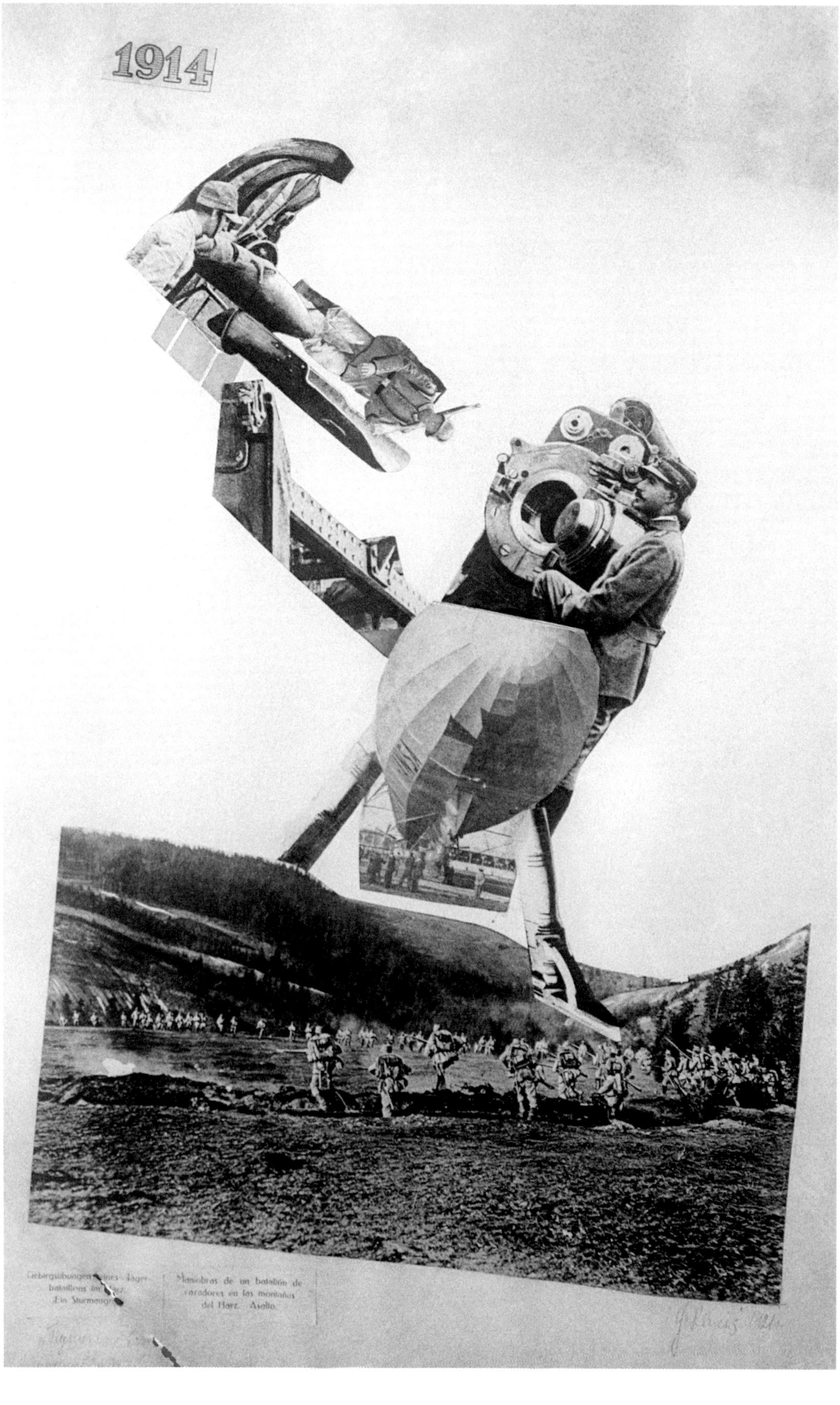
1914
Maniobras de un batallón de
cazadores en las montañas
del Harz. Asalto.

Universal War

What a misunderstanding by a man of the war; here is also a mistake in directing the destructive force not toward the forms of old culture, but toward destruction of a body.

—Kazimir Malevich to Mikhail Matiushin, April 4, 1916

Gustav Klutsis
Cannon Fodder, 1921

The outbreak of World War I in 1914 intensified Russians' awareness of the political significance of their cultural revolt. Malevich declared, "We should use the war for the preparation for a final disintegration of academism."[52] In collaboration with Mayakovsky, he designed antiwar political posters in imitation of folk lithographs called *lubki* that, with a callous mockery associated with this form, mobilized his peasants for a merciless fight against German aggression. The solemn *Black Square*, painted in 1915, reflected his "anxiety" and "desire to resist"; it became, simultaneously, his antiwar and antiart emblem.[53] That same year, Duchamp's statement that "the war will produce a 'severe direct art'" not only hinted at his forthcoming *Fountain* but offered a fit description of Malevich's revolutionary canvas.[54] The war resonated in the exhibitions *Tramway V*, organized to benefit an infirmary opened in Petrograd, and *0,10*, which in its pledge to be "the last futurist exhibition" signaled a final separation from the militarism of Italian futurism. As in the case of the Zurich Dadaists, whose formation was an antiwar phenomenon, the consciousness of rebellious Russian artists dwelled between "the battlefield" and the cultural field, or the space that art historian Leah Dickerman describes, in reference to Dada artists, as where

p. 63

52. Malevich to Matiushin, September 13, 1915, in *Malevich o sebe*, ed. Vakar and Mikhienko, 1:69.

53. Ibid. In 1915 Ilia Zdanevich became a war correspondent for Petrograd's *Speech (Rech)* newspaper, and Le Dantiu and Larionov departed to the front.

54. Marcel Duchamp, quoted in Matthew S. Witkovsky, "Chronology," in *Dada*, ed. Dickerman, 422.

"art is imagined in a quasimilitary way."[55] She continues by citing Richard Huelsenbeck: "the goal was to remake oneself in the mold of a soldier—'to make literature with a gun in hand.'"[56] Several letters that Malevich wrote to Matiushin from the warfront convey this kind of context for creativity: "I am sitting on the frontline writing about cubism amid the rattle, roar, and noise of propellers. I will present it as a weapon with which our understanding of a thing as something whole was effaced from our mind."[57] Malevich's substitution of a military term for an art style, as well as his alluding to cubism's distortion and fragmentation of the human body, effectively fits Huelsenbeck's formula.

Kazimir Malevich (designer) and Vladimir Mayakovsky (text) "Wilhelm's Merry-Go-Around," 1914

Kazimir Malevich (designer) and Vladimir Mayakovsky (text) "Look, look, near the Vistula: The German bellies are swelling so they don't feel so good," 1914

Kazimir Malevich *War*, 1914

Kruchenykh's response to the war immediately prompted him, again in collaboration with Khlebnikov, to write *War Opera*, a never finished follow-up to *Victory over the Sun* that would "unmask woe-warrior Wilhelm II and his gang."[58] After he became a member of Malevich's Supremus society—he would later describe Malevich as "an eco-artist" who "for the first time provides a ration (minimum) of paint and lines"—Kruchenykh applied the reductivism of suprematism in a handmade pp. 64–65 book, *Universal War* (1916).[59] The book's otherwise empty white cover has the Cyrillic hard sign, used to indicate masculine forms of verbs and nouns, including names. The sign's eradication was being proposed at the time, which for Kruchenykh signified a shift in language to be relentlessly pursued. The hard sign along with the book's title works to suggest that war is a male invention. Inside, *Universal War* consists of twelve color collages accompanied by minimal transrational poems referring to the ongoing war as well as to "the looming world and interplanetary

55. Leah Dickerman, "Introduction," in *Dada*, ed. Dickerman, 8.

56. Ibid.

57. Malevich to Matiushin, November 6, 1916, in *Malevich o sebe*, ed. Vakar and Mikhienko, 1:97.

58. Aleksei Kruchenykh, "O voine," in *K istorii russkogo futurizma: vospominaniia i dokumenty*, ed. N. Gur'ianova (Moscow: Gileia, 2006), 238. The opera was never finished.

59. A. E. Kruchenykh, "Nosoboika" (1917), in *Malevich o sebe*, ed. Vakar and Mikhienko, 2:109.

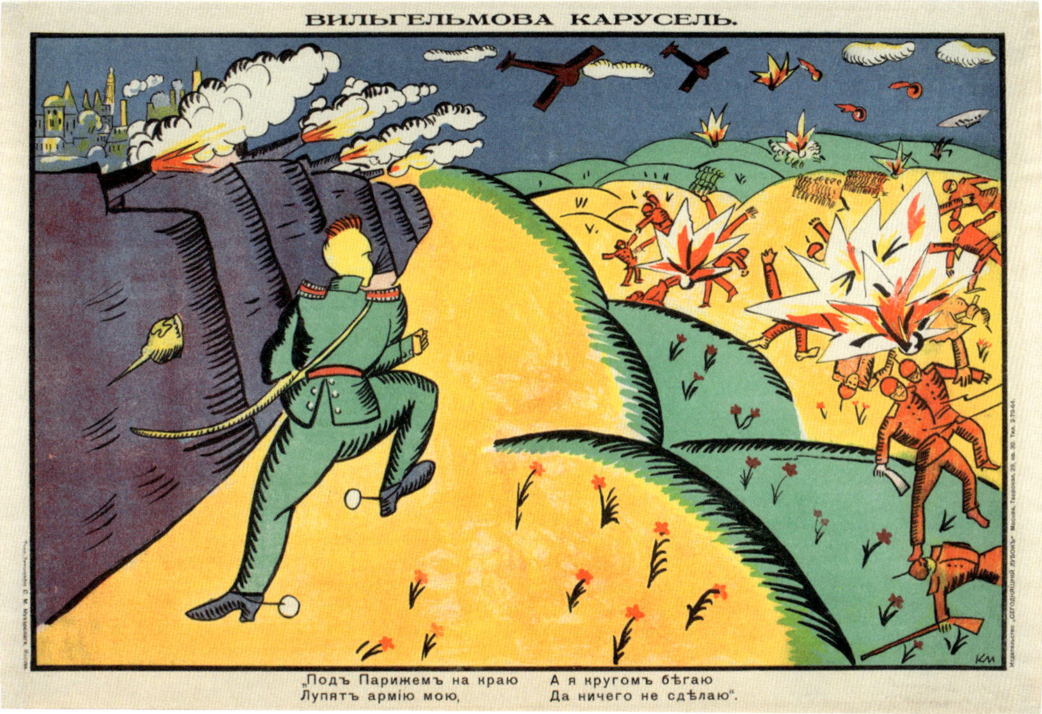
ВИЛЬГЕЛЬМОВА КАРУСЕЛЬ.
КМ
„Подъ Парижемъ на краю
Лупятъ армію мою,
А я кругомъ бѣгаю
Да ничего не сдѣлаю".

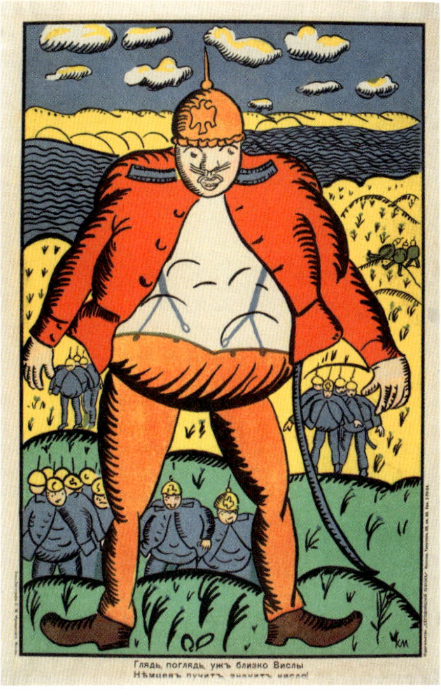
КМ
Глядь, поглядь, ужъ близко Вислы
Нѣмцевъ пучитъ, значитъ кисло!

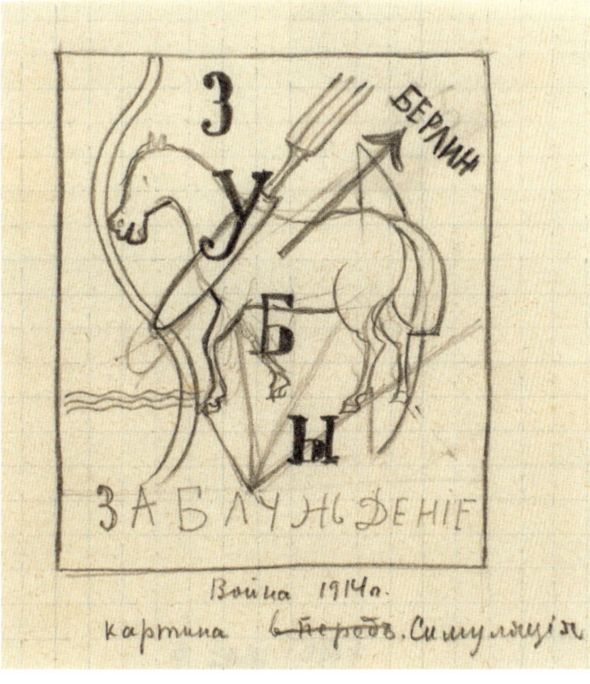
З
У
Б
Ы
БЕРЛИН
ЗАБЛУЖДЕНИЕ
Война 1914 г.
картина в перед. Симуляция

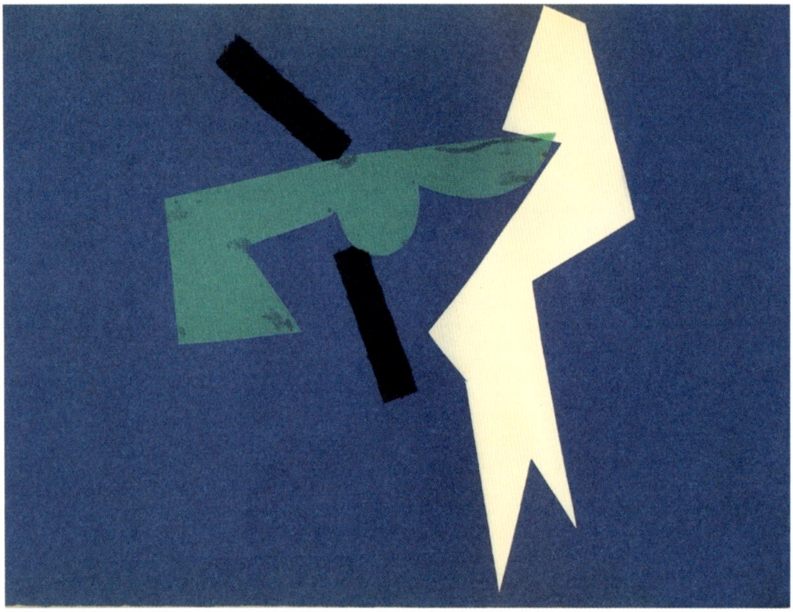

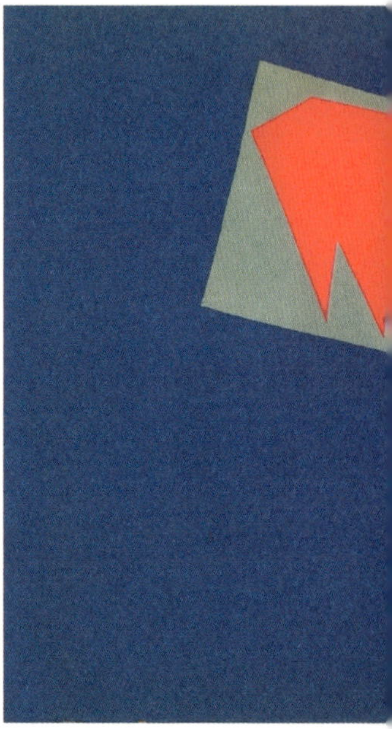

Aleksei Kruchenykh
Illustrations for the book
Universal War, 1916

wars," which Kruchenykh positioned, as had Malevich, as a symbiosis of cultural and actual wars.[60] His introduction hails nonobjective art ("transrational painting," in line with "transrational language") rather than suprematism. Yet Kruchenykh's collages differ from Malevich's strict geometry. They are in line with Olga Rozanova's formally more anarchic nonobjectivity and juxtapose such terms as *explosion*, *destruction*, and *battle*, evoking fragments of broken glass and shell splinters.

pp. 66–67

For the book *War* (1916), Kruchenykh retreated to the album's verbal component, letting Rozanova render the visual arsenal. *War*'s cover repeats the shapes of the collages in *Universal War*, whereas the pages inside mix motifs and styles of folk art primitivism with expressionism (the style that both Russian artists and Dadaists would later defy) and geometry, in line with everythingism's tenets.[61] Goncharova had been the first to appropriate

60. Kruchenykh, "O voine," 238–39.

61. For example, see B. Arvatov, "Ekspressionizm kak sotsial'noe iavlenie," *Kniga i revoliutsiia* 6, no. 18 (1922): 27–29.

62. Kruchenykh, "O voine," 239.

63. Punin, "Vyderzhki iz statei N. Punina," in *O Tatline*, ed. Punina and Rakitin, 25; and Nikolai Punin, "Iz pisem N. Punina A. Arens" (1920), in *O Tatline*, ed. Punina and Rakitin, 13.

64. Aleksei Kruchenykh, "V nogu s epokhoi (Futuristy i oktiabr'), in *K istorii russkogo futurizma*, ed. Gur'ianova, 138.

65. "Kvartira no. 5" from the memoir *Iskusstvo i revoliutsiia* (1930s), in N. Punin, *O Tatline*, ed. Punina and Rakitin, 10.

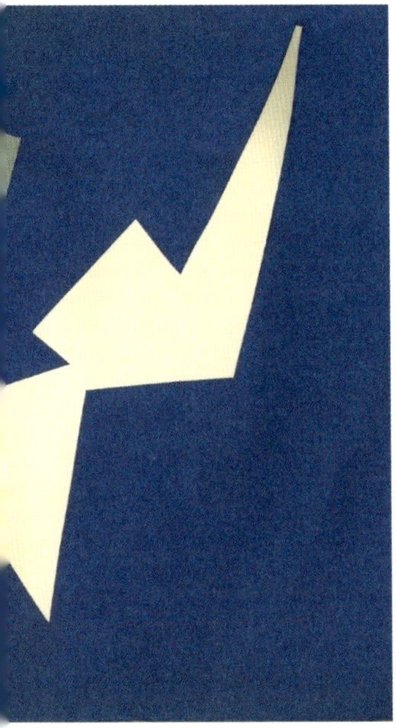

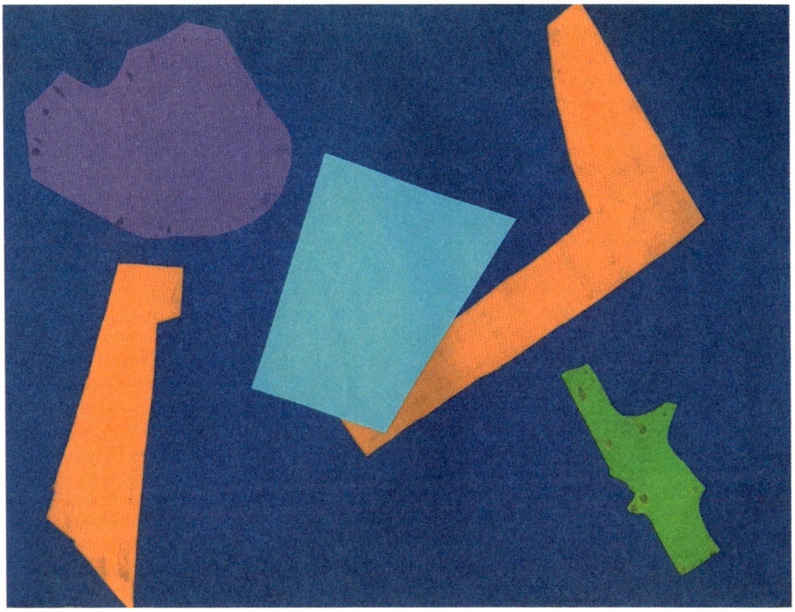

apocalyptic imagery for interpreting war in her black-and-white portfolio *Mystical Images of War* (1914). She undoubtedly had conceived it in response to Larionov's being drafted into the army. He would return from the war wounded. For *War*, Kruchenykh made the radical gesture of including contemporary newspapers' war reportages about "nightmares" and "specific [read "cruel"] 'war tactics.'"[62]

In 1916, in conversation with Tatlin, Punin—whose expression the "ripped consciousness" amply conveys how the avant-garde milieu felt at the time—spoke of the "socialist character of Futurism" that manifests itself "not by being for every worker, but in the fact that the entirety of aesthetic views worked out by socialism had been invested and expressed in Futurist art."[63] On a similar subject, Kruchenykh said, "men of the future [*budetliane*] began their offensive in 1911–12—the years of the new upsurge of the struggle for liberation of the proletariat."[64] Thus, one year before the Russian Revolution, a proto-Dadaist everythingism was "rolling over" into an artistic practice of "uncontrolled shift toward left."[65]

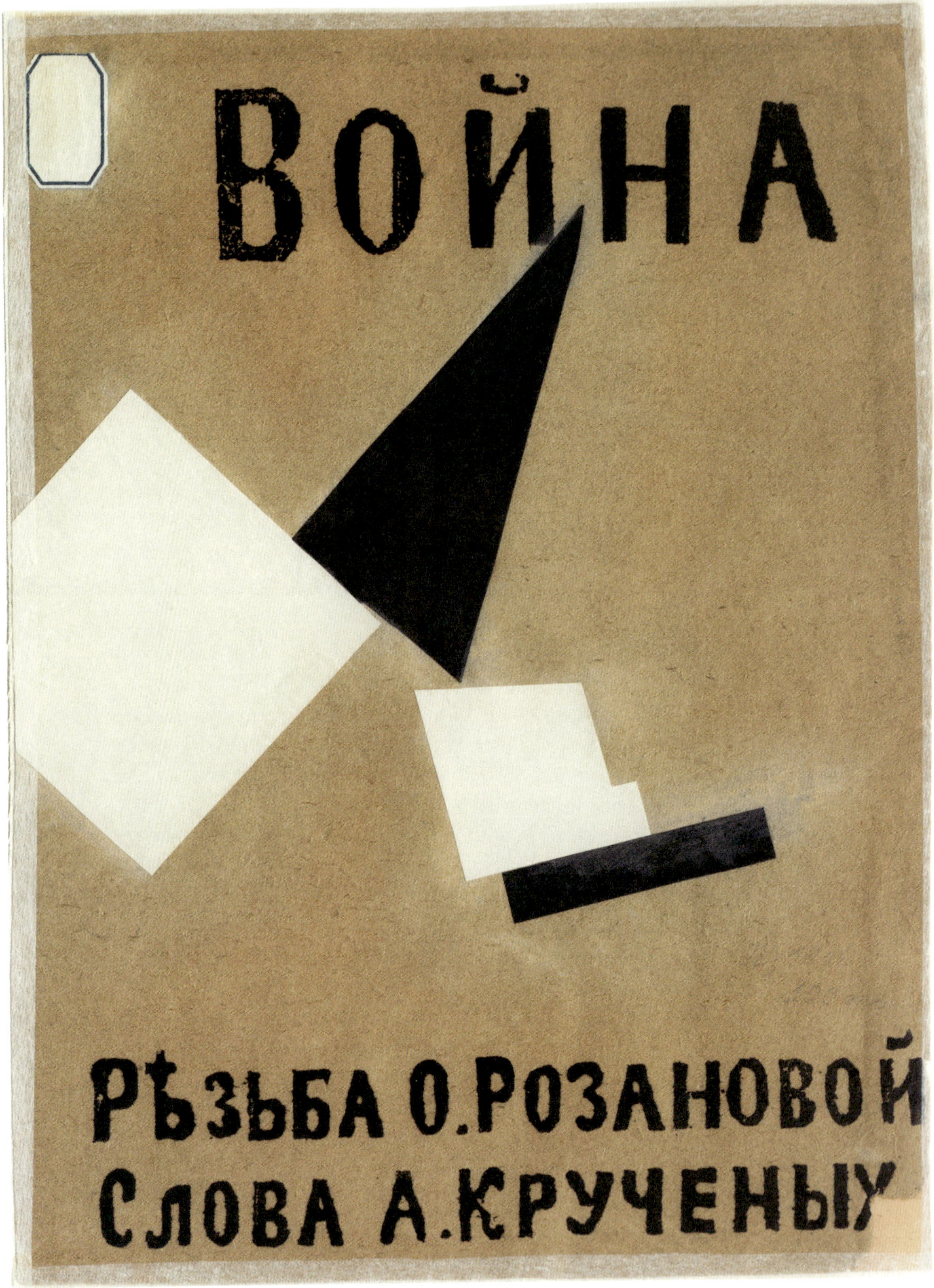
ВОЙНА
РѢЗЬБА О. РОЗАНОВОЙ
СЛОВА А. КРУЧЕНЫХ

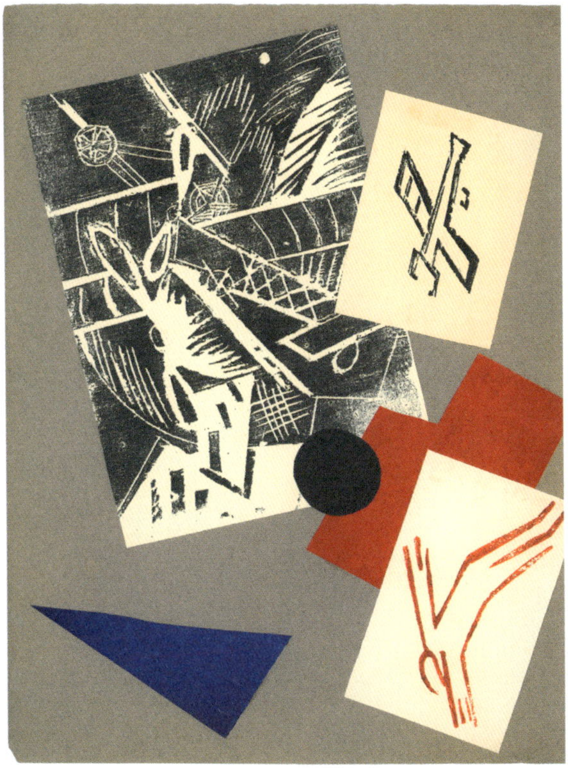

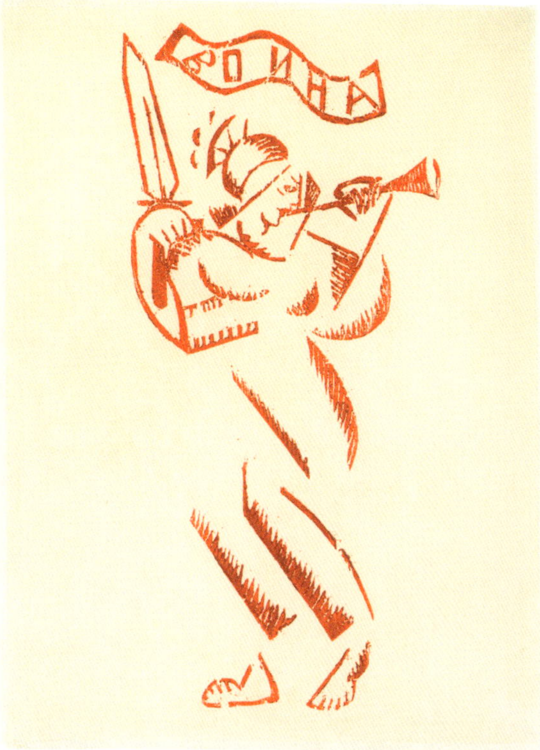

Olga Rozanova
Illustrations for the book *War*
by Aleksei Kruchenykh, 1916

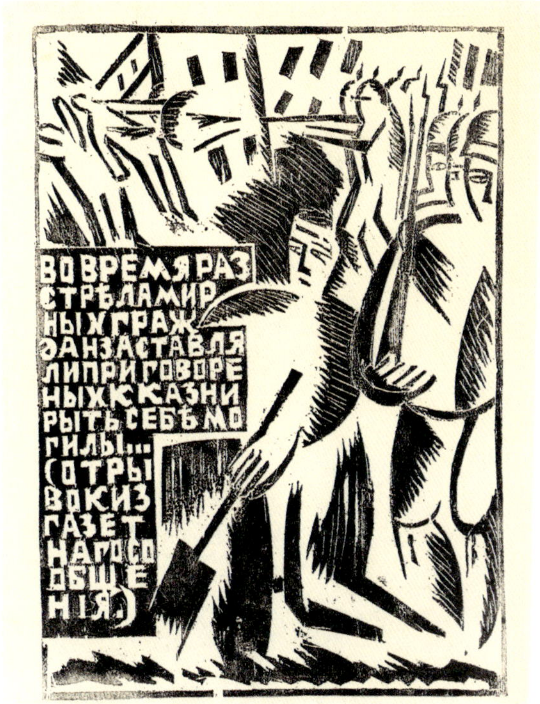

Olga Rozanova
Cover of the book *War* by Aleksei
Kruchenykh, 1916

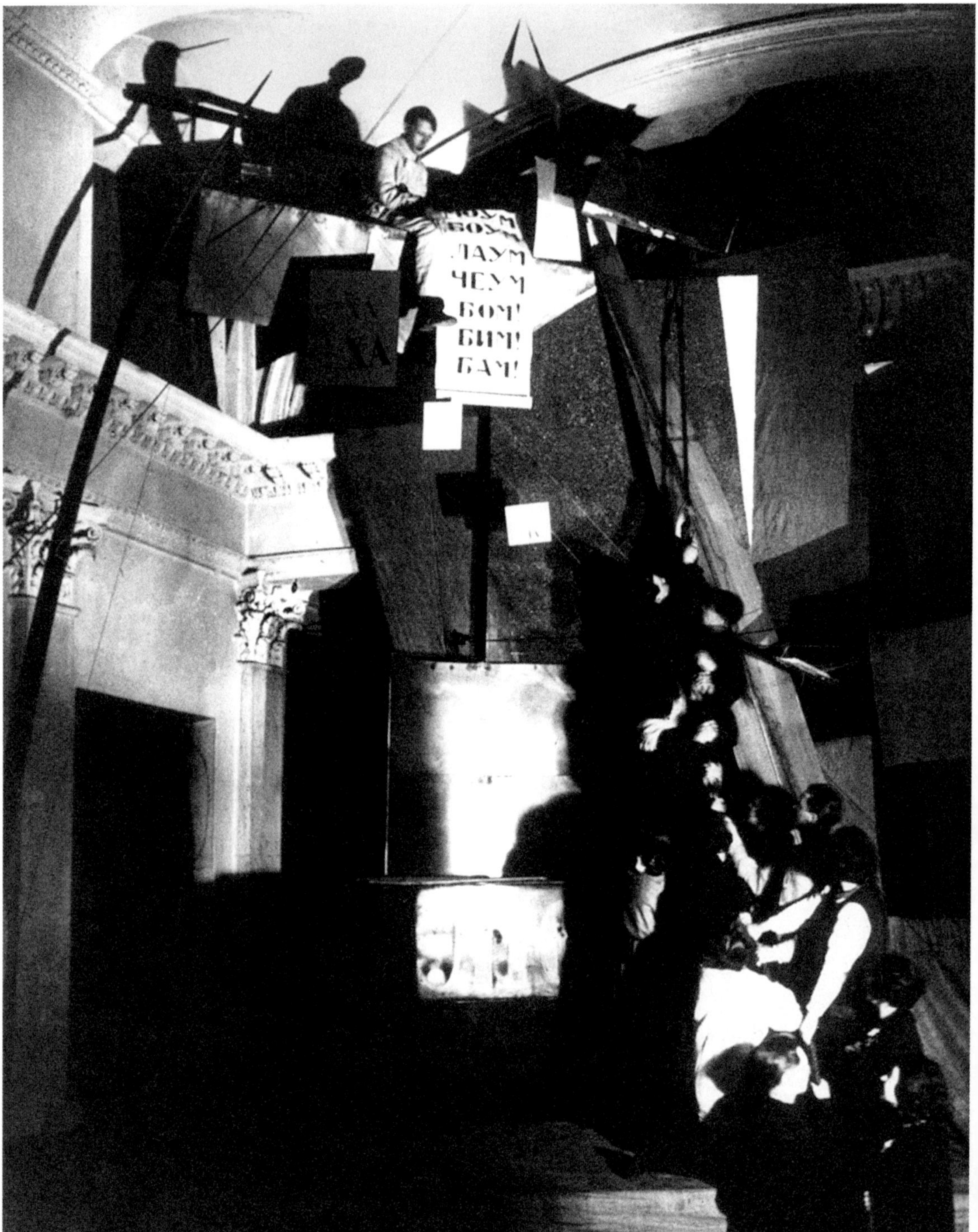
БОУМ
ЛАУМ
ЧЕУМ
БОМ!
БИМ!
БАМ!

Revolutions: Da Da!— Nyet Nyet!

Vladimir Tatlin
Stage design for *Zangezi* by Velimir Khlebnikov, Museum of Material Culture, Leningrad, 1923

> For every "yes" Dada simultaneously sees the "no." Dada is a yes-no.
>
> —Theo van Doesburg, *What Is Dada?*, 1923

> A combative fountain of Dada's founders . . . in Russia was realized in the Revolution.
>
> —Abram Efros, "Dada and Dadaism," 1923[66]

In 1921, prior to Abram Efros's statement above, Jakobson analyzed the Russians as having traveled toward the October Revolution of 1917 "through a realization of the violence of artistic form" that in the West had culminated in Duchamp's *Fountain* (1917).[67] Photographic self-portraits made independently in 1917 by Duchamp and Gustav Klutsis illustrate differences and similarities in Russian and European modernisms that in that year converged on the grounds of Dadaist revolutionary mentality. New York Dadaist Duchamp, dressed in a stylish suit and smoking his pipe leisurely, and soldier of the revolution Klutsis sit "for his trick-mirror photo . . . each man cloned into five, sitting around a table contemplating himselves [*sic*]. Each shows one of them seen from five different vantages in a single photo."[68] The external pp. 70–71 differences between Duchamp and Klutsis underline the fact that although Europeans and Russians concurred in their antiestablishment agendas—often expressed through tomfoolery—one was "bourgeois nihilism" and "anarchism" while the other was directed toward "realization of revolutionary problems" and "connection with the workers" (in the words of "Bolshevik in painting" George Grosz).[69] Yet the fact

66. Abram Efros, "Dada i dadaizm," *Sovremenyi zapad*, no. 3 (1923): 118–25.

67. Roman Jakobson, "Letters from the West. Dada," *Vestnik teatra*, no. 82 (1921), in *Language and Literature*, ed. Krystyna Pomorska and Stephen Rudy (Cambridge, MA: Belknap, 1987), 39.

68. I borrow this description from Allan Antliff's "Anarchy, Politics, and Dada," which tells the story of Henri-Pierre Roché, Duchamp, and Francis Picabia making these kinds of photographs at Rockaway Beach, New York, in 1917. Allan Antliff, "Anarchy, Politics, and Dada," in *Making Mischief: Dada Invades New York* (New York: Whitney Museum of American Art, 1997), 220.

69. Zhorzh Gross, "K moim rabotam," *Lef*, no. 2 (1923): 27, 30. The description of Grosz is by art patron Harry Count Kessler, quoted in John Willett, *Art and Politics in the Weimar Period: The New Sobriety, 1917–1933* (New York: Pantheon Books, 1978), 51.

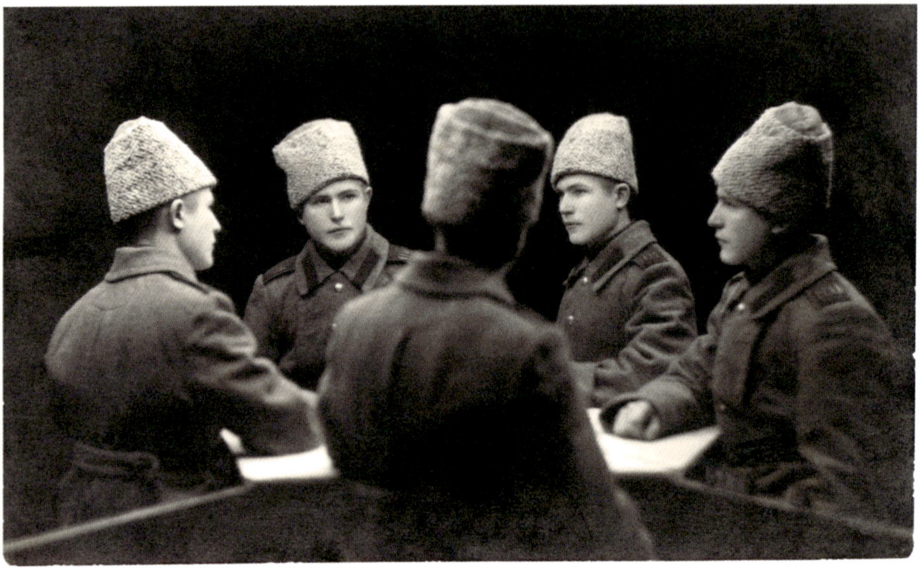

Anonymous
Multiple portrait of Gustav Klutsis, 1917

that critique of culture and critique of regime found expression in compositionally matching photographs means Dadaist tenets had begun to fertilize real politics and expand the movement's international ambitions.

Kruchenykh and Khlebnikov, the authors of *Victory over the Sun* who instigated nihilistic consciousness in the Russian avant-garde, had swiftly reacted to the February Revolution of 1917. Writing from the Caucasus several months after, Kruchenykh stated that, had he been in Petrograd or Moscow, with his "hot head" he would have joined the barricades.[70] Around this time he gave his verdict on contemporary art and politics: "Our epoch is in zero! . . . The world not only has been reshaped (Futurists, *sdvig* [shift], nonsense), but is thrown away. What is left? Nothing. What will come? Something beyond the zero."[71] Kruchenykh viewed the February Revolution as he had the war: as a ground for estrangement (*ostranenie*, a term

70. A. E. Kruchenykh, "O Maleviche," in *Malevich o sebe*, ed. Vakar and Mikhienko, 2:111.

71. Ibid.

72. Vladimir Markov, *Russian Futurism: A History* (Berkeley: University of California Press, 1968), 342.

73. Kruchenykh, "V nogu s epokhoi (Futuristy i Oktiabr')," in *K istorii russkogo futurizma* 144.

74. In his memoirs, Zdanevich writes, "Wherever we put our sight, we saw the new, and the old values were crumbling to dust." Il'ia Zdanevich, *Fragmenty vospominanii: Minuvshee* (Moscow, 1991), 162.

75. This is what Richter wrote on the subject: "The Cabaret Voltaire played and raised hell at No. 1, Spiegelgasse. Diagonally opposite, at No. 12, Spiegelgasse, the same narrow thoroughfare in which the Cabaret Voltaire mounted its nightly orgies of singing, poetry and dancing, lived Lenin. . . . It seemed to me that Swiss authorities were much more suspicious of the Dadaists . . . than of these quiet, studious Russians . . . even though the latter were planning a world revolution and later astonished the authorities by carrying it out." Richter, *Dada*, 16.

76. Ibid., 176.

Shklovsky coined in 1917) and shifts (*sdvigi*); that is, formalist concepts catapulted into politics as the avant-garde artists' and poets' "conscious violations and distortions of traditional aesthetics" manifested themselves in real life.[72] Khlebnikov reacted to the February Revolution more aggressively. He mocked the prime minister of the provisional government, Aleksandr Kirensky, promising him "a slap from the whole Russia" and making a prank call to the Winter Palace (during which he pretended to represent the Academy of Arts).[73] In contrast, Ilia Zdanevich displayed characteristic sagacity by considering the February Revolution a rehearsal of what was to come and embarking on the consolidation of left artists to defend and disseminate avant-garde tenets in the new sociopolitical reality.[74]

Vladimir Lenin had returned to Russia in April 1917 after his exile in Zurich. He remained in Petrograd for only a few months before it became clear that what lay "beyond the zero" was the October Revolution. In Zurich, he had lived near the Cabaret Voltaire, visiting it and contesting with Dadaists in politics and at the chessboard.[75] "The Dadaists failed to convince the workers," but Lenin boarded an armored train to do just that, becoming, among other accusations to come, an agent of Dada.[76] His antiwar speech at a Finnish train station—allegedly delivered from an armored car—employed rhetoric to win the population's trust. Klutsis's photomontages dedicated to the two revolutions of 1917 reflect their

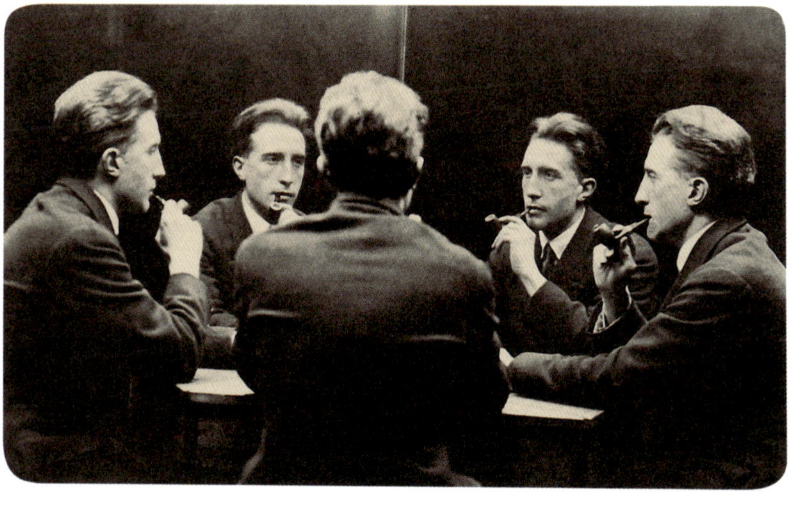

Anonymous
Multiple portrait of Marcel Duchamp, 1917

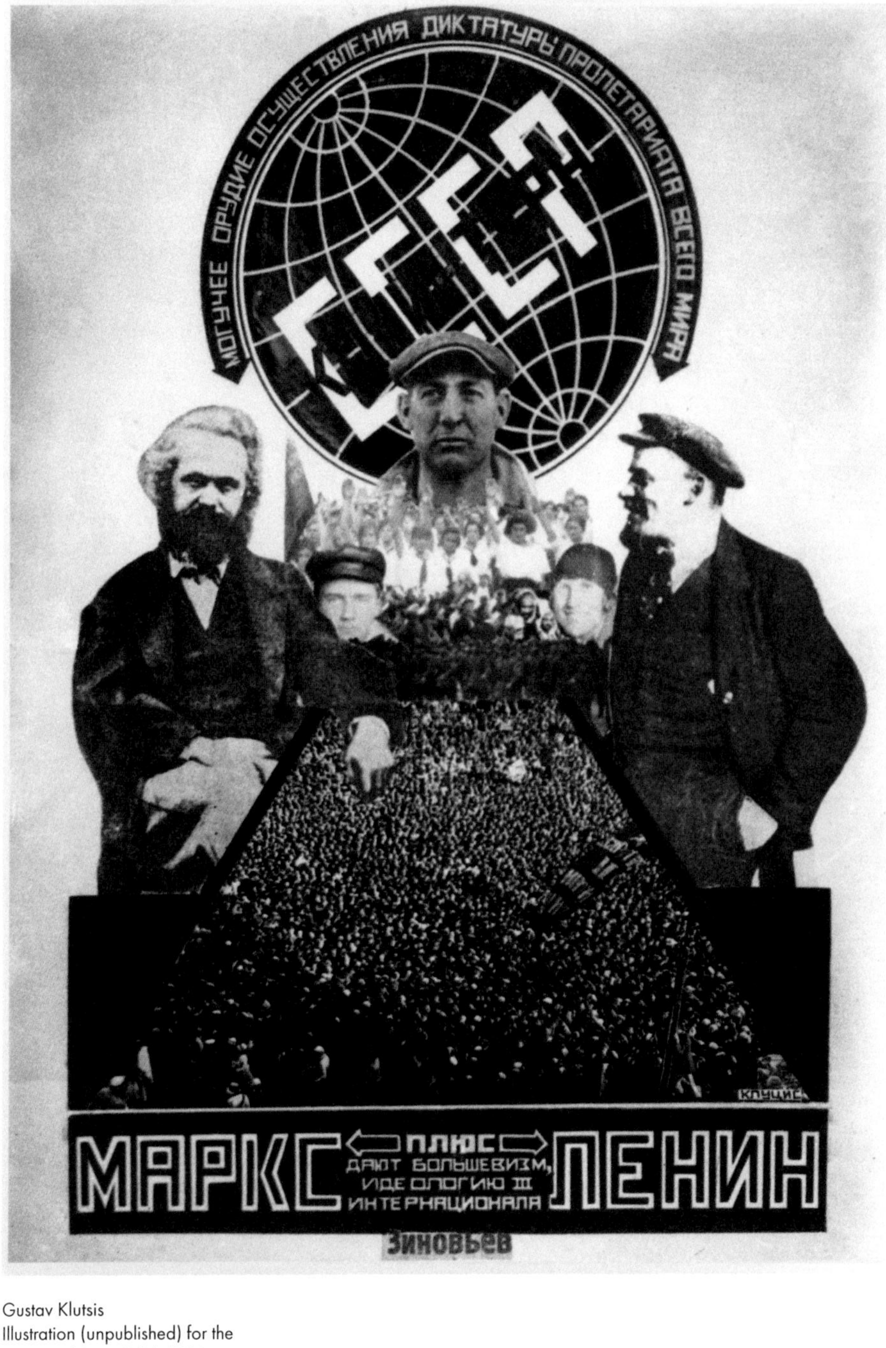

Gustav Klutsis
Illustration (unpublished) for the
History of the VKP(b), 1924

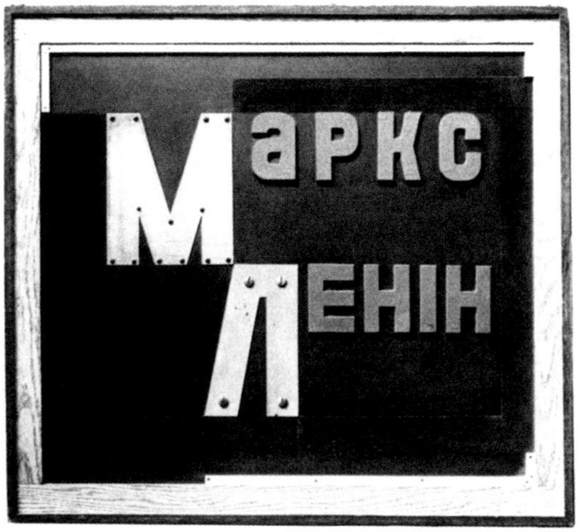

Vasily Ermilov
Memorial board *Marx and Lenin*,
1924

ideological distinctions. His rendition showing the February Revolution—the words are written separately, one along a vertical stripe on the left and another at the bottom—is Dadaist in its negation of the tsar's regime and in its manifestly disjointed imagery; it includes a crossed-out p. 96 portrait of the tsar placed in a black square and connected to the crowds of "proletarians" and "soldiers" whose actions, in Malevich's words, "turned into a huge manifestation. Next day shells were cast and spears sharpened."[77] Here enemies, some disembodied, fall into the barrel of a gun. Next to a black square is a whimsical structure consisting of, among other details, one large and two smaller heads, the latter with speakers from which slogans stream into the streets. As was the case with his earlier cited reports on the war, for his summaries of the February Revolution, published in the newspaper *Anarchy*, Malevich linked the shifts in art and politics: "Cubism, futurism—breaking of objects, abolition of all laws of the old. War, riot, canons, running, movement, crash in the skies, and on the earth. . . . World war, restructuring of states, revolution, new law, etc."[78] In Klutsis's second photomontage, of the October

77. "Chto bylo v fevrale 1917 goda i marte," in *Krasny Malevich: stat'i iz gazety "Anarkhiia"* (Moscow: Common Place, 2016), 185.

78. Ibid., 187.

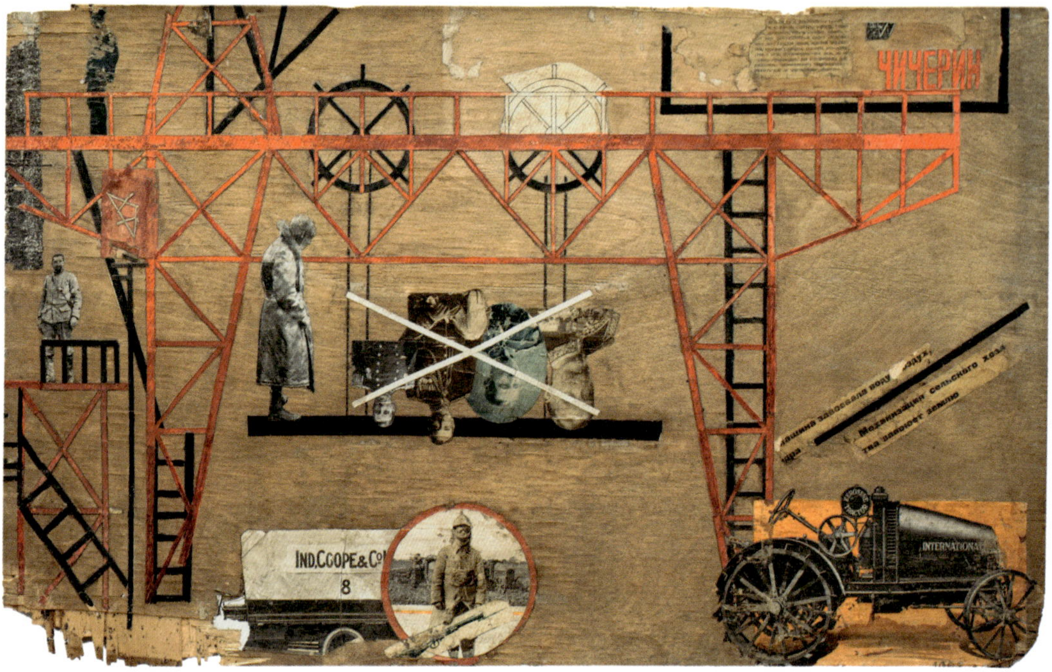

p. 97 Revolution, the heroes, such as a sailor, are affirmed and rendered coherently and on a larger scale. The revolution's enemies, paradoxically placed on the left-hand side, are crossed out. In contrast, Leon Trotsky, Joseph Stalin, Grigory Zinoviev, and Lenin (who is significantly larger) occupy the right side of the composition. Similar scenarios of brutal societal shifts are expressed in the portfolio *October 1917–1918, Heroes and Victims of the Revolution*, issued to commemorate the first anniversary of the October Revolution. p. 98 Its contents include Mayakovsky's "first attempt at 'agitpoetry'" and illustrations by Puni, Boguslavskaia, and others who juxtapose representatives of the toppled classes and those who toppled them.[79] The mockery of the former is balanced by the deeds and misery of the latter in both images and words.

Liubov Popova
Stage design for *Earth in Turmoil* by Sergei Tretiakov, Meyerhold Theater, Moscow, 1923–1924

Aleksei Kruchenykh, Kirill Zdanevich, Vasily Kamensky
Cover of the book *1918*, 1917

Aleksei Kruchenykh
Page from Kruchenykh's scrapbook, n.d.

79. N. I. Khardzhiev, "Fotoshutka Maiakovskogo," in *Stat'i ob avangarde*, ed. Duganov, Arpishkin, and Sarab'ianov, 2:154.

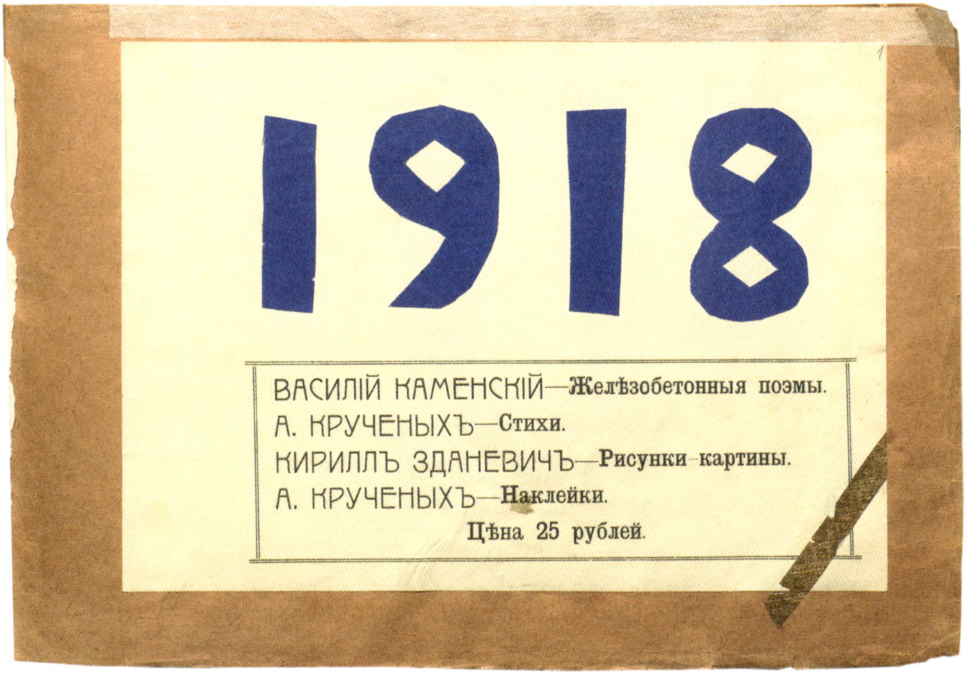
1918
ВАСИЛІЙ КАМЕНСКІЙ—Желѣзобетонныя поэмы.
А. КРУЧЕНЫХЪ—Стихи.
КИРИЛЛЪ ЗДАНЕВИЧЪ—Рисунки-картины.
А. КРУЧЕНЫХЪ—Наклейки.
Цѣна 25 рублей.

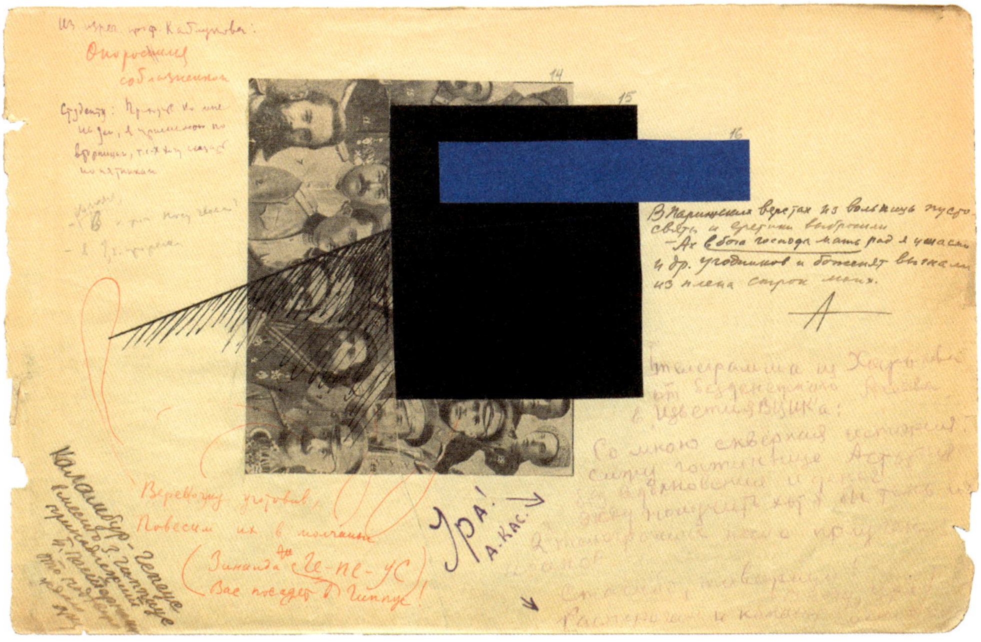

PROLETARIAN NONOBJECTIVITY

Neither *Heroes and Victims*'s expressionism nor Klutsis's photomontage dominated the immediate post-October period. Instead, several paradigms of nonrepresentational art took over the art world: Malevich's suprematism, Tatlin's constructivism, Larionov's rayonism, and Vasily Kandinsky's abstract expressionism. Kandinsky, dubbed the "'father' of Dada," had already made an impact on that movement's founders in Zurich, from Hans Arp to Hugo Ball and Richard Huelsenbeck.[80] To escape author-controlled modernist styles, all nonrepresentational practices were channeled into what can be described as the new concept of nonobjective everythingism, a "Parade of all the Isms" appropriated by the new army of artists.[81] Rooted in *Victory over the Sun* and Dadaism in Zurich, it was artistic practice "imagined in a multimedia context, in which abstraction in language, performance, and the visual arts were seen as integrally related enterprises, and each of great weight."[82]

Unlike Kandinsky's expressionism and psychologism, which faced tangible obstacles on the path of dissemination beyond the aesthetic framework, Malevich's ABC of geometry, Tatlin's "machine art," and Aleksandr Rodchenko's ruler-controlled formalism aspired to be what Shklovsky described as "more set as a task than made"; that is, art that does not depend "on the uninterrupted perception."[83] Mechanical methods of distribution and the framework of collective perception resulted in production that had high potential for copying. With these artists, the imposition of one's ABC was turned into the proposition of an egalitarian ready-made aesthetics that could erase references to the past.[84] Nonobjective forms now signified revolutionary consciousness, catapulting their practitioners into public space and establishing a communicative system among new, proletarian audiences. In Malevich's view, it was an ultra-left social segment that, in carrying his "Suprematist banners," would be able to form an equal opposition to the new "left" as well as to the "center."[85]

Malevich was now ready to objectify nonobjectivity by releasing it into real life and organizing it according to the rules of geometry. Hence, while Kandinsky reached out from Moscow to the masses with a questionnaire on the perception of form and color, Malevich rolled up his sleeves and entered the "Red square of Art."[86] Together with a brigade of younger artists—including Klutsis, Natan Altman, Ivan Kudriashov, El Lissitzky, Pavel Mansurov, and Władysław Strzemiński—he tested pp. 77, 104, 105 his geometric alphabet on squares, streets, buildings, and transport. The goal was not to provide a revolutionary layer over the old world but to build a new one, the pursuit propelling Malevich's students to

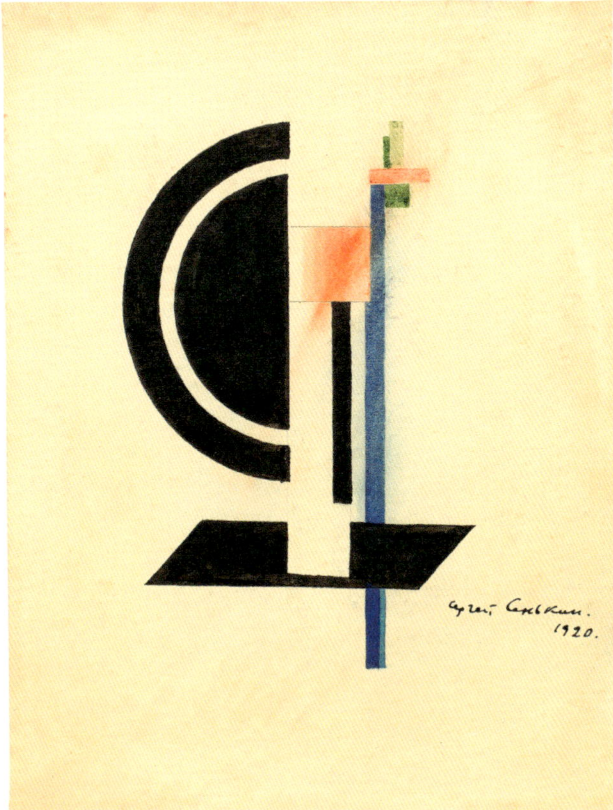

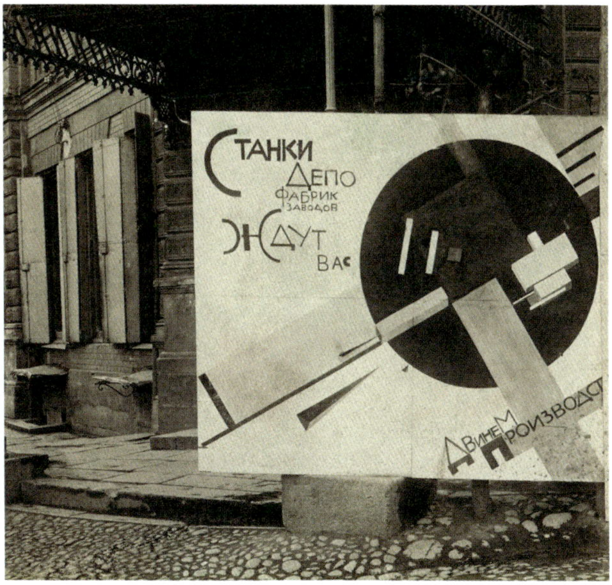

Sergei Senkin
Construction, 1920

Anonymous
View of El Lissitzky's propaganda board "The Factory Workbenches Await You" in front of a factory, Vitebsk, 1920

80. For example, Richter points out that under the influence of Kandinsky, Ball "had taken up the idea of the *Gesamtkunstwerk*." Richter, *Dada*, 39.

81. El Lissitzky to Sophie Küppers, March 23, 1924, in *El Lissitzky: Life, Letters, Texts*, ed. Sophie Lissitzky-Küppers (London: Thames and Hudson, 1968), 48. In 1924, Lissitzky and Arp demonstrated this collectivized approach to visual languages in *The ISMs of Art*, which illustrates several Russian works, including Natan Altman's *Russia, Labor* (1921), Aleksandr Rodchenko's painting from the series *Linearism* (1919), and Tatlin's
p. 110 *Counter-Relief* and *Model for the Monument to the Third International*.

82. Dickerman, "Zurich," 26.

83. Shklovskii, "O fakture i kontrrel'efakh," 2:105. Shklovsky wrote this in 1920 regarding suprematism, which is exactly when Malevich, with UNOVIS students, used suprematism for public decorations in Vitebsk.

84. "ABC" refers to Tzara's phrase "To impose your ABC is a natural thing—hence deplorable." See his Dada manifesto of 1918, available at http://www.writing.upenn.edu/library/Tzara_Dada-Manifesto_1918.pdf (accessed January 25, 2018).

85. Malevich to Stepanova, December 21, 1919, *Malevich o sebe*, ed. Vakar and Mikhienko, 1:119.

86. Malevich to Kruchenykh, September 18, 1920, in *Malevich o sebe*, ed. Vakar and Mikhienko, 1:129.

nonobjective three-dimensional compositions such as Klutsis's *Dynamic City* (1919) and Lissitzky's *Prouns*, an acronym for "project for the affirmation of the new." This conversion of flat nonobjectivity into the three-dimensional eventually led to an entirely new thing (*veshch*), which included communicative apparatuses such as Klutsis's radio orators and his multifunction constructions such as a "screen-tribune-kiosk"; Tatlin's *Monument to the Third International*, or *Tower* (1919–1920);
p. 78 and Lissitzky's *Project for a Tribune on a Square* (1920). Immersion in the transformative qualities of nonobjectivity manifested in artists' antiart ideology, described by Klutsis as "down with art" and by Lissitzky as "overcoming art." Critic Boris Arvatov called such production "proletarian nonobjectivity," distinguishing it from nonobjective practices in capitalist society, considered to depend on the personal goals of the individual artist.[87] In contrast, "the comradely collaboration of artists and theoreticians in the proletarian laboratory will create an atmosphere in which each problem will emerge indispensably and objectively from practical and conscious premises."[88] Forming a universal language, nonobjectivists created an effective method to disseminate the revolutionary agenda both at home and to the international community, within which German Dadaists were most receptive. Klutsis's and Tatlin's works dedicated to the Third Congress of the Communist International (Comintern),
pp. 106–107 Moscow (1921) and the journal *International of Art*, planned in 1919 under Malevich's editorial eye, aspired to the unification of international left cultural communities and the dissemination of an antibourgeois agenda.[89]

Punin helped to build the model of Tatlin's *Monument to the Third International*, and he

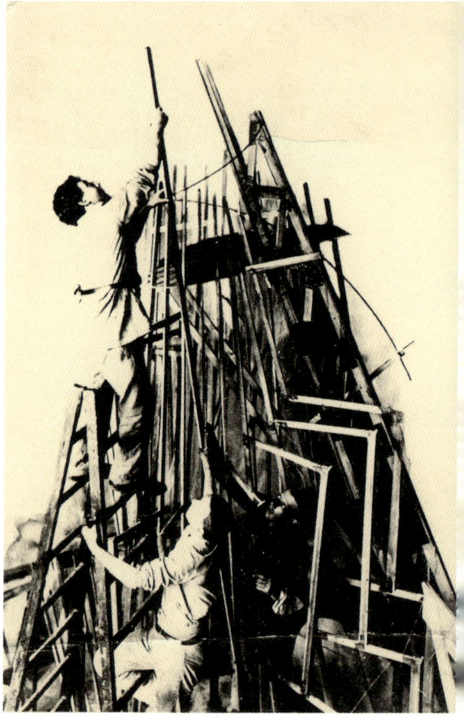

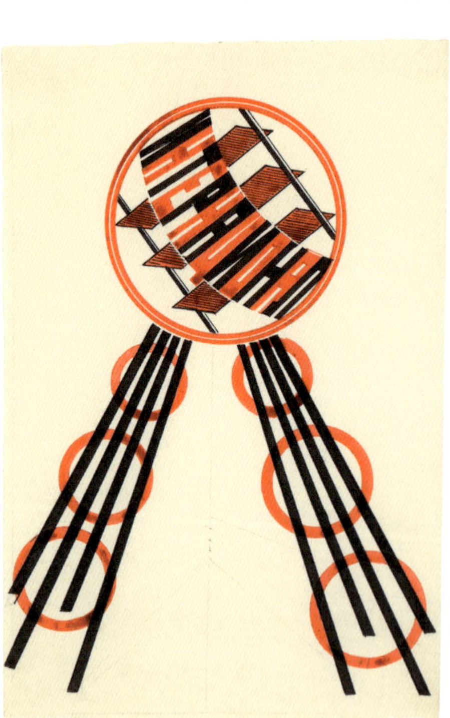

Vladimir Tatlin
Construction of the model of Tatlin's *Monument to the Third International* (left to right: Iosif Meerzon, Tevel Shapiro and Tatlin), 1920

Gustav Klutsis
International, 1922

recalled a Dadaist atmosphere of fun and obscenity, as well as an antiart mood: "They [the collective of builders] are making jokes about painting, art, modernism, etc."[90] Tatlin was saying, "No art . . . Fuck art."[91] On a serious note, Punin described *Tower* as a symbol of class struggle, with its spiral-line movement signifying "liberated humanity."[92] He believed *Tower* was the first revolutionary work that deserved to be sent to Europe. Indeed, *Tower* became "an international event in the art world," with German Dadaists hailing Tatlin as a hero of antiart and machine culture.[93] p. 122

REVOLUTIONARY SHIFTS

Amid the dual atmosphere of mockery and sobriety, in which the "monument-form"—*Tower*—was made, artists were channeling the serious project of public agitation for Marxist ideology and Soviet mass culture into absurdist and chance-based collages and designs. In them, Russian *da da* (yes yes) formed a productive double bind with *nyet nyet* (no no), positioning "transreason" as "the mandatory form for the embodiment of art."[94] This amply concurred with the Dadaists' "central message," the "realization that reason and anti-reason, sense and nonsense, design and chance, consciousness and unconsciousness, belong together as necessary parts of a whole."[95] In his text about Khlebnikov's *Zangezi* (1922; a transrational follow-up to *Victory over the Sun*), Punin addresses the condition as "terrifying, and now victoriously present in art rationalism."[96] He is referring most likely to the constructivism of the Institute of Artistic Culture (INKhUK), formulated in the early 1920s and based on logic. Tatlin's decision to stage *Zangezi* in 1923 challenged INKhUK's homogeneous concept p. 68

87. Boris Arvatov, "Proletariat i levoe iskusstvo," *Vestnik iskusstv*, no. 1 (January 1922): 10.

88. Ibid.

89. Among the texts written for the first issue was Khlebnikov's "Artists of the World" (initially called "The Global Writing Language: A System of Mutual Hieroglyphs for the People of the Earth") and Malevich's "The Appeal of Kazimir Malevich to the Progressive Artists of Italy" [see p. 275 of the present catalogue].

90. Nicolai Punin, "Iz pisem N. Punina A. Arens," in *O Tatline*, ed. Punina and Rakitin, 23.

91. Ibid., 24.

92. Punin, "Pamiatnik III Internatsionala," 20.

93. Ibid.

94. "Manifesto of the '41°'" (1919) [see p. 283 of the present catalogue].

95. Richter, *Dada*, 64.

96. Nikolai Punin, "Zangezi," in *O Tatline*, ed. Punina and Rakitin, 62.

of constructivism. Like Punin, Tatlin valued Khlebnikov's more complex, "weaved" perception of the new reality, where the "materials of his machine" were "death, war, revolution, destruction of Western European science, language," rather than solely technological and social progress.[97]

Gustav Klutsis
Electrification of the Entire Country, 1922

Punin emphasizes *Zangezi*'s "homeyness," "low technology," and amateur acting, which again contrast with Tatlin's concept of *Tower* as the ultimate public structure, built with advanced technology. Likewise, a condition of dialectic opposition was at work in efforts of politically involved avant-gardists such as
p. 81 Klutsis, whose design for the poster *Electrification of the Entire Country* (1920) has an intentional formal awkwardness in its sense of monumentality and montage of three regimes of modernity: artistic (*Proun*), technological (the electricity pylon), and political (Lenin). Similarly, in making his series of "monolithic communist cities where people of the whole world will live" (beginning with *Dynamic City* in 1919), Klutsis at once believed in their potential realization and resisted being guided by pure logic.[98] Thus, he instructed that *Dynamic City* be looked at from all sides and turned, and he placed one such architectural fantasy, or Dadaist riddle, on the cover of Kruchenykh's 1925 book *Kruchenykh Lives!* This same attitude is present in the designs of Klutsis's agit-structures. Their utilitarian content is not in balance with the complexity of formal manipulation.

Like Tatlin and Klutsis, Kruchenykh disrupted propagandistic mass culture and the affirmative political spectacle of the new state, particularly its growing publishing industry, with a dose of Dadaist negativity and (to use his term) "hooliganism." Arvatov helped

97. Ibid. In his "Society of Presidents of Planet Earth," conceived circa 1920, Khlebnikov characterizes Dadaists as students of the Russian futurists. Fascinated with Tatlin's *Tower*, in 1918 Mayakovsky wanted Tatlin to do the decorations for Mayakovsky's play *Mystery Bouffe*, a job he ended up delegating to Malevich, whose designs are lost.

98. This is how Lissitzky described to Malevich, in 1919, the significance of his *Prouns*, a spatial nonobjective structure developed simultaneously by Lissitzky and Klutsis. See *El Lissitzky: Maler, Architekt, Typograf, Fotograf: Erinnerungen, Briefe, Schriften*, ed. Sophie Lissitzky-Küppers (Dresden: VEB Verlag der Kunst, 1976), 15.

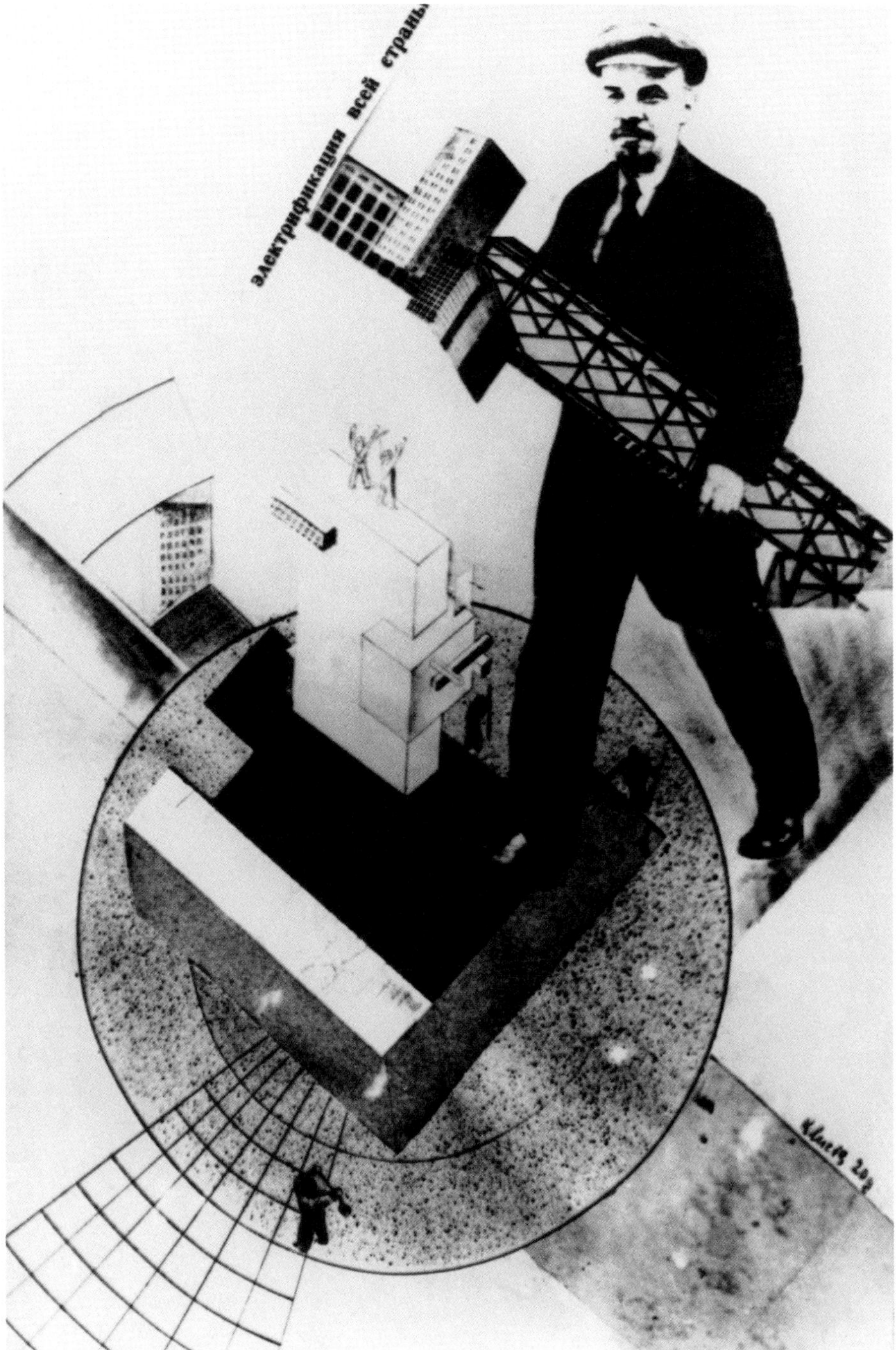
электрификация всей страны

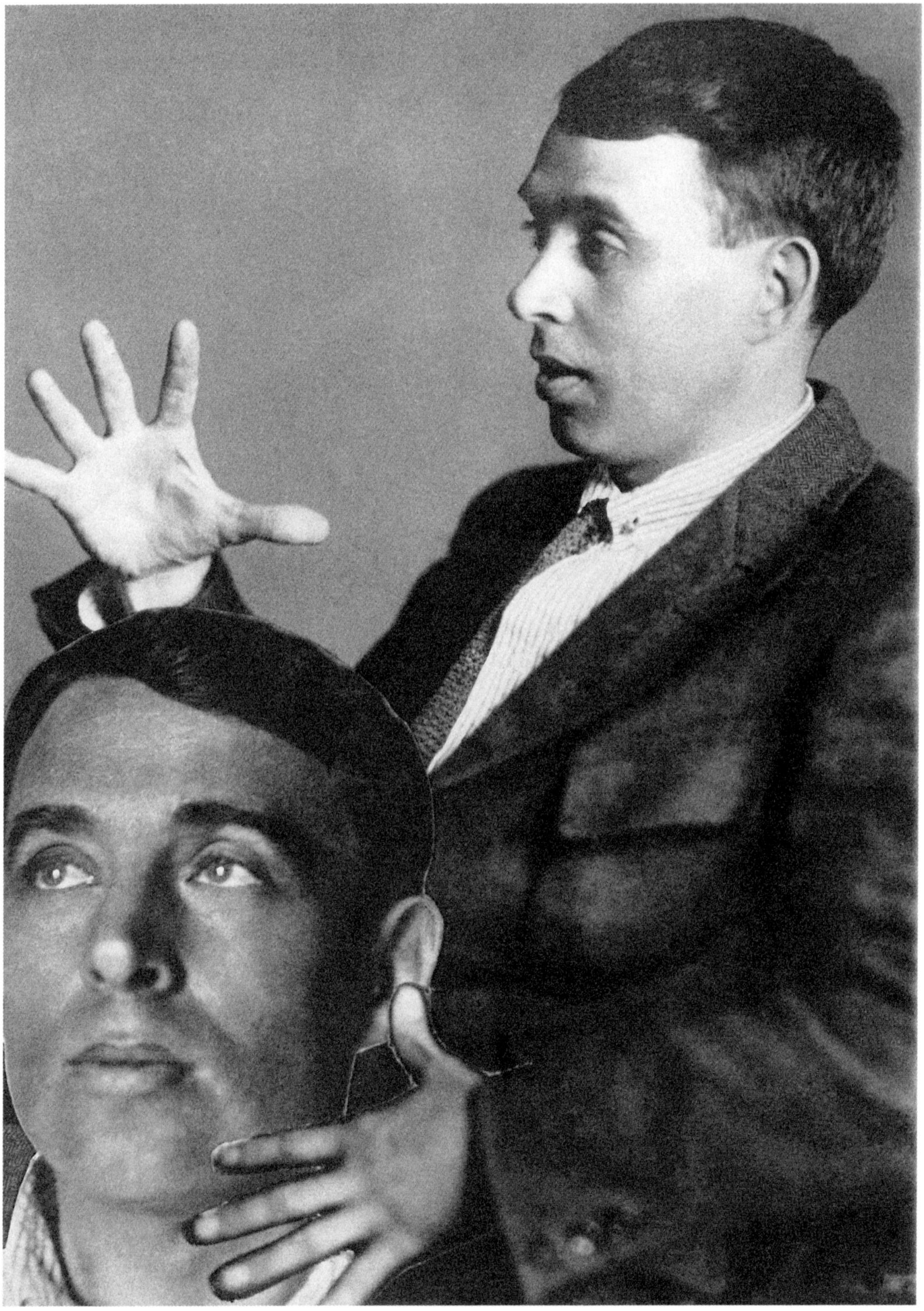

Gustav Klutsis
Kruchenykh Reads His Poetry,
ca. 1925.

introduce Kruchenykh and Khlebnikov's concept of transrational language in the new sociopolitical atmosphere.[99] Kruchenykh's antiwar poems, such as "Air Fortress," published in *Lef* (no. 4, 1924), combine neologisms or literary shifts with excerpts, almost as long as the poem itself, from a speech by the politician Nikolai Bukharin. Khardzhiev compared "Air Fortress" with the "'brutal' grotesques of George Grosz."[100] Kruchenykh's complex frame of politically conscious mind—of dissonant experience and flashes of nonsensical reality—drew major avant-gardists to his literary production. The fact that Kruchenykh lived in the same building at 21 Miasnitskaia Street as Klutsis, Rodchenko, Valentina Kulagina, and Varvara Stepanova only intensified their collaboration, which included book cover designs and mock-heroic impromptu actions in their studios.[101] Some photographs and films record the use of a revolver, an uncanny reminder that the collective laughter disguised danger. Many representatives of the avant-garde, including Klutsis, would be executed in the late 1930s. Significantly, Tristan Tzara, as Sergei Sharshun noted, "dr[ew] a revolver next to his signature," once more hinting at Dada's risky games.[102]

Kruchenykh was popular not only among the artists who lived continuously "in the land of the Bolsheviks." Lissitzky, who stayed in Europe from 1922 to 1925, backed Kruchenykh's concept of transrationality, even when he worked in the space of rational architecture. This is conveyed in one of Lissitzky's letters from 1924: "In a few days I will be finished with the article on architecture. . . . Am now working on a photographic self-portrait. A great piece of nonsense, if it all goes according to plan"[103] Upon his return to Moscow he designed the cover for Kruchenykh's book

99. See Boris Arvatov, "Speech Creation," on pp. 291–293 of the present catalogue.

100. Khardzhiev, "Sud'ba Kruchenykh," 1:305. *Lef*, no. 2 (1923): 27–30, featured Grosz with two drawings under the headline "Works of the Constructivist George Grosz." The
p. 127
accompanying text "About My Work" stresses his anticapitalist moods and faith in the masses, identifies aesthetics with production, and guarantees photography "a big role."

101. See my "Dada on Miasnitskaia Street," in *Gustav Klutsis and Valentina Kulagina: Photography and Montage after Constructivism* (Göttingen: Steidl; New York: International Center of Photography, 2004), 43–47.

102. See Sergei Sharshun, "My Participation in the French Dada Movement," on pp. 314–319 of the present catalogue.

103. Lissitzky to Küppers, December 12, 1924, in *El Lissitzky: Maler, Architekt*, ed. Lissitzky-Küppers, 54.

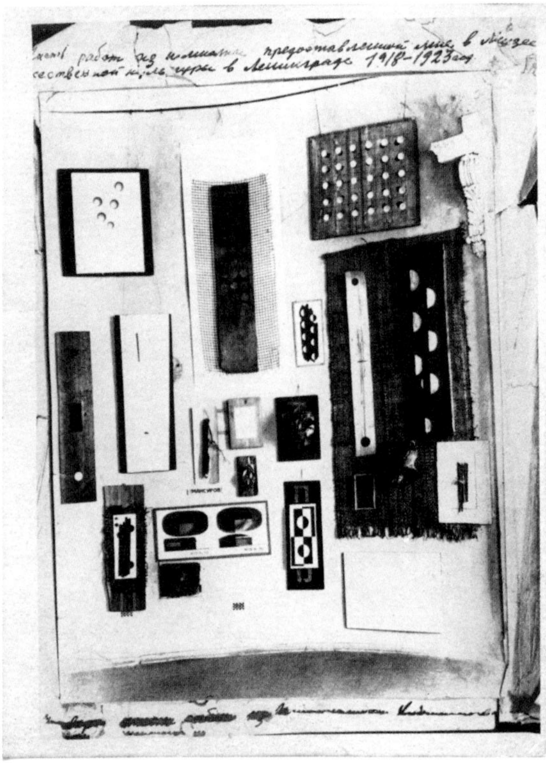

Anonymous
View of Pavel Mansurov's exhibition in the Museum of Artistic Culture, Leningrad, 1923

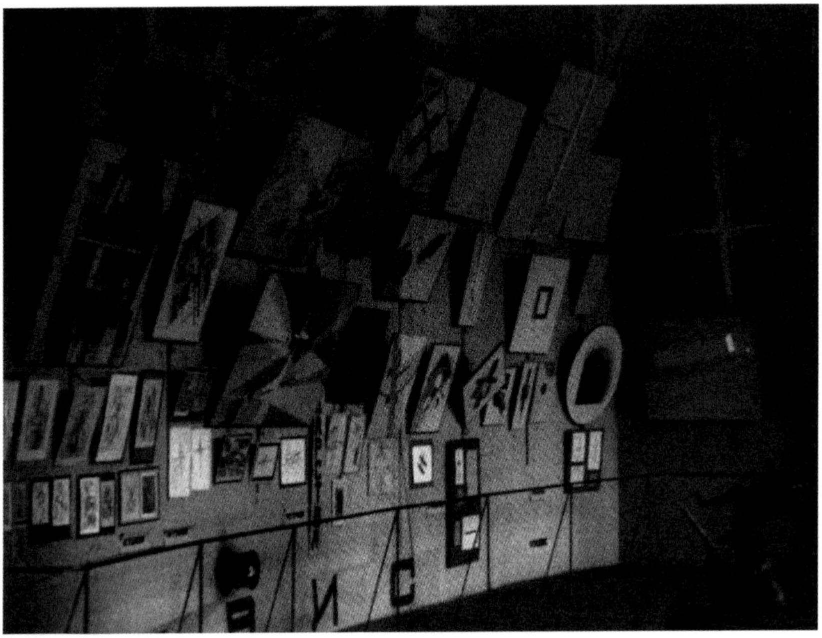

Anonymous
View of the works by the UNOVIS group in the documentary film *Exhibition of Paintings of the Petrograd Artists of All Trends*, 1923

Transrational and also presented him with a series of presents that included a portrait of Arp with the inscription "*Fotopis* portrait of 'Schwalbendada' [Swallowdada] Hans Arp," which he later supplemented with the self-portrait he discussed in his 1924 letter. Another Lissitzky offering to Kruchenykh was a portfolio, *Figurines*, inspired by *Victory over the Sun* and conceived and printed in Hannover in 1923 during a period when Lissitzky was in close contact with Dadaist Kurt Schwitters. This supports Khardzhiev's dubbing Kruchenykh "the first Dadaist" and validates *Victory over the Sun*'s proto-Dadaist status.[104]

p. 178

p. 157

PHOTOMONTAGE AS A NEW KIND OF DADA ART

The signifying capacity and high potential of photomontage for political art was recognized equally by the Dadaists, who deemed it "a medium of Dada art," and by Russian artists.[105] Their shared interest is underscored in the anonymous text "Photomontage," printed in the magazine *Lef*: "In Russia we can point to the works of *Rodchenko* as models of photomontage . . . in the West the works of *George Grosz* and other Dadaists are representative of photomontage."[106] In 1918, when the German Dadaists Raoul Hausmann and Hannah Höch were conceiving of photomontages inspired by the "soldiers' heads and officers' uniforms that they saw on postcards," Klutsis was producing a sketch for an outdoor placard, *Strike on Counterrevolution*, dedicated to the Bolshevik's suppression of the uprising of the Left Socialist Revolutionaries during the Fifth Congress of the Soviets.[107] *Strike*, like his double-sided painting from the period he designated "analytical," reflects his study with Natan Pevzner, Naum Gabo, and Malevich from 1918 to 1920,

pp. 14–15

pp. 108–109

104. Khardzhiev, "Sud'ba Kruchenykh," 1:302. Prior to making *Figurines*, Lissitzky planned to stage *Victory over the Sun* as electromechanical theater. The play was restaged in 1920 in Vitebsk by Malevich's students.

105. Doherty, "Berlin," 93.

106. Gustav Klutsis, "Photomontage," *Lef*, no. 4 (1924), in *Photography in the Modern Era: European Documents and Critical Writings, 1913–1940*, ed. Christopher Phillips (New York: Metropolitan Museum of Art and Aperture, 1989), 212; emphasis in original.

107. Maud Lavin, *Cut with the Kitchen Knife: The Weimar Photomontages of Hannah Höch* (New Haven: Yale University Press, 1993), 17.

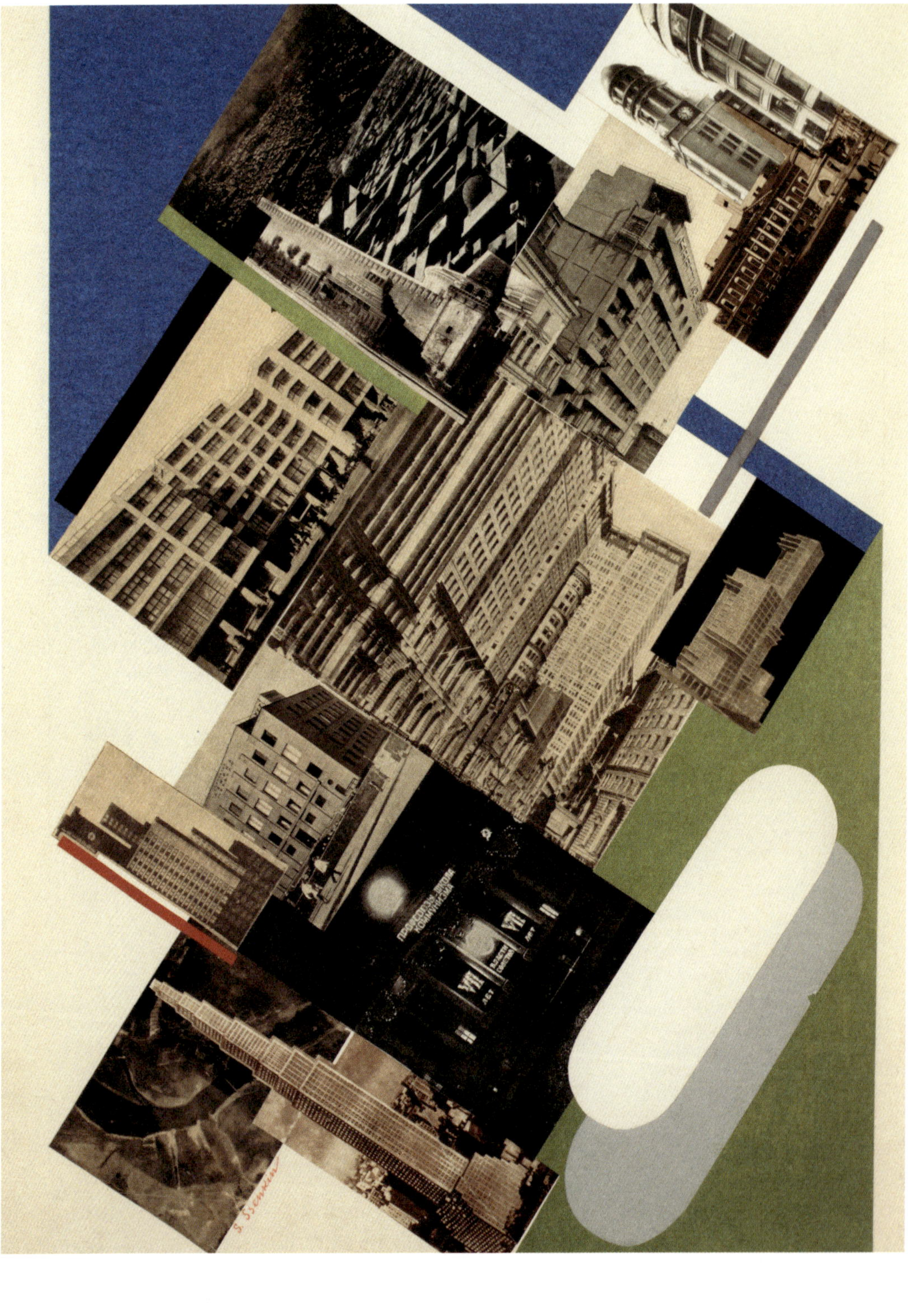

Sergei Senkin
City, ca. 1920

which propelled him from cubo-futurism to nonobjectivity and on to photomontage rendered using formalist methods.

Left critics and filmmakers also aspired to link nonobjectivity to mechanical media, as demonstrated by Aleksei Gan relating the two practices in his magazine *Cine-photo* (*Kino-fot*), launched in 1922, and in Dziga Vertov's adoption of Rodchenko's spatial constructions for the titles in his documentary film *Cine-truth* no. 14 (1923). With a camera, "trans-artistic plots" (*vne-iskusstvennye siuzhety*) were incorporated into artistic practice under the rubric of antiart. One of the earliest examples of the union of the mechanical and the nonobjective can be found in Rodchenko's 1915 *Line and Compass* drawings, followed by his pp. 53, 278 early photomontages. In contrast to Klutsis's soberness and overt political message, Rodchenko inclined to a more immediate social content supported by parody. Thus, as in the case of transrationality paralleling rationality, photomontage production developed in the space of representational dichotomy. At times Rodchenko's photomontages compositionally follow his 1920 theory of linearism (*Liniizm*), according to which he defined line as "the last form," and after which he would disregard painting and embark on spatial constructions and photomontage.

He published his early photomontages in the first issue of *Cine-photo* (1922), calling them "Printed Matter for Criticism" and emphasizing that, like the Dadaists, he saw this technique as a critical rather than purely agitational weapon.[108] The unsigned text that accompanies the photomontages points out that these stand apart from Western and Dada ones, which use printed material "abstractly and for the sake of aesthetic tasks only."[109] This

108. Rodchenko signed his writings in the newspaper *Anarchy* with a pseudonym "Anti," an ultimate antonym that Richter describes as "Dada's original moral credo." Richter, *Dada*, 186.

109. *Kino-fot*, no. 1 (1922): 13.

is perplexing. Aleksandr Lavrentiev, art historian and Rodchenko's grandson, points out that Rodchenko's photomontage production was spurred by Mayakovsky's 1922 visit to Berlin, where the latter bought many magazines and books related to the subject of Dada. Examples of Dadaist works were also available to Rodchenko from his friend Osip Brik, a formalist critic who composed a scrapbook using material collected on trips to Germany. Another influence was filmmaker Lev Kuleshov, whose article in *Cine-photo*, no. 3 (1922) Rodchenko illustrated with photomontages titled *Psychology* and *Detective*. Rodchenko shared Kuleshov's charged wit and interest in mass culture and crime imagery, his blend of technology and primitivism, and his fascination with the circus and Americanisms. All these preferences were consolidated in Rodchenko's photomontages for Mayakovsky's poem "About This" (1923), another departure from constructions of the everyday as exclusively political.

Aleksandr Rodchenko
Cover design for the journal
Lef, no. 2, 1923

pp. 122, 126, 168, 169

pp. 116–117

With Lenin's death in 1924, debates between nonobjectivists and "objectivists" sharpened. The subjects of nonobjectivity, defamiliarization, photomontage, and unconventional regimes of language were prioritized in the commemorative responses. *Lef* dedicated a whole issue to Lenin's language, publishing essays by formalist critics; for example, "Lenin as Decanonizer" by Shklovsky.[110] Analyzing the originality of Lenin's oratorical and written works, Shklovsky states that a political event as significant as Lenin's death inevitably stirs up discussions pertinent to culture and reevaluates its practices; old things get ousted and renamed, and the scale of comparisons changes. Shklovsky shared Malevich's defiance, declared in the latter's essay about Lenin,

110. An excerpt is included elsewhere in this volume, pp. 307–309.

111. Kazimir Malevich, "Appendix: From the Book on Non-objectivity," in *The World as Non-objectivity: Unpublished Writings, 1922–1925*, ed. Troels Andersen, vol. 3 (Copenhagen: Borgen, 1976), 336.

112. See Viktor Shklovsky, "Lenin as a Decanonizer," on pp. 307–309 of the present catalogue.

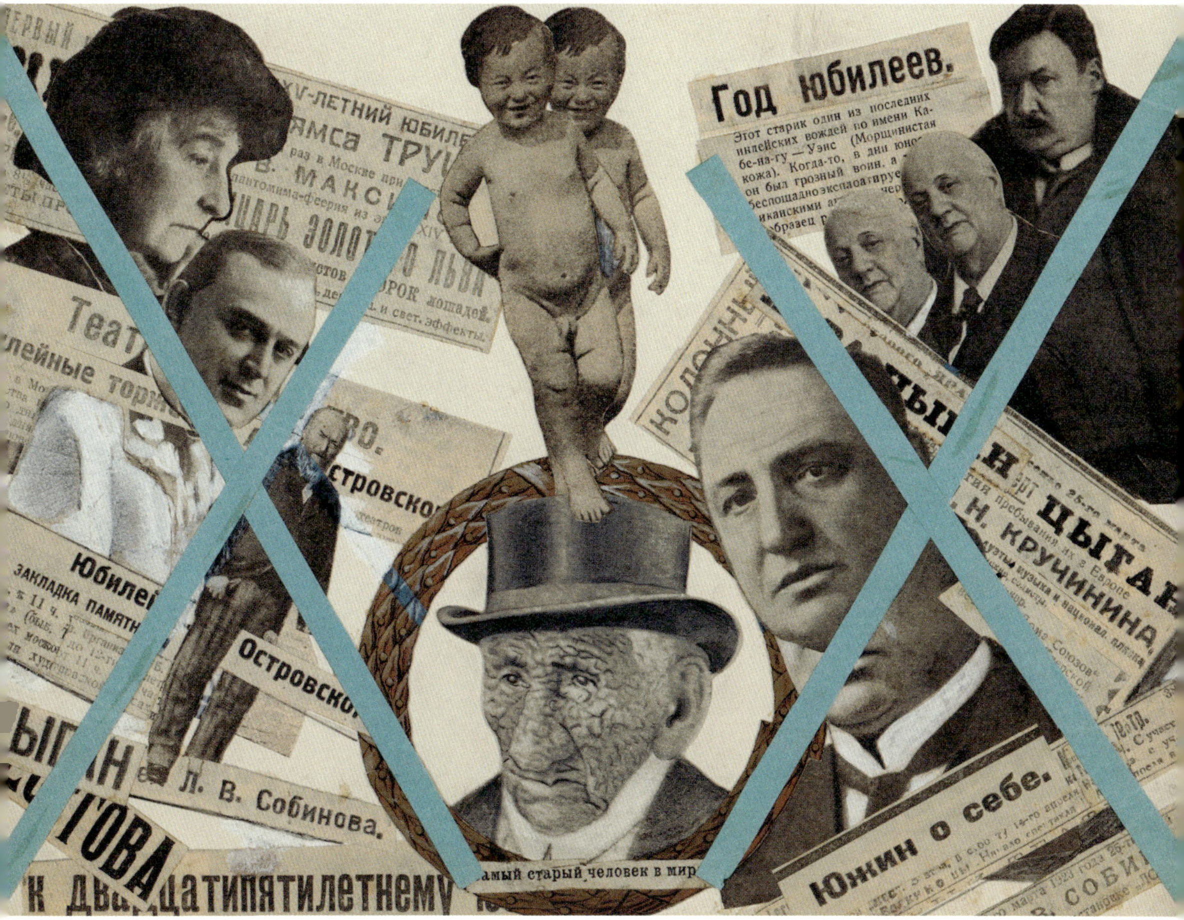

of conventional representations of the Bolshevik leader in "busts or portraits." His face, in Malevich's view, had to be replaced by "non-objectivity and abstraction."[111]

Klutsis's, Rodchenko's, and Sergei Senkin's photomontages executed for the 1924 issue of the magazine *Young Guard* resist "turn[ing] Lenin into a cliché."[112] Senkin and Klutsis in particular make as many shifts from conventional portraiture as the flexible technique of photomontage allows. They clash various periods of Lenin's political activities to the point of paradox, operating through the interplay of scales and severe fragmentation of bodies and objects. The combination of communist red and anarchic black highlights the originality of the graphic designs while also mourning the leader. Slogans boldly cut through the imagery, intensifying its formal character and p. 306

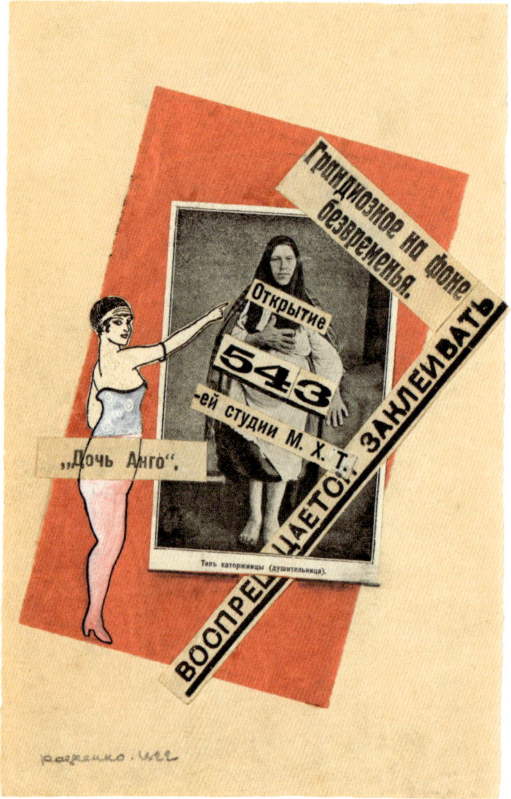

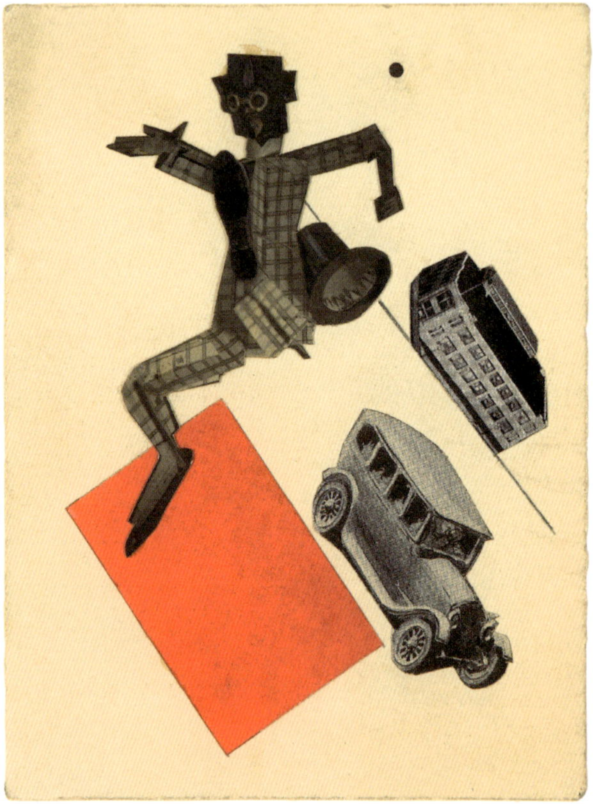

Aleksandr Rodchenko
Type of a Female Convict, 1922

Gustav Klutsis
Untitled, early 1920s

offering new models of junction, between visual and verbal.

p. 93 One laconic composition by Senkin with Lenin's head affixed to a red, gridded background stands out. Lenin's hypnotic gaze evokes his image in Höch's seminal photomontage *Cut with the Kitchen Knife through the Last Weimar Beer-Belly Cultural Epoch in Germany* (1919–1920), in which Lenin's head is placed next to Dadaist Johannes Badaar, among other personalities. The Dadaists' encounter with and interest in Lenin stretched from Cabaret Voltaire to the politically charged Berlin Dada and was validated by Lissitzky when he, while living in Europe, translated and published in *Kunstblatt* at the time of Lenin's death "the extract from Malevich's new work *Lenin*" and

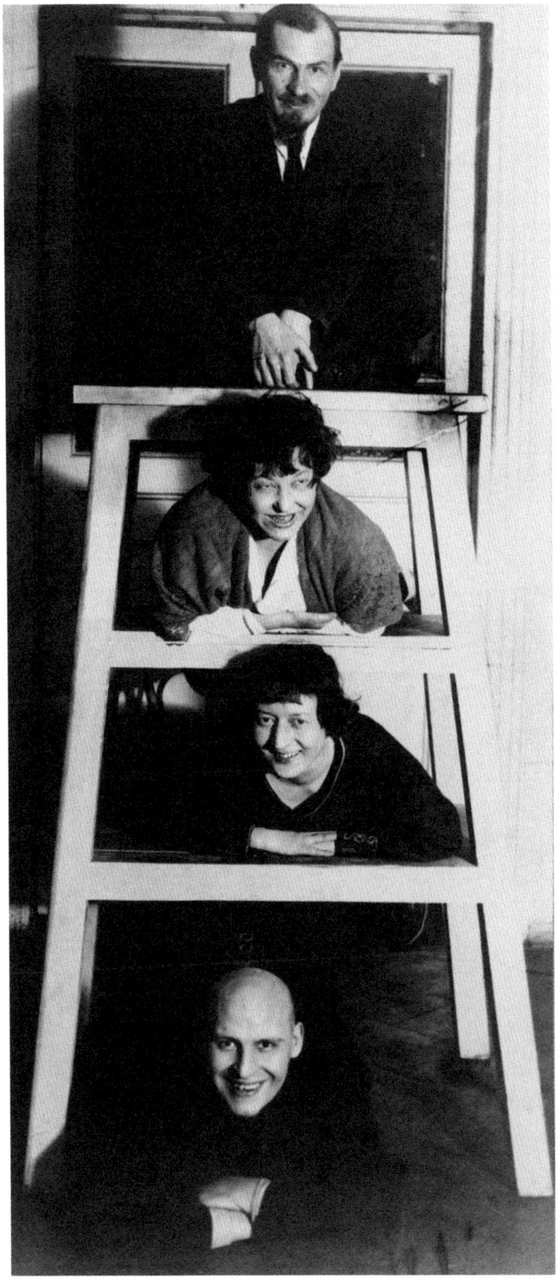

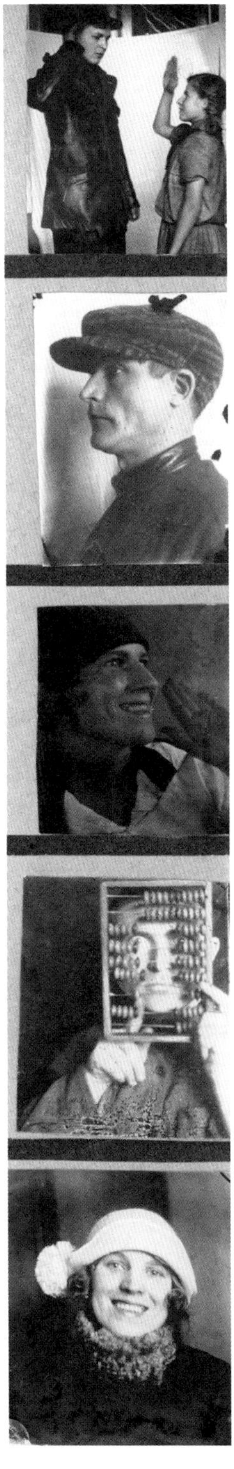

Aleksandr Rodchenko
Family Games (from top to bottom: Boris Shvetsov, Varvara Stepanova, Maria Shvetsova, and Aleksandr Rodchenko), 1924

Gustav Klutsis
Boris Kulagin, Gustav Klutsis, and Valentina Kulagina in various impromptu actions, 1925

p. 94 added Lenin to his earlier design of a speaker's podium.[113] In his words, the remake became "a sensation" at the International Theatrical Exhibition in Vienna in 1924. While translating Malevich, Lissitzky expressed his disappointment at the decline of Dadaism and proposed Malevich's ideas as the replacement for that sensibility: "I don't see anything that excites feeling in Germany any more. . . . 'Dada' had a real passion at the beginning, under the guise of nihilism. The Malevich script at all events stirs the emotions."[114]

Like Badaar, who used Christ as a referent in his works, Malevich repetitively linked Lenin with Christ and even drew an analogy between Gorki, the mansion where Lenin died, and "the hill of Golgotha."[115] In tune with this comparison, Vasily Ermilov assembled a two-square "memorial board," on which the p. 93 word *Gorki* and the date and time of Lenin's death are assembled from real materials, among them metal and sandpaper. The result is a work-sign distinguished by formal austerity and decreeing, "We do not want icons."[116]

Paradoxically, the framework of Russian revolutionary "Dada" mapped here in the duality between rational and transrational, serious and eccentric, culminated in Lenin's physical condition during the last months of his life. Paralyzed, he acquired an insane gaze and produced scribbles while learning how to write using his left hand. He desired to spend time with children, which Klutsis reflected in montages from 1924 that depict him in their company. These works allegorize Lenin's infantile state of mind and inability to communicate or control his body.

pp. 120–121 Klement Redko's painting *Uprising* (1924–1925) is a spectacular summary of the beginning and end of the revolutionary era. The

113. Lissitzky to Küppers, May 11, 1924, in *El Lissitzky*, ed. Lissitzky-Küppers, 50.

114. Lissitzky to Küppers, March 21, 1924, in *El Lissitzky*, ibid.

115. Malevich, "Appendix," 324.

116. Viktor Shklovsky, "Lenin as a Decanonizer," on pp. 307–309 of the present catalogue. E. D. Kashuba writes that in the early 1920s in Kiev, where Ermilov lived, "Dadaist ideas were well known from more than one publication on the pages of periodicals. For example, in 1922 the magazine of the leftist formation 'Semaphore into the Future' published texts by Tristan Tzara and other Dadaists, and materials about Dadaism as one of the radical tendencies in contemporary art." Kashuba also writes about the manifesto of the Ukrainian panfuturists and their idea of "the hegemony of meta-art" that included the new visual form "poetry-painting." In view of Ermilov's adoration of Khlebnikov's poetry, his word pieces, including the ones dedicated to Lenin, might have been inspired by this paradigm. See E. D. Kashuba, "Sotsial'nyi Dadaizm v tvorchestve Viktora Palmova," in *Russkii avangard 1910–1920 v evropeiskom iskusstve* (Moscow: Nauka, 2000), 224.

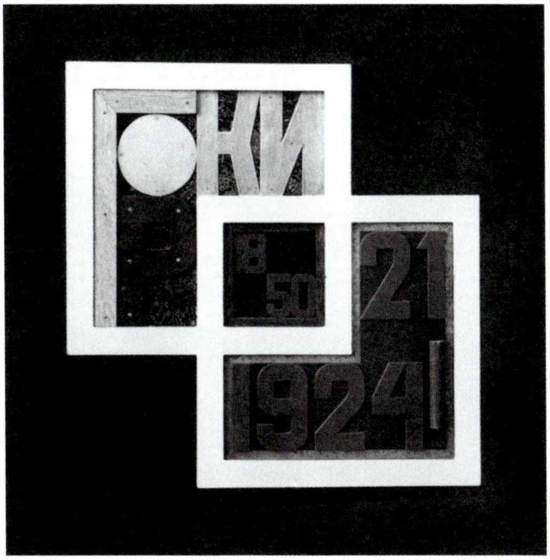

Vasily Ermilov
Memorial board *Gorki*,
1924

Sergei Senkin
Illustration for the journal
Young Guard, 1924

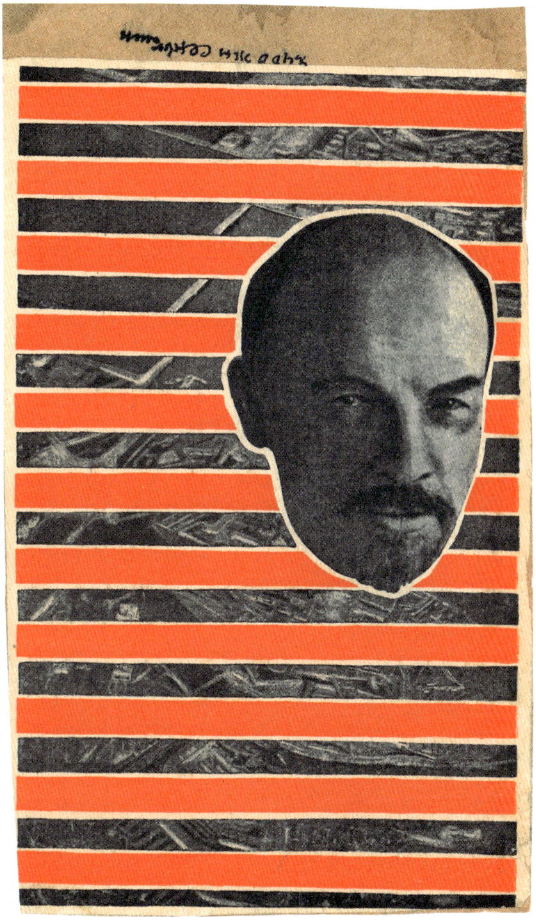

El Lissitzky and Hans Arp
Illustration of Lissitzky's *Lenin Tribune* (1924) in the book *Die Kunstismen / Les ismes de l'art / The Isms of Art: 1914–1924*, Zurich, 1925

Natan Altman
Cover of the book *Lenin: Drawings*, Saint Petersburg, 1921

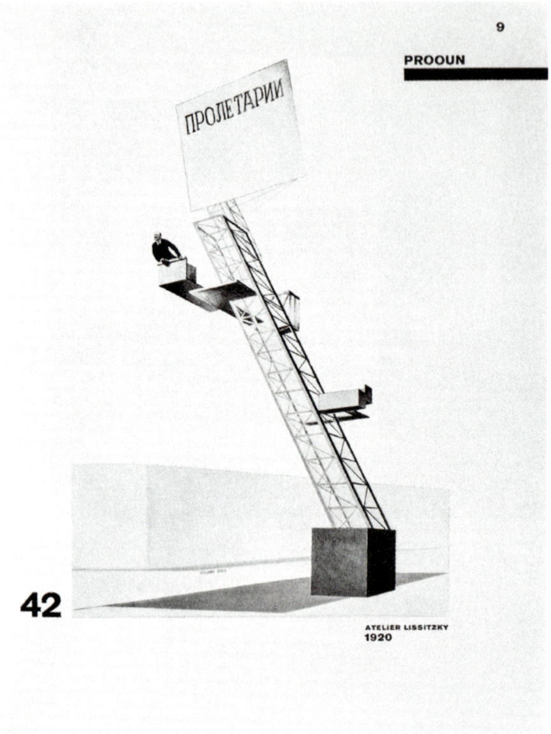

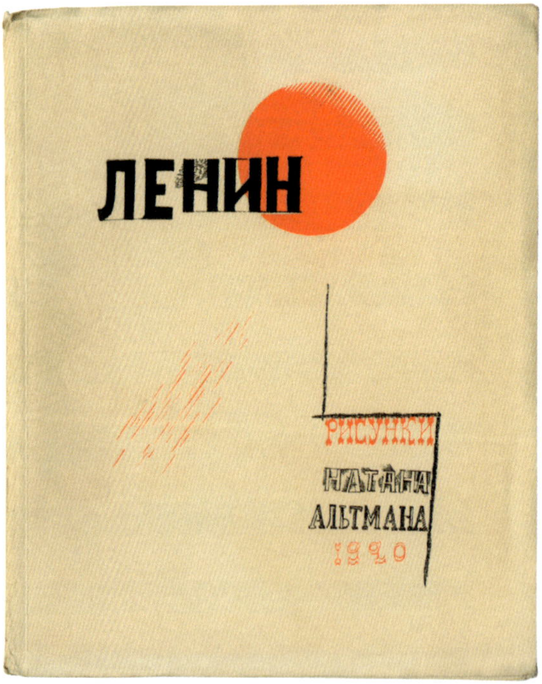

viewer is immediately captivated by the detailed iconography of the original governing iconostases—destined to be purged and effaced from photographs and photomontages. Strangely, the ruthless politics of "démontage" armed Redko's painting with greater documentary power than that held by the photographic media of the Stalin era. Moreover, Redko's formalist education left a deep trace in *Uprising*, for it is structured as a montage of nonobjective techniques invented by the avant-garde artists and surrendered to the revolutionary cause. Redko had studied with Kandinsky at the Higher State Artistic and Technical Studios (VKhUTEMAS) and took from his elder expressionism. From Malevich, another influence, he learned about the signifying power of geometrism, and from Larionov, whose principles of rayonism had been included in the VKhUTEMAS curriculum, he adapted rays of light, placing Lenin at the point of their intersection in the central quadrilateral. This Malevichian shape is deep blood-red inside and black along the edges, where eerie swarms of anonymous agitators and defending agents are marching. Such injection of nonobjective styles is rendered over a gridded wall of windows, signaling the beginning of the conversion of the universal grid structure into concrete window grates, and of unrestrained modernist practices, including Dadaist transgressions, and left politics into symptoms of surreal scenarios and repressive policies.

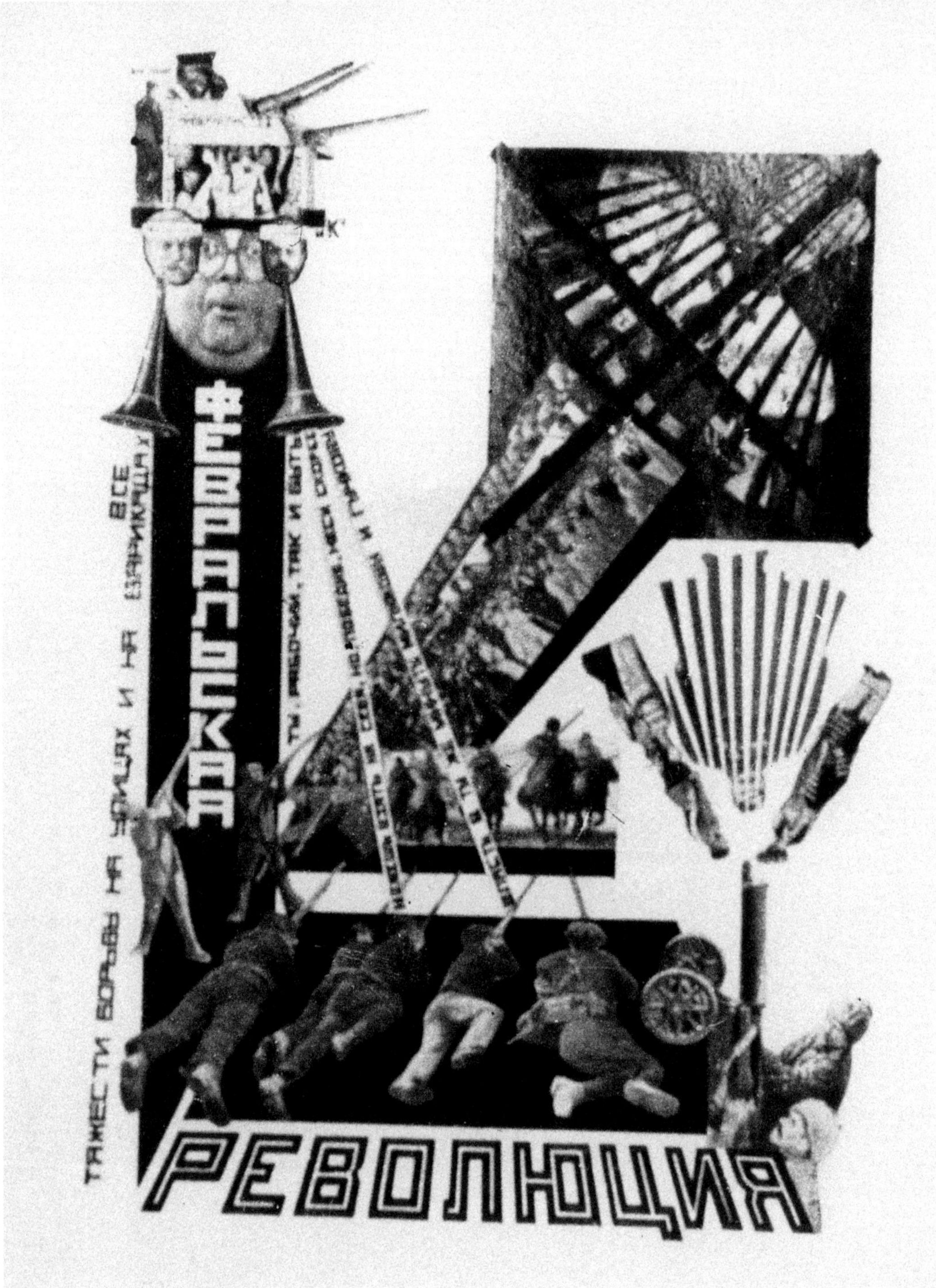

Gustav Klutsis
February Revolution, early 1920s.

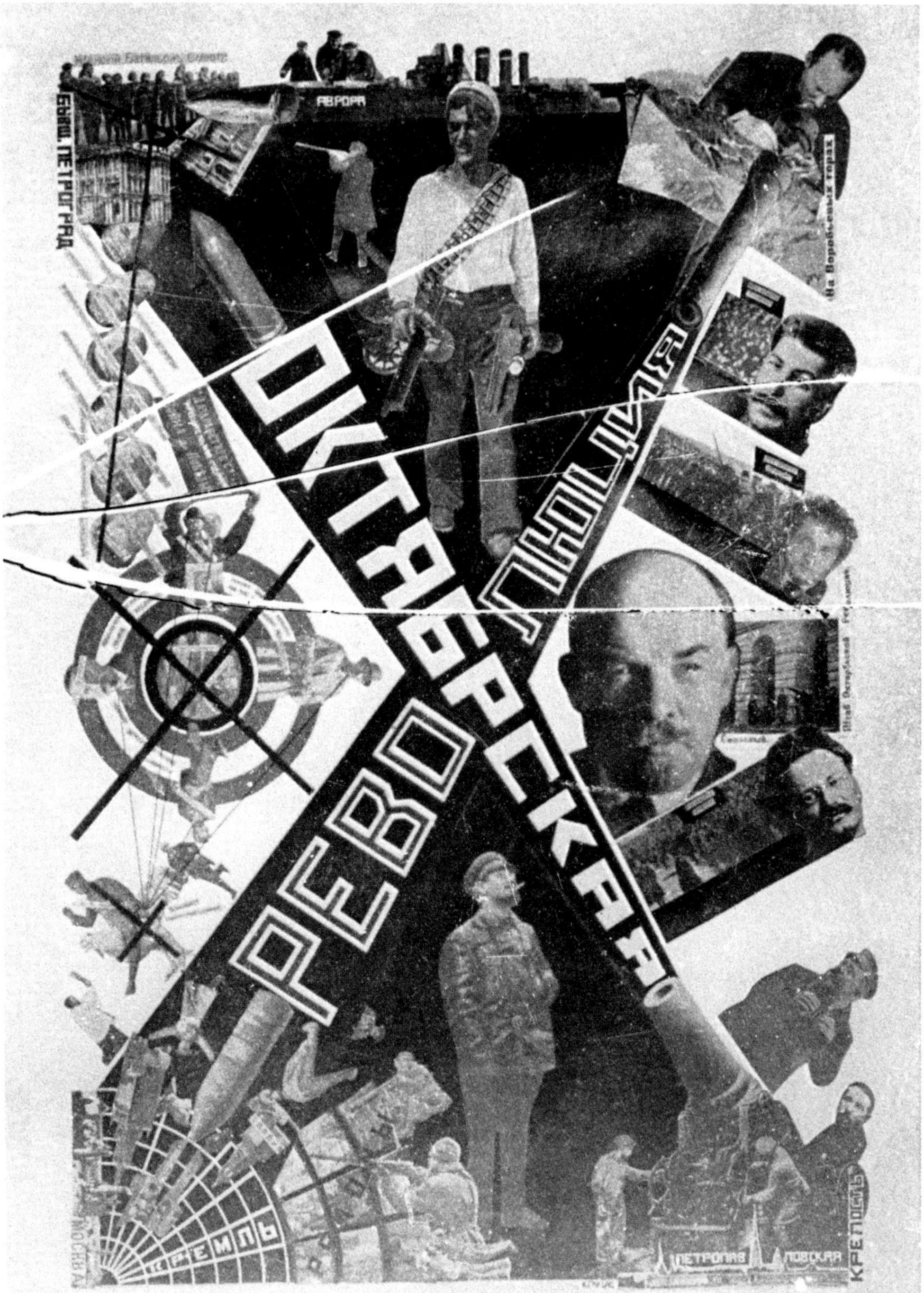

Gustav Klutsis
October Revolution, early 1920s.

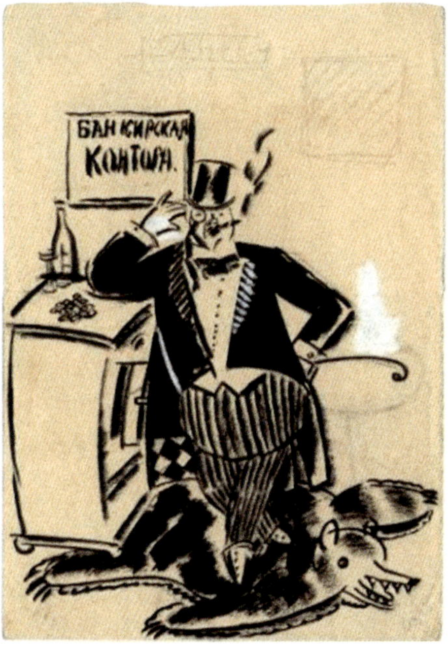

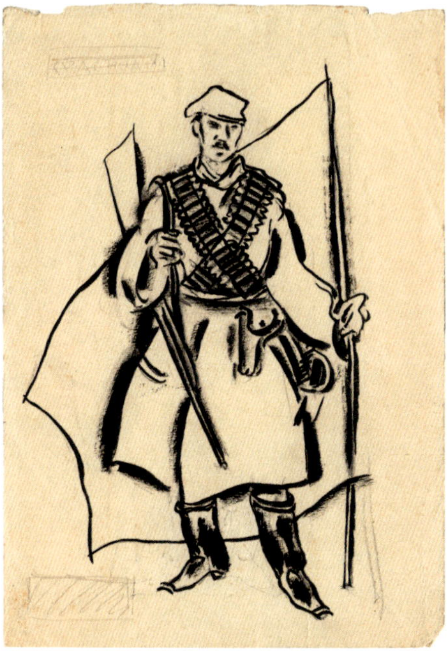

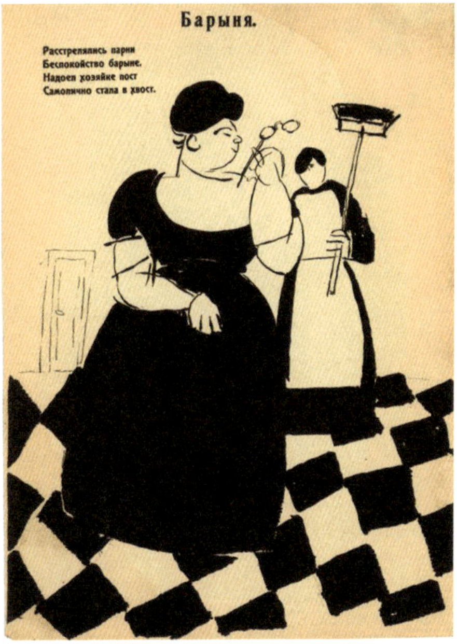

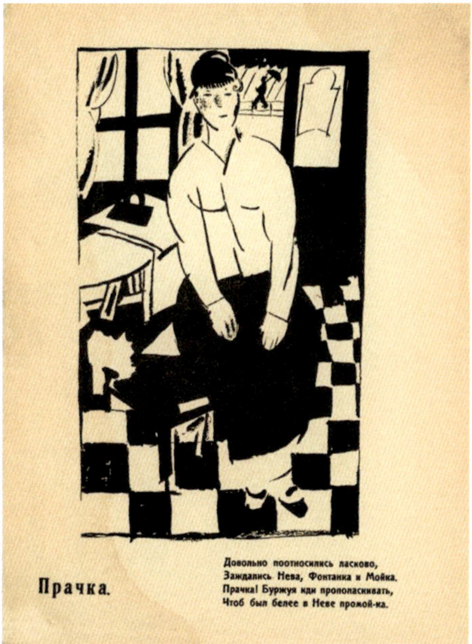

Ksenia Boguslavskaia, *Banker*
Study for an illustration for the portfolio *October 1917–1918: Heroes and Victims of the Revolution* by Vladimir Mayakovsky, 1918

Ivan Puni, *Laundress*
Illustration for the portfolio *October 1917–1918: Heroes and Victims of the Revolution* by Vladimir Mayakovsky, 1918

Ivan Puni, *Red Army Soldier*
Study for an illustration for the portfolio *October 1917–1918: Heroes and Victims of the Revolution* by Vladimir Mayakovsky, 1918

Ivan Puni, *Mistress*
Illustration for the portfolio *October 1917–1918: Heroes and Victims of the Revolution* by Vladimir Mayakovsky, 1918

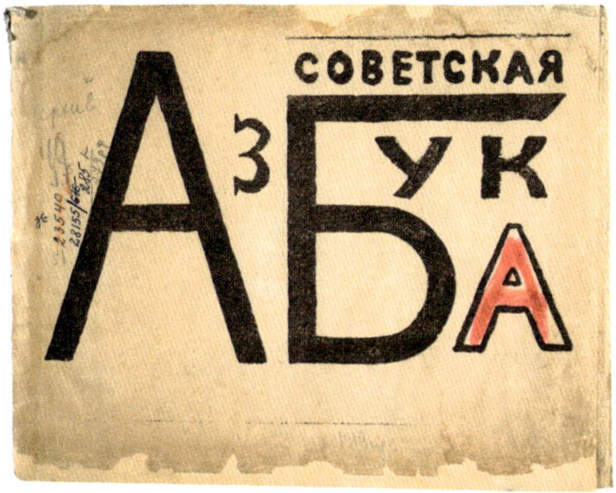

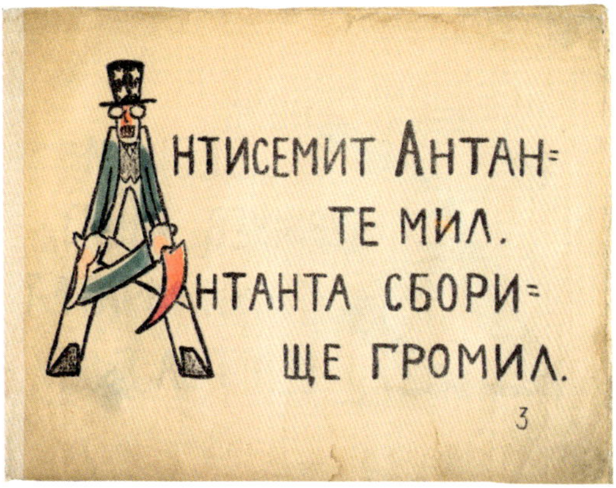

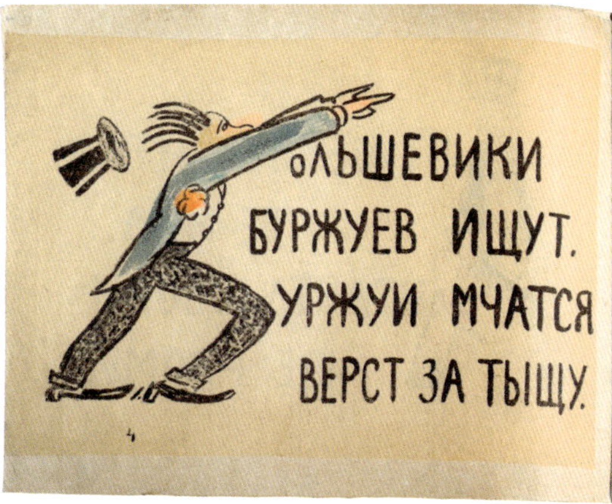

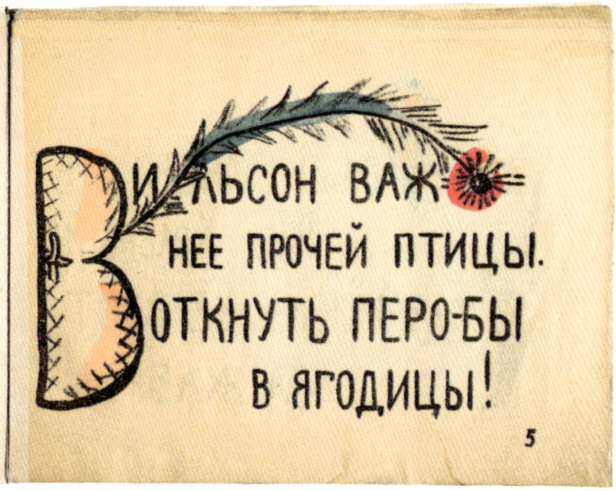

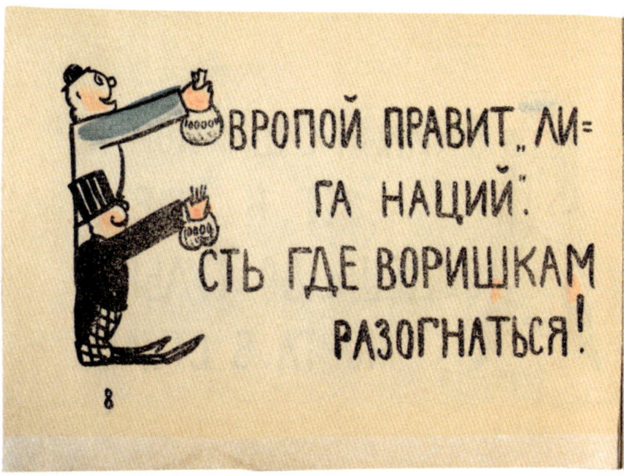

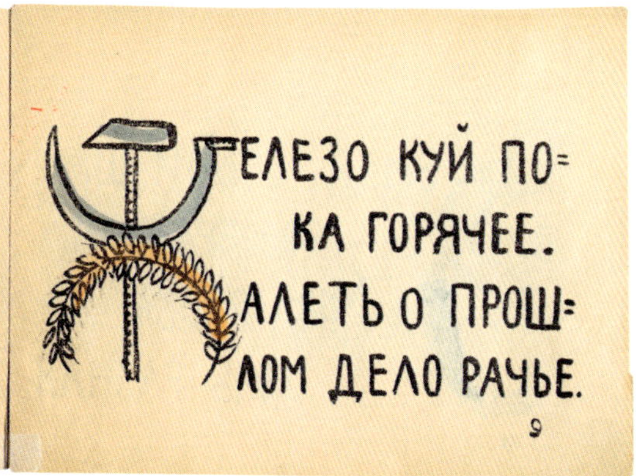

Vladimir Mayakovsky
Soviet Alphabet, 1919

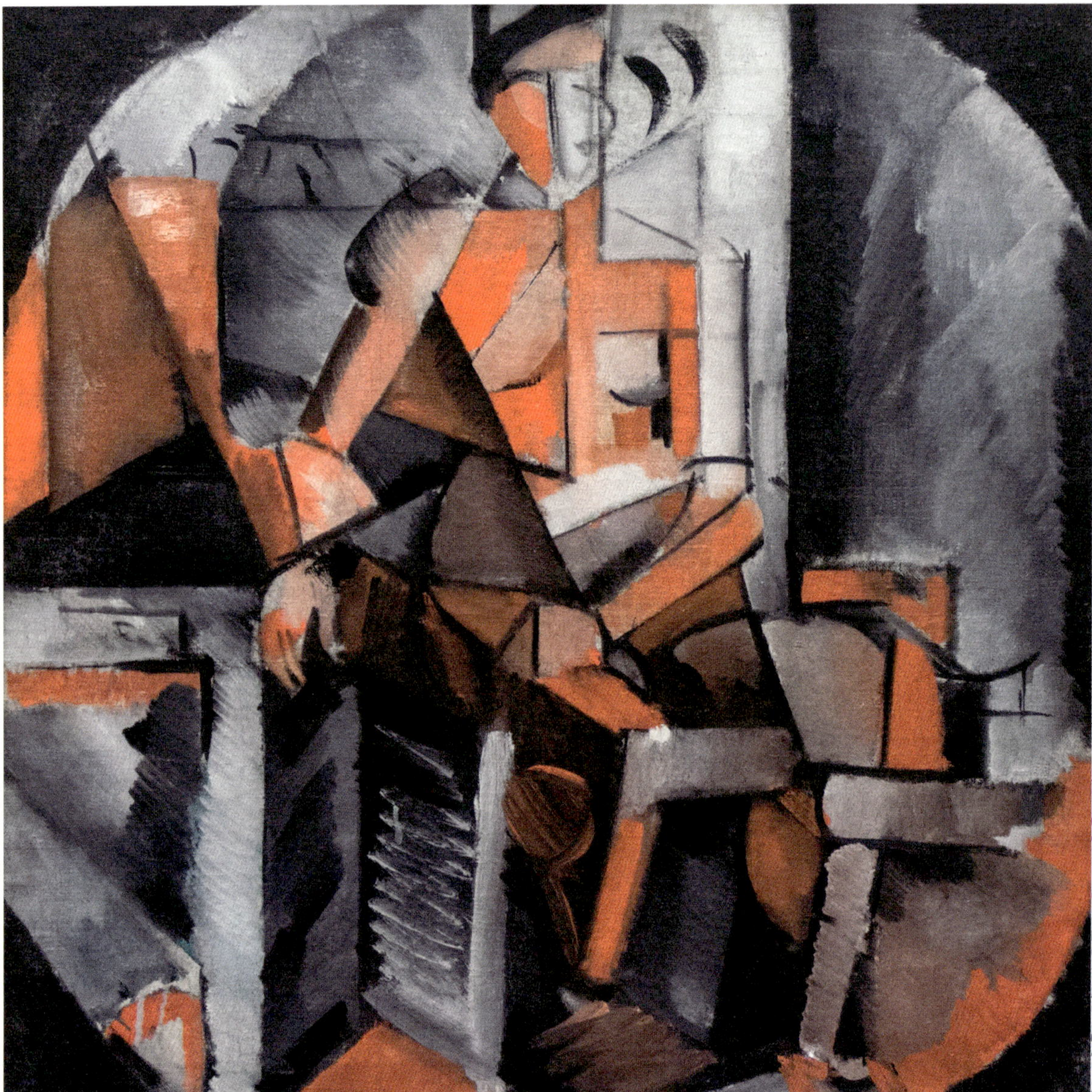

Nadezhda Udaltsova
Red Figure, 1919

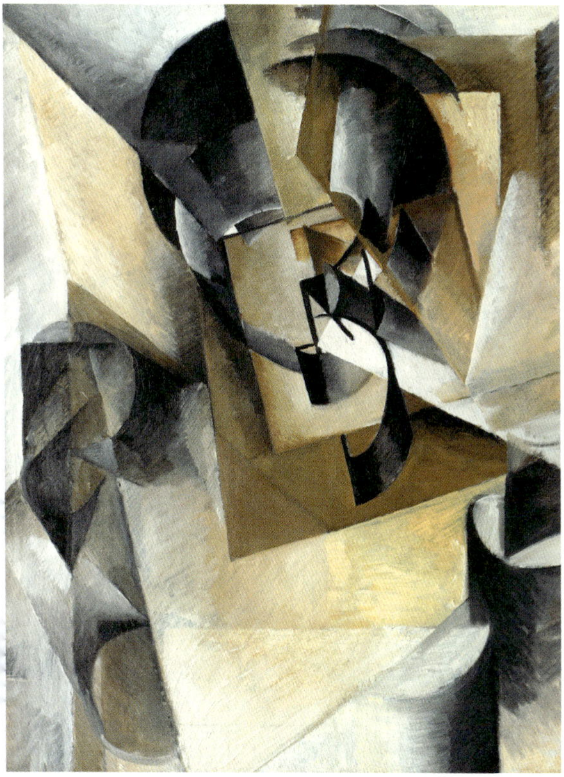

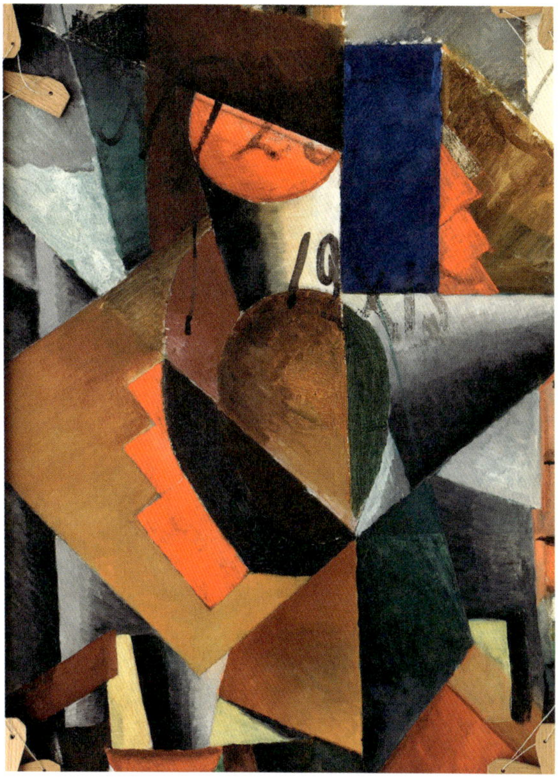

Ivan Kudriashov
Portrait of a Young Lady (recto):
Nonobjective Composition (verso),
ca. 1919

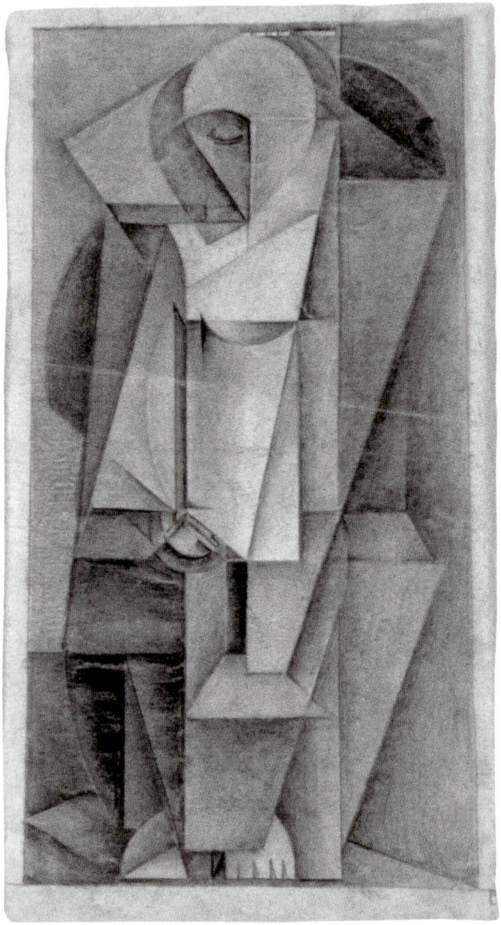

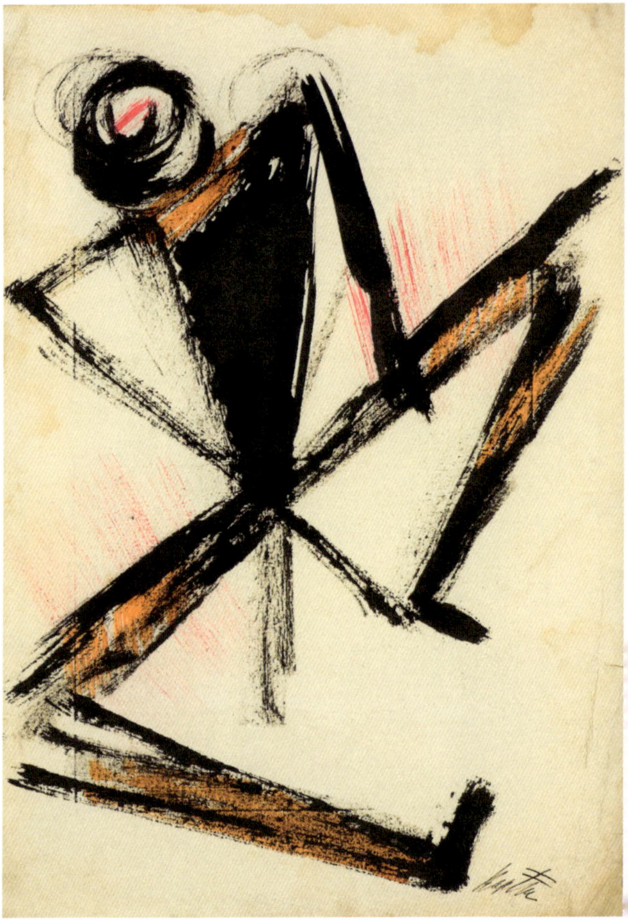

Gustav Klutsis
Red Man, 1919–1920

Varvara Stepanova
Figure, 1921

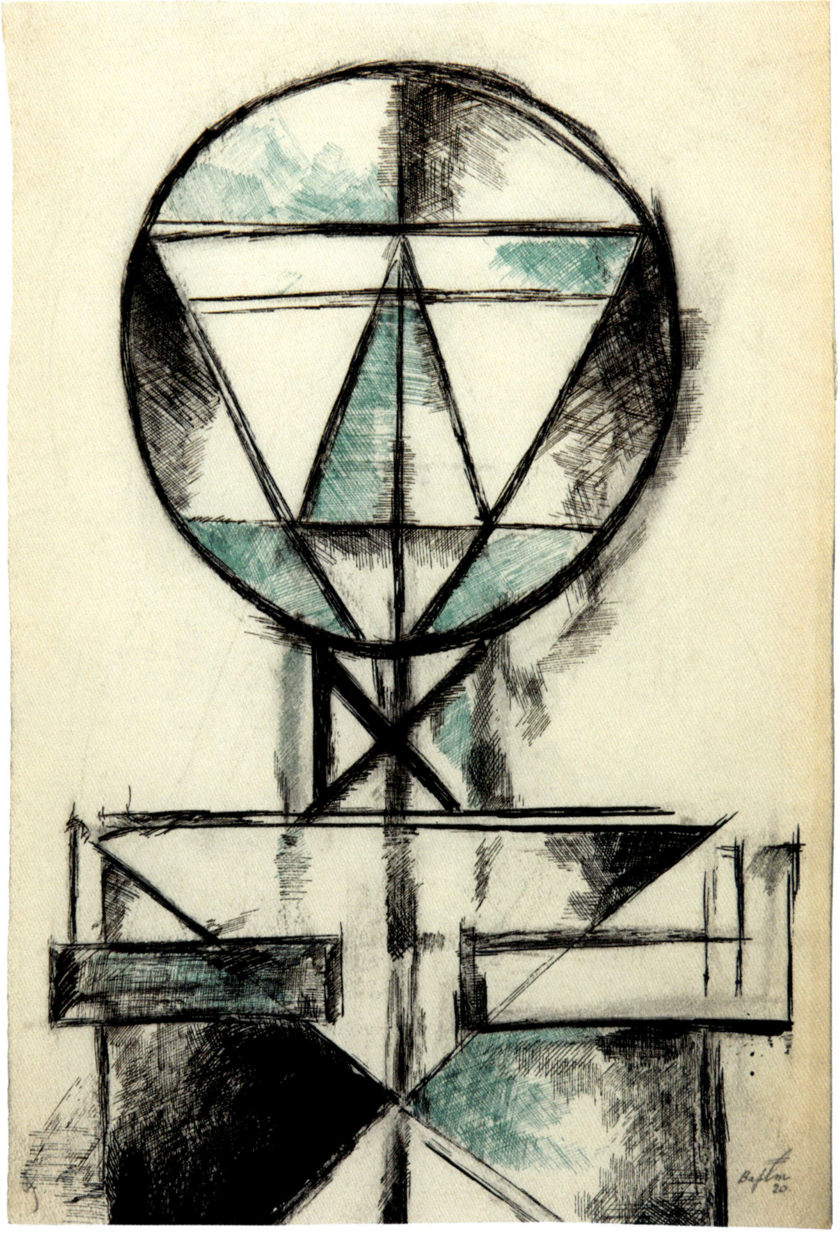

Varvara Stepanova
Torso, 1920

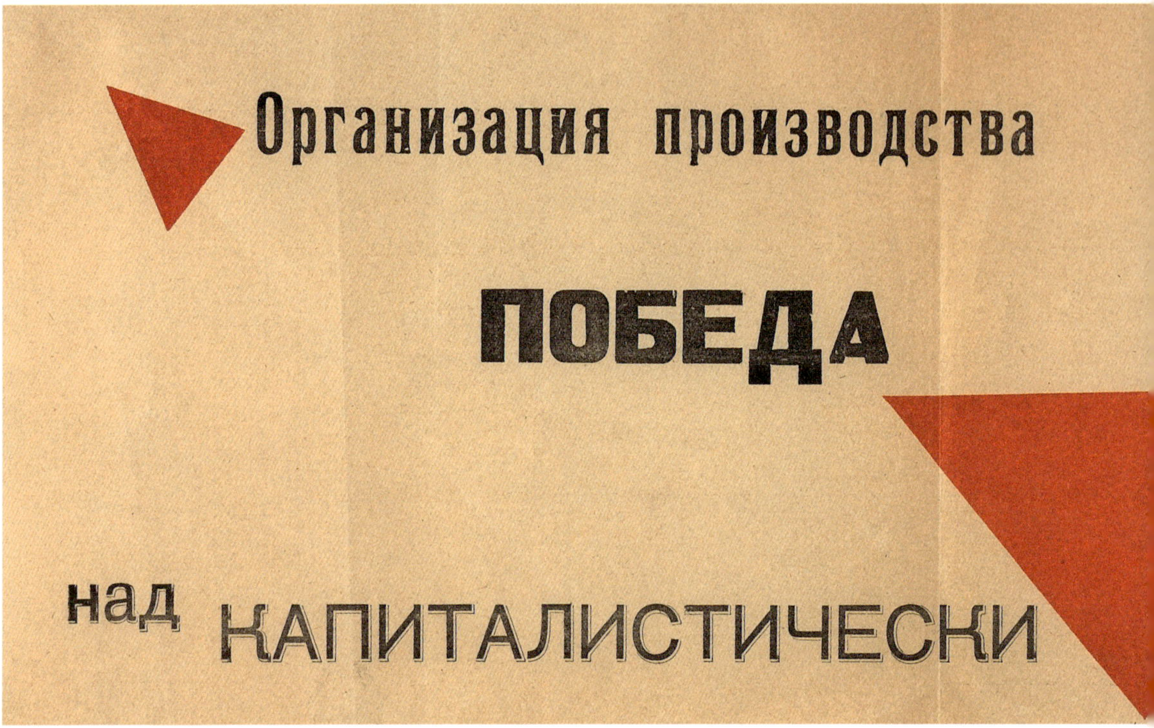
Организация производства
ПОБЕДА
над КАПИТАЛИСТИЧЕСКИ

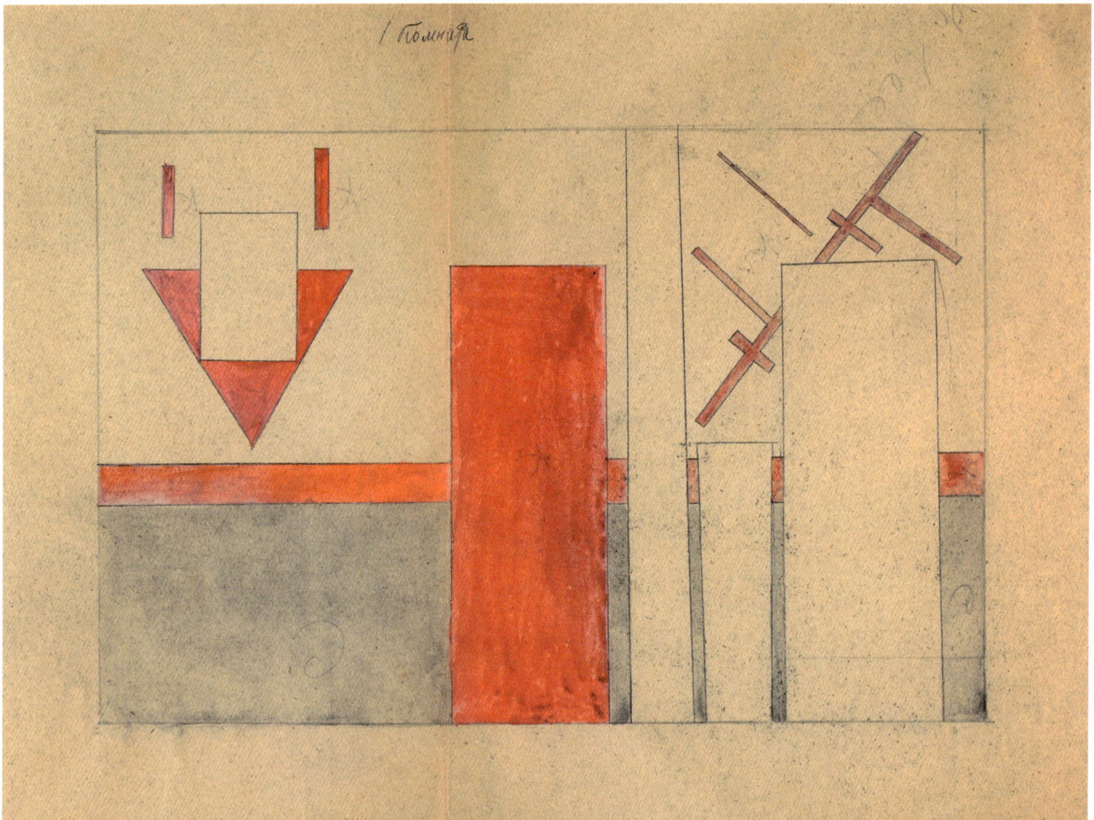

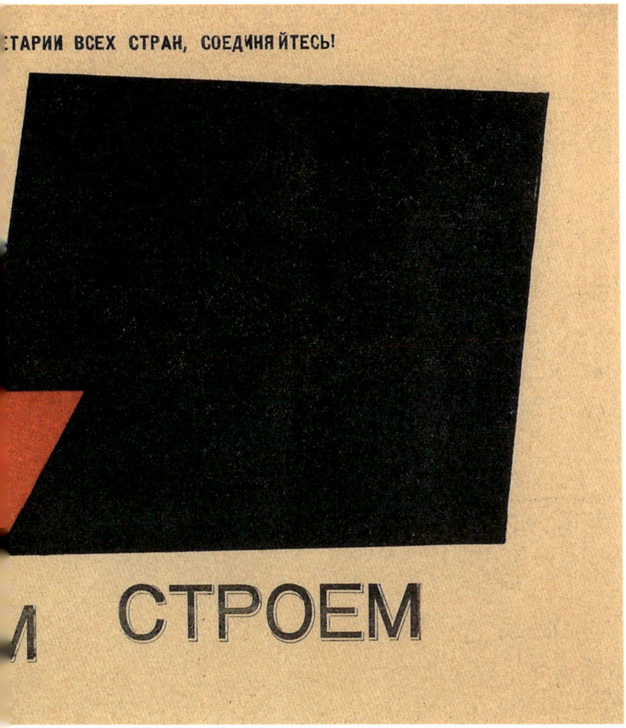

Anonymous
Proletariat of the World Unite: Organization of Production Victory over a Capitalist Structure, early 1920's

Anonymous
Untitled (First Room), early 1920s.

Ivan Kudriashov
Design for the decoration of a motorcar for the First Anniversary of the October Revolution in Moscow, 1918

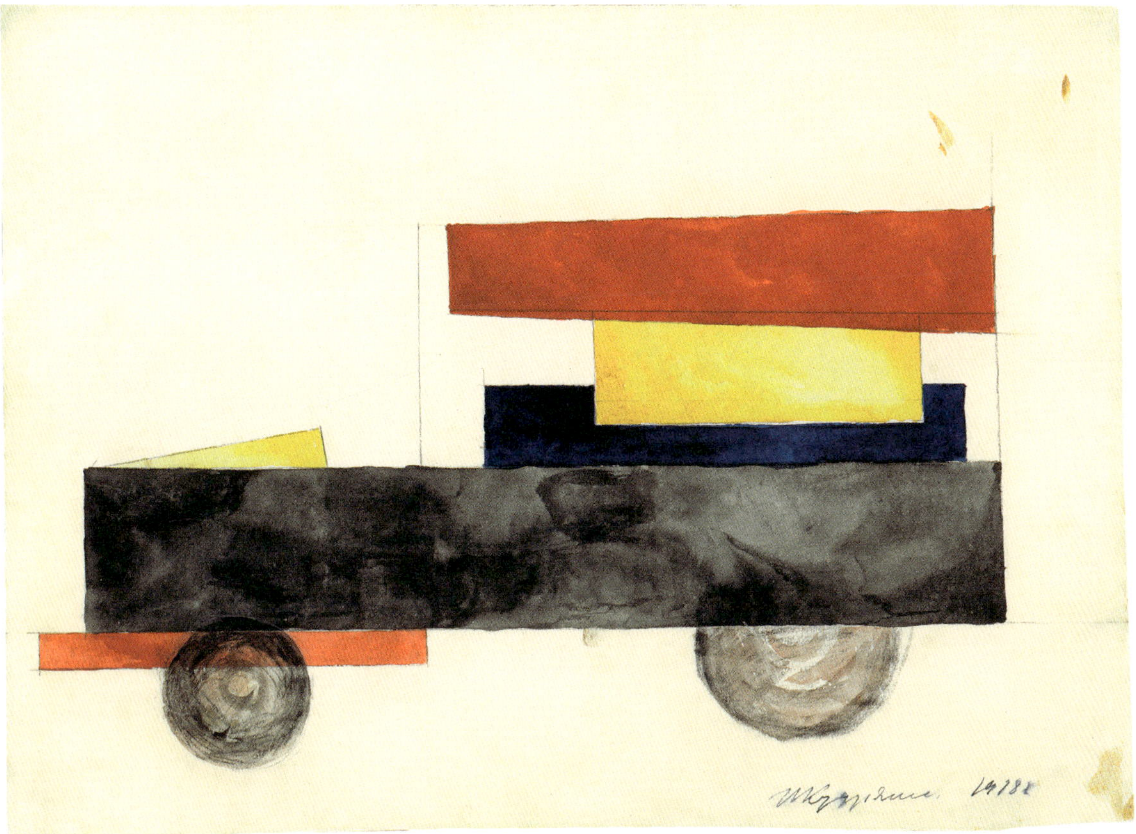

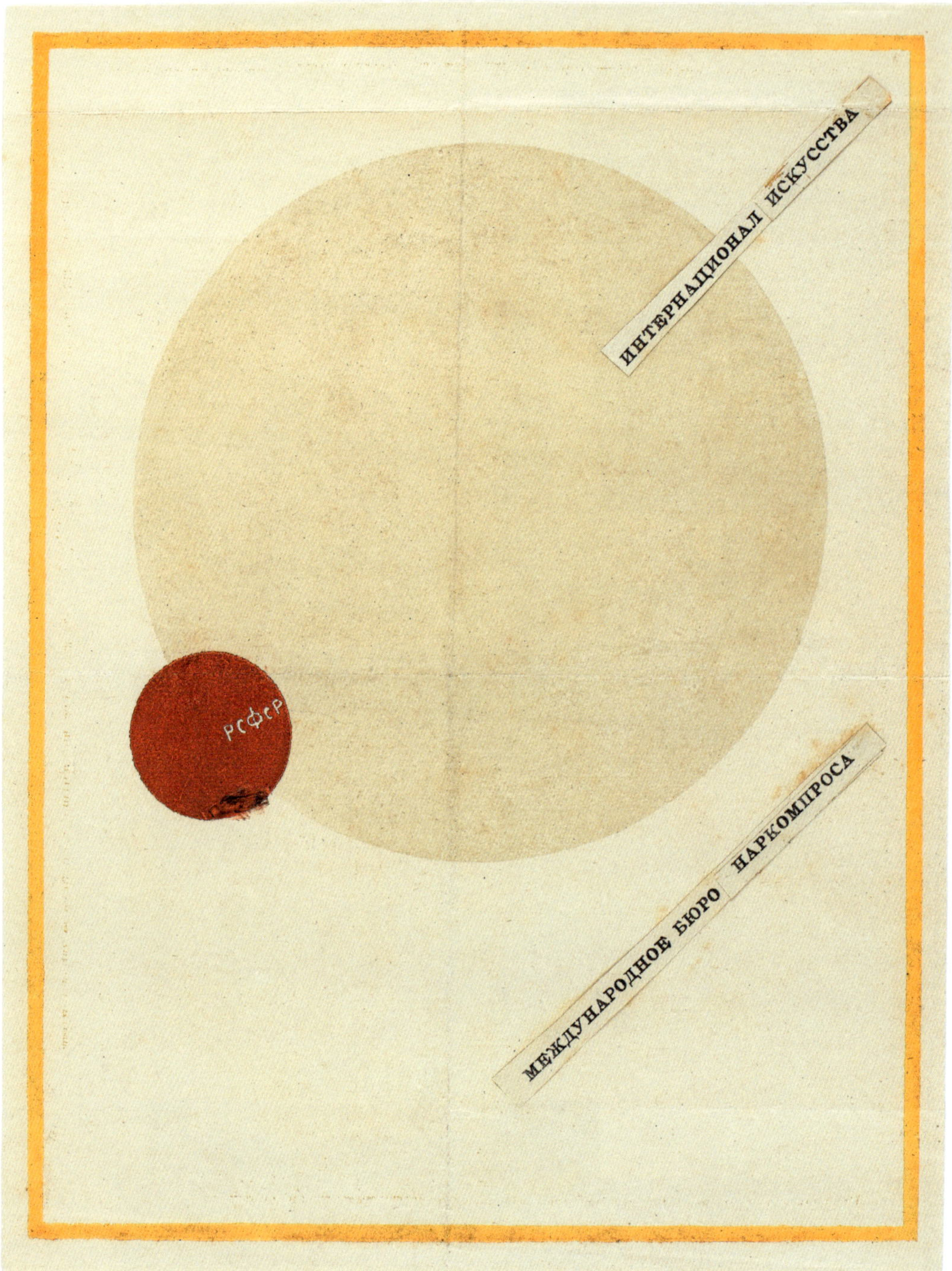

Kazimir Malevich
Cover of the journal *The International of Art*
(unpublished), ca. 1919

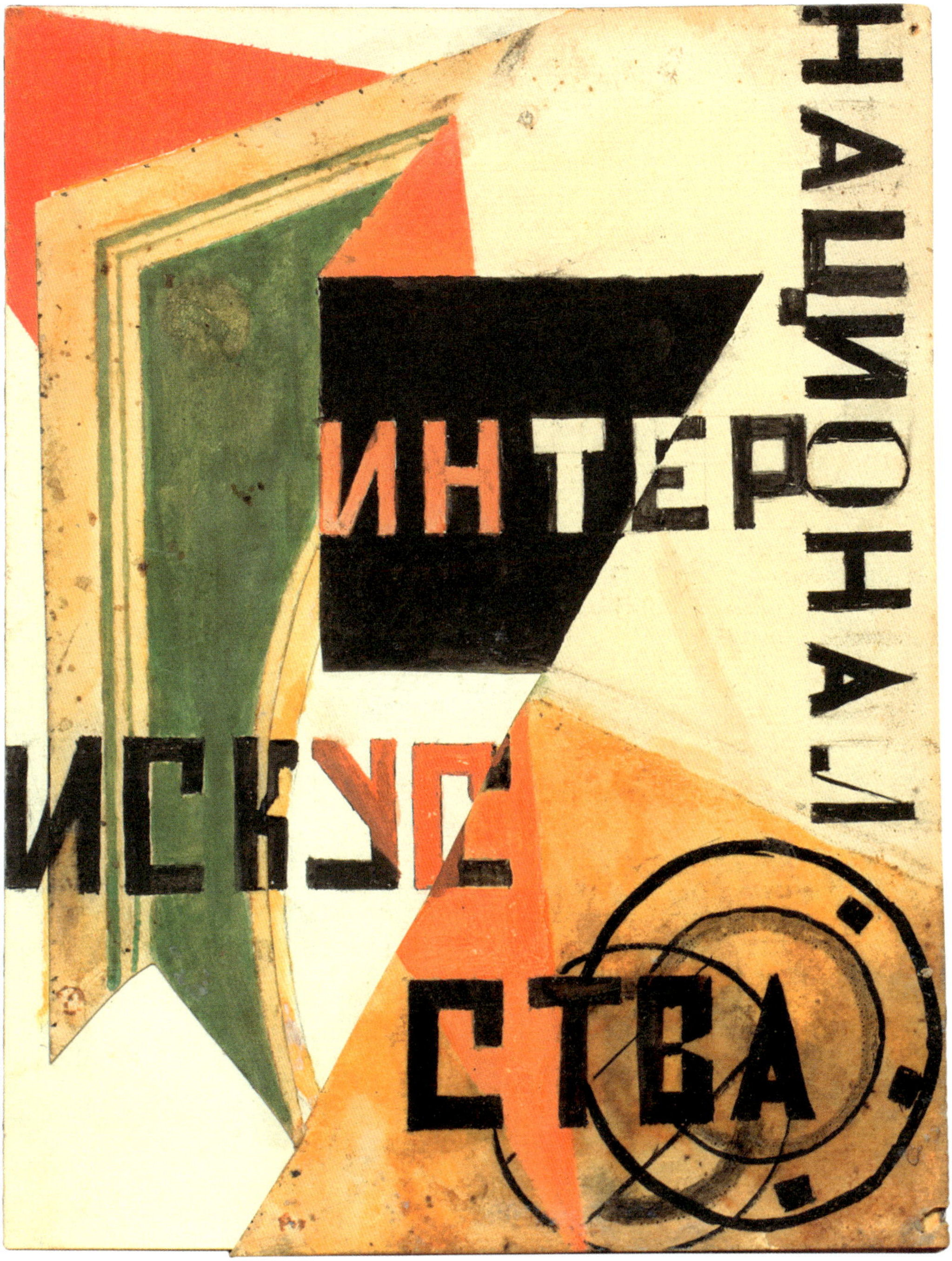

Sofia Dymshits-Tolstaia
Cover of the journal *The International of Art*
(unpublished), 1919

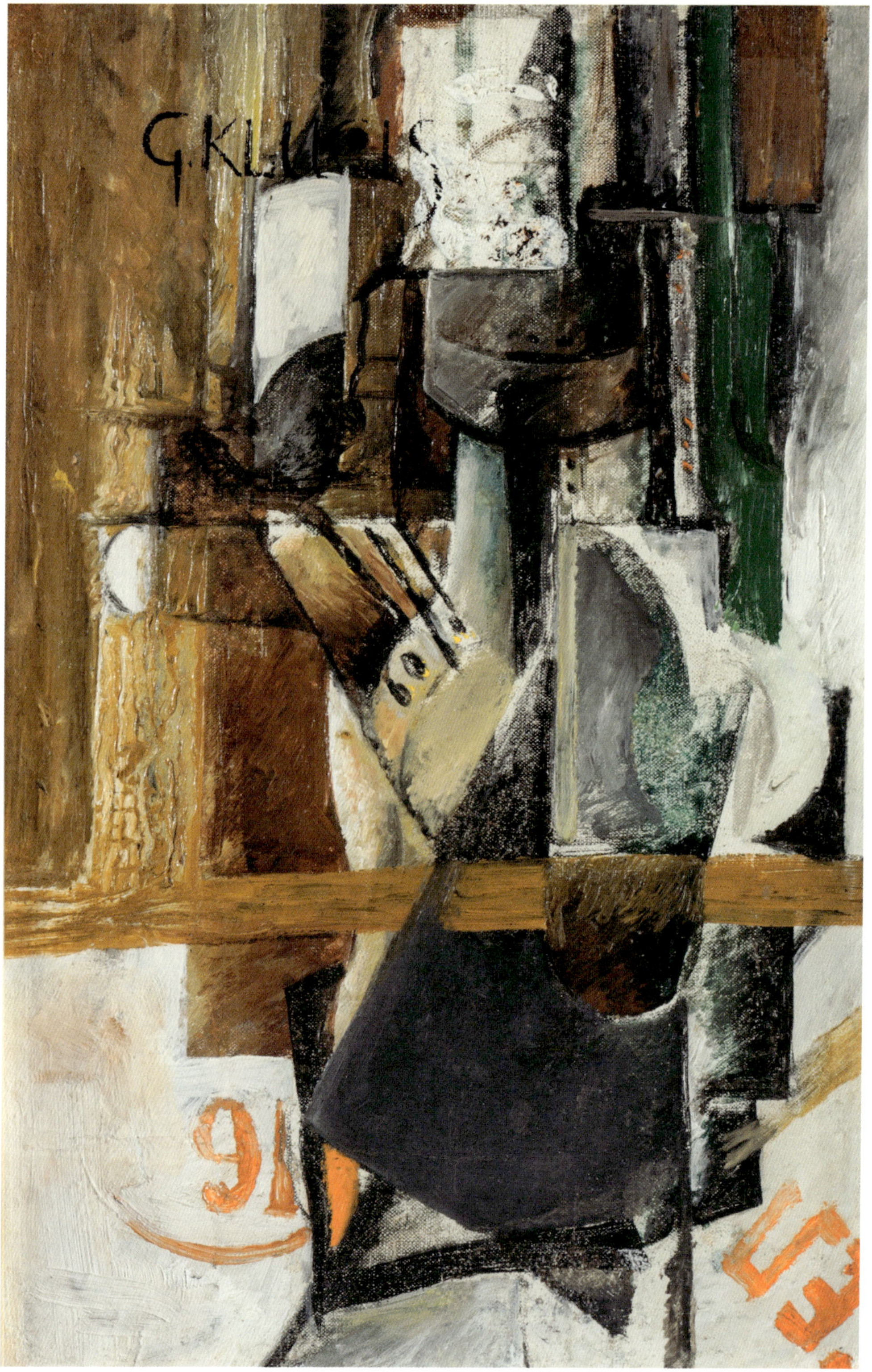

Gustav Klutsis
Untitled (recto and verso), ca. 1920

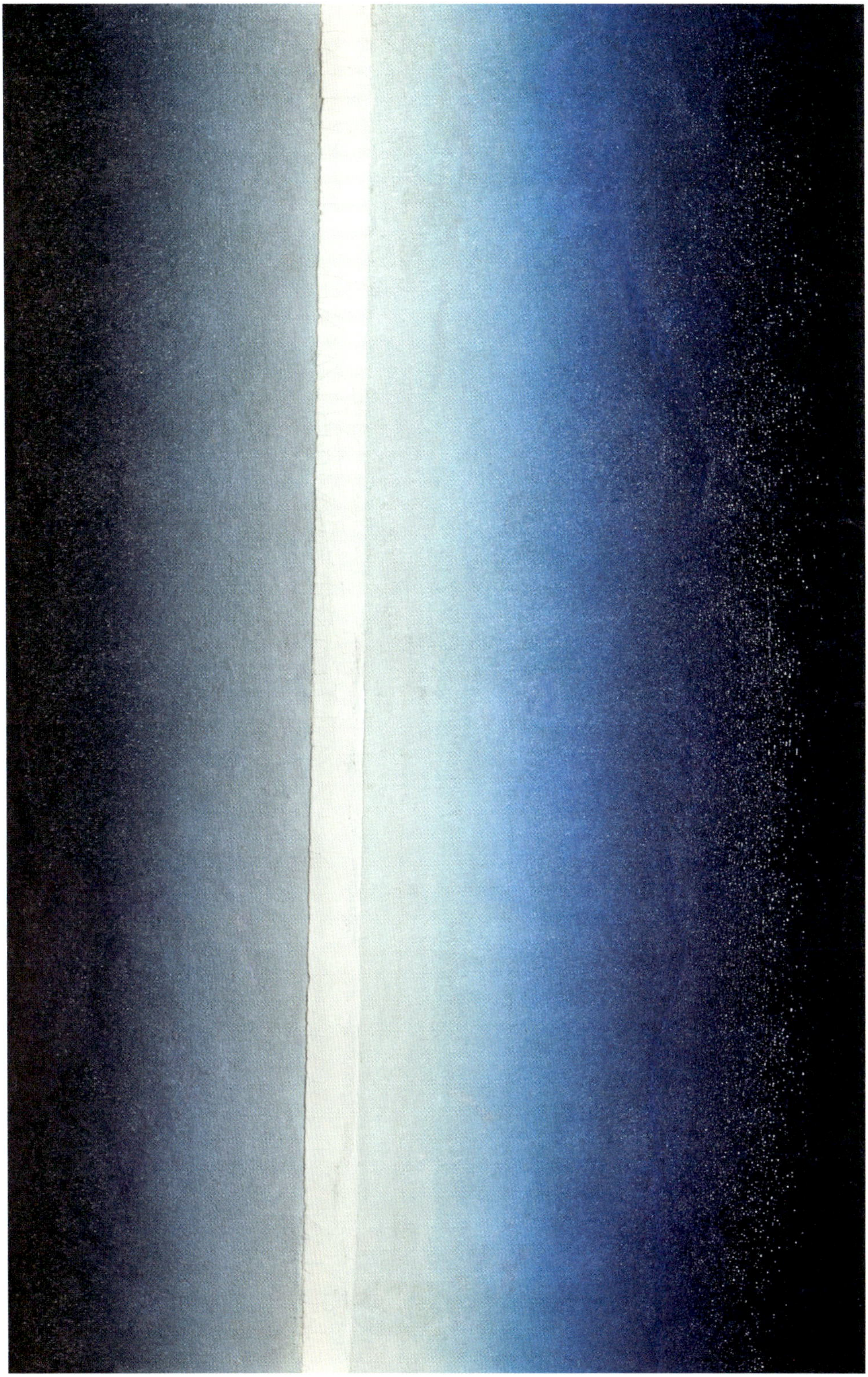

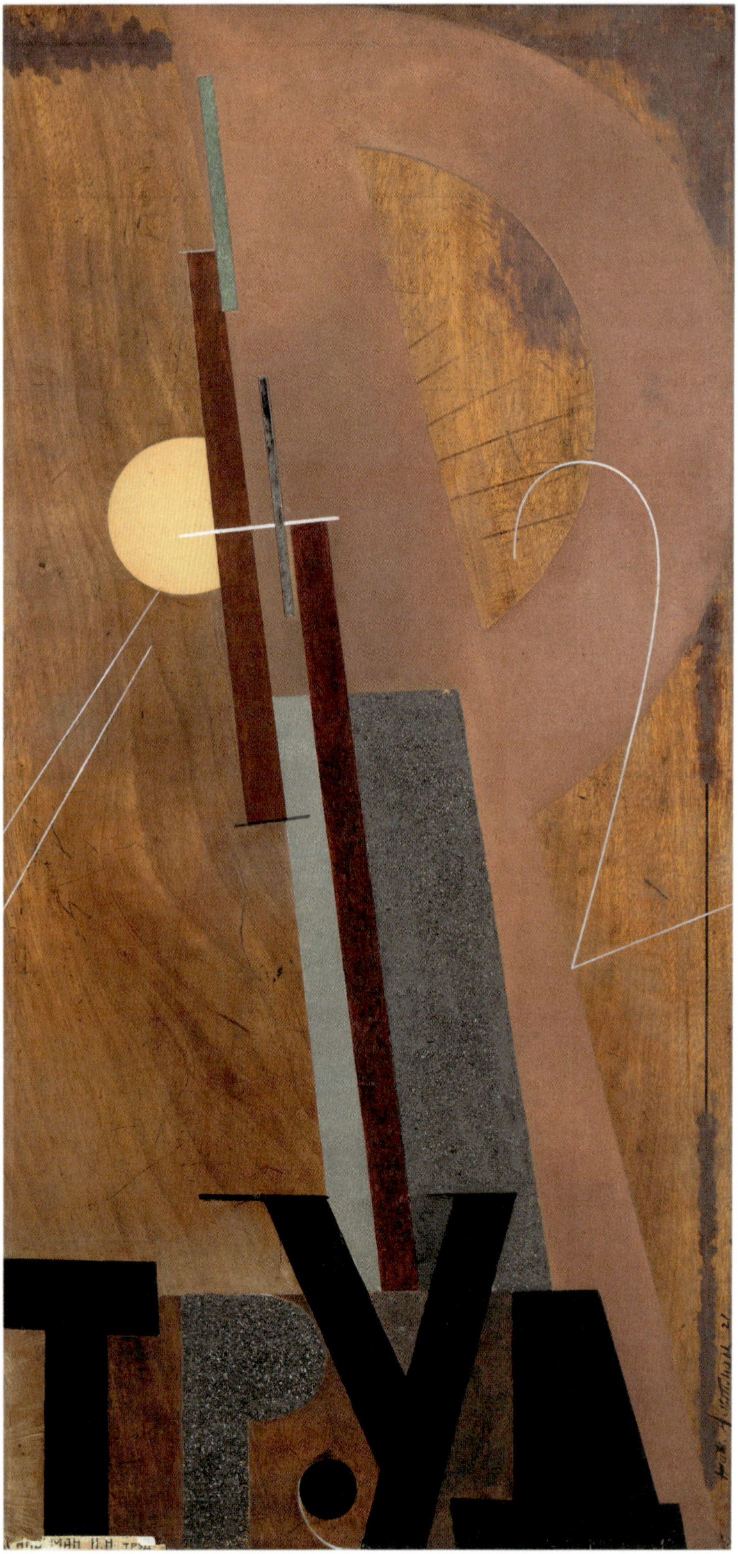

Natan Altman
Russia: Work, 1921

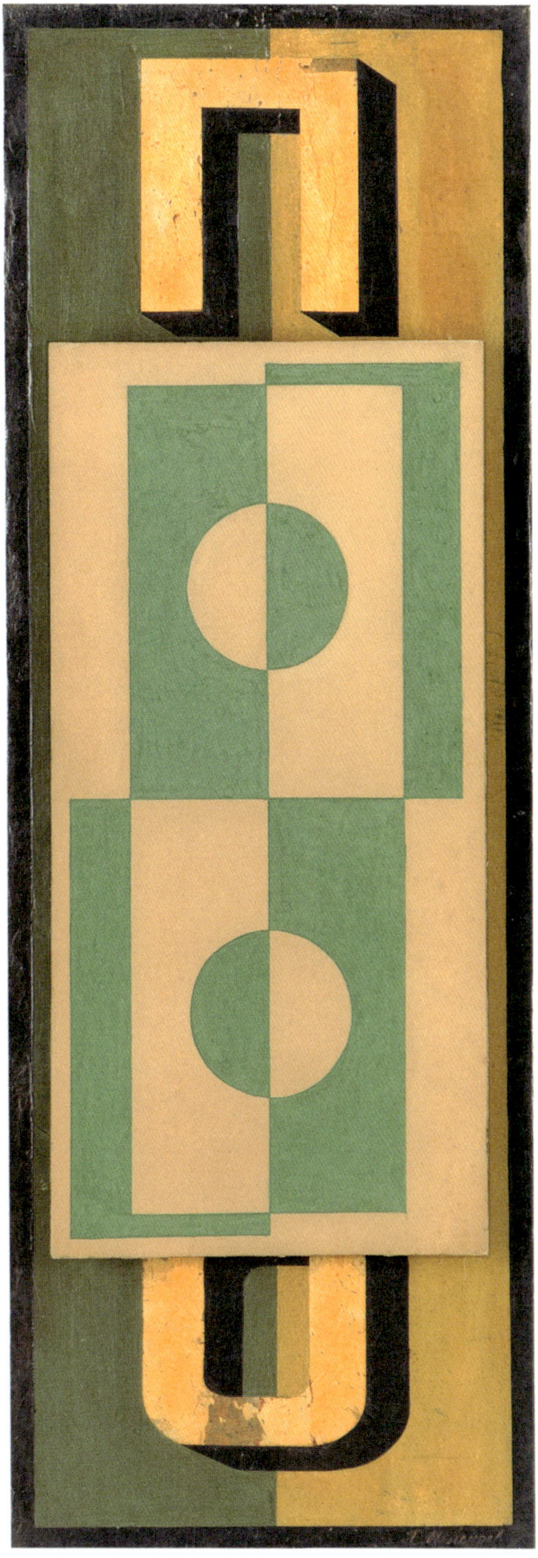

Pavel Mansurov
Beer-Painterly Formula, 1922

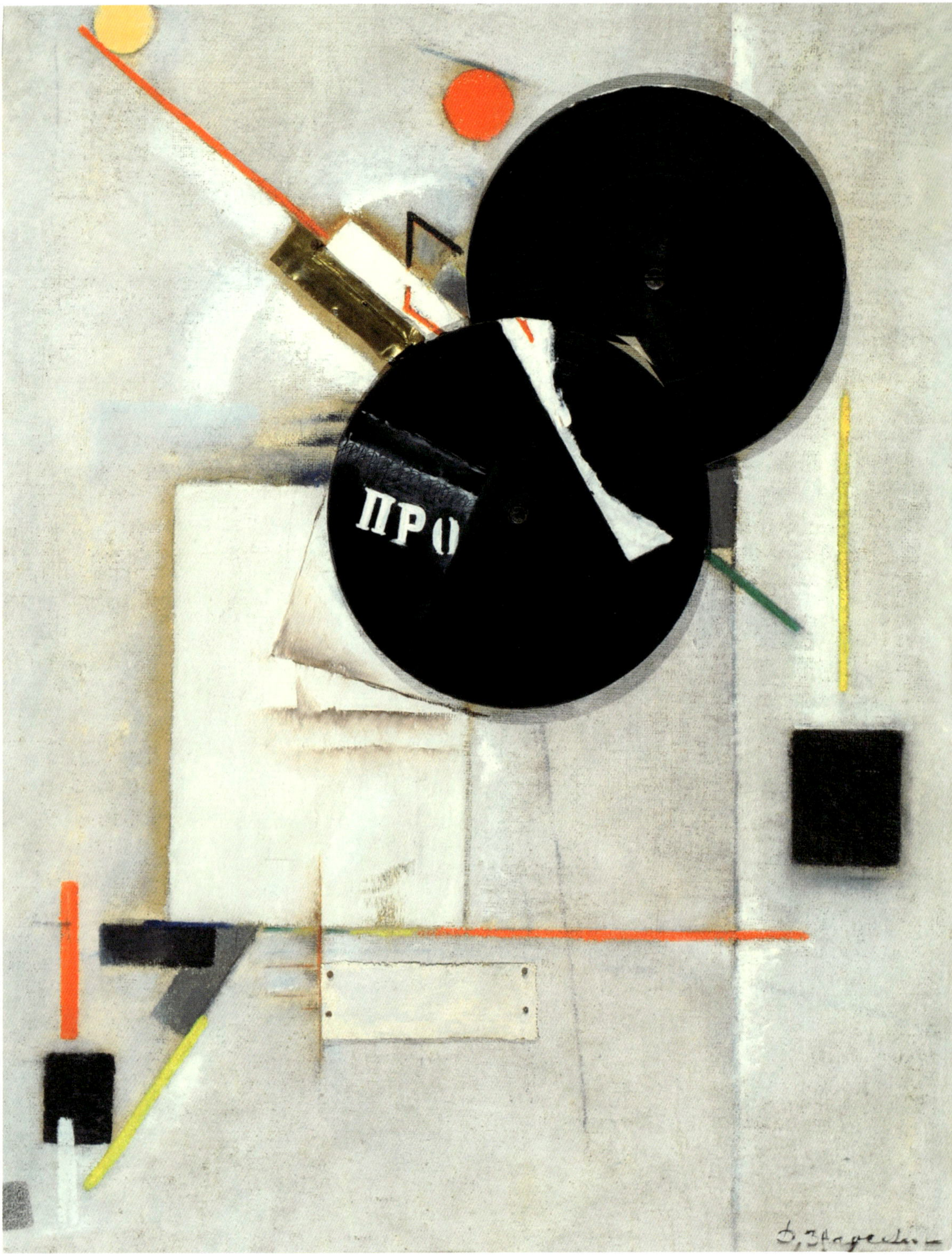
ПРО

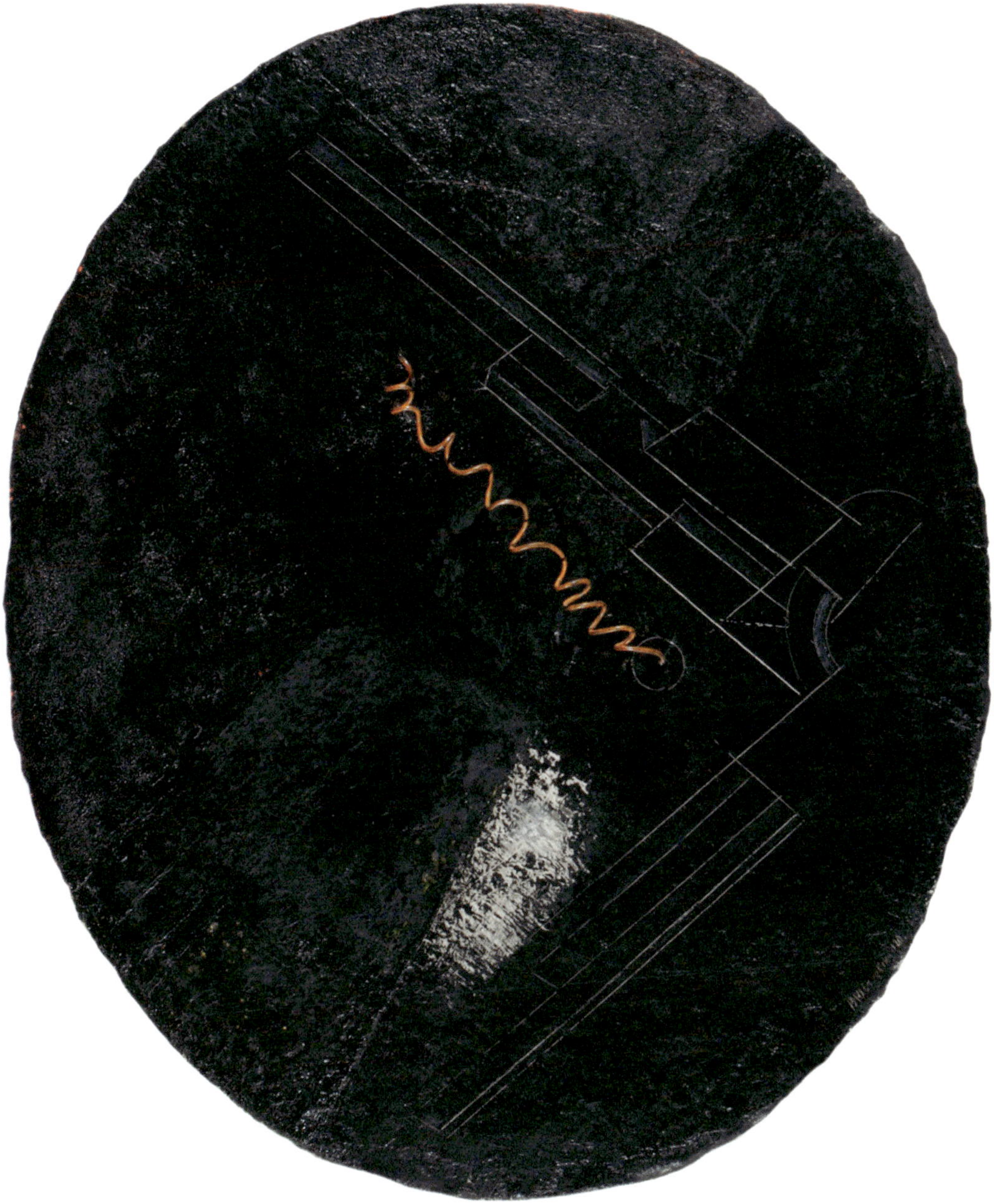

David Zagoskin
Construction, 1921–1922

Valentin Iustitsky
Painterly Construction with Wire, early 1920s

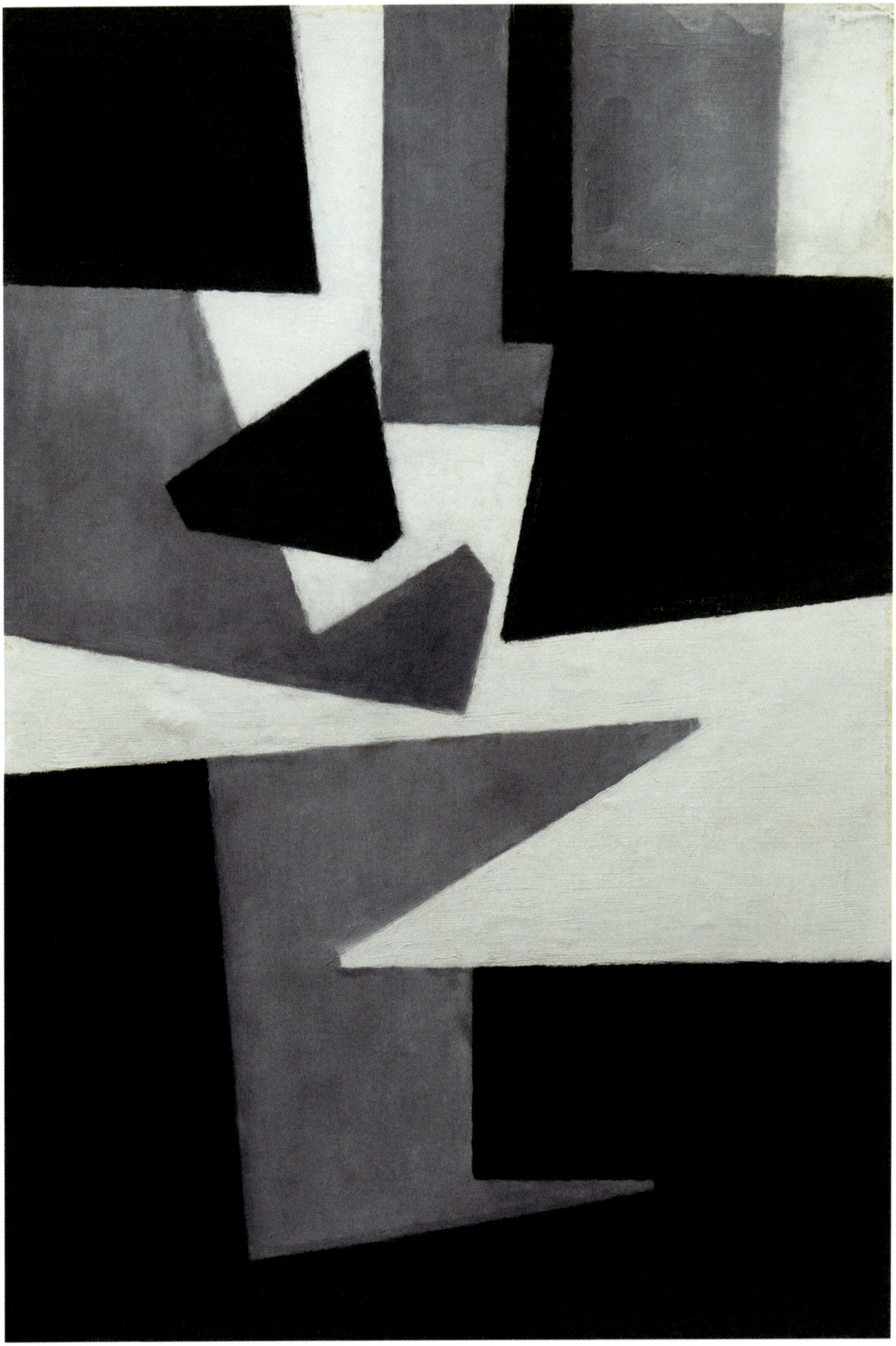

Boris Ender
Karl Liebknecht, 1919

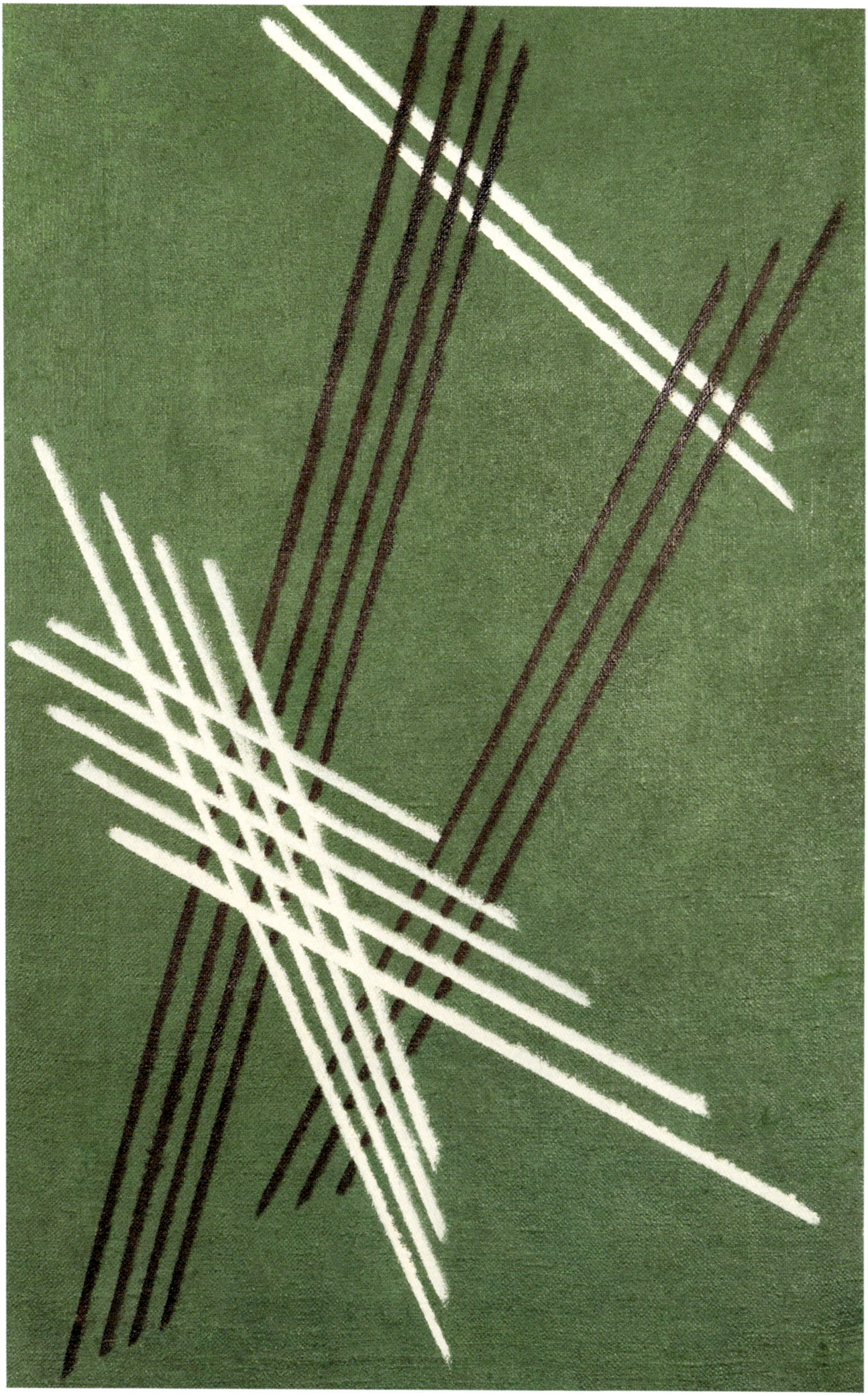

Aleksandr Rodchenko
Construction no. 92 (on Green), 1919

Next double page:
Aleksandr Rodchenko
Detective, 1922

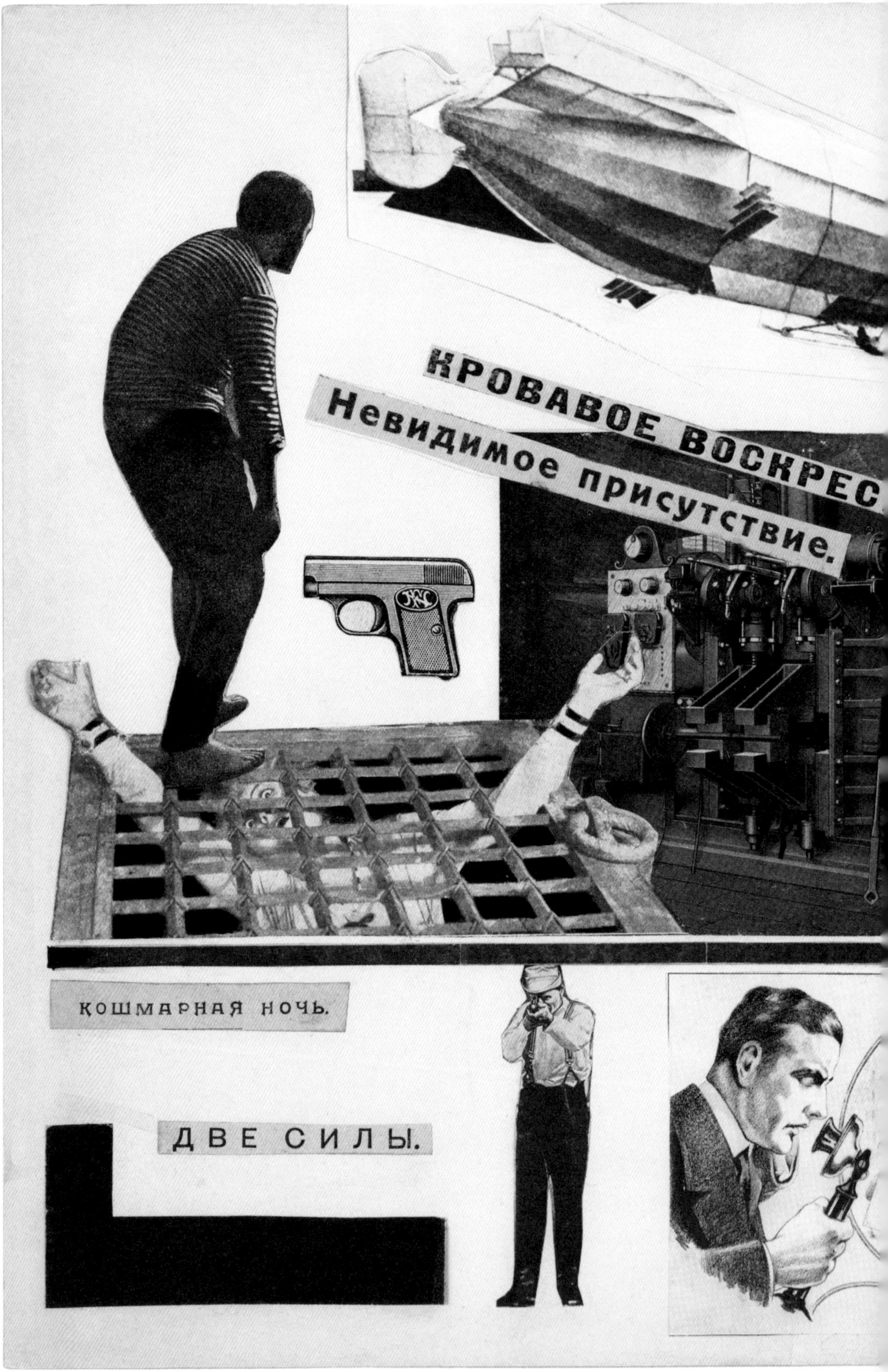
КРОВАВОЕ ВОСКРЕС
Невидимое присутствие.
КОШМАРНАЯ НОЧЬ.
ДВЕ СИЛЫ.

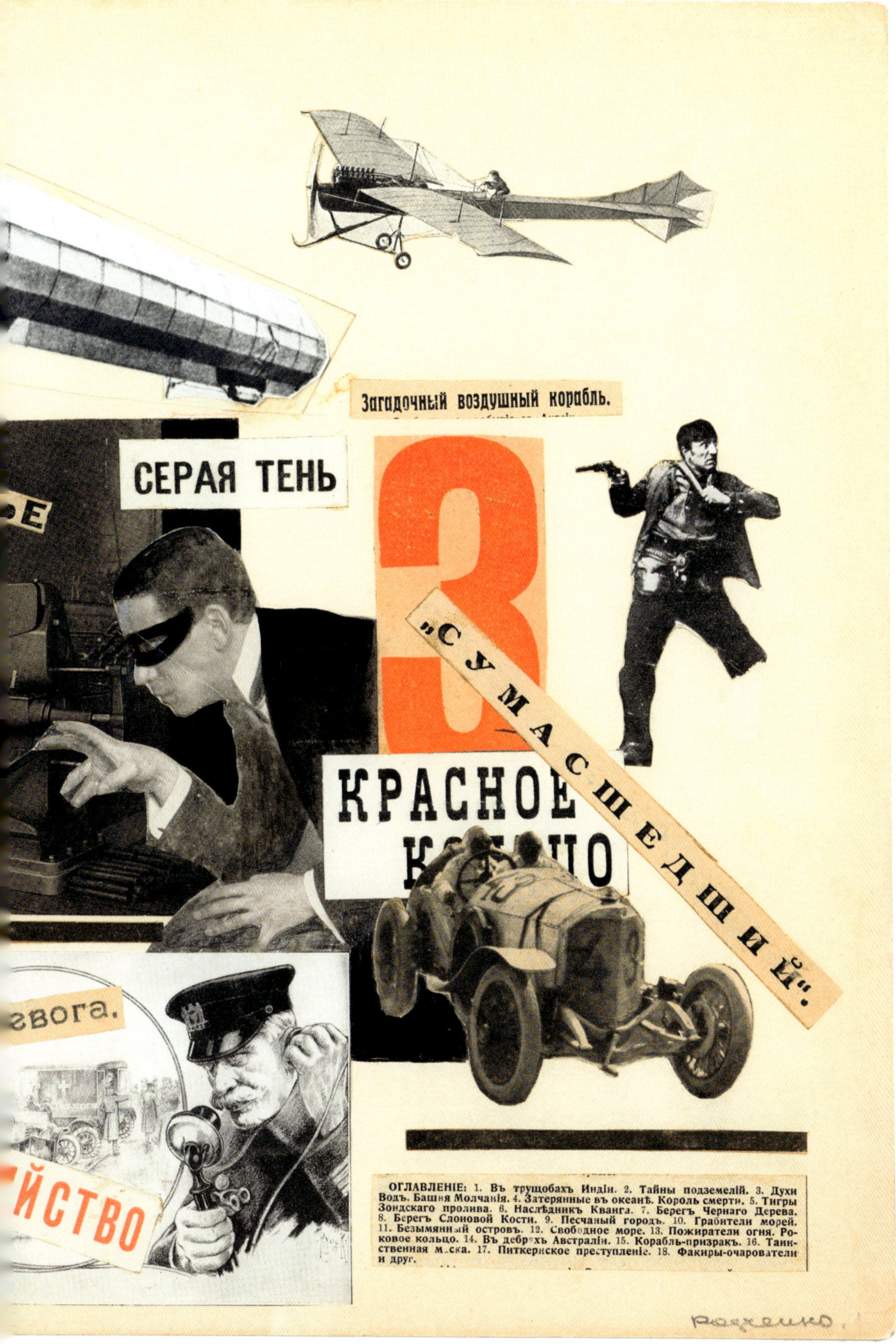
Загадочный воздушный корабль.
СЕРАЯ ТЕНЬ
3
„СУМАСШЕДШИЙ".
КРАСНОЕ
тревога.
ЙСТВО
ОГЛАВЛЕНІЕ: 1. Въ трущобахъ Индіи. 2. Тайны подземелій. 3. Духи Водъ. Башня Молчанія. 4. Затерянные въ океанѣ. Король смерти. 5. Тигры Зондскаго пролива. 6. Наслѣдникъ Кванга. 7. Берегъ Чернаго Дерева. 8. Берегъ Слоновой Кости. 9. Песчаный городъ. 10. Грабители морей. 11. Безымянный островъ. 12. Свободное море. 13. Пожиратели огня. Роковое кольцо. 14. Въ дебряхъ Австраліи. 15. Корабль-призракъ. 16. Таинственная маска. 17. Питкернское преступленіе. 18. Факиры-очарователи и друг.
Родченко.

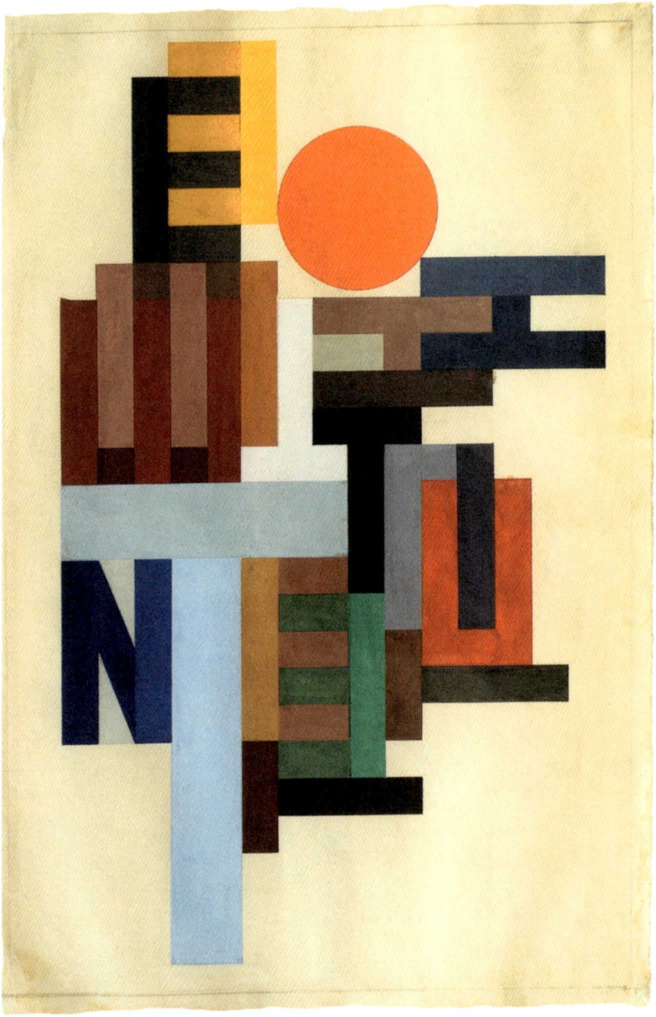

Vasily Ermilov
Untitled (Composition with Letters), ca. 1920

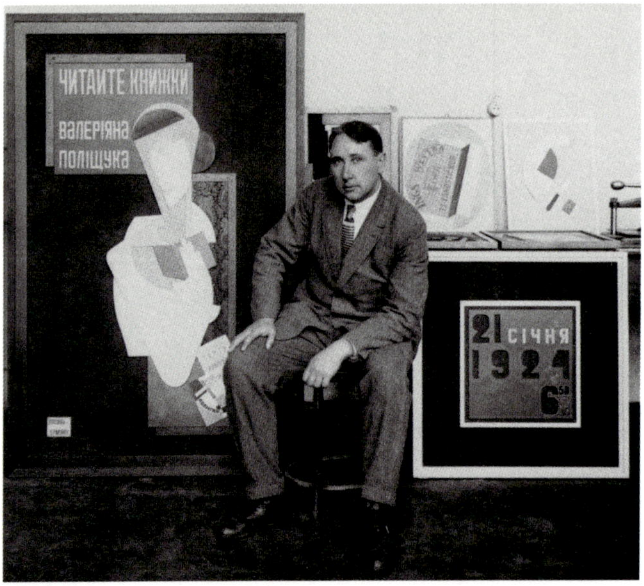

Anonymous
Vasily Ermilov in his studio with an advertising design for "Read Books" by Valerian Polishchiuk (left), ca. 1926

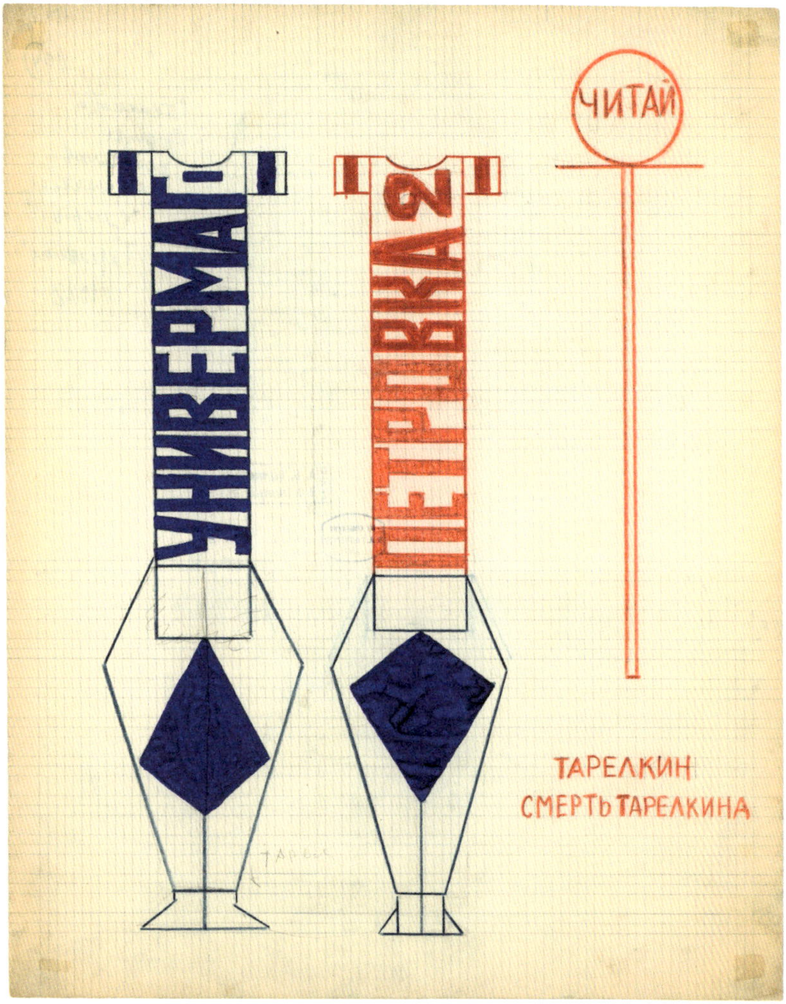

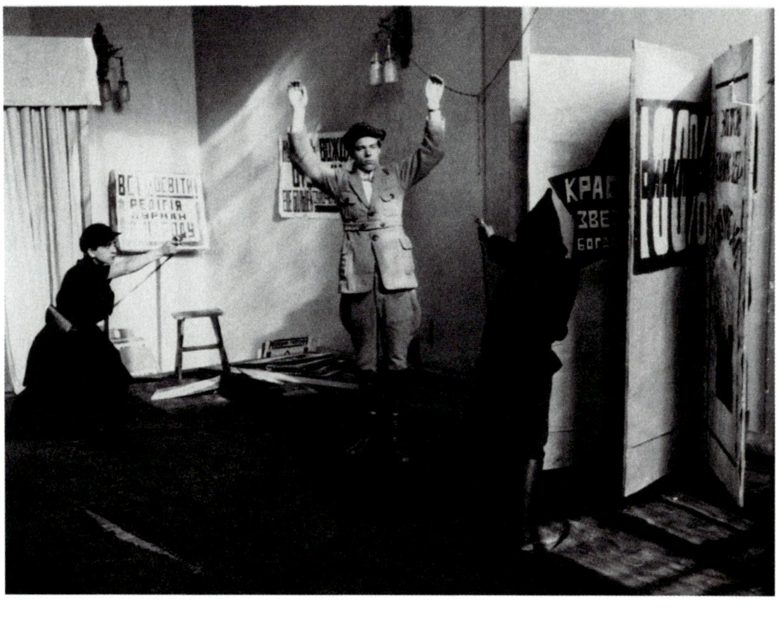

Varvara Stepanova
Costume design for the play *Death of Tarelkin* by Aleksandr Sukhovo-Kobylin for Vsevolod Meyerhold Theater, 1922

Varvara Stepanova
Props design for Vitaly Zhemchuzhny's *Evening of the Book* (Red imps disarm Aleksandr Kirensky), 1924

Klement Redko
Uprising, 1924–1925

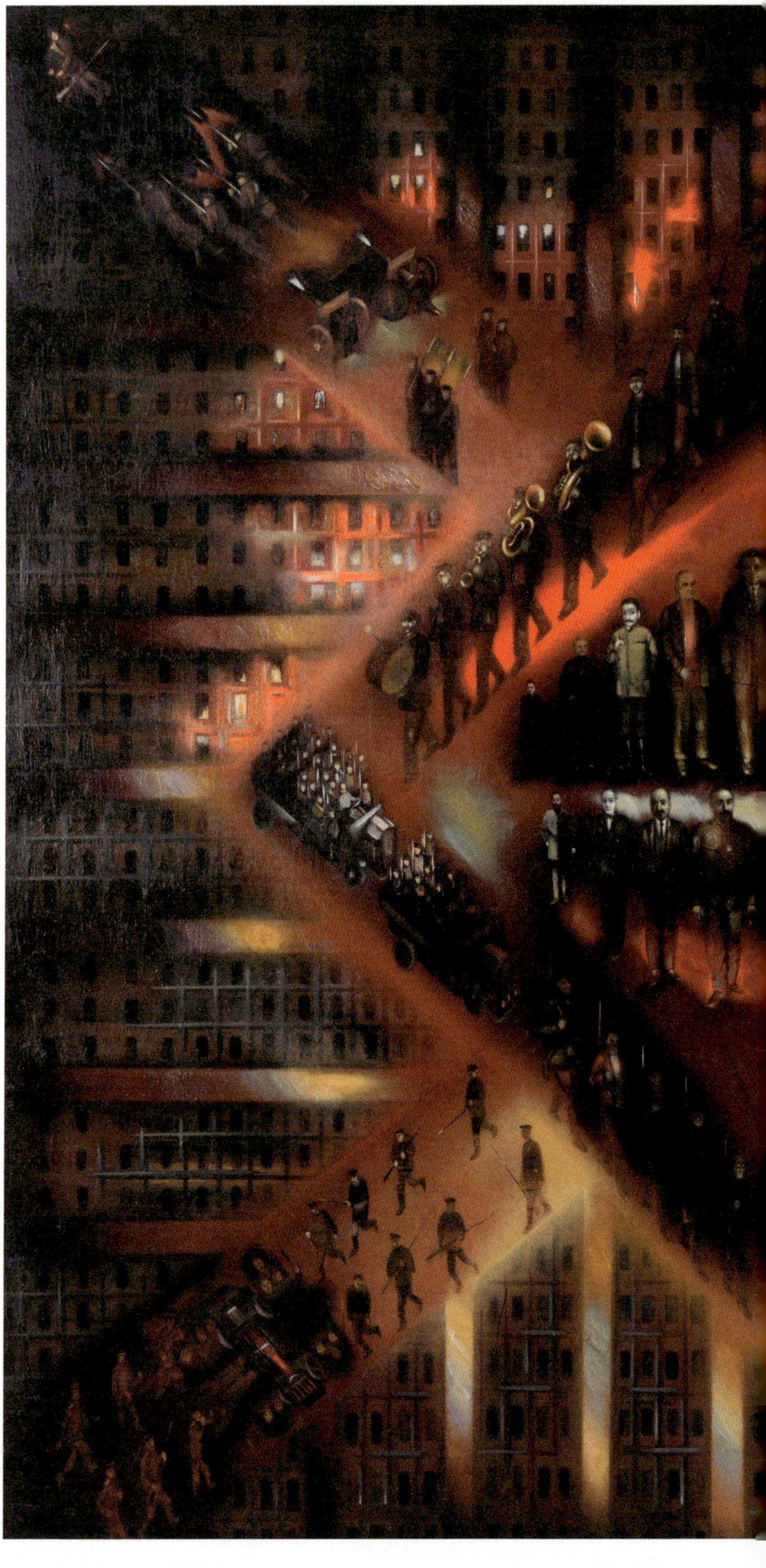

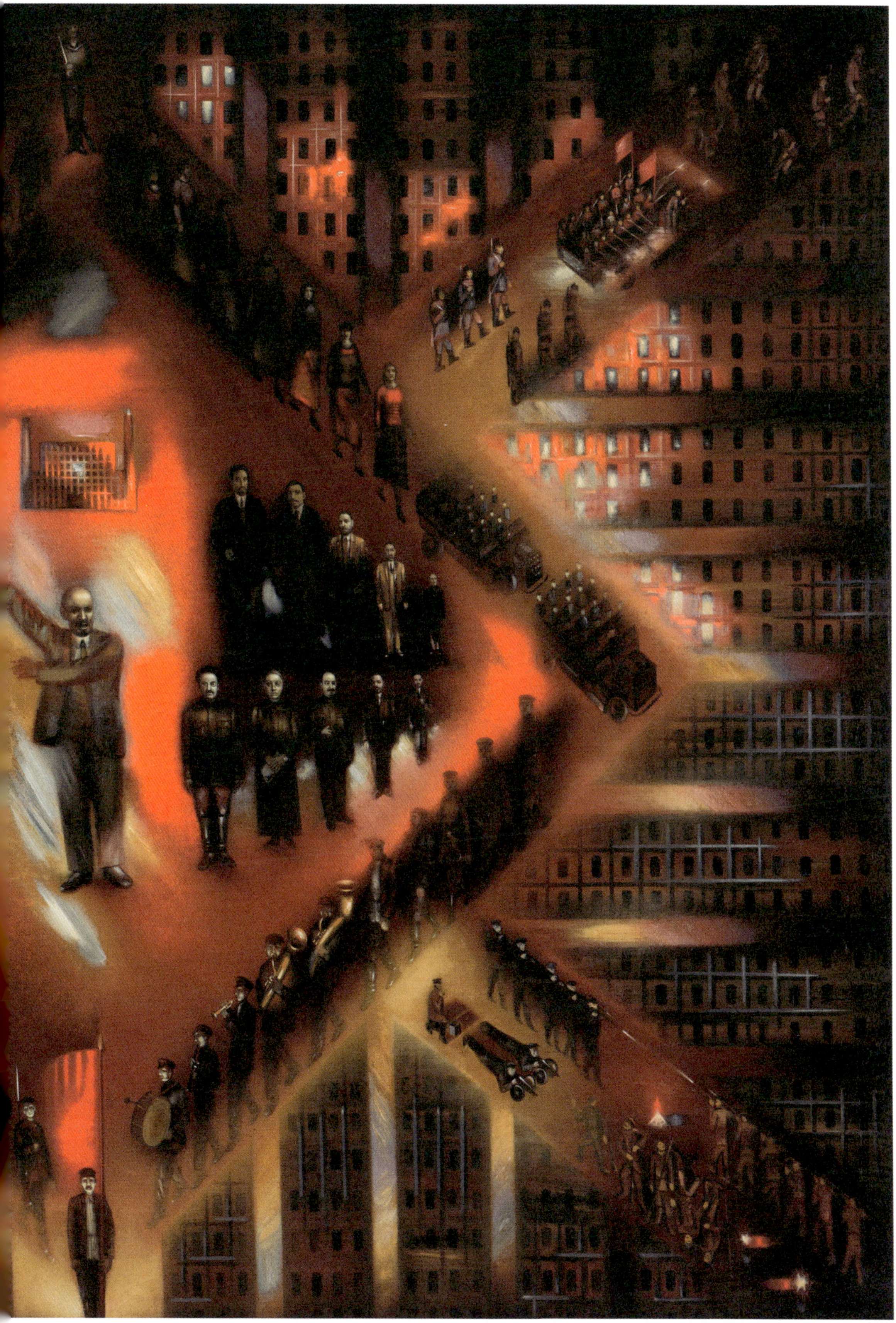

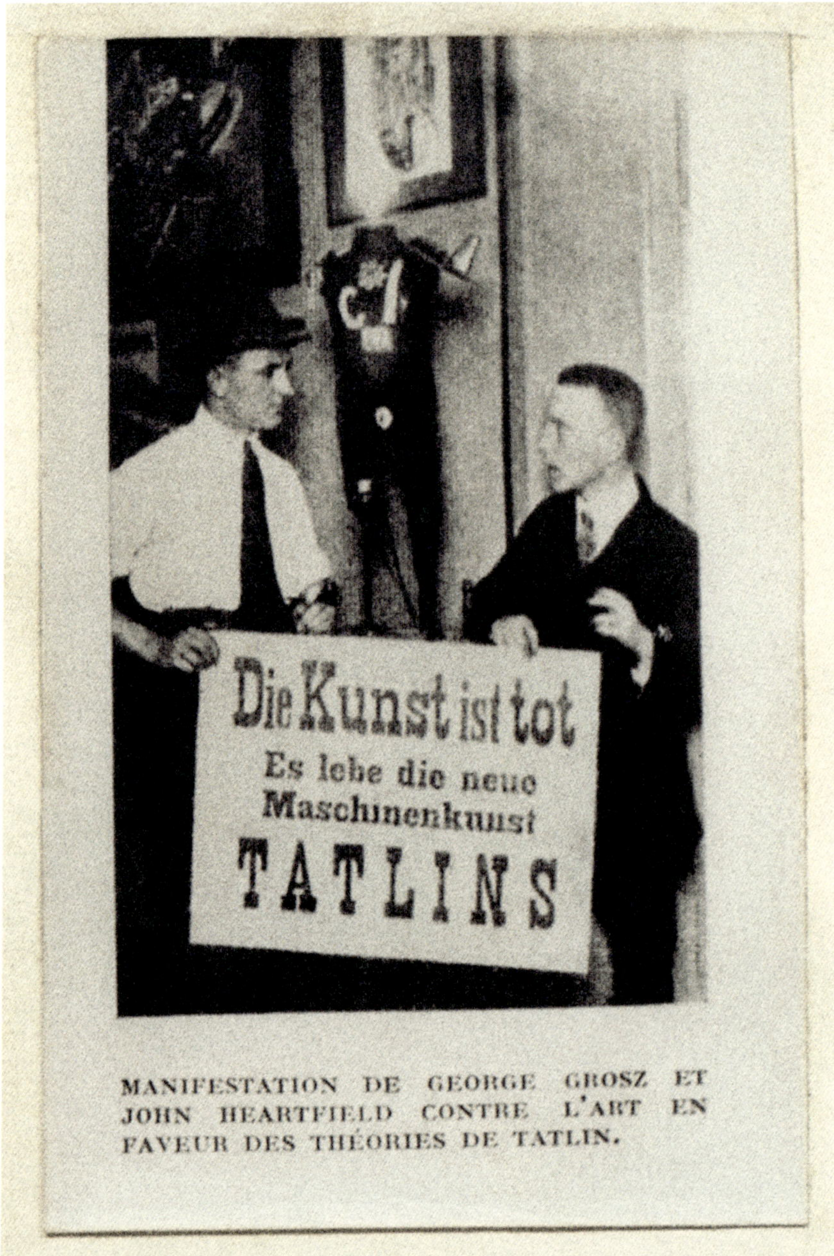

Osip Brik
Scrapbook "Dada," ca. 1923–1924
George Grosz and John Heartfield holding the poster "Art is Dead. Long live Tatlin's Tower"

Dada Bridge

The word Dada expresses
the internationality of the movement.
—Richard Huelsenbeck, cited in Roman Jakobson,
"Letters from the West. Dada," 1921

Dada is Cosmopolitan.
—Sergei Sharshun

Berlin

For his 1922 book *And Yet, It Moves*, Ilya Ehrenburg assesses the recent history of the international avant-garde: "During the war everyone was separated by the barbed wire and by the ears of spies. But in 1918, after a four-year separation, artists and writers saw that without knowing it, they had arrived at the same platform."[117] Ehrenburg's book globalized the significance of Tatlin's *Tower*, referring to it with the phrase "and yet, it moves," Galileo's alleged pronouncement about the earth after his condemnation by the Inquisition. *Tower's* rotational quality positioned it as a new symbol of postwar international art, in contrast to the previous, static separations between East and West. And with this openness, Dadaist tendencies crystalized into the shared platform. These were left politics, involving social critique at once austere and enforced by mechanisms of parody, passionate experimentation, and fanatical agitation for new ideas.

Along with Ehrenburg and Shklovsky, in the 1920s several other significant Russian avant-gardists (Puni, Lissitzky, Zdanevich, Sharshun, Kandinsky, Mayakovsky) moved to or spent time in Europe. All of them came into

117. Il'ia Erenburg, *A vse taki ona vertitsia* (Moscow: Gelikon, 1922), 43.

Anonymous
Vladimir Tatlin, Berlin, 1914

El Lissitzky
Tatlin Working on the Monument to the Third International, illustration in the book *Six Tales with Easy Endings* by Ilya Ehrenburg, 1922

immediate contact with the Dadaists and to different degrees contributed to the expansion of the Dadaist conceptual reservoir. Mayakovsky played a particularly coalescing role between the Russian and European milieus. In the fall of 1922 he departed for Berlin in conjunction with the opening, on October 15, of the *First Russian Exhibition* in that city, which, surprisingly, given the Bolsheviks' antibourgeois attitudes, took place at a private venue, the Van Diemen Gallery. The exhibition included works by all the major nonobjectivists, giving the impression that nonobjective art was endorsed by the Bolsheviks. The popularity of Mayakovsky's political p. 128 Russian Telegraph Agency (ROSTA) posters of 1919–1921, also displayed in the exhibition, was amplified by his poetry readings in anticipation of his forthcoming books *For the Voice*, designed by Lissitzky, and *150,000,000*, with p. 128 a cover by John Heartfield.[118]

Taken at the First International Dada Fair, a photograph of Heartfield and Grosz holding a placard with the slogan "Art is dead / p. 122 Long live the new machine art of TATLIN" registered the beginning of the Dadaists' fascination with Russian avant-gardists.[119] At p. 127 the fair Grosz showed *Tatlinesque Diagram* (1920), which, despite its title, dwells on his characteristic critique of the German bourgeoisie and their pervasive urban alienation. p. 126 Hausmann's since-lost *Tatlin at Home* (1920) was more explicitly relevant to Tatlin's ideas in its juxtaposition of a torso with its organs exposed to effect human physical vulnerability, and a modern man with his brain and eyes replaced by mechanical implants. Such views of Tatlin—as an artist-machine in whose mind the "details are calculated, honestly, with a ruler," or, as Mayakovsky described Tatlin to

118. Several other artists and writers contributed to the production of the ROSTA posters that effectively spread the Bolshevik agenda. Mayakovsky collaborated with Jakobson on at least one poster.

119. M. A. Iziumskaia believes the Berlin Dadaists' knowledge of Tatlin came from the publication in 1920 of Konstantin Umanski's book *Neue Kunst in Rusland 1914–1919*, in which Tatlin's new idea of monuments as "an alive machine" is discussed. See M. A. Iziumskaia, "Nemetskie dadaisty i Rossiia: puti vzaimodeistviia," in *Rossiia-Germaniia: kul'turnye sviazi, iskusstvo, literatura v pervoi polovine dvadtsatogo veka: materialy nauchnoi konferentsii "Vipperovskie chteniia-1996,"* no. 29, ed. I. E. Danilova (Moscow: Pushkin State Museum of Fine Arts, 2000), 56.

120. Mayakovsky quoted in Nikolai Khardzhiev, "Maiakovskii i Tatlin: k 90-letiiu so dnia rozhdeniia khudozhnika," in *Stat'i ob avangarde*, ed. Duganov, Arpishkin, and Sarab'ianov, 1:233. Tatlin visited Picasso's studio during his trip to Europe in 1913 in conjunction with an exhibition of folk art. He appears as part of a band of blind musicians in photographs, playing a bandore with closed eyes, hinting at his future exchange of retinal art for an art of the mind, a shift reflected in Hausmann's and Lissitzky's photomontages. Duchamp, who is credited with the dissemination of the concept of antiretinal art in New York, published a magazine called *The Blind Man* in 1917. p. 125

121. Nikolai Punin, "Tatlin (Protiv kubizma)," in *O Tatline*, ed. Punina and Rakitin, 30.

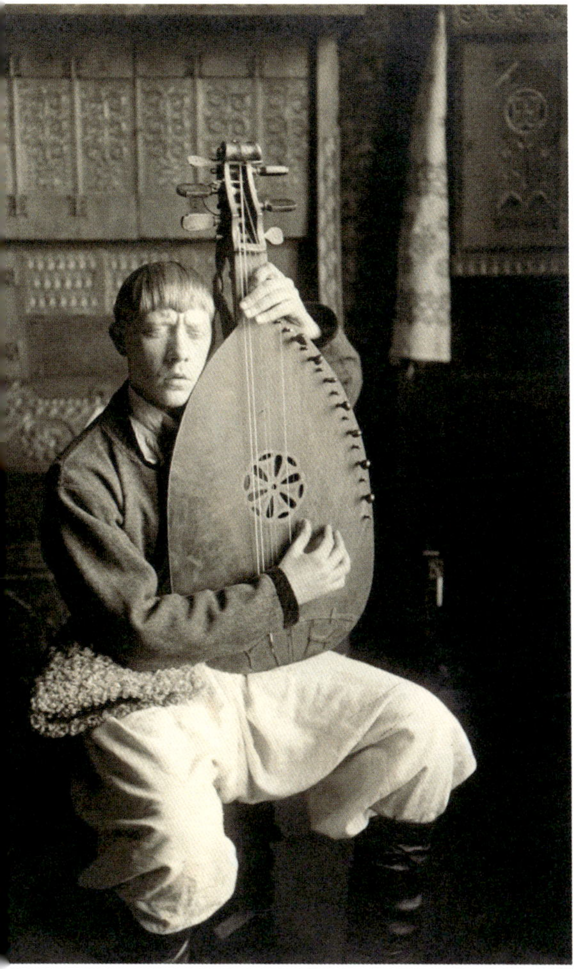

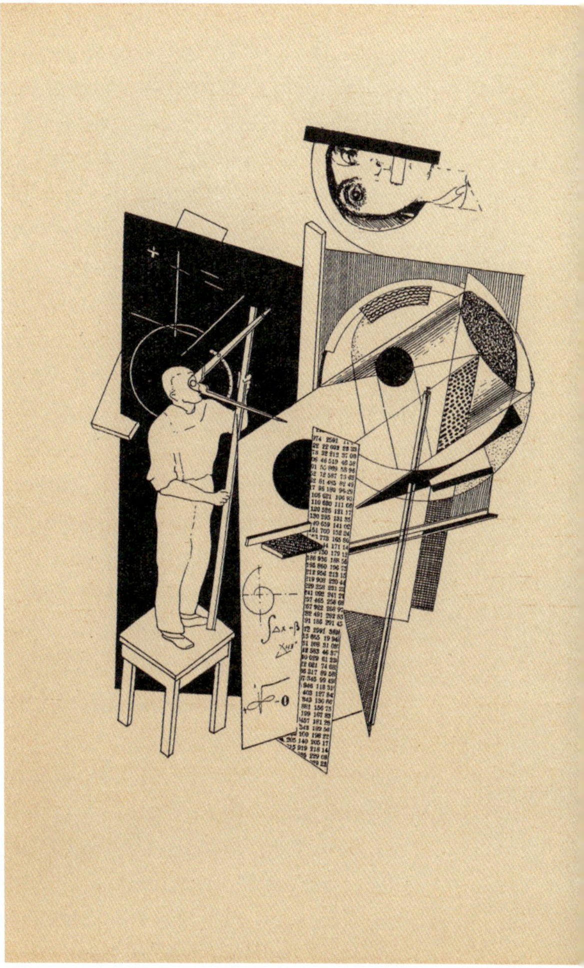

Pablo Picasso in 1922, as an example of an artist who stopped creating art for "pleasing artists' own eyes"—was also reflected in Lissitzky's photocollage *Tatlin Working on the Monument to the Third International*, made for Ehrenburg's book *Six Tales with Easy Endings* (1922).[120] In the photocollage, a ruler is inserted in the place of Tatlin's eye, liberating it from "emotional irritation of the hypertrophied and damaged eye" and "accidental forms" and giving it an "objectively truthful and real viewpoint."[121] p. 125

While Tatlin was the Dadaists' fantasy of a new kind of a progressive modernist, Puni, the organizer of *0,10*, had been physically present in Berlin since the fall of 1920. Puni's exhibition at Herwarth Walden's Der

Sturm gallery in February 1921 put him in contact with German Dadaists associated with the gallery and its eponymous magazine, including Arp, Richter, and Schwitters. Richter later recalled the impact of Puni's exhibition: "Curiously enough, Dada tendencies seem to have made their first appearance in Russia, where p. 47 Futurist influence was still very strong. Puni's *Barber's Shop* [1915] and *Window-cleaner* [1915] are a poetic combination of Simultaneist experience and original experimentation. His empty p. 131 *Hunger Plate* . . . is a piece of defiance that, both in its directness and in its form of expression, can be regarded as a Dada document."[122]

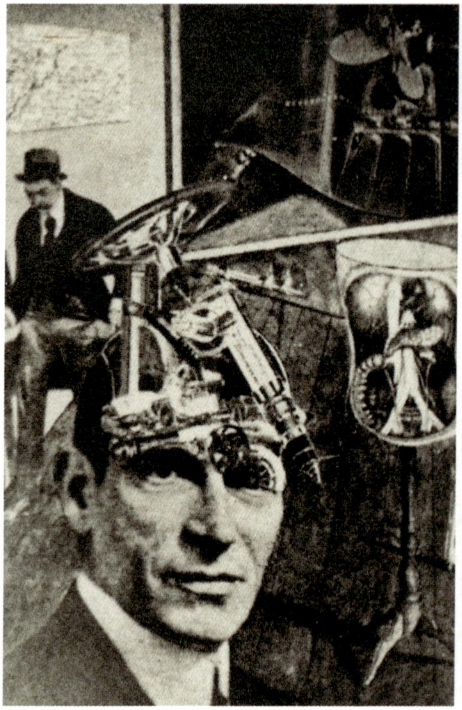

Richter's memoir includes an illustration of *Hunger Plate* dated 1918, with "Petrograd" added to the title—a location that transforms this monochrome with affixed plate into a political allegory. "In Russia in 1918 they were in the middle of a revolution, and one potato a day was a lot. The empty plate was a challenge (to something or someone)," Richter recounts in his memoir.[123] A photograph of the lost assemblage *Hunger Plate*, preserved in the collection of the Mayakovsky Museum in Moscow, was most likely brought back by Mayakovsky from Germany or Paris, where Puni moved in 1924. One of the pair's encounters in Russia resulted in a Dadaist joke by Mayakovsky, described by Khardzhiev as a "photographic trick" and "one of the first examples of photomontage."[124] In p. 35 a group photograph called *Easter at Futurists* (1915), featuring Mayakovsky, Vasily Kamensky, Kulbin, Arthur Lurie, and Rozanova, the poet pasted next to himself Puni's head set against a flowery hanging fabric. This was payback for Puni's refusal to be photographed with him during the exhibition *Tramway V*. The accompanying text lists Easter wishes, one of which (Malevich's) reads, "Reason is a penal

122. Richter, *Dada*, 198–99.

123. Ibid., 206. Puni participated in creating street decorations for the Soviet anniversary and taught at SVOMAS, showing his initial loyalty and interest in the revolution. This is reflected in his membership in the German November Group, with whom he exhibited in Cologne in 1922.

124. Khardzhiev, "Fotoshutka Maiakovskogo," 1:153–54.

Osip Brik
Scrapbook "Dada,"
ca. 1923–1924
Raoul Hausmann,
Tatlin at Home, 1920

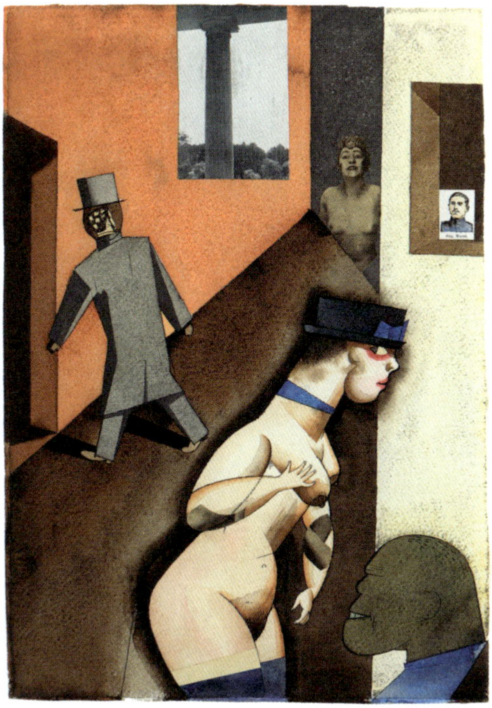

George Grosz
Tatlinesque Diagram, 1920

George Grosz
Two works by the artist reproduced to accompany his article "About My Work, *Lef,* no. 2, 1923

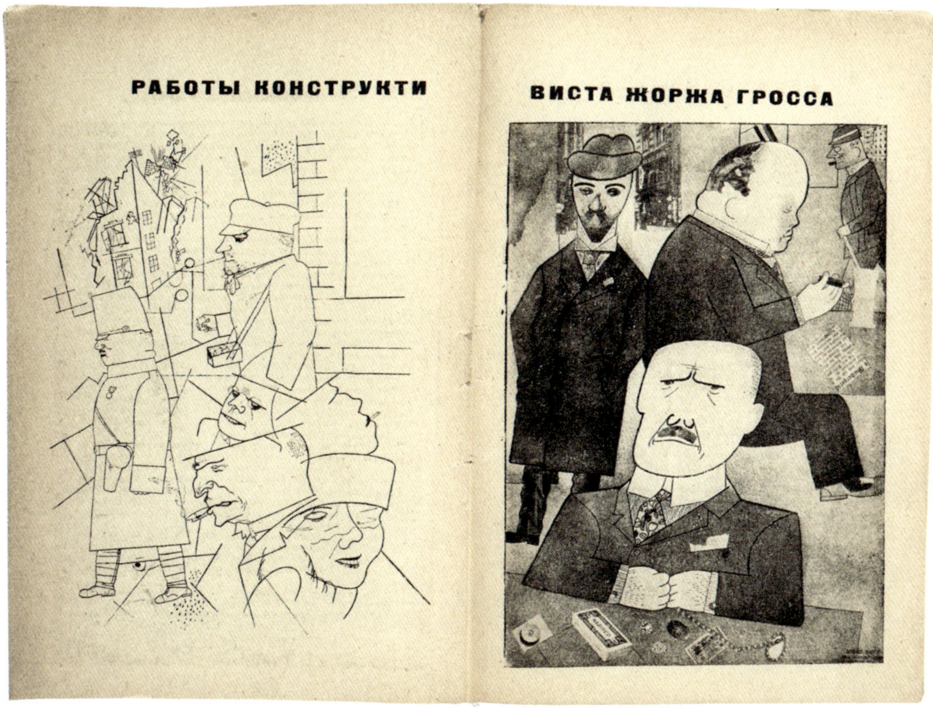

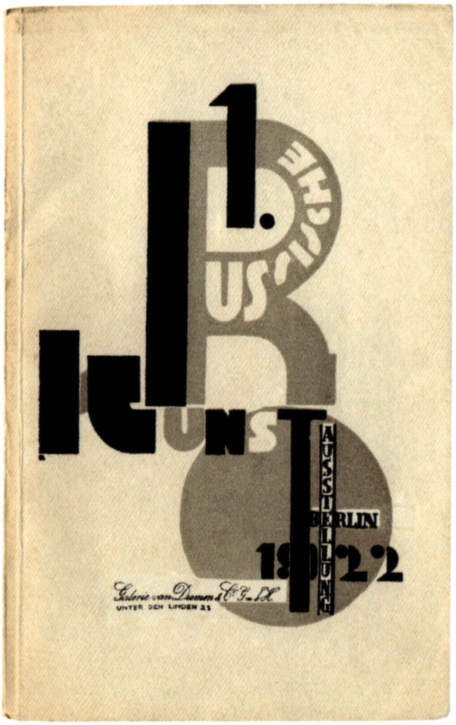
1. Russische Kunstausstellung
Berlin 1922
UNTER DEN LINDEN 21

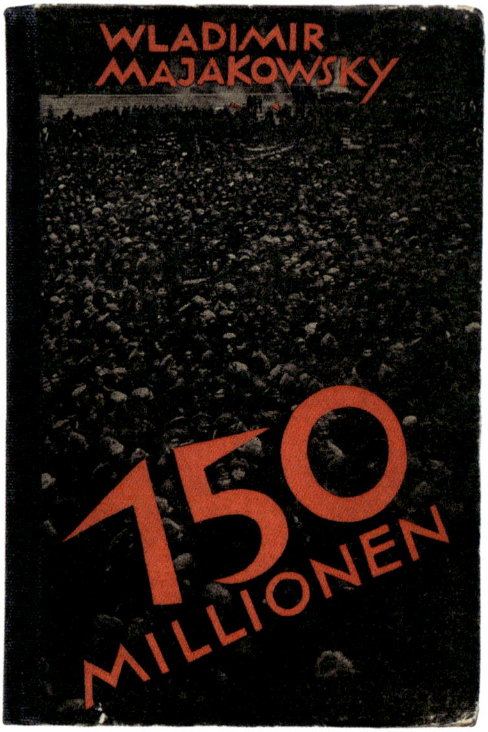
WLADIMIR MAJAKOWSKY
150 MILLIONEN

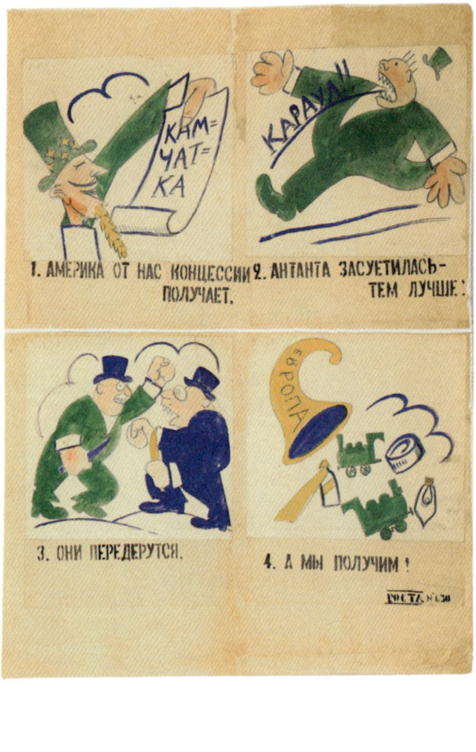
КАМ=ЧАТ=КА
КАРАУЛ!!
1. АМЕРИКА ОТ НАС КОНЦЕССИИ ПОЛУЧАЕТ.
2. АНТАНТА ЗАСУЕТИЛАСЬ- ТЕМ ЛУЧШЕ!
ЕВРОПА
3. ОНИ ПЕРЕДЕРУТСЯ.
4. А МЫ ПОЛУЧИМ!

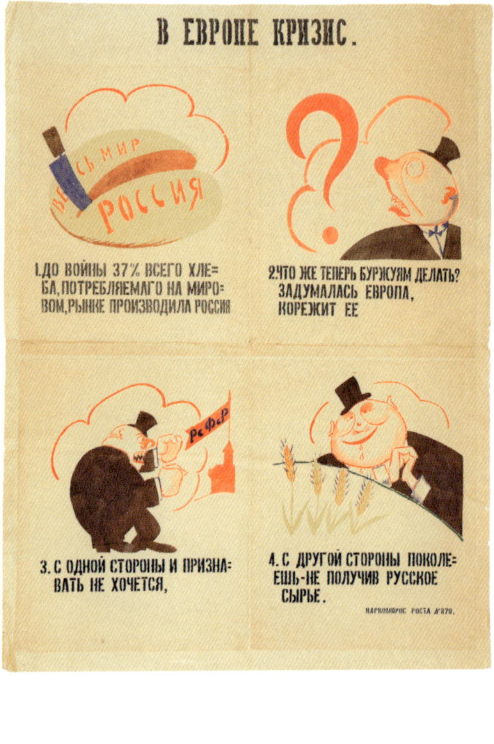
В ЕВРОПЕ КРИЗИС.
ВЕСЬ МИР
РОССИЯ
1.ДО ВОЙНЫ 37% ВСЕГО ХЛЕ= БА,ПОТРЕБЛЯЕМАГО НА МИРО= ВОМ,РЫНКЕ ПРОИЗВОДИЛА РОССИЯ
2.ЧТО ЖЕ ТЕПЕРЬ БУРЖУЯМ ДЕЛАТЬ? ЗАДУМАЛАСЬ ЕВРОПА, КОРЕЖИТ ЕЕ
РСФСР
3. С ОДНОЙ СТОРОНЫ И ПРИЗНА= ВАТЬ НЕ ХОЧЕТСЯ,
4. С ДРУГОЙ СТОРОНЫ ПОКОЛЕ= ЕШЬ-НЕ ПОЛУЧИВ РУССКОЕ СЫРЬЕ.

El Lissitzky
Cover of the catalogue
The First Russian Exhibition,
Berlin, 1922

John Heartfield
Cover of the book
150,000,000 by Vladimir
Mayakovsky, 1924

Vladimir Mayakovsky
ROSTA no. 630, "America
gets concessions from us,"
November 1920

Vladimir Mayakovsky
ROSTA no. 870, "Crisis in
Europe," January 1921

chain for an artist, thus we wish for all artists to lose their minds."

A photograph of Puni's exhibition at Der Sturm impresses with the installation's inventiveness and stylistic diversity, ranging from figurative expressionism, which Puni had practiced while teaching at the beginning of 1919 at Marc Chagall's studio in Vitebsk (and applied in the *Heroes and Victims* portfolio), to nonobjective *Proun*-like compositions and geometric assemblages. Puni hung some of his framed works over walls painted with oversized Russian letters adopted from his painting *Flight of Forms* (1919), in which he accomplished an equilibrium between visual and verbal transrational morphologies (threatened by easily decipherable communicative models such as Mayakovsky's *Soviet Alphabet* [1919]. The overall layered effect of Puni's installation would have evoked Schwitters's 1919 exhibition of mixed assemblages and collages at Der Sturm. Schwitters, like Puni, emphasized the importance of transgressive poetic language, which, as Dorothea Dietrich points out, "put Schwitters and Hannover on the Dada map."[125] This helps to explain why Lissitzky found shelter with Schwitters in Hannover, making, as his first project there, a portfolio of *Figurines* based on Kruchenykh's *Victory over the Sun*.

p. 130

p. 99

Puni's membership in the radical November Group, formed under expressionist leadership but including Berlin Dadaists; his friendship with Shklovsky, then living in Berlin; and his collaboration with László Moholy-Nagy on the manifesto "A Call to Elementary Art—To the Artists of the World," published in *De Stijl* in October 1921, reflect his openness to *everything*. Moholy-Nagy had mounted an exhibition of his work at Der Sturm just before

125. Dietrich, "Hannover," 159. She refers to Schwitters's parodic love poem "An Anna Blume" (1919), published in *Der Sturm* at the time of his exhibition.

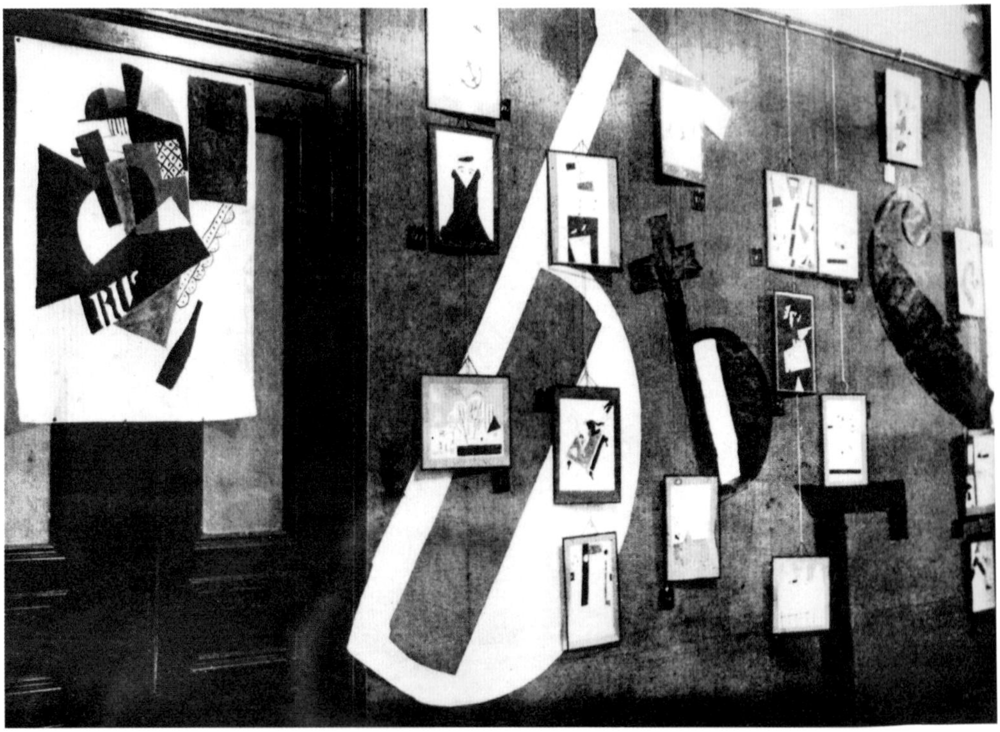

Anonymous
View of Ivan Puni's exhibition in Der Sturm Gallery, Berlin, 1921

Ivan Puni
Untitled (Hunger Plate), ca. 1918

Puni's. The timing, coupled with Moholy-Nagy's preoccupation with nonobjective art and photography, made their interest in each other inevitable. Moholy-Nagy's subsequent *Constructions in Enamel* (1923), which he ordered over the telephone from a local factory by dictating their composition (they are often called his "Telephone Pictures"), attests to the influence, through Puni, of Malevich's democratization of formal inventions through reliance on art's mechanical requisites.[126]

Puni's and Moholy-Nagy's appeal to the international art community was to establish nonobjective art as a platform for unification, an effort that predated the announcement in Düsseldorf of the "Declaration of the International Faction of Constructivists" at the First International Congress of Progressive Artists

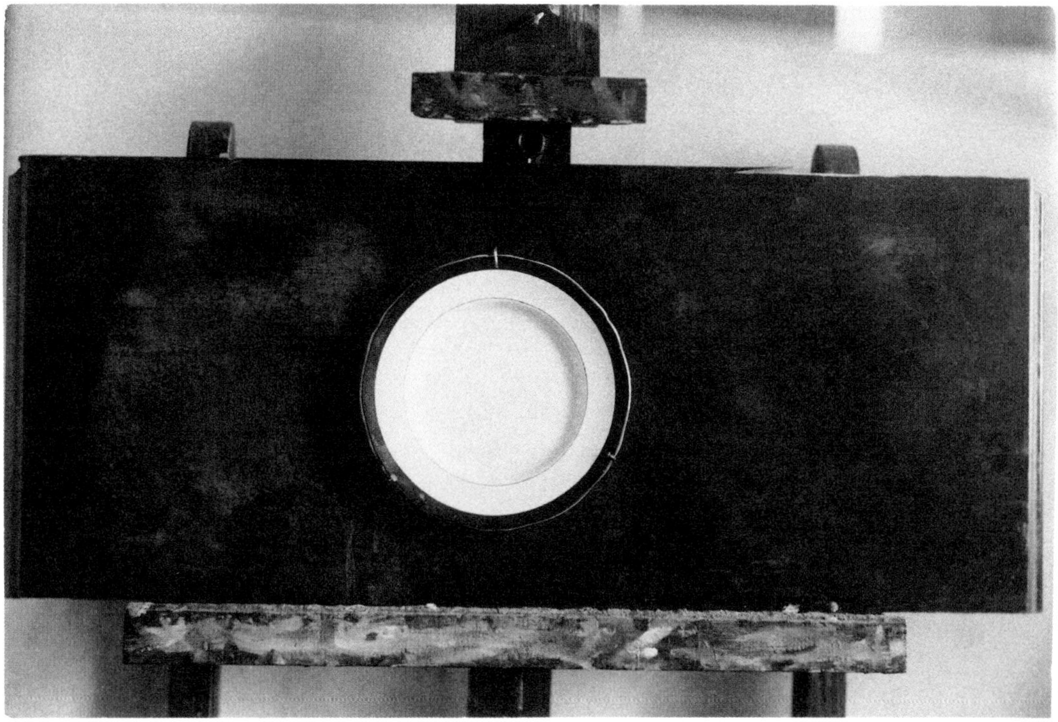

126. Even as left artists in Germany and Russia distanced themselves from expressionism in the early 1920s, the *First Universal German Art Exhibition*, mounted in Moscow and Leningrad in 1924, was overwhelmingly expressionist. However, there were notable exceptions, including seven of Moholy-Nagy's works, among them *Construction in Enamel 3* and *Construction in Enamel 4* (both 1923). On the relationships between Russian artists and Moholy-Nagy, see Margarita Tupitsyn, "Colorless Field: Notes on the Paths of Modern Photography," in *Object:Photo: Modern Photographs: The Thomas Walther Collection 1909–1949*, ed. Mitra Abbaspour, Lee Ann Daffner, and Maria Morris Hambourg (New York: Museum of Modern Art, 2014), https://www.moma.org/interactives/objectphoto/assets/essays/Tupitsyn.pdf (accessed January 25, 2018).

on May 30, 1922. Signed by Theo van Doesburg (who had not yet announced his theory of elementarism), Lissitzky, and Richter, the term *constructivism* was a compromise between the three signatories. The term was used again at a larger gathering in Weimar in September 1922, recorded as the Congress of Constructivists and Dadaists, a combination that encompassed all progressive artists and suggested an alliance between constructivists (read "nonobjectivists") and Dadaists.

In a photograph of the congress, Lissitzky stands out in the background thanks to his pipe and checked cap. Tzara is in front, wearing a similar cap and holding a can while raising to his cheek the hand of his female neighbor. Perhaps this impromptu gesture resonant with futurist eccentricity made Lissitzky doubt p. 136

Tzara's potential for originality. Upon Lissitzky's return to Berlin, he told Sharshun, who at the time was translating into Russian Tzara's *The Gas Heart* (1921), that the play had "no interest for the Russians . . . [for them] there were a multitude of similar things before and after the war."[127] In an issue of the magazine *Veshch* that year, Lissitzky likewise defined "Dadaists' tactics of negation, so reminiscent of our first Futurists of the prewar period," as "anachronism."[128]

Lissitzky shared with Schwitters and Arp an investment in defining Dadaism's formal parameters. His analysis of Schwitters's exhibition at Der Sturm was initially critical: "Schwitters has the brain of a literary person, but neither an eye for color nor hands for material. Together this creates a confused thing." Schwitters's *Merz Portfolio* (1923), printed in Hannover simultaneous with Lissitzky's *Proun: 1st Kestner Portfolio*, demonstrated, in Lissitzky's terms, "impregnation by us," an expression he used elsewhere in relation to Moholy-Nagy's withdrawal from expressionism.[129] In Schwitters's portfolio there is an abrupt shift, similar to Moholy-Nagy's, from structural excessiveness to "precise geometrism" and "organization"—to borrow more terms from Lissitzky—and the use of red and black, a palette characteristic of Malevich and his students.[130] Lissitzky's execution of Schwitters's and Arp's portraits in the multi-image technique of the photogram (for which he invented the neologism *fotopis*), mirrors the visual and technical complexity of the former's *Merz* art and of the latter's chance-based non-
p. 133 objectivity.

The *First Russian Art Exhibition* in Berlin opened right after the congress in Weimar and "unleashed the Russian theory of nonobjective

127. Sharshun cites Lissitzky in his letter to Tzara, March 6, 1923, in "Sergei Sharshun, pis'ma k Tristanu Tsara (1921–1923)," in *Literaturnyi avangard russkogo Parizha. Istoriia. Khronika. Antologiia. Dokumenty*, ed. L. Livak and A. Ustinov (Moscow: OGI, 2014), 771.

128. El Lisitskii, "Blokada Rossii konchaetsia," *Veshch*, no. 1 (1922), trans. into Russian in *El Lisitskii, 1890–1941* (Moscow: Gosudarstvennaia Tret'iakovskaia galereia, 1991), 73.

129. El Lisitskii, "Vystavki v Berline," *Veshch*, no. 3 (1922), trans. into the Russian in *El Lisitskii, 1890–1941*, 136–37.

130. While in Berlin Malevich wrote a letter to Schwitters in reaction to his article "Mein Merz und=Meine Merz=Muster Messe im Sturm" (*Der Sturm*, no. 7 [1926–1927]: 106–7). In the letter he admits Malevich as an influence. Malevich to Schwitters, May 10, 1927, in *Malevich o sebe*, ed. Vakar and Mikhienko, 1:189–91.

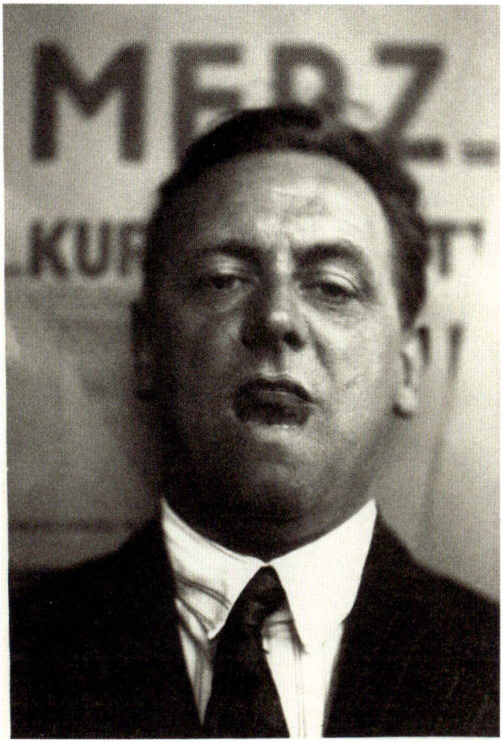

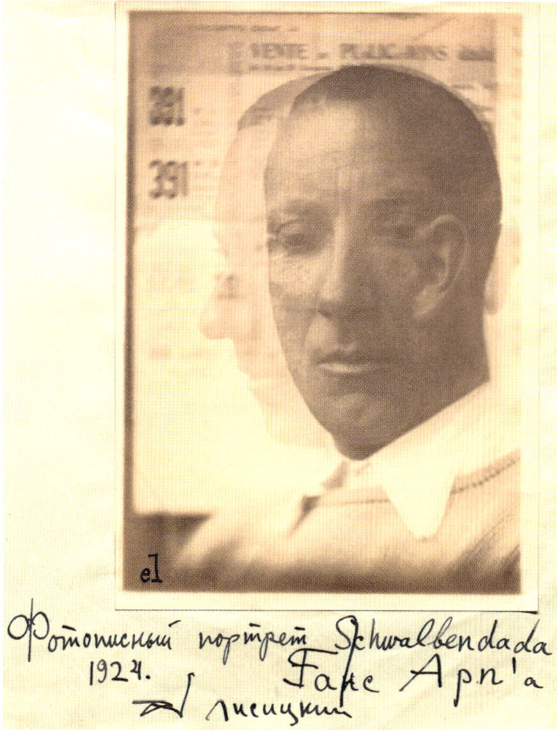

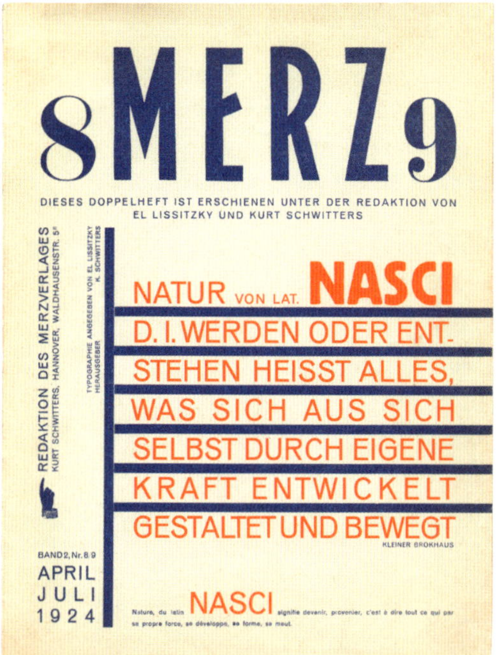

El Lissitzky
Kurt Schwitters, 1924

El Lissitzky
Hans Arp, 1924

El Lissitzky and Kurt Schwitters
Cover of the journal *Merz*, no. 8–9: *Nasci*,
Hannover, April/July 1924

art onto the European artistic scene."[131] The Dadaists Heartfield, Grosz, Hausmann, and Huelsenbeck, associated with the German revolution of 1918–1919, welcomed the exhibition and saw in its participants ideological allies. Hausmann and Huelsenbeck's declaration "What is Dadaism and what does it want in Germany?" (1919) reverberated with Malevich's "Declaration of Human Rights" (1918) in its sociocultural radicalism and far left ideology. Both proposed to transcend the familiar canons of modernist art movements. However, other Dadaists—Arp, Schwitters, Tzara, and van Doesburg—were not entirely supportive of the Russian exhibition, for they disapproved of art practices that committed to one class, be it proletariat or bourgeoisie. Together they signed a "Manifesto of Proletarian Art" to refute the notion of such practice: "Art, made by proletarians, does not exist because the proletarian, when he creates art, no longer remains a proletarian, but becomes an artist."[132] That is, the status of "artist" supersedes other commitments, and artists above all should pursue their own revolutions against artistic convention and restrictive institutions. For these Dadaists, serving the proletarian political cause would mean a loss of control over one's artistic determination and independence.

Yet regardless of some political and conceptual differences, European Dadaists and the Russians who joined them were dedicated to collective practices and the expansion of international alliances. Sharshun is the earliest example of a Russian artist consistently committed to building bridges with the Dadaists. In Moscow, in 1909, he came into contact with proto-Dadaists Larionov and Goncharova, and in Barcelona, where he settled in 1915, he met Arthur Cravan and Francis Picabia, witnessing the launch of the magazine *391*. In Paris, where he returned in 1920, he befriended Tzara, Paul Éluard, and André Breton. And in Berlin, where he stayed from 1922 to 1923 while waiting for a Russian visa, he exhibited at Der Sturm after Puni (in September 1922) and spent time with Schwitters, Ehrenburg, Lissitzky, Mayakovsky, and Brik. From Berlin he corresponded with Tzara, filling him in on art activities and remarking that "many Russians would like to know what Dada is."[133]

The first issue of Sharshun's publication *Transportation* (*Perevoz*), called "Transportation—Dada," was a mere four-page document that announced itself as an "official agency of 3 ½ International" and, on behalf of Europe, told Russia to "come here." In it, Sharshun enthusiastically cites Tzara and advises readers "to go to Paris to see Man Ray, the creator of new visions," and he ridicules Berlin's conservative Russian community, urging its members to exchange their passports for Soviet ones.

He is equally harsh and ironic toward some Russians from avant-garde circles, in particular those who could compete with him for the position of *the* Russian Dadaist. Sharshun dubs "worthless" the newly formed Rostov-on-Don group Nothingists.[134] He bashes Zdanevich's project University 41°, announced right after Zdanevich moved to Paris in 1921, as the place where "students went on hunger strike by refusing to eat rotten *zaum* and *sdvig*"—that is, the key formalist techniques of Russian proto-Dadaists. Lissitzky's rapprochement with the Dadaists resulted in another eruption of scorn from Sharshun: "On the racetrack of Russian artists for the prize of Sameness, E. Lissitzky has come first." A telegram text ends the issue, informing colleagues in Russia—Kruchenykh, poet Grigory Petnikov, and Rodchenko—that "'Transportation—Dada' has sailed with reinforcement into its first voyage."

p. 191

p. 199

Sharshun's visa was denied, depriving him of the voyage to communist Russia, yet his project to transport Dada was taken on by Mayakovsky and Brik (who had accompanied Mayakovsky to Berlin). Upon their return from Europe they launched *Lef* and in the second issue published in German and English an editorial titled "Declaration: Comrades, Organizers of Life!" that is saturated with political and antiart fervor and "summon[s]" progressive artists "to establish a single front of leftist art—the 'Red Art International.'"[135] The issue also includes Grosz's text "About My Work," a reflection on the aforementioned alliance of Dadaists and constructivists. Its two illustrated images are typical Grosz—grotesque depictions of greedy, alienated capitalists and other Berliners. Some of the portraits are cropped and rendered using straight lines that interconnect the negative spaces of the drawing.

p. 127

131. Marc Dachy, "'Life Is an Extraordinary Invention': Doesburg the Dadaist," in *Van Doesburg and the International Avant-Garde: Constructing a New World* (London: Tate Publishing, 2009), 31.

132. Theo van Doesburg, Kurt Schwitters, Hans Arp, Tristan Tzara, and Christof Spengemann, "Manifesto of Proletarian Art" (1923), available at https://libcom.org/library/manifesto-proletarian-art-1923 (accessed January 25, 2018).

133. Sharshun to Tzara, March 30, 1921, cited in "Sergei Sharshun, pis'ma k Tristanu Tsara (1921–1923)," 752.

134. For the group's texts, see pp. 294–299 of the present catalogue.

135. For the complete text, see pp. 303–304 of the present catalogue.

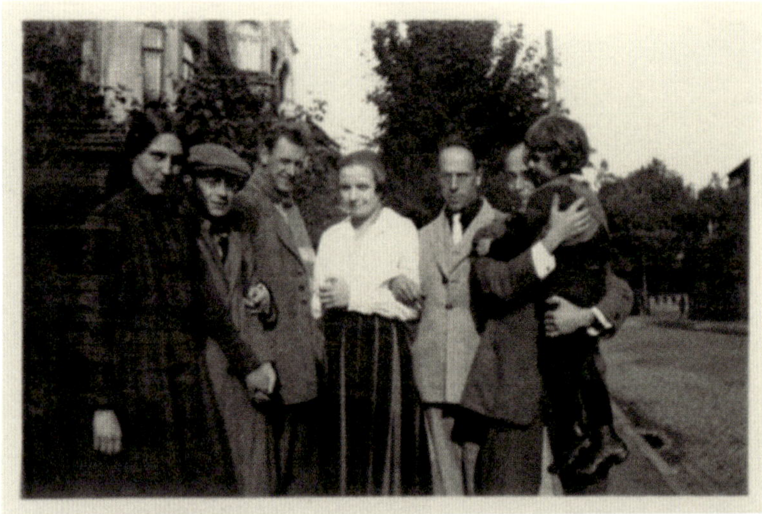

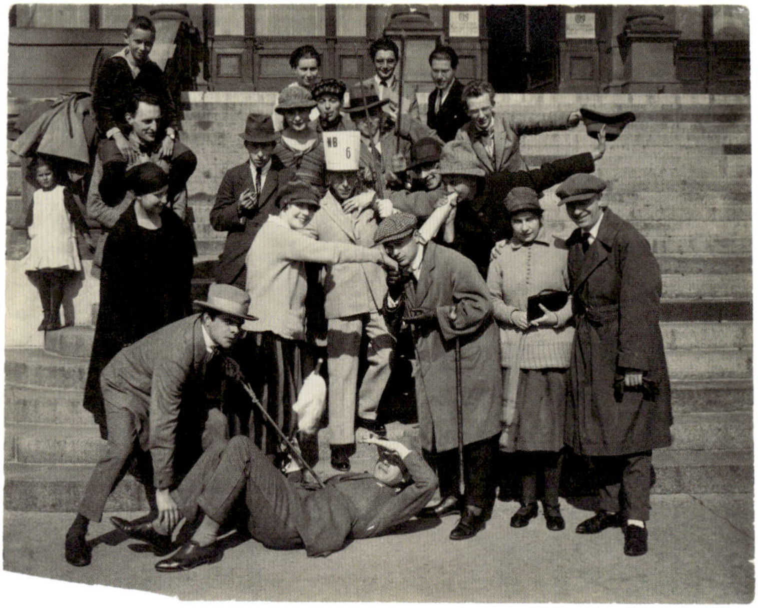

Hans Arp
In front of the Schwitters' house in Hannover (left to right: Helma Schwitters, unidentified, Kurt Schwitters, Nelly van Doesburg, Theo van Doesburg, and El Lissitzky, with Ernst Schwitters), 1922

Anonymous
Congress of Constructivists and Dadaists, Weimar, September 1922

Ivan Puni's Scrapbook
Viktor Shklovsky, Ksenia Boguslavskaia, Ivan Puni, and unknowns (left to right), ca. 1922

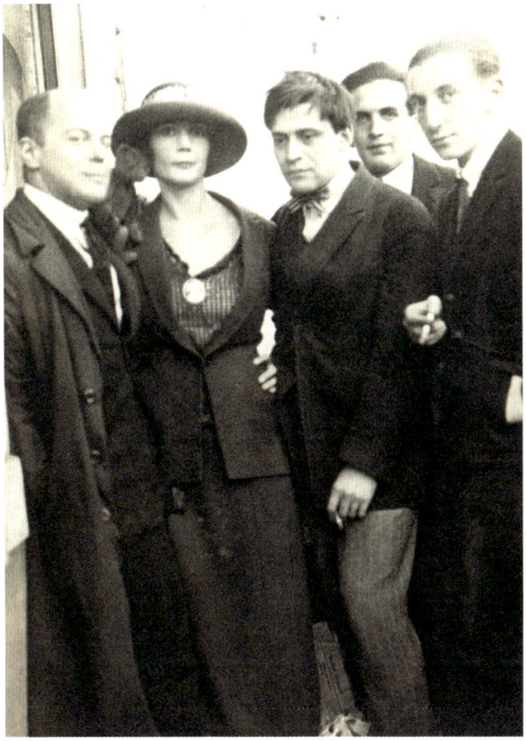

Another important manifestation of the project to transport Dada was Brik's scrapbook laconically annotated by Khardzhiev as "Album 'Dada,'" probably after Tzara's journal *Dada*.[136] Filled with documentation of Dadaist works, publications, and related press collected during Brik's and Mayakovsky's European trips, it includes photographs of the magazines *391* and *Dada*, of *Fountain* and other works by Duchamp, and of Hausmann's *Tatlin at Home* and *ABCD*. The latter work's established date of 1923–1924 indicates either that Brik—described by Soviet Commissar of Education Anatoly Lunacharsky as "the Russian Breton"—assembled his scrapbook over a period of two years or that he made it later than 1922, Khardzhiev's date.[137] Brik's compilation

p. 13

p. 126

136. Khardzhiev received the scrapbook as a gift from Brik.

137. The comparison is made in A. Lunacharskii, "K kharakteristike noveishei frantsuzskoi literatury," *Pechat' i revoluitsiia* 2 (1926): 17–26.

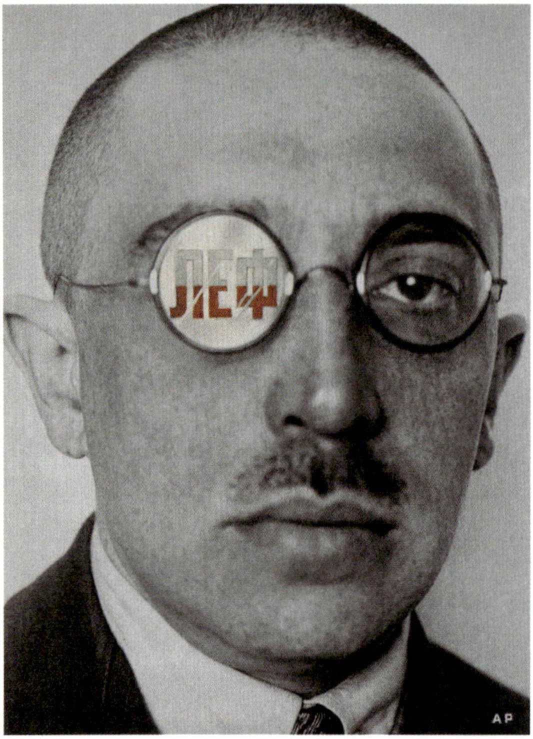

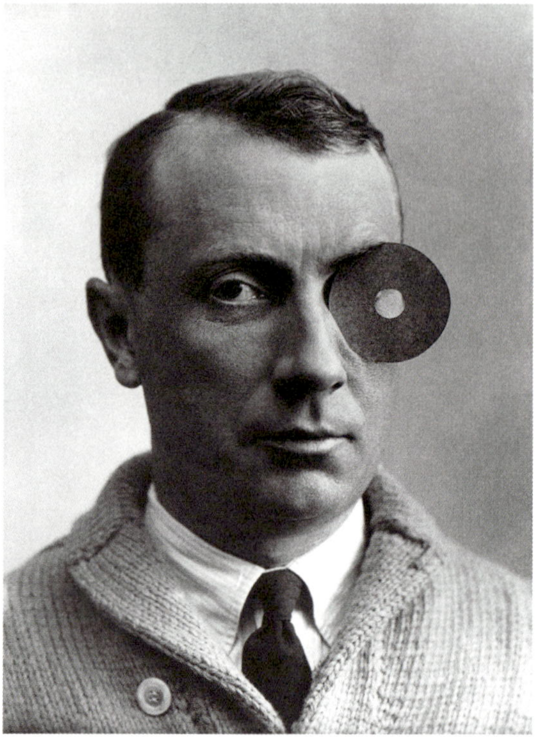

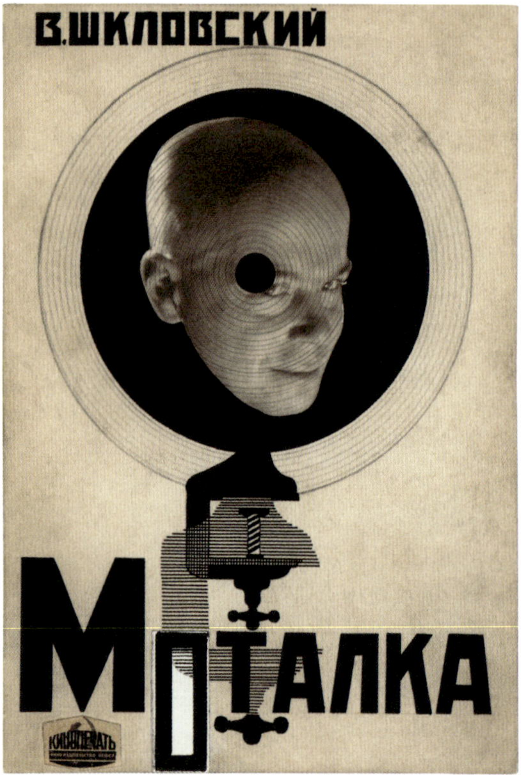

Aleksandr Rodchenko
Cover design for the journal *Lef* (with a portrait of Osip Brik, unpublished), 1924

Anonymous
Arp with naval monocle, 1926

Petr Galadzhev
Cover of the book *Coiler* by Viktor Shklovsky, 1920–1929

138. V. N. Terekhova, "Goncharova, Larionov, Maiakovskii: Parizh, 1922 god," in *N. Goncharova i M. Larionov: isledovaniia i publikatsii* (Moscow: Nauka, 2001), 219. "Poetical fantasy" is Terekhova's expression.

139. Ibid., 220.

140. Khlebnikov is quoted in Markov, *Russian Futurism*, 27.

of Dada factography is intertwined on some pages with his own drawings and comments, affirming his conviction that Dadaism suited the productivist agenda of *Lef* that he had helped to theorize. For one of his unpublished cover designs for *Lef*, Rodchenko blocked the left lens of Brik's spectacles with the magazine's logotype, thus prioritizing left ideology over visual apparatuses, including those of a mechanical nature. This image of Brik creates a fascinating pair with a portrait of Arp taken in 1926 by an anonymous photographer who captured him with his eye obstructed by a naval monocle. The two portraits underline the difference between the far left and moderate Dadaists such as Arp. The latter continued to invest their creativity into optical rather than political shifts. pp. 168–169 p. 138

Paris

In Berlin Mayakovsky met Sergei Diaghilev, who invited him to Paris. Mayakovsky agreed most likely because, among other opportunities, it meant reuniting with his fellow avant-gardists Larionov and Goncharova, who, since settling in Paris in 1915, had gained acclaim in avant-garde circles, first in 1912 for Larionov's exhibition at Der Sturm (which included rayonism), and then for the couple's exhibition at Galerie Paul Guillaume in Paris in 1914. (Guillaume Apollinaire contributed the introduction to the exhibition catalogue.)

Mayakovsky's reunion with Larionov resulted in a collaboration: the publication of *Sun* (1923), a poem in book form illustrated by Larionov. Its theme corresponds with Mayakovsky's preoccupation with the symbolism of the ray as elaborated in his "poetical fantasy" titled "IV International" (1922).[138] Expanding on Larionov's arsenal of metaphoric powers for the ray, and dreaming of the revolution's diffusion, Mayakovsky writes that it "scatters in the form of a five-edge star . . . a ray climbs the Apennine Mountains. And a ray shines over the Pyrenees."[139] In Mayakovsky's mind, Khlebnikov's "new breed of people-rays" had resurfaced as the revolutionaries amassed on Heartfield's cover for Mayakovsky's book *150,000,000*.[140] *Sun*'s cover shows radiant beams of light overlapping an anthropomorphic form that Larionov had used earlier that year in his design for the invitation to Le Grand Bal Transvestite-Transmental in Paris, on February 23, to benefit the Relief Fund of the Russian Artists Union in the presence of the major cubists Picasso, Albert Gris, and Albert Gleizes, as well as Fernand Léger. Although the titular theme confirms that Larionov's inclination p. 143

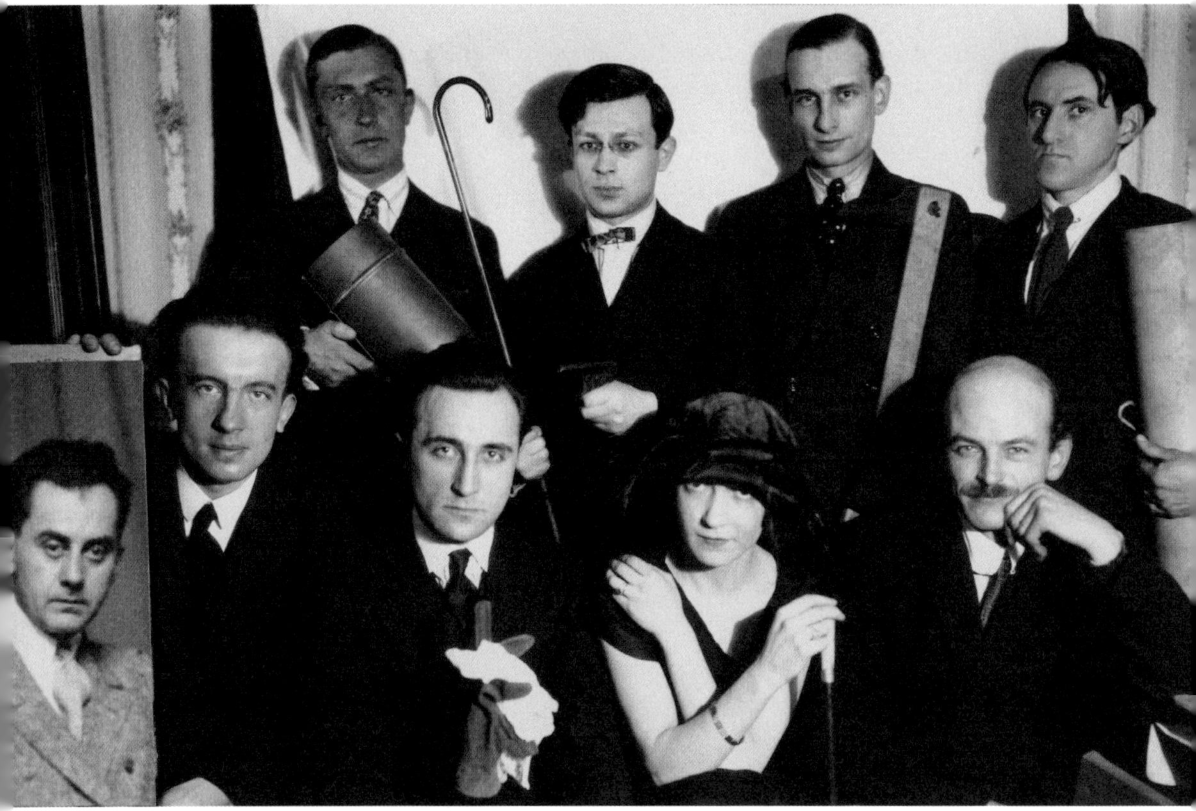

for provocation and transgression remained intact, in the image his gender-ambiguous figure lacks the sexual explicitness demonstrated in Dadaist works on the same subject, such as Johannes Baargeld's photomontage *Vulgar Mess: Cubistic Transvestite at an Alleged Crossroads* (1920). Larionov, like his colleagues in Russia, continued to rely on the disguised iconography of nonobjectivity to articulate his reaction to cultural and political transformation as well as to express indecencies that had long infiltrated his art.

Man Ray
A Dada alliance (top row, left to right: Paul Chadourne, Tristan Tzara, Philippe Soupault, Sergei Sharshun; bottom row, left to right: Paul Éluard, Jacques Rigaut, Mick Soupault, Georges Ribemont-Dessaignes), Paris, November 1921

In Paris from November 1921, Zdanevich created, through his public activities, a background for Mayakovsky's successful arrival in the city in November 1922. In this he repeated

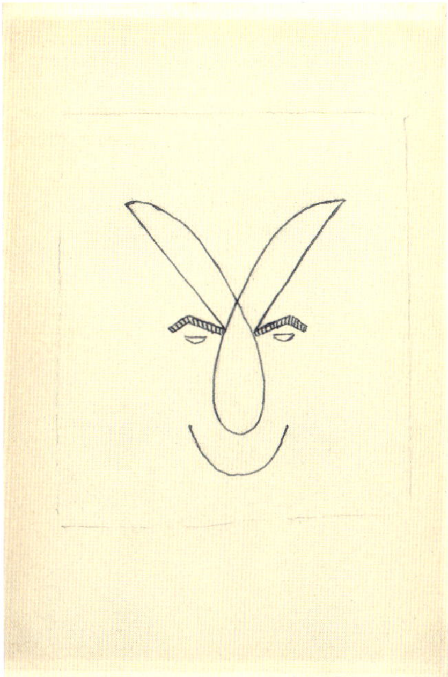

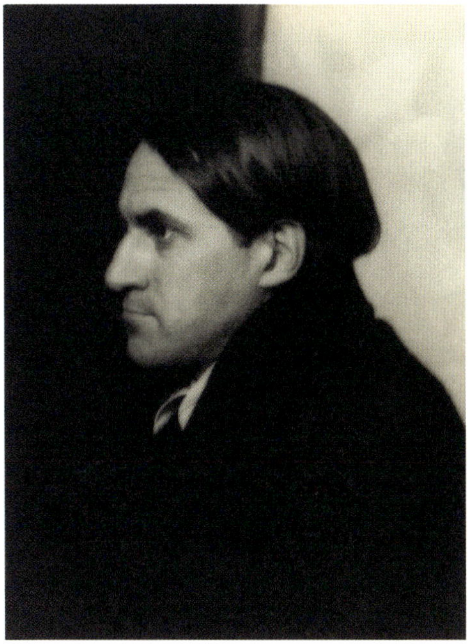

Sergei Sharshun
Self-Portrait as Devil,
ca. 1921–1922

Man Ray
Sergei Sharshun,
ca. 1922–1925

the role Sharshun had played in laying the groundwork for Zdanevich in Paris.[141] The highlight of Sharshun's interaction with Paris Dadaists was his participation in the making of Picabia's *The Cacodylic Eye* (1921).[142] Zdanevich's lecture "New Schools in Russian Poetry," delivered less than two weeks after his arrival, equally benefited Russian poets and artists, demonstrating absurdist techniques relevant to Russian proto-Dada. Zdanevich displayed his hunger for public disorder by sending invitations for the lecture to monuments of Victor Hugo and Honoré de Balzac, whose names he also included in the program. "But life is unpredictable," he grumbled while lecturing. "A postman, a contemporary guard of order, returned the letters to me because the form of the specified addressees does not correspond to the postal rules."[143] Zdanevich described everythingism as "an answer to a fanatical narrowness of Futurism" and in detail

141. On Sharshun's activities in Paris, see his "My Participation in the French Dada Movement," on pp. 314–319 of the present catalogue.

142. Ibid., p. 316.

143. Il'ia Zdanevich, "Novye shkoly v russkoi poezii," in *Literaturnyi avangard russkogo Parizha*, ed. Livak and Ustinov, 795.

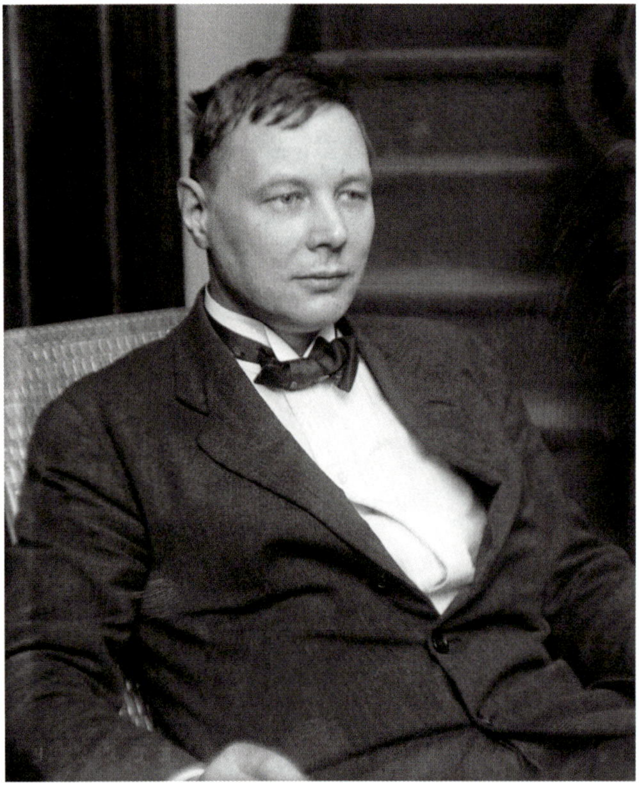

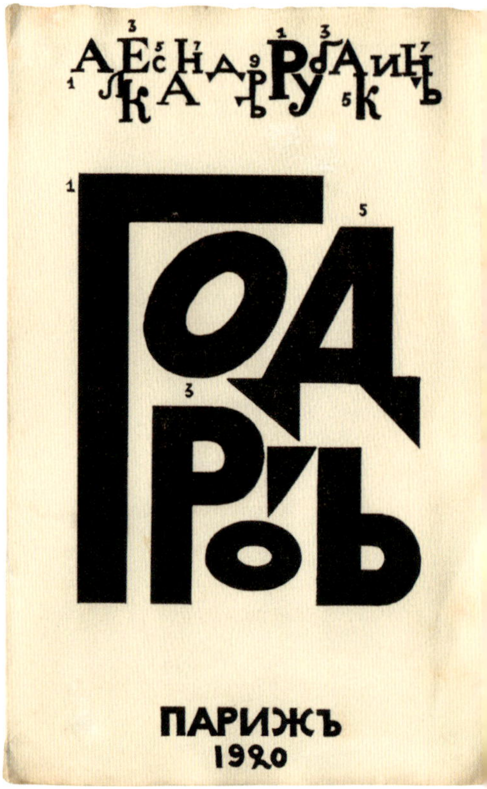

analyzed the formalist techniques of "shift" (*sdvig*) and "estrangement" (*ostranenie*) so central to the formal innovations of the visual and verbal avant-gardes.[144]

When Mayakovsky came to Paris, Zdanevich was already known and respected by key Dadaists, as testified in several letters written p. 147 to him in 1922: by Picabia (January 30), Tzara (February 17), and Éluard (November 18).[145] These correspondences are about meetings. Picabia's invitation to Zdanevich to visit his studio is particularly significant, for it was the center of "the internationalism of Dada" and the place where the Dadaists regularly met "to thrash out new ideas."[146] The degree of conceptual novelty that Zdanevich brought to such gatherings, as well as his endorsement

Man Ray
Mikhail Larionov, 1923

Natalia Goncharova
Cover of the book *The City: Verses* by Aleksandr Rubakin, Paris, 1920

Mikhail Larionov
Poster for *The Grand Ball of Transvestite-Transmental Artists*, Paris, 1923

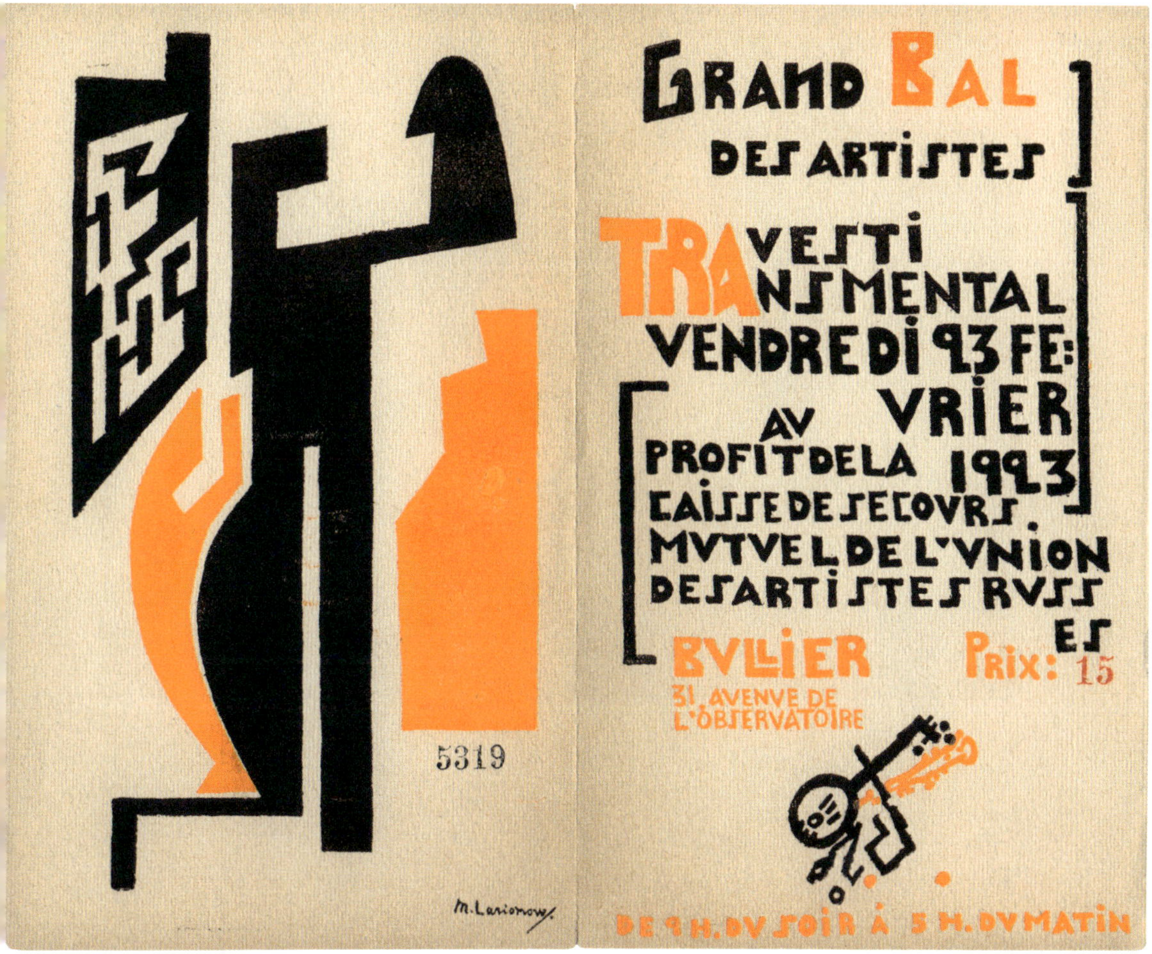

as a Dadaist, is revealed in the writer and literary critic André Garmain's lecture "Ilia Zdanevich and Russian Surdadaism," delivered on November 28 (a few days after Mayakovsky's departure). By combining surrealism and Dada in his title, Germain hints at recruiting the Russian into the surrealists' camp just as the competition between the two groups was heating up.

For Germain, the most significant event in Zdanevich's biography was the "wish of a despotic mother" to dress him as a girl until

144. Ibid. In his lecture, Zdanevich suggested that the process of destruction of logical language is "a key to understanding dreams, to their interpretation, similar to that proposed by professor Freud." Ibid., 808. Sigmund Freud's theories interested the Tiflis group "41°," whose agenda Zdanevich was committed to continuing by creating an informal University 41°.

145. These are in the Archives Iliazd France.

146. Richter, *Dada*, 183.

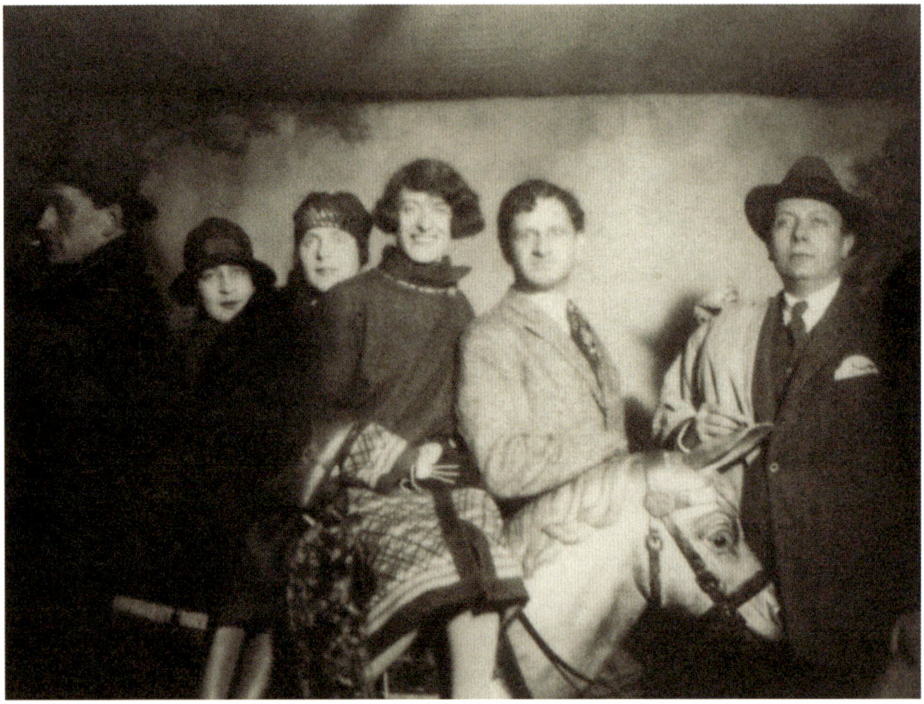

Anonymous
Vladimir Mayakovsky, Valentina Khodasevich, Elza Triolet, Klara Goll, Ivan Goll, Robert Delaunay (left to right), Paris, 1924

he was twelve years old. "'A very beautiful girl,'" he added.[147] Several months prior to this lecture, Zdanevich had changed his name to "Iliazde," but he promptly dropped the French female ending to become "Iliazd." This was at exactly the time that Man Ray's photographs of Duchamp as Rrose Sélavy were becoming known in Paris.[148] Zdanevich was familiar with Duchamp's female character: along with Rrose Sélavy and Sharshun, he had signed, still using "Ilia Zdanevich," Tzara's manifesto "The Bearded Heart," issued in the spring of 1922. Was it *after* he became familiar with Rrose Sélavy that he swiftly adopted and dropped his female alter ego, doing so as a way to establish a dialogue with Duchamp?

147. Zhorzh Ribmon-Dessen', "Predislovie k frantsuzkomu perevodu 'Lidantiu faram,'" in *Literaturnyi avangard russkogo Parizha*, ed. Livak and Ustinov, 817.

148. Man Ray's known photographic portraits of Sharshun (1922) and Larionov (1923) are evidence of his favorable disposition toward them. Larionov's rayonism must have fascinated Man Ray, who around this time invented the "rayograph." pp. 141–315

149. Richter, *Dada*, 181.

150. Ibid.

151. Terekhova, "Goncharova, Larionov, Maiakovskii," 232.

152. Sharshun to Tzara, December 12, 1922, cited in "Sergei Sharshun, pis'ma k Tristanu Tsara (1921–1923)," ed. Livak and Ustinov, 766.

153. Éluard's letter to Iliazd, written in the beginning of July 1923, right before the soirée *The Bearded Heart*, indicates he had agreed to write an introduction but changed his mind due to Iliazd's support of and participation in Tzara's event. The letter is in the Ilia Zdanevich Archive.

Man Ray's photographs of Rrose Sélavy would have triggered in Zdanevich unpleasant childhood memories of an enforced female alter ego, a concept Duchamp was now willingly proposing as art. Zdanevich responded to Duchamp's concept of cross-dressing and cross-naming by subverting Rrose Sélavy through an act of a linguistic cutting—just as he had done with his childhood alter ego when he "cut off his curls." On May 26, 1920, a year before Duchamp's arrival "at the monster gathering at the Salle Gaveau" in Paris, the Dadaists had announced they "would have their hair cut off on the stage."[149] Richter deemed this a scandalous but successful event. Involving the participation of Breton, Éluard, Tzara, Louis Aragon, Georges Ribemont-Dessaignes, and the recently arrived Sharshun, it was "the climax of the Paris Dada movement" because, finally, "Dada was taken seriously!"—which nevertheless contradicted its antimovement, anarchic status.[150]

Mayakovsky and Zdanevich were perfect, super energetic agents for the management of international Dada. A banquet in honor of Mayakovsky, organized by the editors of the émigré magazine *Strike* (*Udar*) on November 24, 1922, became a platform to propose such a project, in the presence of guests including Sonia Delaunay and Robert Delaunay, Goncharova, Larionov, and Tzara. The formation of a "tactical group" followed, called "Across" (Cherez). Its defined goal was "strengthening connections between left emigrants, the like-minded in Soviet Russia, and French colleagues."[151] Tzara's signature, left in the banquet's guest book with a heart pierced by an index finger, testifies to his favoring such exchanges, which he was already conducting through correspondence with Sharshun. Under the umbrella of *Strike* Zdanevich planned his version of (never realized) compilation projects such as Huelsenbeck's *Dadaco* (1919) and Tzara's *Dadaglobe* (1921). Zdanevich asked Sharshun to collect from German Dadaists "poems, prose, photos, chronicles, reflections," a request Sharshun could not fulfill since "no one is left here but Hausmann."[152] Zdanevich did report to *Lef*'s editors on various Dadaist events and on his own achievements, among them the publication of his book *Lidantiu as a Beacon* (*Lidantiu Faram*, 1923), with a cover by Naum Granovsky and an introduction by Ribemont-Dessaignes.[153] Amid "the typographic verdure" with which the interior of this "transrational drama" was stenciled, one finds the word *dada* made to stand out with descending letters and varied typefaces. Because *Lidantiu Faram* was made in homage to the late Le Dantiu, Zdanevich's collaborator on the theorization of everythingism, the book's reference to Dada reinforced everythingism's

p. 195

proto-Dadaist pedigree.[154] A copy of *Lidantiu Faram* with Iliazd's dedication to Brik was delivered to Russia in 1924.

Despite such ambitious intentions, the intensifying rifts among Dadaists had by this time reached a climax, and it was becoming hard not to take sides as Tzara and Breton wrestled over leadership.[155] As the arguments became personal and at times raucous, Dadaists including Iliazd and Sharshun cosigned Tzara's manifesto p. 149 "The Bearded Heart," and on July 6, 1923, in the Théâtre Michel, Iliazd contributed to the organization of the soirée *The Bearded Heart*. He had designed the poster for the evening (as pp. 168–169 well as the cover of the only issue of the newspaper *The Bearded Heart*, published by Tzara in April 1922), and further participated by reciting excerpts from *Lidantiu Faram* accompanied by Igor Stravinsky and other composers, with actors wearing costumes designed by another compatriot, Sonia Delaunay.[156] But it was the restaging of Tzara's *The Gas Heart* that triggered Breton's protest and provoked Éluard—who in a letter had expressed to Zdanevich his dismay at the inclusion of his name in the list of participants in *The Bearded Heart* soirée—to jump onstage, followed by audience members.[157] A riot ensued, resulting in damage to furniture, injuries to those in attendance, and requiring the intervention of the police.[158] To compensate for the damages and the cancelation of a second performance, Tzara filed a lawsuit, further distressing Éluard, who lamented to Iliazd, "I am in advance sad and discouraged. Such an affair humiliates me more than one could imagine."[159]

To Zdanevich, everything that happened around *The Bearded Heart* was a déjà vu experience, reminiscent of the proto-Dadaist public spectacles and scandals in Russia, some of which he had personally instigated.

154. Zhorzh Ribmon-Dessen', "Predislovie k frantsuzkomu perevodu 'Lidantiu faram,'" in *Literaturnyi avangard russkogo Parizha*, ed. Livak and Ustinov, 832, 827. Given that the plot of Iliazd's *Lidantiu Faram* contains a contest between a realist and a modernist, the inclusion of the word *dada* indicates Iliazd's identification with Dadaism.

155. On this last Dada period, see Richter, *Dada*, 179–88.

156. Marc Dachy writes, "Van Doesburg was personally involved in the event, producing scenery for interpretations of Ilya Zdanevitch's [*sic*] *Zaoum* poems by the dancer Lizica Codreano, with costumes by Sonia Delaunay." Dachy, "'Life Is an Extraordinary Invention,'" 29.

157. The letter is in the Archives Iliazd France.

158. Richter, *Dada*, 190.

159. Éluard's letter to Iliazd was written shortly after the soirée *The Bearded Heart* and is now in the Archives Iliazd France. Tzara's lawsuit was a materialization of the mock trial of Maurice Barrès that the Dadaists staged on May 13, 1921, with Breton as one of the judges and Tzara among the witnesses.

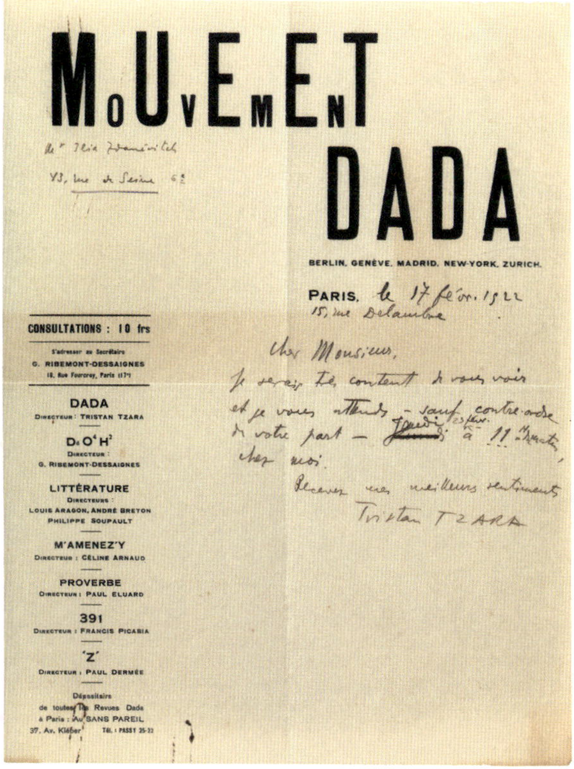

MOUVEMENT DADA

BERLIN, GENÈVE, MADRID, NEW-YORK, ZURICH.

CONSULTATIONS : 10 frs

S'adresser au Secrétaire
G. RIBEMONT-DESSAIGNES
18, Rue Fourcroy, Paris (17e)

DADA
DIRECTEUR : TRISTAN TZARA

D. O⁴ H²
DIRECTEUR :
G. RIBEMONT-DESSAIGNES

LITTÉRATURE
DIRECTEURS :
LOUIS ARAGON, ANDRÉ BRETON
PHILIPPE SOUPAULT

M'AMENEZ'Y
DIRECTEUR : CÉLINE ARNAUD

PROVERBE
DIRECTEUR : PAUL ELUARD

391
DIRECTEUR : FRANCIS PICABIA

'Z'
DIRECTEUR : PAUL DERMÉE

Dépositaire
de toutes les Revues Dada
à Paris : Au SANS PAREIL
37, Av. Kléber   Tél. : PASSY 25-22

PARIS, le 17 févr. 1922
15, rue Delambre

Cher Monsieur,
Je serais très content de vous voir et je vous attends – sauf contre-ordre de votre part – ce soir à 11 h. matin, chez moi.
Recevez mes meilleurs sentiments
Tristan TZARA

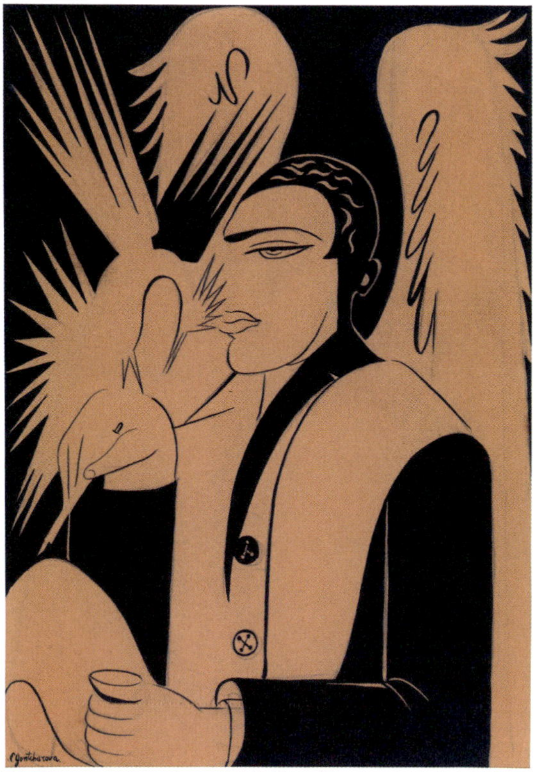

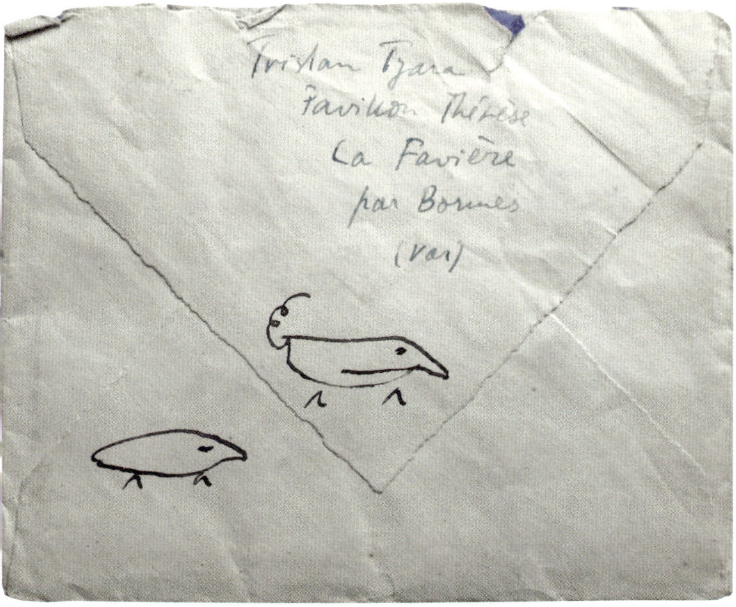

Tristan Tzara
Letter to Illia Zdanevich on Dada stationary "Movement Dada," 17 February 1922

Natalia Goncharova
Ilia Zdanevich as Angel, ca. 1921

Tristan Tzara
Envelope for a letter to Ilia Zdanevich, 1924

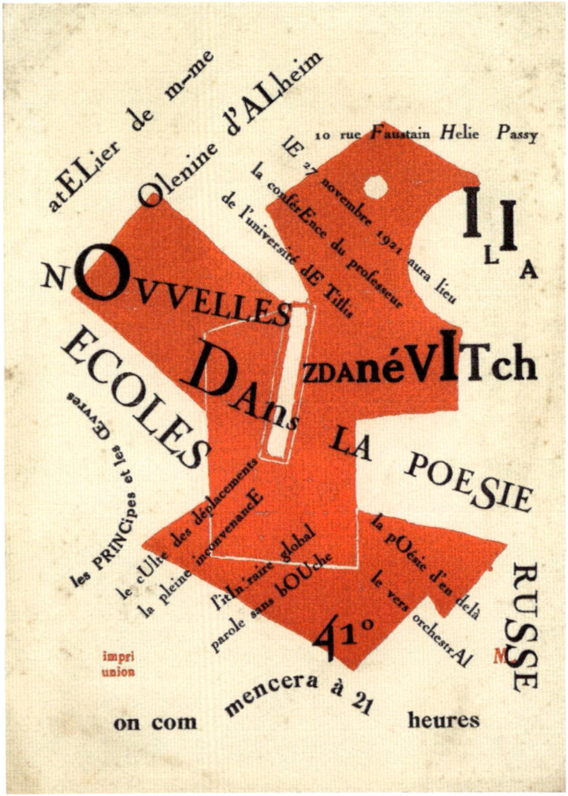

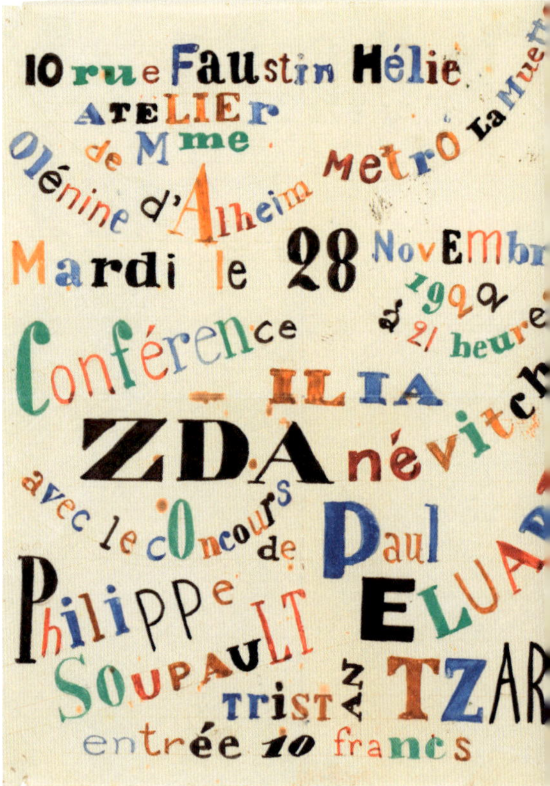

Ilia Zdanevich
Poster for Ilia Zdanevich's lecture *New Schools in Russian Poetry*, 1921

Ilia Zdanevich
Poster design for a conference on the Russian avant-garde, November 28, 1922

Now he was involved in organizing, as "a help to Tzara," an event that would prove fatal for Dada and "marked," in his words, "the end of the 'Across' movement," Dada's agent in Russia.[160] Russian ardency for transrationality, first publicly manifested in the proto-Dadaist production *Victory over the Sun*, loudly reverberated at *The Bearded Heart*, where it signaled that the curtain was closing on the extraordinary adventures of Russian Dada in the land of European Dadaism (to paraphrase the title of
pp. 224–225 Kuleshov's film of 1924).

In 1930, in the first issue of the magazine *Surrealism in the Service of the Revolution*, Breton pledged to be more politically engaged. As part of this commitment (and not without

160. Iliazd, "En approchant Éluard," *Carnets Iliazd-Club*, no. 1 (1990).

161. The script is reminiscent of Picabia's "Manifeste Cannibal Dada" (1920), which similarly plays with death and money. Moreover, Picabia's text is comparable to the Nothingists' "Russia's Nothingists to the West's Dada," written at the same time (see p. 299 of the present volume). In 1939 Aragon married Elsa Triolet, Brik's sister-in-law.

Ilia Zdanevich (Iliazd)
Leaflet for *The Bearded Heart* soirée, 1923

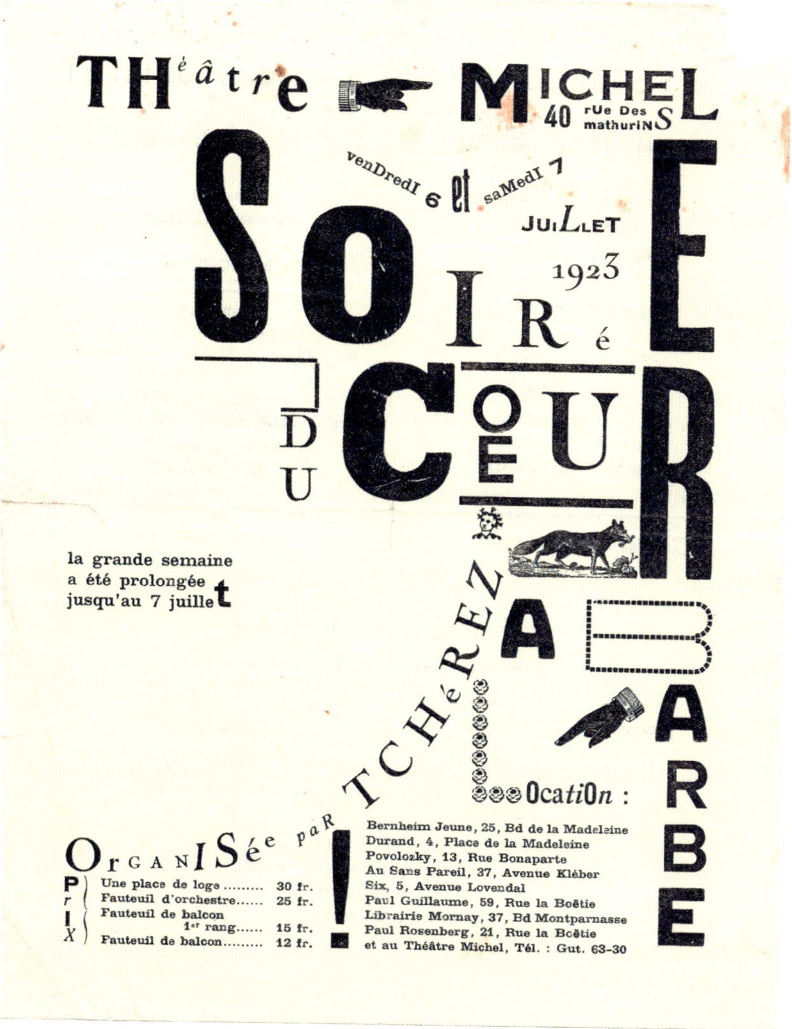

pressure from Aragon, who had met Mayakovsky during his last trip to Paris), Breton, at the end of 1928, printed a still from the now lost film *Not for Money Born* (1918).[161] The script, based on Jack London's *Martin Eden* (1909), was written by Mayakovsky and Burliuk, who acted in the film along with Kamensky. The still shows Mayakovsky dressed in an elegant suit and top hat as he teases Death in true "sur-dadaist" manner, an uncanny scene imagined in the postrevolutionary period and apt for publishing in the surrealist journal two months after Mayakovsky's suicide on April 14, 1930. p. 170

New York

I am thinking of going abroad in the spring. On a donkey to Paris to Larionov and Goncharova, and then somehow to you to New York. I will come with a donkey, maybe you will let me in.

—Kazimir Malevich to David Burliuk, October 20, 1926[162]

In his essay "Anarchy, Politics, and Dada," Allan Antliff observes, "Historically, most of Dada in New York is subsumed into a category called 'proto-Dada,' but when the goofy word finally shows its face here, in the 1921 magazine *New York Dada*, it is to declare . . . that God and my toothpaste are Dada, and New Yorkers can be Dada too."[163] This interpretation of the status of the Dada movement in New York is phenomenally similar to the Russian case, even in terms of chronology, for in 1920 the Nothingists also used "the goofy word," opening the door to an assessment of the Russians' long-existent Dadaist state of mind as part of the international Dada movement.

Michael R. Taylor's analysis of Dada in New York concludes, "New York Dada effectively came to an end in the summer of 1921, when Man Ray and Duchamp departed for Paris."[164] But this is an overstatement, because, as Taylor details, the curator and collector Katherine S. Dreier was committed to promoting the movement in New York and placed at its core the stable of artists Walden was exhibiting at Der Sturm. The gallery even became a model for the founding of the Société Anonyme in New York in 1920. Man Ray and Duchamp joined Dreier as secretary and president, and although they left for Paris a year after, joining the European Dadaists, they became Dreier's agents for her own project of transporting Dada to New York.

162. *Malevich o sebe*, ed. Vakar and Mikhienko, 1:178.

163. Allan Antliff, "Anarchy, Politics, and Dada," in *Making Mischief: Dada Invades New York*, ed. Francis M. Naumann and Beth Venn (New York: Whitney Museum of American Art, 1997), 215.

164. Michael R. Taylor, "New York," in *Dada*, ed. Dickerman, 296.

165. On the destruction of the anarchists, see Olga Burenina-Petrova, "Anarchism and the Russian Avant-Garde," on pp. 226–257 of the present volume.

166. Markov, *Russian Futurism*, 9.

167. One such project was the exhibition *Russian Painting and Sculpture* at the Brooklyn Museum (January 23–March 4, 1923), in which Burliuk was invited to participate with forty-four works. He likely urged the organizers to include his fellow avant-gardists Goncharova, Larionov, and Lado Gudiashvili. Also included, and well-known to the Société Anonyme, were Kandinsky (he was an advisor to Dreier) and Archipenko (the subject of the society's first show).

168. According to art historian Irina Vakar, these were *Black Square*, *Black Cross*, and *Black Circle* (1923–1924). See *Malevich o sebe*, 1:179. The month of this letter has been questioned, and Malevich is not likely to have promised to send his works as late as October; that is, only one month before the exhibition's opening. See ibid., 1:178. Perhaps as compensation for a lack of Malevich's works, Russian artist Constantin Aladjalov (with whom Dreier collaborated on the design of the catalogue) placed red and black squares, Malevich's nonobjective signature shapes, on the title page. In her introduction, Dreier notes, "Malevich represented here by Lissitzky with his group of the Suprematists." Katherine S. Dreier, *International Exhibition of Modern Art Assembled by Société Anonyme* (New York: Brooklyn Museum, 1926), n.p.

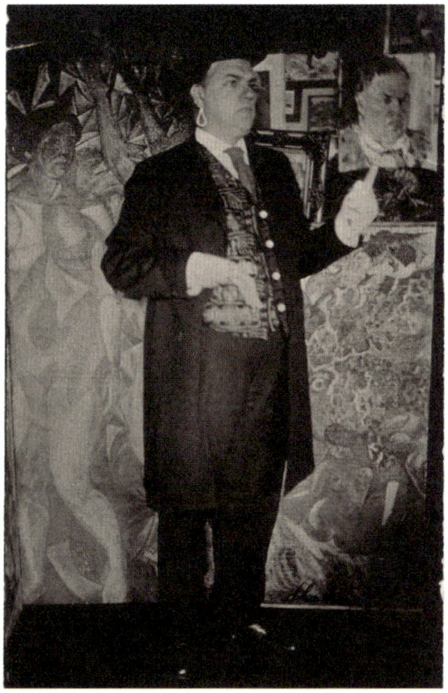

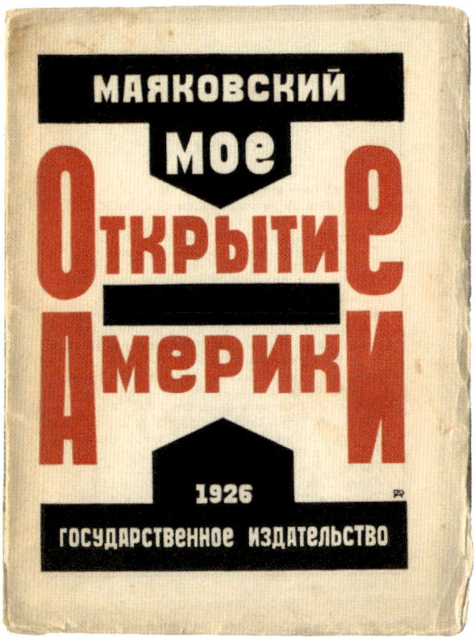

Anonymous
David Burliuk, New York, 1924

Aleksandr Rodchenko
Cover of the book *My Discovery of America* by Vladimir Mayakovsky, 1926

Fleeing Moscow as a result of the Bolsheviks' crushing of the anarchists in 1918, artist and poet Burliuk arrived in New York (after a long journey via Japan and Canada) on September 2, 1922.[165] Historian Vladimir Markov describes Burliuk as "the man without whom there probably would have been no Russian futurism."[166] But prior to Burliuk's gaudy career in Russia, he had become a member, in 1912, of Der Blaue Reiter (The Blue Rider) and in 1914 had an exhibition under the auspices of Der Sturm. Dreier's ambition to fuse European and American progressive modernists into one collective made Burliuk's arrival in New York pivotal. Like Zdanevich in Paris, he was an energetic propagandist of the Russian avant-garde's theoretical and practical tenets. Burliuk's correspondence with Malevich attests to his commitment and his swift integration into New York's avant-garde milieu. He almost immediately enjoyed the fruits of collaboration with Dreier.[167] She and the American critic and Dada supporter Christian Breton remarked in their writings on Burliuk's radical outfits and earring and on how his madcap personality matched his paintings. Much like Tzara, Burliuk had an ability to enthrall his audiences.

Malevich revealed to Burliuk that he had hoped to participate in and even attend the opening, on November 19, 1926, of the *International Exhibition of Modern Art Assembled by Société Anonyme* at the Brooklyn Museum.[168] Unable to send his works in time, he was not included, which is unfortunate, as he would have exemplified the exhibition's concept of the fusion of progressive movements: Dadaists (Arp, Duchamp, Schwitters, Picabia), surrealists (Ernst), and nonobjectivists (Alexander Archipenko, Gabo, Piet Mondrian, Natan Pevzner, Kandinsky, and Lissitzky). At the

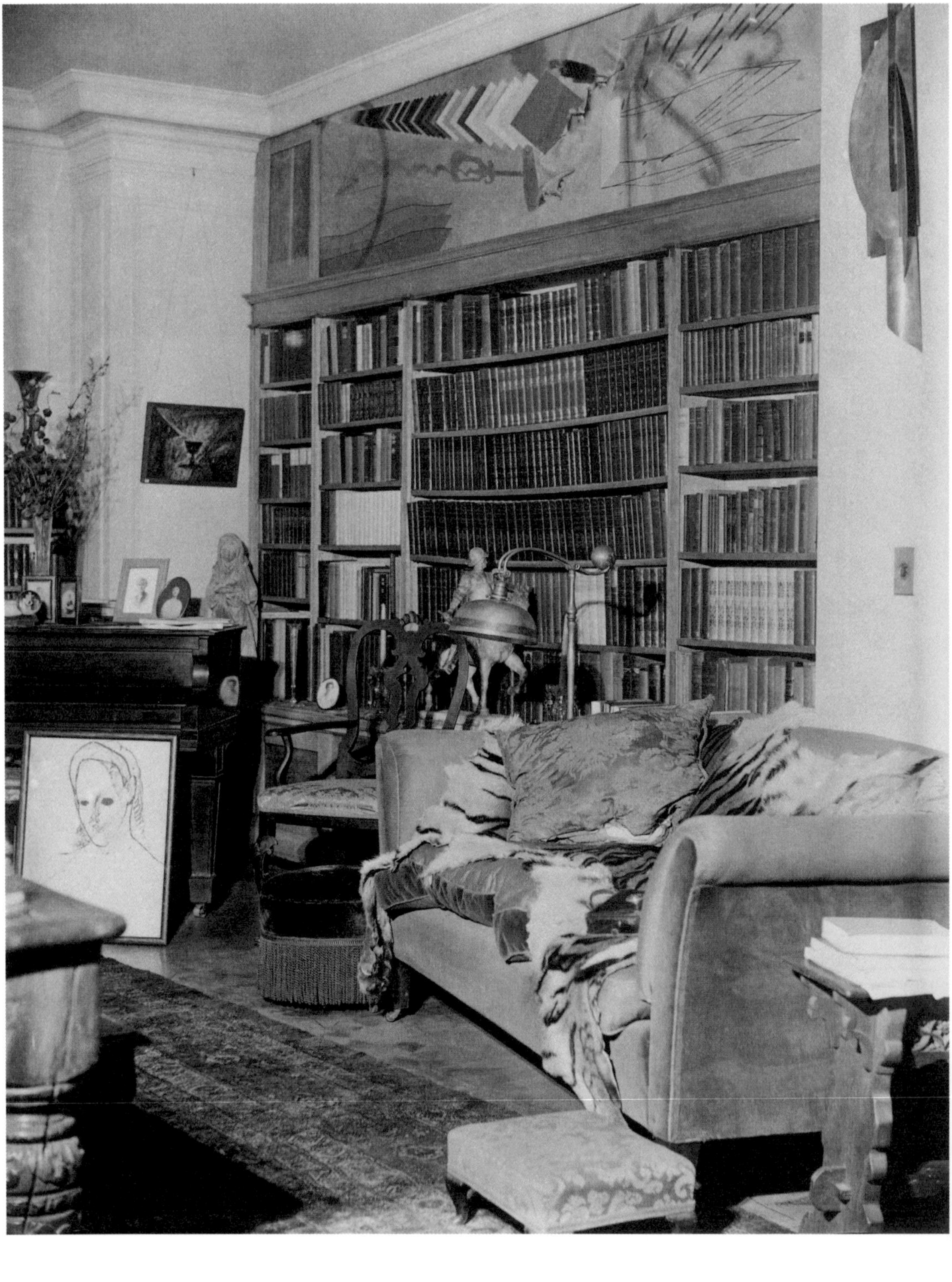

Man Ray
Living room of Katherine S. Dreier with works of David Burliuk, Marcel Duchamp, Pablo Picasso, New York, 1927

David Burliuk's *Forces of Spring*, 1922 [location unknown], from Katherine S. Dreier's private collection, ca. 1945–1946 photograph by John Schiff

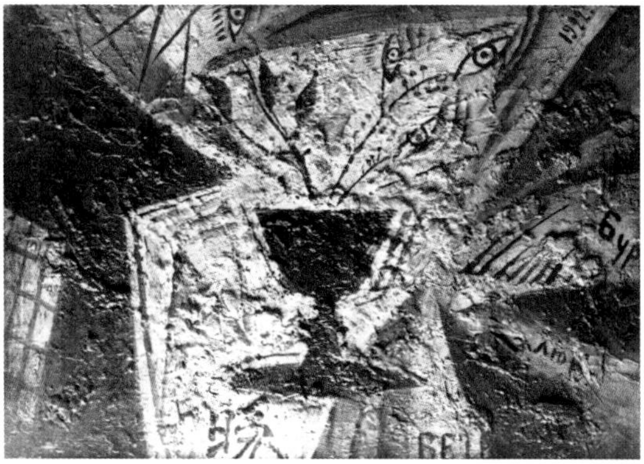

International Exhibition of Modern Art, Burliuk exhibited the paintings *The Eye of God* (1923–1925) and *The Coming of a Mechanical Man* (1926), p. 155 a "surdadaist" pair, with each work registering shifts between the depersonalized and the mechanical, concepts that were equally associated with Russian constructivism and Dada and here subverted by a representation of the eye stripped of all mechanical aids. But Burliuk also responded, most likely inadvertently, to Picabia's *Cacodylic Eye*, conceived as a result of ophthalmic illness. The mass of comments that compassionate friends began to inscribe on a canvas prepared by Picabia with a rendition of an eye turned into a collective assault on its imperfection and vulnerability, with language functioning as remedy to visual impairment. Burliuk's one-eye painting offered a reminder of his own ophthalmic injury: During his childhood he had lost an eye and had since worn an ocular prosthesis. His glass eye was Burliuk's *objet d'épater*—he at times removed it to shock an opponent. Burliuk spoke French and German but not English, and *The Eye of God* depicts the seeing eye rather than the épater eye, revealing Burliuk's need of *visionary* power due to his communicative deficiency in New York.

The Eye of God entered Dreier's private collection, and so did the now lost *Forces of Spring* (1922), populated by multiple eyes, which Bur- pp. 152, 153 liuk most likely executed upon his arrival in New York. *Forces of Spring* affected Dreier so much that she displayed it in her apartment next to Duchamp's *Tu m'* (1918) and a small Picasso assemblage. Perhaps recalling Zdanevich's promotion in Paris of the formalist techniques of "shift" and "estrangement," *Forces of Spring* parades the specifically Russian modernist tool of hyperbolic textures (*faktura*). *Forces of Spring* is, by means of extreme impasto, a painting that accomplishes a collaged

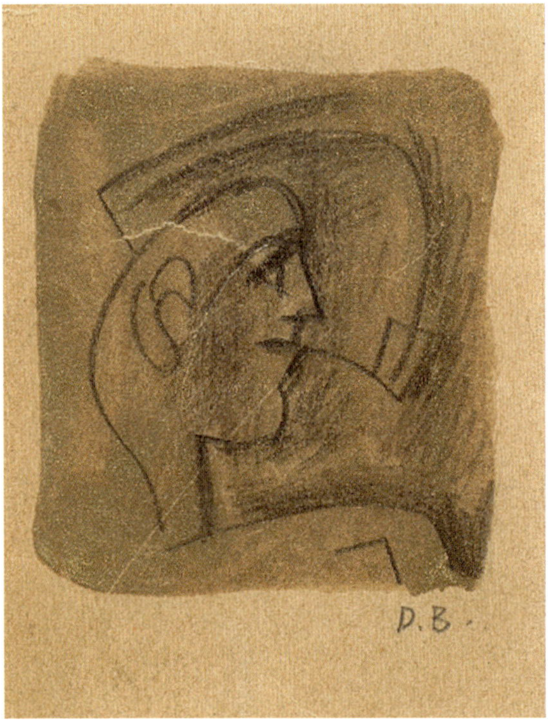

Anonymous
David Burliuk, n.d.

appearance that competes with such all-over collages as Schwitters's *Mz460 Two Underdrawers* (1921), which Drier also acquired.

Dreier asserts in her foreword to the catalogue of the *International Exhibition of Modern Art*, "The service which Soviet Russia rendered to the rest of the world has been chiefly that it scattered most of its creative and living spirits over the whole world." She then adds in a separate entry on Burliuk, "few men have so long and constantly worked for modernism as Burliuck [*sic*]."[169] Regardless of her stress on aesthetic parameters and her appreciation of the apolitical Dada of Duchamp and Man Ray, Dreier's interest in the political wings of Dada, such as the German one, and her efforts to exhibit Grosz and Heartfield indicate that Burliuk's engagement in left politics as he continued in America was not likely to affect her support. Burliuk joined pro-Soviet groups, including the John Reed Club, lectured in workers' clubs, collaborated with the communist publishing houses, and painted Lenin's portrait (with Leo Tolstoy's) as well as Mayakovsky's and Sergei Eisenstein's.[170]

Richard Boix's caricature *Da-Da (New York Dada Group)* (1921) is unexpectedly relevant to the theme of Russian Dada. In it *Dada* is written

David Burliuk's *Eye of God*, 1923–1925, from Katherine S. Dreier's private collection ca. 1945–1946 photograph by John Schiff

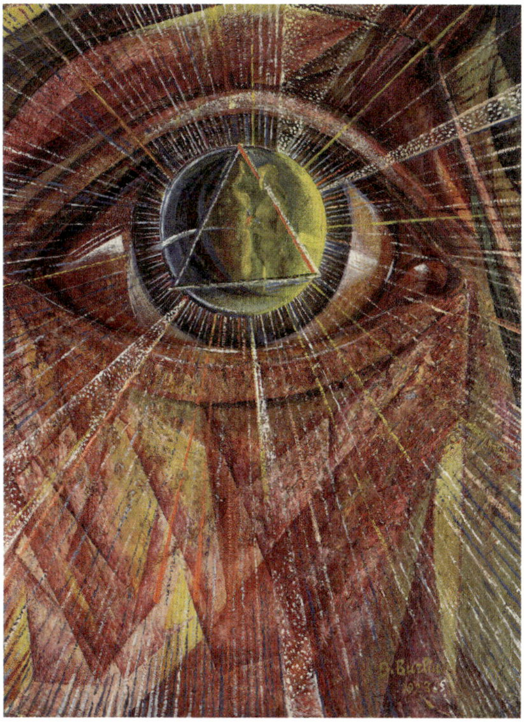

as *da-da*. The addition of the hyphen makes it a Russian double affirmation. Dreier is in the picture and so is Duchamp, playing chess on the floor by himself.[171] This Dadaist game, which had at Cabaret Voltaire placed Tzara and Lenin—and, by extension, the discourses of art and politics—face to face, was now turning into Duchamp's personal obsession, shielding him from breaking the pledge to antiart. In Russia, Vsevolod Pudovkin's film *Chess Fever*—released in 1925, a year after Lenin's death (which itself coincided with Breton's first surrealist manifesto)—constructs a perfect metaphor of a maniacal Dadaist mind able to operate only at an elevated temperature that can drop as quickly as it rises.

169. Katherine S. Dreier, *International Exhibition of Modern Art Arranged by Société Anonyme* (New York: Brooklyn Museum, 1926), 69, 72.

170. Mayakovsky visited New York and other American cities in 1925, after being invited to show his ROSTA poster. After Mayakovsky's return from America, he published the book *The Discovery of America* . 151 (1926) with a cover by Rodchenko.

171. Duchamp would later help Dreier select illustrations for her book about Burliuk. See Katherine S. Dreier, *Burliuk, Part I: Russia. In Collaboration with Nicholas Burliuk, Part II: Twenty Years in America* (New York: Société Anonyme, 1944).

El Lissitzky
"The New Man," from *Figurines: The Three-Dimensional Design of the Electro-mechanical Show "Victory over the Sun"*, 1920–1923

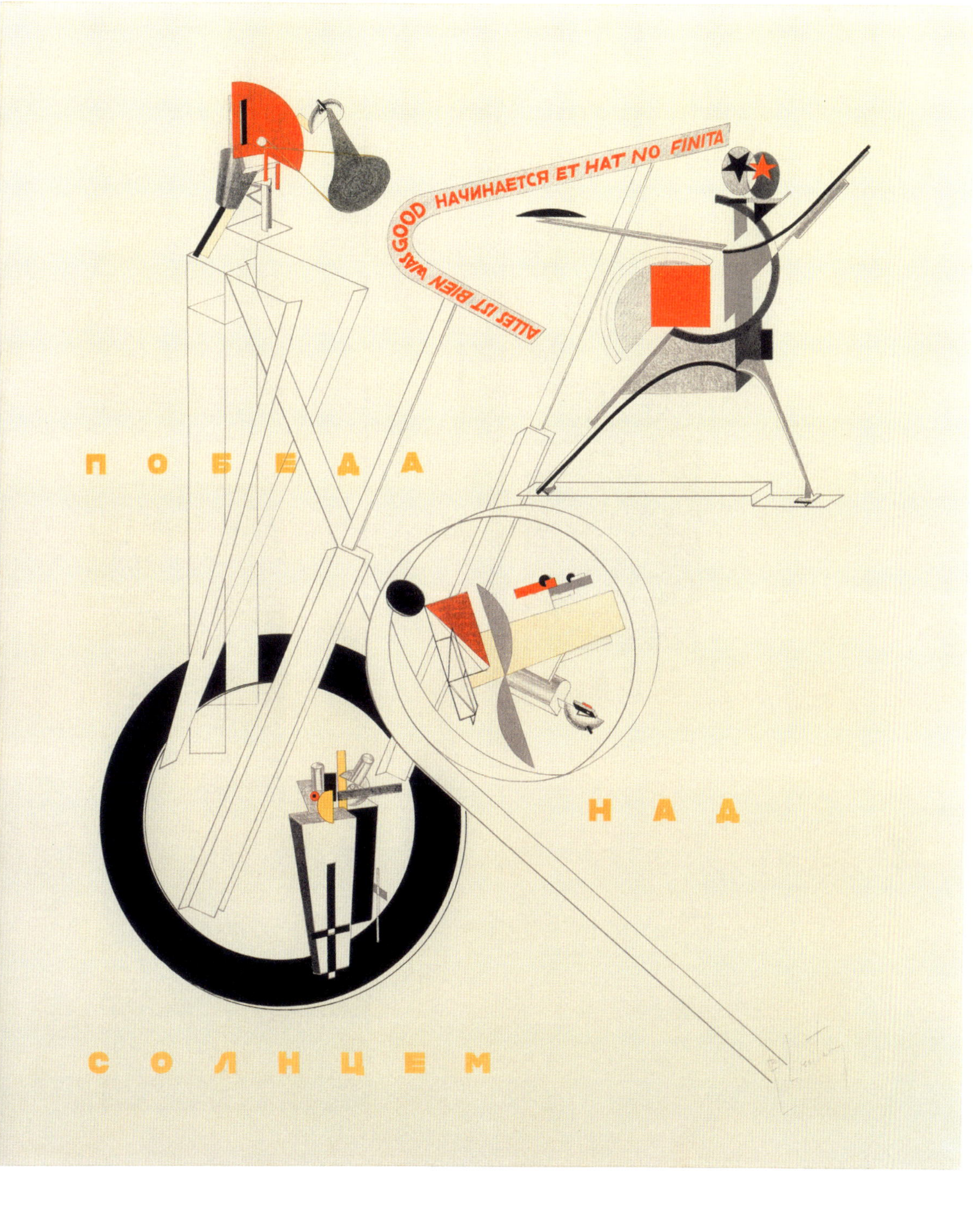
ALLES IST BIEN WAS GOOD НАЧИНАЕТСЯ ET HAT NO FINITA
ПОБЕДА
НАД
СОЛНЦЕМ

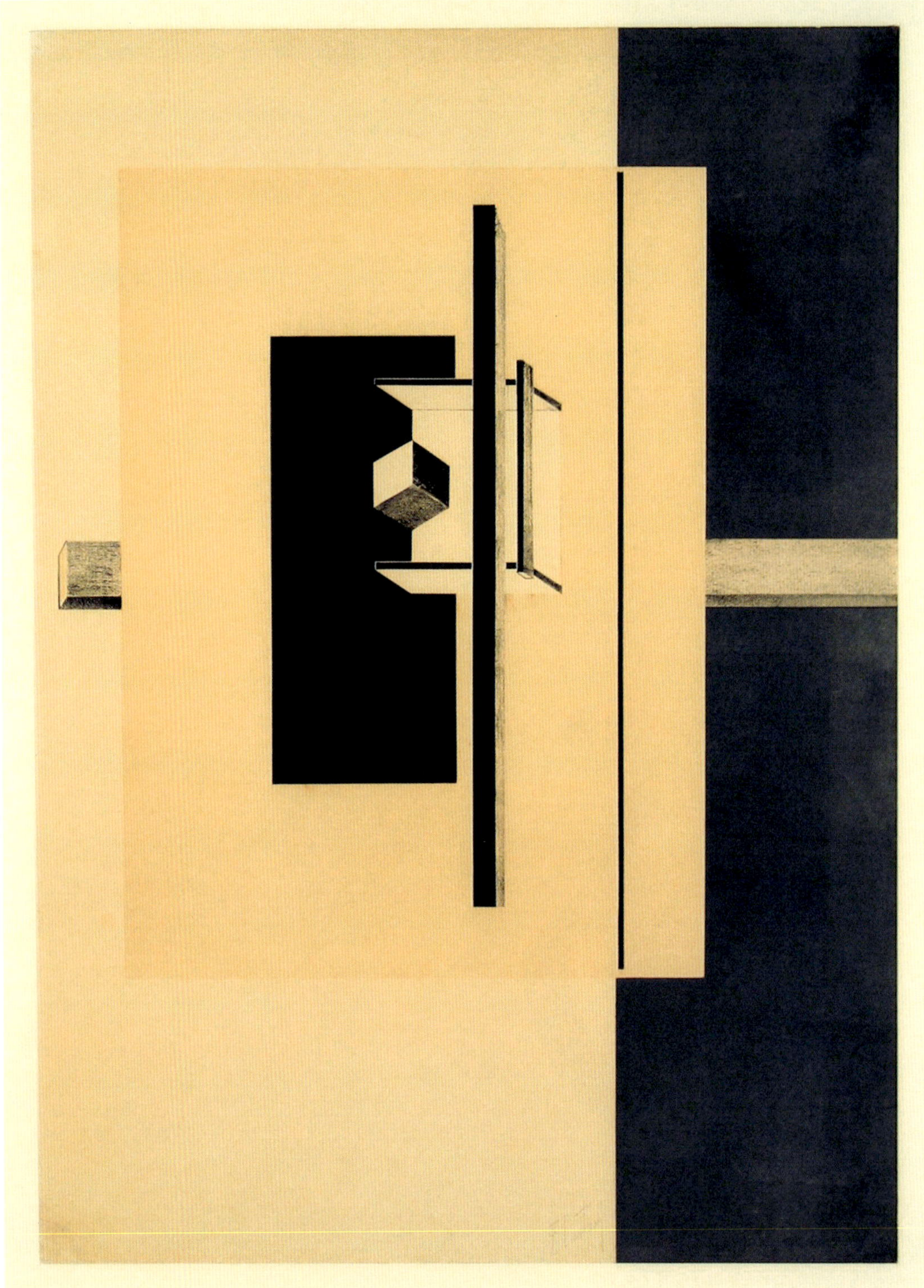

El Lissitzky
First Kestner portfolio *Proun*,
print no. 2, 1919–1923

Kurt Schwitters
Plate 4 from *Merz 3, Merz Portfolio: 6 Lithos*, 1923

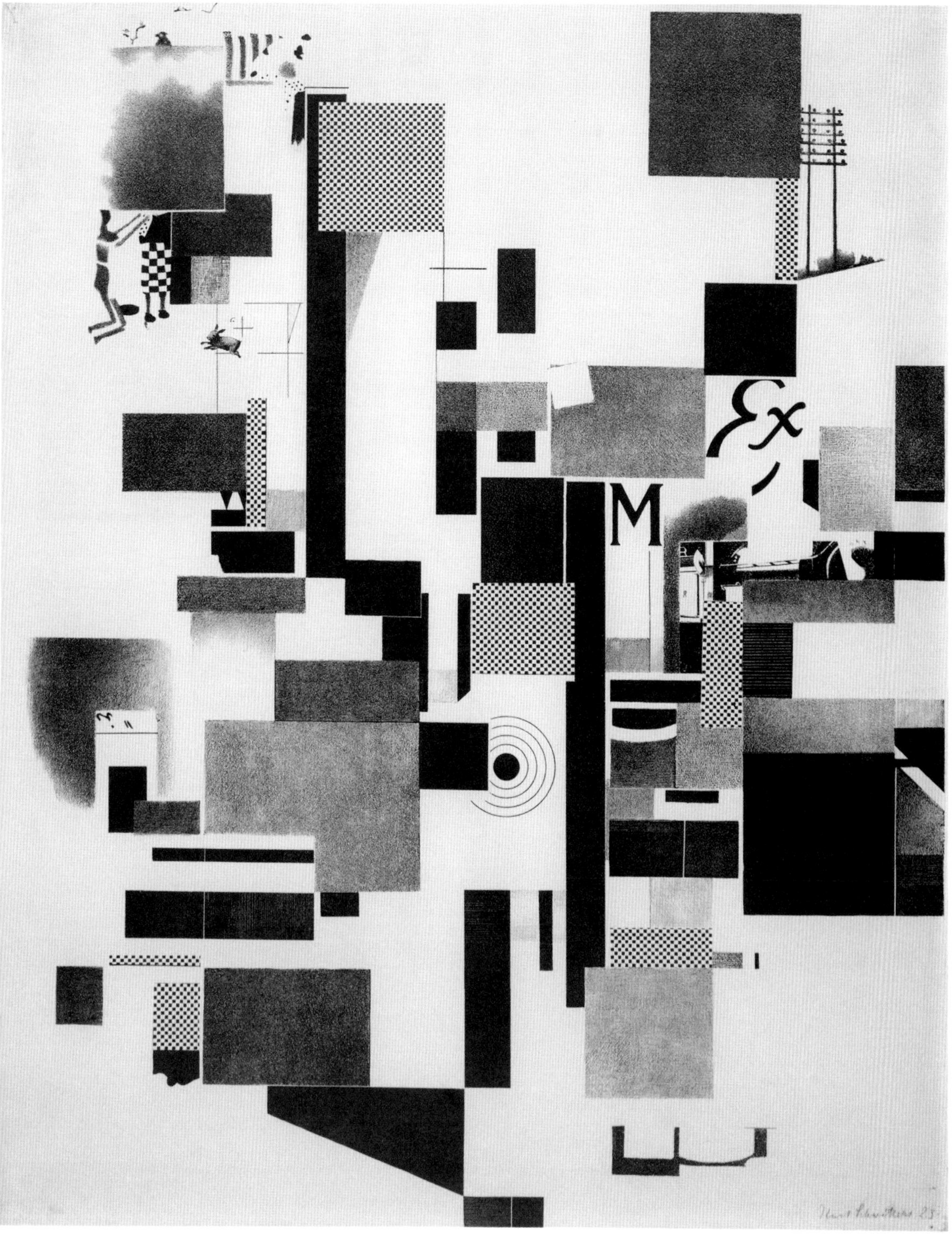
Ex
M

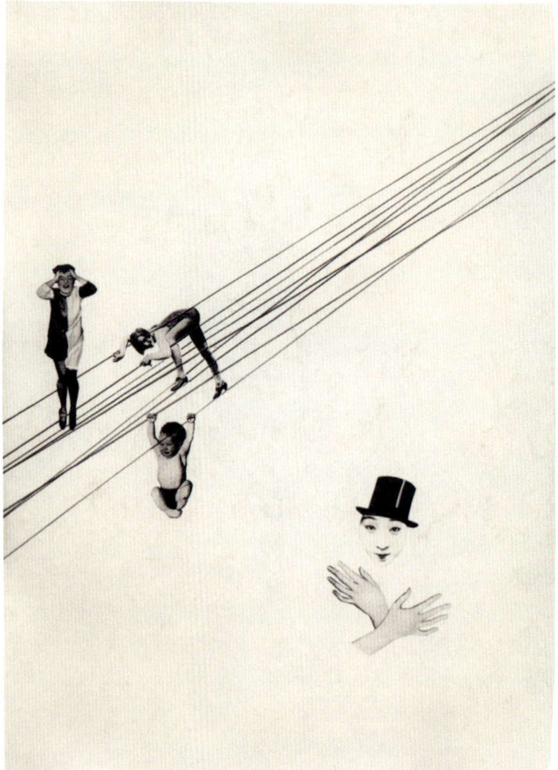

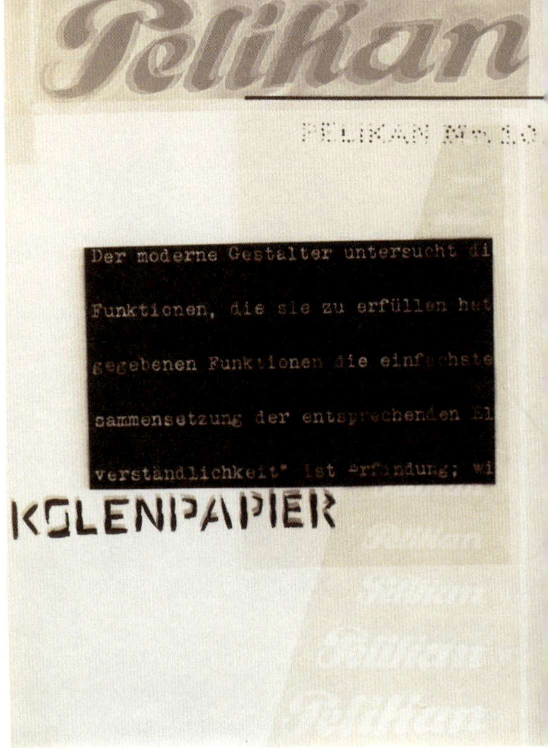

László Moholy-Nagy (with artist's autograph to Vladimir Mayakovsky)
Untitled, 1922

El Lissitzky
Pelikan Carbon Paper, 1924

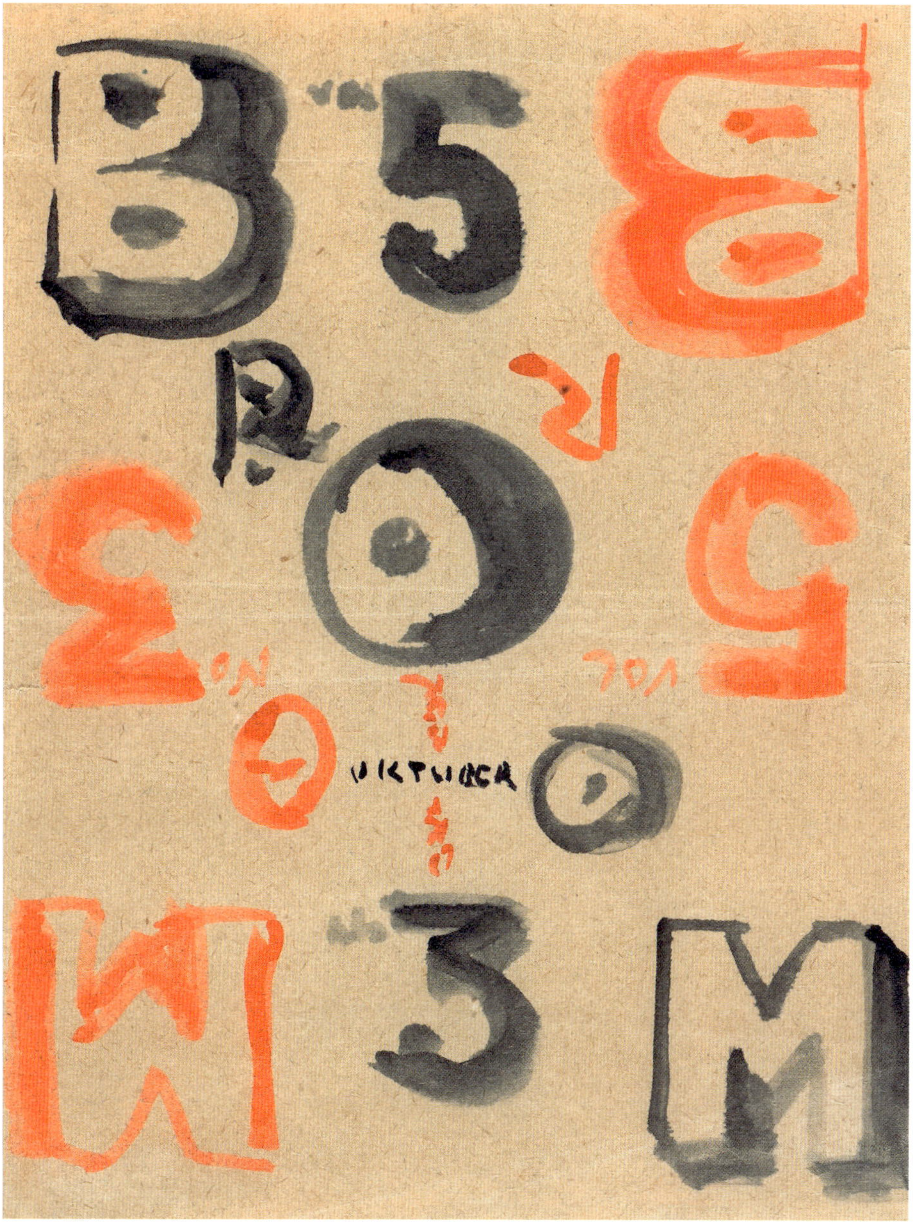

El Lissitzky
Cover design for the journal *Broom*,
no. 3, 1922

Sergei Sharshun
Ornamental Cubism,
1922–1923

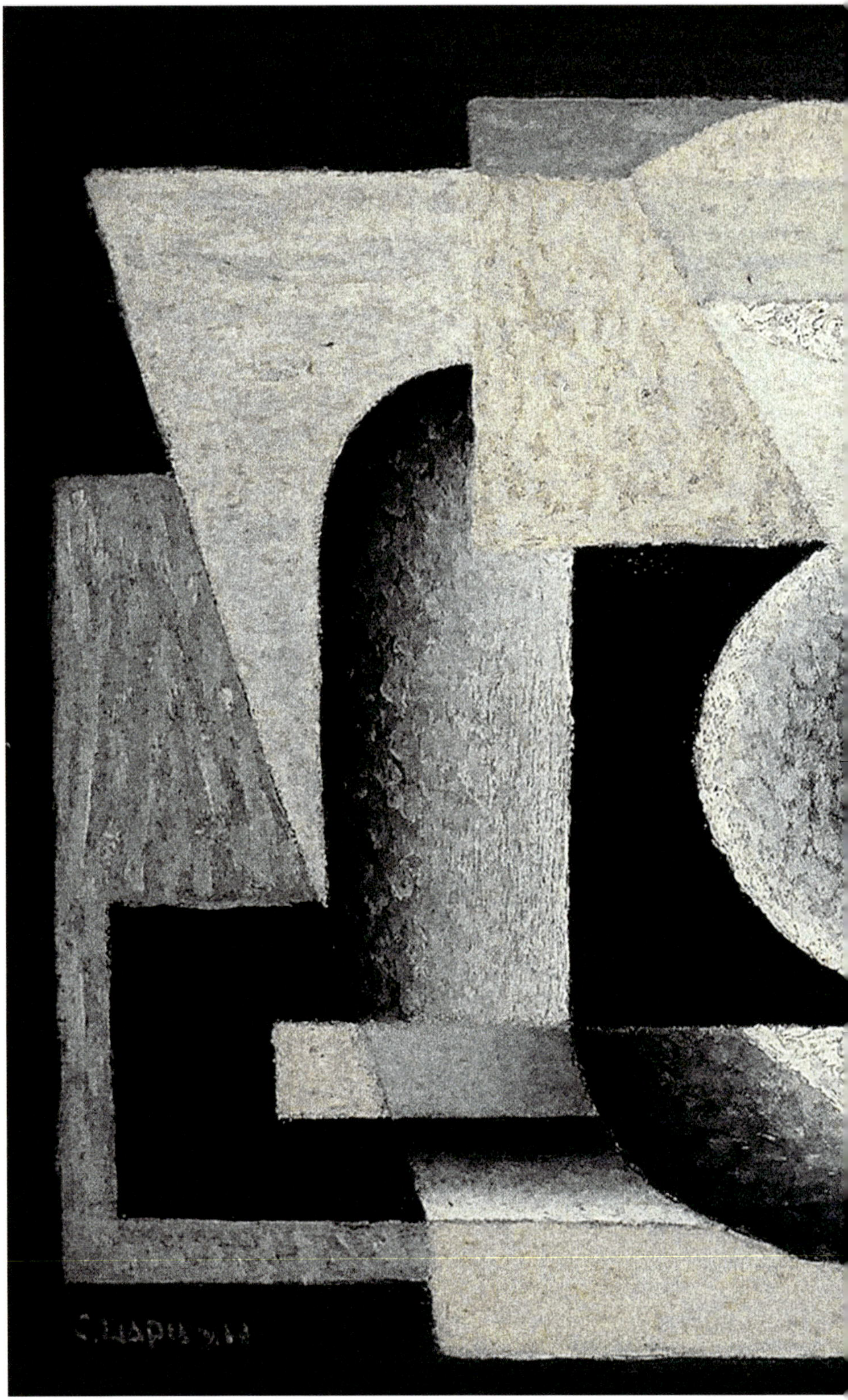

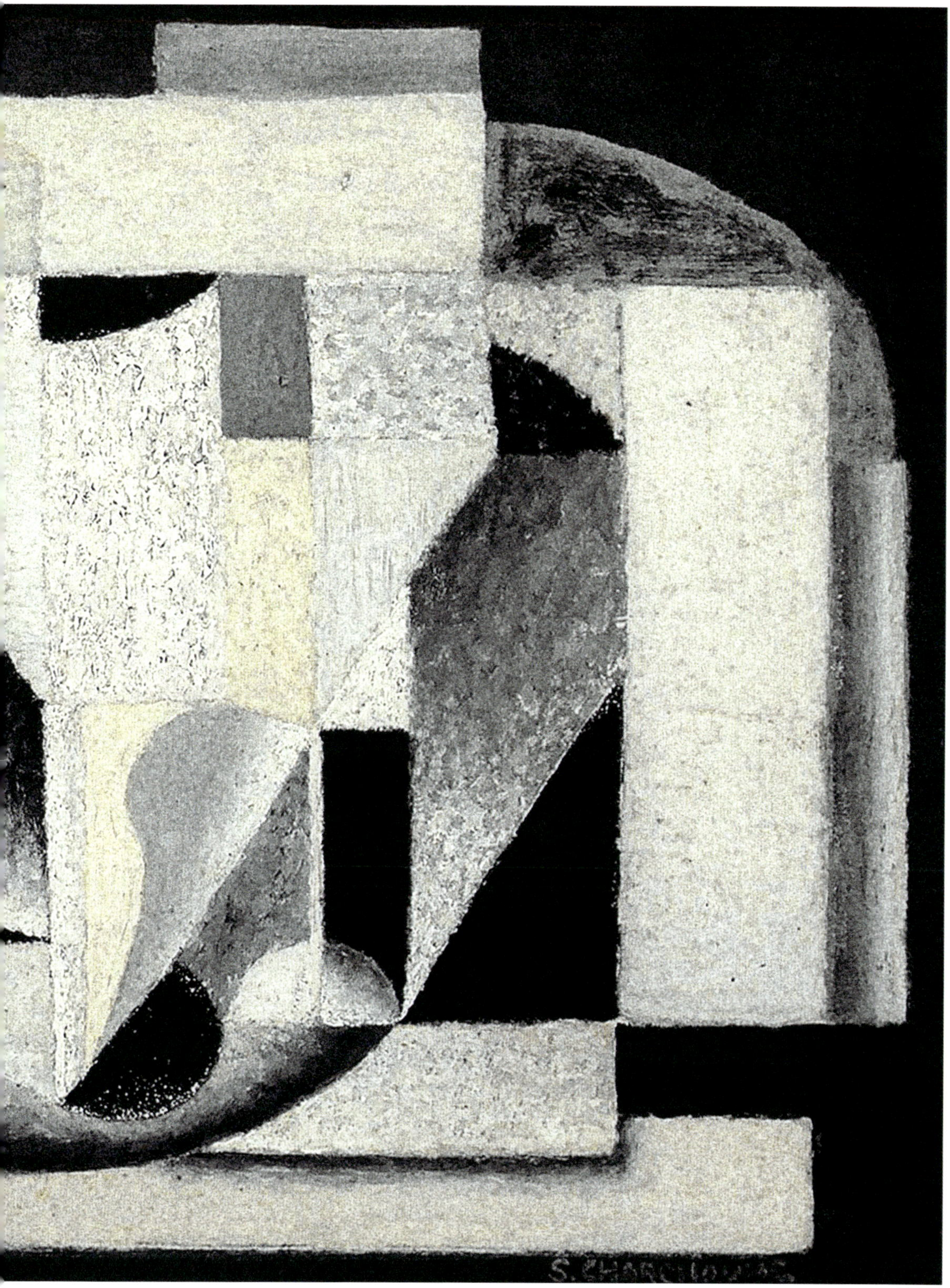

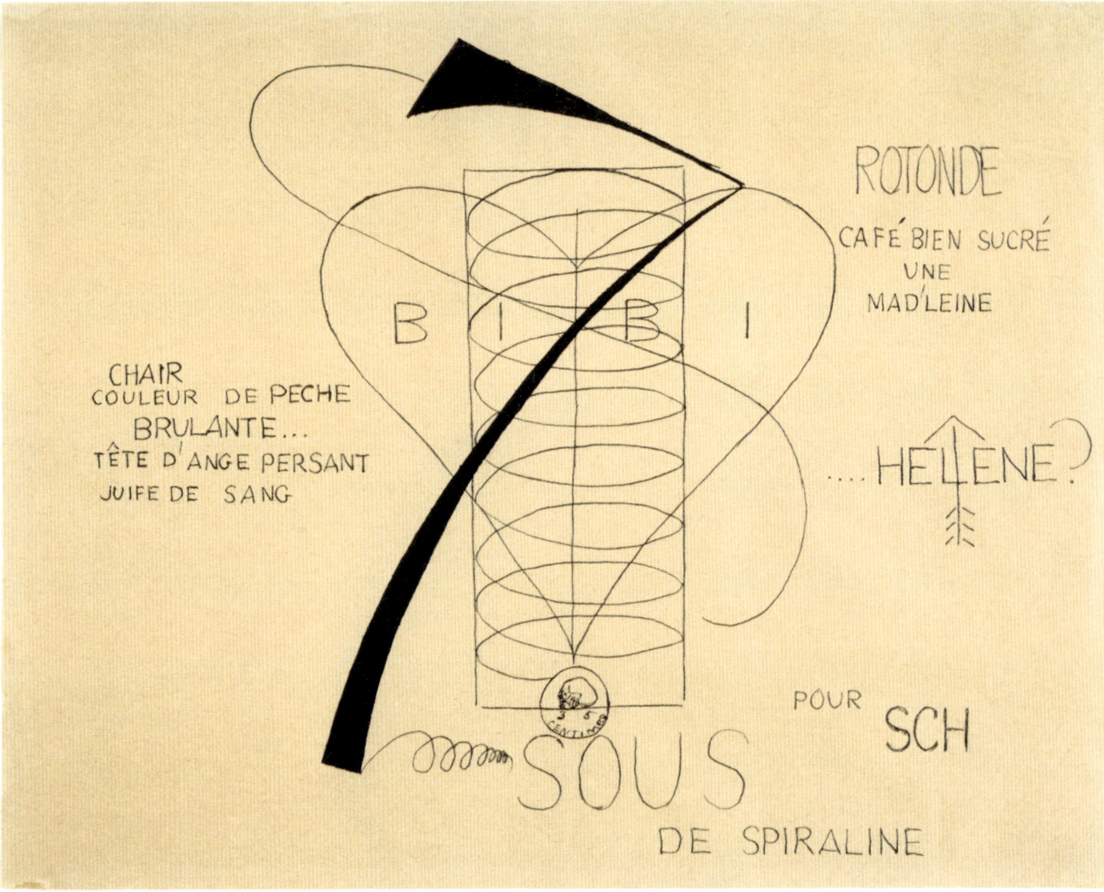

Sergei Sharshun
Bibi, 1921

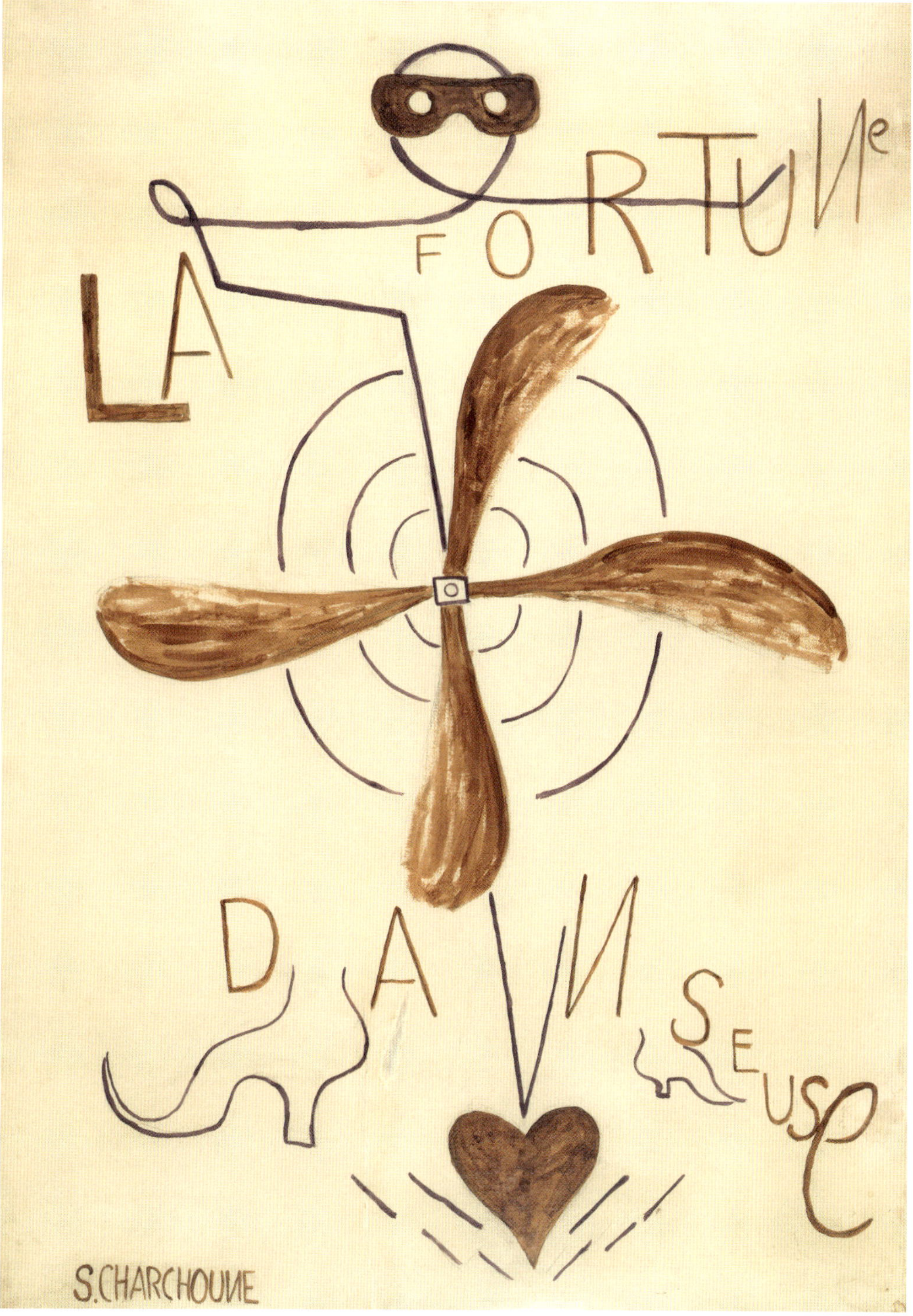

Sergei Sharshun
The Fortune Dancer, 1922

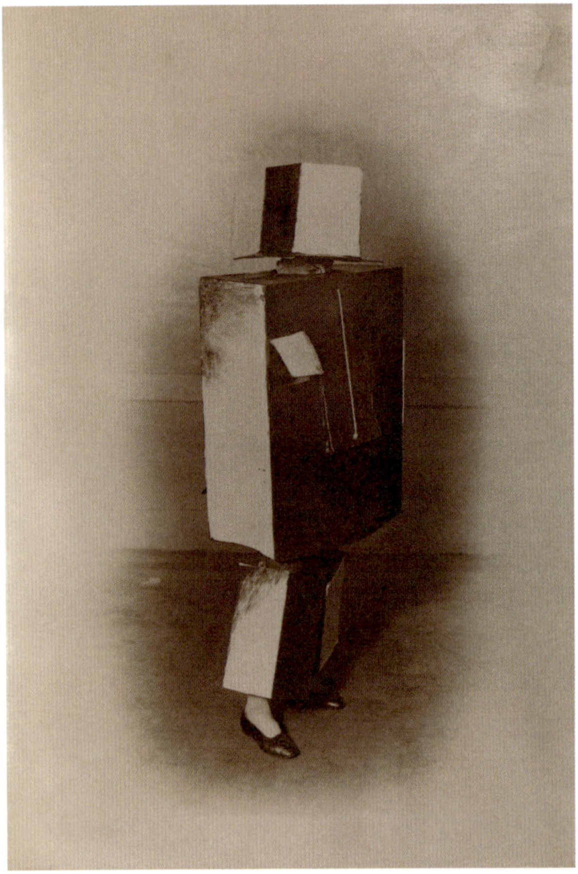

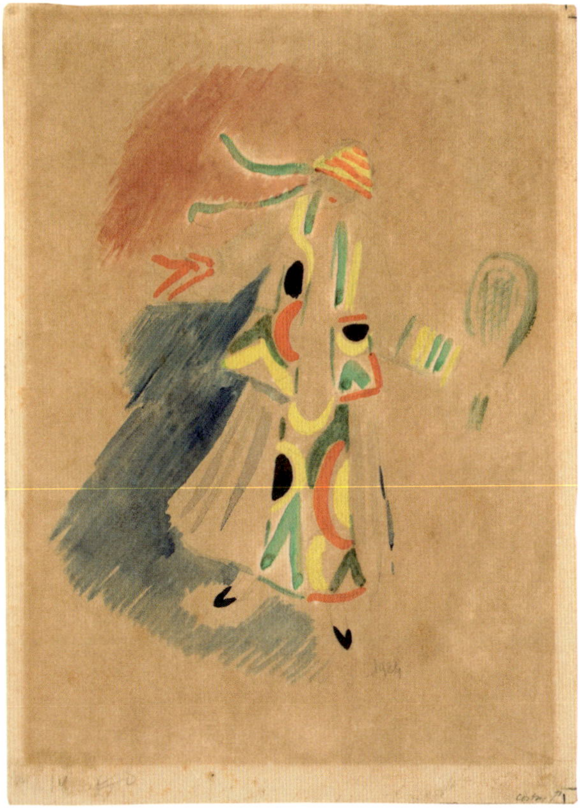

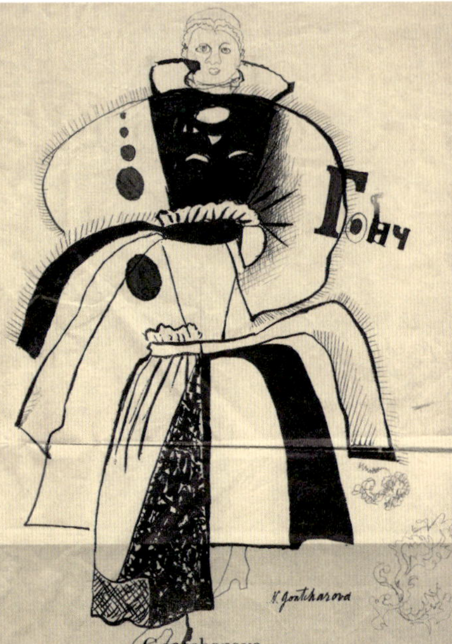

Gontcharova

Projet de Costume pour le Bal Olympique
pouvant servir aux deux sexes; recommandé
aux personnes pressées.
Matière : Papier ou calicot coloriés.

PROGRAMME

Colonnes sculptées — Le miroir décoré
Décor par projections en mouvement
Le divan mobile — Le plafond vivant
Cercles et spirales de lumière
Rubans d'air parfumés
DANSE
par dessus deux paniers

Juger Frus et Jean Borlin
Ballets Suèdois — Danses sportives.

Marie Wassilieff,
Jean Borlin, et Eric Viber
Danses du Homard, Crabe et Crocodile
Costumes du Homard et du Crabe
de *Marie Vassilieff*.
du Crocodile de
Fernand Léger

Mme Sasonoff Slonimsky
Théâtre de Marionnettes de Pétrograde
Un moment Espagnol
avec un Lion
Maquette des costumes et des poupées
par Gontcharova, exécutés par Mr Garine

Thamare Svirskaya
in Métropolitain -- opéra — New-York
Danse Gymnopédie *Musique d'Eric Satie*

Larionow
nouveau système de projections
fantastiques
Dessins coloriés de *Tchelitcheff,*
Chazmann Terechkowitch, Berline Barthe,
Sitrynowitch, Pikelny et Mme Vassilieff

Koussikoff Mariengof
Poésie

Romanoff, Vladimiroff

Panneaux
Pevzner, Pougni, Bogouslavskaia, Mane-Katz, Kicoen, Kotlar, Lanskoy, Granovsky, Chazman, Frenkel, Tchilichtcheff, Choubine, Sterling.

Comité de l'Union des
Artistes Russses à Paris

Widhopf	*Président*
Larionow	*Vice-Président*
Fotinsky	*Secrétaire*
Bogoutsky	*Trésorier*
Mme Marie Vassilieff	*Membres*
Mr Barthe	*du*
Mr Berline	*Comité*

Barmann, Kisling
Foot Ball général
avec des ballons multicolores
spécialement préparés par
Fotinsky et Bogoutsky
Costumes sportifs modernes ou anciens.
Même le costume de bain sera admis.
En tous cas le costume n'est pas obligatoire.

Mlle Lizica Codreano
Danses

Mme Koklova
Danses

Foujita
Sports japonais
Lutte et Boxe masculines et féminines

Zamoyski
prestidigitation

Bohslav Martinou
Musique du Village Tchèque
Quator

Sokol Tchécoslovaque
Gymnastique rythmique populaire

Cherchoun
La Reine des Forains Russes Pola Chentoff. Les danses de la création "La Discrétion" et "La timidité foudroyante".

Tristan Tzara
présentera
Spectacle sur l'Echelle
deux actrices, un acteur et l'auteur.

Comedia dell Cinéarte
Intensification des motifs
sportifs italiens.
Scénario et mise en scène de
Georges Kroll

Iliazde et Kakabadze
poèmes en relief

Vernon Duke
le célèbre compositeur américain
a composé pour cette occasion
plusieurs nouveaux fox-trot
1° No-one-to-Kids
1° Dancy-y our too fancy
3° Olympic Jazz

Panneaux décoratifs
littéraires
Geo Charles, 1er prix des Jeux Olympiques,
Fels, Paplavski, Terechkovitch,

Vazary
poèmes futuristes

Panneaux décoratifs
Sterling, Koyanagui, Coloenesco.

Comité du Bal :
Princesse Penkinas Benn Rott, Rossostoïeff, Rikaldy, Rolf de Maré, Raynal, Mr et Mme Vanek, Paul Guillaume. Povolotzky, Fels, Kessel, Marcel Hiver, Bernouard, Kaplan, Mme Mils, Mlle Bertillon, Epstein, Cogniat, Posener, Mr et Mme Murphy, Romoff, Slivinsky, Kavrenka, Metchaninoff Mandel Mojoukine

Prix d'entrée : 30 fcs
Pour les Artistes : 15 fcs

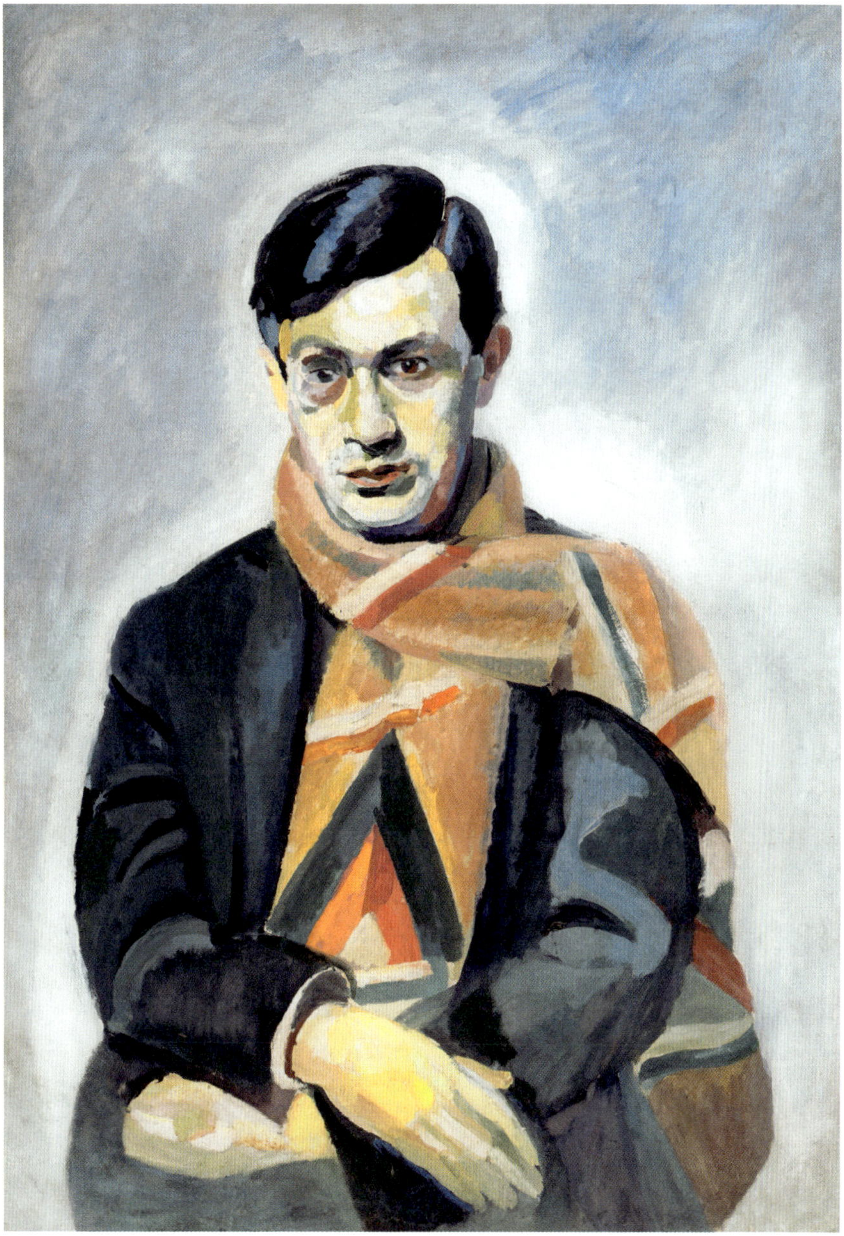

Anonymous
Ilia Zdanevich performing as live painting *The Triumph of Cubism* in the *Banal Ball*, Paris, March 1924

Natalia Goncharova and Ilia Zdanevich
Program for *Olympic Ball*, July 1924

Sonia Delaunay
Design for a tennis dress, 1924

Robert Delaunay
Tristan Tzara, 1923

Next double page:
Osip Brik
Scrapbook "Dada," ca. 1923–1924
left to right: Ilia Zdanevich's cover for the journal *The Bearded Heart*, no. 1, 1922, and a page of the journal *391*, no. 14, 1920, with an illustration of Sergei Sharshun's drawing (top)

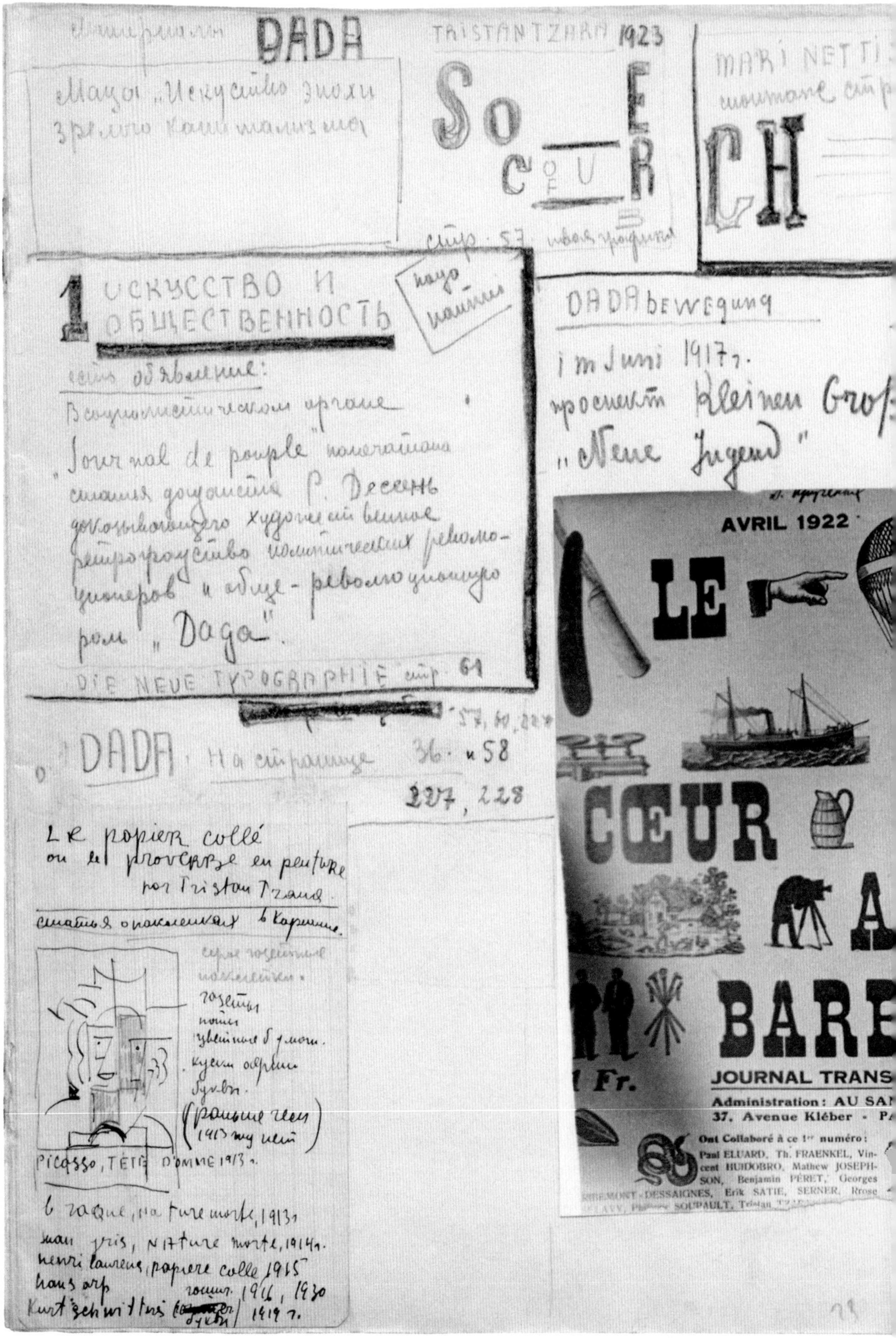
DADA
TRISTAN TZARA 1923
MARINETTI
стр. 57 новая графика
1 ИСКУССТВО И ОБЩЕСТВЕННОСТЬ
DIE NEUE TYPOGRAPHIE стр. 61
DADA bewegung
im Juni 1917 г.
„Neue Jugend"
DADA На странице 36. и 58
227, 228
Le papier collé ou le proverbe en peinture par Tristan Tzara
PICASSO, TETE D'HOMME 1913 г.
AVRIL 1922
LE CŒUR À BARBE
1 Fr.
JOURNAL TRANS
Administration : AU SAN
37. Avenue Kléber - PA
Ont Collaboré à ce 1er numéro :
Paul ELUARD, Th. FRAENKEL, Vincent HUIDOBRO, Mathew JOSEPHSON, Benjamin PÉRET, Georges
RIBEMONT-DESSAIGNES, Erik SATIE, SERNER, Rrose
Philippe SOUPAULT, Tristan
Juan Gris, nature morte, 1914 г.
Henri Laurens, papiere collé 1915
Hans Arp 1916, 1930
1919 г.

стр. 58

Marinetti 1909. Rush

"Les mots en liberté futuristes" (1909).

У Кручёных листовки

фотомонтажи „дада"

Foto ед. стр.

Экспрессионизм стр. 22 и другие.

Hans Arp.

и Tristan Tzara le mouvement DADA, à Zurich, en 1916.

A publié, en collaboration avec Lissitzky le livre sur les ISM.

Бесформенная скульптура.

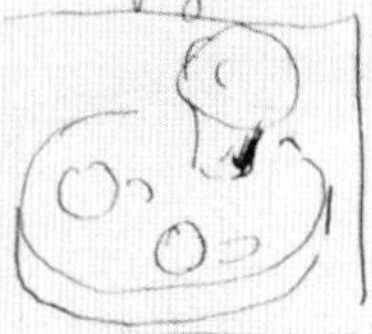

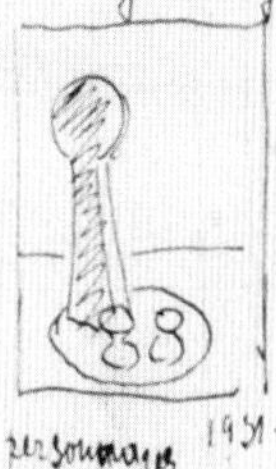

personnages 1931.

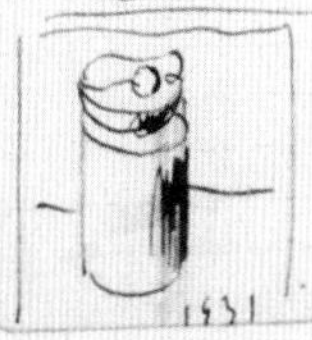

1931 gravate et nombril

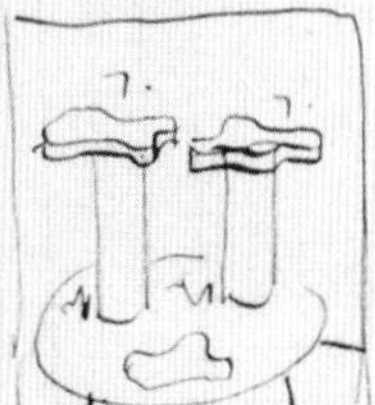

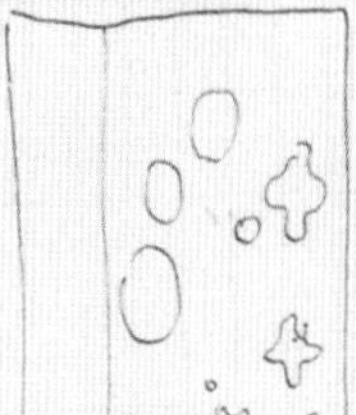

Feuilles 1931. composition 1931.

S. Charchoune

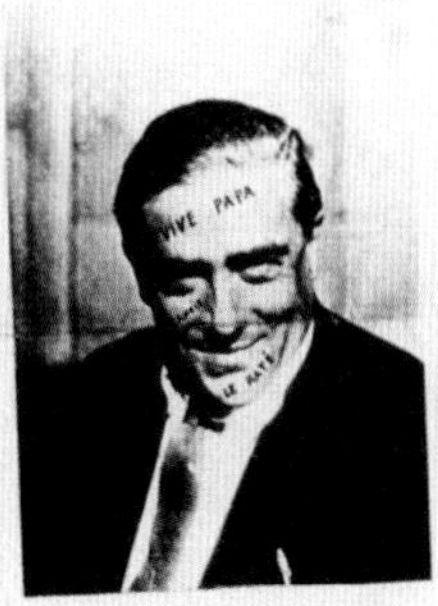

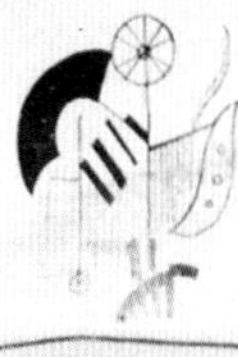

...stitutrice de campagne est comme l'autobus ... garniture en cygne qui borderait la Seine. M. B.

...rancis chante le Coq — Auric — haut. M. B

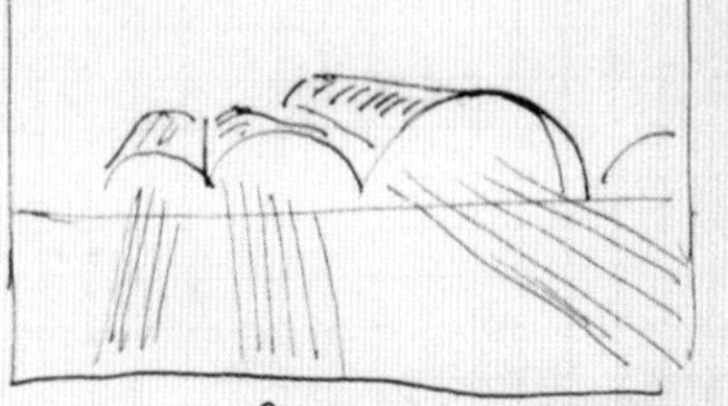

Gare de MILAN.

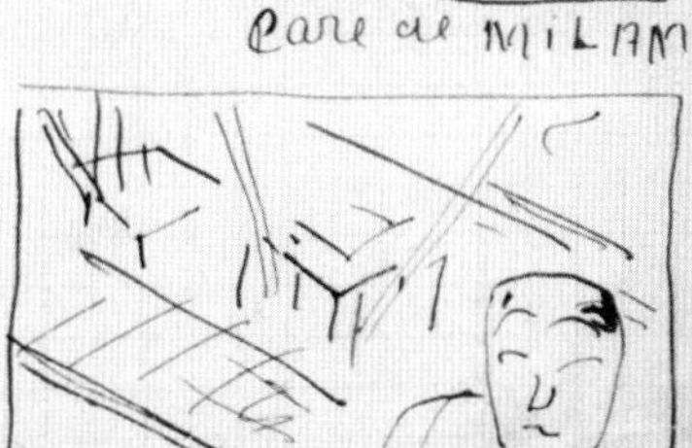

NEW-YORK vu par F. LEGER

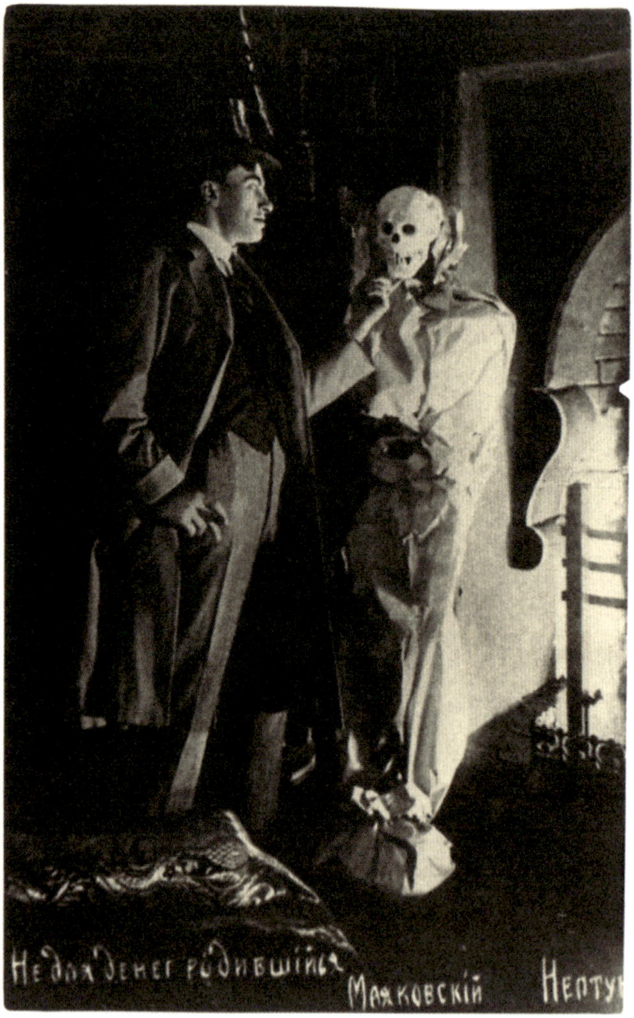

Evgeny Slavinsky
Still from Nikandr Turkin's film *Born Not for the Money* (Vladimir Mayakovsky), 1918

Tristan Tzara
Untitled, May 1931

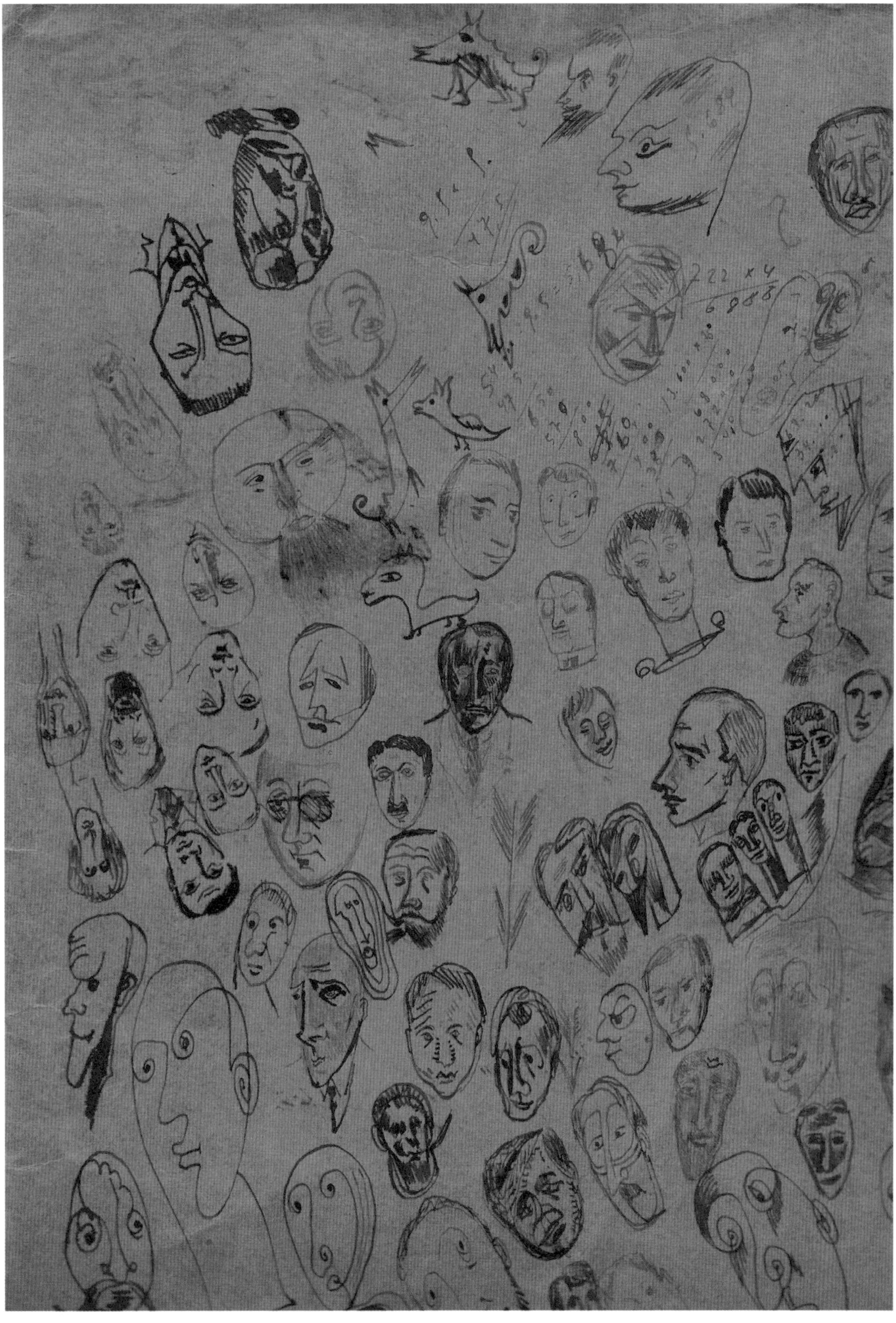

DADA IN CYRILLIC

Victor Tupitsyn

Anonymous
Vasily Kamensky, Kazan, 1914

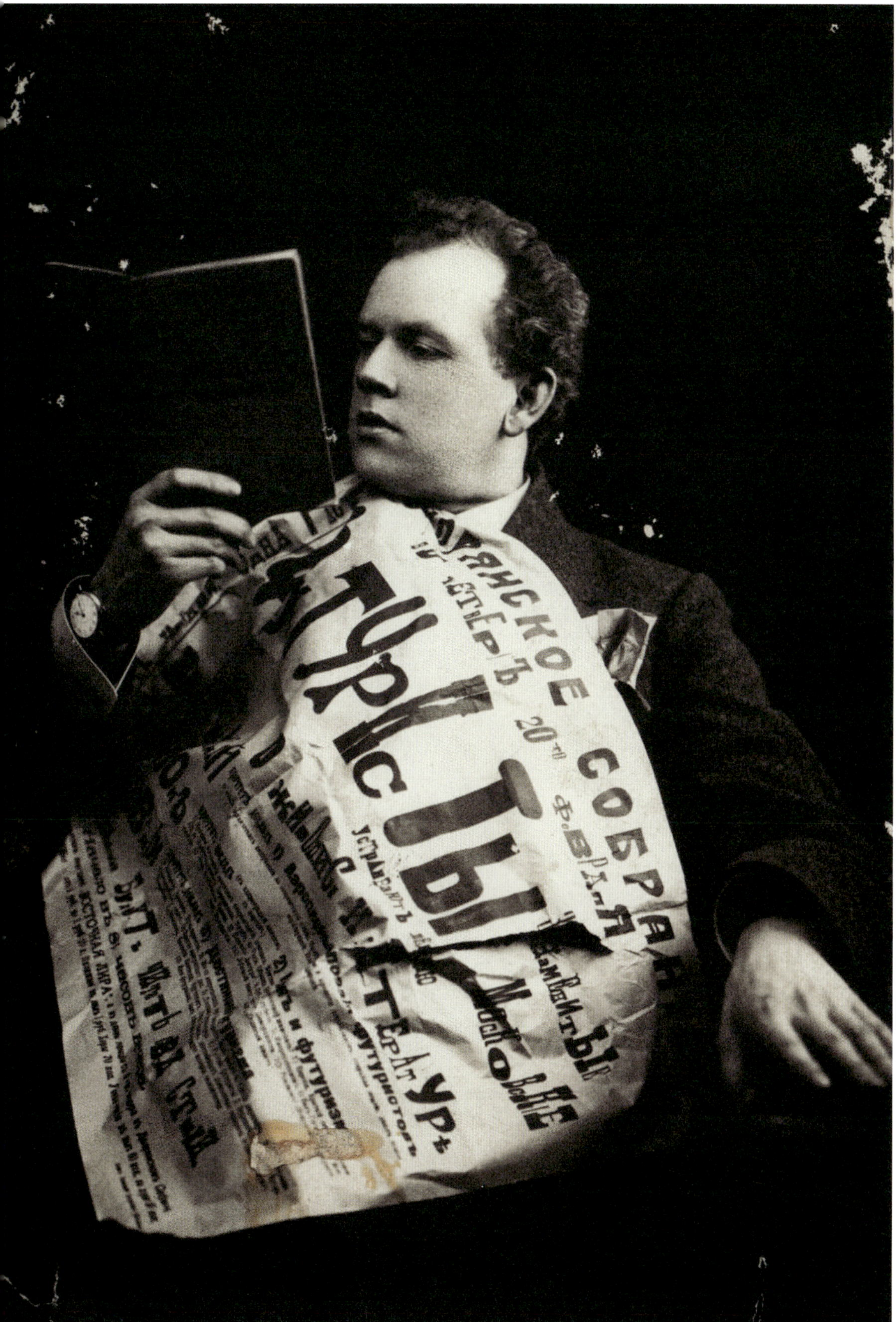

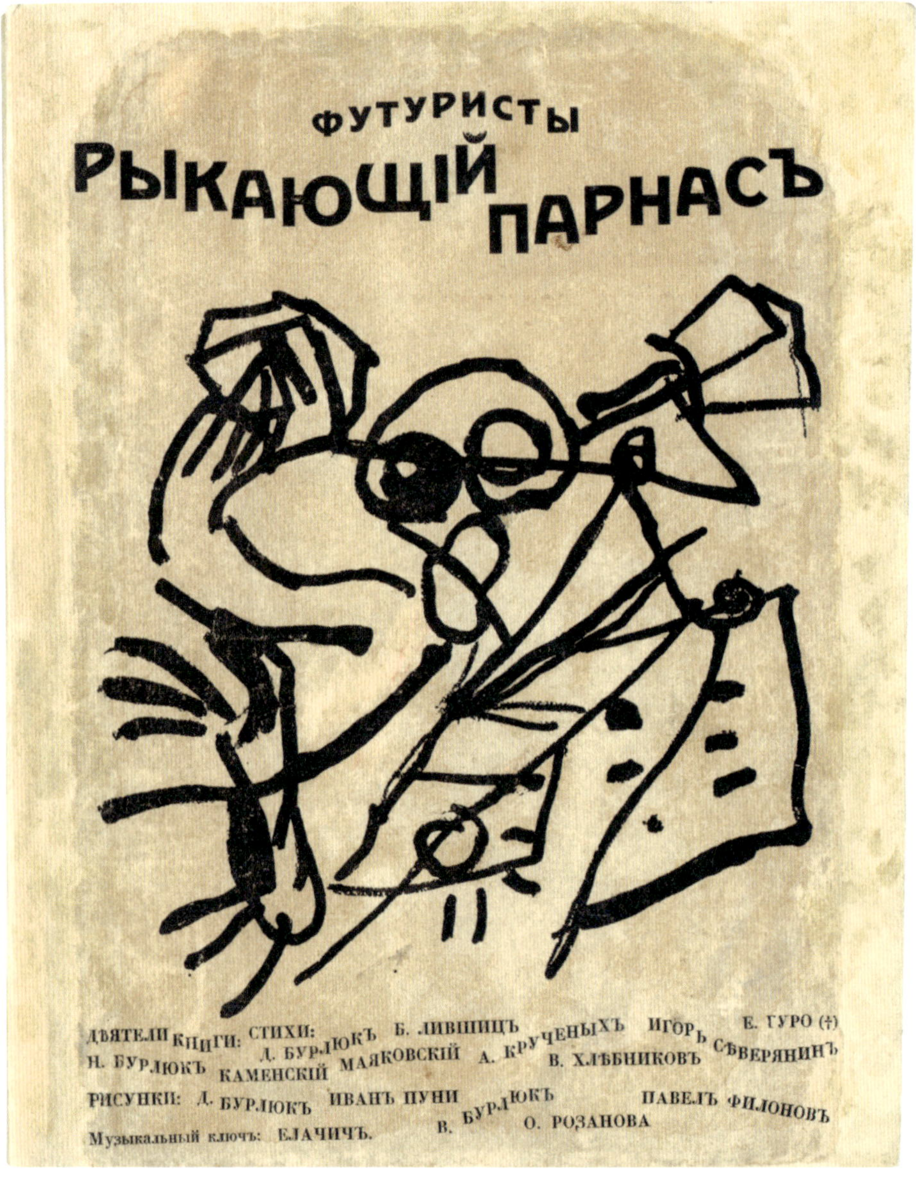

Ivan Puni
Cover of the book *Futurists: Roaring Parnassus* by David Burliuk, Velimir Khlebnikov, Igor Severianin, Aleksei Kruchenykh et al., 1914

> There comes a moment when real life, saturated with art to the brim, will spew it as unnecessary
>
> Nicolai Chuzhak, 1923

1. "It's Not What Is Said That's Important, but to Whom and under What Circumstances"

This comment by Vladimir Mayakovsky characterizes his poetry as intentional; that is, directed at an "object" to which the poetic gesture and the poetic message are addressed. No less important is the context of perception and the related "dispositives" (*dispositifs*) that must undergo objectification. There is nothing new about this, although it was none other than Mayakovsky who brought to this process not only a high level of effectiveness but the ability to see the audience as a situative object.[1] In that sense, he was a situationist long before Guy Debord.

Mayakovsky's early verses and long poems such as "The Cloud in Trousers" and "Backbone Flute," attest to the author's talent, as do some of his plays, including *Mystery-Bouffe*, produced by Vsevolod Meyerhold with lost stage design by Kazimir Malevich (1918). Being "travel-approved" (because of his loyalty to the Bolsheviks), Mayakovsky acted as a link between the Western and Soviet avant-gardes. Starting in 1923, all of his verse texts were constructed in "staircase" form. Critics regarded this style as commercial (the more lines, the higher the fees), but the "staircase" and, consequently, reading as descent down

1. The "objectness" of the audience was something *always already* assumed by Mayakovsky, which helped him brilliantly defend himself from nasty comments in a matter of seconds.

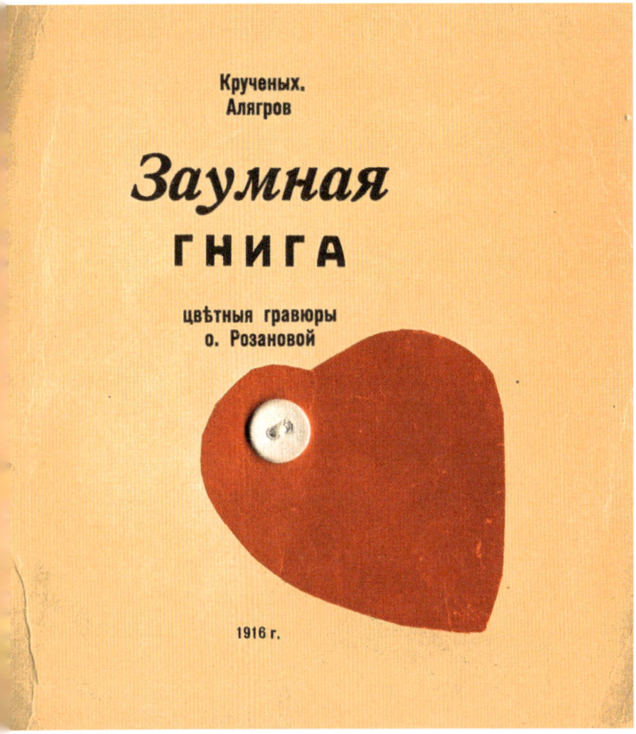

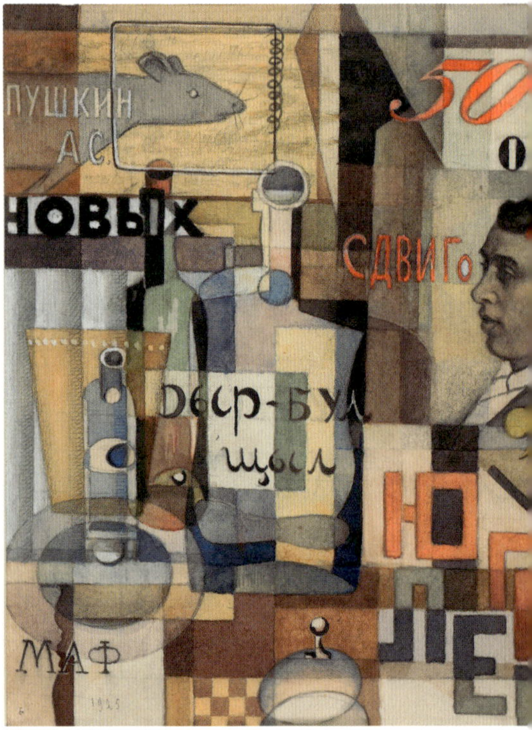

the steps follow Hugo Ball's Dadaist formula, according to which "Dada = word as motion."[2] During the period of the New Economic Policy (NEP, 1922–1928), the poet did commercial advertising, which is much in accordance with Tristan Tzara's thesis that "Advertising and business are also elements of poetry."[3]

In late December 1912, Mayakovsky and David Burliuk, who considered themselves *budetliane* ("men of the future"), published the collection titled *A Slap in the Face to Public Taste*. One cannot call the "perpetrator" of such a slap anything other than a proto-Dadaist. Thus, the term *proto-Dadaism* is more appropriate here. In this context, public taste is abolished, and what enters the arena instead is the *taste* for scandal and for the theatrical manifestation of the state of mind that Anatoly Lunacharsky, in his text *The Foundations of Positive Esthetics* (1904), defines as "negative affectional"—a term he borrows from the philosopher Richard Avenarius.[4] Returning to proto-Dadaism, Vasilisk Gnedov, who gained notoriety with his "Poem of the End" in the book *Death to Art* (1915), should also be given his due. The poem is a blank page with not a single letter or mark on it, other than the title. When "reading" it, the

Olga Rozanova
Cover of the book *Transrational Book* by Aleksei Kruchenykh and Aliagrov (Roman Jakobson), 1916

Ivan Kliun
Untitled (Aleksei Kruchenykh), 1925

author made a "hook-like" gesture without uttering a word. The hand motion was the entirety of the poem. As for the end of art, in the words of Velimir Khlebnikov, "Gnedov was the first to know about it . . . the cuckoo of the alphabet in the pine-forest of names."[5]

2. Aleksei Kruchenykh: Transrationalism and Shiftology

In his essay "On the History of Russian Futurism,"[6] Aleksei Kruchenykh dates the creation of transrational language to 1912, when he wrote the following poem:

Dyr-bul-shchyl
Ubeshchur
Skum
Vy-so-bu
R-l-ez.

This poem was published in January 1913 in his book *Lipstick*. That same year, he published transrational poetry in the anthologies *The Little Garden of Judges II* and *The Union of Youth III*. In April 1913, he published "The Declaration of the Word as Such," in which he introduces and explains the term transrationalism (*zaum*). The declaration expresses the idea that thought and speech cannot keep up with emotional experience, and therefore artists should be free to express themselves not only with common phrases but with a language that has no definite meaning and is not fixed—*transrational* language.[7] "Is

2. Hugo Ball's "Dada Manifesto" was read at the first public Dada soirée, in Zurich, July 14, 1916. Mayakovsky's poetic descent down the staircase echoes Marcel Duchamp's *Nude Descending a Staircase* (1912).

3. Tristan Tzara, "Dada Manifesto 1918," in *The Dada Reader: A Critical Anthology*, ed. Dawn Ades (London: Tate Publishing, 2006), p. 38.

4. In Avenarius's terminology, the "affectional" is the positive or negative tint in which sensations are perceived by consciousness. "The Theater of the Mind" was a phrase used by Stéphane Mallarmé.

5. In the poem "Blue Chains" (1922), Khlebnikov mentions Gnedov's poem "Kuk" (1913) and calls its author "the cuckoo of the alphabet." Gnedov, whom Khlebnikov included among the "chairmen of the earth," was arrested in the 1930s and then spent twenty years in the gulag.

6. Aleksei Kruchenykh, "Otkuda i kak poshli zaumniki?," in *K istorii russkogo futurizma: vospominania i dokumenty*, ed. N. Gur'ianova (Moscow: Gileia, 2006), 301.

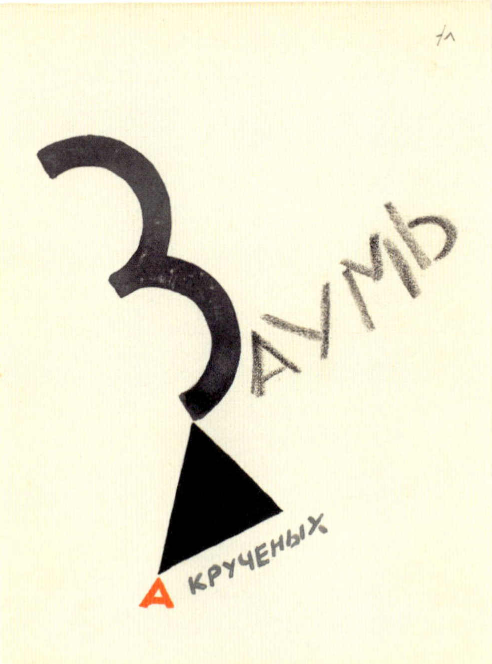
Заумь
А КРУЧЕНЫХ

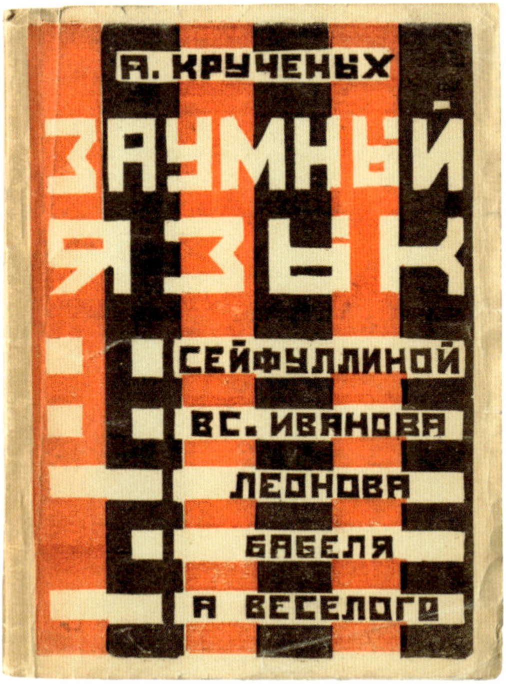
А. КРУЧЕНЫХ
ЗАУМНЫЙ
ЯЗЫК
СЕЙФУЛЛИНОЙ
ВС. ИВАНОВА
ЛЕОНОВА
БАБЕЛЯ
А ВЕСЕЛОГО

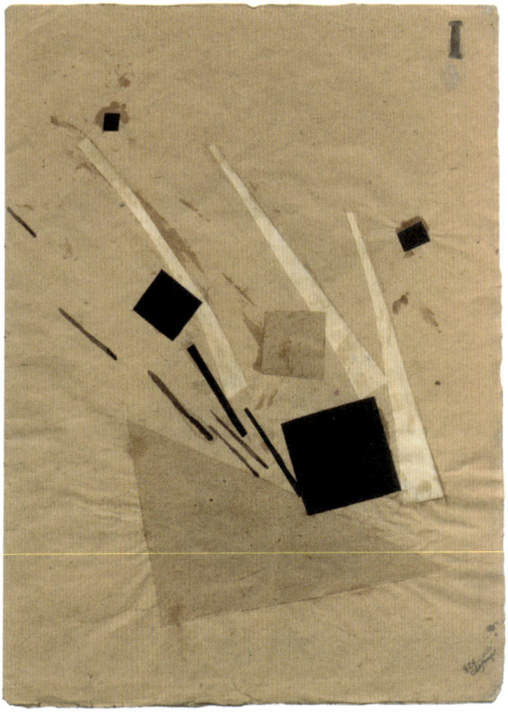

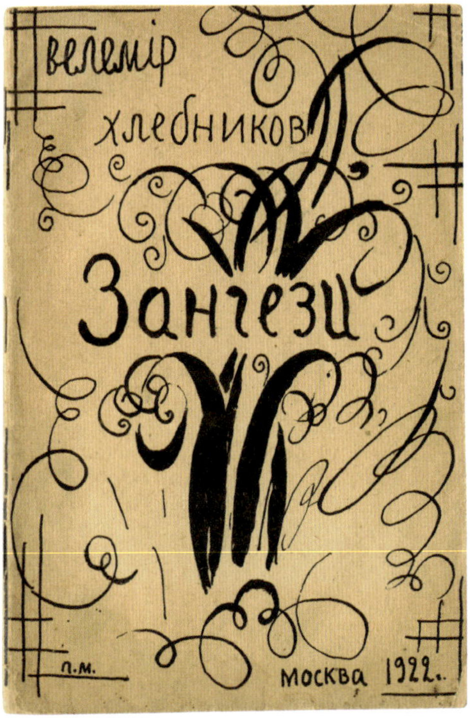
велемiр
хлебников
Зангези
П.М.
Москва 1922.

El Lissitzky
Design for the cover of the book *Transrational* by Aleksei Kruchenykh, 1925

Valentina Kulagina
Cover of the book *Transrational Language* by Aleksei Kruchenykh, 1925

Sergei Gorodetsky and Velimir Khlebnikov
Spinny-Spin-Spin, anniversary book dedicated to Aleksei Kruchenykh, 1920

Petr Miturich
Cover of the book *Zangezi* by Velimir Khlebnikov, 1922

transrationalism the language of the future or the language of the past (savagery, the primitive)?" Kruchenykh asks. He then answers his own question: "For now, this is my opinion and my faith: transrationalism is new art given by a new Russia to the entire shocked and bewildered world."[8] Besides Kruchenykh, the transrational school includes the poets Velimir Khlebnikov, Elena Guro, Vasily Kamensky, Sergei Tretiakov, Olga Rozanova, Ilia Zdanevich (aka Iliazd), Igor Terentiev, and Aleksandr Tufanov. Not everyone in the avant-garde circles became a convert to the theory Kruchenykh preached, however. "The poet has failed to learn the causes of the liberation of the letter," Malevich wrote to Mikhail Matiushin on June 23 and July 5, 1916. "The word as such must be transubstantiated 'into *something*,' but many . . . were compelled to get mired in that meat. So far, Kruchenykh is struggling [against it], not allowing his feet to remain in one place for a long time . . . but if he can't find that '*something*,' he'll inevitably get sucked into the same meat. When you have the sounds '*dyr bul shchyl*,' you . . . have to listen, not think."[9] Malevich's words recall Tzara's comment about "vowels as the essence, the molecule of the letter, and therefore primitive (or pure) sound."[10]

The elements of transrational language can also be found in Khlebnikov's early works, starting with the lyrical miniature "*Bo-beh-oh-bee* Is the Lipsong" (1908).[11]

Bo-beh-oh-bee is the lipsong
Veb-eh-oh-mee is the eyesong
Pee-eh-eh-oh is the eyebrowsong
Lee-eh-eh-ay is the looksong
Gzee-ßzee-gzeh-oh is the chainsong
On the canvas of such correspondences

7. Essays exploring transrational language include Viktor Shklovskii, "O poezii i zaumnom iazyke," *Poetika* (Petrograd, 1919); and Boris Arvatov, "Rechetvorchestvo (po povodu 'zaumnoi' poezii)," *Lef*, no. 2 (April–May 1923): 79–81. [For an English translation of the latter, see pp. 291–293 of the present catalogue.].

8. Kruchenykh, "Otkuda i kak poshli zaumniki?," 304.

9. Malevich to Matiushin, June 23, 1916, in *Malevich o sebe, sovremenniki o Maleviche: pis'ma, dokumenty, vospominaniia, kritika*, ed. I. Vakar and T. Mikhienko, 2 vols. (Moscow: RA, 2004), 1:88.

10. Martin Heidegger, who in old age was friendly with Jacques Lacan, described Lacan's texts as baroque. The same may be said of Tzara, who asserted (in the spirit of François Rabelais) that "thoughts are produced in the mouth." See Tristan Tzara, *7 manifestov dada* (Moscow: Gosudarstvennyi muzei im. V.V. Maiakovskogo, 2016), 24.

11. Nikolai Khardzhiev believed that "besides being a transrationalist (*zaumnik*), Khlebnikov was also a brilliant thinker (*umnik*)." Thus, the "critique of transrational reason" (with apologies to Immanuel Kant) is only half applicable to Khlebnikov, if at all.

somewhere beyond all dimensions
the face has a life of its own.

Even though transrationalism (most likely) began with this poem, Kruchenykh turned out to be a more *systemic* transrationalist than Khlebnikov. In his tract "The Shiftology of Russian Verse" (1922), Kruchenykh uses the concept of "shift" to refer to "the merger (during reading) of two or more words (phonemes) into one sound blot." In his view, "shifts can be conscious or nonconscious (or unconscious). A successful shift strengthens and enriches the sound of the verse, while an improper one breaks up its construction." With regard to the poetic text and what he calls the "texture of the word," Kruchenykh uses performatively engaged concepts, such as "shifts," "shifts-apart," and "under-shifts." "The shift, as the fountainhead of language games, is extremely prone to give birth to verses," he writes in "Declaration No. 4," adding that his "shiftology" (the science of shifts) is based on the thesis that "shifts are one of the most important impulses of modern poetic technique." In his view, the shift is not so much a rhetorical form as "a super-trope, the trope of all tropes."[12]

The "biomechanics of the shift" that Meyerhold and Nikolai Foregger embraced in the 1920s echo Kruchenykh's opinion of the opera *Victory over the Sun* (1913), for which he wrote the libretto.[13] The opera proved to be not so much futuristic as Dadaist.[14] "How did this happen in the opera?" Kruchenykh asks. "It's almost constant dissonances and sudden leaps, and the boldest phonetics, such as songs made up only of vowels or only of consonants—in other words, the most unexpected turns and passages. . . . The plot has several

12. Kruchenykh, "Deklaratsiia no. 4 (O sdvigakh)," *K istorii russkogo futurizma; vospominania i dokumenty*, ed. N. Guz'ia nova, 305–7. A "shift" is defined as a lexical deformation of the phrase and its texture, as a syntactic inversion or relocation (according to Ilia Zdanevich), and also as the effect of homonymy (according to Aristotle). Kruchenykh attributed the shift to the status of a universal category. See T.V. Tsvigun, "Iskusstvo oshibki v russkom avangardizme," Vestnik Baltiiskogo federal'nogo universiteta im. Kanta (Kaliningrad, 2011), 157.

13. For more on the influence of constructivism on the art of dance and theatrical plastics, see E. Surics, "Soviet Ballet of the 1920s and the Influence of Constructivism," *Soviet Union* 7, no. 1–2 (1980): 112–37.

14. "At the dress rehearsal," Kruchenykh recalls, "when everyone was already wearing the costumes (made from a sturdy wire carcass and thick cardboard painted by Malevich), one of the actors shot another with a rifle. It was supposed to be a blank shot, but our enemies (who were part of the theater management) put some hard wadding in the rifle, and it was only thanks to the sturdy costume that the actor was only slightly bruised." Kruchenykh, "Ob opere 'Pobeda nad solntsem," 271.

15. Ibid., 273–74.

16. Franz Brentano, *Psychology from an Empirical Standpoint* (London: Routledge, 1973), 88–89. Brentano's term *intentionality* (adopted by Husserl) derives from the Latin verb *intendere*, which means "to point to" or being "directed toward some object."

storylines: first of all, if there has already been a 'dead moon,' why not a vanquished sun? In the years when symbolism was in bloom, there was a very widespread declaration, 'Let's be like the Sun,' which in turn rhymed primarily with money—gold, hard currency, riches, of which most of the 'Sun people' dreamed at the time."[15] Mikhail Matiushin, who composed the music for the opera, explained to students that, as an antithesis of "art for art's sake," *Victory over the Sun* symbolized victory over the old, familiar notion of the sun as beauty. For Malevich, his *black square* on the curtain "signified the beginning of victory." The *square* is an ideal object that becomes a symbol of *objectlessness*. Recall Franz Brentano's "intentional inexistence of the object" in his *Psychology from an Empirical Standpoint* (1874), which states that "every mental phenomenon includes [intentionally] something as object within itself . . . (which is not to be understood here as meaning a thing)."[16] The premiere of *Victory over the Sun* took place at the Luna-Park theater in December 1913, several months after the publication of the futuristic anthology *The Dead Moon*. The moon and the sun are both round, and since the square is a "competing" *eidos*, we are dealing with the confrontation of ideal Platonic figures. In 1920, this "universal war" of *eidoi* was joined by El Lissitzky in the poster *Beat the Whites with a Red Wedge*, in which the Whites (who were fighting against the Bolsheviks) are identified with a circle. The *budetliane's* attitude toward the culture of the past (including Aleksander Pushkin, who was often called "the Sun of Russian poetry") was akin to the siege of Troy, and in that sense they were not that different from the Dadaists. The mention of "universal war" is not accidental; it is a reference to the twelve-collage series of the same name by Olga Rozanova and Kruchenykh (1916). Their titles—"The Battle of the *Budetliane* and the Ocean," "The Battle of Mars and the Scorpion," pp. 64–65 "The Battle with the Equator," "The Battle of India and Europe," "Germany in the Dust," "Heavy Weapon," "Plea for Victory," "The War State," and so on—speak for themselves. The intervention of language eidetics into what Edmund Husserl, in *Origin of Geometry*, calls "the horizon of the geometric future," leads to the formation of so-called interlocked idealities, which cannot be easily "unlocked" since text and image have already exchanged significations. That is precisely what assisted the proliferation of modernism and its visual rhetoric in the first three decades of the twentieth century. Typical of the entire series are four lines from *Universal War*: "Like a thunderbolt, fell the big box, / And like fluff exploded the rocks; / Eyes shut, I saw the bullet flying; / It came in for a kiss, so quiet."

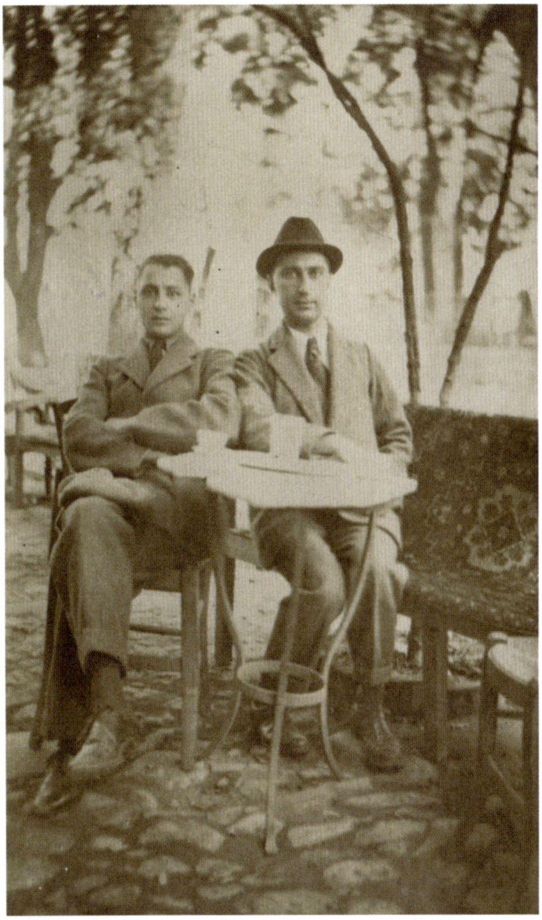

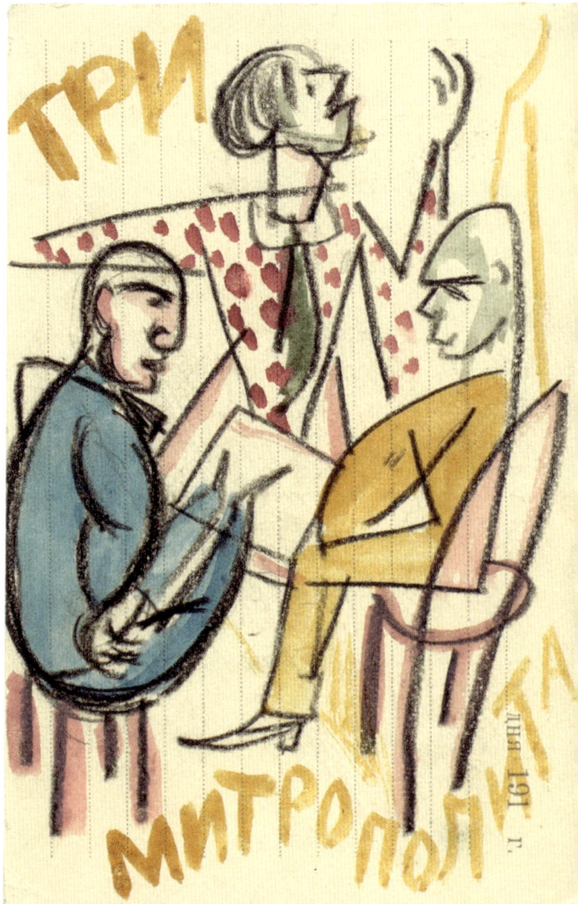

Anonymous
Ilia and Kirill Zdanevich, Tiflis, ca. 1917

Igor Terentiev
Three Archbishops (Aleksei Kruchenykh, Ilia Zdanevich, and Igor Terentiev), 1919

Kruchenykh's series of "Declarations," published in the early 1920s about transrationalism and shifts,[17] are in a dialogue with Boris Arvatov's essay "Speech Creation (On 'Transrational' Poetry)" where he calls for "the renewal of language to be guided not by personal impulses but by the consciously understood needs of the sociolinguistic production process." Arvatov's statement is as symptomatic as his opinion on the *culture of language*, "which was heralded by the *transrationalists* but will be carried out by the proletarian."[18]

3. Dada of Tiflis Vintage

The Tiflis analogue of the Cabaret Voltaire was the Fantastic Pub (1917–1919), which served as a gathering place for the "41°" group: Kruchenykh, Zdanevich, and Terentiev.[19] In their manifesto they point out that "Company 41° . . . affirms transreason as the mandatory form for the embodiment of art."[20] On the p. 282 poster for their event in Borzhom Park (Tiflis, 1919), members of the group announce themselves as "the famous corkscrews of futurism" and as "the word-founders." Kruchenykh studied the theory and practice of phonetic shifts ("shiftology") and, in particular, looked for "caca" and other obscene-sounding shifts in the works of various authors.[21] His studies in "cacology" (poor choice or use of words), in which he was joined by Terentiev, were mediated by interest in Sigmund Freud's theories regarding various "displacements" and deformations of speech in dreams. This interest was expressed, for example, in play with "anal-canal" themes as applied to the words "annals" and "canal." In his text "Philosophical Trinity," Kruchenykh writes, "Kant, Nietzsche, and Schopenhauer form a circle of dancing, foggy deities who have nothing lighthearted about them except their feet."[22]

Mikhail Le Dantiu, a young artist and theorist who was involved in everythingism and had been in contact with Mikhail Larionov and Natalia Goncharova in Moscow, stayed in Tiflis in 1912–1913. After Le Dantiu's tragic death in 1917, Zdanevich (also a proponent of everythingism) dedicated his play *Lidantiu* p. 195 *as a Beacon*, which (cacologically) plays with the artist's French last name, to his memory. The "Manifesto of Everythingism, MV" says that "uppity letters, unsatisfied with their role

17. Kruchenykh's various "Declarations" are published in *K istorii russkogo futurizma*, 285–97.

18. See Boris Arvatov, "Speech Creation (on 'Transrational' Poetry)," on pp. 291–293 of the present catalogue.

19. Nikolai Cherniavsky is also mentioned as a member of the group. In addition to the "41°" group, Tiflis also had the literary associations Blue Horns and H2SO4.

20. Ilia Zdanevich, Aleksei Kruchenykh, Igor Terentiev, and Nikolai Cherniavsky, "Manifesto of the '41°'" (1919), on p. 283 of the present catalogue.

21. See A. Kruchenykh, *Sdvigologia russkogo stikha* (Moscow, 1922), 5.

22. A. Kruchenykh, *Apokalipsis v russkoi literature* (Moscow, 1923), 29.

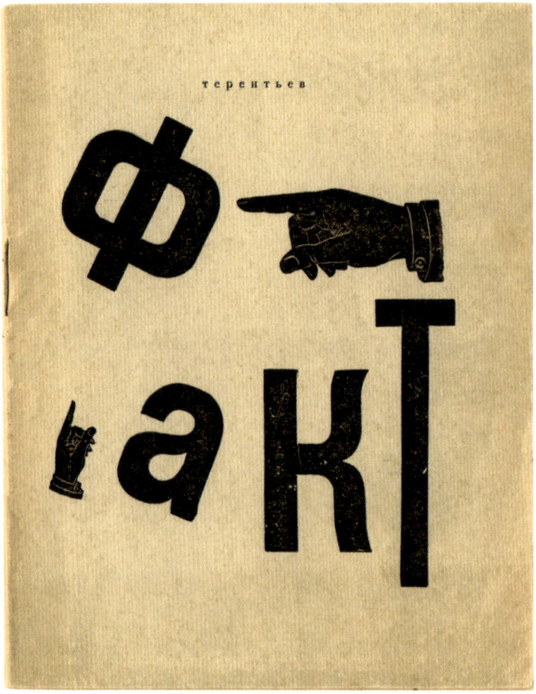

Ilia Zdanevich
Cover of the book *Fact* by Igor Terentiev, 1919

Kirill Zdanevich
Cover of the book *A. Kruchenykh the Magnificent* by Igor Terentiev, 1919

Kirill Zdanevich
Cover of the book *Learn, Artists* by Aleksei Kruchenykh, 1917

as handmaidens, are choking language. . . . Correcting our inadequate mouths, we have arrived at the poetry of *many*, shouting in multitudes, and shouting different things. . . The rocket is ready, we are burning the fuse. Happy travels, until you become an enemy."[23] Everythingism (according to Zdanevich) "makes the war against the past senseless, and thus overthrows futurism. . . .But one can be an everythingist without espousing such beliefs: it doesn't matter whether. . . he regards the public as sheep or not."[24] Kruchenykh, as the author of *Victory over the Sun* (1913), can be called (in the opinion of Nikolai Khardzhiev) the first Dadaist, three years ahead of the emergence of that movement in Western Europe.[25]

Nina Gurianova notes that "the Bergsonian idea of vitality was transformed by Kruchenykh . . . into a shift (explosion) of forms, words and images . . . existing outside any canon."[26] Antiestablishment rebellion and provocation were the norm. The only ism considered permissible was dilettantism. André Breton's phrase, "Beauty will be convulsive or will not be at all," is directly related not only to Kruchenykh but to the OBERIU group who valued his work: Daniil Kharms and Aleksandr Vvedensky.[27]

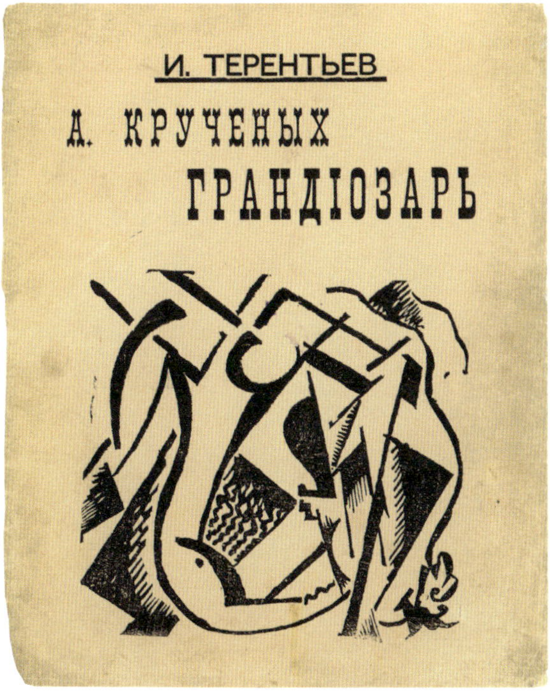

23. Il'ia Zdanevich, "Mnogovaia poeziia," in *Futurizm i vsechestvo, 1912–1914*, ed. Sergei Kudriavtsev, 2 vols. (Moscow: Gileia, 2014), 1:183.

24. For more on everythingism, see Margarita Tupitsyn's article in the present catalogue; and Ilia Zdanevich, "Natalia Goncharova and Everythingism," on pp. 259–261 of the present catalogue.

25. N. I. Khardzhiev, "Polemichnoe imia," in *Ot Maiakovskogo do Kruchenykh: izbrannye raboty o russkom futurizme* (Moscow: Gileia, 2006), 319–92. See also N. I. Khardzhiev, "Sud'ba Kruchenykh," in *Stat'i ob avangarde* (Moscow: RA, 1997), 1:302. In this text, Khardzhiev uses the terms "alogical eccentricity" and "elliptical syntax" with regard to Kruchenykh's poetry.

26. Nina Gur'ianova, "Biografiia dichaishego: vospominaniia Kruchenykh v literaturnom kontekste 1920–1930-ikh godov," in *K istorii russkogo futurizma*, 14.

27. OBERIU (Association for Real Art) included the poets Nikolai Oleinikov, Aleksandr Vvedensky, Daniil Kharms, and Igor Bakhterev. Their transgressive use of transrational language as ready-made contributed to the *victory of nonsense* in the form of *surplus absurd*. In the 1930s and early 1940, the OBERIU group became victims of the Great Terror. "Convulsive beauty" is a phrase that appears in Breton's novel *Nadja* (1928) as well as in *Mad Love* (1937). A similar statement once surfaced in Malevich's letter to Matiushin (July 3, 1913): "You encounter lots of artworks which look as though they were produced in the state of convulsive seizure." In 1993, Hal Foster invoked Freud's notion of the "uncanny," suggesting that "surrealist beauty partakes of the return of the repressed, of the compulsion to repeat." See Hal Foster, *Compulsive Beauty* (Cambridge, MA: MIT Press, 1995), 23. Also see Victor Tupitsyn, "Canny Uncanny," in *Stripped Bare: The Body Revealed in Contemporary Art* (London: Merrel, 2004), 21–42.

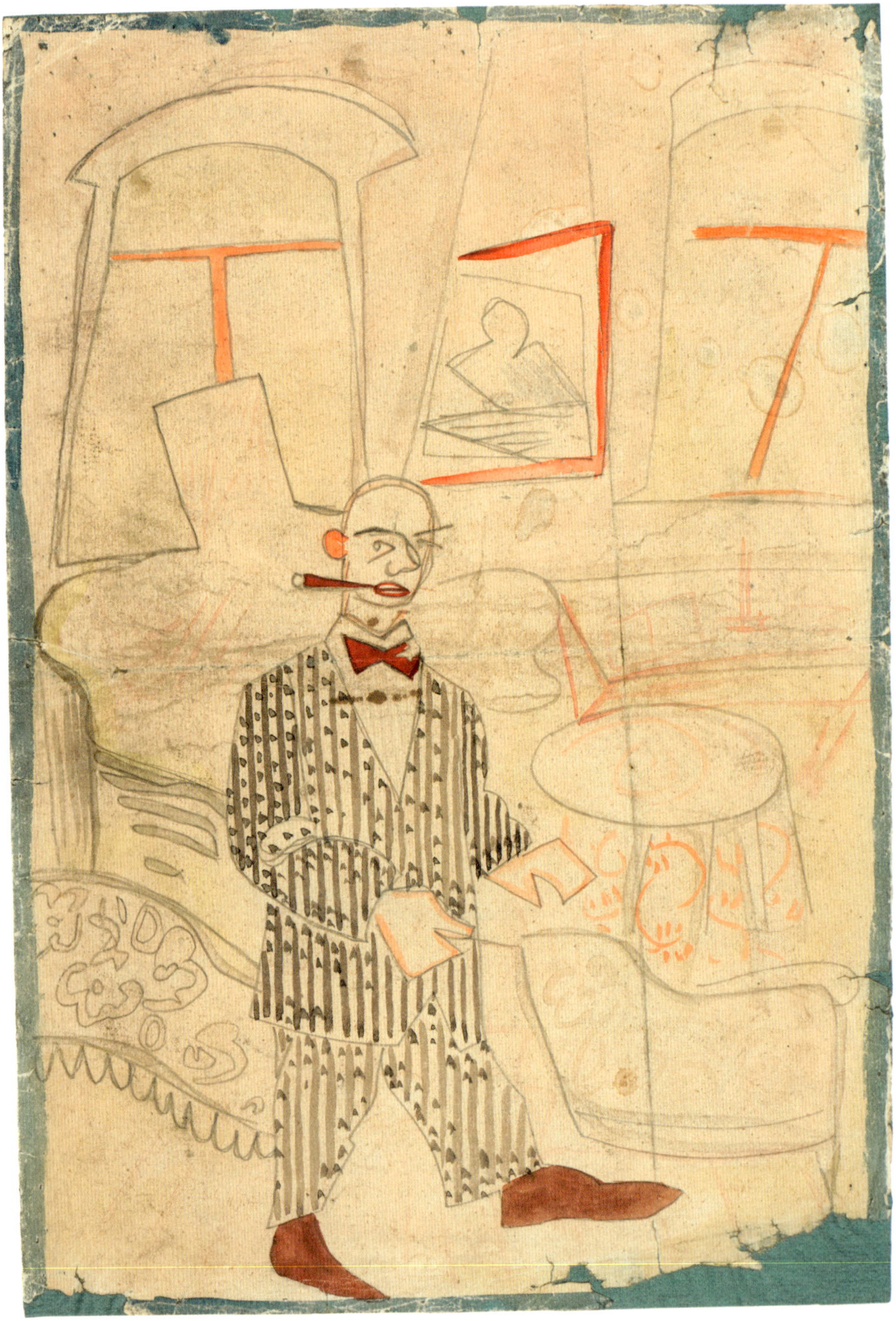

Igor Terentiev
Self-Portrait, ca. 1920

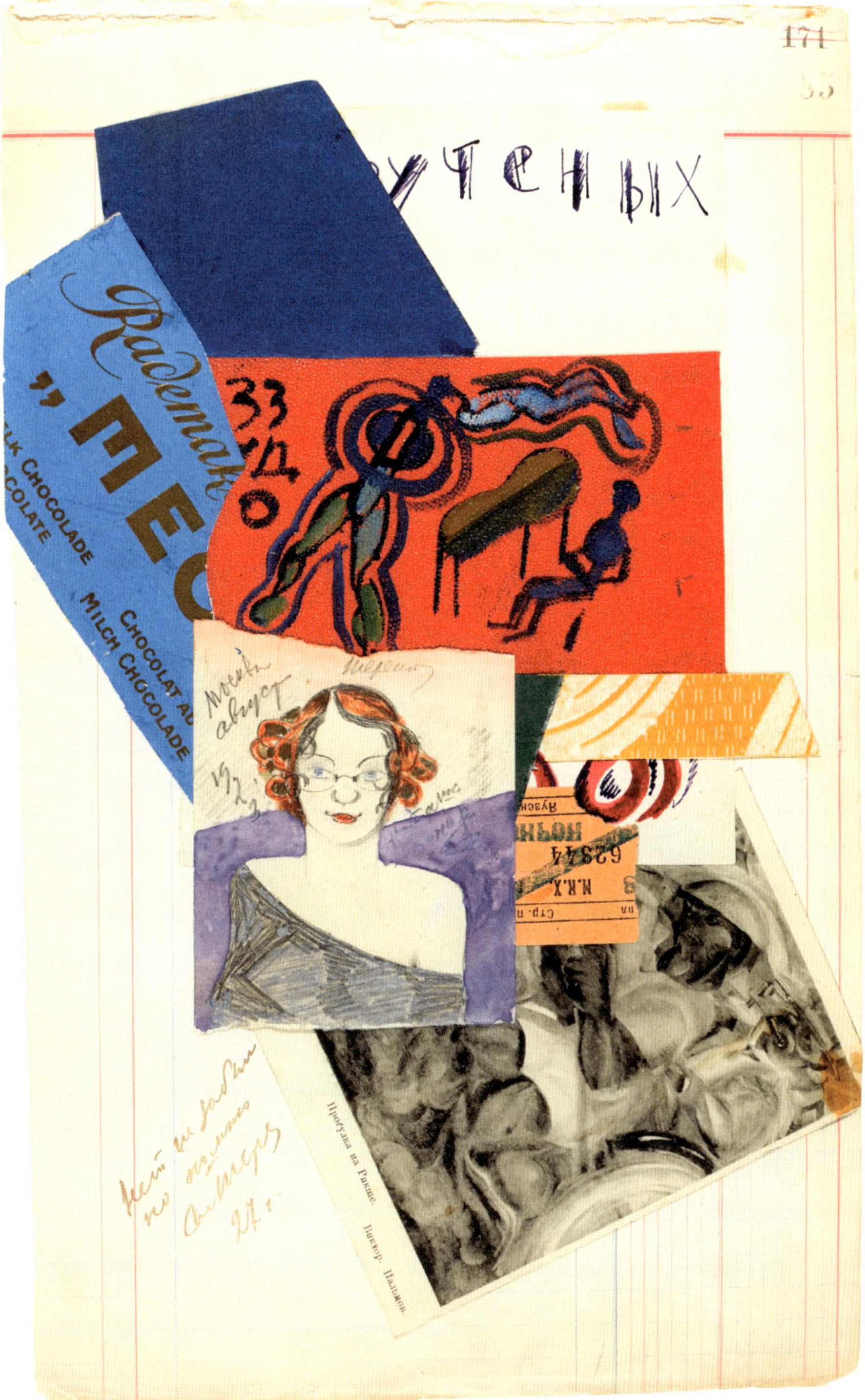

Igor Terentiev
Untitled, 1923

"Never miss an opportunity to say something stupid," Terentiev urged in 1919. Terentiev, a lawyer by training, had lived in Tiflis since 1916. As a poet and an artist, he was formed under the influence of Ilia Zdanevich and Kruchenykh. In 1918, he joined the "41°" group and, by his own admission, "went beyond the bounds of futurism."[28] "Art is nonsense under the command of common sense," Terentiev believed. In 1922, he was unable to emigrate to France to reunite with his wife and daughter, who had managed to go there before France stopped issuing visas to Soviet citizens. The phrase, "Drinking wine after 11 p.m. in solitude," was most likely inspired by thoughts of parting with loved ones.[29] In Tiflis, Terentiev published two books of verses, *The*
p. 184
Cherubim Whistle and *Fact* (1919). His poetic works also appeared in Kruchenykh's book *The Obesity of Roses* (1918). Having settled in Petrograd, Terentiev grew close to Malevich, Matiushin, Vladimir Tatlin, Pavel Mansurov, and Pavel Filonov. In 1924, he began to work as a stage director, producing both his own and other authors' plays, such as *Foxtrot*, *The Knot*, *John Reed*, and Nikolai Gogol's *The Government Inspector*. He regarded himself as a pupil of Meyerhold. His interest in Dadaism began to show when he was still in Tiflis, in his
p. 185
works *A. Kruchenykh: The Magnificent* (1919), *17 Nonsense Instruments* (1919), and *A Tract on Total Indecency* (1920). Terentiev continued to correspond with Ilia Zdanevich, and his tragedy *Iordano Bruno* survives in a letter sent to him in 1924. To illustrate Terentiev's Dadaist aspirations, several passages from his book *17 Nonsense Instruments* should suffice:

28. I. G. Terentiev to M. M. Karpovich, April 8, 1919, in *Moi pokhorony. Stikhi. Pisma. Sledstvennye pokazaniia. Dokumenty*, ed. Sergei Kudriavtsev (Moscow: Gileia, 1993), 23.

29. Terentiev's wife and daughter returned to Russia in the late 1920s.

30. Terent'ev, *17 erundovykh orudii* (Tiflis: 41°, 1919), n.p. Terentiev was arrested in May 1937 and executed three weeks later.

31. Excerpts from the article are published on pp. 310–313 of the present catalogue.

32. R. Iakobson and K. Pomorska, *Raboty po poetike* (Moscow: Progress, 1987), 7. In 1949, Zdanevich published *Poésie de mots inconnus* in Paris; it included Khlebnikov's poetry along with works by such Dadaists as Tzara, Georges Ribemont-Dessaignes, Kurt Schwitters, and Raoul Hausmann.

33. Ibid.

Pieces of dream are good for patches
Zebra gallops Go study Here are exercises
Rewrite, reread, rescind, remove, recycle,
rebound, and run away.[30]

In 1921, while living in Berlin, Roman Jakobson wrote "Letters from the West. Dada," an article in which he surveyed the Dadaist movement for the Soviet audience.[31] Much later, while living in the United States, Jakobson commented, in a dialogue with Krystina Pomorska, on the origins of the Russian proto-Dada period when "avant-garde poetry began to unfold and there appeared an entire string of word-creation revelations from the great Russian poet . . . Khlebnikov . . . who enchanted me forever."[32] In the same text, he calls Kruchenykh "Khlebnikov's enterprising, clever comrade-in-arms."[33] In fact, it was not enterprising cleverness but pragmatism, as well as rejection of the symbolist tendency to treat the text of the Other as a "beautiful lady"—including his own poems and theoretical works. In a poem dedicated to Kruchenykh in 1921, Khlebnikov creates a more complex psychological portrait of his "clever accomplice":

Kruchenykh
Little apparition with a London air,
still a kid at thirty, wing collars and all,
perky, antsy, and brisk.
You keep that Siberian ending, that "chenykh,"
chained to your name like a prisoner on a rock pile.
You take other people's ideas and repeat them
till you beat them to death.
The face of an "Englishman"—
or maybe an indentured bookkeeper
tired of his books.
Skillful editor of scandalous texts,
lazy, unshaven, and slipshod,
but with eyes like a girl's
full of tenderness, sometimes.
Enormous gossip, tricky as they come,
a lover of personal put-downs.
You enchanting writer,
negative double of Burliuk!

4. Nothingists and Nothingism

The Nothingists and the OBERIU group were two branches of Russian Dadaism. The OBERIU sat on two or even three chairs: Dadaism, surrealism, and nonsense (absurdism). The Nothingists (*nichevoki*) were something else altogether. "Nothingists are the Dada of the West," they proclaimed, putting forth such slogans as "We spit on humanity" and "Everything takes its beginning from Nothing."[34] The word *nothing* was used as a universal answer to all questions: Who? What? How? When? Where? Why? What for? For
p. 191
whom? For what reason? Nothingism (*nichevochestvo*) found its capital in Rostov-on-Don, and the Nothingists published their poems, texts, and manifestos in a self-produced pub-
p. 296
lication, *Dog's Box*.[35] Strategic decisions were the responsibility of the Creative Bureau of Nothingists (TvorNichBuro), which included Boris Zemenkov, Susanna Mar, Elena Nikolaeva, Riurik Rok, Sergei Sadikov, and Oleg Erberg. However, its activity proved to be short-lived, and the Nothingists lasted only from 1920 until 1922. In the "Decree on Painting," Zemenkov writes, "Any work of art that expresses itself outside the aesthetic laws of correlation but directly demonstrates with its form and content the artist's possession of a spiritual path is considered permitted until further notice."[36] The "Decree on the Nothingists of Poetry" declares that "the crisis is in ourselves, in our spirit" and that

> Nothing: the purpose of eternity = Nothing.
> Hence:
> In poetry, there is nothing; only Nothingists.

34. See "Decree on the Nothingists of Poetry," on pp. 295–297 of the present catalogue.

35. Ibid.

36. See "Decree on Painting," on pp. 297–298 of the present catalogue.

Nothingists
Leaflets of the group *Nothingists*,
ca. 1924

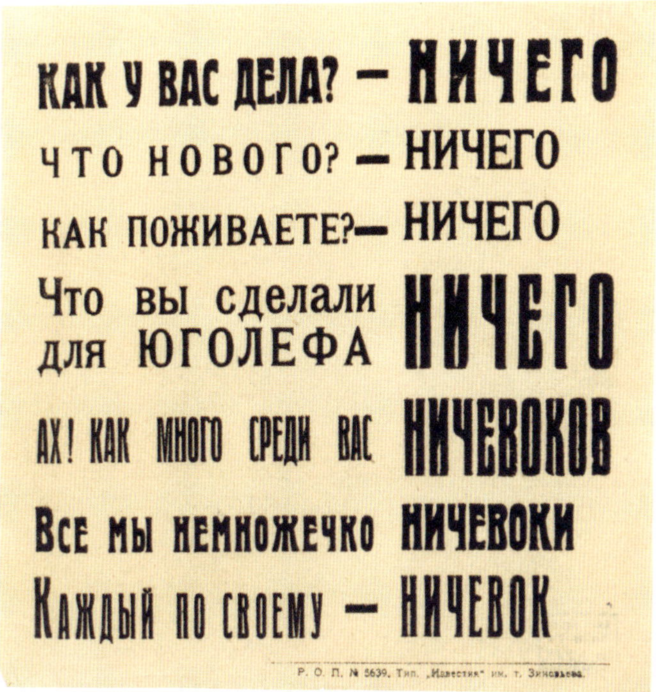

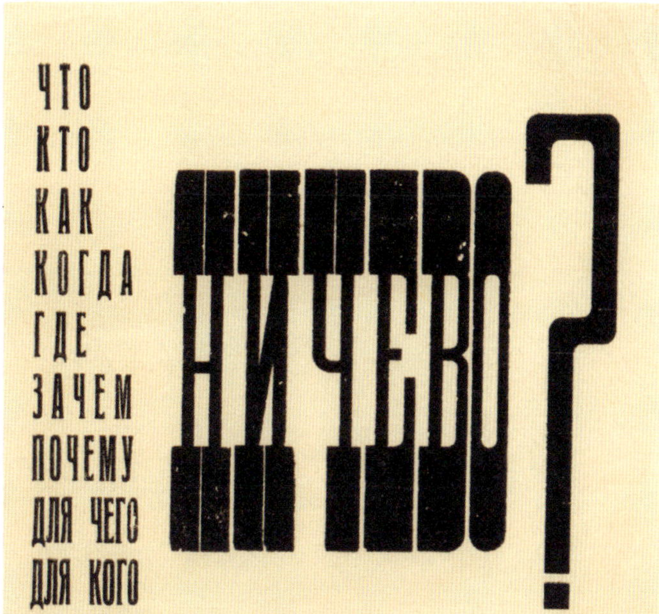

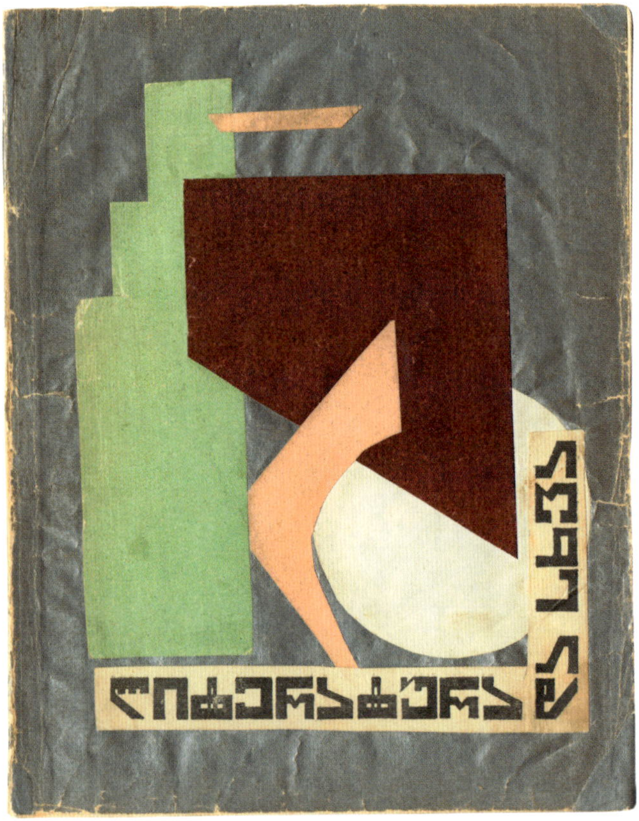

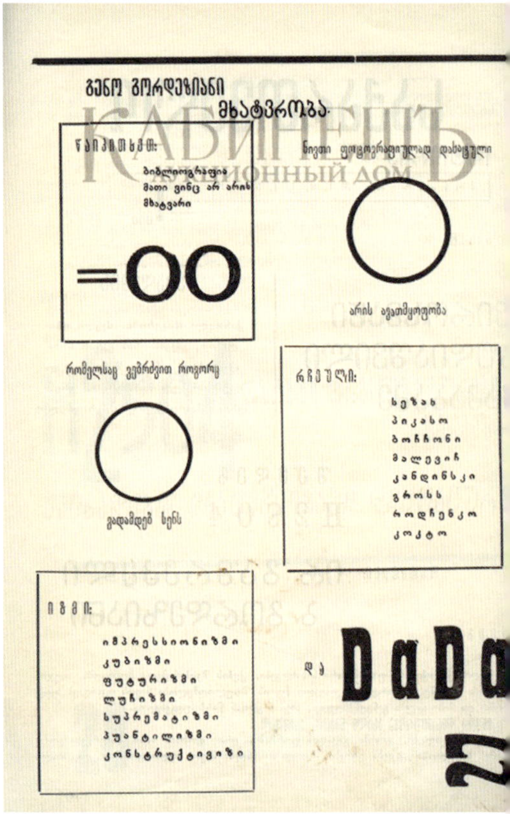

Kirill Zdanevich and H2SO4 Group
Cover of the journal *Literature and the Rest*, no. 1, 1924

Irakly Gamrekeli, Beno Gordeziani, H2SO4 Group
Illustrations for the journal *H2SO4*, no. 1, 1924

37. See "Decree on the Nothingists of Poetry," on pp. 295–297 of the present catalogue.

38. Jean-Paul Sartre, *Being and Nothingness: An Essay in Phenomenological Ontology*, trans. Hazel E. Barnes (New York: Citadel Press, 2001), 44.

39. Malevich's *Black Square* possesses the same quality, although this may be a purely subjective perception.

40. See Maria Granic-White, "The Theatrical Drive: The Unconscious Entering Consciousness," in *Consciousness, Theatre, Literature, and the Arts*, ed. Daniel Meyer-Dinkgräfe (Newcastle: Cambridge Scholars Publishing, 2012), 311–19. See also Herbert Marcuse, *Eros and Civilization: A Philosophical Inquiry into Freud* (Boston: Beacon Press, 1955).

41. This is a nontraditional interpretation of "here-Being" (*Dasein*, in Heidegger) in conjunction with Freud's "fort/da" ("here/there").

42. In the USSR, a grotesque form of Marxism was in power. Now, it's an equally grotesque capitalism.

> Life is heading toward the realization of our slogans:
> Write nothing!
> Read nothing!
> Say nothing!
> Print nothing![37]

Adopting Jean-Paul Sartre's position, one may surmise that Nothing is abstraction, since "one abstracts when one imagines separately that which cannot exist apart."[38] Many scholars link this term to Sartre's novel *Nausea*, written in 1938. A sensation of "nausea" does, in fact, arise when a person leans over an abyss or tries to peer into nothingness, into a vacuum. Nothingness is hypnotic.[39] Its contemplation, if such is possible, plunges us into a trance the panacea for which is "the thinging of nothing" (objectification of nothingness or its imaginary reification).

In his essay *Beyond the Pleasure Principle* (1920), Freud concludes that the death drive is balanced by the libido through their mutual participation in the children's game "fort-da." Maria Granic-White argues that one of the mechanisms that ensures the legitimate presence of the unconscious in the regions of consciousness is the "theatrical drive," which plays a fundamental role in the neutralization of the "death drive" (*Todestrieb*) and in the battle against Thanatos on the side of Eros.[40] For Heidegger, Being (*Dasein*) is always here (*Da*), while what is there (*Fort*) is nothingness.[41] Thus, Dada can be interpreted as a *porto franco* (a "customs-free zone" for the exchange of ideas and preferences between *Dasein* and *Fortsein*).[42]

In late 1924, Mayakovsky brought back from Paris a copy of Tzara's *7 Manifestos of Dada*, which he had received from Ilia Zdanevich with Tzara's autograph: "To Ylya Zdanevitch with all the sympathy of Tristan Tzaranov." If Nothingists managed to see this publication in Moscow, they would have recognized their kinship with Tzara's Dadaism. In its turn, Tzara's russification of his name in the autograph to Zdanevich indicates that the conceptual affinity between the author of *7 Manifestos* and those of *Dog's Box* was mutual.

5. Dada *à la Russe* in Paris

Ilia Zdanevich
Poster for Transrational Ball, 1923

Naum Granovsky
Cover of the book *Lidantiu as a Beacon* by Ilia Zdanevich, 1923

Double page of the book *Lidantiu as a Beacon* by Ilia Zdanevich, 1923

In one of his notes in 1922, Khlebnikov describes the Dadaists as followers of Russian futurists and suggests including Tzara and Ribemont-Dessaignes among "Presidents of Planet Earth." However, as the philosopher René Descartes noted, "I do not wish to know if people existed before me."[43] The Dadaists often followed this prescription. However, Tzara denied that Dadaism, cubism, and futurism had a common background (*baggage culturel*). In 1921, in the manifesto "Dada Raises Everything," Tzara challenged Marinetti—ten years after Khlebnikov and the other *budetliane,* who had been shocked by the Italian futurist's assertion (during his trip to Russia in January 1914) that "war is the only hygiene of the world." Tzara's comment about the birth of the "Parabola of Dada," with the repetition of words and specific sounds (such as "boom boom") echoes more than just the linguistic experiments of the transrationalists.[44] In the book *Critique and Clinic* (1993), Gilles Deleuze writes (with a nod to Henri Bergson and the philosophy of "vitality") that "stuttering is the language of becoming."[45] If so, the transrational speech of Khlebnikov, Kruchenykh, and Tufanov is cut from the same cloth.

Sharshun's and Iliazd's involvement in the Dada scene in Paris and their friendly contacts with Tzara are discussed in Margarita Tupitsyn's article elsewhere in the present catalogue. However, the view of Russia as a provincial empire (a sort of "colossus on clay feet") extended, to some degree, to the Russian Dadaists in Paris. Louis Aragon called Iliazd, in front of Tzara, "an embodiment of Russian stupidity," eliciting a burst of laughter from those present—to which one may respond with Khlebnikov's own verses.[46]

43. Sergei Sharshun attributes this expression to Descartes in his book *Dada (Kompiliatsiia)* (1922).

44. Tzara, *7 manifestov dada*, 26.

45. See Margarita Tupitsyn, "Photography as a Remedy for Stammering," in *Boris Mikhailov, Unfinished Dissertation* (Zurich: Scalo, 1998), 218–20.

46. Louis Aragon, *Projet d'histoire littéraire contemporaine (1922–1923)* (Paris: Digraphe, Mercure de France, 1994), 122–23.

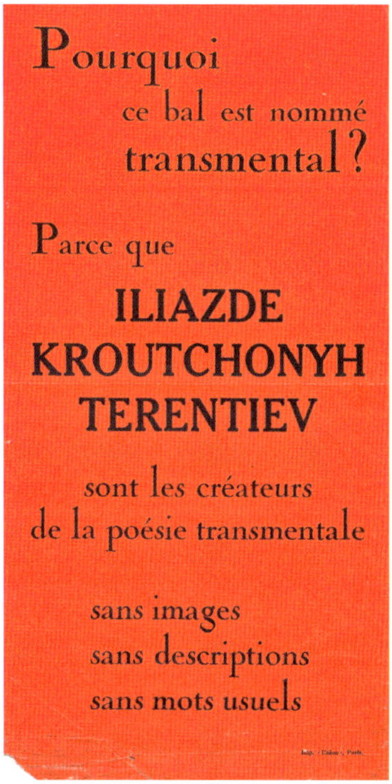
Pourquoi
ce bal est nommé
transmental ?
Parce que
ILIAZDE
KROUTCHONYH
TERENTIEV
sont les créateurs
de la poésie transmentale
sans images
sans descriptions
sans mots usuels

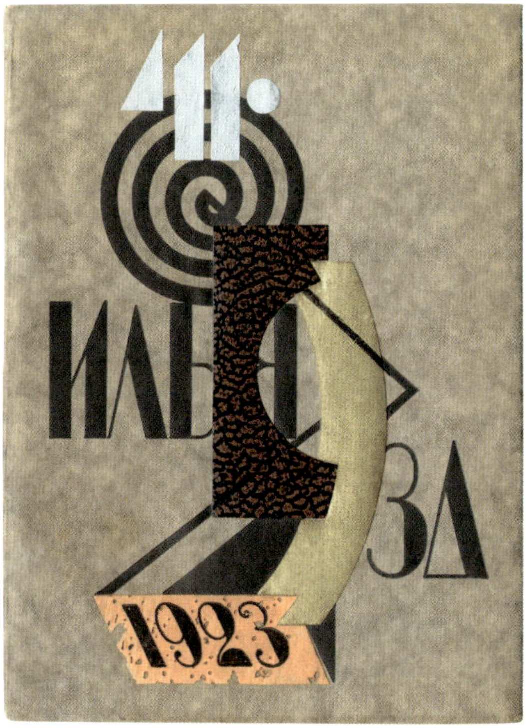
1923

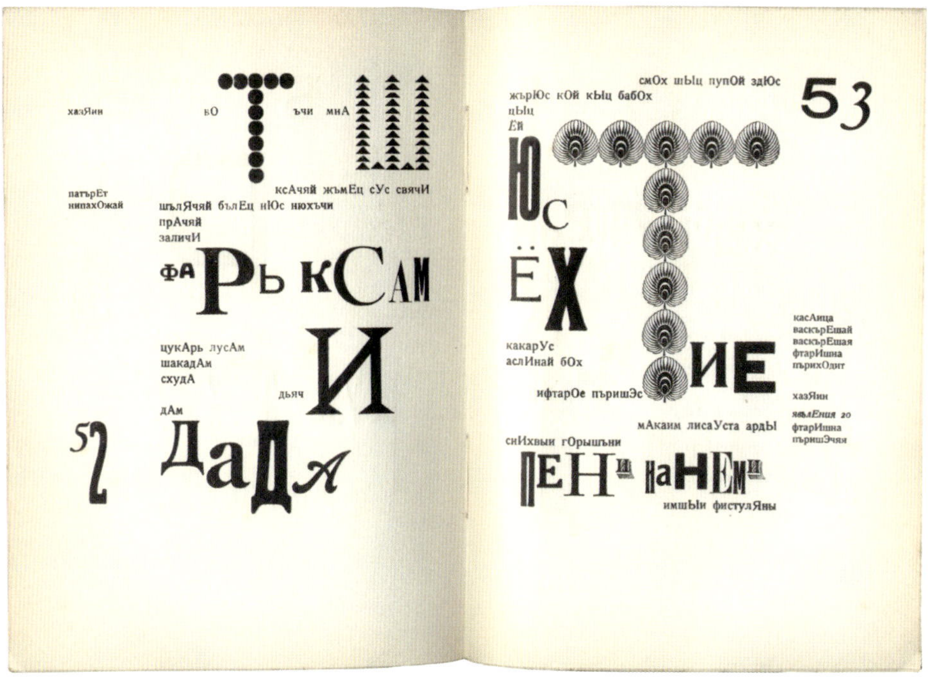
52
53

O, laugh, laughers! . . .
You who laugh with laughs, you who laugh it up laughishly . . .
Uplaugh, enlaugh, laughlings, laughlets . . .
O, laugh out, laughers![47]

In the West, Dada positioned itself as a political, social, and aesthetic demarche on the cultural stage—a demarche mediated by World War I and directed against the elite, using, moreover, the same slogans that have also become highly relevant in the twenty-first century: namely, desegregation and demarginalization. During the period when Dada was able to establish itself as a politically engaged context on the cultural stage in Western Europe, and to some extent in Russia, the slogans *égalité* and *diversité* began to be realized at an accelerated rate. The Zurich and Paris Dadaists were talented poets, so appeals and declarations performed by them (just like Mayakovsky's poetry, which toed the party line) had an effect on the public. The signifier is the foreskin (*praeputium*) of the signified, as one pediatrician put it. Everything that did not fit the definition of proto-Dada had to be negated and ridiculed. Be that as it may, Khlebnikov's "self-made word" and "self-made sound" are substantially different from the Dadaists' theatrical-politicized lexicon.[48] After all, even if a "*budetlianin*" is a proto-Dadaist of sorts, the victorious abolition of the past is not his "cup of tea."

Sentiments toward proletarian culture (as a replacement for the bourgeois one) echo the principle of the organization of chaos into meaningful strands. Members of the principal wing of Dadaism welcomed "the struggle of the proletariat," regarding it as a tool for demainstreaming bourgeois culture, its values, and its moral stereotypes. The German Dadaist Georg Gross referred to himself and his accomplices as followers of total nihilism who oppose attempts to objectify (or reify) nothingness, especially since to turn nothing into something is to "disguise negation without removing it."[49] Thus, for instance, Richard Huelsenbeck urged taking a Dadaist position even toward Dada itself, stopping or ignoring paroxysms of "systemic" attitude toward it. Dadaism is an anarchic mutiny against everything and everyone, including oneself—that is, against any "dispositives" established in our consciousness. The connection between them can be traced in Khlebnikov's early poem, "Monster Living in the Heights" (1908–1909):

Enormous arboreal monster, hanging
high with rump of shocking size,

grips a girl who fetched a pail of water,
rolling at him her cajoling eyes.
Diddled for a moment, she's an apple
on the branches of his shaggy arms.
Enormous monster—rather awful,
really—lolls back and laps. Life has its charms.[50]

Leonid Livak writes, "until 1924, the literary life of the Russian artistic colony [in Paris] had three characteristic traits: (1) the absence of anti-Soviet attitudes among the organizers and members of art groups; (2) the strong popularity in that milieu of the Soviet avant-garde in literature and the visual arts; and (3) close ties to the French Dadaist movement, stemming from the involvement in it of Sergei Sharshun, Valentin Parnakh, and Sergei Romov; their efforts to introduce the young exiles to the Dada aesthetic were supported by Ilia Zdanevich, the veteran of a scandalous avant-garde, who arrived in Paris in November 1921."[51] Sharshun, who had been in Paris since 1920, became a participant in "the 1921 Dada Season," contributed to *391* and Picabia's Cacodylic Eye, and befriended Tzara.[52] He was immediately put to work writing manifestos. One of them (undated) has been preserved in Tzara's archive; it reads, in part, "Art, having filled its belly . . . has birthed the proletarian. . . . Russia is infected with precision. Turn your eyes into a chronometer. Chop off the pharmacist's brains. The hand will knock. The foot will chase and catch up."[53] In 1921, Sharshun published a Dadaist poem, "The Motionless Crowd" (Foule immobile), and Tzara not only reprinted it but began to use the author's name under various proclamations. Jakobson believed that the support for Tzara's group among the Russian

47. Fragment from Velimir Khlebnikov, "Incantation of Laughter" (1908–1909), in *Collected Works of Velimir Khlebnikov*, vol. 3, *Selected Poems*, trans. Paul Schmidt, ed. Ronald Vroom (Cambridge, MA: Harvard University Press, 1997), 30.

48. Michael Fried's reproach of surrealists for theatricality can also be traced to Duchamp's *Rrose Sélavy*, *Étant donnés*, and Dada in general, which (while laying on its death bed) thought surrealism (with its theatrical approach to the so-called imagoes) was worthy enough to succeed it.

49. Sartre, *Being and Nothingness*, 5.

50. Velimir Khlebnikov, "Monster Living in the Heights" (1908–1909), in *Collected Works of Velimir Khlebnikov*, 3:31.

51. L. Livak, "Geroicheskie vremena molodoi zarubezhnoi poezii," in *Literaturnyi avangard russkogo Parizha. Istoriia. Khronika. Antologiia. Dokumenty*, ed. L. Livak and A. Ustinov (Moscow: OGI, 2014), 16.

52. Sharshun and his countrymen the journalist and critic Romov and the poet, translator, and dancer Parnakh were also active participants in various Dada events, including the trial of Maurice Barrés.

53. Dossier Tzara, 847. See Sharshun's manifesto in Livak and Ustinov, *Literaturnyi avangard russkogo Parizha*, 24.

diaspora in Paris was influenced by Dadaism's proximity to the aesthetics and the anarchist aspirations of Russian futurism.[54]

At the scandalous Dada soirée at the Galerie Montaigne on June 10, 1921, Parnakh gave a demonstration of the poetry of dance while lying on his back. "I stamp my ribs in perfect score," he later wrote in a poem about the episode. Livak notes that Sharshun, Romov, and Parnakh became "the main organizers of the young exiles" from the "land of the Soviets"—poets and artists who had emigrated to France.[55] Parnakh, Romov, and Sharshun undoubtedly kept their Russian colleagues up to date on the happenings in the French avant-garde, including the "Dada season." For Sharshun, contacts with the Dadaists made sense not only in his capacity as an artist but also as a writer. Besides participating in exhibitions, he belonged to the Montparnasse associations the Chamber of Poets and Gotarapak, the first of which was founded by Parnakh and the second by Dovid Knut, and also to Romov and Iliazd's group, Across (Cherez). The idea of starting the latter group arose on November 24, 1922, at a banquet organized by Iliazd in honor of Mayakovsky, who was visiting Paris and was directly connected to the upcoming launch of *Lef* (January 1923), with which the Across group was going to be in close cooperation.[56] Besides Iliazd, Sharshun, Romov, Parnakh, Boris Poplavsky, Vladimir Pozner, and Mark Talov, members of the Paris avant-garde—Paul Éluard, Ribemont-Dessaignes, Tzara, and others—were also involved in the group. Its modus operandi included art exhibitions, open discussions, and performances. Sharshun's poetry evening was held at the Chameleon café on December 21, 1921. He himself called his style

Ilia Zdanevich
Poster for Ilia Zdanevich's lecture "41°," Paris, May 12, 1922

54. See Roman Jakobson, "Letters from the West. Dada," on pp. 310–313 of the present catalogue.

55. Livak and Ustinov, *Literaturnyi avangard russkogo Parizha*, 37.

56. In the first issue of *Lef*, Nikolai Chuzhak asserts, "there comes a moment when a real life, saturated with art to the brim, will spew it as unnecessary." *Lef*, no. 1 (1923): 12–39.

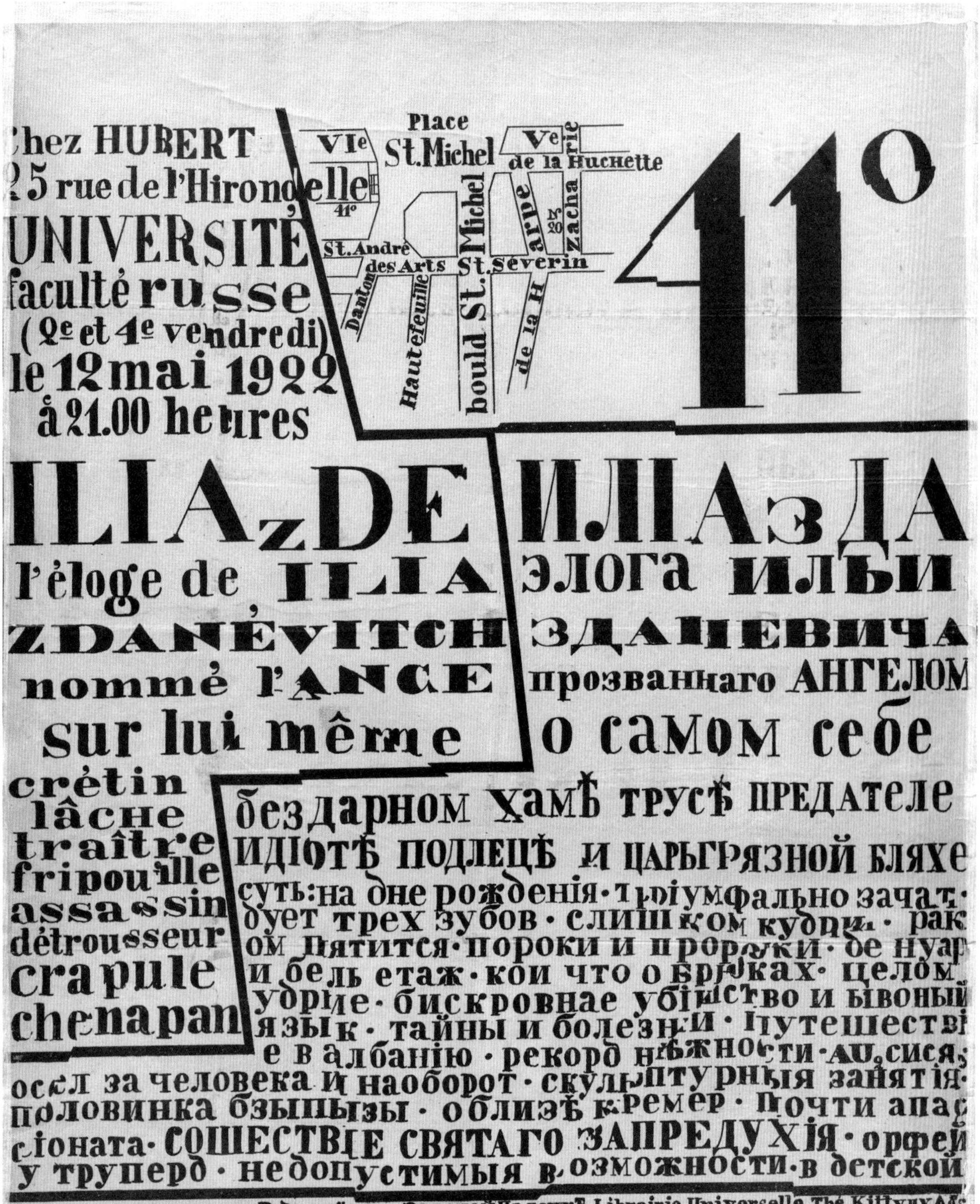
Chez HUBERT
25 rue de l'Hirondelle
UNIVERSITÉ
faculté russe
(2e et 4e vendredi)
le 12 mai 1922
à 21.00 heures
Place
St.Michel
VIe
Ve
de la Huchette
Hirondelle
41o
St.André des Arts
Danton
Hautefeuille
bould St.Michel
St.Séverin
de la Harpe
Zacharie
No 20
41o
ILIAzDE
l'éloge de ILIA ZDANÉVITCH nommé l'ANGE sur lui même
crétin
lâche
traître
fripouille
assassin
détrousseur
crapule
chenapan
ИЛIАЗДА
элога ильи здаНевича прозваннаго АНГЕЛОМ о самом себе
бездарном хамѣ трусѣ предателе идiотѣ подлецѣ и царьгрязной бляхе
суть: на днe рожденiя · трiумфально зачат · бует трех зубов · слишком кудри · раком пятится · пороки и пророки · бе нуар и бель етаж · кои что о брюках · целом, убрiе · бискровнае убiйство и ьвоный язык · тайны и болезни · путешествiе в албанiю · рекорд нежности · аu, сися; осел за человека и наоборот · скульптурныя занятiя · половинка бзыпызы · облизѣ кремер · почти апассiоната · СОШЕСТВIЕ СВЯТАГО ЗАПРЕДУХIЯ · орфей у труперд · недопустимыя возможности · в детской
билеты у Поволоцкаго, Родштейна, в Зеленой Палочкѣ, Librairie Universelle, The Kitty и у Ага

of poetry "Dada-lir-kan"—lyricism, a Dadaist-style chirping. Breton, Philippe Soupault, and Man Ray attended the event.

The Chamber of Poets also included Poplavsky, one of the most brilliant members of the Russian diaspora in Paris. In the early and mid-1920s, he was in regular contact with Iliazd and other Dadaists and later authored the *Dadafonia (1924–1927)* anthology, which collected "astounding examples of Russian Dada."[57] Poplavsky, who died in Paris in 1935, summarized his impression of 1920s Europe in, "Pity for Europe" (1930):

> Europe, Europe,
> your gardens are crowded.
> Ophelia reads the newspaper about it
> in a white white taxi,
> and Hamlet in the tram dreams
> of going free under the wheels
> with the smile of a snail
> in a deadly transit.[58]

Livak was correct when he noted that the "orientation toward the mixing of the arts (Everythingism) was no accident. The same was done by French Dadaists when they presented astonished audiences with hybrid shows whose content included literature, theater, music, sculpture, painting, graphic art, and dance. Thus, Romov, the critic and journalist, works 'outside his field,' organizing an exhibition of Russian artists and sculptors; Poplavsky and Sharshun are torn between poetry and painting; Parnakh prides himself on combining literature, dance, and jazz music in their creative work."[59] From 1922 to 1923, Romov published the literary journal *Strike* (*Udar*), whose editorial board included Lunacharsky and Ilya Ehrenburg. In 1928, Romov returned

57. Boris Poplavskii, *Dadafoniia: Neizvestnye stikhotvoreniia, 1924–1927*, ed. I. Zhelvakova and S. Kudriavtsev (Moscow: Gileia, 1999).

58. First printed in *FLAGI* (*Chisla*, Paris, 1931); translated from Russian by Victor Tupitsyn. The last lines of this fragment echo the death of a character named Berlioz, who was run over by a streetcar in Mikhail Bulgakov's novel *The Master and Margarita*, on which Bulgakov was working around the same time.

59. Livak and Ustinov, *Literaturnyi avangard russkogo Parizha*, 37.

60. Romov was arrested in 1936 and executed in 1939.

61. Sergei Romov, "Ot dada k siurrealizmu," *Vestnik inostrannoi literatury*, no. 3 (1929): 178–208.

62. Livak and Ustinov, *Literaturnyi avangard russkogo Parizha*, 90.

63. Iliazd's confession reflected the dominant attitude in Russian-speaking literary and artistic circles (in Paris), with the exception of Dmitry Merezhkovsky, Ivan Bunin, Vladislav Khodasevich, and other writers who were regarded as "Orthodox." The scandal at the Theatre Michel was instrumental in drawing attention to the fact that agonistic dialogues eventually turn into antagonism, without which cultural life is doomed to stagnation. In this context, antagonism, which had to a large extent been adopted as the modus operandi of the Dada movement, played a healing role. To be precise, Dada was a "Pharmakon."

64. An allusion to the prerevolutionary Russian anthem, "God Save the Tsar." The artist Vagrich Bakhchanian came up with this line regarding Tzara. The irony is based on the similarity (in Russian pronunciation) between Tsar and Tzara. The poet Aleksandr Vvedensky, who used the same line as his drinking toast, was arrested because his accusers had no idea he probably meant "Tzara" (not "Tsar").

65. An allusion to Harald Szeemann's exhibition *When Attitudes Become Form*, Bern Kunsthalle, 1969.

to the USSR.[60] His essay "From Dada to Surrealism," is one of the most reliable primary sources.[61]

Iliazd's role in the Dada scene in Paris is beyond any doubt. He admitted his inability to foresee the turn of events, however, the culmination that, in his words, "put an end to many things."[62] That culmination was the soirée *The Bearded Heart*, organized by Iliazd and Romov at the Théâtre Michel in July 1923. A brawl (or "hand-to-hand combat") between followers of Breton (i.e., surrealists) and Tzara's supporters broke out, signifying the end of Dada. The Russian group was on Tzara's side. Recalling this later, Iliazd admitted that the *Bearded Heart* blow-up showed to what extent we were deluded in thinking that the union of left-wing forces in art had a future.[63]

6. "God Save the Tzara": Dada and the Aesthetic of Funerals[64]

The incident at *The Bearded Heart* soirée did not prevent Breton and Tzara from mending their relationship—not immediately, but seven years later and under the banner of surrealism. Every banner has its front and its reverse side. The aesthetic of funerals and the melancholy trance are an inalienable part of modern art, but now, in contrast to Dada, eschatologically oriented artistic practices and functions risk becoming a marathon that generates more and more new cycles and repetitions, until the funerary format and our attitude toward it "become form."[65] The funeral services industry and the art world connected to it create a suitable environment filled with "melancholy objects" à la Marcel Proust or Walter Benjamin—that is, ones directed toward the wistfully "lost time" and at the same time directed forward, but with one's back to the past, as it were (if one considers "back-of-the-neck vision"). That's the eschatological context and the soil on which the new aesthetics will blossom in abundance. By "will blossom," I refer to something "always already blossoming" and, in some sense, not dependent on temporality.

In the cultural space, Dadaism is a kind of death drive, and in that sense it is not without its appeal, especially when combined with the

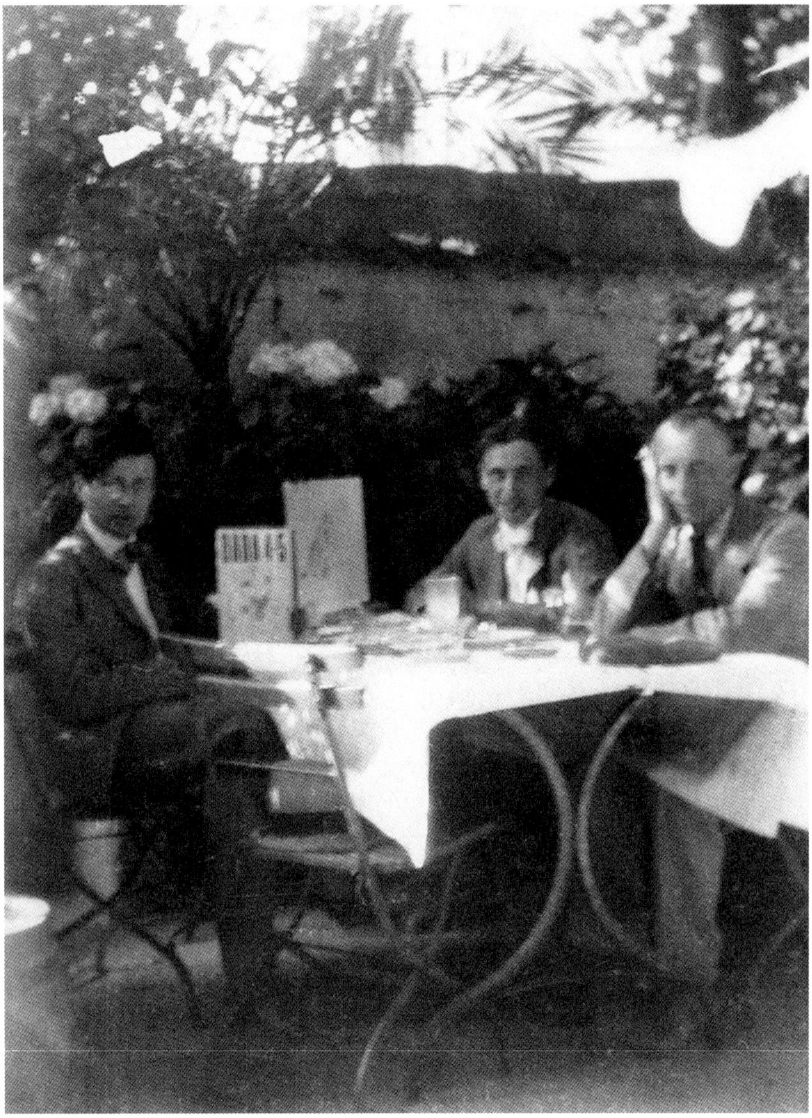

Ivan Puni's scrapbook
Tristan Tzara (left) with two unknowns, ca. 1922

Sergei Sharshun
Tristan Tzara, ca. 1921–1922

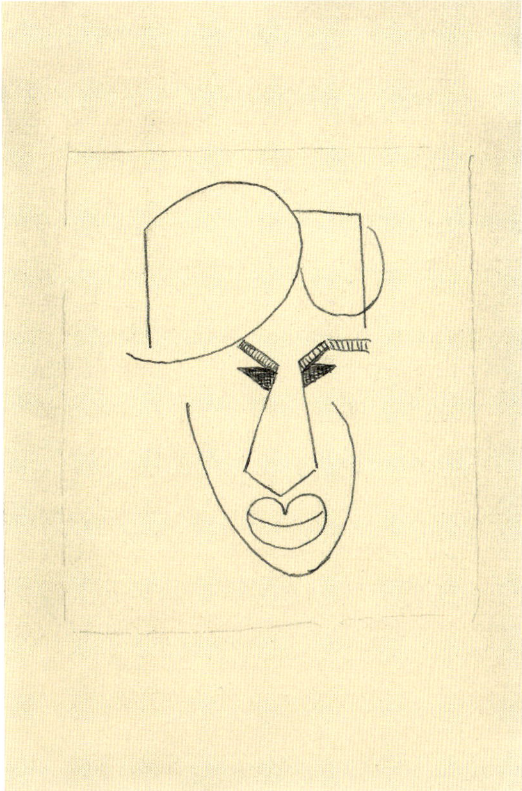

"theatrical drive" that balances the relationship between Eros and Thanatos. And if that is the case, theatricality in moderate doses is still necessary for visual art—at least so it can "seem" alive. This might already have become a part of the postmodern cultural landscape, especially since nostalgia for Dadaism manifested itself in the second half of the twentieth century. In response to the question, "Which exercises of the symbolic function should get top billing, the verbal-audial or the visual?" I will note that for as long as our consciousness is constantly oscillating between *seeing speech* and *listening to the gaze*, the insistence on their segregation is presumptuous. Yet, their power over our lives and appropriation of the "capital" they accumulate create reasons for the "expropriation of expropriators."

Of special interest are situations in which not means but codes are appropriated. The collection of Khlebnikov's prose works includes a chapter titled "May upon the Gravestone" (1904), which says "there are quantities with the alteration of which the blue of the bluebell will . . . after passing through ruptures unknown to us humans, transform into the sound of a cuckoo's song or a child's cry, and become that sound. At the same time, changing continuously, it will form a sort of single-row multiplicity all the points of which, except those near the first and the last, will remain in the realm of unknowable sensations, as though they were from a different world."[66] No one who has read *A Thousand Plateaus* (1980) by Deleuze and Félix Guattari, can fail to see in Khlebnikov's words an analogy to the "rhizome"—production without filiation, identification, imitation, or regressive-progressive tendencies.[67] That the bluebell and the cuckoo become a wasp and an orchid in Deleuze and Guattari makes no difference.

The seminal traveling exhibition *Dada: Zurich, Berlin, Hannover, Cologne, New York, Paris* (2005–2006), also warrants mention. The most striking thing about it (besides the high quality of the works presented at the exhibition) was the "partiality" of negation: having fallen out of love with art, the Dadaists remained captives of the creative imperative, or creativity. The formulas "Dada is nothing" and "*Creo ergo sum*" seem not to contradict each other in the slightest, especially since the Dadaist effect can be achieved regardless of working method.

Of some interest is the link between Dada and utopia. Consider Ernst Bloch, who in conversation with Theodor Adorno described utopia as a project meant to complete the creation of an incomplete world.[68] Or to create it "backward," which is in fact the main goal-setting of Dadaism, its endgame (τη῀λος and έσχατος). In his memoirs, the music scholar Leonid Sabaneev notes that, as early as 1912, Aleksandr Scriabin had theorized about pauses in music and spoke of the "magical" nature of such "emptiness." "It is not impossible that someday the music of total silence will have its turn," Scriabin predicted.[69] That John Cage knew of Sabaneev's book is doubtful; nonetheless, his *4′33″* and *Waiting* (1952) are a realization of the same ideas.[70]

Recurrences of antiart in artists' visual practices manifested themselves in the postwar culture of the 1950s and 1960s—first in the language games of the absurdists, then in the Situationist International (Debord and others), although these were merely episodic "victories of nonsense over surrealism." Once minimalism and conceptualism entered the scene, forms of contact with nothingness became institutionalized. Cage was able to "resurrect" Duchamp, whom many had forgotten, and together, with a joint effort, they were able to influence the young generation of neo-Dadaists united (by George Maciunas) in the Fluxus group.[71] To dot the *i*, I will end by mentioning the frivolous portrait of Joseph Stalin painted by Pablo Picasso at Aragon's request in 1953. When the portrait was printed in a newspaper, it caused a scandal that Tzara himself would have envied.

66. Velimir Khlebnikov, *Proza* (Moscow: Sovremennik, 1990).

67. Gilles Deleuze and Félix Guattari, *A Thousand Plateaus* (1980), trans. Brian Massumi (Minneapolis: University of Minnesota Press, 1987).

68. Bloch and Adorno argue that "the essential function of utopia is a critique of what is present" (Bloch) and that "utopia is essentially in the determined negation of that which merely is" (Adorno). Ernst Bloch and Theodor W. Adorno, "Something's Missing," in *The Utopian Function of Art and Literature: Selected Essays by Ernst Bloch*, trans. Jack Zipes and Frank Mecklenburg (Cambridge, MA: MIT Press, 1988), 12.

69. L. L. Sabaneev, *Skriabin* (Moscow: Gosudarstvennoe izdatelstvo, 1923).

70. Long before Cage, Malevich had the opportunity to "reach" Nothing in his black and white squares. Thanks to these works, Nothingness finally gained the status of context and ceased to be merely a subtext in the cultural space.

71. In 1981, I befriended Jean Brown, the collector of Dada and Fluxus art. She lived in Springfield, Massachusetts, where Margarita Tupitsyn and I visited her to see her collection and share information about contemporary Russian art, including conceptualism and APTART (collective art projects in Moscow, 1982–1984). Jean was the first to underscore their affinity with Fluxus, which she considered an heir to Dada. In 1982, Jean gave us a copy of memoirs authored by Leokadia Maciunas, George Maciunas's mother, and written in her native Russian. Years later, we published this opus in the Saint Petersburg magazine *Kabinet #8* (1994). In 1997 this text was published in English under the aegis of the Stedelijk Museum Amsterdam. See Leokadia Maciunas, "My Son," in *Kabinet, an Anthology*, ed. Victor Mazin and Olesia Turkina, with a postscript by Margarita and Victor Tupitsyn (Amsterdam: Stedelijk Museum, 1997), 149–66.

HUMOR AS PARODY, ECCENTRISM, AND SATIRE IN SOVIET FILM AFTER WORLD WAR I

Natasha Kurchanova

Varvara Stepanova
Cover of the journal *Cine-Photo*, no. 3, 1922

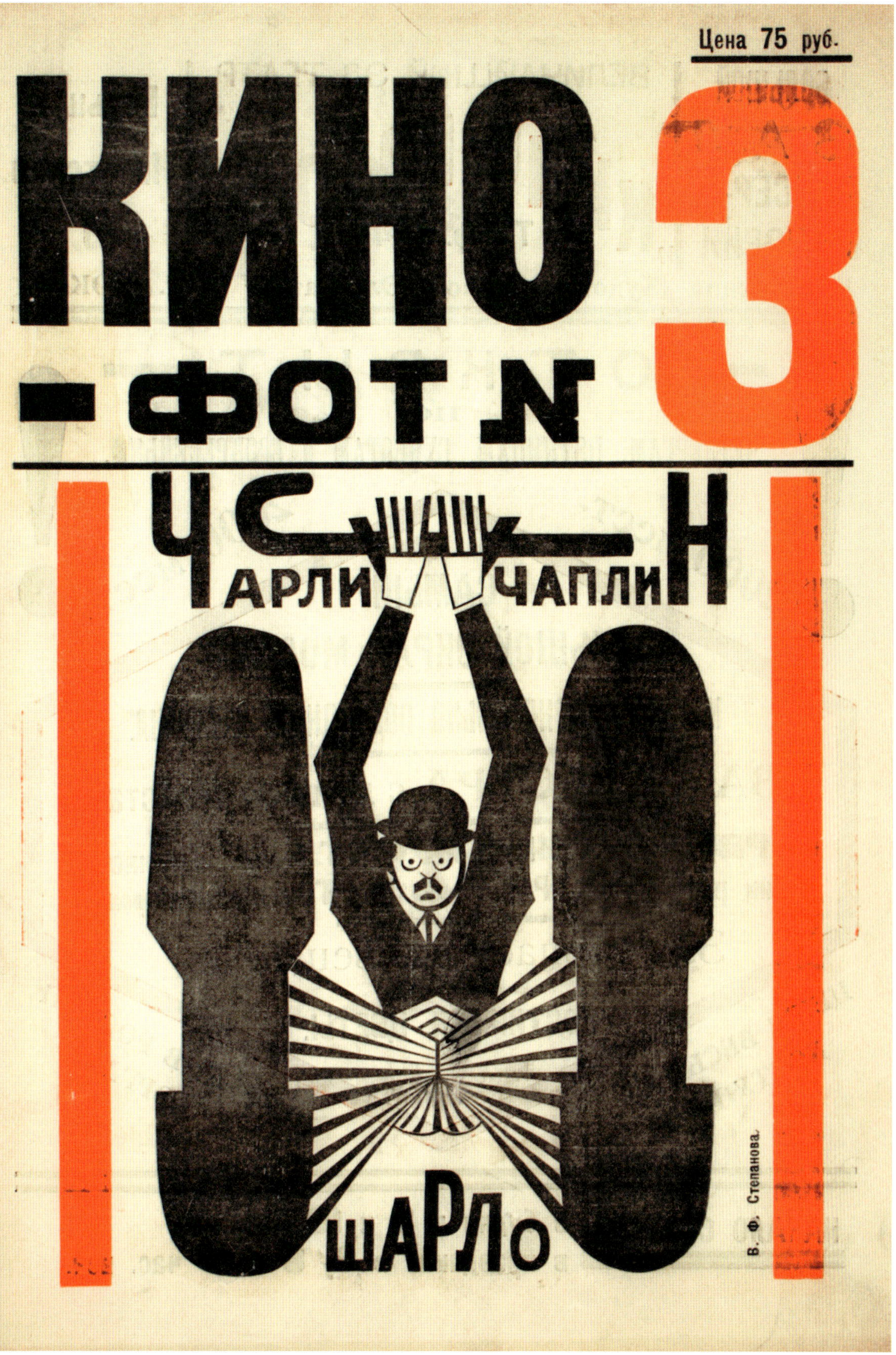
Цена 75 руб.
КИНО
-ФОТ N 3
ЧАРЛИ ЧАПЛИН
ШАРЛО
В. Ф. Степанова.

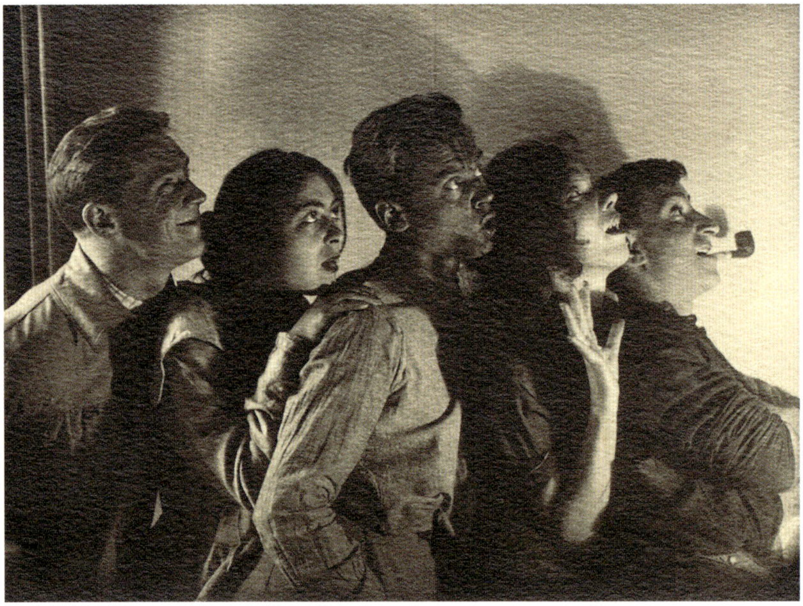

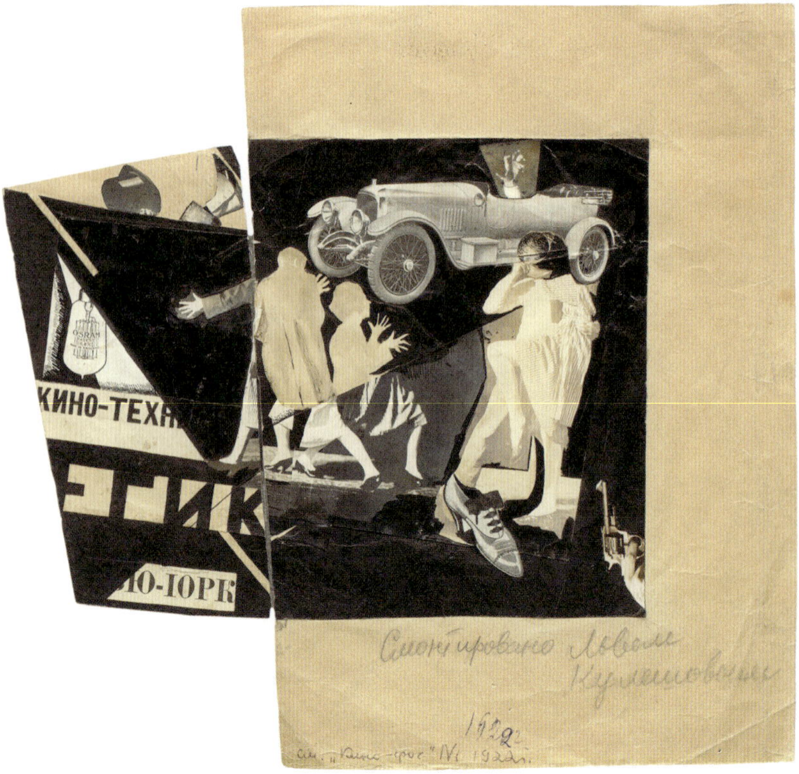
КИНО-ТЕХН
Ю-ЮРК

Lev Kuleshov's Workshop
Boris Barnet, Valentina Lopatina, Vladimir Fogel, Aleksandra Khokhlova, and Petr Galadzhev (left to right), 1923

Lev Kuleshov
Design for the journal *Cine-Photo*, no. 1, 1922

"Engineering of art is based on the spirit of gaiety," wrote Viktor Shklovsky, an influential critic of emergent Soviet film and a leading figure in the Russian formalist circle.[1] Although explicitly referring to Soviet director Sergei Eisenstein, Shklovsky's insight can be applied to much of avant-garde art in Russia. This essay considers explicit manifestations of this "spirit of gaiety" in the works of Eisenstein, Lev Kuleshov, and other prominent filmmakers in Bolshevik Russia, such as the founders of the Factory of the Eccentric Actor (FEKS), Leonid Trauberg and Grigory Kozintsev, who made their first films during the period covered by the exhibition. Because the exhibition explores the links between Dada and the Russian art of the period, these films serve as the basis for investigating possible crosscurrents that may have reached pioneering Soviet directors in their search for a new film language. After all, many Russian artists and critics visited Berlin in the early 1920s, when the Dada movement was gaining momentum. Shklovsky lived in Berlin from 1922 until 1923 and may p. 137
have been aware of Dada's existence through his friend Ivan Puni, whom he knew from Russia and who was close to the Der Sturm circle.[2] This essay manifestly excludes Dziga Vertov, the creator of the mesmerizing documentary newsreel *Cine-Truth* (*Kinopravda*), now canonized as the first instance of constructivism in film.[3] Despite an apparent "spirit of gaiety" pervading Vertov's production, Shklovsky criticized it at the time for Vertov's resistance to introducing elements of plot construction in his films, which corresponded to the lack of hints of psychological conflict in his productions.[4] While creating their own versions of a film language, Eisenstein, Kuleshov, and FEKS retained the seeds of plot construction

1. Viktor Shklovskii, "Eizenshtein" (1927), in *Za sorok let: stat'i o kino* (Moscow: Iskusstvo, 1965), 74. I thank Margarita Tupitsyn, Stuart Liebman, and Naum Kleiman for their help and advice on this article.

2. Shklovsky writes about Puni in *Zoo or Letters Not about Love*, trans. and ed. Richard Sheldon (Ithaca: Cornell University Press, 1971), 55–58.

3. *Cine-Truth* was produced by Vertov, Elizaveta Svilova, and Mikhail Kaufman throughout the 1920s. The trio made twenty-three issues of the cinematic journal, the first of which was shown to the public on May 21, 1922. See Jay Leyda, *Kino: A History of the Russian and Soviet Film* (New York: Collier Books, 1973), 161.

4. Shklovskii, "Vertov," in *Za sorok let*, 70–73, Vertov's gaiety came from the gut, expressing uninhibited energy and a joy of life, without the element of self-reflection and parody apparent in films in this essay.

through their pervasive use of such specific forms of humor as parody, eccentrism, and satire, rendering their work more acceptable to Shklovsky as an expression of cinematic art.[5]

On the larger scale of the development of the film industry in Russia, the avant-garde had to compete with the popularity of commercial films made on the foreign market, Hollywood in particular. The Russian Revolution and the concomitant end of World War I marked the beginning of a period of intensive growth for the Soviet film industry. The Bolsheviks understood film's enormous potential for propaganda, entertainment, and, ultimately, control of the masses, and issued foundational decrees in support of the new art form. From October 1917 until Vladimir Lenin's death in January 1924, the Bolshevik government nationalized the film industry, established film schools, and set up a rudimentary production and distribution network for foreign and Soviet films.[6] This period coincided with the flourishing of constructivism and suprematism in Russia and of the Dada movement in the West. Whereas the influence of the former on Western art has been investigated at length—including, for example, considerations of the great interest Western artists such as George Grosz, John Heartfield, and Hans Richter displayed toward Vladimir Tatlin and Kazimir Malevich—only recently have scholars attempted to examine the inroads Dada made in Russia.[7] Results of this investigation appear inconclusive. Russia at the time was an inspiring and emerging force, which intrigued and captivated the imagination of the avant-garde in the West. However, this fascination worked only at a distance. Upon a closer look, the once-revered Russians disappointed the Westerners.[8] The reaction the other way around was similar: To the Russians, the impressive artistic achievements of the West often looked like a form of subterfuge.[9]

In the sphere of performance, including theater and film, a similar dynamic of mutual attraction and repulsion defied a common ground of relationship according to the degree of "radical criticism, nihilistic denial, and abstraction in aesthetics."[10] Seemingly similar explorations of "strategies, conditions of formation and usage of literary and artistic languages and meaning on paradigmatic . . . and syntagmatic . . . levels," frequently compared to a child-like, naive attitude toward the world, ran against fundamental contextual differences in which the artists were operating.[11] When Hugo Ball, Emmy Hennings, and Tristan Tzara sang, played musical instruments, recited poetry, or dressed in wild costumes in Zurich's Cabaret Voltaire shortly after the outbreak of World War I, they opposed the dominant capitalist culture by provoking it, thereby distancing themselves from the violence and philistinism of the world outside.[12] However, because they could not extricate themselves from this culture, their humor tended toward its wry variant: irony. The protest by Dada artists was largely ironic because it both ridiculed and elevated the artists as representatives of capitalist culture who rebelled against its aggression. Even though the advent of the New Economic Policy in 1922, which gave a green light to private enterprise, put a stop to the unfettered dominance of Vertov's ideological euphoria, in Soviet Russia artists and filmmakers invented other devices to promote the dominant Soviet proletarian and peasant culture, making fun of only those elements that were extrinsic to it, such as the bourgeois, kulaks, or ignorant foreigners. At that time, Soviet artists were not part of the culture they despised; on the contrary, they were building a culture that could be sustained and admired. Instead of irony, they used parody, eccentrism, and satire to laugh at the common enemy, the philistine bourgeois.[13]

Glumov's Diary (1923) was Eisenstein's first film. p. 213 He made it as a cinematic insert into his theatrical adaptation of Nikolai Ostrovsky's comedy *Enough Stupidity in Every Wise Man*, after having studied the craft of theatrical production with the fabled director Vsevolod Meyerhold. The production was staged at the Proletkult Theater. At the time of Eisenstein's training, Meyerhold elaborated his theory of biomechanics, which his talented student highly admired. In opposition to the classical acting technique, which called for "inward," nearly indiscernible feelings and emotions, biomechanics emphasized theatrical pantomime—physical movements and facial expressions that were controlled and carefully rehearsed by each actor for each character. In Meyerhold's system of biomechanics, the

5. Shklovsky, "Kuda shagaet Dziga Vertov?," in *Antologiia russkogo formalizma*, ed. Sergei Ushakov (Moscow-Ekaterinburg: Kabinetnyi uchenyi, 2016), 1:247. On Shklovsky and the development of his theories, see also Il'ia Kalinin, "Viktor Shklovskii kak priem," in ibid., 63–106.

6. All of this was set in motion by a decree Lenin signed on August 27, 1919. For details on the Bolsheviks' nationalization of the Russian film industry, see Vance Kepley Jr., "Soviet Cinema and State Control: Lenin's Nationalization Decree Reconsidered," *Journal of Film and Video* 42, no. 2 (Summer 1990): 3–14.

7. Tomáš Glanc, "Dada izdali," in *"Vy gniete, a pozhar nachalsia": reseptsiia dadaizma v Rossii*, ed. Tomáš Glanc (Moscow: Gosudarstvennyi muzei im. V. V. Maiakovskogo, 2016), 7–23. See also Margarita Tupitsyn, *Malevich and Film* (New Haven: Yale University Press, 2002), 55–69; and Timothy Benson and Aleksandra Shatskikh, "Malevich and Richter: An Indeterminate Encounter," *October* 143 (Winter 2013): 52–68.

8. Glanc, "Dada izdali," 10.

9. Ibid. See also Roman Jakobson, "Letters from the West. Dada," on pp. 310–313 of the present catalogue; and Sergei Sharshun, "My Participation in the French Dada Movement," on pp. 314–319 of the present catalogue.

10. Glanc, "Dada izdali," 8.

11. Ibid.; and Grigorii Bammel', "Dada Almanach," in *"Vy gniete, a pozhar nachalsia,"* ed. Glanc, 40.

12. Hans Richter, "Cabaret Voltaire: Its Members and Collaborators," in *Dada: Art and Anti-Art* (London: Thames & Hudson, 1965), 19.

13. As several writers noticed, the differing approaches of Dada and Russian artists were determined by their relationship to reality. Speaking on behalf of the Dadaists, Georges Ribemont-Dessaignes described their attitude as "refusal to believe in the sameness of things," wreaking havoc on the idea of logical causation. "One and one becomes two only when they want it." Zhorzh Ribmon-Diussen', "Umer li Dada?," in *"Vy gniete, a pozhar nachalsia,"* ed. Glanc, 45. On the Russians' side, Abram Efros emphasized the difference between Velimir Khlebnikov's life-affirming speech creation (*rechetvorchestvo*)—based on live tradition and having as a goal revival of the Russian language—and Tzara's nihilistic "je-m'en-foutisme." Abram Efros, "Dada i Dadaizm," in ibid., 83. Glanc explained the Russians' reluctance to accept Dada as their own by the latter's "refusal of the category of truth," which seemed deficient to the Russians, who, despite their seeming destruction of history and tradition, were always returning to them, whether under the guise of the truth of abstraction, novelty, or beyond-sense reality. Glanc, "Dada izdali," 18.

"psychology" of a character had to be clearly visible in the actor's physical appearance, so that the aesthetic "excitation" could be conveyed to the viewer: "All psychological states are determined by specific psychological processes. By correctly resolving the nature of his state physically, the actor reaches the point where he experiences the excitation, which communicates itself to the spectator and induces him to share in the actor's performance. It is this excitation that is the very essence of an actor's art. From a sequence of physical positions and situations there arise 'points of excitation,' which are informed with some particular emotion."[14] Eisenstein had a chance to become familiar with the technique not only in its theoretical but its practical aspects. In 1922, he witnessed rehearsals of Henrik Ibsen's *A Doll's House* in Meyerhold's theater, and he assisted his teacher in the staging of Aleksandr Sukhovo-Kobylin's play *The Death* p. 119 *of Tarelkin*, with sets designed by Varvara Stepanova.

After leaving Meyerhold and embarking on his own path, Eisenstein incorporated his teacher's emphasis on active outward expression and movement into his own performing theory, called "montage of attractions." In pique to his teacher's devotion to theater as an art form, Eisenstein's theory of action took a sharply ideological turn, calling for the overthrow of "'the values of the past'" and "the abolition of the very institution of the theatre as such, replacing it with a show-place for achievements in the theatre or with an instrument for raising the standard of training of the masses in their day-to-day life."[15] From the beginning of his independent career, then, Eisenstein's aesthetics aimed at a practical goal: mobilization of the masses in support of the Bolshevik cause. The "attractions" unfolding on stage would be "any aggressive aspect of the theatre; that is, any element of the theatre that subjects the spectator to a sensual or psychological impact, experimentally regulated and mathematically calculated to produce in him certain emotional shocks which, when placed in their proper sequence within the totality of the production, become the only means that enable the spectator to perceive the ideological side of what is being demonstrated—the ultimate ideological conclusion."[16]

Consequently, the twenty-five attractions that constituted Eisenstein's production of Ostrovsky's play ranged from narrational soliloquys to musical-eccentric acts to clownery, farcical scenes, and singing performances. *Glumov's Diary* was screened near the beginning of the performance; it followed the first attraction where Glumov (played by Grigory Aleksandrov, Eisenstein's assistant at the time and later a prominent director in his own right) presents the audience with a story of his

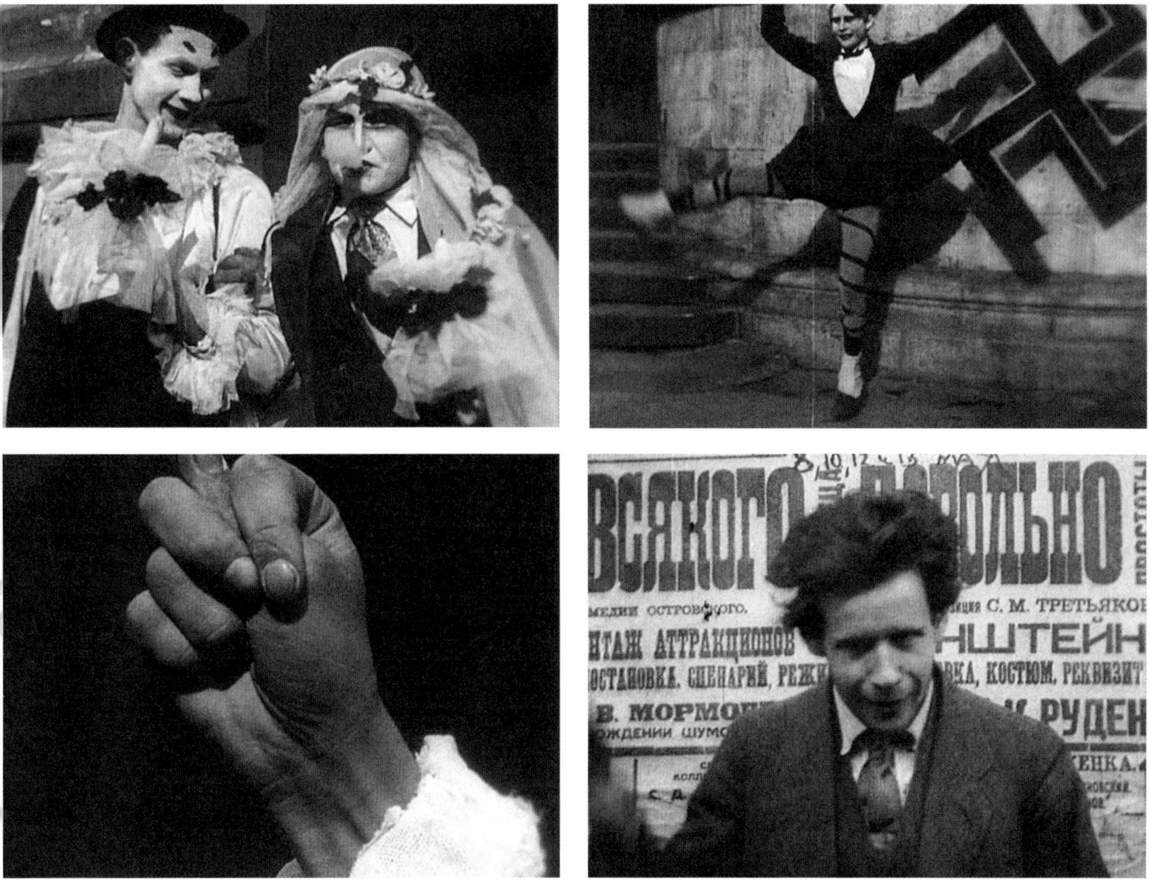

Sergei Eisenstein
Glumov's Diary (conceived as part of the adaptation of Aleksandr Ostrovsky's 1868 comedy *Enough Stupidity in Every Wise Man*, which he realized at the Proletcult Theater), 1923

14. Meyerhold's lecture on biomechanics, cited in V. Fedorov, "Akter budushchego," *Ermitazh*, no. 10 (1922).

15. Sergei Eisenstein, "Montage of Attractions for *Enough Stupidity in Every Wiseman*," trans. Daniel Gerould, *Drama Review* 18, no. 1 (March 1974): 77; available online at http://www.jstor.org/stable/1144865 (accessed December 21, 2017).

16. Ibid., 78.

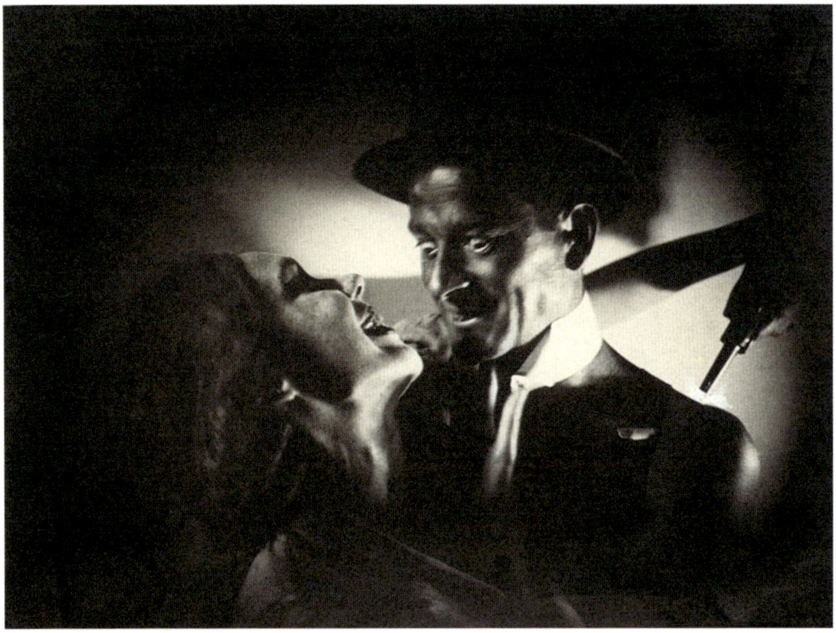

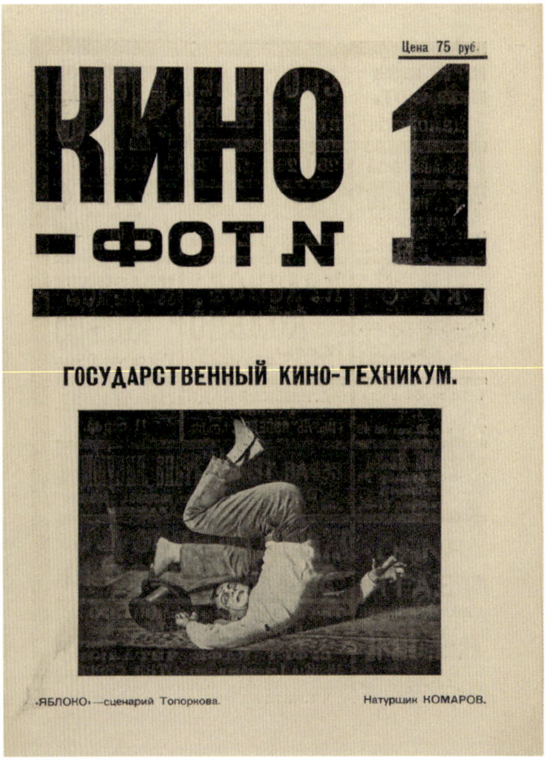

Lev Kuleshov's Workshop
Aleksandra Khokhlova and
Petr Galadzhev, 1923

Aleksandr Rodchenko
Cover of the journal
Cine-Photo, no. 1, 1922

stolen diary. According to Eisenstein, *Glumov's Diary* was a parody of an American detective film. It comprises a series of frames that alternate quickly and appear to lead to a resolution of a mystery. First, we see a car driving by a mansion with an impressive ornamented arch on Vozdvizhenka Street in Moscow—home of Arseny Morozov, scion of a famous merchant family. A man in a top hat jumps out of the car while it is still in motion. He runs up the stairs with his back toward us, turns around suddenly, and stops long enough for us to see he is wearing a black mask over his eyes. From Eisenstein's notation, we know the man is Golutvin, "a man with no particular occupation," who will steal his friend's diary to extort money from him. With a swift gesture, he takes off the hat, waves to us while holding it in his hand, and disappears under the arch. In the following shot, we see Glumov in clown face poking his head out of a roundel in one of the mansion's towers. He screams silently, opening his mouth widely, and disappears from the window. Then the top-hatted Golutvin appears in his place, catches a rope conveniently hanging in front of the roundel, and climbs up the ornaments of the tower to the top balcony surrounded by columns crowned by spiraling cones.

Golutvin hangs his hat on one of the cones and waves his hand. Glumov reappears in the roundel, looks up, sees the hat and then an airplane in the sky. The next shot shows us a crowded street, a moving automobile, and a masked Golutvin landing in the car (supposedly after having jumped down from the airplane). Then there is a close-up of his hands, unraveling a roll of film, and his made-up face, which mimes a smile followed by an expression of fear. A series of heavily made-up clownish characters follow, some wearing dresses and other female-signifying paraphernalia, such as prominent breasts. The clowns gesticulate widely and smile profusely. Glumov approaches each of them, and, trying to adjust to the demands of each character, transforms through a somersault (an acrobatic trick) followed by a fade-in (a montage trick) into something that the character might like: a stack of playing cards for his clown-mother; a *mitrailleuse* for a clown-general; a baby for a clown playing the wife of his relative who likes younger men. The last scene shows Glumov's wedding, in which he amusingly but decisively folds his fingers into an insulting configuration, roughly synonymous with raising a middle finger in the United States. The ending thus metaphorically dots the *i* by conveying the creators' message about American detective stories. In Eisenstein's interpretation of Ostrovsky's play, the hero is the same as the villain, and the only way to combat the evil is through parodic laughter.

The same spirit of gaiety reigned supreme in the productions of FEKS, which Kozintsev and Trauberg formed in 1921 in Petrograd to bring the "eccentrism of the music hall" onto the stage. According to their manifesto, FEKS was created to enliven theater with "hyperbolically crude, overwhelming, nerve-wrecking, overtly utilitarian, mechanically precise, instantaneous, rapid" art, in which the apex of an actor's production would be a "trick" taken from the circus. The play would then resemble a "pile of tricks," and the actor would become a combination of an "inventor-fabricator" and a "mechanized movement," who would not "play" but "give himself airs"; would not "mimic" but "grimace"; would not speak but shout.[17] Shklovsky credited FEKS with influencing Eisenstein's first independent production and its theory: "In any case, the theory of the montage of attractions (moments filled with meaning) is connected with the theory of eccentrism. Eccentrism is based on a choice of impressive moments and their new connection, which defies automatism. Eccentrism is the struggle with life's routine nature, refusal of its perception and rendering based on tradition."[18] In 1924, Kozintsev and Trauberg directed *The Adventures of Oktiabrina*, in which their eccentric method of acting and stage production was introduced on screen. Because the film is lost, we can only imagine its eccentricity in action based on a few remaining frames. In one of them, Oktiabrina appears in an opening of a door on which we see a mysterious inscription: "1,000,000 rubles in gold cur[rency]." She is wearing her signature *budenovka* and determinedly aiming a revolver at two men cowering on the rails of a stairwell. The scene reads like one from an adventure movie, with a clear demarcation between the good Oktiabrina and

17. Grigorii Kozintsev, Georgii Kryzhitskii, Leonid Trauberg, and Sergei Iutkevich, *Eksentrizm* (Eksentropolis-Petrograd, 1922), 3–4.

18. Viktor Shklovskii,, "O rozhdenii i zhizni 'Feksov,'" in *Za sorok let*, 92.

19. Evgeni Gromov, "Lev Kuleshov," in *Lev Kuleshov, Selected Works: Fifty Years in Film*, trans. Dmitri Agrachev and Nina Belenkaya (Moscow: Raduga, 1997), 7.

the bad counterrevolutionaries who are trying to misappropriate the money of the Bolshevik collective.

Reminiscing about his first film from the position of a recognized director, Eisenstein wrote wryly that *Glumov's Diary* "had nothing to do with cinema," dismissing his directorial debut as a student exercise. The film was made two years before the release of *Strike* and *Battleship Potemkin,* which took over the world nearly instantaneously, and in which clownery, farce, and gymnastics were replaced by an all-pervasive ideological pathos. Regardless of Eisenstein's dismissive remark, *Glumov's Diary* uses some basic montage techniques, such as fade-ins and juxtaposition of panoramic and close-up shots. He could have learned about them from the films and writings of his colleague Kuleshov, who, although a year younger than Eisenstein, began a career in cinema much earlier.

At the age of seventeen, Kuleshov was hired as a designer by Aleksandr Khanzhonkov, one of the most established prerevolutionary film producers.[19] In 1918, he directed his first film, *Engineer Prite's Project,* at Khanzhonkov's studio. After having left Khanzhonkov and joined the film and photography department of Narkompros, Kuleshov directed newsreels at the military front and taught at the newly founded State School of Cinematography. At that time, he elaborated key concepts of his theory, including that of montage, also known as "the Kuleshov effect," demonstrating that proper editing and juxtaposition of shots created the films' meaning. He also organized the "Kuleshov Collective," consisting of his students and collaborators—Boris Barnet, Vsevolod Pudovkin, Aleksandra Khokhlova, Sergei Komarov, and Vladimir Fogel among others. The exhibition features two films from this period in Kuleshov's career: *Taras's Dream* (1919), a short agitational feature directed by Iury Zheliabuzhskii, with Kuleshov in charge of montage, and *Extraordinary Adventures of Mr. West in the Land of the Bolsheviks* (1924), which became a marker of Kuleshov's achievement as an innovative film director.

Taras's Dream, which lasts eleven minutes, is a slapstick rendition of a Red Army soldier named Taras, who gets drunk, falls asleep, and has a dream about his former service in the tsarist army, where his days were spent being humiliated by his superiors, performing hard labor, and enduring harsh punishment. A typical absurdist comedy, it includes an exaggerated facial and gestural pantomime by key characters played by classically trained theater actors—the simpleton Taras (Vladimir Riabtsev), pp. 220–221
a sadistic sergeant-major (Anatoly Nelidov), and a jealous and vengeful general (Dmitry Gundurov). The film was made on the occasion of the first anniversary of the Red Army and carried a rudimentary message

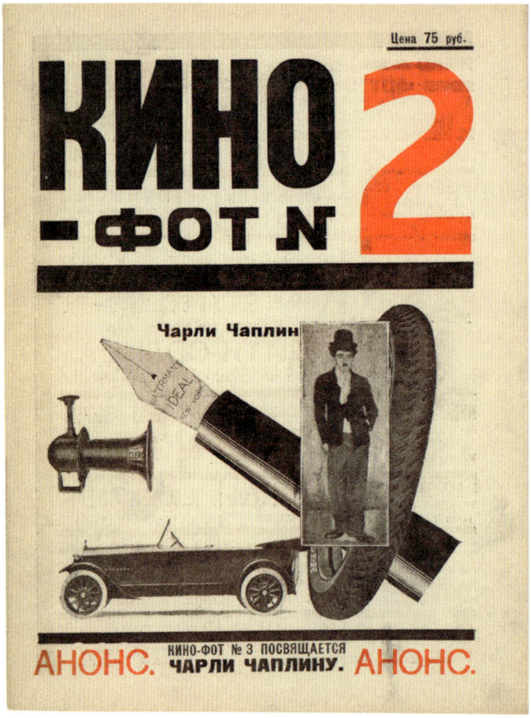

Varvara Stepanova
Cover of the journal *Cine-Photo*, no. 2, 1922

about the superiority of the Red Army—at least where the well-being of its soldiers was concerned—over its tsarist counterpart. Kuleshov was in charge of montage and was concerned with what he called "American shots," or a proper use of editing, which made the action suitably filmic, as opposed to theatrical, literary, or pictorial.[20] The film incudes subtle fade-ins, masterful alteration of medium-range and close-up shots, and an emphasis on smooth frame transitions to convey differences between the "actual" and "dream-induced" realities lived by Taras. In its subject matter and elements of slapstick, the film resembles Charlie Chaplin's films, in particular *Soldiers Arms*, which was released in 1918, a year before *Taras's Dream*. Like the Russian film, *Soldiers Arms* tells the story of a soldier, which at the

20. Lev Kuleshov, "The Banner of Cinematography" (1920), in *Lev Kuleshov, Selected Works*, 37–55.

21. Lev Kuleshov, "David Griffith and Charlie Chaplin" (1928), in *Kuleshov on Film: Writings by Lev Kuleshov*, ed. Ronald Levaco (Berkeley: University of California Press, 1974), 144–45.

22. "Pis'mo L. V. Kuleshova Charl'zu Chaplinu" (1924), in Lev Kuleshov, *Sobranie sochinenii v trekh tomakh, pedagogika* (Moscow: Iskusstvo, 1987), 1:418–20.

23. Lev Kuleshov, "O zadachakh khudozhnika v kinematografe" (1917), in *Sobranie sochinenii v trekh tomakh*, 1:30–31; Lev Kuleshov, "O ssenariiakh" (1917), in ibid., 1:34; Lev Kuleshov, "Znamia kinematografii" (1922), in ibid., 1:38–45; and Lev Kuleshov, "Spravka o naturshchikakh" (1922), in ibid., 1:46–50.

24. Lev Kuleshov, "Prakticheskie raboty nad montazhem i nabliudeniia" (1922), in *Sobranie sochinenii v trekh tomakh*, 1:41–45.

end is revealed to be his dream. Chaplin's film might have been screened in Moscow shortly after its release. Chaplin was widely admired by Western Dadaists and Russian artists and filmmakers. Kuleshov, in particular, expressed his admiration in writing. For him, what made the actor stand out was Chaplin's extraordinary ability to "demonstrate the deportment of a person in various aspects of his life by means of his relationships to things, to objects," rather than by "the elementary portrayal of emotion communicated facially."[21] In 1924, the Kuleshov Collective even wrote a letter to Chaplin, calling him their "teacher" in the way he managed to "precisely and clearly delineate every movement and positioning of the actor in relation to an exacting and harmonious montage" and explaining to him the principles of the work they had elaborated on the basis of his method.[22]

Extraordinary Adventures of Mr. West in the Land of the Bolsheviks pp. 224–225
was the first film the Kuleshov Collective made following this method. Different from *Taras's Dream* in that it used a more refined satire as opposed to slapstick, it was also the first film directed by Kuleshov with his collective and according to the principles of his theory. The plot of the film is rather simple: Mr. John West, the president of the YMCA, arrives for an extended stay in Moscow. He comes there with a skewed image of the Bolsheviks as unwashed and murderous savages, an image propagated by the American media. Upon his arrival, he is promptly set up by a group of swindlers who extort money from him by playing on his fear of the Bolsheviks. Through a series of hilarious tricks, the group succeeds in fleecing the naive American of large amount of cash. This merciless robbery is stopped only through the intervention of a real Bolshevik, represented by a benevolent Cheka commander. At the end of the film, the transformed Mr. West enthusiastically promotes Bolshevism in a letter to his beloved wife.

Although the goal of the film was properly comic—to ridicule a clueless American for his foreignness—the presentation of the comedy was tailored to the properties of the cinematic medium as formulated by Kuleshov in his writings. From his first texts on film, written in 1917, Kuleshov propagated the uniqueness of cinema as an artistic medium. He argued this point in a series of articles on the roles of designers, writers, photographers, and actors in film.[23] A photographer had to give up his monopoly on reproducing reality in a single picture to a film editor, a specialist on montage—an art of "assembling" separate filmed pieces, including the splitting of individual scenes into separate elements and their skillful juxtaposition, with the editor's effort to adjust the filming to the

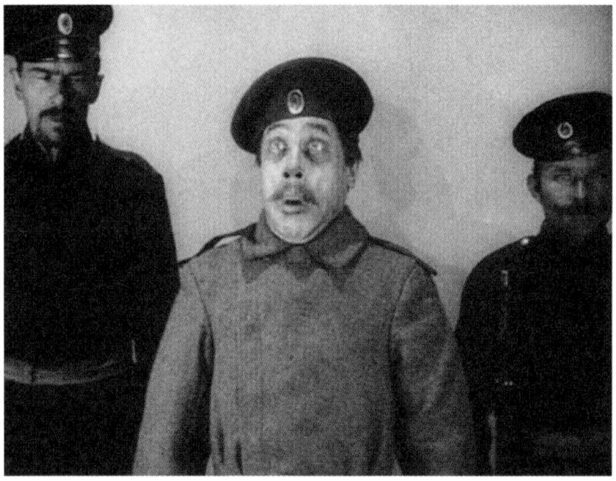

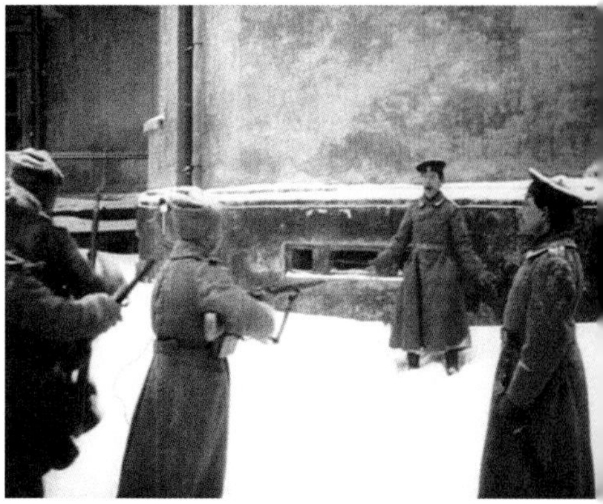

Lev Kuleshov
Taras's Dream, 1919

viewer's perception and on a harmonious transition of shots.[24] Kuleshov completely redefined the role of film actors, asserting that "while the theatre is unthinkable without actors, the cinema does not need actors, . . . but requires models instead."[25] Because film works with reality as material by creatively transforming it into a work of art, in cinema, it is "wrong to 'perform' a script; the thing to do is to place the characters in certain situations . . . in such a manner that the character is perceived not as an actor playing a part but as a model, a genuine type fitting the setup, and then the events he lives through can be played."[26] Thus, the only way for a film actor to look authentic on the screen is to display genuine individuality. Any theatrical role-acting would look contrived and false.

In keeping with the principles stated in the Kuleshov Collective's letter to Chaplin, this display of individuality required rigorous training. For actors, this meant possession of complete control over their facial and gestural expressions at any moment of the shooting and awareness of the camera recording their every move.[27] A good sense of the training received by actors in pp. 208, 214 Kuleshov's workshop can be gained from his description of its graduation requirements: "Upon

25. Kuleshov, "Spravka o naturshchike," 47.

26. Ibid.

27. See "Pis'mo L. V. Kuleshova Charl'zu Chaplinu" (1924).

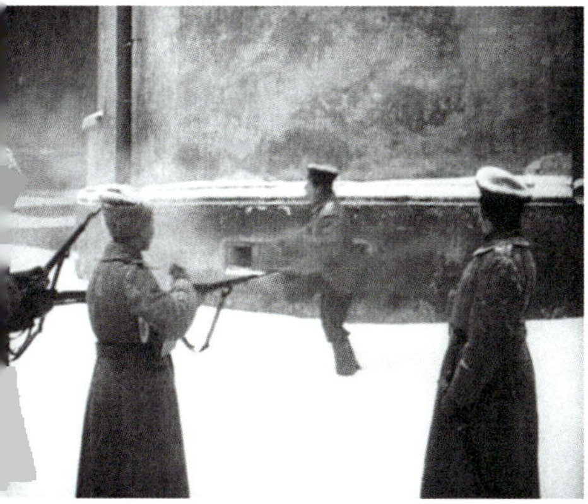

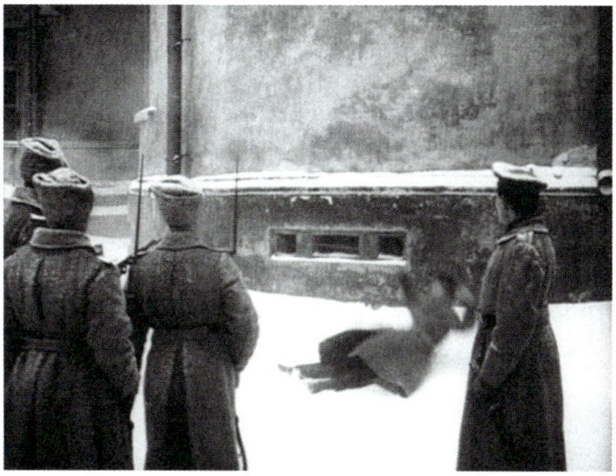

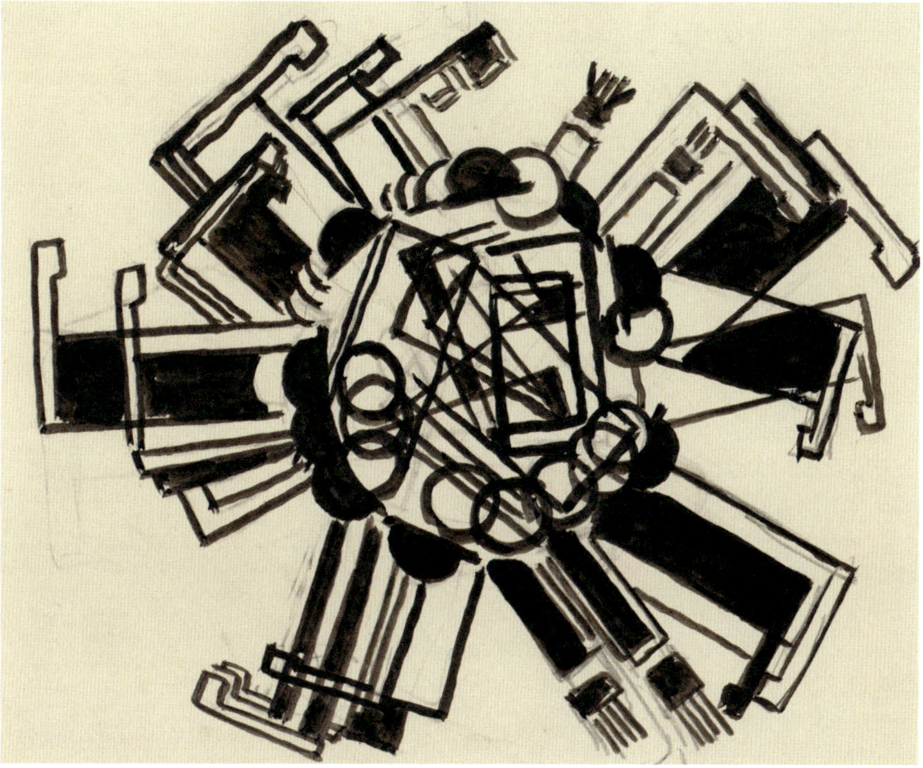

Varvara Stepanova
Charles Chaplin Turning Somersault,
1922

graduation, a model must meet the following requirements: 1) to have the capacity to control the body and face muscles consciously and promptly retain the director's plastic assignments; 2) to have the necessary skill to solve, unassisted, any plastic problems arising from the scenario or the directorial assignment; . . . 4) to have a good knowledge of the specific traits of his or her face and body in terms of photogenicity, depending on the particular light and movement."[28] In practice, this translated into repeated rehearsals to hone the actor's every move and expression and adjust it to the technical possibilities of camera recording. While watching *Mr. West*, one is captivated by the rapidity of action, the changing scenes, and the mechanical precision with which the actors portray their characters. Khokhlova, in particular, attracts attention with her incomparably rich facial mimicry and her angular figure, which she folds and unfolds effortlessly depending on the required movement and the flow of action.

All of the films considered above are comedies, using parody, eccentrism, and satire to make the audience laugh. At first glance, it might seem remarkable that at the birth of Soviet cinema, comedy appears to have been the only alternative to Vertov's cinematic constructivism. In his writings, Shklovsky wondered about this phenomenon, questioning why it was "eccentrism, filtered through Eisenstein, the FEKS, and partly Meyerhold, that created new devices for the art of the post-October period" and not any other current.[29] Elsewhere, he remarked on the significance of parodic laughter for the development of the Soviet aesthetic, because it contributed to conveying "tension in the social field, created by new phenomena."[30] He remarked in this respect that "to create his heroic style, Eisenstein had to go through

28. Lev Kuleshov, "Programma kinematograficheskoi eksperimental'noi masterskoi po klassu naturshchikov" (1923), in *Sobranie sochinenii v trekh tomakh*, 1:95.

29. Shklovskii, "O rozhdenii i zhizni 'Feksov,'" 92

30. Viktor Shklovskii, "O Dzhige Vertove", in *Antologiia*, ed. Ushakov, 1:251–52.

31. Shklovskii, "Eizenshtein," 74.

32. Iu. Tynianov, "O FEKSakh," *Sovetskii ekran*, April 2, 1929, 10, translated and reprinted in *The Film Factory: Russian and Soviet Cinema in Documents, 1896–1939*, ed. Richard Taylor and Ian Christie (London: Routledge, 1988), 257–58.

33. Richter traveled to Moscow to work on *Metal* (1931–1933), a film about a workers' strike in an iron factory in Hennigsdorf, Germany. See Tupitsyn, *Malevich and Film*, 62–65. According to Marion von Hofacker, Richter was prompted begin work on this film, the only political feature of his career, by the rise of the Nazi Party in Germany. Marion von Hofacker, "Richter's Films and the Role of the Radical Artist," in *Hans Richter: Activism, Modernism, and the Avant-Garde*, ed. Stephen C. Foster (Cambridge, MA: MIT Press, 1998), 122–59. Richter met Eisenstein in 1929 in La Sarraz, Switzerland, at the 29th Congress of Independent Cinema. See ibid.; and *Travelling: Documents cinémathèque Suisse* 55 (1979), dedicated to this congress.

34. Shklovsky begins his article on Eisenstein by stating, "he shuns such words as 'inspiration', art" and continues, "if he has anything 'eccentric' about him, it's the eccentricity of a new mechanism." See Shklovskii, "Eizenshtein," 74.

his montage of eccentric attractions."[31] Iury Tynianov, a fellow formalist critic, expanded on Shklovsky's thought when he proposed that "an elementary 'comedy' film," on which the "adventures" of FEKS were reared, still had "traces of cinema as an invention, elements of cinema, which allow one . . . to examine, test, and handle that which the more deferential but less intelligent regard as a taboo—the very essence of the cinema as an art form. Here the FEKS invented what had hitherto been their most valuable feature: freedom from genre, the optional nature of traditions, and the ability to reconcile opposites."[32] Comedy allowed Russian artists in theater and film to bare the device to the maximum, reducing it to its basic building blocks. In this sense, it served the same function in these performance arts as abstraction in painting.

As Dada was a fluid, open-ended international movement, it displayed many choices of aesthetic strategies, highlighting their division according to political lines. Grosz and Heartfield, for example, who were both members of the Communist Party, were close to the Russians in that they used satire to ridicule capitalists as immoral warmongers and money grabbers. The left-leaning Richter became interested in Eisenstein after the Russian director's *Strike* and *Battleship Potemkin* were released in the West. Richter worked on his own saga about a workers' strike in Moscow in the 1930s.[33] Shklovsky's "spirit of gaiety," then, can be traced not only in the early Soviet film but in the satirical and pathos-oriented works of Dada artists who were inspired by the Soviet directors. The difference in context set the frame for their work: Russian artists and filmmakers were at pains to present themselves and everyone involved in the creation of their films as regular "workers" at a film factory.[34] Unless Dada artists consciously affiliated themselves with a certain communist collective or forms of collective production on behalf of a left-leaning political cause, as Grosz, Heartfield, and even Richter did to some extent, their frame of reference remained confined to a culture in which difference and individuality was valued more than similarity and collective action, making irony rather than eccentrism, parody, or satire their artistic device of choice.

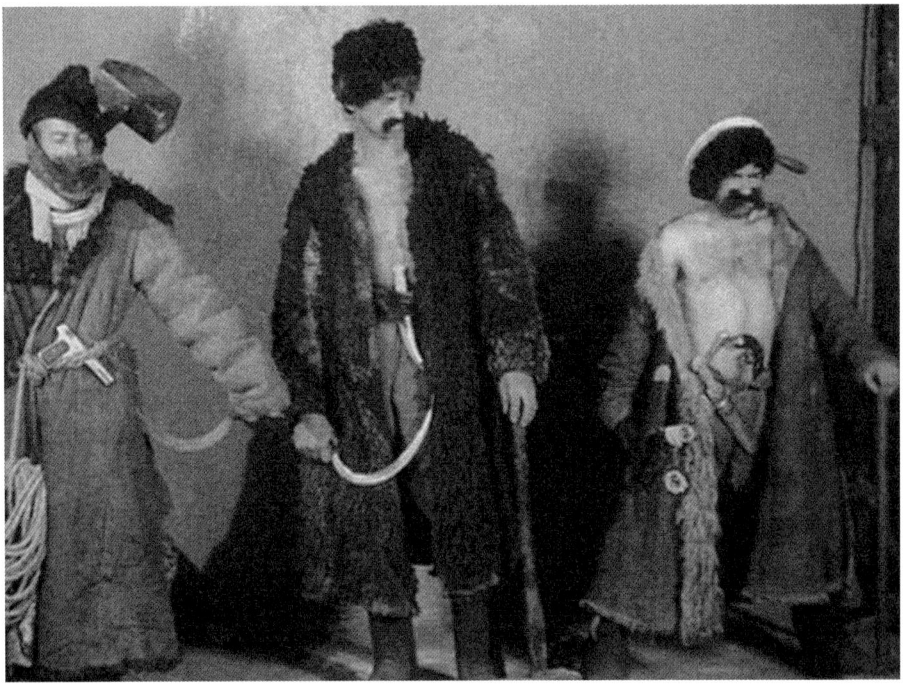

Lev Kuleshov
The Extraordinary Adventures of Mr. West in the Land of the Bolsheviks, 1924

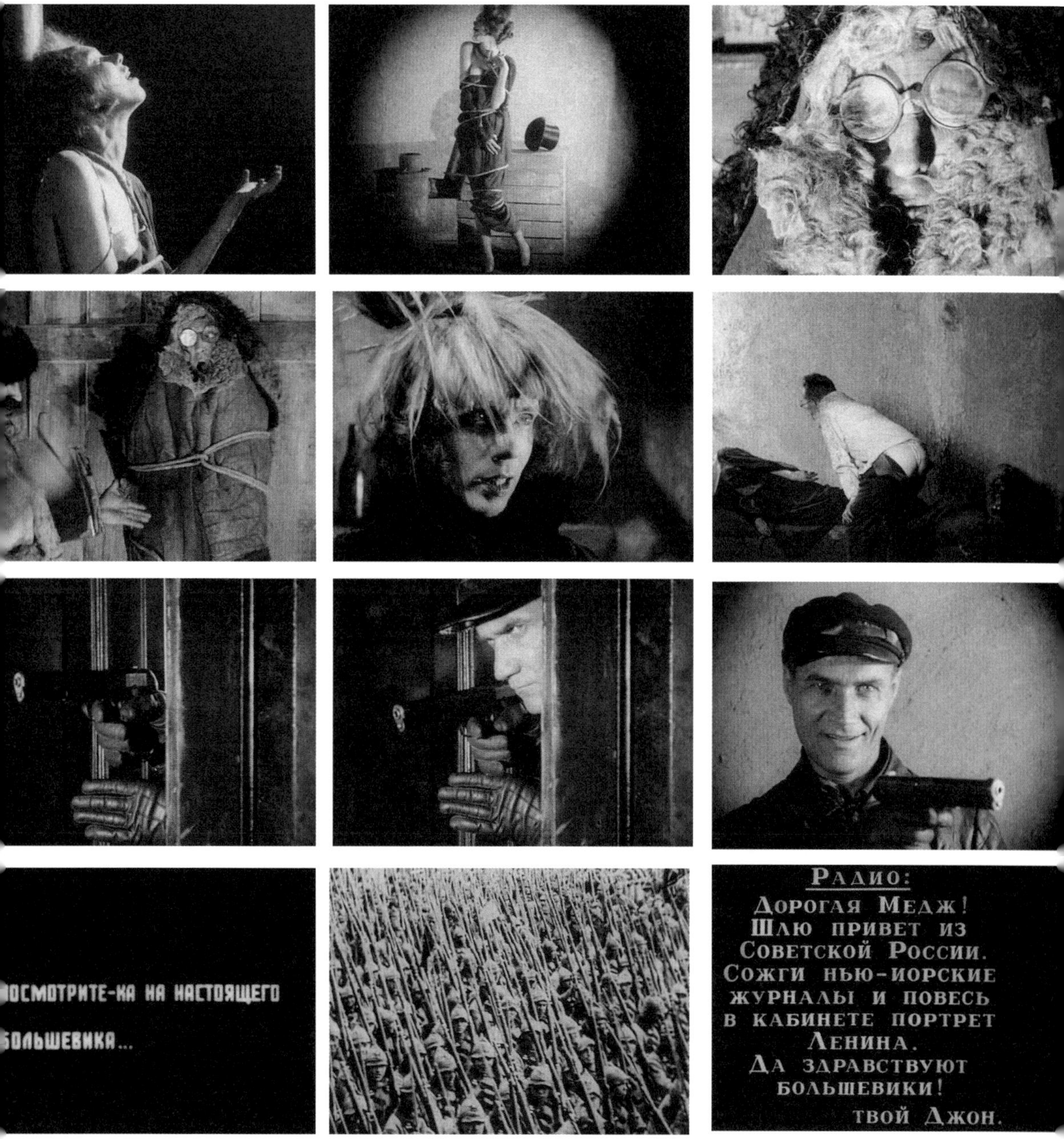
ОСМОТРИТЕ-КА НА НАСТОЯЩЕГО
БОЛЬШЕВИКА...
Радио:
Дорогая Медж!
Шлю привет из
Советской России.
Сожги нью-иорские
журналы и повесь
в кабинете портрет
Ленина.
Да здравствуют
большевики!
твой Джон.

ANARCHISM AND THE RUSSIAN ARTISTIC AVANT-GARDE

Olga Burenina-Petrova

Vladimir Mayakovsky
Cover of the book *Mystery Bouffe* by Vladimir Mayakovsky, Petrograd, 1918

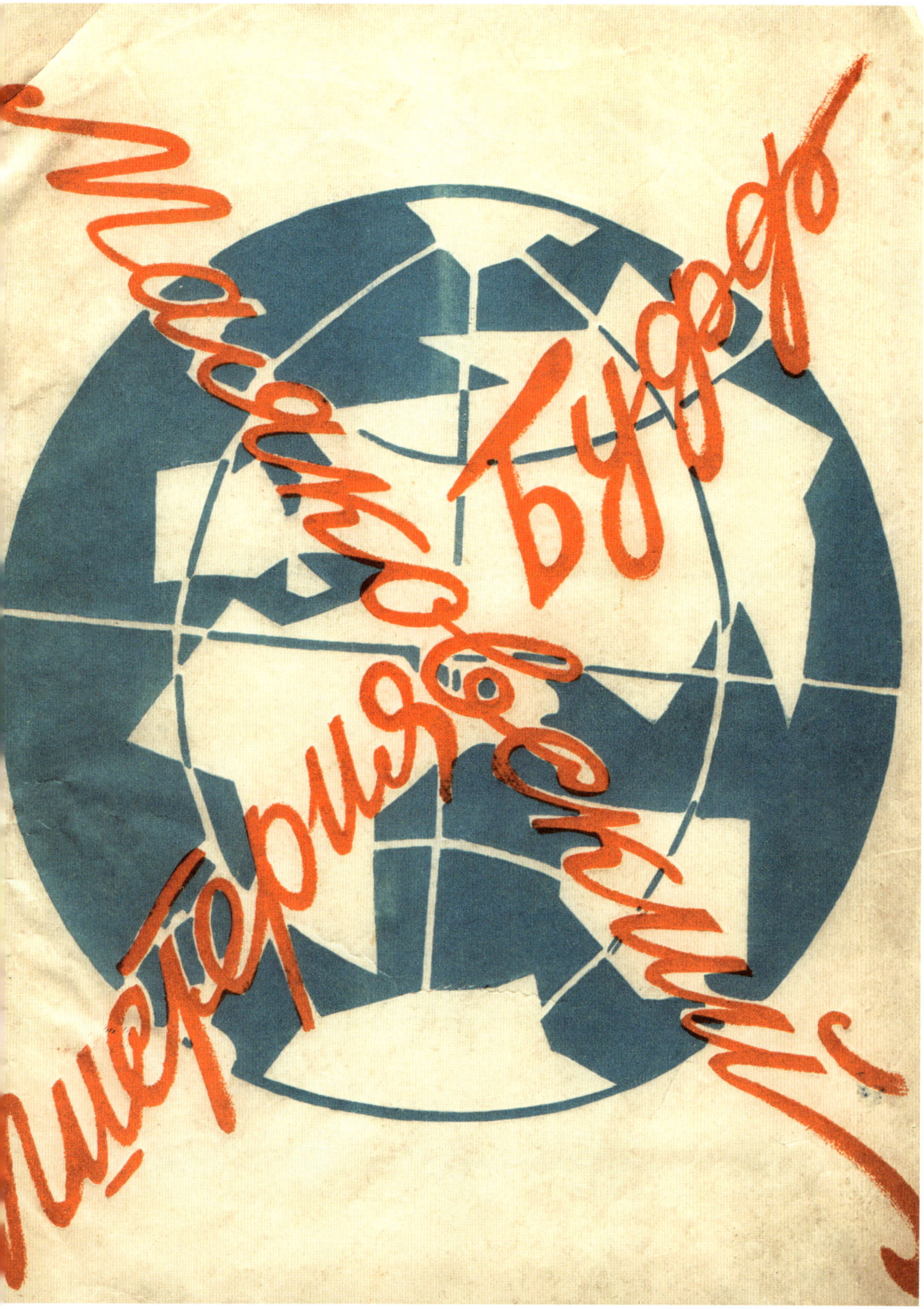

As a political philosophy, anarchism began to take shape at the dawn of the postromantic era, as one of the manifestations of its characteristic nihilism, in the works of Pierre-Joseph Proudhon, who declared that all property is "theft," and Mikhail Bakunin, who rejected all forms of hierarchical power, be they divine or human, collective or individual. Interest in anarchist teachings on the part of artists began in 1910–1916 with the manifestos of Italian and Russian futurists and, especially, of Zurich Dadaists. Many definitions of Dadaism echo the characteristics of anarchism and freedom expounded by Bakunin in his work *Statism and Anarchy*. Bakunin lived in Switzerland from 1872 to 1876 and published this work his main theoretical treatise on anarchism, in Zurich in 1873. The founders of Dadaism who met in Zurich's Cabaret Voltaire in 1916 and were familiar with Bakunin's work—Tristan Tzara, Hans Arp, Marcel Janco, Hugo Ball—were drawn to Bakunin's anarchism, first and foremost, by its rebellious spirit and its power of negation. Ball began to write a book on Bakunin, using materials from the library of the Zurich anarchist, physician, and writer Fritz Brupbacher, with the intent of showing how the program of Dadaism parallels the theoretical views of the great rebel.[1] (He never finished it, however.)

In the Dadaists' work, anarchist negation was aimed at dismantling hierarchy and thus at the destabilization of the genres and conventions of art. Marcel Duchamp's Dadaist experiments are even more complex in this regard: In *Bottle Dryer or Hedgehog* (1914), *Prelude to a Broken Arm* (1915), *Fountain* (1917), and other works he called "readymades," he transposed objects from the space of non-art into the space of art for the first time in

1. Karin Huser, *Eine revolutionäre Ehe in Briefen: Die Sozialrevolutionärin Lidija Petrovna Kotschetkowa und der Anarchist Fritz Brupbacher* (Zurich: Chronos Verlag, 2003).

2. Regarding Stirner's influence on Duchamp, see Allan Antliff, "Anarchy, Politics, and Dada," in *Making Mischief: Dada Invades New York*, ed. Francis M. Naumann, Beth Venn, and Todd Alden (New York: Whitney Museum of American Art, 1996), 212.

3. Leon Trotsky uses the phrase "shift of power" in his book *My Life* (1930); see the chapter "Lenin's Death and the Shift of Power."

4. M. A. Iziumskaia, "Nemetskie dadaisty i Rossiia: puti vzaimodeistviia," in *Rossiia-Germaniia: kul'turnye sviazi, iskusstvo, literatura v pervoi polovine dvadtsatogo veka: materialy nauchnoi konferentsii "Vipperovskie chteniia-1996,"* ed. I. E. Danilova (Moscow: Gosudarstvennyi muzei izobrazitel'nogo islusstva im. Pushkina, 2000), 52–53.

5. Nikolai Khardzhiev, "Poeziia i zhivopis': rannii Maiakovskii," in *K istorii russkogo avangarda / The Russian Avant-Garde* (Stockholm: Hylaea Prints, 1976), 24.

art history. By abolishing aesthetic hierarchy, and with it the mimetic principle in art, Duchamp's "readymades" blurred the lines between intellectual and physical labor and, in general, radically changed artistic practice. Such "deflation" of the object was largely shaped by the influence on Duchamp of Max Stirner's book *The Ego and His Own*, which he had read in the summer of 1912.[2] While Stirner's "ego" liberates the world in order to make it its own property, Duchamp's "fountain/urinal" was intended to show that a painted copy cannot represent an object better than it represents itself by the fact of its existence. Duchamp's readymades are as much a center of the universe as the empirical personality is for Stirner, whose philosophy elevates it to the status of the only and absolute reality.

The time frame of Russian anarchism is marked by the February Revolution of 1917 and by the events of 1921–1924. The leader and principal theorist of anarchism, Petr Kropotkin, died in February 1921, and the leadership of the anarchist movement split into several groups that existed until Vladimir Lenin's death in 1924 and the "shift of power."[3] From 1917 to 1924, philosophical-aesthetic movements that synthesized anarchism and the artistic practice of the avant-garde emerged: the pananarchism of the brothers Abba Gordin and Wolf Gordin; the anarcho-universalism of Apollon Karelin; the anarcho-biocosmism of Aleksandr Sviatogor (the pseudonym of Aleksei Agienko), Aleksandr Iaroslavsky, and Pavel Ivanitsky; the radical anarchism of rebel artists whose aesthetic was similar to Dadaism and whose circle revolved around the *Anarchy* (*Anarkhiia*) gazette. While the prerevolutionary print periodicals of Russian anarchism were mostly authored by anarchist theorists themselves, the postrevolutionary period saw the involvement of avant-garde artists in the movement, along with the theorists/activists of anarchism. The book *Sounds* by anarchist sympathizer Vasily Kandinsky, published in Munich in 1912, had a strong influence on Dadaist poetry. That the Dadaists published Kandinsky's writings in the magazine *Dada* and invited him to appear at the Cabaret Voltaire in 1916 was no accident. Poems from his book were recited at the last Dadaist soirée, held in Zurich in April 1919.[4]

In scholarly literature, Nikolai Khardzhiev was the first to notice the proximity of anarchism and the avant-garde when he wrote that "anarchic mutiny and the overthrow of all authorities" were "equally characteristic of both French and Russian" avant-gardes.[5] Indeed, the anarchist dialectic of negation and the acknowledgment of individual authority turned out to be completely in tune with the avant-garde revolutionary/

nihilistic passion to get rid of all spiritual values and to "throw Pushkin, Dostoyevsky, Tolstoy, etc. etc. etc. off the Steamboat of Modernity."[6]

The diary of the artist Varvara Stepanova contains the following entry, dated 1919: "Russian art is as anarchistic in its principles as Russia is in its spiritual path. We have no schools, and each artist is a creator, each is original and drastically individual, whether he is an innovator, a synthesizer, or a realist."[7] Stepanova's comment refers first and foremost to prerevolutionary avant-garde artists who felt profound sympathy for the anarchist worldview. Furthermore, the thinking and artistic experiments of most of the artists and poets included in this exhibition were formed under the influence of various types of anarchism.

In turn, the theory and practice of postrevolutionary anarchism in 1917–1924 received considerable support from the ideological statements, the artistic and aesthetic theoretical commentary on issues of art and the art world, and the manifestos and declarations of a particular group of these artists that appeared from September 1917 to April 1918 in the pages of the newspaper *Anarchy*, published by the Moscow Federation of Anarchist Groups.[8] The editor-in-chief of *Anarchy* was the anarchist-communist Vladimir Barmash. Initially, the editorial office was located at 12 Moronov Lane (Krymsky Bank). The first seven issues of *Anarchy* had the subhead "Social literary anarchist gazette," underscoring its connection to literary and artistic circles. Starting with issue no. 8, the gazette was declared to be the official organ of the Moscow Federation of Anarchist Groups. After issue no. 10, the gazette briefly went on hiatus, then resumed publication in March 1918. By then, its editorial offices were located in the "Anarchy House"—the headquarters of the Moscow Federation of Anarchist Groups (6 Malaia Dmitrovka).[9]

In late March, the newspaper moved again; its last editorial office was at 1 Nastasinsky Lane.[10] The "Poets' Café" that opened in Moscow immediately after the October Revolution, in December 1917, was in the same building, at the corner. The anarchists were frequent visitors. On March 15, 1918, the *Futurists' Gazette* (*Gazeta futuristov*)—only one issue of which ever came out—published "The Manifesto of the Flying Federation of Futurists" by David Burliuk, Vasily Kamensky, and Mayakovsky, which declared that futurism, as an aesthetic continuation of anarchism, calls upon art to separate itself from the state, come out into the streets, and shut down the Academy of Arts, a state institution. According to the manifesto, the Third Revolution, which the authors called a "Revolution of the Spirit," would free human beings from the shackles of old art. The Third Revolution was a revolution of the anarchist movement

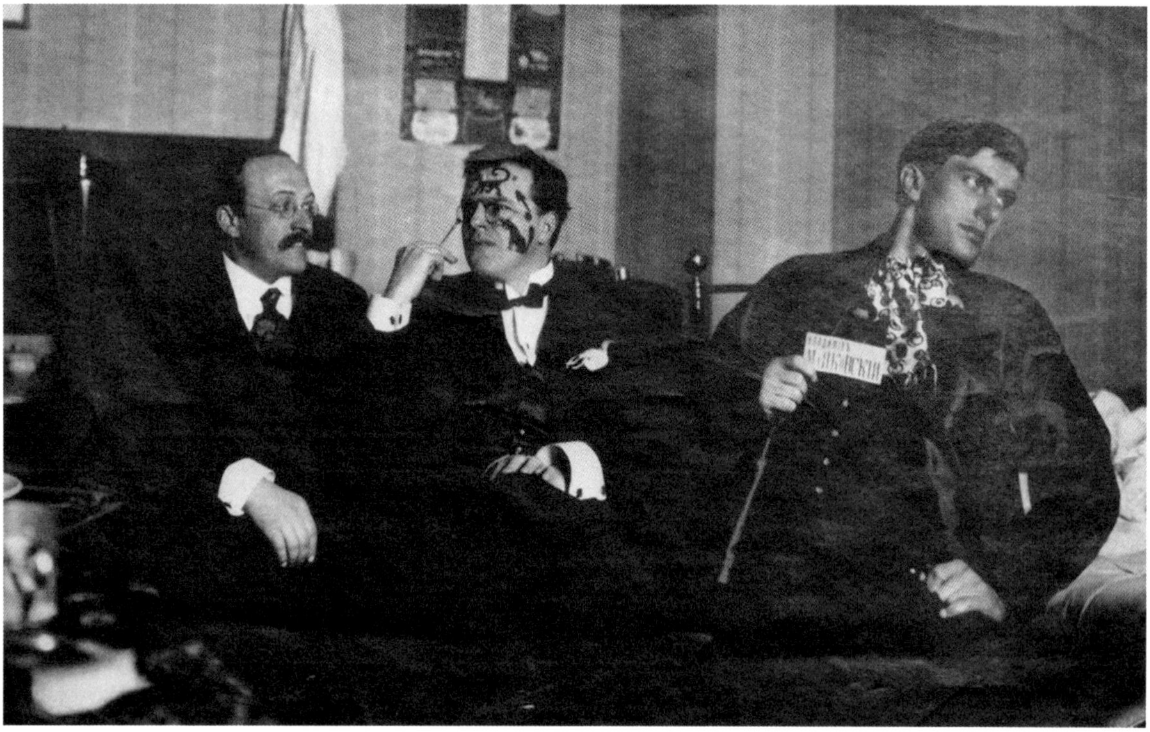

Anonymous
David Burliuk, Vladimir Mayakovsky, and Andrei Shemshurin, Moscow, 1914

6. David Burliuk, Aleksei Kruchenykh, Vladimir Maiakovskii, and Viktor [Velimir] Khlebnikov, "Poshchechina obshchestvennomu vkusu," in *Poeziia russkogo futurizma*, ed. V. N. Sazhin (Saint Petersburg: Gumanitarnoe agenstvo "Akademicheskii proekt," 1999), 617.

7. Varvara Stepanova, *Chelovek ne mozhet zhit bez chuda* (Moscow: Sfera, 1994), 73.

8. For more on the role of this newspaper in artistic and literary circles, see Ol'ga Burenina-Petrova, "Filosofiia anarkhizma v russkom khudozhestvennom avangarde i 'zamknutye konstruktsii' Daniila Kharmsa," in *Kharms-Avangard: materialy mezhdunarodnoi nauchnoi konferentsii "Avangard v deistvii i otmiranii": k stoletiiu so dnia rozhdeniia poeta*, ed. Kornelija Icin and Radko Neschkovic (Belgrade: Izdatelstvo filologicheskogo fakul'teta, 2006), 96–102; and Nina Gurianova, *The Aesthetics of Anarchy: Art and Ideology in the Early Russian Avant-Garde* (Berkeley: University of California Press, 2012).

9. The description of the launch of *Anarchy* and the locations of its offices is based on the materials from A. D. Sarab'ianov, "Stat'i v gazete 'Anarkhiia'" (1918), in *Kazimir Malevich, Stat'i, manifesty, teoreticheskie sochineniia i drugie raboty: 1913–1929*, 5 vols. (Moscow: Gileia, 1995), 1:330–32.

10. The last issue of *Anarchy* (no. 99), was published on July 2, 1918. A few weeks earlier, on April 12, 1918, Barmash was arrested by Moscow Cheka (The All Russian Emergency Commission for Combating Counter-revolution and Sabotage) at "Anarchy House" during the crackdown on anarchists in Moscow. It happened as follows: On April 11, an urgent meeting of Cheka was held in Moscow, and the decision was made to start disarming the anarchists in the early morning hours of April 12. Tanks and armored personnel vehicles were dispatched to take control of the buildings occupied by anarchists. The anarchists fought back as best they could. At the "Anarchy House" on Malaia Dmitrovka, they used machine guns to fire from the windows and the rooftops of adjacent buildings. After the anarchists were arrested, the Cheka announced the closing of *Anarchy*. Shortly after the Moscow raids, the Bolsheviks also smashed all the other anarchist parties.

and, consequently, of the pro-anarchist artistic avant-garde.

Nonetheless, Aleksandr Rodchenko, in his statement addressed to the *Futurists' Gazette* (Gazeta futuristov), regarded Burliuk, Kamensky, and Mayakovsky as insufficient "anarcho-rebels" and dubbed their publication a "gazette of three futurist dictators" and its three publishers "the Bolsheviks of futurism" and "the statists of futurism." He contrasted them to those he called "more than futurists": Velimir Khlebnikov, Aleksei Kruchenykh, Olga Rozanova, Kazimir Malevich, Vladimir Tatlin, Aleksei Morgunov, Nadezhda Udaltsova, and Liubov Popova.[11] In this way, he drew a boundary between artistic anarchism, linked to Dadaism both philosophically and aesthetically, and futurism as it had developed before the Revolution.

In his message "To Comrades Anarchists," Rodchenko expresses the conviction that the spiritual union of anarchism and art (and thus the Revolution of the Spirit as well) is possible only thanks to his artistic brothers in arms: "And we are coming to you, beloved comrades, anarchists, instinctively recognizing in you our hitherto unknown friends! . . . The present belongs to artists who are the anarchists of art."[12]

A short while later, in 1919, Rodchenko graphically depicted the call for a Revolution of the Spirit in the hand-drawn poster *Rejoice, Today the Revolution of the Spirit Is Before You!*

> Rejoice today the Revolution of Spirit
> is before you
> Listen to us,
> who have cast off
> the centuries-old shackles
> of the photographic
> of cliché

11. Aleksandr Rodchenko, "Gazeta futuristov," *Anarkhiia*, no. 31 (March 30, 1918): 4.

12. Aleksandr Rodchenko, "Tovarishcham anarkhistam," *Anarkhiia*, no. 29 (March 28, 1918): 4.

13. See David Burliuk, Vasilii Kamenskii, and Vladimir Maiakovskii, "Manifest letuchei federatsii futuristov," *Gazeta futuristov*, no. 1 (1918): 1; emphasis in original.

14. This club existed for only a week because the premises had to be vacated after all.

of subject
We
are Russian
Columbuses of art
Discoverers of new paths
Of creativity
Today
Is our triumph.

The anarchist artists were convinced that the foremost requirement of their time was support for the primary postulate of anarchism and thus the total opposition of art to state power:

> We demand the recognition of:
> I. *The separation of art and state.*
> The abolition of patronage, privilege, and control in the sphere of art. Down with diplomas, titles, official posts and ranks.[13]

After the October Revolution, one of the key postulates of anarchism—a new attitude toward property—was fulfilled as well. In postrevolutionary times, the first Russian translations (one by E. and I. Leontiev, another by F. Kapeliusha) of Proudhon's 1840 treatise *What Is Property?* became a source for multiple interpretations by anarchists of Proudhon's ideas of property, and for a number of practical actions as well. After the October Revolution, anarchists—influenced by Proudhon, who posited that "property is theft" because it contradicts justice and because not one conception that would justify it can be found in the history of ideas—declared all forms of property to be illegitimate and consequently arrogated to themselves the right to seize premises, mostly ones belonging to wealthy entrepreneurs. Thus, in March 1918, Mayakovsky, Kamensky, and Burliuk, who shared anarchist beliefs about property, occupied the premises of a Moscow restaurant where they planned to start a club for "creative individual anarchism."[14] Also in 1918, Nikandr Turkin's film *Born Not for the Money* was released. The script, based on Jack London's novel *Martin Eden*, was written by Mayakovsky, who incorporated many autobiographical elements. He moved the setting from Oakland to Moscow and changed the names of characters. The story revolves around the lives of the futurists and the Poets' Café, where, as the story progresses, Mayakovsky, Kamensky, and Burliuk appear, essentially playing themselves

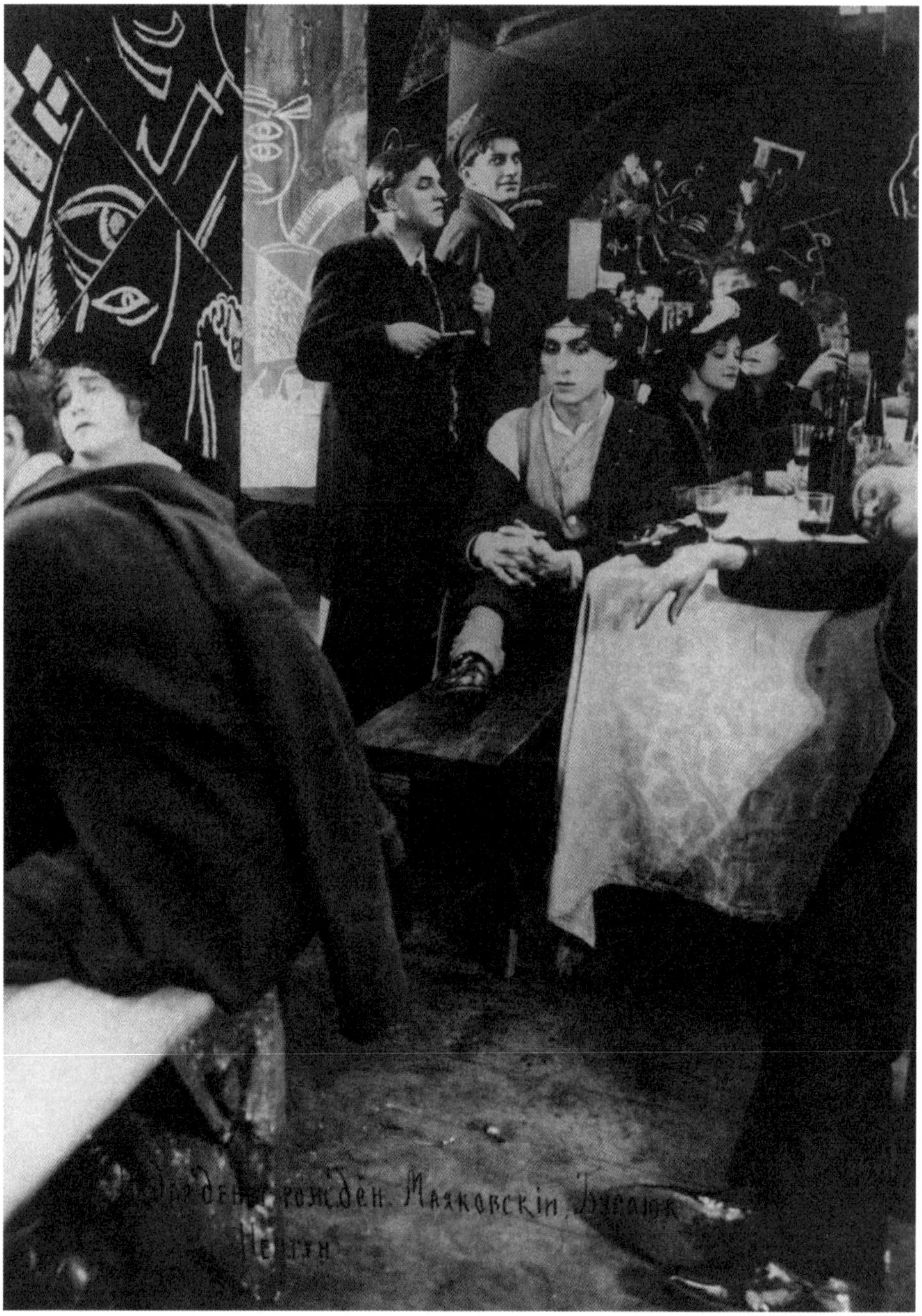

Evgeny Slavinsky
Still from Nikandr Turkin's film *Born Not for the Money*
(David Burliuk and Vladimir Mayakovsky), 1918

and reading their own poetry.[15] The film is believed to be lost; however, photographs made during the filming by operator Evgeny Slavinsky have been preserved. One of them shows the start of the story, against the backdrop of the wall paintings at the Poets' Café.[16] p. 234

Also in 1918, Vsevolod Meyerhold staged Mayakovsky's *Mystery Bouffe*. Written by Mayakovsky for the first anniversary of the October Revolution and included among celebratory events by the Central Bureau for the Organization of Festivities to Commemorate the Anniversary of the Revolution, *Mystery Bouffe*, which premiered on November 7, immediately drew the attention of audiences to the "ultra-anarchism" of the play and its staging.[17] Meyerhold was Mayakovsky's codirector, while Malevich did the stage design (now lost). Mayakovsky, who played several parts in the production—"Just a man," Methuselah, and one of the devils[18]—and instantly transformed himself, demonstrated more circus-like than theatrical methods onstage, methods he had learned both from Vitaly Lazarenko, who also played a devil in the production, and from Meyerhold himself. Lazarenko's trick of instantly changing his appearance and voice could be traced back to Meyerhold's transformations; Meyerhold, in turn, took his cue from the transformations of Leopoldo Fregoli, Ugo Uccelini, and Otto Frankardi, as well as Charlie Chaplin. The play's locations—Act I. The entire universe; Act II. The Arc; Act III, Scene 1: Hell / Scene 2: Paradise / Scene 3: The Promised Land—were conceptualized in such a way that the final scenes of gaining the Promised Land were associated for the audience with the advent of an anarchist world. As for the power of the Bolsheviks, the 1918 version associated it, to a greater degree than the 1919 version, with the tableau of Hell. p. 237 p. 237

15. Vladimir Maiakovskii, *Ne dlia deneg rodivshiisia*, transcribed libretto as told by L. A. Grinberg and Vladimir Maiakovskii, *Polnoie sobranie sochinenii v 13 tomakh* (Moscow: GIKhL, 1958), 11:481.

16. The Poets' Café was decorated by Burliuk, Georgy Iakulov, Valentina Khodasevich, Aristarkh Lentulov, Mikhail Larionov, and Natalia Goncharova.

17. Three years later, Meyerhold included a reworked version of the play in the repertory of the Moscow Theater of the RSFSR Original (Teatr RSFSR pervyi). In this second version, the play was produced in several Russian cities in 1921. A 1921 issue of the newspaper *Theater Messenger* (*Vestnik teatra*) published some information on Mayakovsky's reading of the second version of the play and on the reaction of some Soviet government and Communist Party officials. The "Debates" section reports, "Comrade Karpinskaia: The play has been read to us in entirely different form, its first version was very different. I can only welcome this play; it has futurism and anarchism and so forth, but they have been completely toned down, and the last two acts even make a good impression. However, the first version of the play, before the revisions, was full of ultra-anarchism and we couldn't approve it as suitable for the proletariat." In *Vestnik teatra*, no. 83–84 (February 22, 1921): 18. At the same time, Aleksandr Granovsky staged *Mystery Bouffe* on the premises of the First State Circus on Tzvetnoi Boulevard as a special production for the delegates of the Third Congress of the Comintern who were visiting Moscow. Representatives of the world proletariat watched a production in German, translated by Rita Reit and performed by actors from Moscow theaters who were fluent in German. The libretto, which Mayakovsky wrote for the production program booklet, stated that *Mystery Bouffe* is a "miniature of the world within the walls of a circus." Maiakovskii, *Polnoie sobranie sochinenii*, 2:359.

18. Mayakovsky essentially had to improvise the roles of "Mafusail," "Simply a Man," and one of the "devils," because the actors scheduled to perform these roles did not show up for the premier of *Mystery Bouffe*.

Starting in 1917, anarchism turned from a philosophical/theoretical discourse and a political program into a kind of aesthetic and psychology of artistic creativity. It was precisely as artistic anarchy—above all, nonselection, the rejection of the structural principle of organizing texts, the mixing of phenomena and problems of disparate levels, the establishment of absolute equivalency between nonequivalent phenomena—that anarchism was interpreted by artists who wrote for the newspaper *Anarchy*, which, from the moment of its launch, played an active role in postrevolutionary Moscow.[19] *Anarchy* was particularly supportive of the Left Federation of the Moscow Trade Union of Painters, which was chaired by Tatlin, with Rodchenko as secretary.[20]

Manifestos and statements by avant-garde artists were regularly published in *Anarchy* in the "Creative Art" section, the very name of which was an allusion to Bakunin's thesis, set forth in his 1842 work *Reaction in Germany*, "The joy of destruction is a creative joy!"[21] The "Creative Art" section, which featured articles on art, literature, and theater, appeared in *Anarchy* starting with the publication of critic and artist Aleksei Gan's article "Proletkult" in issue no. 14, arguing that culture-building was possible only thanks to the "association of geniuses and personal initiative."[22]

Also telling is a statement titled "We Want," by the artist Udaltsova. Rejecting the power of old art, she turns not simply to art but to action and "labor," thus paraphrasing Bakunin, who wrote in 1840, "Real life is action, and only action is real life."[23]

> We do not want rich patrons.
> We do not want critics biased in our favor.

Vladimir Mayakovsky
Stage and costume design for *Mystery Bouffe, Seven Pairs of Good*, 1919

Vladimir Mayakovsky
Stage and costume design for *Mystery Bouffe, Seven Pairs of Evil*, 1919

19. For more explanation of the term *nonselection*, see Douwe Wessel Fokkema, *Literary History, Modernism, and Postmodernism* (Amsterdam: Benjamin, 1984).

20. Artists also made political statements in the pages of *Anarchy*. Thus, after the existence of separate federations within trade unions was abolished, the June 27, 1918, issue of *Anarchy*, no. 95, published the text of "The Resolution of the Left Federation at the General Meeting of the Trade Union of Painters," signed by federation chairman Tatlin and secretary Rodchenko, strongly protesting the abolition of federative divisions.

21. The club of "creative individual anarchism" may also have drawn its name from this Bakunin thesis.

22. Aleksei Gan, "Proletkul't," *Anarkhiia*, no. 14 (March 8, 1918): 4.

23. Quoted from A. Koyré, *Mystiques spirituels et alchimistes du XVIe siècle allemand* (Paris: Gallimard, "Idées," 1955), 138.

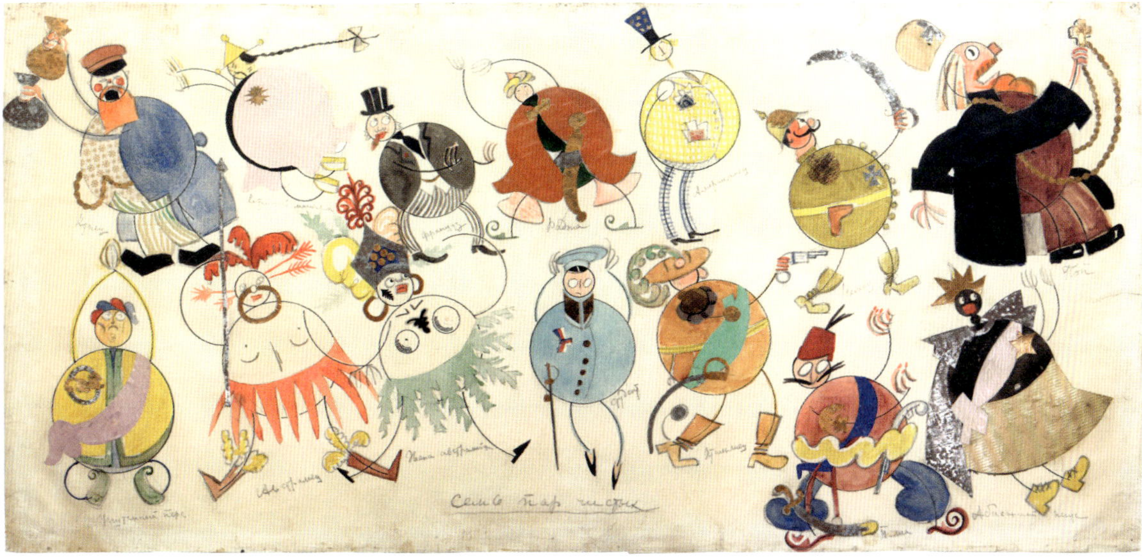
Семь пар чистых

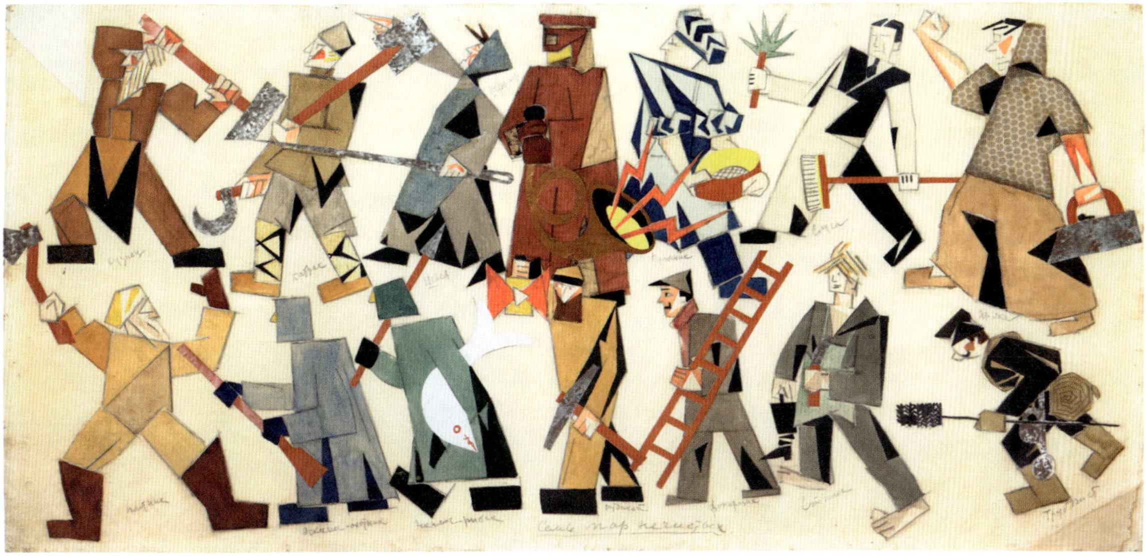
Семь пар нечистых

> We do not want to be privileged.
> We do not want to squelch either those who came
> before us or those who are coming after us.
> We want the right to creativity—to labor.
> We want equality and freedom in art.[24]

In her declaration, Udaltsova rejected the power of wealthy art patrons and hence refused financial support from the powerful. Art, Udaltsova affirmed, is free precisely because it belongs to no one and is not bought or sold. The machinery of the state had forcibly turned art into property. That is why Udaltsova sought for art forms that would make freedom visible and realizable, would resist the inertia and conventionality of the formation of meanings. Udaltsova's statement echoes a collective article published in *Anarchy* much earlier by Gan, Morgunov, and Malevich, entitled "The Tasks of Art and the Role of the Stranglers of Art," which radically extended Gan's statements in "Proletkult" on the role of a union of independent geniuses in culture-building:

> At this moment when the old way of life is being radically broken, when everything new and young is seeking to find its form and declare its "I," the dead are crawling out of their graves and trying to get their cold hands on everything that is alive. The social revolution has broken the shackles of capitalist slavery but has yet to break the old tablets of aesthetic values. And now, when we are embarking on new construction, on the building of new cultural values, it is essential to preserve ourselves from the poison of bourgeois vulgarity. . . . Get out of the way, butchers of art! Gout-ridden old men, you belong in the cemetery. . . . Go away, all of you who drove art into the cellars. Clear the path for the new forces![25]

Morgunov also made his own individual statements in *Anarchy* against state diktat in art: "Enough asking the state for counsel and hope! Any state authority is the butcher of art!"[26] In the article "The Vicious Circle," he dubs artists who are unwilling to compromise with power "anarchist artists" and "great utopians" who are ripping art out of the "vicious circle" of a history founded on power and violence.[27]

In his articles for *Anarchy*, "To the Statists of Art" and "In the State of the Arts," Malevich urged, "Seek a new consciousness and stop being slaves of things"[28] and, describing the state as a ship that "never leaves the Ladoga Ocean and enters the boundless expanse,"[29] spoke out definitively against state control of art: "In art, there must be no state."[30]

Malevich was the first to try to develop an anarchist model by means of the visual arts. The black square motif first arose during his collaborative work with Mikhail Matiushin and Kruchenykh on the staging of the opera *Victory over the Sun* in 1913. In the opera, the *budetliane*—people of the future—conquer the sun thanks to the black square. The conquest of the sun by the square symbolizes the overthrow of closed totalitarian constructions: Elemental anarchist creativity overcomes passive nature and breaks through to the future. In 1915, at *0,10: The Last Futurist Exhibition of Painting,* Malevich presented his painterly version of *Black Square,* which signaled a transition to objectless art and consequently, along with the elimination of "things," ideally represented the elimination of statism. Futurism, according to Malevich, cannot fully explicate the freedom of creative work, and must therefore be supplanted by suprematism: "But futurism's efforts to produce painterly plastics as such were not crowned with success: it could not separate from objectness in general and only destroyed objects for the sake of achieving dynamic movement."[31]

pp. 32–33, 44–45

The square that destroys objectness itself was, for Malevich, also an embodiment of the image of the black banner, the anarchists' main emblem.[32] In his short essay, "Toward a New Frontier," Malevich writes, "The banner of anarchy is the banner of our Self, and our spirit, free as the wind, will stir our creative powers in the vast expanse of our soul."[33] The *Black Square* largely established the representational paradigm for anarchism in art, since, while shedding the old representational logic, it offered the spellbinding possibility of

24. Nadezhda Udal'tsova, "My khotim," *Anarkhiia,* no. 38 (April 7, 1918): 4.

25. Aleksei Gan, Aleksei Morgunov, and Kazimir Malevich, "Zadachi iskusstva i rol' dushitelei iskusstva," *Anarkhiia,* no. 25 (March 23, 1918): 24.

26. Aleksei Morgunov, "K chertu!" *Anarkhiia,* no. 30 (March 29, 1918): 4.

27. Aleksei Morgunov, "Zakoldovannyi krug," *Anarkhiia,* no. 35 (April 4, 1918): 4.

28. Kazimir Malevich, "Gosudarstvennikam ot iskusstva," *Anarkhiia,* no. 53 (May 4, 1918): 4.

29. Kazimir Malevich, "V gosudarstve iskusstv," *Anarkhiia,* no. 54 (May 9, 1918): 4.

30. Ibid.

31. Kazimir Malevich, "Ot kubizma k suprematizmu: novyi zhivopisnyi realizm," in *Kazimir Malevich, Stat'i,* 1:29.

32. *The Black Banner* was, for instance, the title of the magazine founded in 1910 in Geneva by the anarchist I. S. Grossman (Roshchin).

33. Kazimir Malevich, "K novoi grani," *Anarkhiia,* no. 31 (March 30, 1918): 4.

endless quests for freedom in art. For Malevich, anarchism was a special world at the center of which was a free elemental force—that is, a supremely mobile, multidimensional, plastic potential world whose laws allow play with changeable forms and meanings. In his theoretical and artistic experiments, Malevich clearly relied on Bakunin-type anarchism and on Stirner's individualism. According to Malevich, the rejection of the state and its destruction in the name of a religion of art that refuses union with any form of state power appeared to be the only possible attitude of the real artist toward the state. The square, which eschews the concepts of up/down and left/right, as well as traditional representation, became the ideal visual embodiment of anarchist elemental freedom. While it is isomorphic to a certain hypothetical fragment of the universe, it nonetheless does not refer to an image of the whole with which Malevich associated statehood but exists by itself, in its own enclosed space, and symbolizes "the thing in itself." Thus, *Black Square* can be regarded not only as a symbol of the Russian avant-garde but as a sign of the anarchist *equilateral* society, which is not subordinate to any wholeness or statehood.

After the crackdown on anarchism in Moscow, Saint Petersburg, and other Russian cities, a group of rebel artists, although deprived of their mouthpiece, continued to influence others who leaned toward anarchism. The Moscow group of Nothingists (*nichevoki*), which lasted for about two years in 1920–1921, not only took a keen interest in European Dadaism but was guided in its aesthetics by the anarchists' radical understanding of art and culture. In 1921, Boris Zemenkov, Elena Nikolaeva, Aetsy Ranov, Riurik Rok, Oleg Erberg, and Sergei Sadikov published a "Decree on the Separation of Art and State" in the *Dog's Box* almanac. In it they declared "the state to be incompetent in matters of managing the preparation, inventorying, distribution, and oversight of the production of art."[34] Like many anarcho-futurists, they saw art as always linked to the established power structures. Therefore, they called for liberation from all the art that came before, which was to be thrown away into the *Dog's Box*.[35]

Most of the articles published in *Anarchy* can be boiled down to the idea that the interests of art cannot be the same as the interests of the state and thus to the rejection of state power in any form. This rejection was understood by these painters as liberation both from retrograde academicism and from the hierarchy it engendered, and therefore as the abolition of the canonical power of the norm that dictates hierarchy—a norm that can be represented by a literary subject, by the possibility of creating an image of the whole, by color, by object representation, and so on.[36]

One of the key publications in *Anarchy* was the "Letter to Comrade Futurists," a text by Baian Plamen, who accused not only the authorities but the futurists of statism and of selling out to the authorities—that is, of abandoning the main principle of futurism, the essence of which is, "Rebellion in art, revolution in artistic creativity. Anarchy in poetry, in painting, in sculpture, in tragedy. Anarchy in art."[37] One can detect a typological resemblance between Plamen's text and the Dada manifesto issued in Berlin in April 1918. For the Dadaist signatories, including Huelsenbeck and Tzara, expressionism, on which the artists of the new era had pinned huge hopes, had failed to justify those expectations, had become irrelevant, and was to be swept away by Dadaism and its strategy of universal negation: "Has expressionism fulfilled our hopes for an art that would inject into our veins the fire of the essence of being? NO! NO! NO!"[38]

Like the Dadaists, Plamen posits the consistent destruction of any and all aesthetics. Dadaists declared, "The Dadaists are nothing, nothing, nothing; undoubtedly, they will accomplish nothing, nothing, nothing." For anarcho-futurism as interpreted by Plamen, any aesthetic was counteranarchy if only because it rests on confirmed and fixed rules. His article is the manifesto of a movement that never took proper form—apparently because any structure and cataloging relies on authority, which the group of anarchist painters rejected as a matter of principle.

After Malevich, a visual model of an anarchist society that destroys the statist myth was developed by Rodchenko and Stepanova. As a frequent contributor to *Anarchy*, Rodchenko

34. See "Decree on the Separation of Art and State," on p. 298 of the present catalogue.

35. The "Dog's Box" is the negative model of the artists' café "Stray Dog," which existed from December 31, 1911, until March 3, 1915, at no. 5 Mikhailovskaia Square in Petrograd.

36. In 1917–1918, anarchism successfully competed with Bolshevism. Thus, in 1917, rallies by artists protesting state control over art were held in Moscow and Petrograd. Participants in the Moscow rally, held on the premises of the Salamonsky Circus, spoke against the creation of a government agency charged with oversight of the arts. At the rally in Petrograd, held at the Mikhailovsky Theater, a resolution against the establishment of a ministry of the arts was adopted following a report by Ilia Zdanevich. While these rallies did not espouse anarchist slogans, the participants' statements and the resolution on Zdanevich's report were of a clearly anarchist nature.

37. Baian Plamen, "Pis'mo tovarishcham futuristam," *Anarkhiia*, no. 27 (March 26, 1918): 4.

38. Richard Huelsenbeck, "Dadaistisches Manifest" (1918), in *Dada Almanach*, ed. Richard Huelsenbeck (Berlin: Erich Reiss, 1920), 35.

published a programmatic article, "The Dynamism of the Surface" (a month before his first solo exhibition, held in May 1918 in the club of the Left Federation), in which he argues for the possibility of constructing surfaces of any length and depth, "layering" surface elements on each other: "By projecting vertical surfaces painted with the appropriate color and intersecting them with lines directed deeply inward, I reveal that color serves only as a conditional means of distinguishing the surfaces both from each other and from the indicators of depths and intersections."[39]

In his article "Be Creators," Rodchenko takes as his starting point Bakunin's thesis that destruction is a form of creation: "To you who are in power, to you who are victors, I say: Do not stop on the path of Revolution, keep going forward, and if the limitations of your party or agreements stand in the way of your life-creativity, break them; be creators, do not be afraid to lose something, for the spirit of destruction is also the spirit of creation, and your revolutionary march will give you the strength of creative inventiveness, and bright will be your path of revolutionary creativity."[40]

Stepanova never wrote for *Anarchy*. However, after meeting Rodchenko in late 1914 as a student at the Kazan Art School, she became (in 1916) not only his life companion but a loyal comrade-in-arms. Her diary note on the anarchic nature of Russian painting was a response to the atmosphere in which both were immersed.[41] In her early poetry album, *To the King of My Dreams and Imaginings*, dedicated to Rodchenko, she refers to her beloved as "the black king." One of Rodchenko's means of affirming anarchism was a passion for the color black.[42] His series "Black on Black," presented in 1919 at the exhibition *The 10th State*

39. Aleksandr Rodchenko, "Dinamizm ploskosti," *Anarkhiia*, no. 49 (April 28, 1918): 4.

40. Aleksandr Rodchenko, "Bud'te tvortsami," *Anarkhiia*, no. 61, (May 17, 1918): 4.

41. In 1920, Mayakovsky autographed his book *I Love* for Stepanova with the inscription, "To the fierce Stepanova with tender feelings." Rodchenko's nickname at home was "Anti," which he sometimes also used as a pseudonym. See, for instance, his article under this pseudonym, "Tak podnimites' zhe," *Anarkhiia*, no. 43 (April 21, 1918): 4.

42. On the connection between anarchism and the color black in Rodchenko's work, see Leonid Geller, "Zrenie utopii, zrimost' anarkhii," in *Rossica Lublinensia II. Literatura. Mit. Sacrum. Kultura*, ed. Maria Cymborska-Leboda and Witold Kowalczyk (Lublin: Wyd. UMCS, 2002), 183–90.

43. Nikolai Kulbin associated the first letter of his name, K, with the color black, thus simultaneously coding his sympathy for anarchism: "Language arts are the totality of verbal organisms, of verbal indivisibles. Each consonant has its own color: R for red (gore, war, rancor, misfortune), J for yellow (desire, jealousy, yearning), S for blue, Z for green, H for gray, G for black-yellow, K for black." See Nikolai Kul'bin, "Chto est' slovo (II-ia deklatarsiia slova kak takovogo," in *Russkii futurizm. Teoriia. Praktika. Kritika. Vospominaniia*, ed. V. N. Terekhina and A. P. Zimenkov (Moscow: Nasledie, 1999), 45.

44. Stepanova, *Chelovek ne mozhet zhit bez chuda*, 88–89.

45. Iurii Tynianov, "Ob osnovakh kino," in *Poetika. Istoriia literatury. Kino* (Moscow: Nauka, 1977), 335.

Exhibition: Nonobjective Creation and Suprematism together with other black color abstractions, was not only a polemical rejoinder of sorts to Malevich's *White on White* but another visual affirmation of the anarchist emblem: the black banner.[43] Stepanova wrote in her diaries, "In the 'black,' he gave what the West dreamed of: a genuine easel painting taken to its ultimate point."[44] Her admiration for the "black" canvases was rooted in her sympathy for anarchist color symbolism. All these nonobjective compositions convey the atmosphere of the primeval state of humanity, which can be regained through anarchy.

By the early 1920s, Rodchenko's and Stepanova's artistic anarchism began to manifest itself on deeper levels. Consider the photograph titled *Wandering Musicians*—the first double portrait of the two artists, dated 1921. In the background of this photographic portrait are Stepanova's works from the "Figures" series created in 1920–1921. However, the artists do not look like demiurges. Rather, they reserve to themselves the humbler role of "coauthors" of the material. Stepanova's and Rodchenko's postures look as artificial and figurative as the postures of the little stick figures on the walls of their workshop. Taking their cue from the "Figures," the artists demonstrate the constructive basics of the human body, as if laying themselves flat on the surface.

p. 244

p. 102

Several important techniques used by the author of this photoduet—Rodchenko, who affirms anarchism in his work—are in evidence. First, the anarchist way of thinking explicates the very fact of turning to photography, which, as Iury Tynianov writes, "exaggerates the individual features of a type to the millionth degree and thus actually creates the effect of 'non-resemblance.'"[45] Thus, according to Tynianov, the photographic frame underscores the fact that individuality is the only reality, subject to nothing and no one. For Rodchenko, what also matters is that the photographic frame removes the hierarchy characteristic in, for instance, academic painting. Everything that happens to be within the frame is important. Thus, the photograph, unlike the painting, removes the division into primary and secondary subjects.

A year later, Rodchenko created a montage self-portrait based on the *Wandering Musicians* photoduet. In it, he demonstrates the constructivist principle of the development of labor into art by cutting out his own image and then connecting it to a wheel and a cogwheel. Rodchenko's turn to industrial art, to spatial and optical projects involving household objects, fabrics, covers, and so on, was, among other things, a nod to anarchism. The program of "industrial art" took shape as a

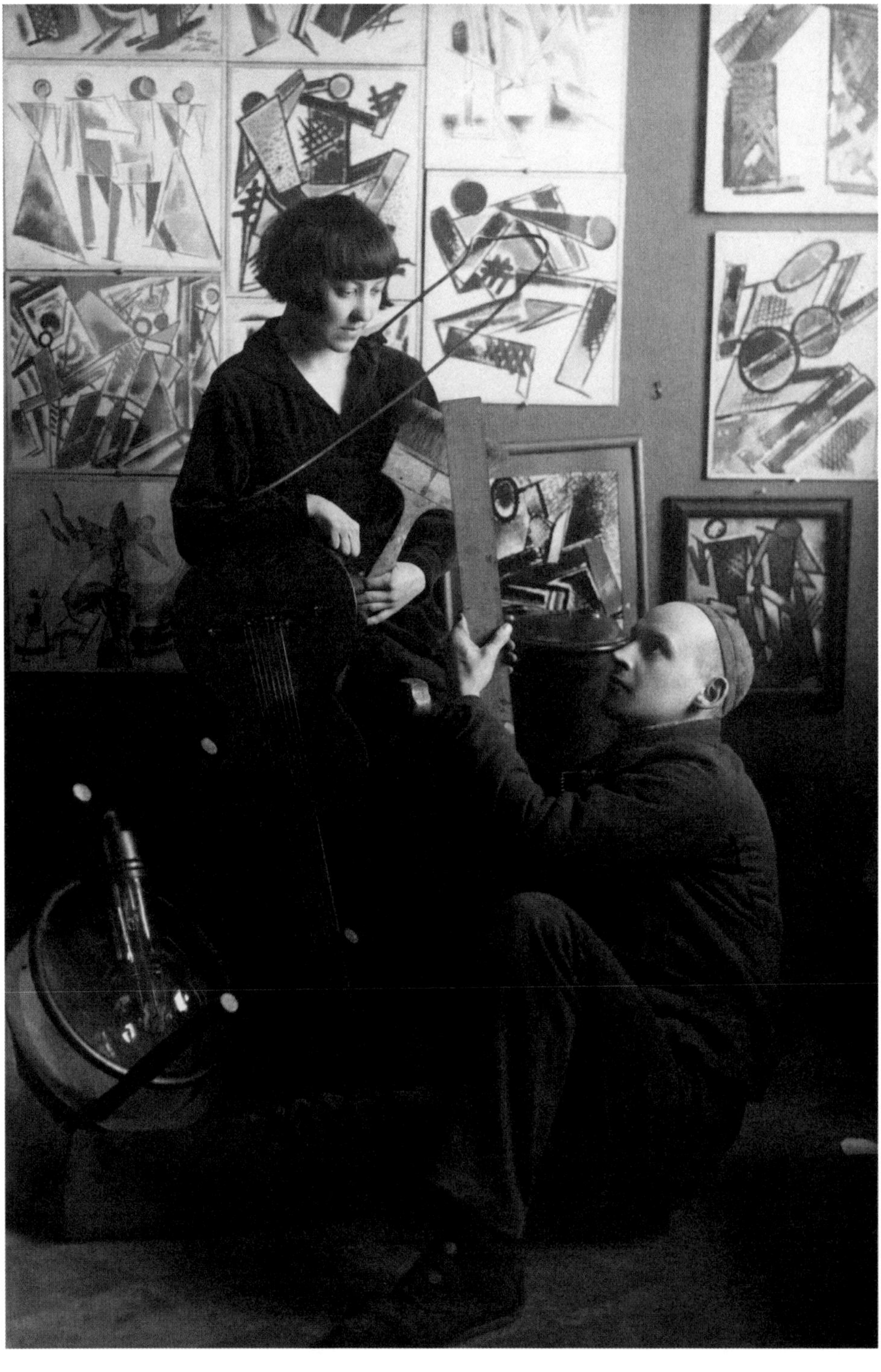

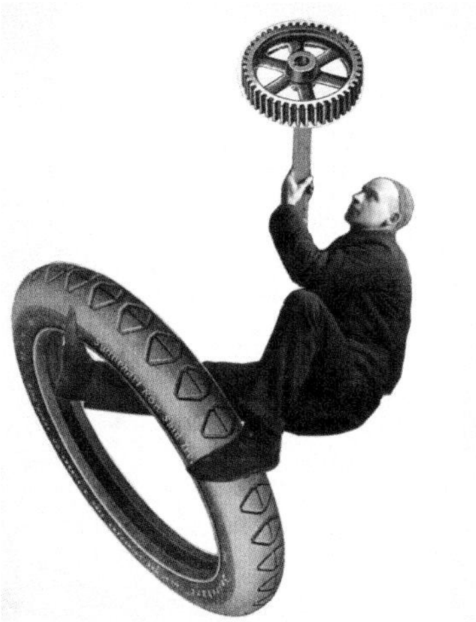

Aleksandr Rodchenko
Self-Portrait, 1922

Anonymous
Wandering Musicians (double portrait of Aleksandr Rodchenko and Varvara Stepanova), 1921

program of "everybody's art." That is, art was to develop through the effort of all workers, not just specially trained persons. Thus, the theory of "industrial art" as a universal form of creativity that would prospectively edge out all established art genres was consonant to anarchist notions about the possibility of a society not divided into the specially trained and those under their command. Those connected to elite art accessible to a small privileged minority of society have power. "Our painting," wrote Stepanova, "should be taken out to the streets, to fences and rooftops."[46]

Just as Duchamp's views were shaped by the relativism and solipsism of Stirner's philosophy, in which the individual is the only reality and *something* has value only insofar as it serves the self, Rodchenko was a devout reader of Stirner's *The Ego and His Own* and a follower of the ideas set forth in that book.[47] Rodchenko explicated his interest in Stirner's philosophy in the epigraph to his essay "The Rodchenko System" (1919). "At the foundation of my work I placed nothing."[48] Next to this statement by Stirner is one from Kruchenykh's play *Gly-Gly*—where, incidentally, the *budetliane* heroes are given the names of Khlebnikov and Malevich—"Paints are disappearing, everything is mixing up black," thus emphasizing the significance of anarchist color symbolism for Rodchenko's artistic system while simultaneously placing Kruchenykh on the same level as Stirner, the theorist of anarchism, and the poet Whitman and the philosopher Weininger, who were close to anarchism in their views.

Gly-Gly was published in 1918 with Ste- pp. 246–247
panova's "black" collages as illustrations. The title of one of them, *Soot and Smoke*, doubles the symbolism of the color black. The black

46. Stepanova, *Chelovek ne mozhet zhit bez chuda*, 85.

47. "I decide what is right for me; except for me there is no right," the German philosopher asserted. See Max Stirner, *Der Einzige und sein Eigentum* (Stuttgart: Philipp Reclam jun. GmbH Verlag, 1981), 208.

48. Aleksandr Rodchenko, *Opyty dlia budushchego* (Moscow: Grant Publishing, 1996), 66.

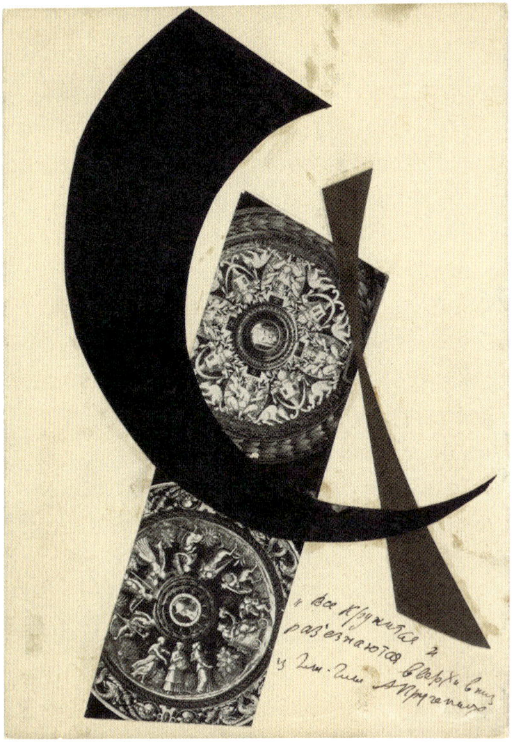

Varvara Stepanova
Illustration for *Gly-Gly* by Aleksei Kruchenykh, 1918

geometric figures in the composition *Everything Revolves* evoke black sails—another anarchist symbol, from the manifesto, *The Trumpet of Martians*: "Flap, black sails of time!"[49] The "woman with golden eyes" conveys the process of the disappearance of the object. Whereas Kruchenykh's play had "real" members of the avant-garde as its dramatis personae, Stepanova's illustrations hint at the artistic mannerisms of rebel painters such as Malevich, Rozanova, and Popova. Thus, those artists too became characters in the play.

The connection between Rodchenko's *Self-Portrait* (1922) and the anarchist worldview can also be seen in the fact that it has been interpreted as a critical response to Tatlin's
pp. 78, 245, 249 *Tower* (Monument to the Third International).

49. Velimir Khlebnikov, Mariia Siniakova, Bozhidar, Grigorii Petnikov, and Nikolai Aseev, *Truba marsian: poeziia russkogo futurizma*, ed. V. N. Alfonsov and S. R. Krassitskii (Saint Petersburg: Akademicheskii proekt, 1999), 624.

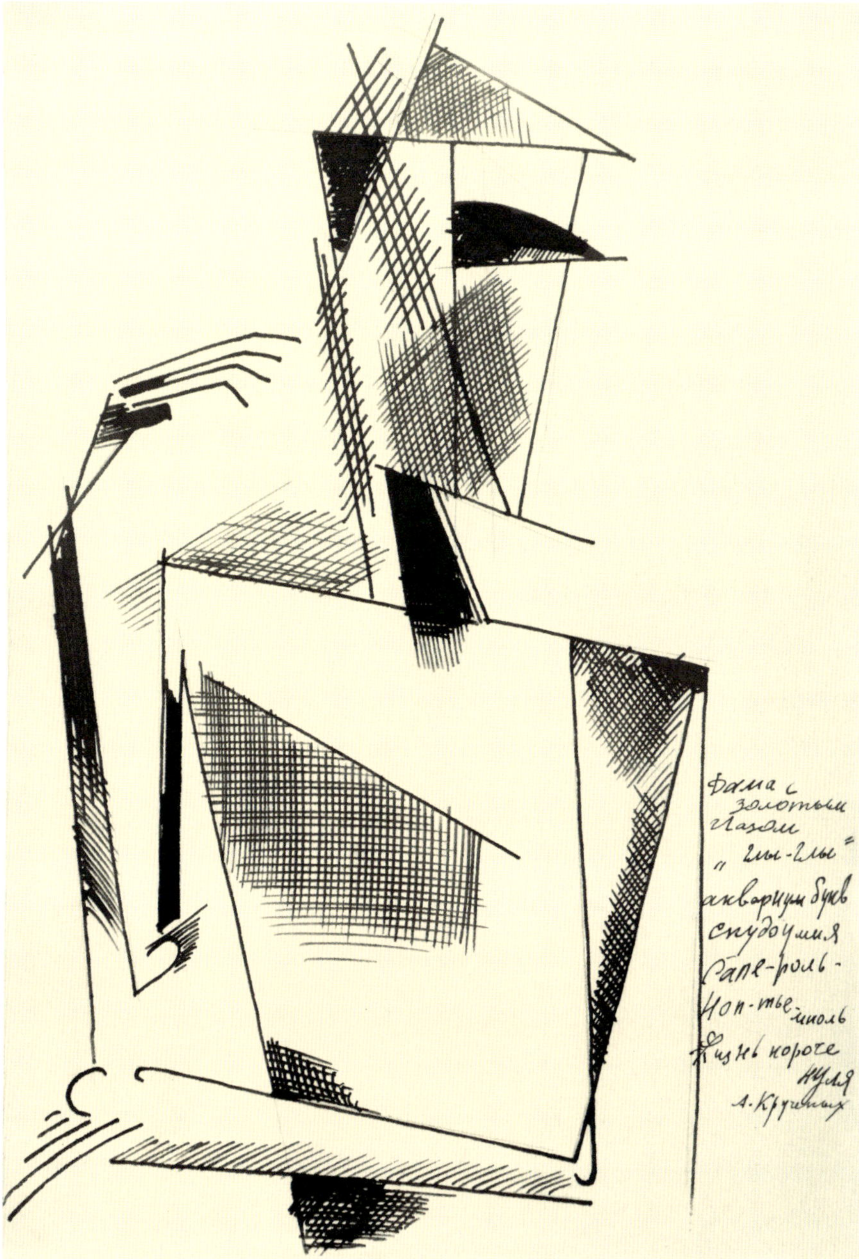

Varvara Stepanova
Illustration for *Gly-Gly* by Aleksei Kruchenykh, 1918

In Rodchenko's view, the construction of monuments is a process that literally demolishes the individual's self. Building monuments to literary greats or to the theoreticians of anarchism is akin to death since it presupposes the loss of individuality, of one's own self: "May all monuments disappear! . . . Why these absurd bronze idols, why these ridiculous puppets—perhaps made by talented people? You may say: It's sculpture, it's art; but you tell me: can art be made to order, made to fit a theme, a standard, a size? Of course not! . . . When something is commissioned by tsars, party leaders, or the people, what you get is a made-to-order work—but not art."[50] Rodchenko also hotly disputed the Hegelian idea of a spiral, which Tatlin made not only the decisive factor in constructing the visual and material environment (along with other geometric constructions: the hyperbole and the parabola), but also a metaphor for the dialectic of historic movement toward the absolute.[51] The silhouette of the artist seated atop a wheel in his *Self-Portrait* seeks the geometrism of the straight line.

The polemics with Tatlin—who, from Rodchenko's point of view, represented the powers that be—are also reflected in the pages of *Anarchy*. On the one hand, Rodchenko was fiercely opposed to the Petrograd Arts Section of the People's Commissariat for Education (Narkompros) extending its activity to Moscow: "A new commissariat: a commissariat for the arts. . . . They want to organize art in accordance with a political party program. . . . Do the Moscow bosses and the St. Petersburg 'terrorists' really believe that setting up an office with blank forms and stamps marked 'Left art' is enough to make the routine disappear, to make rigidity disappear, to make slavery

50. Aleksandr Rodchenko, "O pokoinikakh," *Anarkhiia*, no. 52 (May 4, 1918): 4.

51. On the idea of the spiral in Tatlin's work, see *Vladimir Tatlin: Leben. Werk. Wirkung. Ein internationales Symposium*, ed. Alexander Flaker and Jürgen Harten (Cologne: DuMont Buchverlag, 1993), 469-74.

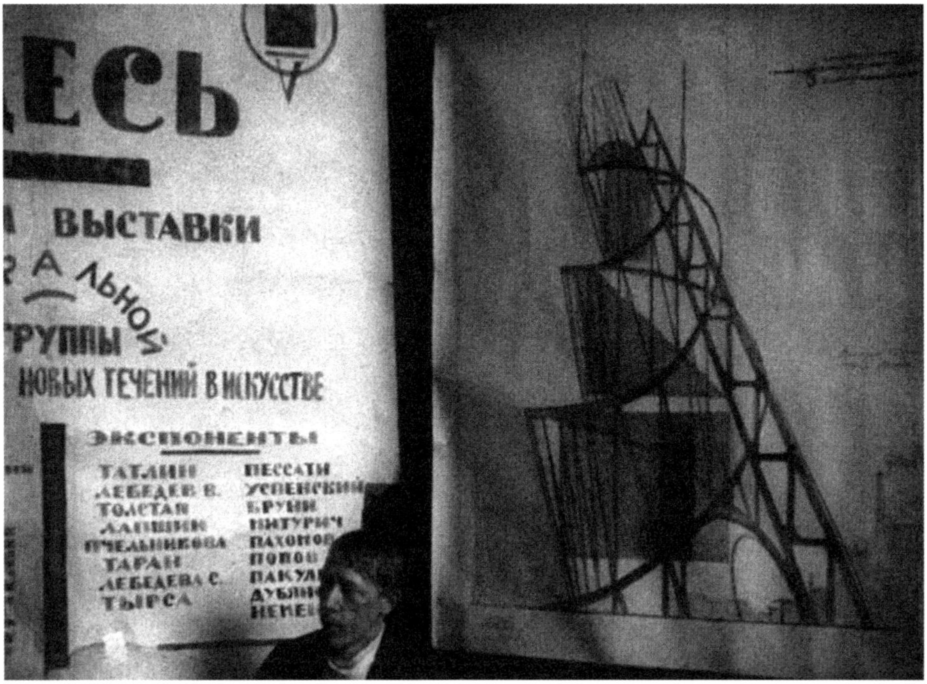

Anonymous
Vladimir Tatlin in the documentary film
Exhibition of Paintings of the Petrograd Artists of All Trends, 1923

and chains for the new art disappear? . . . The rebel artist, the anarchist artist will never agree to this new kind of hidden compromise, this new kind of exploitation and stifling of art."[52] On the other hand, he also condemned Tatlin, who had been appointed the Moscow commissar for the art section. Rodchenko writes, "Look: here's an aquarium, and artists that we ourselves have chosen are respectably swimming inside it, but we are separated by thick glass. . . . How horrible for us is such a victory. Dress up in rags and rejoice: One of us has indeed become the chosen and the authority."[53]

Tatlin, in his response in *Anarchy* to Plamen's "Letter to Futurists," asserts that "in order for the spirit to become anarchic," it is necessary to create "well-equipped art depots where the artist's psychic machinery could receive appropriate repairs."[54] His statements, with advice to artists to "improve the eye," do not contain radical anarchist theses on the destruction of state and property. And yet, Tatlin's views fit quite well into the anarchist paradigm. Tatlin saw an anarchic revolutionary spirit both in anarcho-universalism (in particular, in the theories of Karelin, who allowed the possibility of cooperating with the Bolsheviks since state power was going to make itself obsolete after the victory of the revolution) and in pananarchism. Roughly from the end of the 1917, the Gordin brothers' theories constructed first the architectonic of pananarchism, then of universalism, and finally of "Soviet anarchism," which took a moderate stance toward state power and recognized the idea of a global Communist revolution. In the stories, fairytales, and poems written by the Gordins, one can sense the coexistence of all these models rather than the priority of one of them. The second and third issues of *Anarchy* published the Gordins' sonnets which aestheticized freedom and anarchy. In the sonnets, artistic creativity is shown as a process that simultaneously destroys the objects of its creation as a completed whole.[55] The Gordins wanted to build both a united anarchist society and a global anarchist social network. To this end, Wolf Gordin attempted in 1918 to create an artificial language called AO, a kind of universal language of a united anarchist community. In 1923, he wrote "The Grammar of the Pan-methodological Language AO," in which he formulates the general grammatical rules of the language of future humanity—the language of neologisms. Gordin wrote his "Grammar" under the pen name "Beohbi," a transparent reference to Khlebnikov's poem "*Bo-beh-oh-bee* Is the Lipsong" (1908–1909). Gordin's "universal language" was close to the linguistic experiments of Khlebnikov's transrationalism while also echoing the language games in the work of the Dadaists.[56]

Tatlin's *Tower* was conceived as a kind of architectural embodiment of pananarchism, which would reunite humanity divided during the construction of the Tower of Babel. Like the AO language as an embodiment of the world tree and the foundation of the universe, the enormous radio masts that crowned Tatlin's construction were to become the foundation of a global network for storing and transmitting information. German Dadaists understood Tatlin's works as a genuine revolution in art. In the photograph of Georges Grosz and John Heartfield holding a placard that reads, "Art is dead / Long live the new machine art of TATLIN." Tatlin is greeted as a genuine Dadaist artist.[57] Nonetheless, Rodchenko interpreted spiral-like construction as an image of state power and state control in art and contrasted it to his own montage construction of geometric lines and circles.

p. 122

For Stepanova and Rodchenko, the geometric line, like other closed geometric forms, was a primary factor in any type of construction, including art. In his 1921 text "On the Line," Rodchenko writes, "The line is the first and last, both in painting and in any construction at all. The line is the path of passing through, movement, collision, edge, attachment, joining, sectioning. Thus, the line conquered everything and destroyed the last citadels of painting—color, tone, texture, and surface. The line crossed out painting with a red cross."[58] Furthermore, for Stepanova and Rodchenko, the line (like other closed constructions) was a geometric sign signifying the negative in the Hegelian dialectic of historical development.

Closed constructions become, in the works of Stepanova and Rodchenko, an "optimal projection" (Aleksandr Flaker's term) of anarchism, a graphic model of an anarchist society

52. Aleksandr Rodchenko, "Novyi komissariat (khudozhestvennaia kollegiia)," *Anarkhiia*, no. 43 (April 21, 1918): 4. The visual arts section of the People's Commissariat of Education was established by a decree of the State Commission on Education on May 22, 1918. Even earlier, on January 29, 1918, the artist David Shterenberg was appointed head of the visual arts section by a decree of the commissariat. The section's arts board comprised Shterenberg, Natan Altman, Nikolai Punin, and Sergei Chekhonin, as well as Mayakovsky and Osip Brik. A short time later, a similar board, with the same prerogatives as the Petrograd one, was set up in Moscow. Its members were Tatlin (deputy director of the visual arts section and the board chairman), Morgunov, Malevich, Sofia Dymshits-Tolstaia, Udaltsova, Rozanova, and Kandinsky.

53. Anti, "Tak podnimites' zhe," 4. See also Rodchenko's brief article in *Anarkhiia*, no. 50 (April 30, 1918), in which he criticizes Morgunov and Tatlin for "climbing" into "cushy commissariats."

54. Vladimir Tatlin, "Otvechaiu na 'pis'mo k futuristam,'" *Anarkhiia*, no. 30 (March 29, 1918): 4.

55. Abba Gordin and Wolf Gordin, "Sonety," *Anarkhiia*, no. 3 (September 25, 1917): 2.

56. On the typological kinship of transrationalism and Dadaism, see the collection *Zaumnyi futurizm i dadaizm v russkoi kul'ture*, ed. Luigi Magarotto, Marzio Marzaduri, and Daniela Rizzi (Bern: Peter Lang, 1991).

57. In 1922, paraphrasing this slogan by Grosz and Heartfield, Aleksei Gan called for "death to art" in his book *Konstruktivizm*] (Tver', 1922), 18.

58. Aleksandr Rodchenko, *Experiments for the Future: Diaries, Essays, Letters, and Other Writings*, ed. Alexander N. Lavrentiev, trans. Jamey Gambrell (New York: Museum of Modern Art, 2005), 113.

that is not subject to any state power whatsoever.[59] Stepanova's visual poetry from the collections *Zigra ar* and *Rtny khomle*—whose titles are anagrams not only of the second part of the pseudonym of the artist V. Agarikh but of the word *anarkhism*, and whose contents echo the p. 280 Dadaists' language experiments—is rich with imagery of closed forms. Stepanova's drawings and collages dedicated to Charlie Chaplin, an an- pp. 207, 218, 221 archist loner who does not recognize the laws of authority, is also made of closed constructions.

In the context of the work of anarchist artists in 1917–1924, yet another key figure stands out: El Lissitzky. While not a member of the group of rebel artists who were published in *Anarchy*, he was nonetheless friendly with them and shared their anarchist views of art. When he was in Germany in 1922–1925, Lissitzky worked with Kurt Schwitters, Arp, Raul Hausmann, and Tzara. He also participated in the Congress of Dadaists and Constructivists in Weimar in September 1922. The contact with Dada artists was mutually influential. In particular, one can see parallels between Lissitzky's exhibition designs in the 1920s and Schwitters's *Mer-* p. 255 *zbau*. In 1924, Lissitzky made *Self-Portrait* by photographing his hand clutching a caliper against the backdrop of millimeter-lined graphic paper, then overlaying the hand with his own photographic portrait from another negative—an example of the organo-poetics of anomalous bodiliness. What, then, is the meaning of the anomaly presented in this photomontage?

First, the artist depicted two fragments of the human body: the hand and the head. The use of fragments is a departure from the canonical norm, signaling the incorrectness of text in relation to all canonical genres that lay claim to completeness and wholeness. Therefore, the depiction of the hand and the head as fragments of the body in this montage already belongs to the organo-poetics of anomaly. The human body parts that are captured here and that occupy a significant part of the visual surface ultimately become autonomous "excerpts" from the artist's body. Yet, fragmentation also produces further deformation. The overlaying of two body parts (hand and head) engenders an entirely new body. We are looking at a new, bodiless corporeality created by montage—or, to use a concept from Maurice Merleau-Ponty's theory of the phenomenal body, we are observing a "potential body" of the human being of the future.[60] The hand loses its ordinary meaning as a human extremity and a symbol of human labor. The hand here is not an object or a sum of objects but a new anatomical formation: a hand that acquires vision. The eye from the artist's face is visible through his palm.[61]

The meaning of a "hand that acquires vision" can be understood if we take Edmund Husserl's interpretation of the body as a starting point. In contrast to the classical philosophy of the body, Husserl draws attention to the fact that there are two kinds of body: the physical body and the experiencing subject. The subject/object body, which Husserl ponders in his treatise "Philosophy as Rigorous Science," overcomes the dichotomy between "self" and "the other" and penetrates spheres inaccessible to reflexive analysis. In Lissitzky's *Self-Portrait*, the "hand that acquires vision" is a place where the material (the hand itself) interacts with the contemplative (the eye). This image illustrates new horizons of the artist's experience—the experience that results from the mutual interaction of his mobile bodily activity directed at the outside world and the simultaneous impact of the outside world on him.[62] By depicting an anomalous hand—a hand with an eye—Lissitzky tries to overcome the subject-object dichotomy so typical of classic philosophy of the body. His montage composition represents the metaphorical image of a magical or carnival-like, grotesque (in the Bakhtinian sense) body in which antinomies are removed. Such an anomalous hand is perceived as perfect, and the artist who possesses it as a creator of new culture. The artist who has overcome—in the sense of Stirner's three-part dialectic—both the realistic stage of childhood, with its materialistic limitations, and the weakness of youth, with its idées fixes of ideologies and religions becomes, in *Self-Portrait*, a true Dadaist constructor. Acquiring personal self-government, the constructor symbolizes the concluding part of Stirner's three-part dialectic: He is genuinely free from all internal and external limits.

59. See the chapter "Optimal'naia proektsiia" in Aleksandr Flaker, *Zhivopisnaia literatura i literaturnaia zhipovis'* (Moscow: Tri kvadrata, 2008).

60. Maurice Merleau-Ponty, *Phénoménologie de la perception* (Paris: Gallimard, 1945).

61. Compare this to the Maurits Cornelis Escher's graphic drawing *Hand with Reflecting Sphere*, where the hand, deformed on a glass orb, produces a new optic.

62. See also Martin Heidegger: "The hand both gives and receives, and not only things; it also gives itself, and receives itself with the other hand." Martin Heidegger, *Was heißt Denken?* (Frankfurt: Vittorio Klostermann, 2002), 18–19.

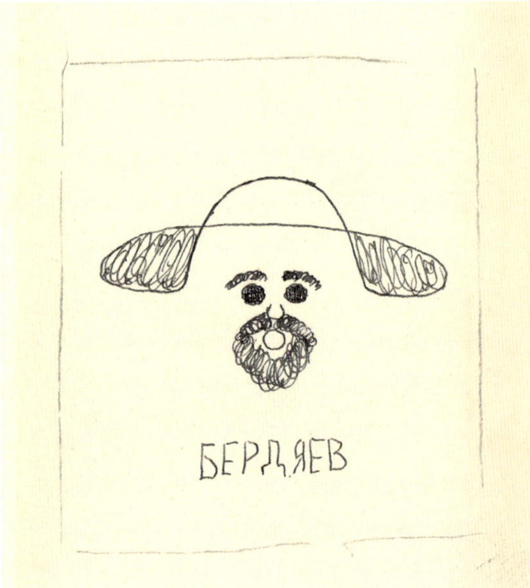

Sergei Sharshun
Nikolai Berdiaev, ca. 1921–1922

The Russian philosopher Nikolai Berdiaev, who lived in Berlin in 1922–1924 and published several of his works there, wrote in 1946 that "the Russian pathos of freedom was more connected to a principled anarchism."[63] Thus he repeated a point often argued by the rebel painters in the era of anarchist utopias. The image of the era that united Dadaism and anarchism was given an unexpected and witty rendition in Sergei Sharshun's Dadaist drawings,
pp. 203, 254 made in Berlin in 1921–1922, of Berdiaev and Tzara, both of whom he knew personally. The Russian philosopher of freedom and anarchy and the leading theorist of Dadaism are represented in such a way that, for all their external divergence, they nonetheless demonstrate a resemblance. Thus Sharshun gives Dada and anarchism the status of phenomena from the same category.

63. Nikolai Berdiaev, "Russkaia ideia: Osnovnye problemy russkoi mysli XIX i nachala XX veka," in *O Rossii i russkoi filosofskoi kul'ture: filosofii russkogo posleoktiabr'skogo zarubezh'ia* (Moscow: Nauka, 1990), 171.

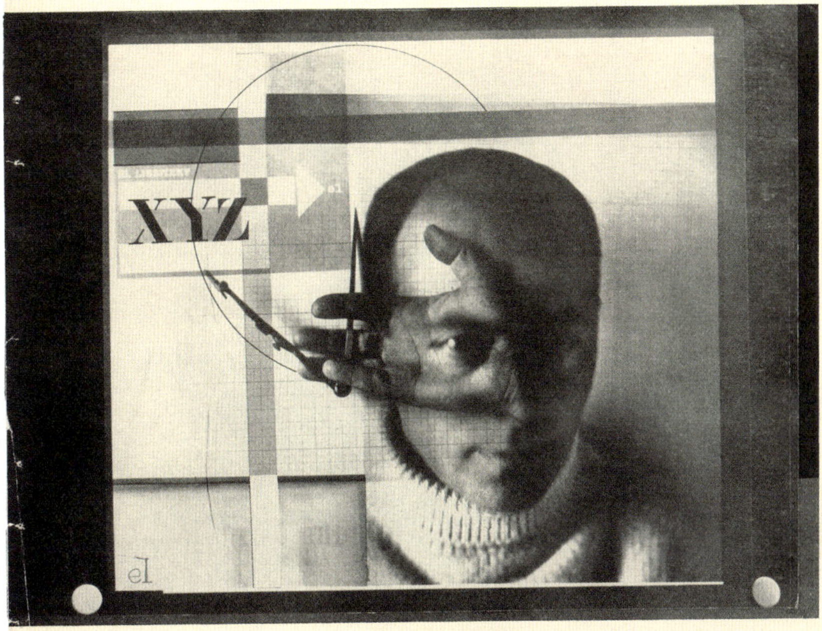

Portrait of himself (Photo-Painting) 1923
Selbstporträt (Photomalerei) 1923

TRAUGOTT SCHALCHER

el LISSITZKY, MOSKAU

DAS Land der Russen mit der Seele suchend — so tastet man sich vorsichtig und genießerisch durch das Werk dieses Künstlers. Lenin spricht. Vor dem Kreml stauen sich unabsehbar die Massen des Proletariats. Eine Karte von Rußland wird ausgebreitet. Sie verliert sich hinter statistischen Tabellen. Der 25. Oktober 1917 wird uns als „Großer Tag der Sowjets" eingehämmert. Noch und noch und noch. Dort ist ein Plakat für die Rote Armee, aber nicht weit davon wirbt der Künstler für Pelikantinte. So ist in Lissitzky Russisches und Deutsches, Merkantiles und Kommunistisches seltsam gemischt. Bei aller

"SEEKING the land of Russians with the soul —" to adapt the poet's words, cautiously and enjoying every step, one feels one's way through the work of this artist. Lenin is speaking. The proletarian masses stand in dense throngs before the Kreml. A map of Russia lies spread before us. It is almost concealed behind tables of statistics. October 25, 1917 is being celebrated as the "Great Day of the Soviets." Here is another striking effect, here another and another. Here is a poster for the Red Army and cheek by jowl with it the artist calls our attention to Pelikan inks. Such is the singular mixture of Russian and

49

El Lissitzky
Self-Portrait, illustration in the journal
Gebrauchsgraphik, 1928

PRIMARY TEXTS

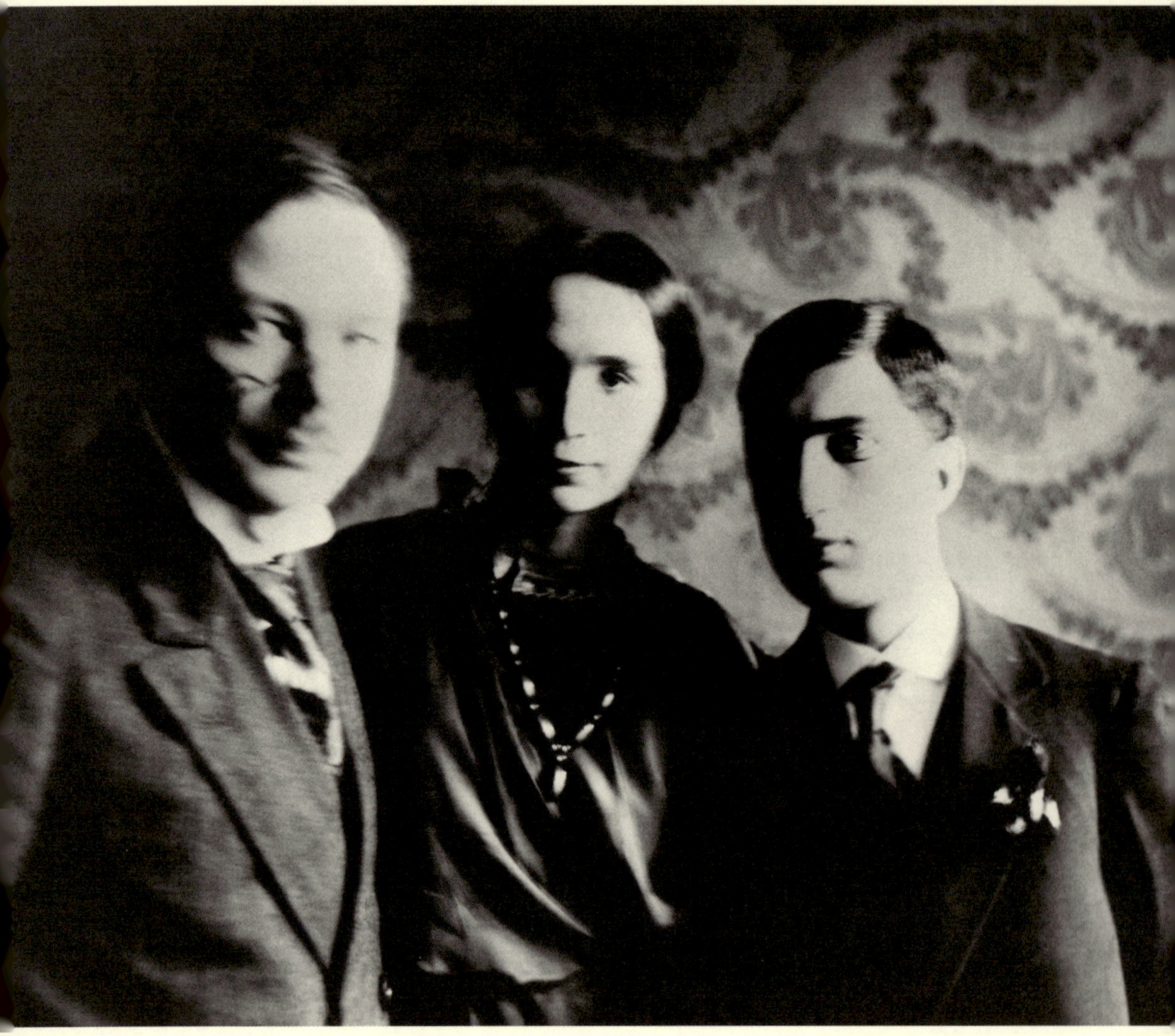

Anonymous
Mikhail Larionov, Natalia Goncharova,
and Ilia Zdanevich, Moscow, 1913

ILIA ZDANEVICH
NATALIA GONCHAROVA AND EVERYTHINGISM, 1913

Truly brief was the reign of futurism. But a great deal was accomplished. Just as the soul always dances on the eve of a dizzying endeavor, so futurism made the impossible possible. And who could have thought that—after all the unheard-of brazen stunts, the trampled values, the transformation of a brain into an airplane, the beauteous revelations and riots—something even more impossibly brazen, crushing, and riotous would come, something that would make no distinction between futurism and its enemies and throw everyone into the same heap of herd-like mindlessness.

You are always blind, deaf, and utterly ignorant until the rocks come crashing down on you. But there's nothing to be done. Your attachment has blindfolded you with a handkerchief and stopped your ears with dirty cotton. . . . To begin with, let us cast aside several words and related concepts: the words *time, space, new, old,* and everything that follows from them. There is no audience but this one, no time but the present. I have in my head a series of books of diverse contents and a series of works to some of which we will now turn. These books and works contain judgments of art, which boil down to this: art grows and falls, artworks age, knowledge is transmitted from generation to generation, etc.; in other words, art lives in history. From these assumptions, one deduces several valuable laws: Art is based primarily on aesthetic emotion, which changes along with the evolution of its bearer. Therefore, if the combination of certain esthetic norms can be defined as style, one can assert that the more conservative and hidebound an environment is, the more constant the style of the state of the ancient world, the state of the most constant styles. With progress and the acceleration of development, styles change faster and faster; today, they rise and fall by the hour. To establish a fixed style for our time is impossible. This is the sort of curious thing they write in those little books. And then they also write that the more hidebound the environment, the slower its development, the less one generation differs from the

Il'ia Zdanevich, excerpts from "Nataliia Goncharova i vsechestvo," lecture presented November 5, 1913, Moscow, in State Russian Museum, Archive of the Department of Manuscripts, Fond 177.

next, the sooner new masters are recognized, the less intense the struggle for recognition and the hostility to innovators, the stronger and more durable authorities are. In ancient times, there was no notion of innovators at war with the crowd; in our time, every new direction is met with more and more hostility. This past spring, you attacked us at the Polytechnic Museum[1]—one of the first instances of fisticuffs over aesthetics. Then: the more hidebound the environment, the more stable tradition is; hence, the less need [for] the theoretical study of art, the less theory and individuality, and vice versa. Then: the more hidebound the environment, the more homogeneous aesthetic beliefs are, the more art belongs to the entire people, the fewer parties and cells; and vice versa. Conclusion: in our time, there can be no stable style, no school, no tradition, no truly universal popular art. Conclusion: ours is a time of cross-breeding and ephemeral styles, of theory, of differentiation in art. For ours is a time of speed and progress, dizzying and hasty.

The books in which these historical laws of art are formulated have been written by me and have never existed. Their precepts are strictly logical and scientific; they are the creed of futurism, which grew out of them and has rested on their foundation. But futurism never suspected that its creed and its logic could be thrown out the window; that both common sense and lack of common sense could be replaced by yet another principle that mocks both common sense and its absence.

There is nothing but this audience and nothing but the present. Yet our gaze pierces the walls like X-rays and takes possession of the world; our thoughts stand guard over it and pass judgment on its evolution. We create the time and the place. There are many worlds beyond this audience, many hours beyond this hour. But no further. Do not return to new paths. We affirm that time exists just like space exists, but there are no relations within them. Relations are created by human beings, and the distant can become near while the near can become distant. There is no historical perspective, no perspective or space as such. There are only systems created by human beings. To wage war against the past is absurd because there is no past. To aspire toward the future is absurd because there is no future. The future can become the past and vice versa, time and place are human material created for better construction, and the master can use this material any way he pleases. Such is the foundation of everythingism [*vsechestvo*]. . . . Everythingism is a special school of mastery; it makes war against the past senseless and thus overthrows futurism. But it is not related to any par-

1. A reference to a fight at the Polytechnic Museum in Moscow during the "Target" debate on the subject "East, Nationality and West," which took place on March 23, 1913.

ticular aesthetic; thus, it does not conflict with the belief that the boot is still more beautiful than Venus,[2] women are still contemptible, etc. That is beside the point, since these are not the tasks of mastery as such. But one can be an everythingist [*vsek*] without espousing such beliefs. Whether the master is a woman-hater matters not. Whether he regards the public as sheep matters not. Only his mastery matters. Futurism's main flaw was not its beliefs, many of which are valuable and are still being affirmed, but in the dilution of mastery by everyday concerns, moods, and so forth. This is a serious problem among the French. As for our St. Petersburg and Moscow poets, those lowlife camp followers have completely forgotten mastery. They seemed, and seem, extravagant and rebellious only by dint of the stupidity of their audiences, even though their rebellions never made any difference.

2. Zdanevich's lecture "About Futurism" was presented at the "Target" debate on March 23, 1913, at the Polytechnic Museum in Moscow and involved the demonstration of a boot. This is how it was reported in the press: "Displayed on the screen, an image of Venus de Milo; displayed by the lecturer, a worn-out old boot. 'Now, here's Venus. Why is she beautiful? Because that's what we've been taught. The beauty of the boot is greater because it is autonomous, because one is not aware of it.' The young man stands there for a long time with the boot in his hands, while the audience is in an uproar. 'Get this boot out of here! To hell with the boot!' 'Traveling salesman!' There is whistling, stamping of feet, wild yelling; finally, he is forced to put the boot away." "Sovremennyi bashmak i Venera (Disput 'Mishen')," *Golos Moskvy*, no. 70 (March 27, 1913): 5.

НОВЬ

Въ розничной продажѣ повсюду. 2 коп.

ЕЖЕДНЕВНОЕ ИЗДАНІЕ.

№ 11. Воскресенье, 26 января 1914 г.
МОСКВА.

Редакція: Б. Дмитровка, 26. Тел. 4-51-42. Пріемъ ежедневно 3 — 6 час. вечера.

Контора: Кузнецкій Мостъ, 11. Тел. 4-51-41.
ПОДПИСНАЯ ЦѢНА: на 1 годъ—5 р. 50 к., на полгода—3 р., на 3 м.—1 р. 60 к., на 1 м.—60 к. Разсрочка: при подпискѣ — 2 р. 50 к., 1 мая — 1 р. 50 к., 1 іюля — 1 р. 50 к. Для учителей, студентовъ, священниковъ, почт.-телегр. служащихъ льготная подписка: въ годъ—5 р., полгода—2 р. 70 к., 3 мѣс.—1 р. 40 к., 1 мѣс.—50 к. За границу вдвое.
ОБЪЯВЛЕНІЯ: 80 коп. строка нонпарели. Печатаются среди текста. Телеф. 2-63-27.

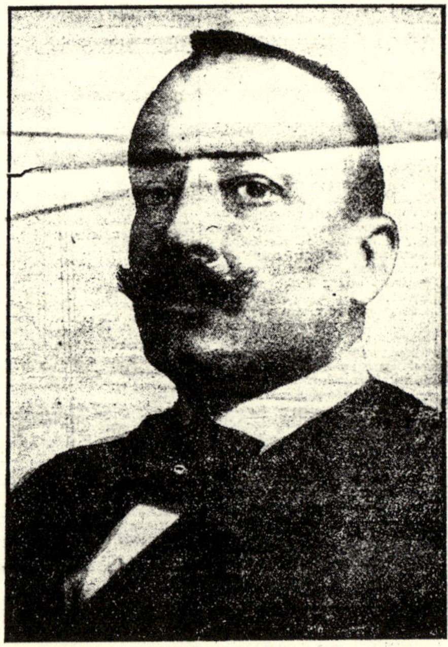

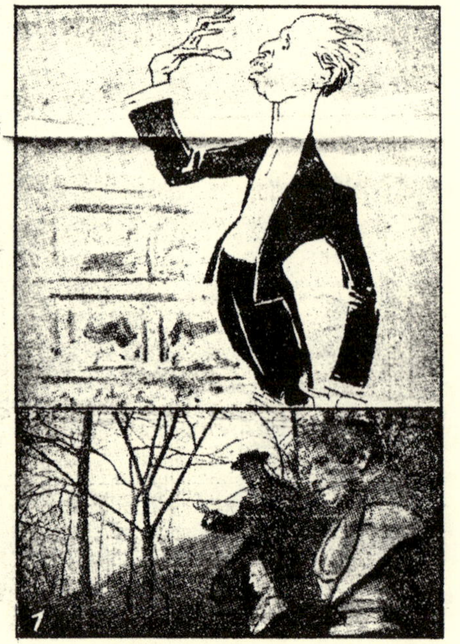

Anonymous
Filippo Tommaso Marinetti, illustration in the newspaper *Nov*, January 26, 1914

ILIA ZDANEVICH TO FILIPPO TOMMASO MARINETTI, 1914

D[ear] S[ir],
Regrettably, I am presently in the South, far away from Moscow, and unable to attend your conference or to say publicly what needs to be said about your visit. I have to resort to writing a letter, and since this is an open letter that affects more than just the two of us, I am sending a copy to the editors of the newspaper *Russkie vedomosti* [Russian News].[1]

My friend, *peintres, M-me Gontcharoff* [Goncharova], *Larionoff* [Larionov], *Le-Dentu* [Le Dantiu] *et moi,* were among the first to preach futurism in Russia, and I believe we contributed in no small measure to its epidemic spread in our day. Futurism was dear to us as the only direction that art truly needed, and, setting the interests of art above everything else, we fought for futurism. But the very same interests of art, the need for its renovation compared to recent past, forced us last year to break away from futurism—above all, because it no longer satisfied our artistic demands and turned out to be in need of a radical transformation in order to be at least somewhat compatible with the growth of artistic culture.

At present, we accept futurism only as a necessary historical stage. But your current propaganda, your current tactics, futurism in the form in which you propagandize it now—that I not only do not accept but regard as simply destructive to art, as a complete surrender of the position you used to hold, a surrender in the name of academicism, so that your futurism is now no more than a mask and, if you will, is more academic than the academy itself. And if the name of futurism is to be applied only to the ideology and tactics wh[ich] you currently espouse, forgetting the broad and anti-a[ca]demic futurism the way it used to be when it was born, it will have to be said that futurism was born yesterday and only yesterday, only as a ghost of unrealized possibilities—it doesn't matter why—and abandoned fortresses.

January 23, 1914, Tiflis

Department of Manuscripts of the State Russian Museum, f. 177, ed. kr. 66, l. 2-2ob.

1. Because Marinetti stayed in Russia longer than planned, the meeting between Zdanevich and Marinetti did take place.

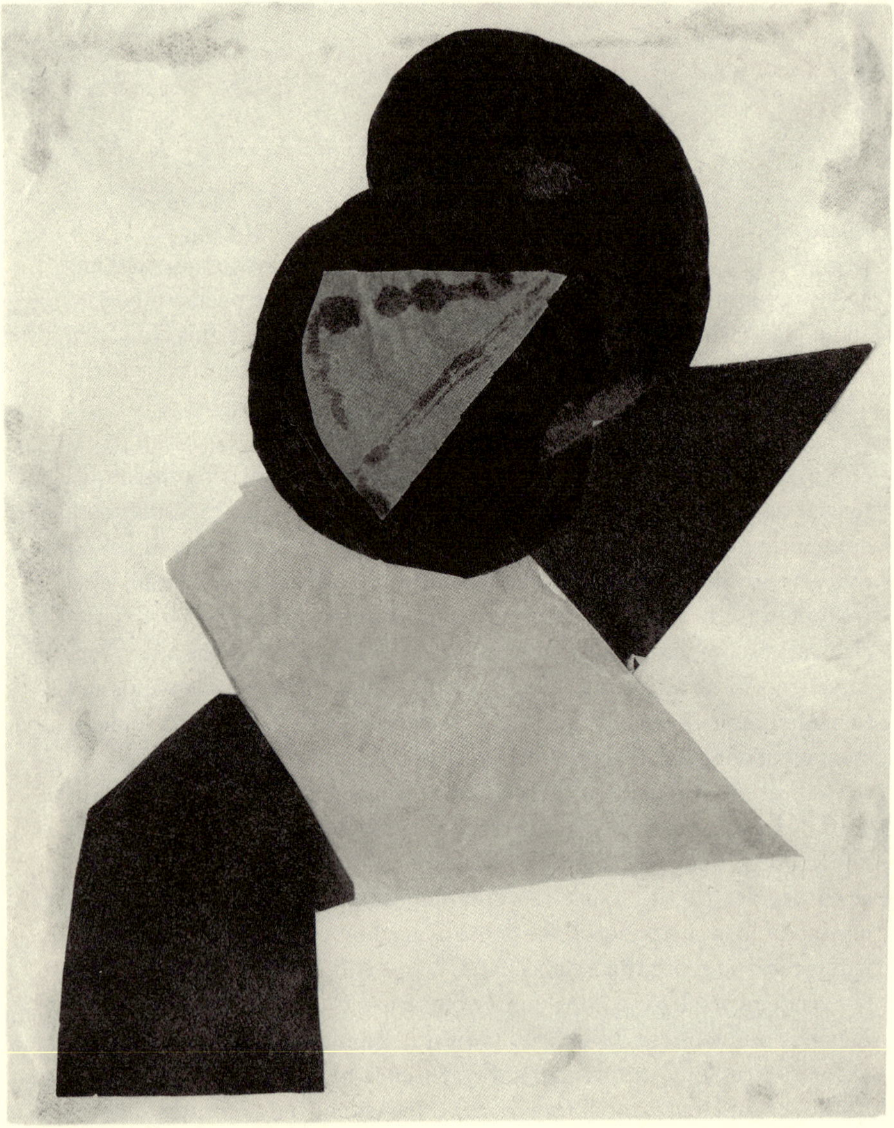

Olga Rozanova
Composition, 1915

OLGA ROZANOVA

THE BASIS OF THE NEW CREATION AND THE REASONS WHY IT IS MISUNDERSTOOD, 1913

For the majority of the public nurtured by pseudo artists on copies of nature, the conception of beauty rests on the terms "Familiar" and "Intelligible." So when an art created on new principles forces the public to awaken from its stagnant, sleepy attitudes crystallized once and for all, the transition to a different state incites protest and hostility since the public is unprepared for it. . . .

The disgusting roars of laughter at exhibitions of the leading trends can be explained only by a reluctance to be educated.

The bewilderment at pictures and titles expressed in technical language (directrix, color instrumentation, etc.) can be explained only by crass ignorance. . . .

Only modern Art has advocated the full and serious importance of such principles as pictorial dynamism, volume and equilibrium, weight and weightlessness, linear and plane displacement, rhythm as a legitimate division of space, design, planar and surface dimension, texture, color correlation, and others. Suffice it to enumerate these principles that distinguish the New Art from the Old to be convinced that they are the Qualitative—and not just the quantitative—New Basis that proves the "self-sufficient" significance of the New Art. They are principles hitherto unknown that signify the rise of a new era in creation—an era of purely artistic achievements.

—The era of the final, absolute liberation of the Great Art of Painting from the alien traits of Literature, Society, and everyday life. Our age is to be credited with the cultivation of this valuable world view—an age that is not affected by the question of how quickly the individual trends it has created flash past.

Olga Rozanova, excerpts from "Osnovy novogo tvorchestva i prichiny ego neponimaniia," *Soiuz molodezhi*, no. 3 (March 1913): 14–22, in *Russian Art of the Avant-Garde*, ed. and trans. John E. Bowlt (New York: Viking Press, 1976), 102–10.

After elucidating the essential values of New Art, one cannot help noting the extraordinary rise in the whole creative life of our day, the unprecedented diversity and quantity of artistic tends.

Messrs. art critics and veterans of the old art are being true to themselves in their fatal fear of what is beautiful and continually renewing itself; they are frightened and tremble for the little caskets of their meager artistic achievements. In order to defend publicly this pitiful property and the positions they occupy, they spare no effort to slander the Young Art and to arrest its triumphant procession. They reproach it further with frivolity and instability.

It is high time that we realized that the future of Art will be assured only when the thirst for eternal renewal in the artist's soul become inexhaustible, when wretched individual taste loses its power over him and frees him from the necessity of continually rehashing. . . .

Each moment of the present is dissimilar to a moment of the past, and moments of the future will contain inexhaustible possibilities and new revelations!

How can one explain the premature spiritual death of the artists of the Old Art, if not by laziness?

They end their days as innovators before they are barely thirty, and then turn to rehashing.

There is nothing more awful in the World than repetition, uniformity.

Uniformity is the apotheosis of banality.

There is nothing more awful in the World than an artist's immutable Face, by which his friends and old buyers recognize him at exhibitions—this accursed mask that shuts off his view of the future, this contemptible hide in which are arrayed all the "venerable" tradesmen of art clinging to their material security!

There is nothing more terrible than this immutability when it is not the imprint of the elemental force of individuality, but merely the tested guarantee of a steady market.

It is high time that we put an end to the debauch of critics' ribaldry and confessed honestly that only "Union of Youth" exhibitions are the pledges of art's renewal. Contempt should be cast on those who hold dear only peaceful sleep and relapses of experience.

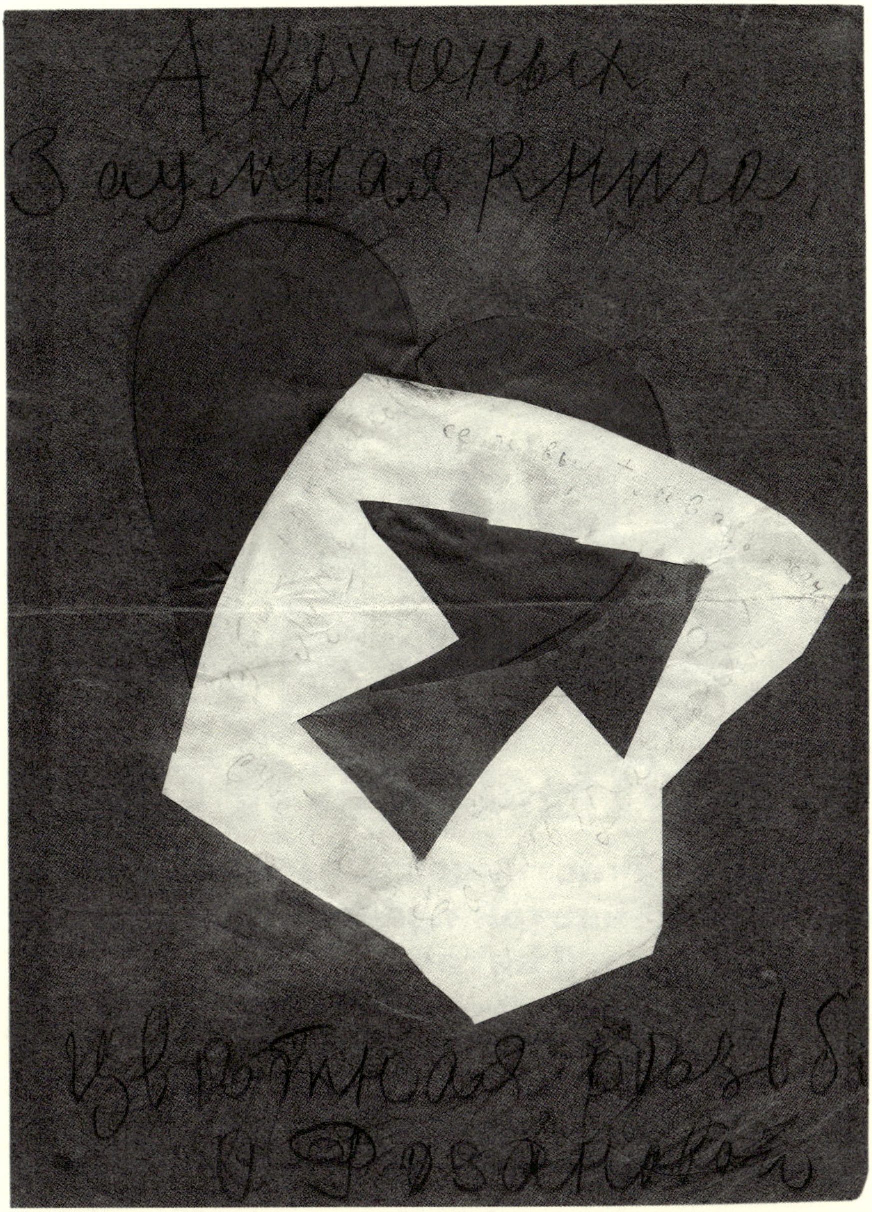

Olga Rozanova
Cover design for the book *Transrational*
by Aleksei Kruchenykh and Aliagrov
(Roman Jakobson), 1915

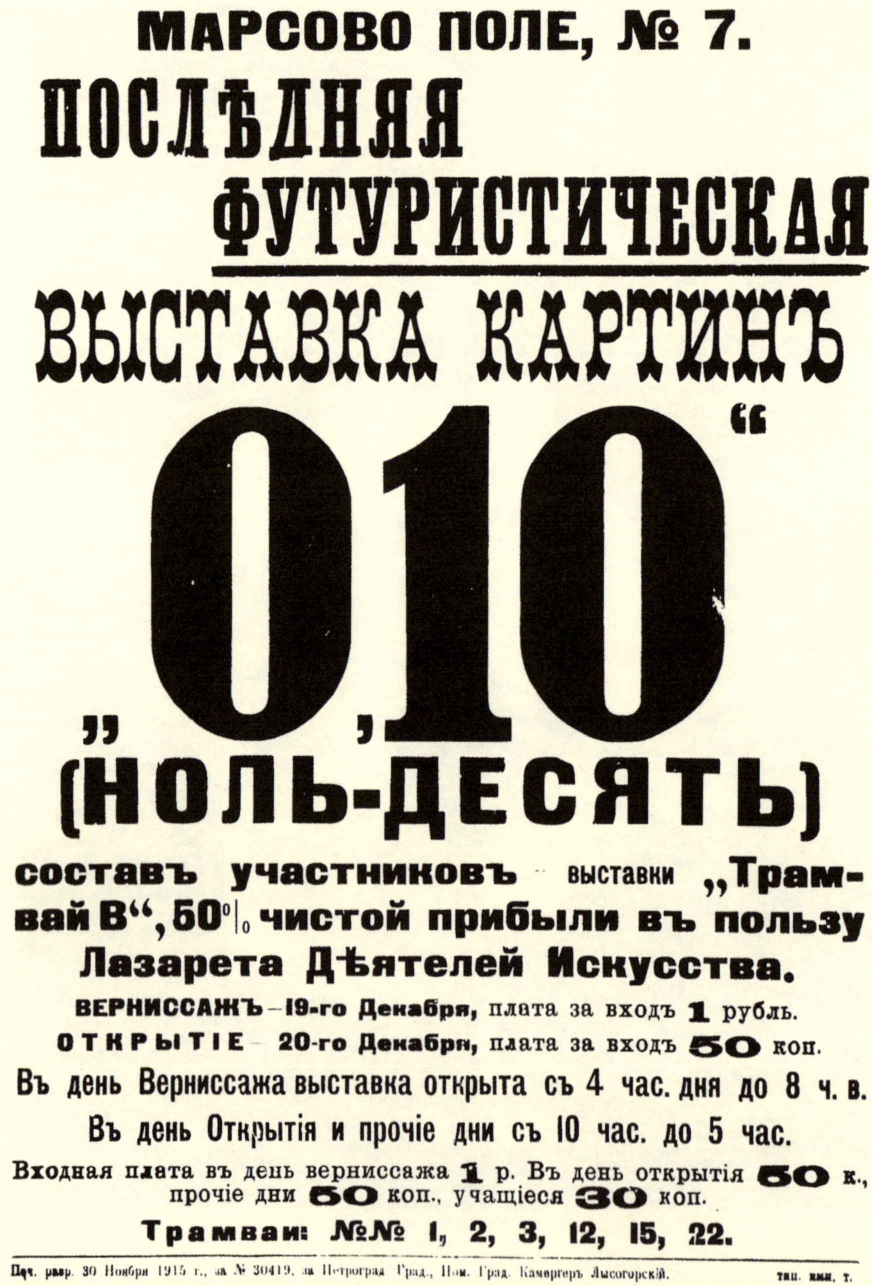

Ivan Puni
0,10: The Last Futurist Exhibition of Painting, 1915

IVAN PUNI AND KSENIA BOGUSLAVSKAIA
LEAFLET, 1915

1) An object is the sum of real units, a sum that has a utilitarian purpose.

> (Utility is the purpose of the sum of real elements to depict *something*. Example: a certain sum of elements is a stone, another man, etc.)

2) The substance of an object (reality) and the being of an object like a chair, a samovar, a house, etc., are not the same thing.

A) Freedom of the object from meaning, the destruction of utility.

B) A picture is a new conception of abstracted real elements, deprived of meaning.

3) 2 × 2 is anything you like, but not four.

C) (The aesthetic thing in itself.)

An object (a world) freed from meaning disintegrates into real elements—the foundation of art.

B. 2) The correlation of elements discovered and revealed in a picture is a new reality, the departure point of the new painting.

Ivan Puni and Kseniia Boguslavskaia, leaflet, distributed in *0,10: The Last Futurist Exhibition of Painting* (Petrograd, 1915), in *Russian Art of the Avant-Garde*, ed. and trans. John Bowlt (New York: The Viking Press, 1976), 112.

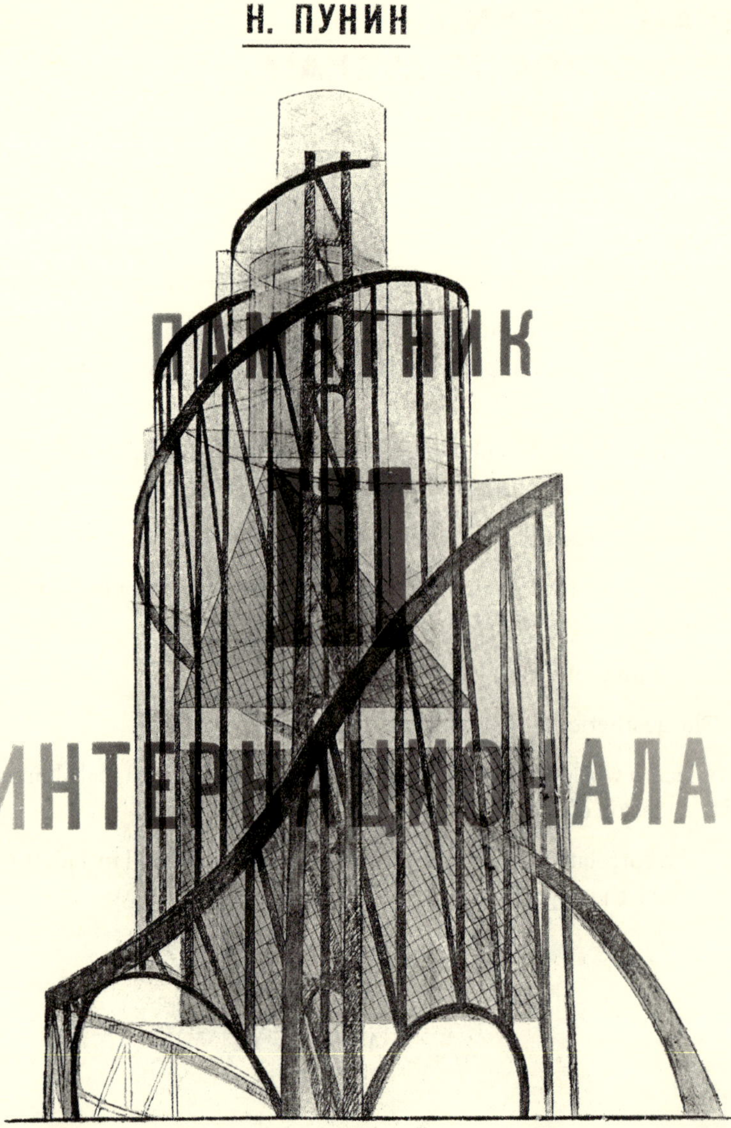

Vladimir Tatlin
Cover of the book *The Monument to the Third International* by Nikolai Punin, 1920

NIKOLAI PUNIN
APARTMENT NO. 5, 1930s

In Apartment No. 5, isms were condemned once and for all; no one used them as a cover for one's work. The only ones that were ever mentioned were terms that had actual meaning and that one could not do without: impressionism, futurism, cubism.

When Malevich brought suprematism along with the *0,10* exhibition, no one was tempted by the new "ism" simply because it was new. The time of futurism had passed. None of us wanted to ride at a gallop while lopping off the heads of clay dolls without slowing down. . . .

Our search was not for something new; it was for means to capture reality, ways to grab it in a vice grip without tormenting it or being tormented by it—by its convulsions and its groans, by its agony on the canvas. Artists needed a sharp eye and a well-trained hand and a hunter's keen senses, agility, and habits. The beast was a terrifying one, and no one expected or wanted mercy after a missed shot or a nonlethal wound. There was a severity in everything that was done then: people were serious and honest. We were all insanely tired of the imprecision of aestheticism and just as tired of the swift-footed experimentation of futuristic derby races. We were looking for art that would be sturdy and simple, as simple as it could be in those years of transition and upheaval. . . . We cherished the present—or, at the very least, none of us wanted to get ahead of our time or peer over people's heads; we were not tempted by poses. . . . And we believed that our art was simple, comprehensible, and needed. We had believed it earlier, in 1915, and we believed it later, in late 1916, when we had already moved on to cubism and even to Tatlin's constructivism, because each of those was not an ism or a movement for us but only a method. War had done its work; it came down between our lives in apartment No. 5 and the "first futurist battles"; it ripped away from us pieces of the past that should have belonged to us, shortening one part and lengthening another, just like a candle shortens or lengthens shadows falling on a wall; and, having changed the speed of the entire world, it laid underneath our lives

Nikolai Punin, excerpts from "Kvartira No. 5," from the memoir *Iskusstvo i revoliutsiia* (1930s); first published in *Panorama iskusstva* 12 (1989): 162–98.

a sinister backdrop against which everything began to seem both tragic and petty. We understood early on that the tactic, which the pioneers of the futurist movement had used with stunning success, but also to excess—*épater les bourgeois*—was harmful and inappropriate in the situation of 1915–1916. It was harmful because it inculcated the habit of viewing art as scandal, removing the quality and the actual meaning of the creative struggle; it was inappropriate because the "bourgeois" were already in such shock from the war—that futurist marching across the planet in the bloody shirt of never-ending sunsets—that it was simply foolish to try to shock them further. And, by and by, we developed an ironic attitude toward everything connected to the first futuristic campaign. . . . For the entire duration of 1916, there was intensive work going on in apartment No. 5 on comprehending the principles of "cubism." Both under Tatlin's guidance and without it, but within the framework of solving the tasks he had set, the apartment's denizens sweated over the construction of spatial models, over the selection of materials of different kinds, qualities, and forms. They sawed and shaved, they cut and polished, they stretched and bent. Painting was almost forgotten. The talk was only of contrasts, of combinations, of tensions, of cross-sections, of textures. From the outside, this could all look like a mania, but in reality it was the creative intensity of people who thought their efforts would finally displace age-old canons and that a "new Renaissance would arise." . . . The war slowly rolled over into revolution. When the revolution began, we do not know: The war never ended.

KAZIMIR MALEVICH

2ND DECLARATION OF THE SUPREMATISTS, FROM THE "DECLARATIONS OF HUMAN RIGHTS," 1918

Let there be the nonobjective Suprematist world of phenomena.
Pulverized, the objects of Cubism as a system have lost their elements.
The colored square section of the color mass engenders, in the minds of many individuals, an impulse toward nonobjectness.

At every corner, backs flattened by the force of Suprematism's laws lie trembling with the bursting of muscles.

The grunting of voices, the stamping of feet—twisted, the throat hurls its peculiar extravagances into the skulls of people of a different mettle.

We, the Suprematists, who have hurled a new law into the space of structures, into the structure of rubble, whilst slicing through the breast of space in endless motion, have broken free of the race.

The color of cross-section—the law of the guaranteed sign—is our distinction from the entirety of nonobjective pseudo-Suprematist numbers.

Now at each crossroads of backs [*sic*] is an aesthete-painted canvas of pink and violet blossoms like feminine bloomers, corsets, and brassieres; these canvasses show the inner essence of artists who have defected to the new art from old and worn ways of painting.

To the banner of movement, they bring individualism under the mask of the color of mediocre lines.

Behind us is heard the stamping of running feet, the steps of a cohort of artists, enveloping in the resilient system of suprematist constructions.

Maimed by touch, flattened, they lie amidst the vulgar ramps of coffeehouses and theaters.

Kazimir Malevich, "2-ia deklaratsiia Suprematistov" (1918), from the project "Deklaratsii prav cheloveka"; first published in *Kazimir Malevich: proizvedeniia raznykh let. Stat'i. Traktaty. Manifesty i deklaratsii. Proekty. Lektsii. Zapisi i zametki. Poeziia,* ed. Aleksandra Shatskikh, vol. 5 (Moscow: Gileia, 2004), 104–5.

We are crowned by the consciousness of new intuitive cross-sections; we move toward the new signs of real phenomena.

Our death and the death of things are united in the matter of cuneiform writing. The world of matter disappears, divided by space.

We divide the division of the new path of movement, leaving the blue cap of the sky like a lid on the skull of the old world.

The world, we preach, will be painted in colorlessness: the mad fire, the color-thrower of burning colors, will reveal the hue of things amidst the dome of the brain, being a sign of the new order.

But amidst the innumerable corridors of the mind, under the onslaught of roiling forces, I already see a new image beyond the world of color.

Proudly, like a serpent in arc-like coils, it burst from the body into space; it carries away the voices of new dotted lines; it moans like a trumpet amidst abysses.

In the vortex of belts of moments, the intuition of new numbers and sums will descend into the white center of color.

Sums without weight, volume, or color will lie at the foundation of the first formations.

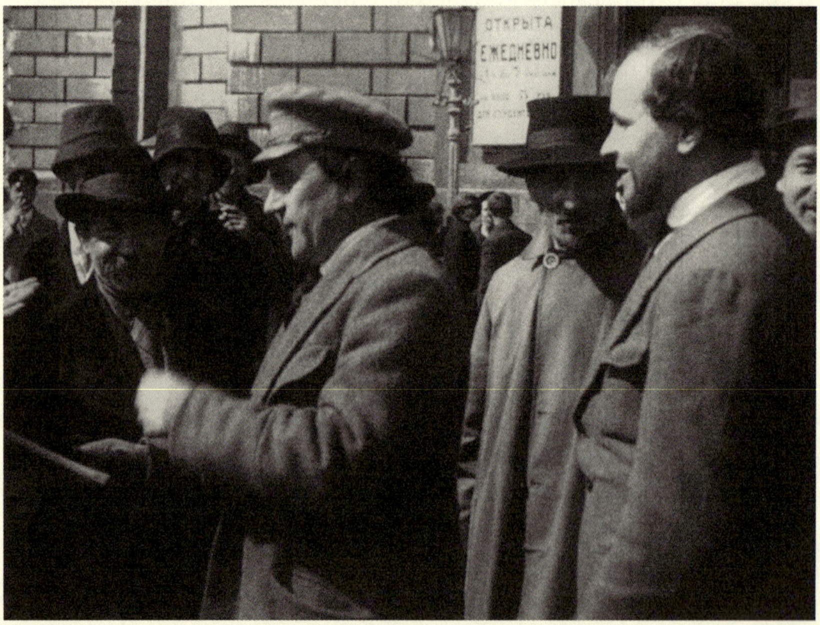

Anonymous
Kazimir Malevich in the documentary film
Exhibition of Paintings of the Petrograd Artists of All Trends, 1923

KAZIMIR MALEVICH

THE APPEAL OF KAZIMIR MALEVICH TO THE PROGRESSIVE ARTISTS OF ITALY, 1919[1]

You, who stood at the craters of Mt. Vesuvius and Mt. Aetna and flung at the globe the language of sacrilege toward old relics! You, who spat on the altar on yesterday's sacred values of art, and the sun in your hands became a polished brass basin so that the fingers of futurism banging against its bottom burst the eardrums of the system of Beethoven, Wagner, Chopin!

You who turned inside out the skull of Holy Rome and exposed the graveyard of reason's pitfalls, of the philistine logic of the maestros' art.

The running footsteps of the old day was drowned out by futurism; the instant clang of the wheels of the express train formed the rhythm of the new musical ear that holds thousands of orchestras of the moving noises of things.

Your call flattened the old day on its back, and the new morning was lit up by the brass basin of new wisdom.

Now, electrical wires have been stuck into the forehead of the earth, and the arcs of futuristic speed are growing.

Everywhere, the banners of rebellion have been affirmed, and just as you were calling once, we are calling upon you to raise a new blaze of art's banners.

Blow into the trumpets of Vesuvius and Mt. Aetna! Shout from the tops of radio and telegraph towers! Send words of steel-reinforced concrete, and crisscross the lining of the sky with multicolor projector beams!

Let the grinding of teeth on old jawbones turn to dust—in our whistle and whirlwind, in our victorious global dance.

We, your northern friends, amid snows and stars glittering in the cold, amid the noise and roar of factories, have restored the world citadel of art and planted the banner of international forces.

We are waiting for you to build an international base for the world expresses of art amid the Southern heat, and to plant a banner in the throats of Mt. Vesuvius and Mt. Aetna.

Kazimir Malevich, "The Appeal of Kazimir Malevich to the Progressive Artists of Italy" (1919), in N. I. Khardzhiev, "'Internatsional iskusstva': iz materialov po istorii Sovetskogo iskusstva," in *Stat'i ob avangarde*, vol. 1 (Moscow: RA, 1997), 258–59.

1. Written for the unpublished magazine "International of Art," 1919.

Aleksandr Rodchenko
Untitled (Change of Milestones), 1922

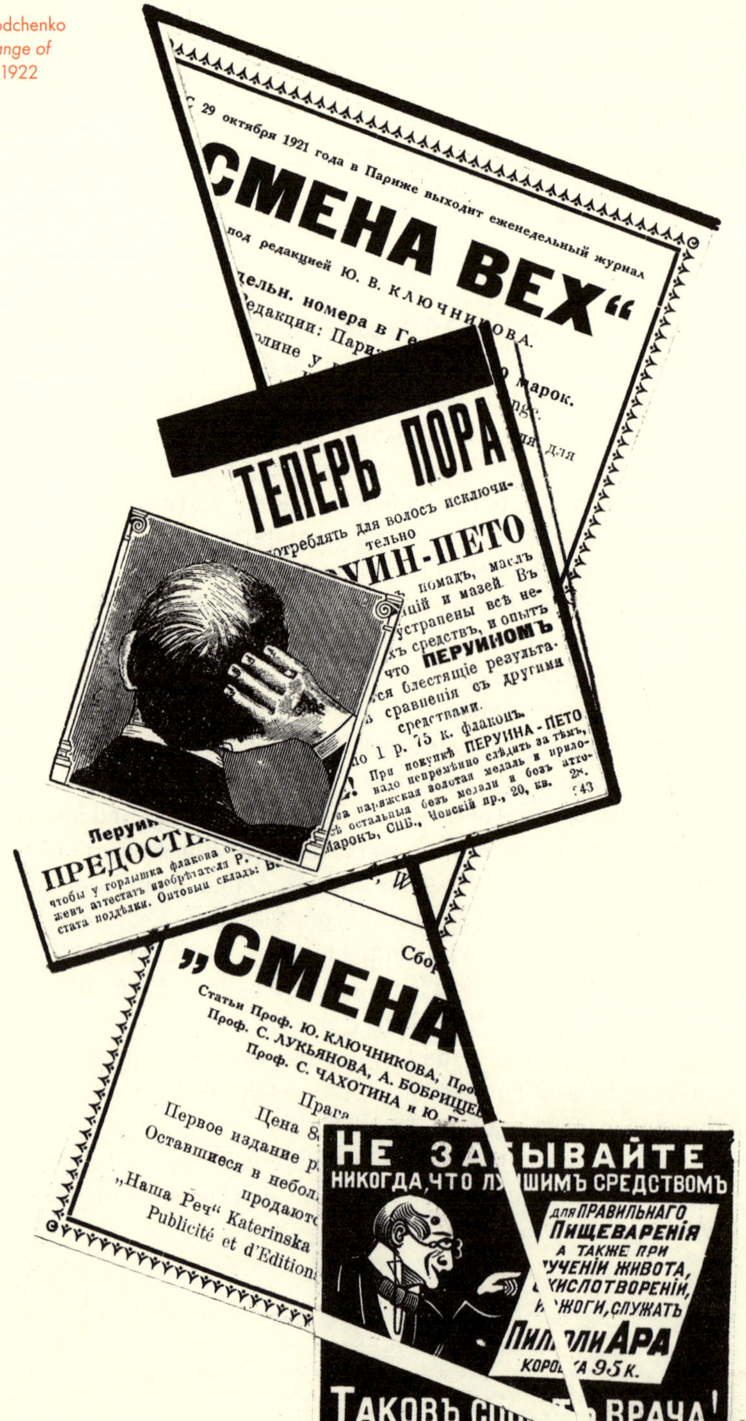

ALEKSANDR RODCHENKO
TO ARTISTS-PROLETARIANS, 1918

We—are the proletarians of the brush! Creator-martyrs! Oppressed artists!

We—are the inhabitants of cold attics and damp cellars!

We, who carry the blazing fire of creativity, walk hungry and barefoot!

We, who do not have the opportunity to create, are giving our best energy and time to earn the means for a miserable subsistence.

We, whose position is worse than the oppressed workers, for we—both work for our subsistence and create our art at one and the same time!

We, who are cooped up in kennels, often without either paint or light, on the time for creative work.

Proletarians of the brush, we must come together, we must organize a "free association of oppressed artist-painters" and demand bread, studios, and the right to exist.

Enough!

The art patrons oppressed us, they forced us to fulfill their whims. . . .

Aleksandr Rodchenko, "Khudozhnikam-proletariiam," *Anarkhiia*, no. 41 (April 11, 1918), trans. Jamey Gambrell, in *Aleksandr Rodchenko: Experiments for the Future, Diaries, Essays, Letters and Other Writings* (New York: Museum of Modern Art, 2005), 82.

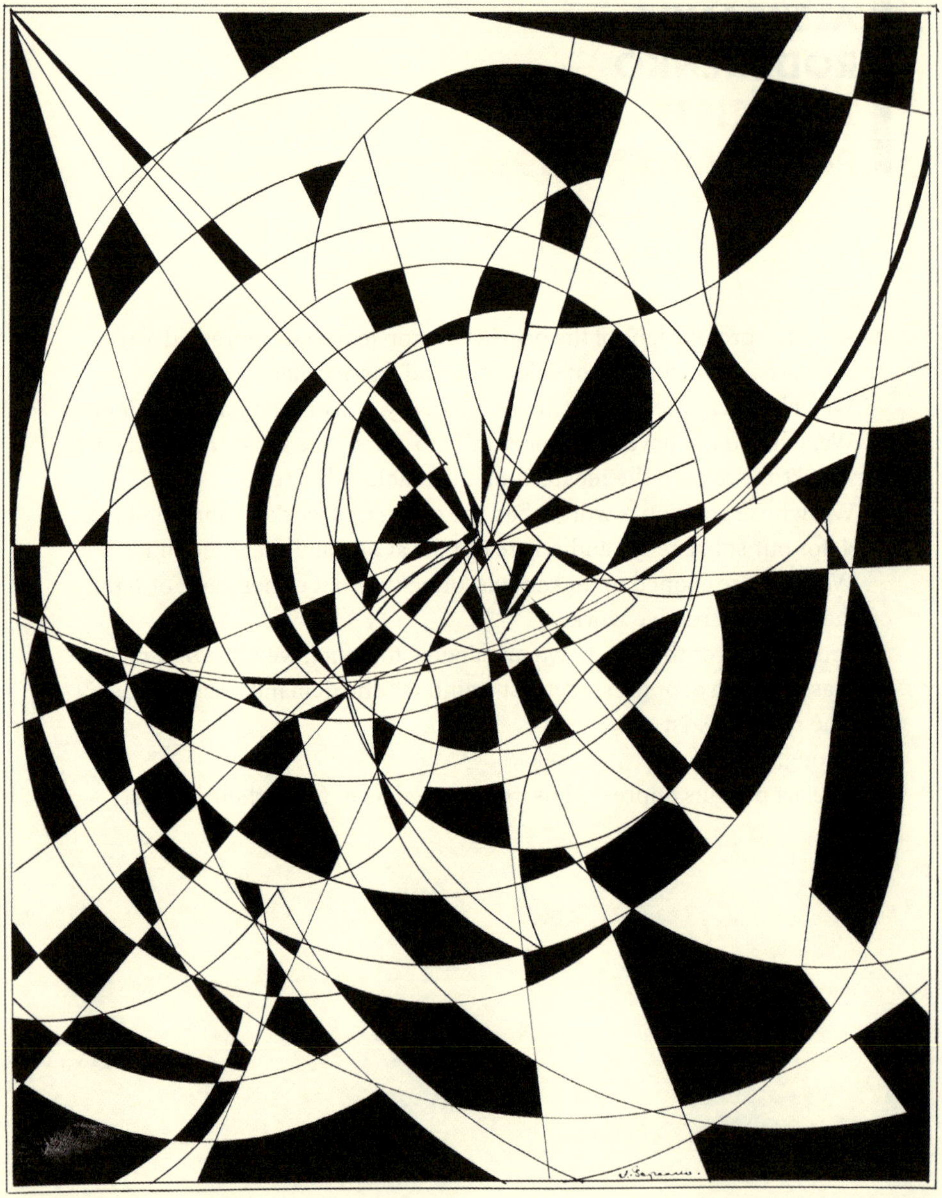

Aleksandr Rodchenko
Line and Compass Drawing, 1915

ALEKSANDR RODCHENKO
RODCHENKO'S SYSTEM, 1919

At the foundation of my work I placed nothing.
Max Stirner, *The Ego and His Own*

Paints are disappearing—everything
is mixing up black.
A. Kruchenykh, *Gly-Gly*

The collapse of all "isms" in painting was the beginning of my ascent. To the toll of the funeral bells of colorist painting, the last "ism" is laid to eternal rest here, the last hope and love collapse, and I leave the house of dead truths.

Synthesis is not the engine, the engine is invention (analysis).

Painting—is the body, creativity—the spirit. My work—is to create the new out of painting, so look at my work in action. Literature and philosophy are for specialists in this work, but I—am an inventor of new discoveries deriving from painting.

Christopher Columbus was not a writer or a philosopher, he was only a discoverer of new countries.

Aleksandr Rodchenko, "Sistema Rodchenko," in *X Gosudarstvennaia vystavka: bespredmetnoe tvorchestvo i suprematizm* (Moscow, 1919), trans. Jamey Gambrell, in *Aleksandr Rodchenko: Experiments for the Future, Diaries, Essays, Letters and Other Writings* (New York: Museum of Modern Art, 2005), 84.

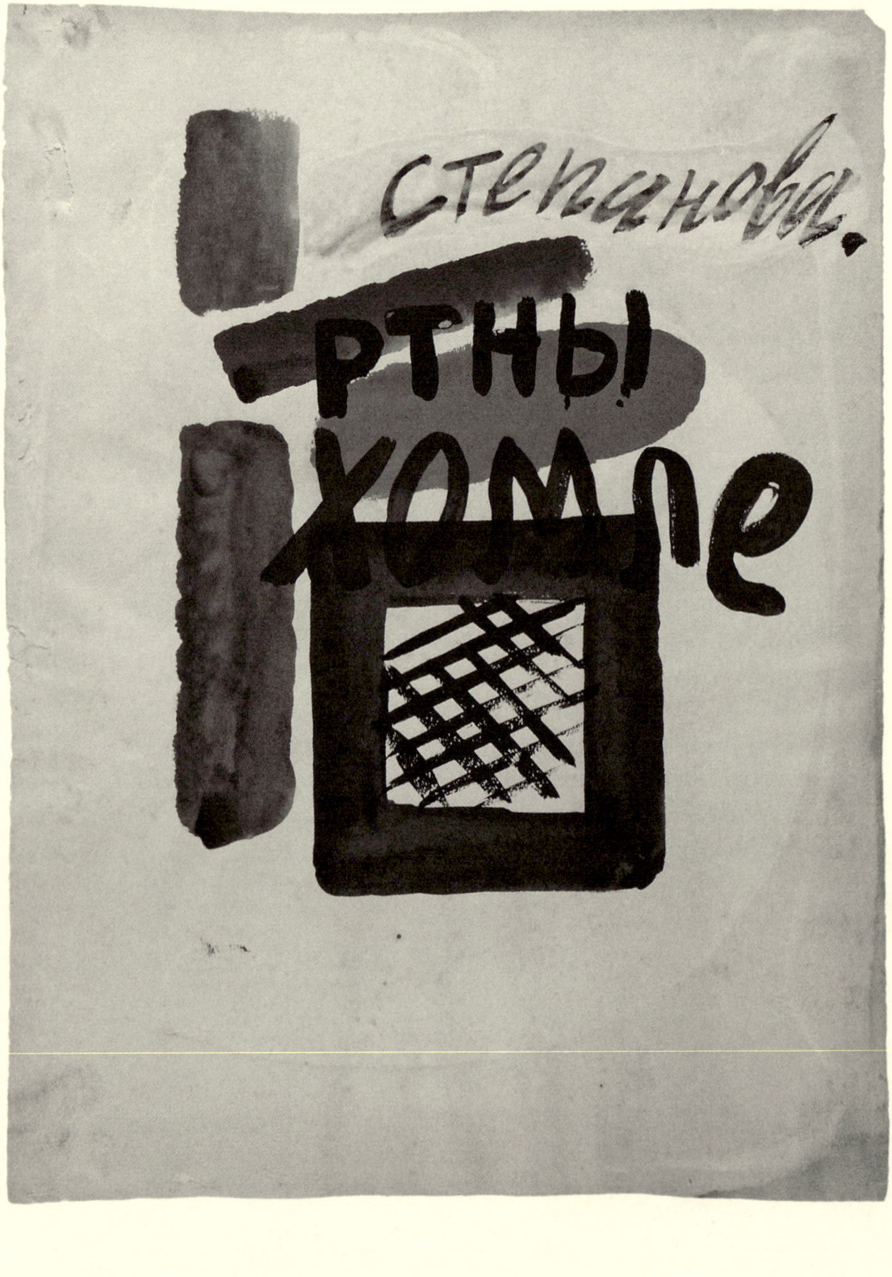

Varvara Stepanova
Cover of *Rtny Khomle: Nonobjective Poetry* by Varvara Stepanova, 1918

VARVARA STEPANOVA
NONOBJECTIVE CREATION, 1919

The ordinary "cultured" spectator who is slow to evolve in his understanding of new achievements finds it difficult to keep up with the development of the nonobjectivists, for they move along a revolutionary path of new discoveries and have behind them the transitional attainments of futurism and cubism. But if we accept "continuity" as an axiom, then nonobjective creation becomes the logical and legitimate consequence of the preceding stages of painterly creation. However, the same spectator—not being corrupted by pictorial subject matter and not being "cultured" enough to demand always and everywhere figurativeness in art—should, through his feeling and uncorrupted intuition, conceive this creation as a new beauty, the beauty of explosion, the beauty of painting's liberation from the age-old curse: from subject and depiction of the visible.

In nonobjective creation you will not find anything "familiar," anything "comprehensible," but don't be put off by this, grow fond of art, understand what it is to "live art," and don't just investigate it and analyze it, don't just admire it casually, don't just search for intelligible subjects in it or depictions of themes you like....

Varvara Stepanova, excerpts from "Bespredmetnoe tvorchestvo," in *X Gosudarstvennaia vystavka: bespredmetnoe tvorchestvo i suprematizm* (Moscow, 1919), in *Russian Art of the Avant-Garde*, ed. and trans. John E. Bowlt (New York: Viking Press, 1976), 141–42.

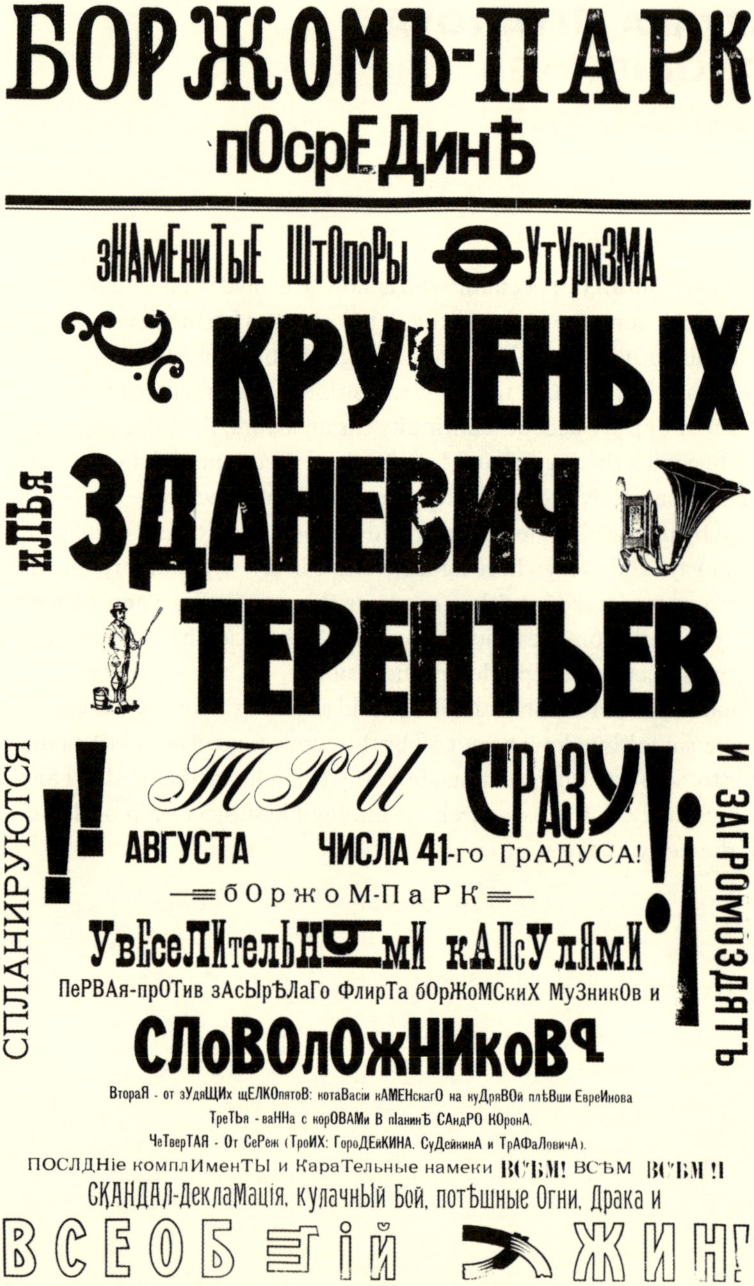

Ilia Zdanevich
Poster for a performance by Kruchenykh, Zdanevich, and Terentiev in Borjomi, Georgia, 1919

ILIA ZDANEVICH, ALEKSEI KRUCHENYKH, IGOR TERENTIEV, AND NIKOLAI CHERNIAVSKY

MANIFESTO OF THE "41°," 1919

Company 41° unifies left-wing Futurism, and affirms transreason as the mandatory form for the embodiment of art.

The task of 41° is to make use of all the great discoveries of its contributors, and to place the world on a new axis.

This newspaper will be a haven for happenings in the life of the company as well as a cause of constant trouble.

Let's roll up our sleeves.

I. Zdanevich, A. Kruchenykh, I. Terent'ev, and N. Cherniavskii, in the newspaper *41°* (Tiflis, 1919) in *Russian Futurism through Its Manifestoes, 1912–1928,* ed. and trans. Anna Lawton and Herbert Eagle (Ithaca: Cornell University Press, 1988), 177.

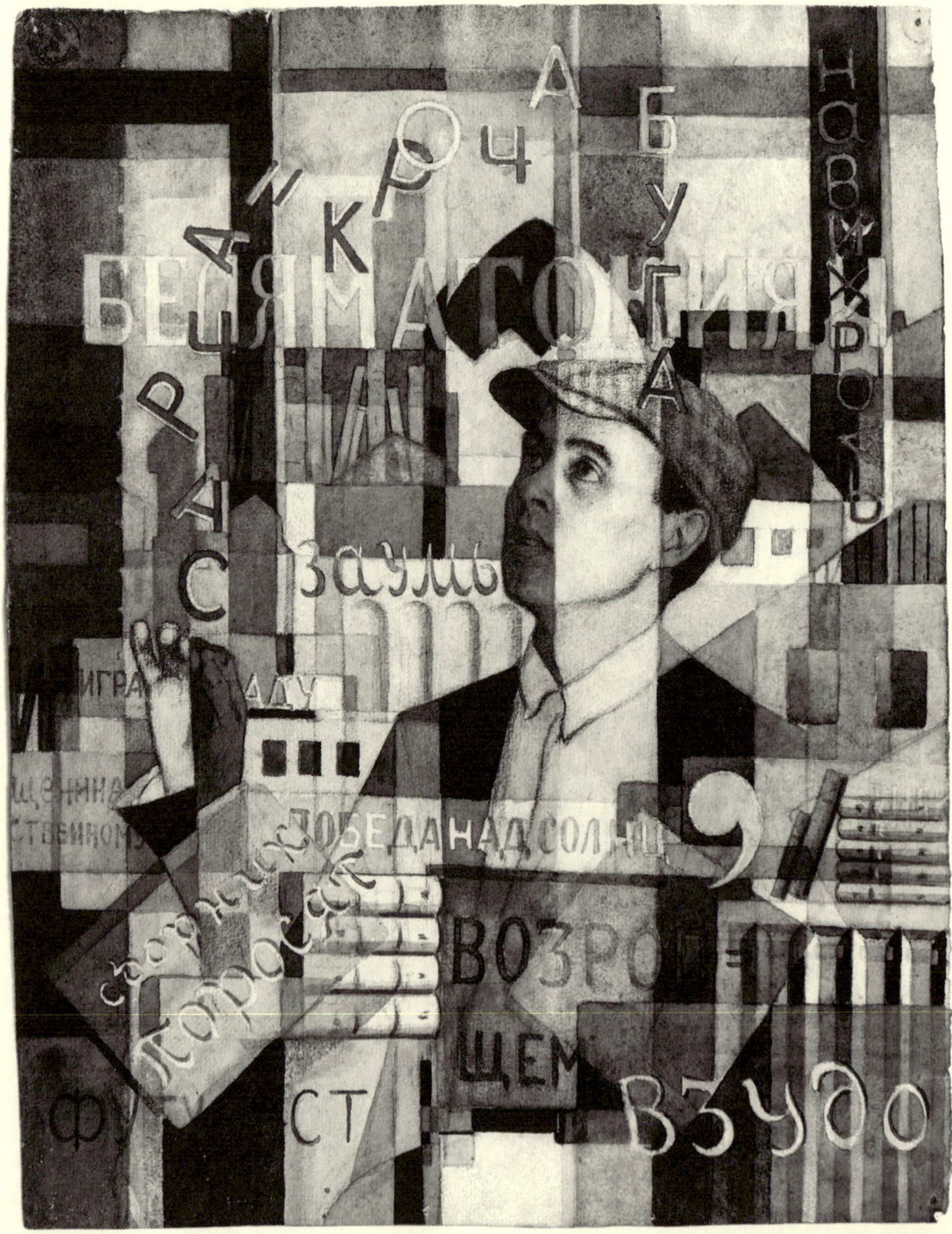

Ivan Kliun
Aleksei Kruchenykh, 1925

ALEKSEI KRUCHENYKH

IN LOCKSTEP WITH THE MARCH OF TIME (FUTURISTS AND THE OCTOBER REVOLUTION), N. D.

The frontlines of the *budetliane*[1] war for new art became, from the very start, one of the points of the general assault of societal forces on the bastions of autocracy, on the landowner-capitalist society with all its superstructures, with its religion and art.

We declared war on the fat-assed sculpture that flattered the crowned oppressors, on the syrupy art and literature that transformed the flabby, ruddy-faced, bloated flesh of Mr. Moneybags and his "missus" into Mitrofan of Belvedere and Queen Ortruda.[2]

The wrapping paper and wallpaper of our first collections, books, and declarations were our attack on the pompous vulgarity of philistine ribbed paper in gold-leaf binding, with their stuffing of nice quiet boys, languidly ailing pearls, and drunken lilies.

Over the fences of the tombs of thick journals, over the cordons of the academies, smashing the shop-windows of the institutions of beauty, accompanied by the warning whistles of the bank-owned yellow press, we entered the stage and faced a living audience that yearned for a breath of fresh air. We consciously linked our anti-aesthete "slaps in the face" to the struggle for the destruction of the environment that had nurtured the hothouses of Acmeism, Apollonism, . . . So what if we only ripped the flags and emblems from the well-fed mansion of the shopkeepers. It was still an insult, a mutiny. And that's exactly how our explosive work was seen by the police state. The yellow press hounded us, openly and shamelessly acting as informants: there they are, the rioters! The censors defaced our books with pockmarks of ellipses and blank spaces. Policemen stood at the ready behind our backs during debates . . .

Everyone knows how [Vladimir] Mayakovsky, that "drummer of the Revolution," welcomed October 1917. For him, as for other Moscow futurists, there was not even a question of "whether to accept it or not." . . .

Aleksei Kruchenykh, excerpts from "V nogu s epokhoi (Futuristy i Oktiabr')," in Aleksei Kruchenykh, *K istorii russkogo futurizma: vospominaniia i dokumenty* (Moscow: Gileia, 2006), 138–46.

1. Throughout this text Kruchenykh uses this neologism that the Russians coined to distinguish themselves from the Italian futurists. 2. References to a satirical line from Aleksandr Pushkin and a 1909 novel by Fedr Sologub.—Trans.

[Velimir] Khlebnikov's attitude toward those events is clear from his poem "October on the Neva" (1917–1918).

"In these days," he wrote, "there is a strange pride in the sound of the word *bolshevichka*."[3]

Khlebnikov's pre-October behavior was interesting as well, with the poet's eccentricity and his affinity for popular, carnivalesque buffoonery on full display.

"Is there one person who doesn't find [Aleksandr] Kerensky ludicrous and pathetic?" Khlebnikov would ask under the provisional government. He saw Kerensky as a personal insult and kept inventing projects that would "destroy" him, as the impractical fantasist he was. For instance:

> • Have toymakers make squeaky little imps with the head of Mrs. Insect-in-Chief. (Khlebnikov persistently referred to Kerensky as "Alexandra Fedorovna," the name of the deposed Tsarina.) "It's going to be a huge hit," Velimir would say. "Mrs. Kerensky sulks and dies squeaking."
>
> • Make a Mrs. Kerensky effigy and carry it in a solemn procession to the Field of Mars, where she will be put down near the common grave and whipped soundly enough that her cries will be heard by those who died in February with her name on their lips. (Khlebnikov called this a "bewhipping"—as in "beheading"—to underscore the solemnity of the proceedings.)
>
> • And, finally, the third and most radical project for Kerensky's "overthrow" was to have one of the members of the then-inseparable trio of Khlebnikov, Dm[itry] Petrovsky, and [Grigory] Petnikov, selected by drawing lots, go to the palace, call Kerensky out into the hallway, and slap his face in the name of Russia.

. . . Of course, Khlebnikov did not limit himself only to sarcastic gibes at the provisional government. He dreamed of taking to the barricades with the workers. But he was too absent-minded and ill-fit for combat, and his friends could not allow him to join the fray. It's not even that he was courageous; he somehow lacked any sense of awareness of danger. In the days of the October Revolution in Moscow, where he had moved from St. Petersburg, he calmly showed up in the most dangerous spots, amid street battles and shooting, observing these happenings with intense interest. This behavior was all the more reckless since, in that environment, he often became oblivious to what was around him, completely absorbed in his creative plans.

3. "Female Bolshevik."—Trans.

Here's how V[asily] Kamensky describes the work of the *budetliane* in Moscow in the first days after the October Revolution:

> Stubborn, vulgar rumors were openly going around: the Bolsheviks will stay in power "no more than two weeks." The fact that "the futurists were the first to recognize Soviet power" cost us many supporters.
>
> Those people were now gaping at us with undisguised horror and revulsion, as if we were wild-eyed lunatics who, like the Bolsheviks, had "no more than two weeks left."
>
> Even some good friends actually stopped saying hello to me, so as not to come under suspicion of Bolshevism after those prophesized "two weeks."
>
> And some openly said, "Oh, you crazy people, what are you doing? Listen, another two weeks, and they'll hang you right next to the Bolsheviks, you poor wretches!"
>
> But we knew very well what we were doing.
>
> What's more: using our broad influence on progressive young people, we led our young army toward the path of October's victories.
>
> (*The Path of the Enthusiast*)[4]

But what's the threat of the gallows! The October hurricane swept away all the barriers that had stood in the way of new art. The field had been cleared, and the *budetliane* rushed in without hesitation, rolled up their sleeves, and set to work on a huge task. We had to "give a march" to the revolution's soldiers and arm millions with a battle song that would mobilize the masses and lift them up in a surge of joy. The mastery of the poet and the artist had to give sound and color to the first revolutionary triumphs, to the harsh days of battles and privations. Mayakovsky clearly formulated these tasks in his "Orders to the Army of the Arts."

Budetliane put tremendous energy into carrying out these slogans, put forth by the spirit of the time. This was possible not only because they welcomed the revolution at once but because they instantly found their own place in it.

4. V. Kamenskii, "Put' entuziasta," in V. Kamenskii, *Sochinennia: reprintnoe vosproizvedenie izdanii 1914, 1916, 1918 s. prilozhenien*, ed. M. Ia. Poliakova (Moscow: Kniga, 1990), 522.

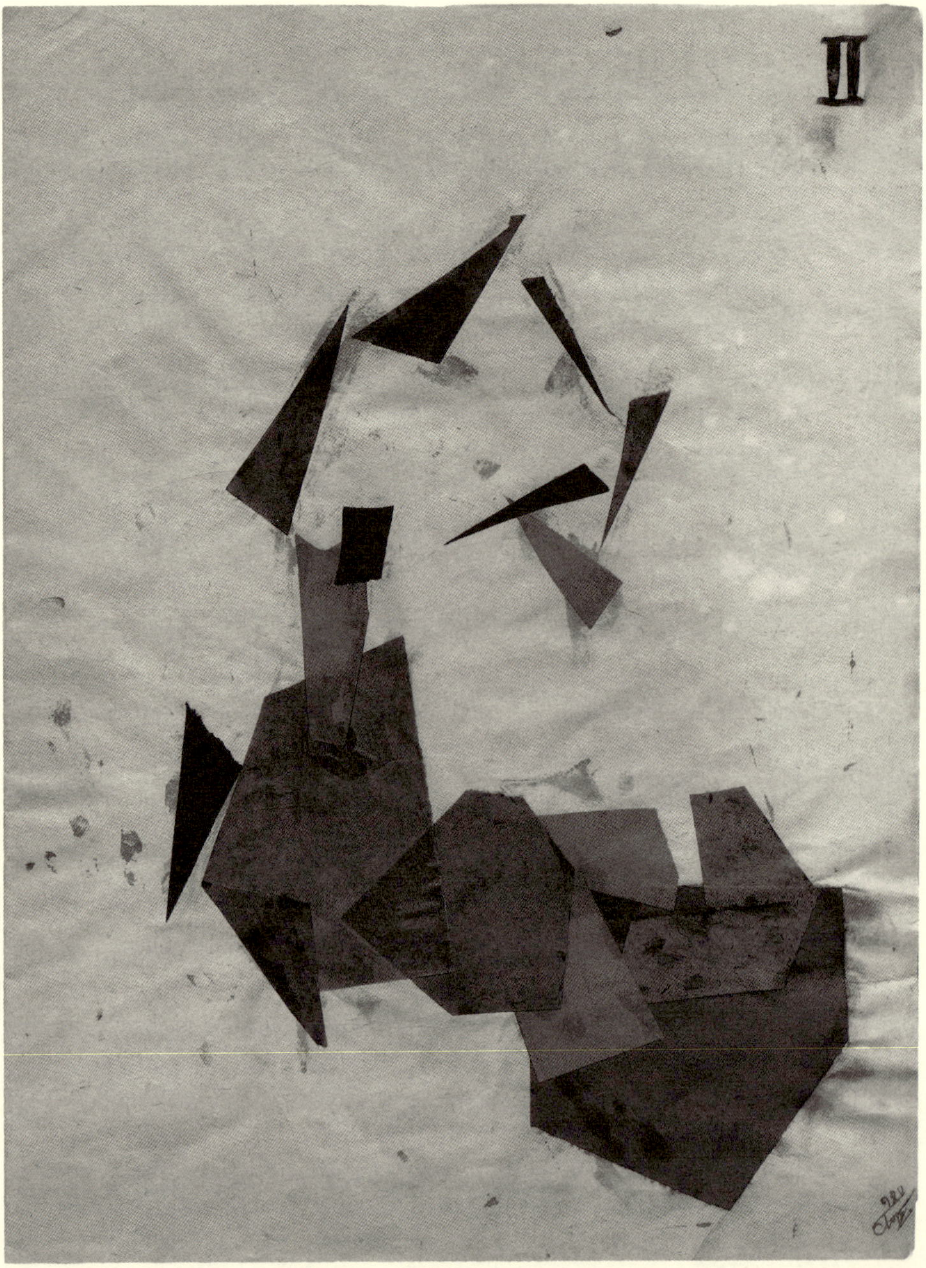

Sergei Gorodetsky and Velimir Khlebnikov
Spinny-spin-spin, anniversary book dedicated to Aleksei Kruchenykh, 1920

ALEKSEI KRUCHENYKH
DECLARATION NO. 6 ON THE ARTS TODAY (THESES), 1925

3) The painting has croaked. It made the journey from the monumentalism of antiques and bedrooms to the here-and-now of the streets (that's where the demand was): the poster, the placard, the photomontage. From the aestheticism of the mansion to the square and the factory workstation. The painters abolished by Lef ran off to AKhRR [the Artists' Association of Revolutionary Russia]—a hybrid of a vat of blood and a bucket of shoe polish, of bad photography and oleography, of the paralytic and the para-academic. AKhRR tries to be "scary" but succeeds only in being boring and laughable. . . . Rotting somewhere in some back yard are the World of Art crowd and the candy Blue Roses.

4) CINEMA. The public has been thoroughly corrupted by Deaf-Mute Cinema. Instead of a shock-work style, it has given us broken necks; instead of powerful gestures, clownish slaps in the face.

As an art form, cinema is still in the future.

But even now, where it uses the techniques of Lef (speed, shift, "cross-fade," double exposure, sharp montage), the Mute beats the mumbling *acs* [academicians].

The business of art is to invent and implement (standard, synthesis) the appropriate technique. The material will be provided in abundance by life around us.

Only the technique (form, style) makes the face of the era. (The maudlin song technique, Gypsy or academic, will make any revolutionary song suitable for a private study. The Lef technique will make even laboratory work revolutionary.)

That is why it is a question of EITHER academicism OR Lef—and no BASTARDS . . .

Moscow, October 1925

A. Kruchenykh, excerpt from "Deklaratsiia no. 6 o segodniashnikh iskusstvakh (tezisy)," in Aleksei Kruchenykh, *K istorii russkogo futurizma: vospominaniia i dokumenty* (Moscow: Gileia, 2006), 312–13.

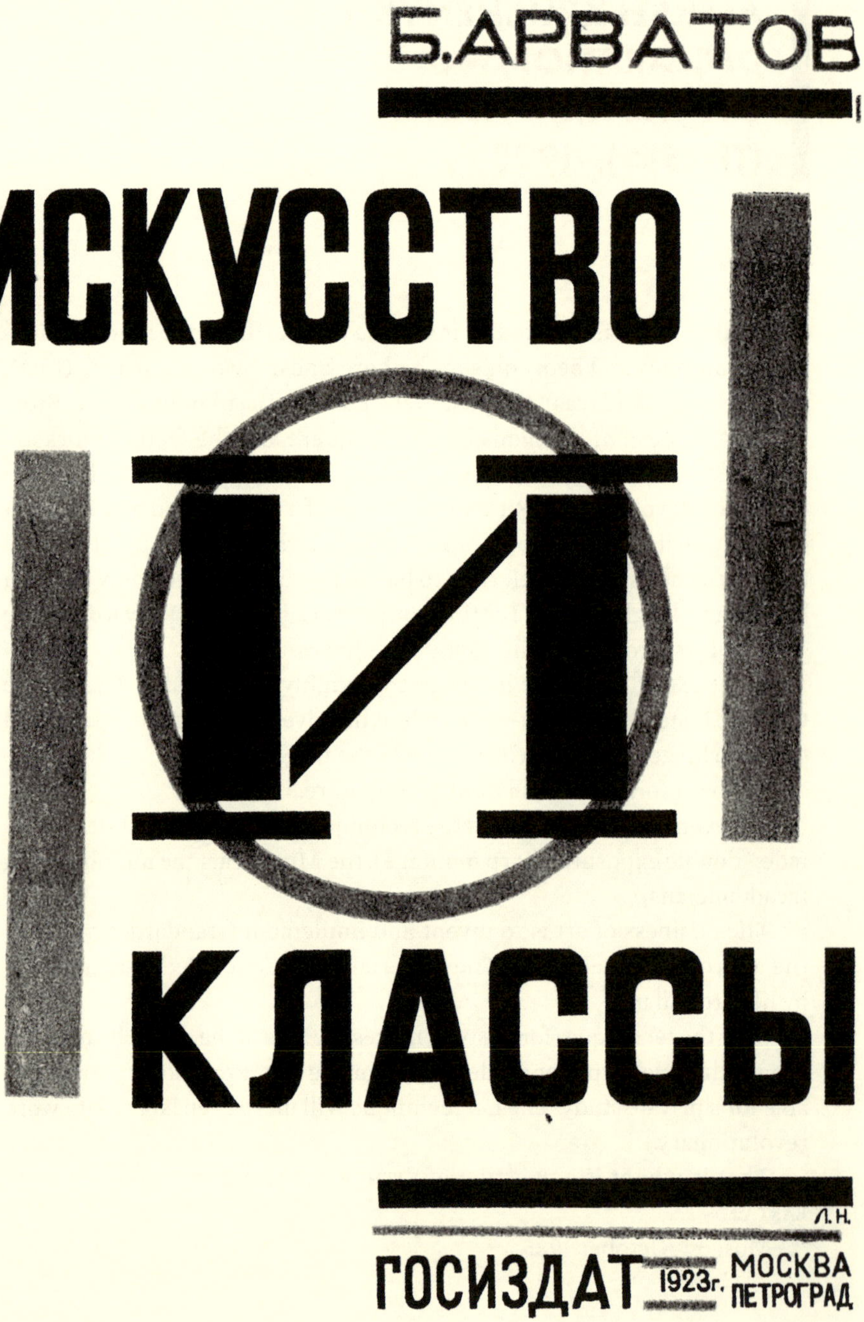

L. Nikitin
Cover of the book *Art and Classes* by
Boris Arvatov, 1923

BORIS ARVATOV
SPEECH CREATION (ON "TRANSRATIONAL" POETRY), 1923

When the works of the "transrationalists" [zaumniki] *(Khlebnikov and Kruchenykh) first appeared, both the public and the vast majority of scholars received them as:*

(1) a hitherto unprecedented fact;

(2) a fact possible only in poetry;

(3) a phenomenon of purely phonetic nature (sound play, "a collection of sounds");

(4) a phenomenon of decay of poetry and poetic language;

(5) a novelty with no independent, positively organizational meaning; i.e., something pointless.

. . . "Zaum'" ("the transrational") is usually seen as a "collection of sounds," and if it is acknowledged to have any formal meaning, it is only a musical, acoustic one. The "transrational" turns out to be an abstract phonetical composition. This alone should have excluded "transrational" forms from the category of sound forms, since language in any manifestation has three inseparable and necessary aspects: phonetics, morphology/syntax, and semantics. And yet we speak of "transrational" language and speech forms. Indeed, the problem of "transrational" itself would never have arisen if it was not a fact of language. The "transrational" is interesting precisely because it is not a mere combination of sounds (recitative, melody, vocal music) but a spoken form that has social applications (verse, conversations, the ecstatic ramblings of religious sectarians, the "cooing" of lovers, etc.)—that is, a form of language.

The critics' main error is this: Any human action is carried out in a very specific environment and is entirely dependent upon it. That is, any singular phenomenon has its function defined by the presence of a general, collective, legitimized stereotype of similar phenomena. In the same way, any spoken/sound composition is inevitably perceived in the context of the present language system and thus enters it as a new element, obeys all its norms, and turns out to be effective solely because we associate it with accustomed forms of our speechmaking.

B. Arvatov, excerpts from"Rechetvorchestvo (po povodu "zaumnoi" poezii)," *Lef*, no. 2 (April–May 1923): 79–91.

In this sense, no purely phonetic form exists or can exist. This or that combination of sounds is inevitably connected to the familiar meanings of these sounds and similar combinations, with analogous morphemes, etc. That is why the "transrational" is not a phonetic phenomenon but a phonological one ([Roman] Jakobson's term), or even a morphological one. . . .

In other words, transrational forms share the qualities of the language system to which they are attached. They are complete speech facts, formally no different from existing linguistic material. To emphasize this, I put "transrational" in quotation marks: speech that is completely senseless, completely beyond sense, is impossible. An individual is the product and crystallized form of the collective, and all its activity is social: The "incomprehensible" murmurs of someone half asleep and the babbling cries of a lunatic are just as social as an ordinary conversation about the weather. The only difference is the degree to which we understand it—a quantitative rather than qualitative difference (parents understand their children's "transrationality" far better than other people). . . .

Kruchenykh defines transrational forms as forms with an indeterminate meaning; it would have been more accurate to say "indeterminate purpose." This definition is . . . entirely correct, but insufficient. A negative definition circumscribes but does not "define." The principal and positive element of "transrational" is the innovative nature of its forms. Any "transrational" introduces unusual constructions into the system of practical language, taking it beyond the boundaries of "pleasant" cliché. . . . "Transrational" is everything that adds to the general mass of verbal constructions in everyday use new constructions that have no precise communicative function. (*Cheka* is not a "transrational" word, since it has a fixed "object" meaning, not necessary for carrying out its specific utilitarian tasks.) Thus understood, pure "transrationality" is only an extreme expression of speech creation taken to its outer limits. . . . From this point on, I will speak not of "transrational" but of compositional speech creation as a universal phenomenon that includes pure "transrational" as an element. I use the phrase "compositional speech creation" as a phenomenon distinct from "communicative speech creation," which produces linguistic forms that have already acquired a precisely fixed purpose in practical language (Boborykin's "intelligentsia,"[1] the modern "Sovdep,"[2] etc.). By contrast, compositional speech creation has no practical fixed place and, superficially, seems to be its own purpose. The main forms of such speech creation are literature and all kinds of everyday "wordplay" (see above).

1. The Russian journalist and essayist Petr Boborykin introduced the word *intelligentsia* into the Russian language as a term for the class engaged in intellectual activity.—Trans. 2. An abbreviation for *soviet deputatov*, or "Council of Deputies."—Trans.

We may ask what social meaning compositional speech creation, particularly of the everyday kind, may have.

Any language system has two aspects: content and the forms in which that content is bound. Language is the living, fluid energy of society, which evolves together with and depending on the latter. But like any energy, language can find a social use only when it acquires "commonly understood"—that is, firmly fixed—skeletal forms, when it solidifies into unchanging constant crystals. Naturally, such social clichés deaden language, make speech energy static, and are thus in obvious contradiction with the need of language to evolve. The evolutionary tendencies of language clash with the petrification of its forms and force a breakthrough past these forms—their breakdown, alteration, or at least partial shift. However, for forms to change at all, to be capable of being changed, they absolutely must have one quality: plasticity. On the other hand, practical forms of speech that require clear definitions do not allow for any freedom or "plasticity," which is the same thing. Utilitarianism always demands strictly fixed constructions. And so bourgeois society spontaneously and unconsciously achieves plasticity of construction outside strictly utilitarian acts: in punts, witticisms, sayings, "illustrative" metaphors, and so on. From this everyday mass speech creation are born millions of new constructions, forms, neologisms, new roots, etc., etc. This entire newly created supply of turns of speech that still lack a precise, objective usage enters the sphere of practical action, undergoes a meticulous spontaneous selection, and works as a kind of "reserve army" of language from which new practical forms are drawn—forms of what becomes communicative rather than compositional speech creation.... Thus, poetry has always been nothing less than an experimental laboratory of speech creation. But until futurism came along, this social role of poetry was not consciously understood; it remained hidden under the fetishized cover of poetic canons and other "intellectualisms." Experimentation happened spontaneously, chaotically, partially.

The historic significance of the "transrationalists" lies precisely in the fact that for the first time, this always-existing role of poetry has been revealed by the form of the creative work itself. The "transrationalists" laid bare, and began to do openly and consciously, what had been done unconsciously before them. This expanded the sphere of creativity, its methods, and the sum of its achievements. Poets became conscious organizers of linguistic material. Simultaneously, the boundaries of speech creation collapsed. The poet was no longer bound by inescapable traditional norms, and freedom of experimentation—that sole condition of purposeful organizing activity—was achieved. That many of Khlebnikov's inventions were made by him outside the poetical canon and offered in their pure form as experiments is no accident (see, for instance, his essay about neologisms formed from the word "to fly" in the collection *A Slap in the Face to Public Taste*).

NOTHINGISTS
DOG'S BOX, OR THE WORKS OF THE CREATIVE BUREAU OF NOTHINGISTS IN 1920–1921

INTO THE DOG'S BOX

Introduction

Our method of picking a title was inspired by Dadaists. They themselves complain that "Dada means nothing!" Our path is almost the same as theirs. They have to go right, we have to go left.

Or the other way round!

Our choice was guided by just. Just like that. We liked the combination of two words, hence Dog's Box.

It is compiled as an accessible guide to the home study of Nothingism. "How you yourself can become a Nothingist in the shortest possible time, without resorting to medicines or costly mechanical devices such as the Spanish boot," etc., etc.

The material is an operative summary of snatches from a grandiose cinematographic shoot under the general title, "12 months of struggle for the dictatorship of Nothingism over the arts."

"The Dog's Box" has been manufactured for purposes of undermining and demoralizing fine literature, in accordance with the resolution of Creative of Bureau of Nothingists of December 5, 1920.

Moscow, September 25, 1921. Khitrov Market, Soviet Water-Boiler.

Excerpts from *Nichevoki. Sobachii iashchik ili trudy tvorcheskogo biuro nichevokov v techenie 1920–1921*, vypusk pervyi, ed. S. V. Sadikov (Moscow: "Khobo," 1921).

DECREE ON THE NOTHINGISTS OF POETRY

In the name of the Revolution of Spirit, we declare:

1. Any poetry that does not offer an individual approach to creativity, that does not define a special worldview and sense of the world possessed only by the individual, that does not deal with the inner meaning of phenomena and things (meaning is nothing from the standpoint of matter), of both objects and words, is at this point in time, starting in August 1920,

ANNULLED

2. Persons caught trafficking in annulled units of poetry or forging units of Notpoetry (Nothingist Poetry) will be subject to trial by the Revolutionary Tribunal of Nothingists, composed of Boris Zemenkov, Riurik Rok, and Sergei Sadikov.

3. It is time to forcibly purge poetry of traditional and artisanal-poetic, dung-like elements of life, in the name of collectivization of the entire being of the universal spirit and of the Mask of Nothing. This spirit does not exist for materialists and cliché-bound idealists: For them, it is Nothing. We are the first to raise the bricks of rebellion for Nothing.

WE ARE NOTHINGISTS.

4. The Nothingist sees in clear focus the modern crisis in the realities and perceptions of the world: the crisis is in ourselves, in our spirit. In poetical works, this crisis can be solved through refinement of image, of meter, rhythm, instrumentation, and ending. (The only currently viable school of poetry, Imaginism,[1] is viewed by us as a partial method.) Refinement will obliterate art and destroy it, reduce it to nothing and lead it into Nothing. Our goal: the refinement of poetical works in the name of Nothing. It is to take the verbal fabric and embroider upon it the experience of oneness with the world and insight into it, into its image, color, smell, taste, etc.

Thus, Everything takes its beginning from Nothing. The means of representation through the formula $n + 1$ (where n = the element of representation until this point in time and 1 = the new representation) must bring us to the equation $n + 1 = \infty$; that is, Nothing: the purpose of eternity = Nothing. Hence:

5. In poetry, there is nothing; only Nothingists.

6. Life is heading toward the realization of our slogans:

1. Imaginism was founded in 1918 in Moscow by a group of poets that included Anatoly Mariengof, Vadim Shershenevich, and Sergei Esenin, who wanted to distance themselves from the futurists.

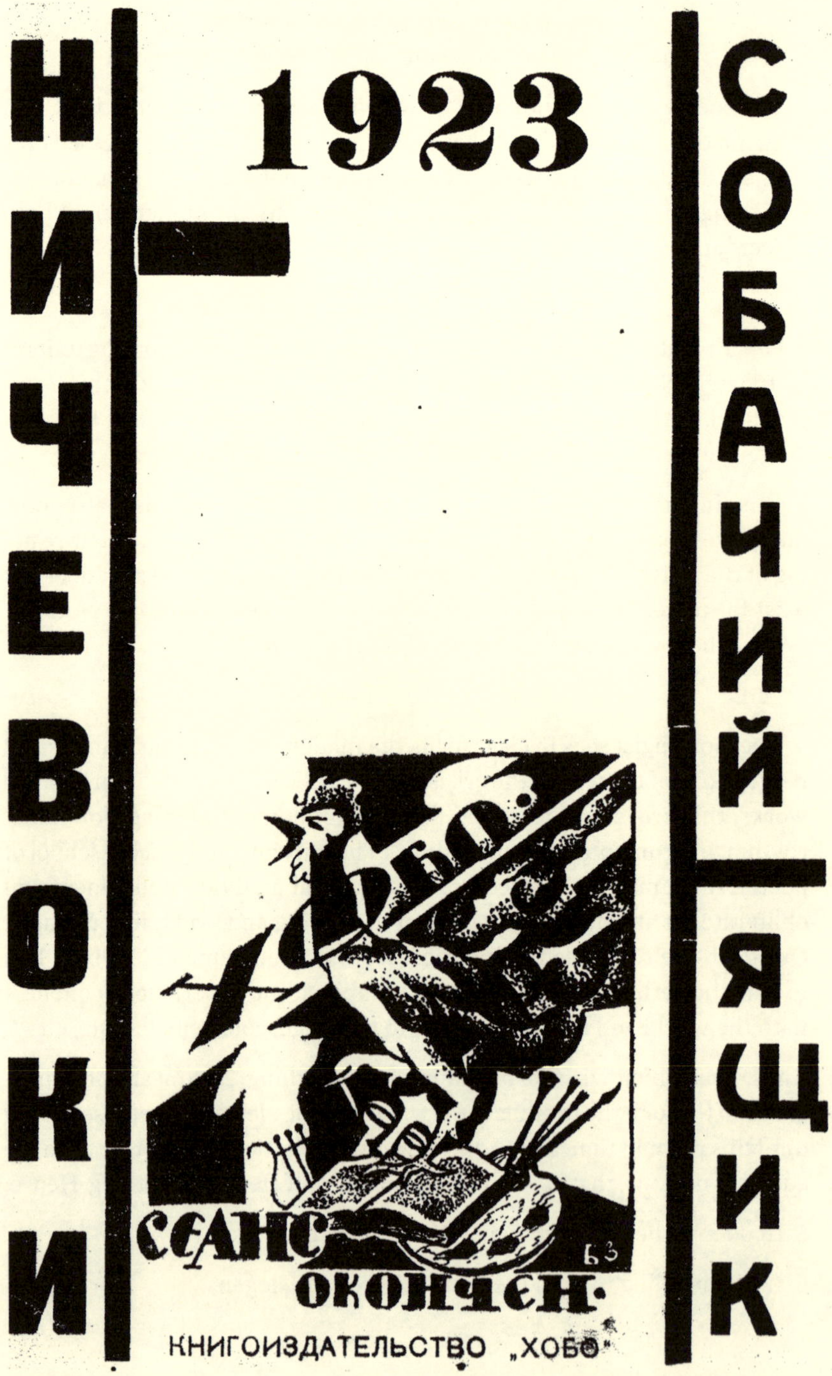

Anonymous
Nothingists: Dog's Box, 1923

Write nothing!
Read nothing!
Say nothing!
Print nothing!

Creative Bureau of Nothingists: Susanna Mar, Elena Nikolaeva, Aetsy Ranov, Riurik Rok, Oleg Erberg

Chief Secretary: Sergei Sadikov

Rostov-on-the-Don, August 1920

The present decree was signed on April 17, 1921, in Moscow by the expressionist Boris Zemenkov, who joined the Russian Encampment of Nothingists and became a member of the Creative Bureau of Nothingists (TvorNichBuro).

DECREE ON PAINTING

In the name of Nothing!

In the name of the Liberation of the Uniqueness of Human Personality, we declare:

1. Because empirical culture must move from the sphere of matter to the sphere of spirit, any work of art that expresses itself outside the aesthetic laws of correlation but directly demonstrates with its form and content, the artist's possession of a spiritual path, is considered permitted until further notice.

2. Every work of art based on the principles of discrediting art acquires market value only upon being presented to the Nothingists' Revolutionary Tribunal for the purpose of considering its fitness for relevant patents confirming its authenticity.

3. All forms of art not covered by paragraphs 1 and 2 of this decree are annulled as of the date of its publication.

4. From the moment of the publication of this decree, every citizen has a duty, on pain of being charged as an accomplice, to immediately report to the Nothingists' Revolutionary Tribunal any sightings of theories, opinions, or artworks disseminated with the purpose of preserving art's authority and value.

Note: All products of thought that serve the above-mentioned criminal purposes must be immediately confiscated while their owners must be subjected to disciplinary reeducation through the ideas of Nothing.

5. In order to combat the degradation of the tangibility of our environment, admission to any museum, exhibition, or art storeroom without an appropriate pass issued by the Nothingist Revolutionary Tribunal is considered unacceptable.

On behalf of the TvorNichBuro,
Extraordinary Nothingist of Art, Boris Zemenkov
This decree issued on July 4, 1921
Moscow, Simonov Monastery

DECREE ON THE SEPARATION OF ART AND STATE

1. Declared today is the full separation of art and state.

2. As part of the orderly enforcement of this decree, we declare the state to be incompetent in matters of managing the preparation, inventorying, distribution, and oversight of the production of art.

3. The entire system of management, preparation, inventorying, distribution, and oversight of production units of art is entirely transferred, upon the determination of current stocks and remainders, to the TvorNichBuro.

4. All registrations of artworks undertaken by the state with the purpose of determining their value are no longer mandatory for anyone as of June 3 of this year.

5. The resolutions in Points 1 through 4 should be considered valid only with the signatures and seal of the TvorNichBuro and the Secretariat of the Russian Encampment of Nothingists.

6. This Decree is to be translated into all the world's languages, sent to all national associations and agencies of state authority, and presented to the All-Russian Central Executive Committee, the Large and Small Soviets of People's Commissars, and the next congress of the Comintern.

TvorNichBuro: Boris Zemenkov, Elena Nikolaeva, Aetsy Ranov, Riurik Rok, Oleg Erberg

Chief Secretary: Sergei Sadikov

Address to the Dadaists

"Dada ne signifie rien!"

"That's right:
'Requiem Aeternam,' you will write."

RUSSIA'S NOTHINGISTS TO THE WEST'S DADA

Upon the marked cards of the map of Old Europe, we throw down:
"Long live the last International of the 'Dada of Light!'"
In our time, when every "new" art shamelessly begs for a slap in the face from creative Sadism,
When the crumbling bars of charlatanism are no longer able to protect poetry from the lynch mobs of a hell-bent reality—we will not rise up in defense of the slandered Homer.
Because that too, like many other holy relics, has only one destination left: the sausage of World Nothingism.
We say: "There is nothing in art."
Our only creed is the ink-and-pen program of verbal terror.
To someone's gentle, "Art is ahead of life, art teaches us . . ."—we club them over the head.
We sound the alarm: "Watch out, citizens! Art is still safe!"
And furthermore: We know the value of our mastery. Once born, we inevitably perish, struck down by the rocks of our works, not made by human hands.
To be translated into all the languages of the globe.
TvorNichBuro
Moscow, April 7, 1921.

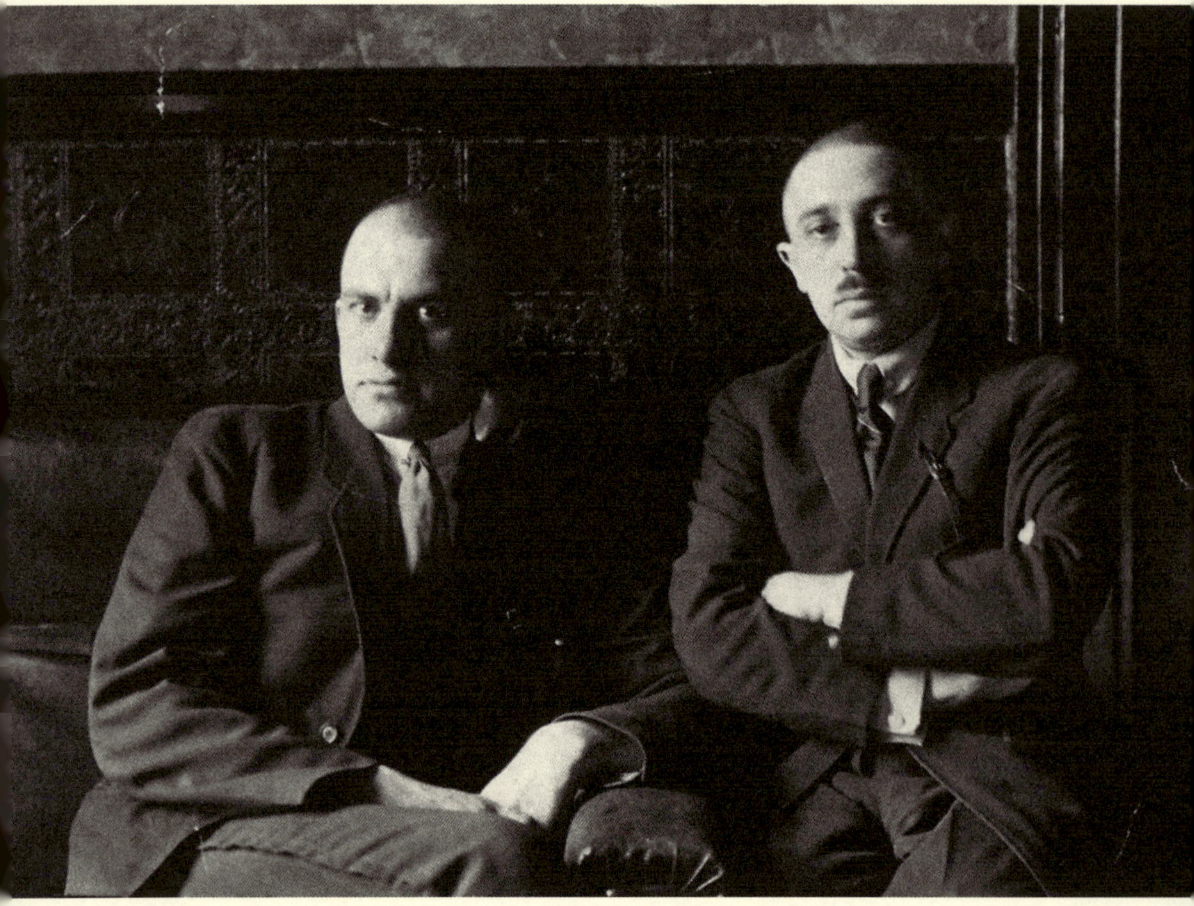

John Sraubenz
Vladimir Mayakovsky and Osip Brik, Berlin, 1923

VLADIMIR MAYAKOVSKY AND OSIP BRIK
OUR LINGUISTIC WORK, 1923

We work on the organization of language sounds, on the polyphony of the rhythm, on the simplification of verbal constructions, on the accuracy of verbal expressiveness, on the manufacture of new thematic devices.

All this *work for us is not an aesthetic end in itself, but a workshop for the best expression of the facts of the contemporary era.*

We are not priest-creators, but master-executors of the social demand.

Our practice printed in *Lef* is not "absolute artistic revelations," but examples of work in progress.

Aseyev. Experiment in linguistic flight into the future.

Kamensky. Wordplay in all of its resoundingness.

Kruchenykh. Experiment with the use of jargon phonetics to give form to antireligious and political themes.

Pasternak. Use of dynamic syntax to fulfill the revolutionary task.

Tretyakov. Experiment with march constructions to give an organization to revolutionary anarchy.

Khlebnikov. Achievement of maximal expressiveness by means of conversational language cleansed of all previous poetic elements.

Mayakovsky. Experiment with polyphonic rhythm in narrative poems with broad social scope.

Brik. Experiment with laconic prose on a contemporary theme.

Vittfogel. Experiment with communist agit-skits without the usual imperialistic craziness of revolutionary mysticism.

V. V. Mayakovsky and O. M. Brik, "Nasha slovesnaia rabota," *Lef*, no. 1 (1923): 40–41, in *Russian Futurism through Its Manifestoes, 1912–1928*, ed. and trans. Anna Lawton and Herbert Eagle (Ithaca: Cornell University Press, 1988), 202–3.

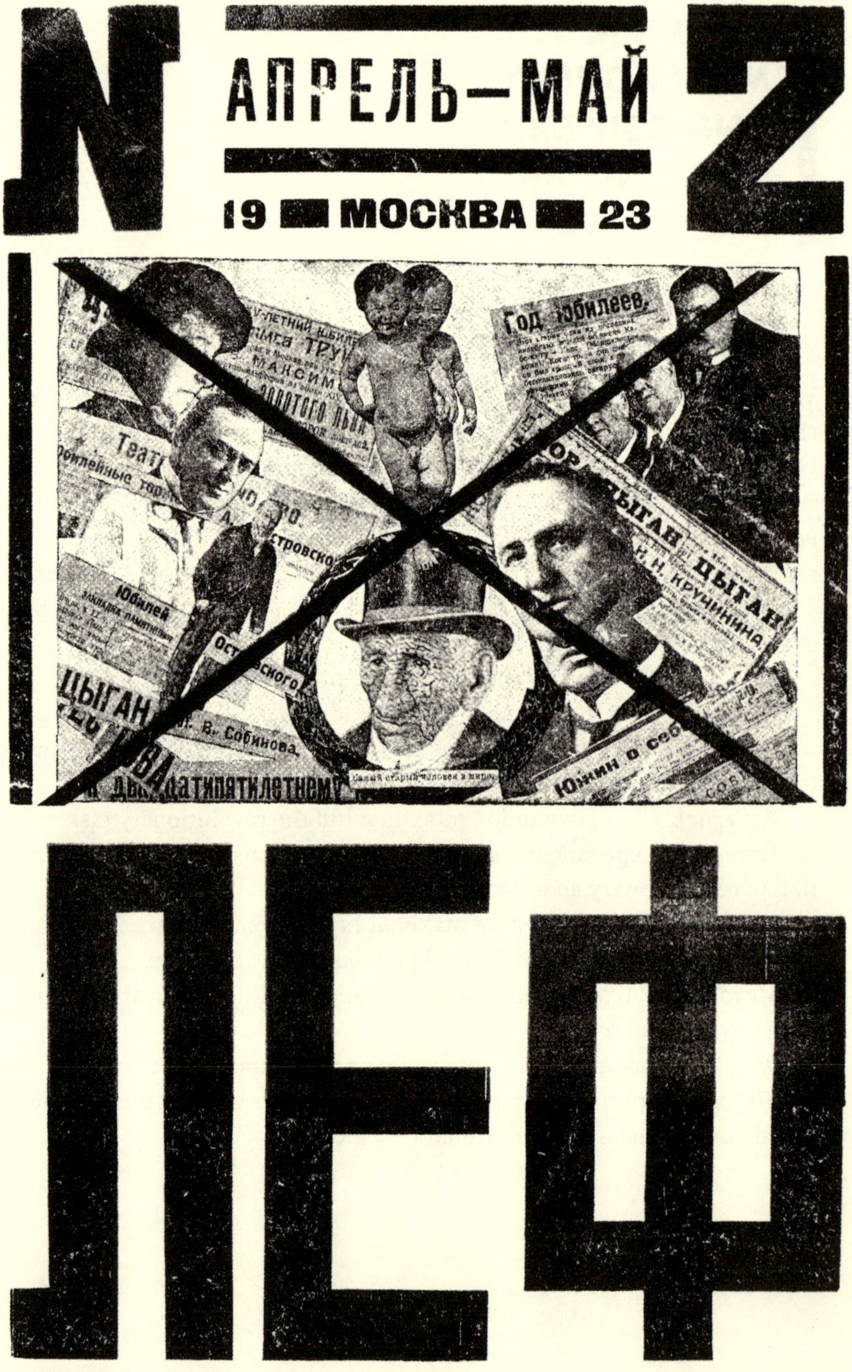

Aleksandr Rodchenko
Cover of the journal *Lef*, no. 2, 1923

LEF
DECLARATION: COMRADES, ORGANIZERS OF LIFE!, 1923

Today, the *First of May*, the workers of the world will demonstrate in their millions with song and festivity.

Five years of attainments, ever increasing.

Five years of slogans renewed and realized daily.

Five years of victory.

And—

Five years of monotonous designs for celebrations.

Five years of languishing art.

So-called Stage Managers!

How much longer will you and other rats continue to gnaw at this theatrical sham?

Organize according to real life!

Plan the victorious procession of the Revolution!

So-called Poets!

When will you throw away your sickly lyrics?

Will you ever understand that to sing praises of a tempest according to newspaper information is not to sing praises about a tempest?

Give us a new *Marseillaise* and let the *Internationale* thunder the march of the victorious Revolution!

So-called Artists!

Stop making patches of color on moth-eaten canvases.

Stop decorating the easy life of the bourgeoisie.

Exercise your artistic strength to engirdle cities until you are able to take part in the whole of global construction!

"Tovarishchi—formovshchiki zhizni!," *Lef*, no. 2 (April–May 1923): 3–4, in *Russian Art of the Avant-Garde*, ed. and trans. John E. Bowlt (New York: Viking Press, 1976), 199–202.

Give the world new colors and outlines!

We know that the "priests of art" have neither strength nor desire to meet these tasks: they keep to the aesthetic confines of their studios.

On this day of demonstration, the First of May, when proletarians are gathered on a united front, we summon you, organizers of the world:

Break down the barriers of "beauty for beauty's sake"; break down the barriers of those nice little artistic schools!

Add your strength to the united energy of the collective!

We know that the aesthetics of the old artists, whom we have branded "rightists," revive monasticism and await the holy spirit of inspiration, but they will not respond to our call.

We summon the "leftists": the revolutionary *futurists*, who have given the streets and squares their art; the *productivists*, who have squared accounts with inspiration by relying on the inspiration of factory dynamos; the *constructivists*, who have substituted the processing of material for the mysticism of creation.

Leftists of the world!

We know few of your names, or the names of your schools, but this we do know—wherever revolution is beginning, there you are advancing.

We summon you to establish a single front of leftist art—the "Red Art International."

Comrades!

Split leftist art from rightist everywhere!

With leftist art prepare the European Revolution; in the U.S.S.R. strengthen it.

Keep in contact with your staff in Moscow (Journal *Lef*, 8 Nikitsky Boulevard, Moscow).

Not by accident did we choose the First of May as the day of our call.

Only in conjunction with the Workers' Revolution can we see the dawn of future art.

We, who have worked for five years in a land of revolution, know:

That only October has given us new, tremendous ideas that demand new artistic organization.

That the October Revolution, which liberated art from bourgeois enslavement, has given real freedom to art.

Down with the boundaries of countries and of studios!

Down with the monks of rightist art!

Long live the single front of the leftists!

Long live the art of the Proletarian Revolution!

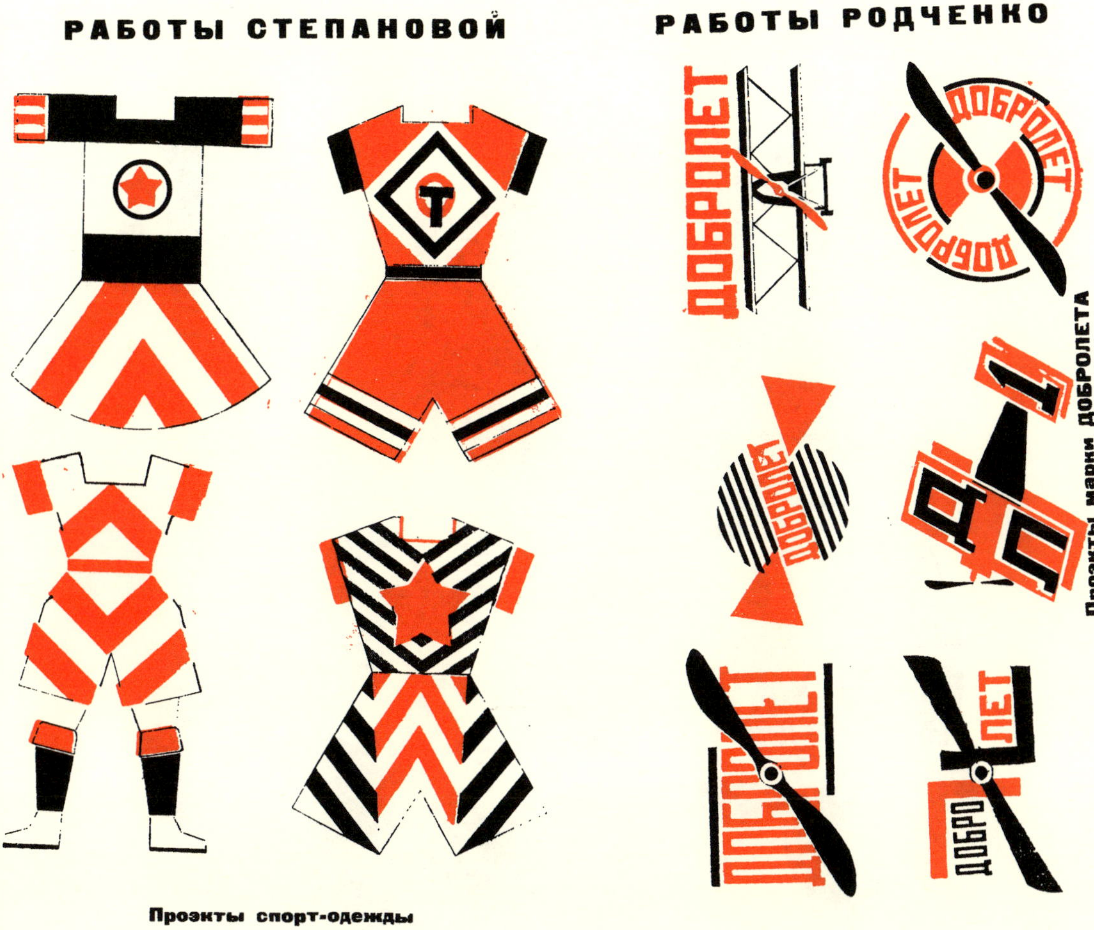

РАБОТЫ СТЕПАНОВОЙ

Проэкты спорт-одежды

РАБОТЫ РОДЧЕНКО

Проэкты марки ДОБРОЛЕТА

Varvara Stepanova's sports clothing
and Aleksandr Rodchenko's designs
for insignia for the state airline Dobrolet
Double page of the journal *Lef*, no. 2, 1923

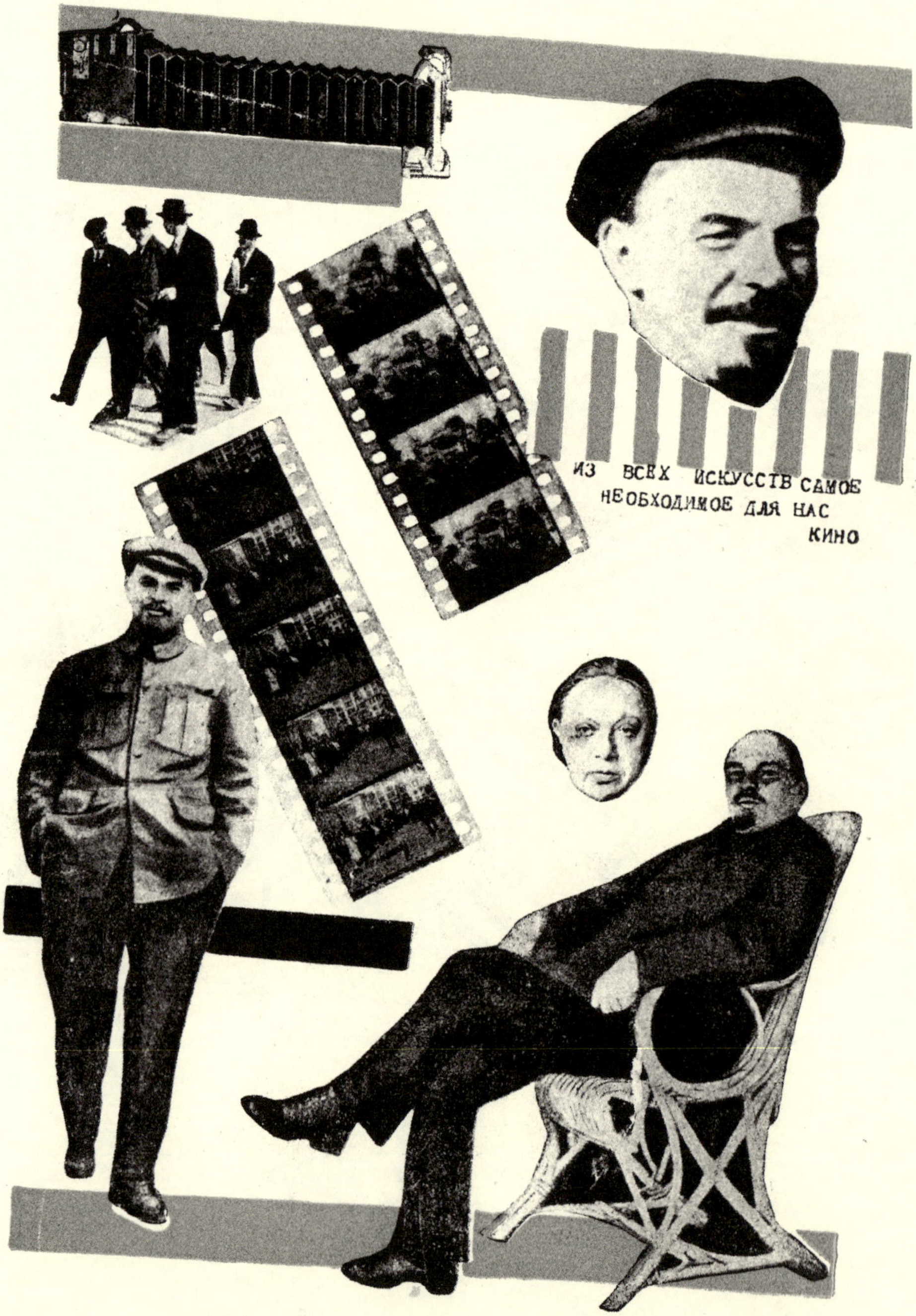

Фото-монтаж.—*С. Сенькина.*

Sergei Senkin
Illustration for the journal *Young Guard*, 1924

VIKTOR SHKLOVSKY

LENIN AS A DECANONIZER, 1924

Lenin's style is characterized, in particular, by the absence of incantation.

Every speech or article seems to start from scratch. There is no preset terminology; it appears only in the middle of each piece, as a specific product of the analytical work.

Lenin's arguments with his opponents—be they enemies or fellow party members—usually begin a debate on "words"—an assertion that words have changed.

As for the "element of language," which Lenin understood quite well, he had a peculiar attitude toward it that could be described as ironic push-back.

"I would very much like, for instance, to take several *gostrests*[1] (as we say in that beautiful Russian language [Ivan] Turgenev praises so highly) and show how we can manage a business" ("The Principal Tasks of the Party under NEP," p. 137). Here, the irony seems to be directed at the coinage *gostrest*.

But here's another example.

"Of this, we are unaware; there is still a remnant of Communist smugness, or comsmugness, as we'd say it in that same great Russian language" (ibid., p. 139). Fascinatingly, in this instance, the word is created before our very eyes, even as it is deliberately shown to be in conflict with the "element of language"—which, actually, exists for the sole purpose of being in conflict with it.

The formula, when it appears in Lenin's agit-work as an agitator, is constructed in a way that keeps it from becoming fixed.

Lenin despises people who have memorized books. The essence of his style is to bring revolutionary rhetoric down to earth, to replace its traditional words with everyday synonyms.

In this sense, Lenin's style lies close, in its principal technique, to that of Leo Tolstoy. Lenin opposes naming; each time, he establishes a new re-

Viktor Shklovskii, excerpts from"Lenin kak dekanonizator," *Lef*, no. 1 (1924): 53–56.

1. State trusts.—Trans

lationship between word and object, without naming things and without making the new name stick. . . .

DO NOT TRADE IN LENIN!

The following announcement has appeared in our newspapers:

"ANNOUNCEMENT:

BUSTS OF V.I. LENIN

plaster, patina, bronze, marble, granite

LIFE-SIZE OR DOUBLE-LIFE-SIZE

made from the original, authorized for reproduction and distribution by the Commission on Preserving the Eternal Memory of V. I. LENIN

MADE BY THE SCULPTOR

S. D. MERKULOV

OFFERED BY STATE PUBLISHING

for government offices, party and professional organizations, cooperatives, etc.

EACH UNIT IS AUTHORIZED

can be viewed and ordered

at the Department of COMMERCIAL PUBLISHING, Moscow, Rozhdestvenka, 4

Illustrated brochures will be mailed free of charge upon request.

UNAUTHORIZED REPRODUCTION AND COPYING WILL BE PROSECUTED UNDER THE LAW."

We are against this.

We agree with the railway workers of the Kazan Railroad who asked an artist to design their club's Lenin Room with no busts or portraits of Lenin, saying, "We do not want icons."

We insist:

Do not turn Lenin into a cliché.

Do not print his portraits on posters, tablecloths, plates, tea mugs, or cigar holders.

Do not bronze Lenin.

Do not take away his living step, his humanity, which he was able to preserve even as he steered history.

Lenin is still our contemporary.

He is still among the living.

We need him as a living man, not a dead man.

That is why:

Learn from Lenin but do not canonize him.

Do not create a cult in the name of a man who spent his entire life fighting against all sorts of cults.

Do not trade in objects of this cult.

Do not trade in Lenin!

ROMAN JAKOBSON
LETTERS FROM THE WEST. DADA, 1921

The word *dada* expresses the internationality of the movement," Huelsenbeck writes. The very question "What is Dada?" is itself un-dadaistic and sophomoric, he also notes. "'What does Dada want?"—Dada doesn't want anything. "I am writing a manifesto and I don't want anything . . . and I am on principle against manifestoes, as I am also against principles," Tzara declares.

No matter what you accuse Dada of, you can't accuse it of being dishonest, of concealment, of hedging its bets. Dada honorably perceives the "limitedness of its existence in time"; it relativizes itself historically, in its own words. Meanwhile, the first result of establishing a scientific view of artistic expression, that is, the laying bare of the device, is the cry: "The old art is dead" or "Art is dead," depending on the temperament of the person doing the yelling. The first call was issued by the Futurists, hence "Vive le futur!" The second, not without some stipulations, was issued by Dada—what business of theirs, of artists, is the future?—"A bas le futur!" So the improviser from Odoevsky's story, having received the gift of a clarity of vision which laid everything bare, ends his life as a fool in a cap scrawling transrational verses. The laying bare of the device is sharp; it is precisely a laying bare; the already laid-bare device—no longer in sharp confrontation with the code (à la langue)—is vapid, it lacks flavor. The initially laid-bare device is usually justified and regulated by so-called constructive laws, but, for example, the path from rhyme to assonance to a set toward any relationship between sounds leads to the announcement that a laundry list is a poetic work. Then letters in arbitrary order, randomly struck on a typewriter, are considered verses; dabs on a canvas made by a donkey's tail dipped in paint are considered a painting. With Dada's appeal, "Dilettantes, rise up against art," we have gone from yesterday's cult of "made things" (say, refined assonance) to the poetics of the first word let slip (a laundry list). What is dada by profession? To use an expression from

Roman Iakobson, "Pis'ma s zapada Dada," *Vestnik teatra*, no. 82 (February 8, 1921): 3–7, trans. Stephen Rudy in *Between Worlds: A Sourcebook of Central European Avant-Gardes, 1910–1930*, ed. Timothy O. Benson (Cambridge, MA: MIT Press, 2002), 359–63.

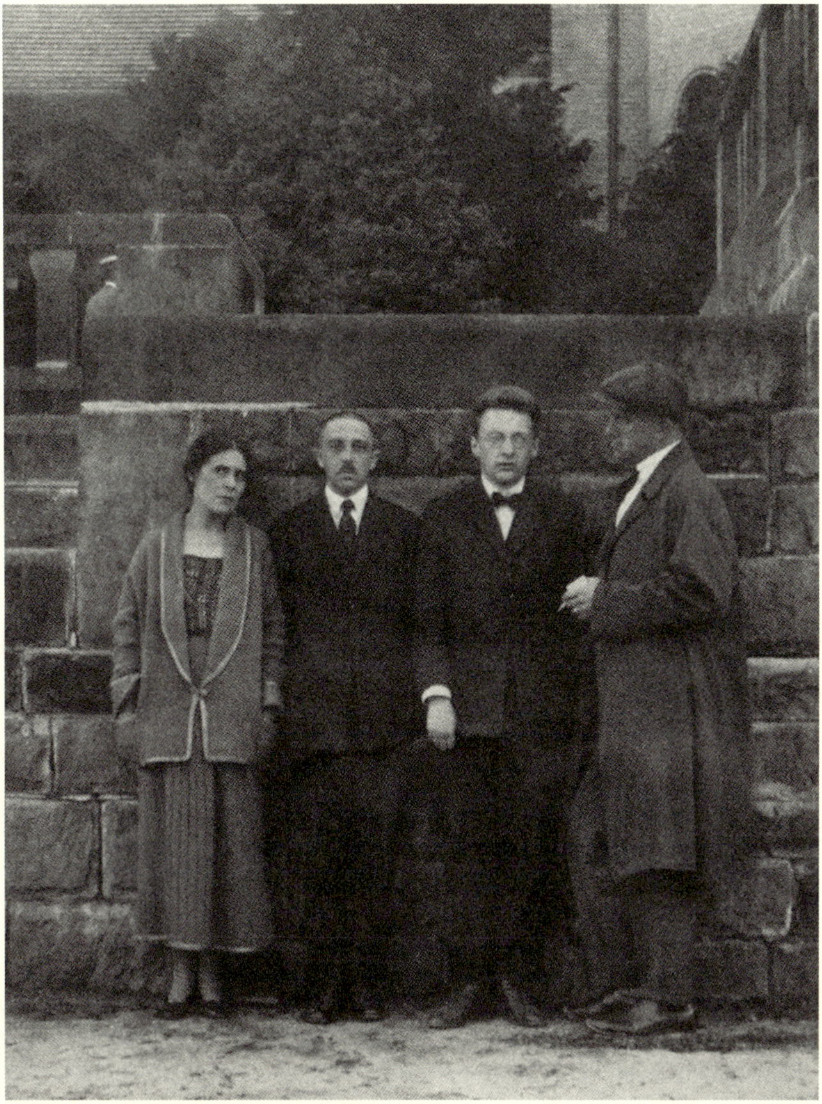

Anonymous
Lili Brik, Osip Brik, Roman Jakobson, and Vladimir Mayakovsky, Bad Flinsberg, Germany, 1923

Moscow artistic jargon, the Dadaists are "painters of the world." They have more declarations than poems and pictures. And actually in their poems and pictures there is nothing new, even if only in comparison to Italian and Russian Futurism. Tatlin's *Maschinenkunst*, universal poems made up of vowels, round verses (Simultaneism), the music of noise (Bruitism), Primitivism—a sort of poetic Berlitz:

Meine Mutter sagte mir verjage die Hühner
Ich ober kann nicht fortjagen die Hühner.
(Tzara)

Finally, paroxysms of naive realism: "Dada has common sense and in a chair sees a chair, in a plum—a plum."

But the crux of the matter lies elsewhere, and the Dadaists understand this. "Dada is not an artistic movement," they say. "In Switzerland Dada is for abstract [nonobjective] art, in Berlin—against." What is important is that, having finished once and for all with the principle of the legendary coalition of form and content, through a realization of the violence of artistic form, the toning down of pictorial and poetic semantics, through the color and texture *as such* of the nonobjective picture, through the fanatic word of transrational verses *as such,* we come in Russia to the blue grass of the first celebrations of October and in the West to the unambiguous Dadaist formula: "Nous voulons nous voulons nous voulons pisser en couleurs diverses." Coloring *as such*! Only the canvas is removed, like an act in a sideshow one has grown tired of.

Poetry and painting became for Dada one of the acts of the sideshow. Let us be frank: poetry and painting occupy in our consciousness an excessively high position only because of tradition. "The English are so sure of the genius of Shakespeare that they don't consider it necessary even to read him," as Aubrey Beardsley puts it. We are prepared to respect the classics but for reading prefer literature written for train rides, detective stories, novels about adultery, that whole area of "belles-lettres" in which the *word* makes itself least heard. Dostoevsky, if one reads him inattentively, quickly becomes a cheap best seller, and it is hardly by chance that in the West they prefer to see his works in the movies. If the theaters are full, then it is more a matter of tradition than of interest on the part of the public. The theater is dying: the movies are blossoming. The screen ceases bit by bit to be the equivalent of the stage; it frees itself of the theatrical unities, of the theatrical *mise en scène*. The aphorism of the Dadaist Mehring is timely: "The popularity of an idea springs from the possibility of transferring onto film its anecdotal content." For variety's sake the Western reader is willing to accept a peppering of self-valuable words. The Parisian newspaper *Le Siècle* states: "We need a literature which the mind can savor like a cocktail." During the last decade, no one has brought to the artistic market so much varied junk of all times and places as the very people who reject the past. It should be understood that the Dadaists are also eclectics, though theirs is not the museum-bound eclecticism of respectful veneration, but a motley cafe *chantant* program (not by chance was Dada born in a cabaret in Zurich). A little song of the Maoris takes turns with a Parisian music hall number, a sentimental lyric—with the above-mentioned color effect. "I like an old work for its novelty. Only contrast links us to the past," Tzara explains.

One should take into account the background against which Dada is frolicking in order to understand certain of its manifestations. For example, the infantile anti-French attacks of the French Dadaists and the anti-German attacks of the Germans ten years ago might sound naive and purposeless. But today, in the countries of the Entente there rages an almost zoological nationalism, while in response to it in Germany there grows the hypertrophied national pride of an oppressed people. The Royal British Society contemplates refusing Einstein a medal so as not to export gold to Germany, while the French newspapers are outraged by the fact that Hamsun, who according to rumor was Germanophile during the war, was given a Nobel Prize. The politically innocent Dada arouses terrible suspicion on the part of those same papers that it is some sort of German machination, while those papers print advertisements for "nationalistic double beds." Against this background, the Dadaist Fronde is quite understandable. At the present moment, when even scientific ties have been severed, Dada is one of the few truly international societies of the bourgeois intelligentsia.

By the way, it is a unique Internationale; the Dadaist Bauman lays his cards on the table when he says that "Dada is the product of international hotels." The environment in which Dada was reared was that of the adventuristic bourgeois of the war—the profiteers, the nouveaux riches, the Schieberen, the black marketeers, or whatever else they were called. Dada's sociopsychological twins in old Spain gave birth to the so-called picaresque novel. They know no traditions (*"je ne veux même pas savoir s'il y a eu des homes avant moi"*); their future is doubtful ("à bas le futur"); they are in hurry to take what is theirs ("give and take, live and die"). They are exceptionally supple and adaptable ("one can perform contrary actions at the same time, in a single, fresh breath"); they are artists at what they do ("advertising and business are also poetic elements"). They do not object to the war ("still today for war"); yet they are the first to proclaim the cause of erasing the boundaries between yesterday's warring powers ("me, I'm of many nationalities"). When it comes right down to it, they are satisfied and therefore prefer bars ("he holds war and peace in his toga, but decides in favor of a cherry brandy flip"). Here, amid the "cosmopolitan mixture of god and the bordello," in Tzara's testimonial, Dada is born.

"The time is Dada-ripe," Huelsenbeck assures us. "With Dada it will ascend, and with Dada it will vanish."

SERGEI SHARSHUN
MY PARTICIPATION IN THE FRENCH DADA MOVEMENT, 1967

I made my first acquaintance with the French Dadaists in Barcelona in 1916.

I organized an exhibition of my paintings, which allowed me to reconnect or connect with the Parisian Boheme.

Among them was Otho Lloyd, with whom I had spent two years studying at the cubist Académie La Palette. He considered himself the nephew of Oscar Wilde. He was married to the Russian artist Olga Sakharova.[1]

Also in Barcelona was the poet Maximilien Gauthier later an art critic. (He too had a Russian wife.) He was the editor-in-chief of the journal *391*, published by the Bohemian snob Francis Picabia, who had by then moved from Barcelona to New York; after four issues the journal stopped publishing (but was later revived).

Then, Otho Lloyd's brother Arthur Cravan, whose Dadaist life was the subject of much discussion in Paris, arrived. He was planning to turn all of Barcelona upside down. Not long after, his life ended tragically.

Also living in Barcelona was the painter Marie Laurencin, who had married a German artist before the war.

After my return in Paris, I was present at the Dadaist showing at the Salle Gaveau.[2] After that, I sent a drawing to Francis Picabia by mail.

Later, I ran into him at Povolotsky's Russian bookstore, where a Dadaist exhibition was being prepared.[3]

Someone asked him for permission to attend the opening. Then I mustered the courage to do the same. "What's your name?" he asked. "Sharshun." "You can come, your drawing is printed in the journal."

At the opening of the exhibition, Jean Cocteau was "exposing" the Parisians to jazz band music.

In response, Tristan Tzara—not a creator but a destroyer, the man who truly inspired Dadaism—spent a long time honking a vehicle horn by his ear at deafening volume.

Sergei Sharshun, "Moe uchastie vo frantzuskom dadaisticheskom dvizhenii," *Almanakh Vozdushnye puti* 5 (1967).

1. Olga Sakharova was a painter and a graphic artist. In 1917–1924, she belonged to the circle of the international avant-garde journal *391*. 2. The Dada festival was held at the Salle Gaveau on Rue La Boétie in Paris on May 26, 1920. It was one of the Dadaists' most scandalous actions. 3. The Picabia exhibition at Povolotsky's shop (Galerie Povolotsky) was held from December 10 to December 25, 1920.

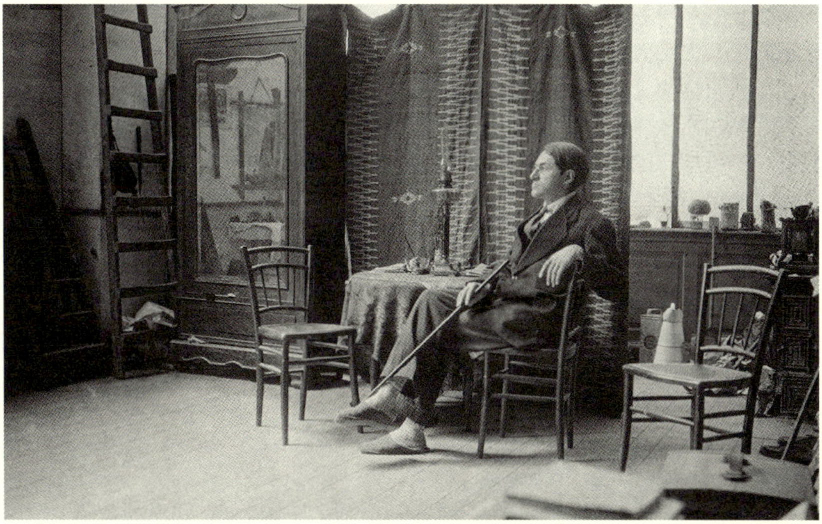

Man Ray
Sergei Sharshun in His Studio, 1925

I started coming to Picabia's Sunday gatherings dressed in a Russian army uniform dyed black.

Once, Picabia lamented that he hadn't found a partner for sneaking across the Spanish border during the war.

"I wouldn't have said no to that, *mon vieux*!" I blurted out. There followed an awkward silence, which Picabia finally broke with a brief exclamation of approval.

Another time, someone mentioned Einstein. "Einstein . . . isn't that so?" Picabia responded. That was the end of it.

Once or twice, the "young ones" played cards. One of them, when losing, would take out his wallet, hold it open, and then hide it again.

The composers [Francis] Poulenc and [Georges] Auric were frequent visitors.

By then, I had published my first printed work: the poem "Foule immobile" [The Immobile Crowd], kindly edited by Philippe Soupault and illustrated by six of my own drawings.

Once, I showed several of my drawings. Cocteau declared that only [Georges] Braque could draw like that. I did not find it appropriate to give him one of them as an expression of gratitude for such a comment; but another time he made drawings, merrily and mockingly scattering them across the table, of dozens of scenes from the love life of a sophisticated couple, and I asked his permission, not without embarrassment, and took five or six of them.

But then Picabia invented the painting-collage *L'oeil cacodylate* [The Cacodylic Eye].

A blank canvas about one-and-a-half meters high, with the title "L'oeil cacodylate" scrawled at the very top and an eye painted in the lower right part, was set up in the reception hall, to be filled with the signatures of fashionable celebrities.

Everyone signed politely.

The Napoleonic Tzara, however, handled it differently. He wrote, "I consider myself very . . ." (the phrase was completed in another part of the canvas: "likeable"). Of course he signed off with a huge flourish, then glued an aspirin pill onto the canvas and drew an index finger. (Usually, he would draw a revolver next to his signature.)

The honor was soon offered to me as well, fairly early on; the canvas was still more or less empty.

Like all of humanity in those days, I was, of course, "delighted" by the Bolshevist revolution and was hoping to go to the Paradise on Earth.

A quiet man by ethnicity and heritage, and therefore little-noticed (I was tolerated only for my "looks" and external appearance), I probably surprised everyone by outlining a fat "S. Charchoune" right underneath the eye, then, to the left of it, a vertical "Sharshun," Mongolian-style, and underneath it all, in a descending slanted line, "*Soleil Russe*" [The Russian Sun].

The anarchist snob Picabia seemed rather perplexed by my stunt, saying, "This will get me in trouble."

However, he probably soon calmed down: as the painting filled with signatures, my exclamation was lost in the general mass.

Although someone did tell me that he saw my painting *L'oeil cacodylate* at the restaurant Boeuf sur le toit [Bull on the Roof], which had acquired the work.

A retired major (*commandant*) who also left his signature advised me to offer my services as an interpreter to an author who was planning to make a flight along the Russian borders.

I went to see him at the Issy-les-Moulineaux airport, but the job had already been filled.

"Give my greetings to Lenin," Roland Dorgelès told me sardonically. "I most certainly will," I replied.

"Give [Henri] Gilbeaux a trashing for me," said Tzara.

Picabia asked Isadora Duncan for her signature, and she expressed interest in finding out through me how to travel to Russia.

I was slightly acquainted with one particular Bolshevik Party member and, after making inquiries with him, went with Picabia to see Duncan.

This led to her "vulgar" marriage to [Sergei] Esenin.

On Thursdays, I also visited the La Certa coffeehouse near the Grand Boulevards, which served as a gathering place for Dadaists (other than Picabia). Once, "[Pierre] Drieu de la Rochelle. showed up. However, I was present only as a silent observer/eyewitness; the regulars hardly even knew the sound of my voice.

While preparing for the arrival of the German artist Max Ernst in Paris, Tzara organized an exhibition of his work at the bookshop Au san Pareil.

He asked me to come to such-and-such place, on such-and-such day, at such-and-such hour.

Ernst's paintings were being hung for display.

The only ones present were André Breton, Philippe Soupault, Benjamin Péret, Jacques Rigaut, and me.

Breton, who had walked from the Latin quarter to Etoile, passing dozens of bakeries on the way, asked the owner of the bookshop, who was involved in the arts, to bring him "a croissant."

He took this in stride and quickly brought one for each of us.

Such is the tradition of the relationship between master and apprentice.

The six of us (including the owner) had our photograph taken for the press.

A while later, an exhibition of Dadaist antiart was organized at the gallery of the Comédie des Champs-Élysées theater—and, of course, there was also an antiliterary performance.

I exhibited *The Virgin Mary of Salpingite*, composed of the only sculpture I had made in my life—the small, wooden futuristic sculpture *The Dance*—with shirt collars and neckties hung on it and around it.

Overhead, there was paper tape glued all along the cornice under the ceiling, covered with exclamations and sayings.

I wrote in Russian, "I'm here!"

One of the evening's numbers was a performance by an itinerant faience pottery repairman whom Tristan Tzara had brought over, and who squeaked out a professional-quality song on a pipe.

Also performing was my friend Valentin Iakovlevich Parnakh, the Russian poet and dancer; he lay down on the table and danced to music by jerking and bouncing.

In the third number, four or five participants, led by Frenkel, walked single file through the hall past the public, and each solemnly received a gift from the author: a match.

I felt that I should participate in this and joined at the back of the line, but I was told in a whisper to leave the group, and so I went backstage.

The walls of the corridor that led to the hall were covered with Dadaist magazines, almost all published by Tzara.

I went in there "during the show."

One of the movement's hangers-on, the one who had so conscientiously paid his gambling debts, was ripping the magazines down shouting, "*Boche!*"[4]

I don't remember how I met Marcel Duchamp, who never attended any gatherings. He was favorably disposed toward me.

Then, once again, Tristan Tzara told me to come to the hall of the Société Savante.[5]

I had often attended Russian social gatherings, which took place in that hall, selling (without much success) émigré books.

The security guards were surprised to see me among "these gentlemen."

This time, the planned event was the "Trial of Barrès."[6] Participants donned white doctor's gowns and four-cornered black caps.

I was given the role of calling witnesses. Picabia was sitting in the audience.

The chairman, Andre Breton, would turn to me and ask me to call a witness—for instance, Monsignor Giuseppe Ungaretti. I would go to the door that led to the hall and call out, "Signor Giuseppe Ungaretti!" Or "bring the "German Unknown Soldier," and I'd call out, "der Unbekannte Soldat!" (The French public saw this universalism as Dadaist.)

André Gide, who was then collecting material for his novel *Les faux-monnayeurs* [*The Counterfeiters*] and who, I think, attended the trial, called his heroes' little magazine *Fer* à *repasser* [The Clothes Iron], borrowing it from one of my drawings for the poem "La foule immobile."

I don't like drawing, but Tzara asked me to illustrate his poem "Coeur à gaz" [The Gas Heart], and I gave him 7 or 8 drawings.

However, Max Ernst's drawings were unquestionably better.

Eventually, Tzara had in his possession several of my drawings and paintings, which he intended to get published in magazines in several countries. (They all ended up being lost.)

As the commander of the Dadaist army, he had, of course, no compunction about building his Nietzschean career on the "dead bodies" of others.

From Michel Samouillet's work *Dadaïsme à Paris* [Dadaism in Paris], published in 1965, I learned that Tzara had issued leaflets signed with my name, that he had reissued 25 copies of "Foule immobile," and that he had used my name whenever he needed to.

Such things were common practice in those days.

4. French slur for "German." 5. "Learned Society." 6. The "Trial of Maurice Barrès" (May 13, 1921) was one of the key theatricalized actions of the Dada movement, held at the Hall of the Learned Society. Auguste-Maurice Barrès was a French nationalist writer whose work and extremist ideology during World War I were at odds with the "new spirit" of Dada. Participants in the trial included well-known Dadaists as well as Sergei Sharshun and Sergei Romov.

At the time, there were two émigré groups on Montparnasse: "The Gatarapak" and "The Chamber of Poets." The latter was created by the aforementioned V. Ia. Parnakh. It was made up of five people: G. S. Evangulov (the founder), A. S. Ginger, M. Talov, and me.

The refugee tradition of holding benefit events flourished.

I called mine "Dada-lyr-can" (lyricism, Dadaist-style chirping) and asked the Dadaists to participate.[7]

For that event, I wrote a booklet on Dadaism, which I had printed later in Germany in a batch of 1,500 or 2,000 copies, intending to take it back to Russia with me. But because of the collapse of the deutschmark I was unable to collect it and could only "extract" a few copies from the printing shop (I don't have a single copy for reissuing it).

Some Dadaists read their works, including Paul Éluard, who recited his both in the "common" and in the inverted sense.

An American Dadaist who had just arrived from New York—I think it was Nicholson—recited several German poems by the sculptor Hans Arp. Members of the audience deemed it wise to express their protest with weak booing.[8] A few weeks later, nearly all of those in attendance were in Berlin.

Finally, in 1921 I started to take action to realize my plan to go back to Russia and came to Berlin, but after 14 months, obeying instinct, returned to Paris.

During that time, Dadaism had run out of steam.

Picabia and Tzara had exhausted themselves and lost the fighting spirit.

The throne of newly created surrealism had been occupied by A[ndré] Breton, who had rewarded all of his allies with red cards.

For that reason, I did not renew my contacts with any of my former friends.

Personal discipline was enough for me. My involvement with Dadaism happened only because I was so young.

P.S. Several of my drawings were reproduced in *Manomètre* and *Merz*.

Not a single one of my texts was published. Only on one occasion did Tzara inform me at Café Certa that he was gathering material for a Dadaist poetry collection. But the submissions deadline had expired the day before.

Out of sheer naïveté, when I got home I sent him something by pneumatic post.

7. The event was held on December 21, 1921, at the Café Caméléon. 8. Paul Éluard, in a letter to Tristan Tzara (January 4, 1922), described this evening as follows: "You have probably heard about Sharshun's soiree. The most swinish of Russians had boredom reflected in their eyes." Quoted in Samouillet, *Dada in Paris*, p. 279.

LIST OF WORKS

Anonymous
Ilia Zdanevich, 1912
Gelatin silver print
11.2 x 8.6 cm
Archives Iliazd
France
p. 22

Anonymous
Mikhail Larionov, Natalia Goncharova and Ilia Zdanevich, Moscow, 1913
Gelatin silver print
16.8 x 21.2 cm
Archives Iliazd
France
p. 258

Anonymous
David Burliuk, Vladimir Mayakovsky, and Andrei Shemshurin, Moscow, 1914
Gelatin silver print
12 x 18 cm
The State Mayakovsky Museum, Moscow
10925
p. 231

Anonymous
Filippo Tommaso Marinetti in Moscow, illustration in the newspaper *Nov*, January 28, 1914
Offset
19 x 28.5 cm
The State Mayakovsky Museum, Moscow
BG-1914/101

Anonymous
Filippo Tommaso Marinetti, illustration in the newspaper *Nov*, January 26, 1914
Offset
29 x 30 cm
The State Mayakovsky Museum, Moscow
BG-1914/102
p. 262

Anonymous
Vasily Kamensky, Kazan, 1914
Gelatin silver print
13 x 8.5 cm
The State Mayakovsky Museum, Moscow
29866
p. 173

Anonymous
Vladimir Tatlin, Berlin, 1914
Gelatin silver print
37 x 29.5 cm
Russian State Archives of Literature and Art
f. 2089, op. 2, ed. khr. 31, l. 1
p. 125

Anonymous
"Easter at Futurists" and "Tramway V" illustration in the journal *Blue Journal*, no. 12, 1915
Offset
30 x 22 cm
The State Museum of Contemporary Art-Costakis Collection
2 objects AB059 and CDA-0145
pp. 35–36

Anonymous
"0,10: The Last Futurist Exhibition in Petrograd," illustration in *Ogonek*, no. 1, 1916
Printed 2018
Russian State Library
p. 42

Anonymous
Gustav Klutsis as a soldier in the Latvian rifles detachment, 1917
Gelatin silver print
14 x 8.7 cm
Private Collection

Anonymous
Ilia and Kirill Zdanevich, Tiflis, ca. 1917
Gelatin silver print
14 x 9 cm
Archives Iliazd
France
p. 182

Anonymous
Leaflet to the Russian citizens about the fall of the provisional government and Bolsheviks seizing power, 25 October, 1917
Letterpress
15.9 x 13.9 cm
Archivo Lafuente
010990/000

Anonymous
Multiple portrait of Gustav Klutsis, 1917
Gelatin silver print
8.5 x 13.5 cm
Private Collection
p. 70

Anonymous
Multiple portrait of Marcel Duchamp, 1917
Gelatin silver print (printed 2018)
20 x 33 cm
Courtesy of Francis M. Naumann Fine Art
p. 71

Anonymous
Cover of *Final Dissolution: Dada Manifesto* by Walter Serner, Hannover, 1920
Letterpress
22 x 14.5 cm
The State Mayakovsky Museum, Moscow
И-784

Anonymous
Cover of the book *Zaum* by Aleksei Kruchenykh, 1921
Ink and color pencil on paper
18.3 x 15.7 cm

The State Mayakovsky Museum, Moscow
33345(40)

Anonymous
Leaflet of the manifesto *Dada Raises Everything*, Paris, 1921
Letterpress
27.5 x 21 cm
The State Mayakovsky Museum, Moscow
10691

Anonymous
View of Ivan Puni's exhibition in Der Sturm Gallery, Berlin, 1921
Gelatin silver print
18.5 x 24 cm
Private Collection
p. 130

Anonymous
Wandering Musicians (double portrait of Aleksandr Rodchenko and Varvara Stepanova), 1921
Gelatin silver print
23.5 x 16.5 cm
Private Collection
p. 244

Anonymous
Vladimir Mayakovsky, Berlin, 1922
Gelatin silver print
22 x 16.2 cm
The State Mayakovsky Museum, Moscow
11222

Anonymous
Exhibition of Paintings of the Petrograd Artists of All Trends, 1923
16 mm film transferred to DVD, b/w, silent, 32"
Russian State Documentary Film and Photo Archive, Krasnogorsk
pp. 84, 249, 274

Anonymous
Lili Brik, Osip Brik, Roman Jakobson, Vladimir Mayakovsky, Bad Flinsberg, Germany, 1923
Gelatin silver print
13.6 x 8.7 cm
The State Mayakovsky Museum, Moscow
31000
p. 311

Anonymous
Nothingists: Dog's Box, 1923
Letterpress
24.3 x 15 cm
The State Mayakovsky Museum, Moscow
28155(543)
p. 296

Anonymous
Page from the journal *Clarté*, no. 39, with Maurice Pirijianine's review of *The Bearded Heart* soiree, "Le Dadaisme boxeé par les siens" [Dadaism is boxing with itself], 13 July 1923
Letterpress
29 x 22.7 cm
Archives Iliazd France

Anonymous
View of Pavel Mansurov's exhibition in the Museum of Artistic Culture, Leningrad, 1923
Gelatin silver print
23.5 x 17.5 cm
Private Collection
p. 84

Anonymous
David Burliuk, New York, 1924
Gelatin silver print
13.5 x 8.6 cm
The State Mayakovsky Museum, Moscow
32086
p. 151

Anonymous
Leaflet of the group Nothingists, ca. 1924
Letterpress
18 x 18 cm
The State Mayakovsky Museum, Moscow
9844
p. 191

Anonymous
Leaflet of the group Nothingists, ca. 1924
Letterpress
18 x 18 cm
The State Mayakovsky Museum, Moscow
9843
p. 191

Anonymous
Leaflet of the group Nothingists, ca. 1924
Letterpress
19 x 22.5 cm
The State Mayakovsky Museum, Moscow
9845

Anonymous
Vladimir Mayakovsky, Valentina Khodasevich, Elza Triolet, Klara Goll, Ivan Goll, and Robert Delaunay (left to right), Paris, 1924
Gelatin silver print (postcard)
9 x 13.8 cm
The State Mayakovsky Museum, Moscow
11144
p. 144

Anonymous
Ilia Zdanevich performing as live painting *The Triumph of Cubism* in the *Banal Ball*, Paris, March 1924
Gelatin silver print
18 x 13 cm
Archives Iliazd France
p. 166

Anonymous
Vladimir Mayakovsky and David Burliuk, New York, 1925
Gelatin silver print
13.5 x 11.5 cm
The State Mayakovsky Museum, Moscow
И-929

Anonymous
Aleksandr Rodchenko, and Varvara Stepanova, and Olga Rodchenko, in an impromptu action ca. 1925
16 mm film transferred to DVD, b/w, silent, 21"
Private Collection

Anonymous
Arp with naval monocle, 1926
Gelatin silver print (printed 2018)
Stiftung Arp e.V., Berlin/Rolandswerth
p. 138

Anonymous
Vasily Ermilov in his studio with an advertising design for "Read Books" by Valerian Polishchiuk (left), ca. 1926
Gelatin silver print, ca. 1926 (printed 2018)
Central State Archives, Museum of Literature and Arts of Ukraine
p. 118

Anonymous
David Burliuk, n.d.
Cut-and-pasted papers, gold paint, and pencil on paper
13.7 x 13.5 cm
Russian State Archives of Literature and Art
f. 1334, op. 1, ed. khr. 1085, ll. 109–110
p. 154

Anonymous
Proletariat of the World Unite: Organization of Production Victory over a Capitalist Structure
Lithograph
17.9 x 45.5 cm
The State Museum of Contemporary Art-Costakis Collection
139.80-244
pp. 104–105

Anonymous
Scenes from World War I documentary, n.d.
16 mm film transferred to DVD, b/w, silent, 6'08"
Russian State Documentary Film and Photo Archive, Krasnogorsk

Anonymous
Untitled (First Room/Ceiling), n.d.
Watercolor and graphite on paper
37.7 x 57.8 cm
The State Museum of Contemporary Art-Costakis Collection
C207-258

Anonymous
Untitled (First Room), early 1920s.
Watercolor and graphite on paper
37.9 x 57.6 cm
The State Museum of Contemporary Art-Costakis Collection
C205-259
p. 104

Samuil Adlivankin
Cover of the book *Songs for Workers* by Vladimir Mayakovsky, Moscow, 1925
Letterpress
18.1 x 13 cm
Archivo Lafuente
007018/000

Natan Altman, Natalia Goncharova, Nikolai Kulbin (cover), Kazimir Malevich, and Olga Rozanova
Cover and illustrations for the book *Explodity* by Aleksei Kruchenykh, Saint Petersburg, 1913
Lithograph
17.8 x 12.4 cm
Archivo Lafuente
006848/000
p. 29

Natan Altman
Cover and illustrations for the book *Lenin: Drawings*, Saint Petersburg, 1921
23.4 x 19.1 cm
Lithograph
Archivo Lafuente
006920/000
p. 94

Natan Altman
Russia: Work, 1921
Charcoal on paper mounted on mahogany
98.2 x 49.3 cm
State Tretyakov Gallery, Moscow
ЖС-696
p. 110

Iury Annenkov
Cover of the journal *Modern West*, no. 3, 1923
Saint Petersburg/Moscow: s.e.
Lithograph
26.8 x 18.5 cm
Archivo Lafuente
006981/000

Hans Arp
Cover of the journal *Die Wolkenpumpe*, Hannover, 1920
Letterpress
23.4 x 15.5 cm
The State Mayakovsky Museum, Moscow
И-785

Hans Arp
In front of the Schwitters' house in Hannover (left to right: Helma Schwitters, unidentified, Kurt Schwitters, Nelly van Doesburg, Theo van Doesburg, and El Lissitzky, with Ernst Schwitters), 1922
Gelatin silver print
4.5 x 6.5 cm
Archivo Lafuente
005687/000
p. 136

Arseny Avraamov
Symphony of Factory Sirens, composed to celebrate the fifth anniversary of the October Revolution, performed in Baku in 1922 and Moscow in 1923
28'10"
Published by ReR Megacorp, London, 2008
Courtesy Miguel Molina Alarcón, Universitat Politècnica de València

Ksenia Boguslavskaia, Ivan Puni, Vladimir Kozlinsky, and Sergei Makletsov
Cover of the portfolio *October 1917–1918: Heroes and Victims of the Revolution*, 1918
Lithograph
35 x 53 cm
Vladimir Dahl Russian State Literary Museum
GLM KP 12210/1

Ksenia Boguslavskaia
Banker, illustration for the portfolio *October 1917–1918: Heroes and Victims of the Revolution* by Vladimir Mayakovsky, 1918
Lithograph
33.5 x 23.7 cm
Vladimir Dahl Russian State Literary Museum
GLM KP 12210/21

Ksenia Boguslavskaia
Dressmaker, illustration for the portfolio *October 1917–1918: Heroes and Victims of the Revolution* by Vladimir Mayakovsky, 1918
Lithograph
33.7 x 24 cm
Vladimir Dahl Russian State Literary Museum
GLM KP 12210/24

Ksenia Boguslavskaia
Kulak, illustration for the portfolio *October 1917–1918: Heroes and Victims of the Revolution* by Vladimir Mayakovsky, 1918
Lithograph
33 x 24.2 cm
Vladimir Dahl Russian State Literary Museum
GLM KP 12210/22

Ksenia Boguslavskaia
Merchant, illustration for the portfolio *October 1917–1918: Heroes and Victims of the Revolution* by Vladimir Mayakovsky, 1918
Lithograph
33 x 23.5 cm
Vladimir Dahl Russian State Literary Museum
GLM KP 12210/23

Ksenia Boguslavskaia
Study for *Banker*, illustration in the portfolio *October 1917–1918: Heroes and Victims of the Revolution* by Vladimir Mayakovsky, 1918

Ink and white
paint on paper
33.3 x 24 cm
Vladimir Dahl
Russian State
Literary Museum
GLM KP 7309/1
p. 98

Osip Brik
Scrapbook "Dada,"
ca. 1923–1924
Cut-and-pasted
papers and gelatin
silver prints, ink-and-
pencil drawings
27.5 x 21.9 cm
The State
Mayakovsky
Museum, Moscow
10595
pp. 10, 122, 126,
168, 169,

Karl Bulla
Mikhail Matiushin, Aleksei Kruchenykh, and Kazimir Malevich, 1913
Gelatin silver print
17.8 x 23.8 cm
The State Mayakovsky
Museum, Moscow
И-708
p. 31

David Burliuk
Cover of the book
Burliuk Shakes Woolworth Building's Hand, New York, 1924
Letterpress
22.5 x 15.5 cm
The State Mayakovsky
Museum, Moscow
P-5414

Charles Chaplin
Shoulder Arms, 1918
35 mm film
transferred to DVD,
b/w, silent, 36"
(extract 2'45")
Roy Export S.A.S.

Giorgio de Chirico
Iliazd, ca. 1927
Ink on paper
25.5 x 19.5 cm
Private Collection
France

Mikhail Le Dantiu
Igor Severianin's March to Berlin, 1914
Watercolor and
graphite on paper
26.2 x 42.2 cm
Vladimir Dahl
Russian State
Literary Museum
GLM KP 46627
p. 30

Robert Delaunay
Vladimir Mayakovsky,
Paris, 1922
Autolithograph
12.6 x 10.3 cm
The State Mayakovsky
Museum, Moscow
13148

Robert Delaunay
Tristan Tzara, 1923
Oil on cardboard
104.5 x 75 cm
Museo Nacional
Centro de Arte
Reina Sofía
AD00372
p. 167

Sonia Delaunay
Design for a tennis
dress, 1924
Gouache and pencil
on cardboard
31 x 23 cm
Museo Nacional
Centro de Arte Reina
Sofía. Extended
Loan from Pedro and
Ary Altamiranda,
Panama, 2010
DO01215
p. 166

Sonia Delaunay
Design for a costume
with umbrella, 1925
Gouache and pencil
on cardboard
33 x 22.5 cm
Museo Nacional
Centro de Arte Reina
Sofía. Extended
Loan from Pedro and
Ary Altamiranda,
Panama, 2010
DO01216

Sofia Dymshits-
Tolstaia
Cover of the
journal *The International of Art*
(unpublished), 1919
Cut-and-pasted
papers and gouache
25 x 16 cm
Russian State
Archives of
Literature and Art
f. 665, op. 1, ed.
khr. 36, l. 1
p. 107

Sergei Eisenstein
Glumov's Diary
(conceived as part
of the adaptation
of Aleksandr
Ostrovsky's 1868
comedy *Enough Stupidity in Every Wise Man*, which
he realized at
the Proletcult
Theater), 1923
35 mm film
transferred to DVD,
b/w, silent, 5'
National Film
Foundation of
Russian Federation
p. 213

Boris Ender
Karl Liebknecht, 1919
Oil on canvas
100 x 69 cm
The Nizhny Tagil Art
Museum, provided
with assistance from
the State Museum
and Exhibition
Center ROSIZO
484-X
p. 114

Vasily Ermilov
Untitled
(Composition with
Letters), ca. 1920
Gouache on paper
54.6 x 36.5 cm
Collection V.
Tsarenkov
p. 118

Vasily Ermilov
Memorial board
Gorki, 1924
Gelatin silver print
(printed 2018)
Central State
Archives, Museum
of Literature and
Arts of Ukraine
p. 93

Vasily Ermilov
Memorial board *Marx and Lenin*, 1924
Gelatin silver print
(printed 2018)
Central State
Archives, Museum
of Literature and
Arts of Ukraine
p. 73

Nikolai Evreinov
Storming of the Winter Palace, 1920
35 mm film
transferred to DVD,
b/w, silent, 8'03"
Russian State
Documentary Film
and Photo Archive,
Krasnogorsk

Aleksandra Exter
Cover of the book
Picasso's Environs
by Ivan Aksenov,
Moscow, 1917
Letterpress
27.1 x 20.9 cm
Archivo Lafuente
006900/000

Petr Galadzhev
Cover of the book
Coiler by Viktor
Shklovsky, 1920–1929
Paper, ink, pen
and photomontage
(Printed 2018)
State Central Cinema
Museum, Moscow
p. 138

Petr Galadzhev
Cover of the journal
Spectacles, nos. 73,
74, 77, 1924
Letterpress

25 x 17 cm
The State Mayakovsky Museum, Moscow
10796 (1,2,3)

Petr Galadzhev
Cover of the book *One Minute, 1,000 Episodes, 10,000,000 Faces, 100,000 Kilometers* by Vilbur Gress, Moscow, 1925
Letterpress
17.5 x 13 cm
Archivo Lafuente
007019/000

Irakly Gamrekeli, Beno Gordeziani, H2SO4 Group
Cover and illustrations for the journal *H2SO4*, Tiflis, no. 1, 1924
Letterpress
31.7 x 23.8 cm
Archivo Lafuente
006982/000
p. 192

Efim Golyshev
String Trio, ca. 1914–1925
13'33"
Moscow State Tchaikovsky Conservatory

Natalia Goncharova, Sigizmund Valishevsky, Kirill Zdanevich, Ilia Zdanevich et al.
Cover and illustrations for the book *To Sofia Georgievna Melnikova: The Fantastic Tavern*, Tiflis, 1919
Letterpress
18 x 13.7 cm
Archivo Lafuente
006908/000

Natalia Goncharova
Cover of the book *The City: Verses* by Aleksandr Rubakin, Paris, 1920
Lithograph
25.5 x 16.6 cm
Archivo Lafuente
006919/000
p. 142

Natalia Goncharova
Ilia Zdanevich as Angel, ca. 1921
Ink and pencil on paper
36 x 25.5 cm
Private Collection France
p. 147

Natalia Goncharova and Ilia Zdanevich
Program for *Olympic Ball*, July 1924
Letterpress
64 x 25 cm
Private Collection France
p. 166

Sergei Gorodetsky and Velimir Khlebnikov
Spinny-spin-spin, anniversary book dedicated to Aleksei Kruchenykh
Watercolor on paper and manuscript, 1920
31 x 23 cm
Russian State Archives of Literature and Art
f. 1334, op. 1, ed. khr. 252, ll. 1–24
pp. 178, 288

Naum Granovsky
Cover of the book *Lidantiu as a Beacon* by Ilia Zdanevich, Paris, 1923
Cut-and-pasted papers
19.3 x 14.4 cm
Archivo Lafuente
006951/000
p. 195

George Grosz
Tatlinesque Diagram, 1920
Cut-and-pasted papers, watercolor, and ink on paper
41 x 29.2 cm
Museo Thyssen-Bornemisza, Madrid
570 (1978.6)
p. 127

Raoul Hausmann
Cover of the journal *Der Dada*, no. 2, Berlin, 1921
Letterpress
29 x 23 cm
The State Mayakovsky Museum, Moscow
10896

John Heartfield
Cover of the journal *Der Dada*, no. 3, Berlin, 1921
Letterpress
23.5 x 15.5 cm
The State Mayakovsky Museum, Moscow
И-786

John Heartfield
Cover of the book *150,000,000* by Vladimir Mayakovsky, Prague, 1924
Lithograph
21.4 x 13.5 cm
IVAM, Institut Valencià d'Art Modern, Generalitat
1997.063 (Código 4315)
p. 128

Richard Huelsenbeck
Cover of the book *En avant Dada: Die Geschichte des Dadaismus* [Forward Dada: The history of Dadaism], Hannover/Leipzig/Vienna/Zurich, Poaul Steegemann Verlag, 1921
Letterpress
23 x 15 cm
The State Mayakovsky Museum, Moscow
11113

Ilin (Nal)
Futurism in a Village, 1914
Watercolor on paper
30.5 x 25.2 cm
Vladimir Dahl Russian State Literary Museum
GLM KP 754
p. 27

Valentin Iustitsky
Painterly Construction with Wire, early 1920s
Oil and wire on canvas
70 x 62 cm
The Saratov State Art Museum named after A. N. Radischev, provided with assistance from the State Museum and Exhibition Center ROSIZO
СГХМ КП-11677
ĐЖ-105
p. 113

Vasily Kamensky, David Burliuk, Vladimir Burliuk
Tango with Cows: Ferro-concrete Poems by Vasily Kamensky, 1914
Letterpress on wallpaper
20.5 x 20 cm
The State Mayakovsky Museum, Moscow
28155(1974)
p. 39

Vasily Kamensky
Tiflis: Ferro-concrete Poem, 1917
Cut-and-pasted papers, lithograph
28.8 x 37.8 cm
The State Mayakovsky Museum, Moscow
11332

Vasily Kamensky
Cover of the journal *My Journal*, no. 1, 1922
Letterpress
37 x 28 cm

Vladimir Dahl
Russian State
Literary Museum
GLM KU 4764

Vasily Kandinsky
Kandinsky,
Moscow, 1918
Letterpress
30.9 x 21 cm
Archivo Lafuente
006901/000
Velimir Khlebnikov
Roman Jakobson
reads "Incantation
by Laughter" (1908–1909), a poem by
Velimir Khlebnikov
Recorded 1954 52"
Published by ReR
Megacorp, London,
2008
Courtesy Miguel
Molina Alarcón,
Universitat
Politècnica
de València

Velimir Khlebnikov
*Radio of the
Future*, 1921
Re-creation 2006
CD, 3'45"
Published by ReR
Megacorp, London,
2008
Courtesy Miguel
Molina Alarcón,
Universitat
Politècnica
de València

Nikolai Khodataev
*Interplanetary
Revolution*, 1924
35 mm film
transferred to DVD,
b/w, silent, 8'
National Film
Foundation of
Russian Federation

Ivan Kliun
*Self-Portrait with
a Saw (Nonobjective
Composition)*, 1914
Oil on canvas
71 x 62 cm
The Astrakhan
State Art Museum
named after P. M.
Dogadina, provided
with assistance from
the State Museum
and Exhibition
Center ROSIZO
Zh-460
p. 48

Ivan Kliun
Cover and
illustrations for the
book *The Secret Vices
of Academicians*
by Ivan Kliun,
Aleksei Kruchenykh,
Kazimir Malevich,
Moscow, 1916
Letterpress
20.5 x 17.7 cm
The State Mayakovsky
Museum, Moscow
28155(930)

Ivan Kliun
Aleksei Kruchenykh,
1925
Watercolor and
pencil on paper
38.5 x 30.5 cm
The State Mayakovsky
Museum, Moscow
10907
p. 284

Ivan Kliun
Untitled (Aleksei
Kruchenykh), 1925
Watercolor, charcoal,
and pencil
26.6 x 21.9 cm
The State Museum of
Contemporary
Art Costakis
Collection
91.78-441
p. 176

Gustav Klutsis
Design for the
billboard *Storm: Strike
on Counterrevolution*
for the Fifth Congress
of Soviets, 1918
Gelatin silver print
from a glass plate
negative, 1918
(printed 2018)
12 x 9 cm
Private Collection

Gustav Klutsis
Design for the
billboard *Storm: Strike
on Counterrevolution*,
ca. 1918
Gelatin silver print
11 x 18 cm
Private Collection
p.14

Gustav Klutsis
Red Man, 1919–1920
Pencil on paper
28.5 x 16 cm
Private Collection
p. 102

Gustav Klutsis
*Construction
(City)*, 1920
Gelatin silver print
17 x 17.5 cm
Private Collection

Gustav Klutsis
*Electrification of the
Entire Country*, 1920
Gelatin silver print
18 x 11.5 cm
Private Collection
p. 81

Gustav Klutsis
Untitled, ca. 1920
Oil on canvas,
double-sided
50 x 32.5 cm
The State Mayakovsky
Museum, Moscow
11478
pp. 108–109

Gustav Klutsis
Cannon Fodder, 1921
Gelatin silver print
from a glass plate
negative, 1921
(printed 2018)
12 x 9 cm
Private Collection
p. 60

Gustav Klutsis
Spatial Construction,
1921
Lithograph
20.5 x 13.7 cm
Vladimir Dahl
Russian State
Literary Museum
GLM KP 48568

Gustav Klutsis
Cover of the book
*All-Russian Union of
Poets*, Moscow, 1922
Letterpress
18 x 12.4 cm
The State Mayakovsky
Museum, Moscow
28155(3652)

Gustav Klutsis
Design for *Sport
Suit*, 1922
Linocut on paper
25.2 x 16.2 cm
State Tretyakov
Gallery, Moscow
ГРС-5683

Gustav Klutsis
Design for
*Propaganda
Kiosk, Screen,
and Loudspeaker
Platform*, 1922
Watercolor, ink,
and graphite on
paper
32.9 x 24 cm
The State Museum
of Contemporary Art
Costakis Collection
108.78-187

Gustav Klutsis
Design for
*Propaganda Stand
(Agit-prop for
Communism of the
proletariat of the
whole world)*, 1922
Ink and gouache
on paper
26.5 x 17.2 cm
The State Museum
of Contemporary Art
Costakis Collection
113.78-144

Gustav Klutsis
Design for *Radio-Orator*, no. 7, 1922
Gouache, ink, and pencil on paper
26.9 x 17.7 cm
The State Museum of Contemporary Art Costakis Collection
CC-0384/G. Klutsis-/C623-292

Gustav Klutsis
Double Self-Portrait, 1922
Cut-and-pasted gelatin silver prints
10.5 x 11 cm
Private Collection

Gustav Klutsis
International, 1922
Ink, gouache, and pencil on paper
27.1 x 17.8 cm
The State Museum of Contemporary Art Costakis Collection
110.78-167
p. 78

Gustav Klutsis
Radio-Orator, 1922
Lithograph
10.5 x 8.5 cm
Vladimir Dahl Russian State Literary Museum
GLM KP 48566

Gustav Klutsis
Spatial Construction, 1922
20.5 x 15 cm
Lithograph
Vladimir Dahl Russian State Literary Museum
GLM KP 48569

Gustav Klutsis
Spatial Construction, 1922
Lithograph
11.2 x 9.5 cm
Vladimir Dahl Russian State Literary Museum
GLM KP 48678

Gustav Klutsis
Untitled, ca. 1922
Cut-and-pasted papers and watercolor on paper
4.5 x 8 cm
Vladimir Dahl Russian State Literary Museum
GLM KP 48573

Gustav Klutsis
Untitled, ca. 1922
Cut-and-pasted papers and watercolor on paper
4.5 x 8 cm
Vladimir Dahl Russian State Literary Museum
GLM KP 48572

Gustav Klutsis
Untitled, ca. 1922
Cut-and-pasted papers and watercolor on paper
4.5 x 8 cm
Vladimir Dahl Russian State Literary Museum
GLM KP 48571

Gustav Klutsis
Untitled, ca. 1922
Cut-and-pasted papers and watercolor on paper
4.5 x 8 cm
Vladimir Dahl Russian State Literary Museum
GLM KP 48570

Gustav Klutsis
Illustration (unpublished) for the *History of the VKP(b)*, 1924
Gelatin silver print
16 x 12 cm
Private Collection
p. 72

Gustav Klutsis
Illustrations for the journal *Young Guard*, 1924
Lithograph
21 x 15 cm
The State Mayakovsky Museum, Moscow
12132 (6), 11898, 11903, 11904, 11902, 11900, 11901

Gustav Klutsis
Lenin's Call, 1924
Gelatin silver print from a glass plate negative, 1924 (printed 2018)
12 x 9 cm
Private Collection

Gustav Klutsis
Lenin's Slogan, 1924
Gelatin silver print
17 x 12 cm
Private Collection

Gustav Klutsis
Various designs for children books, 1924
Cut-and-pasted gelatin silver prints
29 x 20 cm
Private Collection

Gustav Klutsis
We Do Not Need Hysterical Bursts, We Need a Measuring Walk, 1924
Gelatin silver print
18 x 12 cm
Private Collection

Gustav Klutsis, Aleksandr Rodchenko, Sergei Senkin
Cover and illustrations for the book *Young Guard*, Moscow, 1924
Letterpress
24.9 x 17 cm
Archivo Lafuente
014541/000

Gustav Klutsis
Boris Kulagin, Gustav Klutsis, and Valentina Kulagina in various impromptu actions, 1925
Cut-and-pasted gelatin silver prints and papers
29.5 x 4.3 cm
Private Collection
p. 91

Gustav Klutsis
Cover of the book *Lenin's Language: Eleven Devices of Lenin's Speech* by Aleksei Kruchenykh, Moscow, 1925
Letterpress
18 x 13.6 cm
The State Mayakovsky Museum, Moscow
10753

Gustav Klutsis
Klutsis and Valentina Kulagina in various impromptu actions, 1925
Cut-and-pasted gelatin silver prints
34.5 x 24.5 cm
Private Collection

Gustav Klutsis and Sergei Senkin
Front (Senkin) and back (Klutsis) covers of the book *In Memory of Fallen Leaders*, Moscow, 1927
Lithograph
35 x 27 cm
Centro de Documentación, Museo Nacional Centro de Arte Reina Sofía, Madrid
CDB.188678 FL 1422
Nº Reg. 188678

Gustav Klutsis
February Revolution, early 1920s
Gelatin silver print
16 x 11 cm
Private Collection
p. 96

Gustav Klutsis
October Revolution, early 1920s
Gelatin silver print
21 x 14 cm
Private Collection
p. 97

Gustav Klutsis
Cover of the book
Kruchenykh Is Alive! by Aleksei Kruchenykh, Boris Pasternak, Sergei Tretiakov, David Burliuk et al., 1925
19 x 14 cm
Russian State Archives of Literature and Art
Библиотека РГАЛИ
Ж-66/91920

Gustav Klutsis
Untitled, early 1920s
Cut-and-pasted gelatin silver prints and papers
12.7 x 9.6 cm
The State Museum of Contemporary Art Costakis Collection
C356-744
p. 90

Gustav Klutsis
Kruchenykh Reads His Poetry, ca. 1925
Gelatin silver print
16.1 x 12 cm
The State Mayakovsky Museum, Moscow
26018
p. 82

George Kobbe
Cover of the *Die Dadaistische Korruption* [The Dadaist corruption] by Walter Petry, Berlin, Leon Hirsche Verlag, 1920
Letterpress
21 x 15.5 cm
The State Mayakovsky Museum, Moscow
И-787

Vladimir Kozlinsky
Producer
Motorist
Priest
Railwayman
Sailor
Illustrations for the portfolio *October 1917–1918: Heroes and Victims of the Revolution* by Vladimir Mayakovsky, 1918
Lithograph
23.5 x 33.6 cm each
Vladimir Dahl Russian State Literary Museum
GLM KP 12210/9;
GLM KP 12210/11;
GLM KP 12210/13;
GLM KP 12210/12;
GLM KP 12210/8

Victory over the Sun, opera by Aleksei Kruchenykh (libretto), Kazimir Malevich (design), and Mikhail Matiushin (music), 1913
Re-creation by Robert L. Benedetti and Douglas Cruickshank, 1981
Super-8 transferred to DVD, color, sound, 45′02″
Courtesy Robert Benedetti

Aleksei Kruchenykh
Cover and illustrations for the book *Universal War*, Petrograd, 1916
Cut-and-pasted papers and letterpress
22.5 x 33 cm
The State Mayakovsky Museum, Moscow
28155(5259)
pp. 64–65

Aleksei Kruchenykh, Kirill Zdanevich, Vasily Kamensky
1918, Tiflis, 1917
Cut-and-pasted papers and lithograph
26 x 38.5 cm
Russian State Archives of Literature and Art
f. 1334, op. 1, ed. khr. 1083, ll. 1–72
The State Mayakovsky Museum, Moscow
10886
p. 75

Aleksei Kruchenykh
Page from a scrapbook with Osip Brik's portraits, 1922–1932
Cut-and-pasted papers and prints, pencil, and watercolor on paper
23 x 35 cm
Russian State Archives of Literature and Art
f. 1334, op. 2, ed. khr. 124, ll. 1–8, 8a, 9–53Aleksei Kruchenykh

Sound poem *Winter*, 1926
CD, 2'40"
Published by ReR Megacorp, London, 2008
Courtesy Miguel Molina Alarcón, Universitat Politècnica de València

Aleksei Kruchenykh
Page from Kruchenykh's scrapbook, n.d.
Cut-and-pasted printed papers, ink, and pencil on paper
22 x 35 cm
Russian State Archives of Literature and Art
f. 334, op. 1, ed. khr. 1084, ll. 13–16
p. 75

Ivan Kudriashov
Design for the decoration of a motorcar for the First Anniversary of the October Revolution in Moscow, 1918
Watercolor and graphite on paper
24.8 x 34.6 cm
State Tretyakov Gallery, Moscow
PC-2896
p. 105

Ivan Kudriashov
Portrait of a Young Lady: Nonobjective Composition, ca. 1919
Oil on canvas, double-sided
67.5 x 50.5 cm
The Vyatka Art Museum named after V. M. and A. M. Vasnetsovs, provided with assistance from the State Museum and Exhibition Center ROSIZO
p. 101

Valentina Kulagina
Dynamic City, 1923
Lithograph after Gustav Klutsis' painting *Dynamic City*, 1919
26.4 x 18.4 cm
The State Museum of Contemporary Art-Costakis Collection
Inv. 101. 78

Valentina Kulagina
Cover of the book *Transrational Language* by Aleksei Kruchenykh, 1925
Letterpress
18.5 x 14 cm
Archivo Lafuente
007021/000
p. 178

Lev Kuleshov
Taras's Dream, 1919
35 mm film transferred to DVD, b/w, silent, (extract 10'54")
National Film Foundation of Russian Federation
pp. 220–221

Lev Kuleshov
Design for the journal *Cine-Photo*, no. 1, 1922
Cut-and-pasted gelatin silver prints, ink, and white paint
24.2 x 26 cm
Russian State Archives of Literature and Art
f. 2679, op. 1, ed. khr. 239, ll. 1–3
p. 208

Lev Kuleshov's Workshop
Petr Galadzhev, 1923
Gelatin silver print
7 x 11 cm
Russian State Archives of Literature and Art
f. 2679, op. 1, ed. khr. 134, l. 3

Lev Kuleshov's Workshop
Boris Barnet, Valentina Lopatina, Vladimir Fogel, Aleksandra Khokhlova, and Petr Galadzhev (left to right), 1923
Gelatin silver print
8.4 x 11.2 cm
Russian State Archives of Literature and Art
f. 2679, op. 1, ed. khr. 158, l. 1
p. 208

Lev Kuleshov's Workshop
Petr Galadzhev, Averbakh, Veintrop (left to right), 1923
Gelatin silver print
7 x 11 cm
Russian State Archives of Literature and Art
f. 2679, op. 1, ed. khr. 134, ll. 5–6

Lev Kuleshov's Workshop
Aleksandra Khokhlova and Petr Galadzhev, 1923
Gelatin silver print
8 x 10.6 cm
Russian State Archives of Literature and Art
f. 2679, op. 1, ed. khr. 158, l. 4
p. 214

Lev Kuleshov
The Extraordinary Adventures of Mr. West in the Land of the Bolsheviks, 1924
35 mm film transferred to DVD, b/w, silent, 94' (extract 19'40")
National Film Foundation of Russian Federation
pp. 224–225

Lev Kuleshov
The Death Ray, 1925
35 mm film transferred to DVD, b/w, silent, extract 22"
National Film Foundation of Russian Federation
pp. 2–3

Mikhail Larionov
Man, 1913
Ink and pencil on paper
13.7 x 10.2 cm
Vladimir Dahl Russian State Literary Museum
GLM KP 11701/4
p. 25

Mikhail Larionov
Cover and illustrations for the book *Pomade* by Aleksei Kruchenykh, Moscow, 1913
Lithograph
15.6 x 10.9 cm
Archivo Lafuente
006824/000

Mikhail Larionov
Cover and illustrations for the book *Half-Alive* by Aleksei Kruchenykh, Moscow, 1913
Lithograph
18.8 x 15.3 cm
Archivo Lafuente
006822/000

Mikhail Larionov
Cover and illustrations for the book *The Sun* by Vladimir Mayakovsky, Moscow, 1923
Lithograph
17 x 13 cm
Archivo Lafuente
006952/000

Mikhail Larionov
Poster for *The Grand Ball of Transvestite-Transmental Artists*, Paris, 1923
Lithograph
22.2 x 27.5 cm
Archivo Lafuente
007472/000
p. 142

El Lissitzky
Cover design for the book *The Spent Sun* by Konstantin Bolshakov, Moscow, 1916
Ink on paper
17.2 x 12.8 cm
The State Museum of Contemporary Art Costakis Collection
441.80-388

El Lissitzky
Cover of the book *The Spent Sun* by Konstantin Bolshakov, Moscow, 1916
Letterpress
23 x 17.3 cm
Archivo Lafuente
006888/000

El Lissitzky and Kazimir Malevich
Title page of the book *On New Systems in Art*, Vitebsk, 1919
Lithograph
24.4 x 20.7 cm
IVAM, Institut Valencià d'Art Modern, Generalitat
1994.014 (Código 18)

El Lissitzky and Kazimir Malevich
Title page of the book *On New Systems in Art*, Vitebsk, 1919
Lithograph
23.5 x 18.5 cm
Archivo Lafuente
006905/000
p. 39

El Lissitzky
"The New Man," from *Figurines: The Three-Dimensional Design of the Electro-mechanical Show "Victory over the Sun"*, 1920–1923
Lithograph
53.5 x 45.6 cm
Stedelijk Museum Amsterdam
A 40295(1-12)
p. 157

El Lissitzky
Cover of *Figurines: The Three-Dimensional Design of the Electro-mechanical Show "Victory over the Sun"*, 1920–1923
Lithograph
53.5 x 45.6 cm
Stedelijk Museum Amsterdam
A 40295(1-12)

El Lissitzky
"The Old," from *Figurines: The Three-Dimensional Design of the Electro-mechanical Show "Victory over the Sun"*, 1920–1923
Lithograph
53.5 x 45.6 cm
Stedelijk Museum Amsterdam
A 40295(1-12)

El Lissitzky
"Troublemaker," from *Figurines: The Three-Dimensional Design of the Electro-mechanical*

Show "Victory over the Sun", 1920–1923
Lithograph
53.5 x 45.6 cm
Stedelijk Museum Amsterdam
A 40295(1-12)

El Lissitzky
"Sportsmen," from *Figurines: The Three-Dimensional Design of the Electro-mechanical Show "Victory over the Sun"*, 1920–1923
Lithograph
53.5 x 45.6 cm
Stedelijk Museum Amsterdam
A 40295(1-12)

El Lissitzky
"Gravediggers," from *Figurines: The Three-Dimensional Design of the Electro-mechanical Show "Victory over the Sun"*, 1920–1923
Lithograph
53.5 x 45.6 cm
Stedelijk Museum Amsterdam
A 40295(1-12)

El Lissitzky
Title page from *Figurines: The Three-Dimensional Design of the Electro-mechanical Show "Victory over the Sun"*, 1920–1923
Lithograph
53.5 x 45.6 cm
Stedelijk Museum Amsterdam
A 40295(1-12)

El Lissitzky
"Globetrotter in Time," from *Figurines: The Three-Dimensional Design of the Electro-mechanical Show "Victory over the Sun"*, 1920–1923
Lithograph
53.5 x 45.6 cm
Stedelijk Museum Amsterdam
A 40295(1-12)

El Lissitzky
"Part of the Mechanical Setting," from *Figurines: The Three-Dimensional Design of the Electro-mechanical Show "Victory over the Sun"*, 1920–1923
Lithograph
53.5 x 45.6 cm
Stedelijk Museum Amsterdam
A 40295(1-12)

El Lissitzky
"The Terrified," from *Figurines: The Three-Dimensional Design of the Electro-mechanical Show "Victory over the Sun"*, 1920–1923
53.5 x 45.6 cm
Stedelijk Museum Amsterdam
A 40295(1-12)

El Lissitzky
"Announcer," from *Figurines: The Three-Dimensional Design of the Electro-mechanical Show "Victory over the Sun"*, 1920–1923
Lithograph
53.5 x 45.6 cm
Stedelijk Museum Amsterdam
A 40295(1-12)

El Lissitzky
"*Budetliane* Strongman," from *Figurines: The Three-Dimensional Design of the Electro-mechanical Show "Victory over the Sun"*, 1920–1923
Lithograph
53.5 x 45.6 cm
Stedelijk Museum Amsterdam
A 40295(1-12)

El Lissitzky
Cover of the magazine *Wendingen*, vol. 4, no. 11, Amsterdam, 1921
Lithograph and letterpress
33 x 33 cm
Archivo Lafuente
006922/000

El Lissitzky
Cover of the book *A Suprematist Story about Two Squares in 6 Constructions*, Berlin, 1922
Letterpress
28.5 x 22.5 cm
Archivo Lafuente
006933/000

El Lissitzky
Cover design for the journal *Broom*, no. 3, Berlin/New York, 1922
Watercolor and ink on paper
10.6 x 13.5 cm
The State Museum of Contemporary Art-Costakis Collection
C500-391
p. 161

El Lissitzky and Ilya Ehrenburg
Cover of the magazine *Veshch-Gegenstand-Object*, no. 1–2, Berlin, 1922
Letterpress
31 x 23.5 cm
Archivo Lafuente
006936/000

El Lissitzky
Cover of the catalogue *The First Russian Exhibition*, Berlin, 1922
Letterpress
22.8 x 15.1 cm
Archivo Lafuente
006926/000
p. 128

El Lissitzky and Olga Forsch
Ravvi, Berlin, Skify, 1922
Letterpress
20 x 13.8 cm
Archivo Lafuente
006935/000

El Lissitzky
Tatlin Working on the Monument to the Third International, illustration in the book *Six Tales with Easy Endings* by Ilya Ehrenburg, Berlin, 1922
Letterpress
21 x 14.5 cm
IVAM, Institut Valencià d'Art Modern, Generalitat
1993.168 (Código 2119)
p. 125

El Lissitzky
Cover and illustrations for the book *For the Voice* by Vladimir Mayakovsky, Moscow/Berlin, 1923
Letterpress
18.8 x 13.3 cm
Archivo Lafuente
006957/000

El Lissitzky
Cover of the journal *Broom*, vol. 4, no. 3, Berlin/New York, February 1923
Letterpress
33.5 x 23 cm
Archivo Lafuente
007578/015

El Lissitzky and Hans Richter
Cover of the journal *G: Material zur elementaren Gestaltung*, no. 1, Berlin, July 1923
Letterpress
45.4 x 59.5 cm
Stedelijk Museum Amsterdam, gift of Elaine Lustig Cohen
KBA 967(1-4)

El Lissitzky
Cover of the book *Das entfesselte Theater* [Unleashed theater]

by Aleksandr Tairov, Potsdam, 1923
Letterpress
25 x 18 cm
Archivo Lafuente
006956/000

El Lissitzky
First Kestner portfolio *Proun*, prints nos. 1, 2, 3, 5, 1919–1923
Lithographs
60 x 43 cm each
Stedelijk Museum Amsterdam
A 40294(1-6)
p. 158

El Lissitzky
First Kestner portfolio, *Proun Room*, 1919–1923
Lithograph
60 x 43 cm
Stedelijk Museum Amsterdam
A 34494

El Lissitzky
Hans Arp, 1924
Gelatin silver print
22 x 33.5 cm
Russian State Archives of Literature and Art
f. 1072, op. 2, ed. khr. 357, ll. 87–88
p. 133

El Lissitzky
Kurt Schwitters, 1924
Gelatin silver print
18.2 x 11.8 cm
Russian State Archives of Literature and Art
f. 1334, op. 1, ed. khr. 1581, l. 1
p. 133

El Lissitzky
Pelikan Carbon Paper, 1924
Gelatin silver print
12.8 x 12.9 cm
Russian State Archives of Literature and Art
f. 2361, op. 1, ed. khr. 5, l. 17

El Lissitzky
Pelikan Carbon Paper, 1924
Gelatin silver print
17.9 x 12.9 cm
Russian State Archives of Literature and Art
f. 2361, op. 1, ed. khr. 5, l. 19
p. 160

El Lissitzky and Kurt Schwitters
Cover of the journal *Merz*, no. 8–9: *Nasci*, Hannover, April/July 1924
Letterpress
30.5 x 23.5 cm
Archivo Lafuente
005449/003
p. 133

El Lissitzky
Design for the cover of the book *Transrational* by Aleksei Kruchenykh, 1925
Gouache and ink on paper
16.4 x 12.6 cm
Stedelijk Museum Amsterdam
4.2001 (594)
p. 178

El Lissitzky and Hans Arp
Die Kunstismen / Les ismes de l'art / The Isms of Art: 1914–1924, Zurich, 1925
Letterpress
26.5 x 20.5 cm
Centro de Documentación, Museo Nacional Centro de Arte Reina Sofía, Madrid
RESERVA 2232
Nº Reg. 123335
p. 94

El Lissitzky
Cover of the journal *G: Material zur elementaren Gestaltung*, no. 4, March 26, 1926
Letterpress
45.4 x 59.5 cm
Stedelijk Museum Amsterdam
KBA 967(1-4)

El Lissitzky
Self-Portrait, illustration in the journal *Gebrauchsgraphik*, 1928
30 x 22.5 cm
Offset
Russian State Archives of Literature and Art
f. 1334, op. 2, ed. khr. 313, l. 1
p. 255

Arthur Lurie
Our March, 1918
Piano piece accompanied by a reading of Mayakovsky's poem "Our March"
5'6"
Deutschlandradio Kultur-Capriccio

Paul Mak (Pavel Ivanov)
Mikhail Larionov, 1914
Ink on paper
22 x 19.7 cm
Vladimir Dahl Russian State Literary Museum
GLM KP 4012

Kazimir Malevich
Alogic Composition, design for *Victory over the Sun* (*Budetlianin Strongman*), 1913
Pencil on graph paper
10.2 x 11.5 cm
Stedelijk Museum Amsterdam, on loan from the Stichting Khardzhiev
4.2001 (122)
p. 32

Kazimir Malevich
Cover of the book *Victory over the Sun*, Saint Petersburg, 1913
Letterpress
23.5 x 16.6 cm
The State Mayakovsky Museum, Moscow
28155(2063)

Kazimir Malevich
Cover of the book *The Three* by Velimir Khlebnikov and Aleksei Kruchenykh, Saint Petersburg, 1913
Lithograph
18.8 x 17.6 cm
Archivo Lafuente
006835/000

Kazimir Malevich
Costume design for *Victory over the Sun*, Budetlianin Strongman, 1913
Pencil on paper
16.2 x 8 cm
Vladimir Dahl Russian State Literary Museum
GLM KP 11701/7
p. 44

Kazimir Malevich
Design for the curtain for the opera *Victory over the Sun*, 1913
Pencil on paper
8.8 x 8 cm
Vladimir Dahl Russian State Literary Museum
GLM KP 11701/6
p. 33

Kazimir Malevich
Stage design for *Victory over the Sun*, 1913
Pencil on paper
11.2 x 12.3 cm
Vladimir Dahl Russian State Literary Museum
GLM KP 11701/5
p. 32

Kazimir Malevich
Curtain design for the opera *Victory over the Sun*, 1913
Ink over pencil on transparent white paper
11.8 x 10.5 cm
Stedelijk Museum Amsterdam, on loan from the Stichting Khardzhiev
4.2001 (016)
p. 45

Kazimir Malevich
Alogic Composition 3 (study for the painting *An Englishman in Moscow*), 1914
Pencil on paper
16 x 9 cm
Stedelijk Museum Amsterdam, on loan from the Stichting Khardzhiev
4.2001 (014)
p. 41

Kazimir Malevich
Cover of the book *A Game in Hell* by Aleksei Kruchenykh and Velimir Khlebnikov, Saint Petersburg, 1914
Lithograph
18.7 x 14 cm
Archivo Lafuente
006881/000

Kazimir Malevich
War, 1914
Pencil on paper
9.8 x 9.7 cm
Stedelijk Museum Amsterdam, on loan from the Stichting Khardzhiev
4.2001 (018)
p. 63

Kazimir Malevich (designer) and Vladimir Mayakovsky (text)
"Look, look, near the Vistula: The German bellies are swelling so they don't feel so good," 1914
Lithograph
55 x 37.5 cm
The State Mayakovsky Museum, Moscow
И-709
p. 63

Kazimir Malevich and Vladimir Mayakovsky
"An Austrian went to Radziwill and landed right on a peasant woman's pitchfork," 1914
Lithograph
39 x 52 cm
The State Mayakovsky Museum, Moscow
29161

Kazimir Malevich (designer) and Vladimir Mayakovsky (text)
"What a rattle, what a thunder from the Germans near the Łomża" 1914
Lithograph
39 x 52 cm
The State Mayakovsky Museum, Moscow
И-719

Kazimir Malevich (designer) and Vladimir Mayakovsky (text)
"Wilhelm's Merry-Go-Around," 1914
Lithograph
39 x 52 cm
The State Mayakovsky Museum, Moscow
12682
p. 63

Kazimir Malevich
Four Squares, 1915
Oil on canvas
49 x 49 cm
The Saratov State Art Museum named after A. N. Radischev, provided with assistance from the State Museum and Exhibition Center ROSIZO
СГХМ КП-10959
Ж-1089
p. 57

Kazimir Malevich
Suprematism: Square on a Diagonal Surface, 1915
Pencil and ink on graph paper
15.4 x 11 cm
Stedelijk Museum Amsterdam, on loan from the Stichting Khardzhiev
4.2001 (020)
p. 52

Kazimir Malevich
Three Irregular Quadrangles, ca. 1915–1916
Pencil on graph paper
17.3 x 20.7 cm
Stedelijk Museum Amsterdam, on loan from the Stichting Khardzhiev
4.2001 (053)
p. 55

Kazimir Malevich
I the Apostle of New Concepts in Art, 1916
Pencil, black crayon, and gouache on paper
26.5 x 15.1 cm
Stedelijk Museum Amsterdam, on loan from the Stichting Khardzhiev
4.2001 (147)
p. 43

Kazimir Malevich
Cover of the journal *The International of Art* (unpublished), ca. 1919
Cut-and-pasted papers and lithograph
25.8 x 20 cm
Stedelijk Museum Amsterdam, on loan from the Stichting Khardzhiev
4.2001 (124)
p. 106

Kazimir Malevich
Cover of the book *First Series of Lectures* by Nikolai Punin, Petrograd, 1920
Letterpress
22.6 x 15.1 cm
Archivo Lafuente
006918/000

Pavel Mansurov
Beer-Painterly Formula, 1922
Oil and tempera on cardboard
76.5 x 27 x 7 cm
Private Collection
p. 111

Filippo Tommaso Marinetti
Der Futurismus, Berlin, 1922
Letterpress
29.4 x 23.1 cm
The State Mayakovsky Museum, Moscow
10693

Filippo Tommaso Marinetti
Letter to Ilia Zdanevich, June 1922
28.4 x 22.6 cm
Private Collection France
p. 24

Filippo Tommaso Marinetti
Manifestos of Italian Futurism, Moscow, 1914
Letterpress
25.8 x 18 cm
Archivo Lafuente
006884/000

Vladimir Mayakovsky
Cover of the book *Mystery Bouffe* by Vladimir Mayakovsky, Petrograd, 1918
Letterpress
24.5 x 18.5 cm
The State Mayakovsky Museum, Moscow
28155(213)
p. 227

Vladimir Mayakovsky
Poster for *Mystery Bouffe*, 1918
Lithograph
91 x 73.5 cm
The State Mayakovsky Museum, Moscow
10966

Vladimir Mayakovsky
Soviet Alphabet by Vladimir Mayakovsky, 1919
Watercolor and lithograph
19.5 x 24.4 cm
The State Mayakovsky Museum, Moscow
28155(285)
p. 99

Vladimir Mayakovsky
Stage and costume design for *Mystery Bouffe, Seven Pairs of Evil*, 1919
Cut-and-pasted papers, fabric, watercolor, and pencil
75.2 x 161.3 cm
Vladimir Dahl Russian State Literary Museum
GLM KP 11760/6
p. 237

Vladimir Mayakovsky
Stage and costume design for *Mystery Bouffe, Seven Pairs of Good*, 1919
Cut-and-pasted papers, watercolor, ink, and pencil
75.8 x 159.1 cm
Vladimir Dahl Russian State Literary Museum
GLM KP 11760/5
p. 237

Vladimir Mayakovsky
An Extraordinary Adventure Which Befell Vladimir Mayakovsky in a Summer Cottage, 1920
Audio, 4'57"
Vladimir Dahl Russian State Literary Museum

Vladimir Mayakovsky
ROSTA, no. 630, "America gets concessions from us," November 1920
Lithograph
105 x 78 cm
The State Mayakovsky Museum, Moscow
И-676
p. 128

Vladimir Mayakovsky
ROSTA, no. 525, "Do you want to free yourself from the burden of war," November 1920
Lithograph
102 x 88 cm
The State Mayakovsky Museum, Moscow
И-738

Vladimir Mayakovsky
ROSTA, no. 836, "We have made a delivery to Don Basin up to 17 December," January 1921
Lithograph
110 x 82 cm
The State Mayakovsky Museum, Moscow
9297

Vladimir Mayakovsky
ROSTA, no. 870, "Crisis in Europe," January 1921
Lithograph
112 x 83 cm
The State Mayakovsky Museum, Moscow
9298
p. 128

Vladimir Mayakovsky
Cover of the book *Mayakovsky Gallery: Those I Have Never Seen* by Vladimir Mayakovsky, Moscow, 1923
Letterpress
19.3 x 13.5 cm
Archivo Lafuente
006961/000

Sergei Makletsov
Laborer
Landowner
Telegraphist, Illustrations for the portfolio *October 1917–1918: Heroes and Victims of the Revolution* by Vladimir Mayakovsky, 1918
Lithographs
33.5 x 24 cm
Vladimir Dahl Russian State Literary Museum
GLM KP 12210/4; GLM KP 12210/7; GLM KP 12210/5

Ruvim Mazel
Cover of the book *About Kursk, Komsomol, Flying, Chaplin, Germany, Oil, Fifth International, etc.*, by Vladimir Mayakovsky, Moscow, Krasnaia nov', 1924
18 x 13.3 cm
Archivo Lafuente
006983/000

Mikhail Menkov
Tramway 6, 1914
Oil on canvas
82 x 51.5 cm
The Samara Regional Art Museum, provided with assistance from the State Museum and Exhibition Center ROSIZO
p. 51

Petr Miturich
Cover of the book *Our March* by Vladimir Mayakovsky, Petrograd, 1918
Letterpress
35.3 x 33.1 cm
The State Mayakovsky Museum, Moscow
28261(12)

Petr Miturich
Cover of the book *Zangezi* by Velimir Khlebnikov, Moscow, 1922
Lithograph
23.7 x 16 cm
Archivo Lafuente
006937/000
p. 178

László Moholy-Nagy (with artist's autograph to Vladimir Mayakovsky)
Untitled, 1922
Gelatin silver print
22.5 x 17 cm
The State Mayakovsky Museum, Moscow
11133
p. 160

Aleksei Morgunov
Aviator's Workroom, 1913
Gouache on canvas
50.5 x 36 cm
The State Museum of Contemporary Art-Costakis Collection
159.78-226
p. 49

Aleksei Morgunov
Composition, 1915
Pencil, watercolor, and gouache on cardboard
47.9 x 31.8 cm
Stedelijk Museum Amsterdam, on loan from the Stichting Khardzhiev
4.2001 (570)

Aleksei Morgunov
Study for *The Barber Set Off for the Bathhouse*, 1915
Watercolor and gouache on paper
31.9 x 22.8 cm
Stedelijk Museum

Amsterdam, on loan from the Stichting Khardzhiev
4.2001 (291)
p. 41

Aleksei Morgunov
Composition no. 1, 1916–1917
Oil on canvas
71 x 62 cm
The Krasnodar Regional Art Museum named after F. A. Kovalenko, provided with assistance from the State Museum and Exhibition Center ROSIZO
p. 56

Aleksei Morgunov
Cover of the journal *The International of Art* (unpublished), 1919
Watercolor on paper
Russian State Archives of Literature and Art
f. 665, op. 1, ed. khr. 35, l. 1

L. Nikitin
Cover of the book *Art and Classes* by Boris Arvatov, Moscow/Petrograd, 1923
Letterpress
23.8 x 16 cm
Archivo Lafuente
006979/000
p. 290

Varsanofy Parkin (Mikhail Larionov) and K. Khudakov (Ilia Zdanevich)
Cover and illustrations for the book *Donkey's Tail and Target*, Moscow, Ts. A. Miunster, 1913
Lithograph
30.6 x 23.6 cm
Archivo Lafuente
006834/000

Vera Pestel
Still Life with Red, 1915–1916
Oil on canvas
77.8 x 70 cm
The Nizhny Tagil Art Museum, provided with assistance from the State Museum and Exhibition Center ROSIZO
345-X
p. 50

Francis Picabia
Cover of the journal *391*, no. 1, Barcelona, 1917
Letterpress
37.2 x 27.1 cm
Centro de Documentación, Museo Nacional Centro de Arte Reina Sofía, Madrid
RESERVA P1-1
N° Reg. 115540

Francis Picabia
Cover of the journal *391*, no. 8, Zurich, February 1919
Letterpress
43.6 x 27.2 cm
Archivo Lafuente
001458/003

Francis Picabia and Sergei Sharshun
Cover of the journal *391*, no. 14, Paris, 1920
Letterpress
49 x 32.2 cm
Centro de Documentación, Museo Nacional Centro de Arte Reina Sofía, Madrid
RESERVA P1-1
N° Reg. 115540

Francis Picabia after Marcel Duchamp, *Dada Picture by Marcel Duchamp: L.H.O.O.Q.*, illustration on the cover of the journal *391*, no. 12, Paris, March 1920
Letterpress
55.6 x 38 cm
Archivo Lafuente
001458/005
p. 21

Liubov Popova
Stage design for *Earth in Turmoil* by Sergei Tretiakov, Meyerhold Theater, Moscow, 1923–1924
Cut-and-pasted gelatin silver prints and printed papers and gouache on plywood
49 x 82.7 cm
The State Museum of Contemporary Art-Costakis Collection
204.78/88
p. 74

Vsevolod Pudovkin and Nikolai Shpikovsky
Chess Fever, 1925
35 mm film transferred to DVD, b/w, silent, 28'
The Blackhawk Films Collection

Ivan Puni
Cover of the book *Futurists: Roaring Parnassus* by David Burliuk, Velimir Khlebnikov, Igor Severianin, Aleksei Kruchenykh et al., Saint Petersburg, 1914
20.6 x 16.3 cm
Letterpress
Archivo Lafuente
006886/000
p. 174

Ivan Puni
Barber, 1915
Oil on canvas
83 x 65 cm
Centre Pompidou, Paris, Musée national d'art moderne / Centre de création industrielle, donation of Mme. Xénia Pougny in 1966
AM4329P
p. 47

Ivan Puni
Poster for the exhibition *0,10: The Last Futurist Exhibition of Painting*, 1915
Lithograph
37.3 x 27.6 cm
Russian State Archives of Literature and Art
f. 2089, op. 2, ed. khr. 15, l. 4
p. 268

Ivan Puni
Relief, 1915
Oil and painted wood on canvas
64.5 x 81 cm
Centre Pompidou, Paris, Musée national d'art moderne / Centre de création industrielle, donation of Mme. Xénia Pougny in 1966
AM 1493 S
p. 59

Ivan Puni
Composition (The Understanding Court), 1915–1916
Pencil on paper
16.7 x 11.8 cm
The State Museum of Contemporary Art-Costakis Collection
C295-141
p. 55

Ivan Puni
Composition, 1916
Pencil and ink on paper
48 x 34.5 cm
Centre Pompidou, Paris, Musée national d'art moderne / Centre de création industrielle, donation of Mme. Xénia Pougny in 1966
AM3448D
p. 52

Ivan Puni
Study for *Red Army Soldier*, illustration in the portfolio *October 1917–1918: Heroes and Victims of the Revolution* by Vladimir Mayakovsky, 1918
Pencil and ink on paper
33.8 x 23.7 cm
Vladimir Dahl Russian State Literary Museum
GLM KP 7309/5
p. 98

Ivan Puni
Laundress
Worker
Mistress
Red Army Soldier
Bureaucrat
General, Illustrations for the portfolio *October 1917–1918: Heroes and Victims of the Revolution* by Vladimir Mayakovsky, 1918
Lithographs
33 x 24 cm each
Vladimir Dahl Russian State Literary Museum
GLM KP 12210/19; GLM KP 12210/14; GLM KP 12210/20; GLM KP 12210/17; GLM KP 12210/18; GLM KP 12210/16
p. 98

Ivan Puni
Untitled (Hunger Plate), ca. 1918
Gelatin silver print
12 x 18 cm
The State Mayakovsky Museum, Moscow
HB-1813
p. 131

Man Ray
Sergei Sharshun, ca. 1922–1925
Gelatin silver print
20.2 x 15.1 cm
Centre Pompidou, Paris, Musée national d'art moderne / Centre de création industrielle
Dation, 1994
AM 1994-339
p. 141

Man Ray
Mikhail Larionov, 1923
Gelatin silver print (printed 2018)
Centre Pompidou, Paris, Musée national d'art moderne / Centre de création industrielle
AM 1994-393 (2445)
p. 142

Man Ray
Raoul de Roussy and Marcel Duchamp, Man Ray's workshop, Paris, 1924
Gelatin silver print (printed 2018)
Man Ray Trust
1573

Man Ray
Sergei Sharshun in His Studio, 1925
Gelatin silver print (printed 2018)
Centre Pompidou, Paris, Musée national d'art moderne / Centre de création industrielle
AM 1994-393 (2616)
p. 315

Man Ray
Living room of Katherine S. Dreier with works of David Burliuk, Marcel Duchamp, Pablo Picasso, New York, 1927
Gelatin silver print
11.3 x 9.2 cm
Centre Pompidou, Paris, Musée national d'art moderne / Centre de création industrielle
Dation, 1994
AM 1994-394 (3586)
p. 152

Klement Redko
Uprising, 1924–1925
Oil on canvas
170.5 x 212 cm
State Tretyakov Gallery, Moscow
ЖС-5009
pp. 120–121

Hans Richter
Rhythmus 21, ca. 1921
16 mm film transferred to video (Digital Betacam and DVD), b/w, silent, 3'25"
Museo Nacional Centro de Arte Reina Sofía
AD04968

Aleksandr Rodchenko
Line and Compass Drawing, 1915
Ink on paper
25.1 x 20.4 cm
Private Collection
p. 53

Aleksandr Rodchenko
Line and Compass Drawing, 1915
Ink on paper
25.1 x 20.4 cm
Private Collection
p. 278

Aleksandr Rodchenko
Construction no. 92 (on Green), 1919
Oil on canvas
73 x 46 cm
The Vyatka Art Museum named after V. M. and A. M. Vasnetsovs, provided with assistance from the State Museum and Exhibition Center ROSIZO
p. 115

Aleksandr Rodchenko
Cover design for the book *Tsotsa* by Aleksei Kruchenykh, 1921
Cut-and-pasted papers and colored pencil on paper
17.8 x 13.8 cm
Private Collection

Aleksandr Rodchenko
Cover design for the book *Transrational* by Aleksei Kruchenykh, 1921
Cut-and-pasted printed papers, colored pencil, and linocut on paper
18.5 x 13.2 cm
The State Mayakovsky Museum, Moscow
28155(2091)

Aleksandr Rodchenko
Cover design for the book *Tsotsa* by Aleksei Kruchenykh, 1921
Cut-and-pasted color papers
18 x 14 cm
The State Mayakovsky Museum, Moscow
28155(5237)

Aleksandr Rodchenko
Cover of the journal *Cine-Photo*, no. 1, 1922
Letterpress
29.6 x 22.1 cm
Private Collection
p. 214

Aleksandr Rodchenko
Narkompros, 1922
Cut-and-pasted printed papers on paper
26.8 x 17.5 cm
The Pushkin State Museum of Fine Arts, Department of Private Collections
КП-391870/ МЛК ГР 2142

Aleksandr Rodchenko
Detective, 1922
Cut-and-pasted

printed papers,
gelatin silver prints,
and ink on paper
29.4 x 41 cm
The Pushkin State
Museum of Fine
Arts, Department of
Private Collections
КП-391903/
МЛК ГР 2176
pp. 116–117

Aleksandr Rodchenko
Self-Portrait, 1922
Cut-and-pasted
printed papers
and gelatin silver
prints on paper
18.5 x 15 cm
Private Collection
p. 245

Aleksandr Rodchenko
Type of a Female Convict, 1922
Cut-and-pasted
printed papers
on paper
27 x 17.5 cm
The Pushkin State
Museum of Fine
Arts, Department of
Private Collections
КП-391869/
МЛК ГР 2141
p. 90

Aleksandr Rodchenko
Untitled (Change of
Milestones), 1922
Cut-and-pasted
printed papers
on paper
27 x 18 cm
Private Collection
p. 276

Aleksandr
Rodchenko and
Varvara Stepanova
Cover design for the
journal *Lef*, no. 2, 1923
Cut-and-pasted
printed papers
and gelatin silver
prints on paper
20.3 x 28.8 cm
Private Collection
p. 89

Aleksandr Rodchenko
Circus, 1923
Cut-and-pasted
printed papers
on paper
35 x 25 cm
Private Collection

Aleksandr Rodchenko
Cover of the journal
Lef, no. 2, 1923
Letterpress
23 x 15.2 cm
Centro de
Documentación,
Museo Nacional
Centro de Arte Reina
Sofía, Madrid
CDB.173118 REVIIA 1
CDB.173120 REVIIB 1
pp. 127, 302, 305

Aleksandr Rodchenko
Cover of the book
About This by
Vladimir Mayakovsky,
Moscow, 1923
Letterpress
23 x 16 cm
Archivo Lafuente
006968/000

Aleksandr Rodchenko
Cover of the journal
Lef, no. 3, 1923
23.5 x 15.8 cm
Letterpress
Centro de
Documentación,
Museo Nacional
Centro de Arte Reina
Sofía, Madrid
CDB.173118 REVIIA 1
CDB.173120 REVIIB 1

Aleksandr Rodchenko
Cover of the book
*Mayakovsky Smiles,
Mayakovsky Laughs,
Mayakovsky Mocks* by
Vladimir Mayakovsky,
Moscow/Saint
Petersburg, 1923
Letterpress
17.6 x 13 cm
Archivo Lafuente
006967/000

Aleksandr Rodchenko
Maquette for
illustrations for
About This, a
book by Vladimir
Mayakovsky, 1923
Cut-and-pasted
printed papers and
gelatin silver prints
on cardboard
35.2 x 22 cm
The State Mayakovsky
Museum, Moscow
И-1108

Aleksandr Rodchenko
Maquette for
illustrations for
About This, a
book by Vladimir
Mayakovsky, 1923
Cut-and-pasted
printed papers and
gelatin silver prints
on cardboard
35.2 x 22 cm
The State Mayakovsky
Museum, Moscow
И-1105

Aleksandr Rodchenko
*Poems about
Revolution* by
Vladimir Mayakovsky,
Moscow, Krasnaia
nov', 1923
17.5 x 13.3 cm
Archivo Lafuente
006966/000

Aleksandr Rodchenko
Varvara Stepanova
posing for a
poster, 1924
Gelatin silver print
30 x 23.8 cm
Private Collection

Aleksandr Rodchenko
Family Games (from
top to bottom: Boris
Shvetsov, Varvara
Stepanova, Maria
Shvetsova, Aleksandr
Rodchenko), 1924
Gelatin silver print
34.5 x 14.7 cm
Private Collection
p. 91

Aleksandr Rodchenko
Cover of the journal
Lef, no. 1, 1924
Letterpress
22 x 14.5 cm
Centro de
Documentación,
Museo Nacional
Centro de Arte Reina
Sofía, Madrid
CDB.173118 REVIIA 1
CDB.173120 REVIIB 1

Aleksandr Rodchenko
Cover design for the
journal *Lef* (with
a portrait of Osip
Brik, unpublished),
1924
Gelatin silver print,
gouache, and pencil
24 x 18 cm
The Pushkin State
Museum of Fine
Arts, Department of
Private Collections
КП-391904/
МЛК ГР 2176
p. 138

Aleksandr Rodchenko
Cover of the journal
Book about Books,
no. 1–2, Moscow,
April 1924
Cover of the journal
Book about Books, no.
3, Moscow, May 1924
Cover of the journal
Book about Books,
no. 5–6, Moscow,
June 1924
Cover of the journal
Book about Books,
no. 7–8, Moscow,
July 1924
Letterpress
25 x 17 cm each
Archivo Lafuente
006987/001;
006987/002;
006987/003;
006987/004

Aleksandr Rodchenko
Cover of the book
*Mess Mend or a
Yankee in Petrograd* by

Jim Dollar (Marietta Shaginian), Moscow, nos. 3, 5 & 9, 1924
Letterpress
18 x 12.5 cm each
Archivo Lafuente
006984/001; 006984/002; 006984/003

Aleksandr Rodchenko
Cover of the book *Through the Russian Revolution* by Albert Rhys Williams (New York, 1921), Moscow/Leningrad, 1925
Letterpress
22 x 15 cm
Archivo Lafuente
007025/000

Aleksandr Rodchenko
Cover of the book *My Discovery of America* by Vladimir Mayakovsky, Leningrad/Moscow, 1926
Letterpress
18.5 x 14 cm
Archivo Lafuente
007144/000
p. 151

Olga Rozanova
The Devil and the Speech Makers, Saint Petersburg, 1913
Lithograph
22.8 x 16.8 cm
Archivo Lafuente
006844/000

Olga Rozanova
Cover of the book *Te Li Le* by Aleksei Kruchenykh and Velimir Khlebnikov, 1914
Hectograph print
23.1 x 16 cm
The State Mayakovsky Museum, Moscow
11109

Olga Rozanova
In the Street, 1915
Oil on canvas
101 x 77 cm
Slobodskoy Museum-Exhibition Center
p. 46

Olga Rozanova
Cover design for the book *Transrational* by Aleksei Kruchenykh and Aliagrov (Roman Jakobson), 1915
Cut-and-pasted papers on paper
18.8 x 13.8 cm
The State Mayakovsky Museum, Moscow
11406
p. 267

Olga Rozanova
Composition, 1915
Cut-and-pasted papers on paper
12.2 x 9.7 cm
The State Mayakovsky Museum, Moscow
11632
p. 264

Olga Rozanova
Cover of the book *Transrational Book* by Aleksei Kruchenykh and Aliagrov (Roman Jakobson), 1916
Lithograph
21.8 x 19.7 cm
The State Mayakovsky Museum, Moscow
28155(5239)
p. 176

Olga Rozanova
Cover and Illustrations for the book *War* by Aleksei Kruchenykh, Petrograd, 1916
Linocut
41.5 x 32.5 cm approx. each.
The State Mayakovsky Museum, Moscow
10954(6); 10954(7); 10954(13); 10954(14); 10954(1); бD98445; 10954(11); 10954(8); 10954(12); 10954(3); 10954(5); 10954(2); 10954(10); 10954(4); 10954(9)
pp. 66, 67

Kurt Schwitters
Plates 2, 3, 4, 5 from *Merz 3, Merz Portfolio: 6 Lithos*, 1923
Lithographs
55.4 x 44.3 cm each
Stedelijk Museum Amsterdam
A 4677(1-6)2; A 4677(1-6)3; A 4677(1-6)4; A 4677(1-6)5
p. 159

Kurt Schwitters
Cover of the journal *Merz*, no. 11, Hannover, November 1924
Letterpress
29 x 22 cm
Archivo Lafuente
005449/004

Sergei Senkin
City, ca. 1920
Cut-and-pasted papers on paper
70.4 x 52 cm
State Tretyakov Gallery, Moscow
PC-12378
p. 86

Sergei Senkin
Construction, 1920
Ink, pencil, and gouache on paper
26.1 x 20.5 cm
Russian State Archives of Literature and Art
f. 1334, op. 1, ed. khr. 896, ll. 1–2
p. 77

Sergei Senkin
Illustrations for the journal *Young Guard*, Moscow, 1924
Lithographs
22 x 15 cm
The State Mayakovsky Museum, Moscow
12127 (1); 12131; 12130; 12128
pp. 93, 306

Robert Sennecke
Hannah Höch and Raoul Hausmann at the First International Dada Fair, Berlin, 1920
Gelatin silver print (printed 2018)
Berlinische Galerie, Berlin's Museum of Modern Art
BG-FS 077/94.4

Sergei Sharshun
Poster design for the exhibition of Elena Gringof and Sergei Sharshun, Galerie Dalmau, Barcelona, 1916
Gouache and ink on paper
35.7 x 28.3 cm
IVAM, Institut Valencià d'Art Modern, Generalitat
1996.004 (Código 5019)

Sergei Sharshun
Bibi, 1921
Ink and pencil on paper
20.9 x 26.9 cm
Centre Pompidou, Paris, Musée national d'art moderne / Centre de création industrielle
AM 1981-628
p. 164

Sergei Sharshun
The Fortune Dancer, 1922
Charcoal and ink on paper
100.3 x 71.2 cm
Centre Pompidou, Paris, Musée national d'art moderne / Centre de création industrielle, Legacy of the artist 1976
AM 1976-606
p. 165

Sergei Sharshun
Tristan Tzara, ca. 1921–1922
Ink and graphite on paper

12 x 8 cm
Fundación MAPFRE
Collection
FM000268
p. 203

Sergei Sharshun
Nikolai Berdiaev,
ca. 1921–1922
Ink and graphite
on paper
12 x 8 cm
Fundación MAPFRE
Collection
FM000264
p. 254

Sergei Sharshun
*Portrait: Dada
Drawing*,
ca. 1921–1922
Ink and graphite
on paper
12 x 8 cm
Fundación MAPFRE
Collection
FM000262

Sergei Sharshun
*Self-Portrait as
Devil*, ca. 1921–1922
Ink on paper
12 x 8 cm
Fundación MAPFRE
Collection
FM000265
p. 141

Sergei Sharshun
Female Portrait,
ca. 1921–1922
Ink and graphite
on paper
12 x 8 cm
Fundación MAPFRE
Collection
FM000267

Sergei Sharshun
Four-page journal
*Transportation-
Dada*, July 1922
Letterpress
14.2 x 27.5 cm
Archives Iliazd France

Sergei Sharshun
*Portrait: Dada
Drawing*, 1922
Ink and graphite
on paper
12 x 8 cm
Fundación MAPFRE
Collection
FM000263

Sergei Sharshun
Ornamental Cubism,
1922–1923
Oil on canvas
24 x 34 cm
Private Collection
pp. 162–163

Sergei Sharshun
Back cover of the
journal *Merz*,
no. 7, Hannover,
November 1924
Letterpress
20.5 x 24 cm
Stedelijk Museum
Amsterdam
1994.7.0251(1-14)05

Maria Siniakova
Cover of the book
Oi konin dan okein!
by Nikolai Aseev's,
Moscow, 1916
Cut-and-pasted
papers
20.2 x 16 cm
The State Mayakovsky
Museum, Moscow
28115(1261)

Evgeny Slavinsky
Still from Nikandr
Turkin's film *Born Not
for the Money* (David
Burliuk and Vladimir
Mayakovsky), 1918
Gelatin silver print
21.9 x 15.9 cm
The State Mayakovsky
Museum, Moscow
И-466
p. 234

Evgeny Slavinsky
Still from Nikandr
Turkin's film
*Born Not for the
Money* (Vladimir
Mayakovsky), 1918
14.8 x 9.6 cm
The State Mayakovsky
Museum, Moscow
И-468
p. 170

Antonina Sofronova
Cover design for the
book *From the Easel
to the Machine* by
Nikolai Tarabukin,
Moscow, 1923
Letterpress
23 x 15.6 cm
The State Mayakovsky
Museum, Moscow
10775

John Sraubenz
Vladimir Mayakovsky
and Osip Brik,
Berlin, 1923
Gelatin silver print
10 x 14.7 cm
The State Mayakovsky
Museum, Moscow
8498
p. 300

Varvara Stepanova
Illustration for
Gly-Gly by Aleksei
Kruchenykh, 1918
Cut-and-pasted
papers and ink
on paper
15.5 x 11 cm
Private Collection
p. 246

Varvara Stepanova
Illustration for
Gly-Gly by Aleksei
Kruchenykh, 1918
Ink on paper
15.5 x 11 cm
Private Collection
p. 247

Varvara Stepanova
Illustration for
Gly-Gly by Aleksei
Kruchenykh, 1918
Ink on paper
15.5 x 11 cm
Private Collection

Varvara Stepanova
Illustration for *Rtny
Khomle: Nonobjective
Poetry* by Varvara
Stepanova, 1918
Gouache on paper
23.3 x 18.5 cm
Private Collection

Varvara Stepanova
Cover of *Rtny
Khomle: Nonobjective
Poetry* by Varvara
Stepanova, 1918
Gouache on paper
23.3 x 17.8 cm
Private Collection
p. 280

Varvara Stepanova
Illustration for
Zigra-Ar by Varvara
Stepanova, 1918
Gouache on paper
23.5 x 18 cm
The Pushkin State
Museum of Fine
Arts, Department
of Private Collections
КП-391788/
МЛК ГР 2060

Varvara Stepanova
Gaust Chaba, 1919
Cut-and-pasted
papers on newspaper
27.5 x 17 cm
Private Collection

Varvara Stepanova
*Nonobjective
Poems*, 1919
Color pencil
and text on paper
23 x 18.4 cm
Private Collection

Varvara Stepanova
Gaust Chaba, 1919
Cut-and-pasted
papers on newspaper
27.5 x 17 cm
Private Collection

Varvara Stepanova
*Nonobjective
Poems*, 1919
Color pencil a
nd text on paper
23 x 18.4 cm
Private Collection

Varvara Stepanova
Torso, 1920
Ink on paper
29 x 22 cm
Private Collection
p. 103

Varvara Stepanova
Figure, 1921
Ink on paper
43 x 30.5 cm
Private Collection
p. 102

Varvara Stepanova
Cover of the journal
Cine-Photo, no. 2, 1922
Letterpress
29.6 x 22.1 cm
Private Collection
p. 218

Varvara Stepanova
Costume designs
for the play *Death of Tarelkin* by Aleksandr
Sukhovo-Kobylin
for Vsevolod
Meyerhold
Theater, 1922
Color pencil and
gouache on paper
36 x 44.5 cm,
37 x 45.8 cm
Private Collection
p. 119

Varvara Stepanova
Charles Chaplin Turning Somersault, 1922
Ink and pencil
on paper
15.8 x 12.9 cm
Private Collection
p. 221

Varvara Stepanova
Cover of the journal
Cine-Photo, no. 3, 1922
Letterpress
29.5 x 22 cm
The Pushkin State
Museum of Fine
Arts, Department of
Private Collections
КП-391647/
МЛК ГРП 27
p. 207

Varvara Stepanova
Props design for
Vitaly Zhemchuzhny's
Evening of the Book
(The heroes of old
books), 1924
Gelatin silver print
23.4 x 17.5 cm
Private Collection

Varvara Stepanova
Poster for Vitaly
Zhemchuzhny's
Evening of the Book, 1924
Gelatin silver print
16 x 12.5 cm
Private Collection

Varvara Stepanova
Props design for
Vitaly Zhemchuzhny's
Evening of the Book (Red imps
disarm Aleksandr
Kirensky), 1924
Gelatin silver print
18 x 24 cm
Private Collection
p. 119

Vladimir Tatlin
Painterly Relief,
ca. 1914
Leather and
metal on wood
63 x 53 cm
State Tretyakov
Gallery, Moscow
Ж-1295
p. 58

Vladimir Tatlin
Cover of the pamphlet
Vladimir Evgrafovich Tatlin, 1915
Letterpress
31 x 24.5 cm
The State Mayakovsky
Museum, Moscow
10776

Vladimir Tatlin
Complex Corner-Relief, 1915
Reconstruction by
Martin Chalk, 1982
Paint, iron,
aluminum, and zinc
78.8 x 152.4 x 76.2 cm
Annely Juda Fine
Arts, London
MC0082W

Vladimir Tatlin
Painterly Relief
(in the exhibition
Moscow Artists to Victims of War), 1915
Gelatin silver print
24.3 x 18 cm
Russian State
Archives of
Literature and Art
f. 998, op. 1, ed.
khr. 3623, l. 2

Vladimir Tatlin
Counter-relief, 1915
Gelatin silver print
15.5 x 11 cm
Russian State
Archives of
Literature and Art
f. 998, op. 1, ed.
khr. 3623, ll. 8–9

Vladimir Tatlin
Cover of the book
The Monument to the Third International by
Nikolai Punin, 1920
28 x 21.9 cm
Letterpress
Centro de
Documentación,
Museo Nacional
Centro de Arte Reina
Sofía, Madrid
RESERVA 2714
p. 270

Vladimir Tatlin
Construction of the
model of Tatlin's
Monument to the Third International
(left to right: Iosif
Meerzon, Tevel
Shapiro, and
Tatlin), 1920
Gelatin silver print
14.9 x 10.2 cm
The State Museum of
Contemporary Art -
Costakis Collection
CDA-0233
p. 78

Vladimir Tatlin
Construction of the
model of Tatlin's
Monument to the Third International
(left to right: Sofia
Dymshits-Tolstaia,
Tatlin, Tevel
Shapiro, and Iosif
Meerzon), 1920
Gelatin silver print
9.8 x 13.3 cm
The State Museum of
Contemporary Art -
Costakis Collection
CDA-0234

Vladimir Tatlin
Stage design for
Zangezi by Velimir
Khlebnikov, Museum
of Material Culture,
Leningrad, 1923
Gelatin silver print
18 x 13.2 cm
Russian State
Archives of
Literature and Art
f. 3070, op. 1, ed.
khr. 1615, l. 1
p. 68

Solomon Telingater
Cover design for the
book *Zudo* by Aleksei
Kruchenykh, 1922
Watercolor and
ink on paper
21.5 x 30.5 cm
Russian State
Archives of
Literature and Art
f. 1334, op. 1, ed.
khr. 1318, ll. 1–2

Igor Terentiev
Cover design for
the book *Obesity of Roses* by Aleksei
Kruchenykh,
Tiflis, 1918
Letterpress
20 x 14.7 cm
The State Mayakovsky
Museum, Moscow
28155(5236)

Igor Terentiev
Three Archbishops
(Aleksei Kruchenykh,

Ilia Zdanevich, and
Igor Terentiev), 1919
Ink on paper
22.4 x 27 cm
Russian State
Archives of
Literature and Art
f. 1334, op. 1, ed. khr.
288, ll. 66–70, 70a
p. 182

Igor Terentiev
Cover of the book
The Cherubim Are Whistling by Igor
Terentiev, 1919
Letterpress
25 x 18 cm
The State Mayakovsky
Museum, Moscow
28155(3787)

Igor Terentiev (cover)
and Kirill Zdanevich
(illustrations)
17 Nonsense Instruments by Igor
Terentiev, 1919
Letterpress
17 x 13.5 cm
The State Mayakovsky
Museum, Moscow
28155(3788)

Igor Terentiev
Cover of the book
Treatise on Total Obscenity by Igor
Terentiev, Tiflis,
1919–1920
Letterpress
21.9 x 17 cm
Archivo Lafuente
006907/000

Igor Terentiev
Self-Portrait, ca. 1920
Watercolor, ink, and
pencil on paper
50.5 x 35 cm
Collection Ildar
Galeyev
p. 186

Igor Terentiev
Untitled, 1923
Cut-and-pasted
papers, pencil, and
crayon on paper
35 x 21.4 cm
Collection Ildar
Galeyev
p. 187

Igor Terentiev
Cover of the book
Zudo by Aleksei
Kruchenykh, ca. 1923
Cut-and-pasted
papers on ruled paper
33.2 x 20.5 cm
Collection Ildar
Galeyev

Tristan Tzara
Letter to Ilia
Zdanevich on
Dada stationary
"Movement Dada,"
17 February 1922
Ink on paper
20.9 x 27.3 cm
Private Collection
France
p. 147

Tristan Tzara
Envelope for
a letter to Ilia
Zdanevich, 1924
Ink on paper
14.4 x 11.5 cm
Archives Iliazd France
218
p. 147

Tristan Tzara
Letter to Ilia
Zdanevich, 1924
Ink on paper
13.4 x 21.1 cm
Archives Iliazd France

Tristan Tzara
Seven Dada Manifestos
(autographed by Tzara
to Ilia Zdanevich in
November 1924: "To
Ylya Zdanevitch with
all the sympathy of
Tristan Tzaranov),
Paris, 1924
Letterpress
19 x 15.5 cm
The State Mayakovsky
Museum, Moscow
10690

Tristan Tzara
Untitled, May 1931
Ink on cardboard
24.5 x 31.5 cm
Private Collection
France
p. 171

Nadezhda Udaltsova
Red Figure, 1919
Oil on canvas
70 x 70 cm
The State Rostov-
Iaroslavl Architectural
and Art Museum
Preserve, provided
with assistance from
the State Museum
and Exhibition
Center ROSIZO
Zh-136
p. 100

Sigizmund
Valishevsky
Untitled (Ilia
Zdanevich lecturing
donkeys), 1915
Ink on paper
19 x 23.5 cm
Private Collection
France
p. 26

Dziga Vertov
Cine-Truth,
no. 14, 1923
35 mm film
transferred to DVD,
b/w, silent, 14'
(extract 6' 57")
National Film
Foundation of
Russian Federation

Dziga Vertov
Cine-Truth, no.
21 (dedicated to
Lenin), 1925
35 mm film
transferred to DVD,
b/w, silent, 23'
Lobster Films

David Zagoskin
Construction,
1921–1922
Oil on canvas
mounted on board,
and a collage
of records
60 x 48 cm
The Saratov State
Art Museum named
after A. N. Radischev,
provided with
assistance from
the State Museum
and Exhibition
Center ROSIZO
СГХМ КП-1097
BZh-106
p. 112

Ilia Zdanevich
Indecent Flyer, ca. 1917
Letterpress
15.5 x 24 cm
Private Collection
France

Ilia Zdanevich
Indecent Flyer, ca. 1917
Letterpress
13.5 x 21 cm
Private Collection
France

Ilia Zdanevich
Cover of the book
Fact by Igor Terentiev,
Tiflis, 1919

Letterpress
17.4 x 14 cm
Archivo Lafuente
006906/000
p. 184

Ilia Zdanevich
Cover of the book
Easter Island by Ilia
Zdanevich, Tiflis, 1919
Letterpress
21.2 x 17.5 cm
Archivo Lafuente
006909/000

Ilia Zdanevich
Poster for a
performance by
Kruchenykh,
Zdanevich, and
Terentiev in Borjomi,
Georgia, 1919
Letterpress
106 x 69.5 cm
Private Collection
France
p. 282

Ilia Zdanevich
Poster for Ilia Zdanevich's lecture *New Schools in Russian Poetry*, 1921
Letterpress
20.4 x 15.4 cm
Archives Iliazd France
p. 148

Ilia Zdanevich
Leaflet for Ilia Zdanevich's lecture in Café Caméléon, Paris, April 16, 1922
Letterpress
14.6 x 22 cm
Private Collection
France

Ilia Zdanevich
Cover of the journal *The Bearded Heart*, no. 1, Paris, April 1922
Letterpress
22.5 x 14.1 cm
Archivo Lafuente
005686/000

Ilia Zdanevich
Poster for Ilia Zdanevich's lecture "41°," Paris, May 12, 1922
Lithograph
53.4 x 44 cm
The State Mayakovsky Museum, Moscow
10934
p. 199

Ilia Zdanevich
Poster design for a conference on the Russian avant-garde, November 28, 1922
Watercolor on paper
26.5 x 20.5 cm
Private Collection
France

Ilia Zdanevich (designer) and Sergei Romov (editor)
Cover of *Strike*, February 1922
Offset
16 x 24.6 cm
Archives Iliazd France

Ilia Zdanevich
Poster design for a conference on the Russian avant-garde, November 28, 1922
Ink on paper
32 x 25 cm
Private Collection
France
p. 148

Ilia Zdanevich
Poster for Ilia Zdanevich's lecture "Berlin and Its Hack Job," 1923
Handwritten
50.2 x 32.5 cm
Private Collection
France
Inv. Number: 16

Ilia Zdanevich
Program for *Transrational Ball*, Paris, February 1923
Letterpress
17.5 cm in diameter
Private Collection
France

Ilia Zdanevich
Poster for *Transrational Ball*, 1923
Letterpress
31.5 x 16 cm
Private Collection
France
p. 195

Ilia Zdanevich
Leaflet for *The Bearded Heart* soirée, 1923
Letterpress
26 x 20.3 cm
IVAM, Institut Valencià d'Art Modern, Generalitat
1995.136 (Código 3984)
p. 149

Kirill Zdanevich
Composition, 1916
Ink on paper
22.5 x 18.2 cm
Russian State Archives of Literature and Art
f. 1334, op. 1, ed. khr. 482, l. 1
p. 25

Kirill Zdanevich
Cover and illustrations for the book *Learn Artists* by Aleksei Kruchenykh, Tiflis, 1917
Lithograph
23.8 x 19.2 cm
Archivo Lafuente
006656/000
p. 185

Kirill Zdanevich and Sigizmund Valishevsky
Cover of the book *Learn Artists* by Aleksei Kruchenykh, Tiflis, 1917
Lithograph
22.5 x 18 cm
The State Mayakovsky Museum, Moscow
33345(1)

Kirill Zdanevich
Cover and illustrations for the book *Record of Tenderness: Life of Ilia Zdanevich* by Igor Terentiev, Tiflis, 1919
Letterpress
13.8 x 15.2 cm
The State Mayakovsky Museum, Moscow
28155(3790)

Kirill Zdanevich
Cover of the book *A. Kruchenykh the Magnificent* by Igor Terentiev, 1919
Letterpress
21 x 17 cm
Vladimir Dahl Russian State Literary Museum
GLM KP 50858/2831
p. 185

Kirill Zdanevich
Untitled, 1922
Ink on paper
21.2 x 156 cm
Russian State Archives of Literature and Art
f. 2563, op. 1, ed. khr. 113, l. 1

Kirill Zdanevich and H2SO4 Group
Cover of the journal *Literature and the Rest*, no. 1, Tiflis, 1924
Cut-and-pasted papers on paper
21.6 x 17.2 cm
Archivo Lafuente
007318/000
p. 192

Kirill Zdanevich
Aleksei Kruchenykh, n.d.
Ink and pencil on paper
28.3 x 21.5 cm
Russian State Archives of Literature and Art
f. 1334, op. 1, ed. khr. 1085, l. 178

OTHER WORKS REPRODUCED IN THE CATALOGUE

Anonymous
Mikhail Larionov, 1913
Gelatin silver print
14 x 9.7 cm
Vladimir Dahl Russian State Literary Museum
p. 34

Anonymous
View of El Lissitzky's propaganda board "The Factory Workbenches Await You" in front of a factory in Vitebsk, 1920
Gelatin silver print
30 x 32.8 cm
Russian State Library
p. 77

Anonymous
Congress of Constructivists and Dadaists, Weimar, September, 1922
Participants: far left: Max Burchartz (carrying son); back row, from left: Lucia Moholy-Nagy, Alfred Kémény, and László Moholy-Nagy; third

row above the poster, El Lissitzky (checked cap); second row: Nelly van Doesburg, Theo van Doesburg (with poster in hat), Tristan Tzara (gloved and manacled), Werner Graeff (with stick), and Han Arp (on ground)
Gelatin silver print
Bauhaus-Archiv Berlin
Inv. no. 7599
p. 136

Kazimir Malevich
Composition with Mona Lisa (Partial Eclipse), ca. 1914–1915
Oil, collage, and pencil on canvas
62 x 49.3 cm
The State Russian Museum, St. Petersburg
p. 54

Man Ray
A Dada alliance (top row, left to right: Paul Chadourne, Tristan Tzara, Philippe Soupault, and Sergei Sharshun; bottom row, left to right: Paul Éluard, Jacques Rigaut, Mick Soupault, and Georges Ribemont-Dessaignes), Paris, November 1921
Gelatin silver print (printed 2018)
Centre Pompidou, Paris, Musée national d'art moderne / Centre de création industrielle
AM 1987-883
p. 140

Ivan Puni (Scrapbook)
Tristan Tzara (left) with two unknowns, ca. 1922
Gelatin silver print
Bibliothèque nationale de France
p. 202

Ivan Puni (Scrapbook)
Viktor Shklovsky, Ivan Puni, Ksenia Boguslavskaia, and unknowns, ca. 1922
Gelatin silver print
Bibliothèque nationale de France
p. 137

John Schiff
David Burliuk's *Forces of Spring,* 1922 [location unknown] from Katherine S. Dreier's private collection, ca. 1945–1946
Black and white photograph
Yale University Art Gallery. Purchase, Director's Discretionary Funds
p. 153

John Schiff
David Burliuk's *Eye of God,* 1923–25 from Katherine S. Dreier's private collection ca. 1945-1946
Black and white photograph
Yale University Art Gallery. Purchase, Director's Discretionary Funds
p. 155

This catalogue is published to coincide with the exhibition *Russian Dada 1914–1924*, organized and held in the Museo Nacional Centro de Arte Reina Sofía from June 6 to October 22, 2018.

EXHIBITION

Curator
Margarita Tupitsyn

MNCARS

Head of Exhibitions
Teresa Velázquez

Exhibition Coordinator
Sofía Cuadrado
Leticia Sastre

Management
Natalia Guaza

Management Assistant
María Inés Álvarez

Registrars
Clara Berástegui
Raquel Esteban
Iliana Naranjo
David Ruiz

Conservation
Eugenia Gimeno
(Conservator in charge)
Blanca Guerra
Pilar Hernández
Mikel Rotaeche
Juan Antonio Sáez
Juan Sánchez

Exhibition Design
Estudio María Fraile

Installation
SIT. Proyectos, diseño
y conservación S.L.

Audio-visuals
Zenit Audio S.L.U

Shipping
Tti (Grupo Bovis)

Insurance
Garantía del Estado,
Ingosstrakh, Poolsegur

Translator of documentation for loans
Elena Kizima

CATALOGUE

Catalogue edited by
Margarita Tupitsyn and the
MNCARS Editorial Activities

Head of Editorial Activities
Alicia Pinteño

Editorial Coordination
Mafalda Rodríguez
Teresa Ochoa de Zabalegui

Translations
From Russian to English
Cathy Young, 23–255,
259–263, 271–275, 285–299,
307–309, 314–319
From Spanish to English
Philip Sutton, 7–13

Copyediting and Proofreading
Christopher Davey

Images Documentation
Alexia Oviedo

Graphic Design
tipos móviles

Production Management
Julio López

Plates
La Troupe

Printing
Brizzolis, arte en gráficas
Madrid, Spain

Binding
Ramos
Madrid, Spain

ISBN: 978-0-262-53639-4
(The MIT Press)

ISBN: 978-84-8026-573-7
(MNCARS)

NIPO: 036-18-017-2
L.D.: M-13383-2018

Library of Congress Control
Number: 2018938300

General Catalogue of Official Publications
http://publicacionesoficiales.boe.es

PHOTOGRAPHIC CREDITS

Archives Iliazd France: 21, 147, 148, 166, 182, 258.

Archivo Lafuente: 21, 29, 39, 94, 133, 136, 142, 151, 174, 178, 184, 192, 195, 290.

A. Rodchenko and V. Stepanova Archive: 53, 89, 91, 119, 218, 221, 244, 245, 246, 247.

Biblioteca Museo Nacional Centro de Arte Reina Sofía, Madrid. Photos: Joaquín Cortés and Román Lores: 94, 127, 270, 302, 305.

Bibliothèque nationale de France: 137, 202.

Central State Archives, Museum of Literature and Arts of Ukraine: 73, 93, 118.

Centre Pompidou, MNAM-CCI, Dist. RMN-Grand Palais: 140, 142, 315 / Photos Georges Meguerditchian: 52, 141, 164, 165/ Photo Guy Carrard: 152 / Photo Philippe Migeat: 59 / Photo Jacqueline Hyde: 47.

Fundación MAPFRE Collection. Photos Fernando Maquieira: 141, 203, 254.

François Mairé Collection: 21, 24, 148, 149, 258. Photos Gerard Dufresne: 26, 147, 166.

Galeyev Gallery: 186, 187.

IVAM, Institut Valencià d'Art Modern: 125.

Lorenzelli Arte, Milano. Photo: Andrea Lazzari: 111.

Museo Nacional Centro de Arte Reina Sofía, Madrid. Photos Joaquín Cortés and Román Lores: 166, 167.

Museo Nacional Thyssen-Bornemisza, Madrid: 127.

Private Collection Margarita Tupitsyn: 70, 72, 81, 84, 91, 96, 97, 102, 130.

Russian State Archive of Literature and Art: 25, 68, 75, 77, 107, 125, 133, 154, 160, 178, 182, 208, 214, 255, 268, 288.

Slobodskoy Museum-Exhibition Center: 46.

State Tretyakov Gallery, Moscow: 58, 86, 105, 110, 120, 121.

Stedelijk Museum, Amsterdam: 32, 41, 43, 45, 52, 55, 63, 106, 157, 158, 159, 178.

The Astrakhan State Art Museum named after P. M. Dogadina, provided with assistance from the State Museum and Exhibition Center ROSIZO: 48.

The Krasnodar Regional Art Museum named after F. A. Kovalenko, provided with assistance from the State Museum and Exhibition Center ROSIZO: 56.

The Moscow Film Archive: 2, 3.

The Nizhny Tagil Art Museum, provided with assistance from the State Museum and Exhibition Center ROSIZO: 50, 114.

The Pushkin State Museum of Fine Arts, Department of Private Collections: 90, 116,117, 138, 207.

The Samara Regional Art Museum, provided with assistance from the State Museum and Exhibition Center ROSIZO: 51.

The Saratov State Art Museum named after A. N. Radischev, provided with assistance from the State Museum and Exhibition Center ROSIZO: 57, 112, 113.

The State Mayakovsky Museum, Moscow: 10, 31, 39, 63, 64, 65, 66, 67, 82, 99, 122, 126, 128, 131, 137, 144, 151, 160, 166, 168, 169, 173, 176, 191, 195, 227, 231, 262, 264, 267, 284, 296, 311.

The State Museum of Contemporary Art-Costakis Collection, Thessaloniki: 35–36, 49, 55, 74, 78, 90, 104, 105, 108–109, 161, 176.

The State Rostov-Yaroslavl Architectural and Art Museum Preserve: 100.

The State Russian Museum, Saint Petersburg: 54.

The Vyatka Art Museum named after V. M. and A. M. Vasnetsovs, provided with assistance from the State Museum and Exhibition Center ROSIZO: 101, 115.

Vladimir Dahl Russian State Literary Museum: 25, 27, 30, 32, 33, 34, 44, 98, 184, 237.

Yale University Art Gallery. Photo: John Schiff: 153, 155.

ACKNOWLEDGMENTS

The Museo Nacional Centro de Arte Reina Sofía, is especially grateful to the curator of the exhibition, Margarita Tupitsyn, for her dedication and help with every aspect of the project.

Our gratitude to the following individuals and institutions without whose collaboration and cooperation neither the exhibition nor the catalogue would have been possible:

Annely Juda Fine Arts ◆ Archives Iliazd, France ◆ Archivo Lafuente ◆ The Astrakhan State Art Museum named after P. M. Dogadina ◆ Bauhaus Archiv Museum für Gestaltung ◆ Berlinische Galerie, Berlin ◆ California Institute of The Arts ◆ Central State Archives, Museum of Literature and Arts of Ukraine ◆ Centre Pompidou, Paris. Musée national d'art moderne / Centre de création industrielle ◆ Colecciones Fundación Mapfre, Madrid ◆ D. G. de Bellas Artes y Patrimonio Cultural (MECD) ◆ Embassy of the Russian Federation in Madrid ◆ Francis M. Naumann Fine Art, New York ◆ IVAM, Institut Valencià d'Art Modern, Generalitat ◆ Los Angeles County Museum, Los Angeles ◆ Moscow Museum of Modern Art ◆ Moscow State Tchaikovsky Conservatory ◆ National Film Foundation of Russian Federation ◆ Man Ray Trust ◆ Museo Thyssen-Bornemisza, Madrid ◆ Russian State Archives of Literature and Art ◆ Russian State Documentary Film and Photo Archive ◆ Slobodskoy Museum-Exhibition Center ◆ Sotheby's, London ◆ State Central Cinema Museum ◆ Stedelijk Museum, Amsterdam ◆ The Krasnodar Regional Art Museum named after F.A. Kovalenko ◆ The MIT Press, Cambridge ◆ The Museum of Modern Art, New York ◆ The Nizhniy Tagil Art Museum ◆ The Pushkin State Museum of Fine Arts, Department of Private Collections ◆ The Samara Regional Art Museum ◆ The Saratov State Art Museum named after A. N. Radischev ◆ The State Mayakovsky Museum, Moscow ◆ The State Museum and Exhibition Center ROSIZO, Moscow ◆ The State Museum of Contemporary Art-Costakis Collection ◆ The State Rostov-Yaroslavl Architectural and Art Museum Preserve ◆ The State Tretyakov Gallery, Moscow ◆ Vladimir Dahl Russian State Literary Museum, Moscow ◆ The Vyatka Art Museum named after V. M. and A. M. Vasnetsovs

And specially to those who have supported the project in various ways: ◆ Larisa Alekseeva ◆ Anna Ashkinazi ◆ Erika Babatz ◆ Reto Balmettler ◆ Robert Benedetti ◆ Yanina Beloshapkina ◆ Kathy Carbone ◆ Roger Conover ◆ Pilar Corchado ◆ Emily Cushman ◆ Ildar Galeyev ◆ Paul Galloway ◆ Elena Gasparova ◆ Régis Gayraud ◆ Margarita Godina ◆ Alejandro Ituarte Climent ◆ Larissa Ivanova ◆ Dmitry Karpov ◆ Ekaterina Khokhlova ◆ Tanja Keppler ◆ Aleksandr Lavrentiev ◆ Matteo Lorenzelli ◆ François Mairé ◆ Miguel Molina ◆ Erik Nurgaleev ◆ José Luis Rodríguez Muñoz ◆ Julia Sadovnikova ◆ Piper Severance ◆ Vladimir Tsarenkov

As well as those who wish to remain anonymous

COLLABORATE

Comunidad de Madrid

With the Support of Abertis

This BOOk

CAME OFF THE PRESS IN MADRID IN MAY 2018